Engaging the Doctrine of Israel

Engaging the Doctrine of Israel

A Christian Israelology in Dialogue with Ongoing Judaism

by
MATTHEW LEVERING

CASCADE *Books* • Eugene, Oregon

ENGAGING THE DOCTRINE OF ISRAEL
A Christian Israelology in Dialogue with Ongoing Judaism

Copyright © 2021 Matthew Levering. All rights reserved. Except for brief quotations in critical publications or reviews, no part of this book may be reproduced in any manner without prior written permission from the publisher. Write: Permissions, Wipf and Stock Publishers, 199 W. 8th Ave., Suite 3, Eugene, OR 97401.

Cascade Books
An Imprint of Wipf and Stock Publishers
199 W. 8th Ave., Suite 3
Eugene, OR 97401

www.wipfandstock.com

PAPERBACK ISBN: 978-1-7252-9110-2
HARDCOVER ISBN: 978-1-7252-9109-6
EBOOK ISBN: 978-1-7252-9111-9

Cataloguing-in-Publication data:

Names: Levering, Matthew.

Title: Engaging the doctrine of Israel : a Christian Israelology in dialogue with ongoing Judaism / Matthew Levering.

Description: Eugene, OR: Cascade Books, 2021 | Series: Engaging Doctrine. | Includes bibliographical references and index.

Identifiers: ISBN 978-1-7252-9110-2 (paperback) | ISBN 978-1-7252-9109-6 (hardcover) | ISBN 978-1-7252-9111-9 (ebook)

Subjects: LCSH: Judaism (Christian theology)—History of doctrines. | Christianity and other religions—Judaism. | Judaism—Relations—Christianity. | Christianity and antisemitism.

Classification: BT93 .L45 2021 (paperback) | BT93 (ebook)

09/13/21

To David Novak

Contents

Acknowledgments | ix

INTRODUCTION | 1

Chapter 1
JEWISH-CHRISTIAN DIALOGUE | 48

Chapter 2
CREATION AND SCRIPTURE | 110

Chapter 3
EXODUS | 147

Chapter 4
TORAH | 194

Chapter 5
TEMPLE | 262

Chapter 6
LAND | 322

Chapter 7
KING | 395

CONCLUSION | 444

Bibliography | 467

Index | 541

Acknowledgments

I benefited from delivering portions of the present volume as lectures. In March 2019, I delivered "Pope Pius IX and the Mortara Case: A Catholic Critique" at a Festschrift conference for David Novak that I organized here at Mundelein Seminary. This paper was incorporated into chapter 7 of this book, and a version of the paper has been published in *The Achievement of David Novak: A Catholic-Jewish Dialogue*, edited by Tom Angier and me (Eugene, OR: Pickwick, 2021), 199–219. In April 2019, I spoke at the University of Notre Dame's McGrath Institute for Church Life, at a conference in honor of Olivier-Thomas Venard, OP. My topic was "Israel's Scriptures and the Doctrine of Creation." A much revised version of this paper appears as chapter 2 of this book. In June 2019, I gave a paper at the annual conference of the University Faculty for Life, on the topic of "Life and Suffering: Lessons from the Book of Exodus"—and a revised version of this paper appears here as part of chapter 3. In October 2019, I gave the A. O. Collins Lecture at Houston Baptist University, where I spoke on "What Was the Purpose of the Exodus?" The material in this lecture likewise forms part of chapter 3. To the biblical studies and theology faculty and students of Houston Baptist, I presented "Psalms and Providence," and a portion of this material found its way into my book's Conclusion. In 2019, too, I was scheduled to speak at a conference in Jerusalem organized by Gavin D'Costa, but a blood clot incurred due to an orthopedic surgery prevented me from going. The impetus for chapter 6 came from preparations for this conference, which I greatly regretted missing. Let me thank Gary Anderson, Ben Blackwell, John Cavadini, the late Joseph Koterski, SJ, Francesca Aran Murphy, Nathan Eubank, and the many other gracious hosts and colleagues who, as part of the above events, posed valuable questions and sharpened my thinking on these topics.

Preparations for the present book began with my doctoral dissertation, published in 2002 as *Christ's Fulfillment of Torah and Temple: Salvation according to Thomas Aquinas*. The book also has roots in my friendship with Rabbi David G. Dalin during my time at Ave Maria University, which bore fruit in a conference and 2008 edited volume titled *John Paul II and the Jewish People*. Most important for the approach taken in the present volume was my *Jewish-Christian Dialogue and the Life of Wisdom: Engagements with the Theology of David Novak*, published in 2010. This work resulted in a series of collaborative lectures and projects with David Novak, and also in a dialogue with Mark Kinzer.

Among Catholic friends, a particular word of thanks with regard to the topics treated in this book should go to Holly Taylor Coolman, Douglas Farrow, Lawrence Feingold, Robert P. George, Bruce Marshall, Matthew Minerd, Roger Nutt, Nathaniel Peters, Mark Reasoner, and Thomas Joseph White, OP. When it came time to revise my manuscript, I received crucial critical feedback and bibliographical assistance from Gavin D'Costa and Matthew Tapie. Indeed, without the benefit of conversations and debates with these two scholars and friends, I could hardly have written this book. My friend and former student David Moser, now a professor of theology at Dordt University, read the whole manuscript and provided countless clarifying suggestions. Jason Paone, now at Word on Fire, skillfully prepared the manuscript for submission to Cascade—an extensive undertaking indeed—and put together the bibliography and index. With their usual skill, Michael Thomson and Rodney Clapp guided the book through the process at Cascade. Thanks to Meghan Duke for doing the Index quickly and capably, and to Ian Creeger for his excellent work in overseeing the final production stages.

I am grateful for the support for Jewish-Christian dialogue offered by Jim and Molly Perry, to whose generosity I am constantly indebted. Fr. Thomas Baima, Provost of the Seminary, is an eminent leader in Jewish-Christian dialogue. I thank him, the Seminary's Rector Fr. John Kartje, Melanie Barrett, and other friends, colleagues, and students here for their support and encouragement. My wife, Joy, and my family have my deepest love and gratitude. For such a wonderful wife and family, "I give thanks to you, O Lord my God, with my whole heart" (Ps 86:12).

This book is very much a work of Catholic theology. Nevertheless, since I here undertake an extensive dialogue with Judaism, it is fitting, I hope, to dedicate the book to one of the giants of our time, a man whom I am privileged to count as a friend and mentor, David Novak. I cannot think of truer words to describe David than to say that he lives by the words of the psalmist: "It is good to give thanks to the Lord, to sing praises to your name, O Most High" (Ps 92:1).

Introduction

This book is the dogmatic sequel to my *Engaging the Doctrine of Marriage*, in which I argued that God's purpose in creating the cosmos is the eschatological marriage of God and his people—the unfathomably glorious consummation that we await. God sets this marriage into motion through his covenantal election of a particular people, the people of Israel. As the Jewish theologian David Novak puts it, this election unto marriage "means that our desire for God has been *awakened* by God's desire for us."[1] Novak perceives that "even the most exalted interhuman relationship, which is the marriage of a woman and a man, is only so exalted because it reflects the more perfect marriage of God and His people."[2]

It makes sense, then, to turn from the doctrine of marriage to the doctrine of Israel. I engage the *Christian* doctrine of Israel, what Ellen Charry has called "the question of Christian Israelology."[3] The Christian doctrine

---

1. Novak, "How Jewish Was Barth?," 16—an excellent summary of what Catholic theologies of nature and grace describe in terms of obediential potency and elicited desire. Novak adds, "true *eros*—as distinct from untrue lust—is only valid when it is in harmony with, when it truly reflects, God's love for Israel" ("How Jewish Was Barth?," 18). For "marriage" as a metaphor for inclusivist, exclusivist, and pluralist perspectives on other religions—with preference given to the inclusivist position that accepts a single divine revelation but insofar as possible appreciates other religions (as Novak does in his work on Barth)—see Brill, *Judaism and Other Religions*, 28.

2. Novak, *Athens and Jerusalem*, 83.

3. Charry, "Toward Ending Enmity," 148; cf. 150n2. Friedrich-Wilhelm Marquardt argues, "Just as there is no Jewish theology comparable to Christian theology, so there is also nothing such as a Jewish doctrine or normative creed. What we call 'confession of faith' is for Jews a unity of prayer, day-to-day conduct, and martyrdom" (Marquardt, "'Enemies for Our Sake,'" 11). With David Novak, I think there is Jewish theology; and truth-claims such as Israel's covenantal election and the oneness of God (among other such claims) function as doctrine. Marquardt proposes that Jewish understanding of God "is not so much a theory about the uniqueness and oneness of God but rather a self-unification or integration with the God of Abraham, Isaac and Jacob always to be accomplished anew by every Jew and by the people of Israel as a whole" ("'Enemies for

of Israel differs, of course, from reflection upon the *State* of Israel. But although Charry holds that "Christian Israelology" does not involve the State of Israel in any way, the importance of the State for the Jewish people means that I will need to give the State of Israel a significant place in my chapter on the land.

In offering a Christian Israelology, the chapters that follow provide extensive meditations on biblical texts drawn from the entirety of Christian Scripture. Yet, the book is not a biblical theology. Readers will not find here a dogmatic theologian's version of Brevard Childs's *Biblical Theology of the Old and New Testaments*, Walter Brueggemann's *Theology of the Old Testament*, or John Goldingay's three-volume *Old Testament Theology*.[4] Instead, my chapters will engage theologically with a few central topics: Jewish-Christian dialogue, creation and Scripture, the exodus, the Torah, the temple, the promised land, and the Davidic kingship.[5]

Many of these topics do not normally have a distinct place in classical Christian dogmatics, with the exception being the Torah (or law) and, of course, creation. I have already covered the doctrine of creation in volume

---

Our Sake," 11). This is a false opposition; there is no need to denigrate the "theory" or (scriptural) propositional judgment that God is one, in order to lift up the existential and participatory elements of Israel's faith. For the same false opposition—a trademark of liberal Protestantism—see Paul van Buren's relativization of doctrine at the outset of his three-volume *Theology of the Jewish-Christian Reality*: "It is possible, as a logical exercise, to analyze a person's trust into propositions implied by that trust. This is, however, an exercise in abstraction which, from the walker's point of view, is a move from the primary and important to the secondary and much less important. Propositional reduction abstracts from the actual walk and the actual Way" (*Discerning the Way*, 19). For further discussion see Novak, "What Is Jewish Theology?" For a Jewish perspective that is the opposite of Novak's, see Meyer, "*Nostra Aetate*," 124: "There is not really such a thing as 'Jewish theology.' Judaism is not a religion of specific dogmas or beliefs but more a religion of practices in which we follow the 613 commandments that God gave to Moses in the text of the Torah." For reflection along Novak's lines, affirming the significance of Jewish doctrine (while denying "the exclusive primacy of dogmas"), see Heschel, *God in Search of Man*, 330–32.

4. Childs, *Biblical Theology*; Brueggemann, *Theology of the Old Testament*; Goldingay, *Israel's Gospel*; Goldingay, *Israel's Faith*; Goldingay, *Israel's Life*. These authors are well aware of the anti-Semitism present within the development of historical-critical Old Testament scholarship, on which topic see Gerdmar, *Theological Anti-Semitism*. I do not think that biblical theology need fall into the (in this case specifically Protestant) problems identified by Levenson in "Not Interested in Biblical Theology," although surely all biblical theology—including Levenson's own version—will be open to criticism.

5. Thus I am certainly not (in the words of Norbert Lohfink, SJ and Erich Zenger) attempting "to 'evaluate' Judaism with categories that are 'allegedly' Christian and alien to what is Jewish" (Lohfink and Zenger, "Theological Context," 5). See also Lohfink, *Covenant Never Revoked*; and Zenger, "Covenant."

INTRODUCTION

3 of my dogmatics, so what is it doing here? In answer, here is the place to reflect upon why divine revelation and scriptural composition took place as they did within God's people Israel. Creation is utterly central to the doctrine of Israel, and yet God allowed ambiguities in Genesis 1 regarding the reality of *creatio ex nihilo*.

The primary goal of the present volume is to undertake, within Catholic dogmatics, a full-fledged treatment of the central realities of God's biblical people Israel. Absent contemplation of the main elements of Israel's covenantal life with God, Catholic dogmatics suffers a twofold deprivation: of the dogmatic place of Israel in its own right, and of the deep and inextricable relationship of Israel to the Christ and, indeed, to all the loci of Christian dogmatics. Thus, my purpose does not entail examining the main elements of Israel's covenantal life with God as though there were no Jesus of Nazareth, fulfilling and transforming Israel's covenants and promises and pouring out his Spirit. Even so, these central elements of God's history with his people deserve full Christian attention in their own right even if not "independently."

As befits a Christian Israelology, I actively seek to learn from Jewish scholars.[6] Each chapter mounts a theological dialogue with one or more

---

6. For a work that similarly "attempts to listen to the voice of the teaching Church, attend to the signs of the time, while engaging in conversation with Jewish and Catholic scholars to advance the project of Catholic theological reflection on the Jewish people," see D'Costa, *Catholic Doctrines* (quotation from 8). I have sought to learn from these modern Jewish scholars in part because they, too, are involved in Jewish-Christian dialogue, and in part because I hope that through them I may obtain a deeper understanding of their sources (including the Oral Torah, in respect to which I am not knowledgeable). I appreciate the easy introduction to the Talmud provided by Rabbi Amy Scheinerman's *Talmud of Relationships*, vol. 1: *God, Self, and Family* and vol. 2: *The Jewish Community and Beyond*, though I often find myself disagreeing when Scheinerman corrects the rabbis!—as she does for example by stating with approval: "Contemporary marital partnerships may be heterosexual or homosexual, the partners may be cisgender or transgender, and the children may be, as the old expression goes, any combination of 'yours, mine, and ours'—or none at all" (vol. 1, 124). Scheinerman at least recognizes that "for the Rabbis, sexual intercourse is an essential aspect of married life because it is necessary for reproduction" (vol. 1, 126), a point that keeps sex grounded in a relationship ordered to male-female parenting, so that children are not unjustly deprived of their right to be raised by their mother and father. Marquardt's "Why the Talmud Interests Me" rightly warns against employing texts from the Talmud "as a heap of fragments, gathered to suit a Christian purpose and end" (72) and against drawing invidious comparisons between these texts and the New Testament. Marquardt adds, "*It is worth* listening to the Talmud, listening to the conversation of the teachers of Israel about the life of God's people living in constant danger from within and from without. It is valuable for us, for our understanding of the Bible and for our self-understanding as Christians, in short, for our Christian identity" ("Why the Talmud Interests Me," 75). To the extent that Marquardt is implying that a Christian doctrine of Israel cannot be

Jewish thinkers. David Novak, from whom I have already learned much in previous works, is my central interlocutor in two chapters, on the land and the Davidic kingship, respectively.[7] Franz Rosenzweig and Abraham Joshua Heschel contribute to the chapter on Scripture and creation *ex nihilo*, Jonathan Sacks to the chapter on the exodus, Joseph B. Soloveitchik to the chapter on the Torah, and Jonathan Klawans to the chapter on the temple. Along the way, I discuss the viewpoints of many other Jewish theologians, philosophers, and exegetes. In setting forth their perspectives for the purposes of my Christian Israelology, I seek "to see things as Judaism sees them as a result of its particular experiences" and to do so appreciatively, "without feeling called to sit in judgment on the way of life of the Jewish people in our own day."[8]

I. The Plan of the Work

Let me briefly introduce the contents of the seven chapters. Chapter 1 examines issues pertaining to Jewish-Christian dialogue itself. I reflect upon the figure of Abraham as understood by Jews and Christians. I pay particular attention to the New Testament texts that have caused pain for the Jewish people, whether due to the rhetorical invective found in the texts or to the polemical criticisms they aim at particular Jewish groups or at ongoing Judaism. I examine these passages in light of my belief that the New Testament was inspired by the Holy Spirit for the salvation of the world but was written in a fully human manner. My goal consists in distinguishing truths that Christians must affirm—for example that Jesus was and is the Messiah of Israel and that the rejection of Jesus by the Jewish leaders and by the people to whom Paul and the apostles preached was a serious mistake—from time-bound elements that pertain to the intra-Jewish polemics of the period in

---

accomplished without extensive reading of Talmud, it is clear that I disagree. In addition, I disagree with Marquardt's application of his point, when he goes on to argue that "Jesus does not need to be perceived differently from any woman, any man, any child of his people.... Jesus is from God for us what his whole people is from God for us" ("Why the Talmud Interests Me," 77).

7. See my *Jewish-Christian Dialogue*; Emon, Levering, and Novak, *Natural Law*; Levering and Angier, *Achievement of David Novak*.

8. Hruby, "Jewish-Christian Dialogue," 92. D'Costa poses a challenging question: which "Judaism" and whose "Judaism"? ("Between Doctrine and Discernment," 74–75). Although I have not ignored Reform Jewish scholars, in general I have privileged "Conservative" or "Orthodox" Jewish voices, since their theological perspectives are rooted in an understanding of divine revelation that is similar to my own. For diverse understandings of Judaism, see Hartman, *Israelis and the Jewish Tradition*; as well as Stanislawski, *Autobiographical Jews*.

which the texts of the New Testament were written. This task of evaluating and sifting controversial passages constitutes a necessary prolegomenon to Christian Israelology.

Chapter 2 asks why God has revealed important truths in a sometimes ambiguous way, with the result that even such a crucial doctrine as creation *ex nihilo* is not made crystal clear in Genesis 1.[9] I suggest that the answer has to do with the theo-dramatic mode, uniting mystical and metaphysical patterns of thought, through which believers come to know and share in the God who reveals himself in history and in Scripture. Central to Israel's patterns of belief and worship is the truth that all things—from angels to worms to stars—are creatures, meaning that all things depend radically upon Israel's God, the Creator, for their finite existence. Learning how to recognize this God in Israel's Scriptures, despite sometimes ambiguous and anthropomorphic language, should be the first step of a Christian Israelology. In this task, Franz Rosenzweig's understanding of divine creative language, and especially Abraham Joshua Heschel's comparison of Rabbi Akiva and Rabbi Ishmael on scriptural anthropomorphism, prove helpful.[10]

---

9. For many biblical scholars and theologians today, the Bible is treated mainly as a repository of human yearnings and power struggles, and as a record of ancient human attitudes to be measured by contemporary movements of liberation. The Old Testament's discourse about God is treated as a hodgepodge of merely human claims. For this approach in a popularized form, see Miles, *God: A Biography*. See also the thoroughgoing historicism—matched with erudition in historical-critical scholarship—of Schmid, *Historical Theology*. For Schmid, it is taken for granted on all topics that "the Hebrew Bible is objectively too plurivocal to allow one to settle on one position. . . . [O]rthodoxy consists of those heterodoxies that were able to become established. One cannot escape the manifold political forces and contingencies guiding the history of reception by means of some supposed logic when investigating the possible unity of the Hebrew Bible. . . . The differentiation between 'true' and 'false,' of 'orthodox' and 'heterodox' is relativized substantially within the framework of non-exclusivist approaches to the question of truth. Truth can appear in various shapes, in various linguistic forms. It can be captured differently from different presuppositions. It cannot be pinned down uniformly" (*Historical Theology*, 440–41). Schmid here posits a (false) choice between believing that the "Hebrew Bible" communicates enduring truths, on the one hand, and appreciating historical developments and contextualization, on the other. Schmid's classically liberal conclusion is built into his historicist lens: "Whatever is stated about God religiously or theologically remains penultimate rather than ultimate. This is also the case for the Bible—it contains, therefore, witnesses of human experiences of God and not divinely revealed truths" (*Historical Theology*, 441). For a better approach, see Moberly's "Bible, the Question of God." See also William Wright IV and Francis Martin's instructive *Encountering the Living God*.

10. I focus on the problem of scriptural ambiguity with regard to creation *ex nihilo*—and, more broadly, the whole debate about how to interpret Scripture's anthropomorphic or philosophically troubling language about God and divine action. Here may be the place to mention Soulen, *Distinguishing the Voices*. Soulen's argument is that Christian supersessionism is fueled by Christian forgetfulness or neglect of the revealed

Christian Israelology relies upon the fact that the Creator God, in Christ, is accomplishing for believers what the biblical scholar Michael Bird terms "a new exodus and a new redemption by entering into the imperishable inheritance of God."[11] In chapter 3, I explore the exodus and the new exodus in Christ. I begin by asking why God, having heard the cries of his suffering people, redeemed them from Egyptian slavery only to immerse them in the terrible sufferings of the exodus journey. God hears his people's cry, redeems his people from suffering, and leads his people toward perfect communal dwelling with him. But why does God allow so much suffering and death to remain? Assisted by Jonathan Sacks's political reading of the exodus, I investigate the question of suffering on the exodus and on the new exodus in light of the way in which the exodus constitutes a specific people or nation. By placing the constitution of a nation front and center, Jewish thinkers can help Christians better understand the new exodus in Christ.

For ongoing Judaism, "It is the Torah that makes Judaism stand out from anything in the human background."[12] In this light, chapter 4 engages the Torah that God gives to Israel.[13] I turn to Joseph B. Soloveitchik's *Halakhic Man* in order to gain insight into what Rabbinic Jews mean when they say, "The Torah is the link between God and man. The ladder, seen by Jacob in his dream (Gen. 28.12), connecting heaven and earth is said to be Sinai on which the Torah was given. The Torah was created before the creation of the world."[14] Christians may suppose that we have left behind

---

name YHWH. Although I disagree with Soulen in certain ways, I find his viewpoint to be stimulating, and I hope to return to it in the projected final volume of this dogmatic series. See also Marshall, "Do Christians Worship the God of Israel?" I agree with Marshall's conclusion, which (without mentioning them) could be directed against Karl Barth and Karl Rahner: "Christians need to be able to locate the Trinity in order to be *Christians*, but not in order to locate God.... [A]s Christian liturgical practice and the New Testament's talk of God indicate, identifying the Trinity presupposes locating the God of Israel" ("Do Christians Worship the God of Israel?," 262–63). For critique of Barth and Rahner on this point—but without sufficient valuation of the revelation of the Trinity—see Merkle, "God of Israel." With attention to the problem of evil, see also Eleonore Stump, "God of Abraham."

11. Bird, *Colossians and Philemon*, 43–44. See also L. M. Morales, *Exodus Old and New*, where Morales argues that the exodus (and thus the new exodus) is the central theme of human history and of biblical theology.

12. Novak, *Jewish-Christian Dialogue*, 129.

13. I do not repeat the attention to Israel's specific laws that, in expositing Thomas Aquinas's theology, I have undertaken elsewhere. See my *Christ's Fulfillment of Torah*; "Thomas Aquinas"; and *Paul in the* Summa, chapter 4. See also F. T. Harkins, "*Primus Doctor Iudaeorum*"; Somme, "L'adoption filiale des juifs."

14. Jacobs, "Significance of the Law," 19.

obedience to the Torah, but in fact this cannot be so.[15] Comparing the New Testament's worldview with that of Soloveitchik, I argue that Christ is Torah in person and that believers fulfill the whole Torah by sharing in his paschal mystery and embodying his love by the Spirit's power.[16] No doubt, "Christ" for Christians does not simply parallel "Torah" for Jews, because Christ is the divine Son. Even so, Christ as the embodiment or fulfillment of Torah stands as the Christian path of life along lines that resonate with Jewish understandings.[17]

Just as the Torah is central for Christian Israelology, so is the temple. Richard Ounsworth rightly observes that Christians "cannot understand their salvation without entering into the imaginative world of that cult."[18]

---

15. For a further approach to this topic, see the work of the Seventh-Day Adventist scholar Roy E. Gane, *Old Testament Law for Christians*. Gane insists throughout his book on the relevance of the Torah's laws for Christians. When Mosaic laws no longer literally apply, they still apply insofar as they shape the Christian worldview. Gane is correct that in giving the law at Sinai, "God offered a relationship based on grace, as shown by the fact that he had already delivered the Israelites (Exod. 19:4; 20:2)" (*Old Testament Law for Christians*, 402n5; cf. 408). He addresses issues such as the existence of Old Testaments laws that "regulate but still tolerate slavery and polygamy," that provide for "unduly harsh" penalties, and that command "corporate capital punishment of the Canaanites" (Gane, *Old Testament Law for Christians*, 141). See also C. J. H. Wright, *Old Testament Ethics*. For the theonomist perspective, which Gane rightly criticizes, see Greg L. Bahnsen, "Theonomic Reformed Approach." See also the questions raised from a Jewish perspective by Adam Gregerman, "Reverence Despite Rejection." Gregerman describes "a distinctively Christian scandal of particularity" in which the early Christians believed in biblical authority but did not impose God's commandments upon believers, with the result that "certain parts of the text, and certain roles for the text, are privileged over others" ("Reverence Despite Rejection," 186). Gregerman has in view the contemporary scholarly rejection of "sharp boundaries" between "Jews" and "Christians" in the centuries after Jesus; and he directs attention to the essays in Becker and Reed, eds., *Ways That Never Parted*.

16. For a stimulating effort in comparative theology, see Joslyn-Siemiatkoski, *More Torah, More Life*, in which Joslyn-Siematkoski strives to offer "a sustained Christian theological reflection upon a rabbinic Jewish text that does not appropriate the text for its own purposes but dwells with its meanings" while also "offer[ing] theological reflections from the Christian tradition" (4). As Joslyn-Siematkoski observes, Mishnah Avot develops a "Torah-centered wisdom" that aims to extend the "wisdom piety" of Sirach and other Second Temple sages (*More Torah, More Life*, 6; cf. 80–81 for comparison of Avot 1:6–7 with Christian texts). Joslyn-Siematkoski is indebted to Tropper, *Wisdom, Politics, and Historiography*.

17. For an emphasis on the discontinuities, see Morgan, "Jewish Perspectives," 16, indebted to Jon D. Levenson. At 22n29, Morgan remarks: "I would say that it is virtually impossible for Jews to grasp the notion of the Trinity and the idea of Jesus as God incarnate. . . . In a similar—but not identical—way, Torah is an essential element in the lexicon that Jews use to describe the world, and it is not exactly translatable into another faith's vocabulary."

18. Ounsworth, *Joshua Typology*, 185.

In chapter 5, I explore the temple and its animal sacrifices in light of the cessation of temple sacrifices and concerns about Christian supersessionism, as recently put forward by Jonathan Klawans. God intended the temple in Jerusalem to be the place where the entire people of Israel would offer worship to God. Jesus enacted a symbolic cleansing of the temple by driving out money-changers; and Jesus and his first followers preached often in the temple precincts rather than dissociating themselves sharply from the temple. As Gerd Theissen notes, in Christianity "the traditional ritual actions (bloody animal sacrifices) were replaced by new (bloodless) rites" organized around "the atoning sacrifice of Jesus."[19]

I argue that the temple's sacrifices are indeed superseded in Christian worship. But this supersession is preeminently a fulfillment, because worship in Christ—who is the eschatological temple—is temple-shaped and sacrificial, in a mode opened up by Christ's self-offering in love on the cross and his gift of the Eucharist.[20] Katherine Sonderegger aptly remarks, "The sacrifice of the altar, and the sacrificial meal, are not left behind when the Old Testament turns toward the New, but are rather underscored, heightened and consummated in the life and death of the Incarnate Son."[21]

Chapter 6 turns to the significance of the land for Christian Israelology, which inevitably means coming to terms with the Christian understanding of Jewish Zionism (the return of the Jewish people to dwell in and govern the promised land) and the State of Israel. Gavin D'Costa has recently put the question: "if the land was part of the covenant that God makes with his people, the Jews, and the covenant is irrevocable, then does that promise still stand? . . . If it does stand, does it apply to post-biblical Israel (of 1948)"?[22] Indeed, the very same question was raised by the Catholic scholar

---

19. Theissen, *Theory of Primitive Christian Religion*, 3. For Theissen this is a veiled renewal of the forbidden practice of human sacrifice. According to Theissen, "Religion is first of all a *semiotic* phenomenon" (*Theory of Primitive Christian Religion*, 2)—an interpretation of the world through signs and sign-systems. On this view, the living Creator God, actual divine action, has nothing to do with "religion" or at least must be bracketed out.

20. See Stubbs, *Table and Temple*.

21. Sonderegger, *Doctrine of the Holy Trinity*, 479.

22. D'Costa, *Catholic Doctrines*, 6. Chapters 3 and 4 of D'Costa's book address this question; and see also his "Catholic Zionism." In general, my position accords with his. In chapter 3 of *Catholic Doctrines*, D'Costa mainly surveys Pontifical Biblical Commission, "Jewish People." From this document—with which Catholics are free to disagree—D'Costa draws the inference that "if we ask about whether the temple should be found in the restored land of Israel if it is the land Promised, the answer could be yes, even though the restoration of the temple is not significant for Christians" (*Catholic Doctrines*, 101). In my view, the problem here is the terrible crisis that would be caused by the disruption of the Muslim holy sites on the Temple Mount. Likewise, D'Costa

Edward Flannery in 1986, and the question needs an answer.[23]

Jewish thinkers have advanced various reasons why Christians should support Zionism, including the fact that the destruction of the Jewish State would be experienced by the Jewish people as a disaster comparable to the Holocaust. In my view, David Novak and his co-authors of *Dabru Emet* are correct that Christians should "appreciate that Israel was promised—and given—to Jews as the physical center of the covenant between them and God" and that this means that the State of Israel is not solely a political matter.[24] From a Christian perspective, however, the land promise also requires

---

infers from his survey that, since the covenant has not been revoked, Catholics can understand the ingathering of the Jewish people to the land as potentially having "eschatological significance, but one that is not clearly timed or signalled precisely because of the long process that may lie ahead" (*Catholic Doctrines*, 104). See also chapter 4 of *Catholic Doctrines*, where D'Costa reviews the twentieth-century development of Catholic magisterial teaching and diplomatic agreements regarding the land and State of Israel, and directs attention to such studies as Lapide, *Last Three Popes*; Boadt and Camillo, eds., *John Paul II*; and Fischer, *Päpste und Juden*. I note in addition Fisher and Klenicki, eds., *Saint for Shalom*; as well as Kluger and Di Simone, *Pope and I*; and Krajewski, "Reception of *Nostra Aetate*." For an unsettling discussion of pre-war Polish Catholic negative understandings of ongoing Judaism, see Łysiak, "Rabbinic Judaism." Although Łysiak finds much derogatory and ill-informed material, she points also to an exceptional figure, Tadeusz Zaderecki. See also the excellent, and fair, presentation of Poland during the Holocaust—detailing the *incredible* suffering of Polish Catholics, the *far greater* suffering of Polish Jews, the fact that Polish Catholics saved many Jews, and the presence of significant anti-Semitism or anti-Judaism among Polish Catholics—in P. Hayes, *Why?*, 250–58.

23. E. H. Flannery, "Israel, Jerusalem, and the Middle East," 85. Flannery points out, "Under Jordanian occupation from 1948 to 1967 no Jew could visit the Old City or the Western Wall; a road was built through the most sacred of Jewish cemeteries; tombstones were desecrated; all synagogues were converted to secular use or razed; and a Hilton-type hotel was built atop the Mount of Olives" ("Israel, Jerusalem, and the Middle East," 83).

24. Novak et al., "*Dabru Emet*," xviii. David Berger points out that Jewish-Christian dialogue does not seem to be having much of a positive impact with regard to the land, despite the land's central theological status in Judaism. Berger states: "Christian attitudes toward Israel in the current crisis [in the year 2002] have once again raised serious questions in Jewish minds about the value of dialogue. Support for Israel in the organized Christian community comes primarily from those who eschew theological dialogue and support conversionary efforts aimed at Jews. Churches and organizations most involved in dialogue are far more ambivalent and even hostile. The very habits of mind that produce the dialogical imperative—the desire to redress grievances and achieve justice for the historically oppressed—produce sympathy for Palestinians. In the view of most Jews (myself decidedly included), this sympathy has led to an inversion of morality in which mass murder in response to an extraordinary peace proposal, education toward *jihad* in the bloodiest sense, and mass dissemination of the vilest antisemitism evoke next to no protest or diminution of sympathy" (Berger, "*Dabru Emet*," 398; cf. Berger, "Jewish-Christian Relations," 356–64). See also Spector,

accounting for the fact that Jesus, as the Messiah of Israel, has fulfilled the covenants, so that all peoples are called to union with him in the inaugurated kingdom. The fulfilled covenantal land includes the whole world, in accord with Paul's understanding that "the promise to Abraham and his descendants" meant that "they should inherit the whole world" (Rom 4:13). Christ's fulfillment of the covenant of land entails a transformation, given that believers, awaiting the fullness of the cosmic new creation, have already "come to Mount Zion and to the city of the living God, the heavenly Jerusalem" (Heb 12:22; cf. Heb 11:16).[25] At the same time, Christians must take into consideration the impact of Christian persecution of the ongoing Jewish people over the centuries, which has produced "invincible ignorance" (which I will describe below) about Jesus' identity as the Messiah. In this light, I make a Christian case for holding that the Jewish people as a whole still possess a covenantal obligation to dwell in and govern the land and should be supported in obeying this obligation, although Christians recognize that the land promise has been eschatologically fulfilled in Christ.[26]

Evangelicals and Israel, which offers a broad background (including seventeenth- and eighteenth-century British sources) combined with a special focus on the years of the presidency of George W. Bush. Spector notes that in 2005, three-quarters of American evangelicals "expressed favorable or very favorable attitudes about the Jewish people," whereas American Jews largely distrusted and disliked evangelicals (*Evangelicals and Israel*, viii). Among the reasons Spector explores for American evangelicals' love of Israel are: shared love for the God of Israel; awe at God's enduring covenant with his chosen people; remorse for how Christians treated the Jews over the centuries; a belief that God has promised to judge all peoples by how they treated his Jewish people; a sense of broad spiritual kinship between Christians and Jews; a sense of indebtedness to the Jewish people; gratitude to have been grafted into Israel in Christ; a belief that God blesses those who bless the descendants of Abraham; concerns about Islam; and end-time prophecies regarding the restoration of Israel to Zion, the second coming of Christ, and the millennial kingdom. See also Hummel, "*His Land*"; and Sandmel, "Philosemitism," 406.

25. See Ounsworth, *Joshua Typology*, 116. See also Schenck, *Cosmology and Eschatology in Hebrews*, though I disagree with Schenck's claim that "it was not a long journey from the author [of Hebrews]'s thought to the Gnosticism of the following century" (184)—since (as I note) according to Hebrews Christ is Creator and the "heavenly" country does not void creation. Schenck suggests that Hebrews's eschatology (which, theologically speaking, must be integrated with the other New Testament portraits) involves a disembodied heavenly kingdom, but I do not see how this interpretation of Hebrews can ultimately be correct, given that Christ is risen in his glorified flesh.

26. See also McGarry, "Land of Israel." I can agree with McGarry that "Christians should neither delegitimize nor sacralize the State of Israel," and I can agree, at least in a certain sense, when he argues that there is no need for Christians "to provide a warrant for Israel's political legitimacy on theological grounds" ("Land of Israel," 219, 223). It is clear that McGarry supports a two-state solution, as do I. He rightly rejects attempts to delegitimize of the State of Israel on theological grounds, such as by the claim that "most contemporary Israelis are not living according to the covenant" or

INTRODUCTION

As a last step in my Christian Israelology, chapter 7 addresses the Davidic kingship, in light of Catholic ecclesiology and, specifically, papal abuse of temporal power. My main question is why God ties himself so tightly to institutions in which power is wielded by fallen humans. According to 2 Samuel 7, God bound himself to the Davidic royal line. Through the prophet Nathan, God tells David, "When your days are fulfilled and you lie down with your fathers, I will raise up your offspring after you, who shall come forth from your body, and I will establish his kingdom. He shall build a house for my name, and I will establish the throne of his kingdom for ever" (2 Sam 7:12–13). God committed himself in this manner even though David had "liquidated Saul's family" and would soon fall into "an independence of the law, a personal lust . . . that results in adultery and murder."[27] Indebted again to David Novak, and in light of Pope Pius IX's forcible removal in 1858 of a Jewish boy from his loving parents on the grounds that he had been secretly baptized as an infant by his nanny, I argue that the Davidic kings' failures in the exercise of divinely granted power can assist in understanding the failures of divinely authorized Catholic leaders.[28] The success of God's covenantal plan through the Davidic kingship, like the success of God's working through the successors of Peter, does not depend upon human sinlessness but rather depends upon the sinless Davidic Messiah whose reign, Christians believe, has been inaugurated in a form that invites our participation but can be obscured by our sins.

In these seven chapters, I do not directly engage the Rabbinic Sages but instead allow that tradition to be mediated to me by numerous Jewish thinkers from the past one hundred years who themselves, in various ways, have been engaged in Jewish-Christian dialogue.[29] Although I give ample

---

by the claim that "Jews lost their right to the land when they denied their Messiah" ("Land of Israel," 223). For further discussion, he directs attention to March, *Israel*; and Merkley, *Christian Attitudes*.

27. Halpern, *David's Secret Demons*, xvi, 6.

28. Cases similar to that of Edgardo Mortara took place after World War II and had a more just outcome. For example, two small Jewish boys were given by their parents to a Catholic convent shortly before the parents were sent to their deaths in a Nazi concentration camp. The boys were baptized by the laywoman who adopted them, who took them to Spain rather than giving them up to their Jewish relatives. Fortunately the Catholic Church helped to ensure that they were returned. John Connelly discusses this case in *From Enemy to Brother*, 234–35, drawing upon E. H. Flannery, "Finaly Case." In addition, as a young priest in Poland, Karol Wojtyła helped to return adopted Jewish children to their Jewish families. See also P. D. Jones, "Finaly Affair." More broadly (involving a Jewish couple who in the 1950s adopted the baby of a Catholic woman, who then demanded the return of the baby, a demand that the Jewish couple resisted), see Glenn, "'Kidnapping' of Hilda McCoy."

29. An important contemporary Jewish thinker who is largely missing from this

space to describing their views, I should reiterate that I am not trying to provide a theological account of the doctrine of Israel that both Jews and Christians could accept. On the contrary, as indicated above, my engagement with the doctrine of Israel is thoroughly Christian, while at the same time affirming (in the words of Walter Moberly) that "the negative attitudes toward Jewishness and Judaism that have generally characterized Christianity are ... perversions and distortions of [Christianity]."[30]

Fortunately, an explicitly Christian perspective is what thinkers such as Novak, Soloveitchik, and Jon D. Levenson would hope for from a Christian theological work. Soloveitchik famously warned against attempts to produce a fusion of Judaism and Christianity, something that arguably would be neither Judaism nor Christianity. He feared that "dialogue" could be a screen for people seeking to unburden themselves of the revelation that God has given. He urged his fellow Jews not to "trade favors pertaining to fundamental matters of faith," and he insisted upon the necessity and goodness of "believing with great passion in the ultimate truthfulness of our views."[31]

---

volume is Peter Ochs. For reflections on his *Another Reformation*, see my review in *International Journal of Systematic Theology*. I think that Ochs's project works better in practice than in theory—which indeed is what he himself might expect—insofar as gathering together for shared scriptural reading does indeed nourish friendships that foster a more adequate view of the "religious other." Ochs movingly offers examples of "the non-conventional communication that SR [Scriptural Reasoning] may foster. To experience this kind of communication, readers would need to experience several sessions of formational SR study" (Ochs, *Religion without Violence*, 44). He also rightly insists upon the incorporation of performative reception (and thus tradition and liturgical practices) within our understanding of Scripture. But Ochs's critique of the place of propositions within religious knowledge strikes me as too sharp. Oddly, while opposing "binarist" outlooks, he offers a firmly "binary" take on religious readers and readings, according to which "monovalent" readers are bad and "polyvalent" readers are good. I recognize, of course, that this binary sometimes is all too accurate, namely when religious persons are stuck in a stance of hatred and persecution vis-à-vis the religious other. Ochs deserves thanks for attempting to stem *"the global increase in specifically religion-related violent conflict"* (*Religion without Violence*, 154). For the complexities of Ochs's position, rooted in a Wittgensteinian denial that there is "a single conventional language" within which propositions may accurately be understood in a monovalent or literalistic way (Ochs especially has in view situations where trauma or "nonpeace" is present)—and rooted at the same time in a rejection of "radical skepticism"—see also Ochs, "To Love Tanakh," (quotations at 82, 85). For reflection upon the place of propositional truth in divine revelation, in light of Vatican II's *Dei Verbum*, see my *Introduction to Vatican II*, especially chapter 1.

30. Moberly, *Old Testament of the Old Testament*, 170.

31. Soloveitchik, *Confrontation and Other Essays*, 85–115, at 110. See also the similar concerns of David Berger in his "Revisiting 'Confrontation.'" Berger gives two examples. First, he himself was criticized for not supporting Jewish rabbis' participation in an interfaith prayer service held in St. Patrick's Cathedral's main sanctuary. Berger was concerned that to do so would be to suggest, however implicitly, that worship of

INTRODUCTION

I very much agree with him. There are truth-claims that Jews cannot relinquish without ceasing to be Jews, and there are truth-claims that Christians cannot relinquish without ceasing to be Christians. If these truth-claims are controversial, this cannot be helped.[32] As Hans Küng puts it, "That the Jews should surrender their unbelief in regard to Jesus seems just as unlikely as that the Christians should abandon their belief in him. For if they did so, the Jews would no longer be Jews, or the Christians Christians."[33]

Although this book is a work of Catholic theology, I also make frequent use of Protestant theology and biblical scholarship, in grateful recognition of the many notable contributions that Protestant scholars have made to contemporary Christian Israelology. By and large, Eastern Orthodox theologians have not been as active in Christian-Jewish dialogue as have Protestants. Over the centuries, Orthodox Christians were generally as responsible for anti-Jewish oppression, pogroms, and blood libels as were Catholics and Protestants; but the Holocaust was largely enacted by Catholics and Protestants.[34] Eastern Orthodoxy has not been entirely absent

---

Jesus was acceptable as a religious practice. Second, a Jewish scholar criticized a Catholic document for maintaining that at the end of time, Jews would recognize that Jesus is the Messiah. But this is a fundamental Catholic belief, one which, as Berger points out, "parallels Rabbi Soloveitchik's assertion of the eschatological confirmation of Judaism" ("Revisiting 'Confrontation,'" 390). In *Jewish-Christian Dialogue*, 6–9, David Novak argues that Soloveitchik should have made clearer that Jewish doctrines and morality can be defended in dialogue with non-Jews rather than solely in intra-Jewish discussion, and Berger—if I understand him correctly—agrees with this point. For Soloveitchik and Heschel on Jewish-Christian dialogue, see Morgan, "Jewish Perspectives," 7–13; Kimelman, "Rabbis Joseph B. Soloveitchik"; and Sherwin and Kasimow, eds., *No Religion Is an Island*. For further discussion, see Breger, "Reassessment of Rav Soloveitchik's Essay."

32. Hruby holds in his "Jewish-Christian Dialogue" that "real contact with Judaism" requires "*full and unreserved recognition of the other party's legitimate theological and existential autonomy*" (88). If this simply means affirming ongoing Judaism as a positive and "active spiritual force" ("Jewish-Christian Dialogue," 89), then Christians certainly should do this, without muting the claim that Jesus is the Messiah. To my mind, it is the question of whether Jesus is the Messiah of Israel and universal Savior that explains why, as Hruby complains, "people fear that the whole structure of Christian doctrine will be made unsafe if attempts are made to do justice to Judaism and recognize it as a theological factor and a valid form of spirituality in the present" ("Jewish-Christian Dialogue," 90).

33. Küng, "Introduction," 14. For a richly detailed treatment that accords with my perspective, see Lévy, *Jewish Church*, chapter 2.

34. See for example Margaroni, "Blood Libel"; and, in the same volume, Surh, "Duty and Ambivalence." Similarly, Paul A. Shapiro shows that in the 1920s and 1930s the Romanian fascists (the "Iron Guard") "moved beyond traditional religious antisemitism to promote economic, cultural, and racial antisemitism and violence against Jews," but did so without "abandon[ing] religious belief, Orthodox symbolism, and spirituality"

from Jewish-Christian dialogue, as can be seen for instance in the volume *Orthodox Christians and Jews on Continuity and Renewal*.[35] Even so, John Pawlikowski is correct when he states that "[Eastern] Orthodox Christians in the main have not bought into the new template on Christian-Jewish relations."[36] Orthodox scholars are present in my book, but not nearly as present as they were in earlier volumes of this dogmatic series.

Let me mention, however, a notable exception to this rule: the Russian Orthodox (and perhaps, at the end of his life, Roman Catholic) thinker Vladimir Solovyov. In the late nineteenth century, Solovyov praised the Jewish people for their adherence to Torah, while he bemoaned Christian lack of adherence to the new commandment of charity. He states, "The Jews have always treated us in the Jewish way [in accord with Torah]; we Christians, on the contrary, have not learned to this day to adopt a Christian attitude to the Jews. They have never transgressed their religious law in relation to us; we, on the other hand, have always broken the commandments of the Christian religion in relation to them."[37] He points out that Christians

---

(Shapiro, "Faith, Murder, Resurrection," 136). Moving backward in time, Robert Louis Wilken notes that John Chrysostom's deeply anti-Jewish *Discourses Against Judaizing Christians* "were excerpted in Byzantine times and incorporated in the Byzantine liturgy for Holy Week. . . . The eight homilies were translated into Russian in the eleventh century at a time when Jewish homes were being plundered and the first pogrom in Russian history was taking place in the grand duchy of Kiev under Prince Vladimir" (Wilken, *John Chrysostom and the Jews*, 162).

35. See Lowe, ed., *Orthodox Christians and Jews*. See also Heldt, "Brief History"; Heldt, "Bibliography of Dialogue." See, however, Kessler, *Introduction to Jewish-Christian Dialogue*, 9: "The Orthodox Church . . . did not participate in these theological revisions [undertaken by Catholics and Protestants since the 1960s vis-à-vis the Jewish people and Judaism], and still have not done so."

36. Pawlikowski, "Fifty Years of Christian-Jewish Dialogue," 100.

37. Solovyov, "Jews and the Christian Problem," 105. Solovyov recognizes the spiritual fecundity of ongoing Judaism, even though he still believes, as a Christian, that the Jewish people should embrace Jesus as the Messiah. He remarks: "Jews are deeply religious and devoted to their God to the point of self-sacrifice" ("Jews and the Christian Problem," 108; cf. 112). Unfortunately, he thinks that the spiritual richness, and the bonds of unity that Jews feel toward each other, coexist with a "materialism" that he connects with "national egoism" and "greediness" ("Jews and the Christian Problem," 116). However, it should be stressed that for Solovyov, "materialism" is not in itself a vice, since he connects it with the incarnation. He observes: "If we now consider the Jews' striving for the materialization of the divine principle and their care to purify and sanctify bodily nature we shall easily understand why it was that the Jewish people presented the most suitable material environment for the incarnation of the divine Word. . . . Clearly, this sacred materialism of the Jews does not in any way conflict with, but on the contrary serves as a direct complement to, their other two qualities—the deep religious feeling and the energy of human self-consciousness and independent activity. . . . The religious materialism of the Jews springs not from disbelief but from

make all sorts of excuses for the lack of charity shown by Christians toward the Jewish people over the course of history. Some Christians, he observes, consider the Jewish people to be under the self-inflicted curse of Matthew 27:25 ("His blood be on us and on our children") and therefore insist that Christians must subjugate Jews. He responds: "That blood is *the blood of redemption*. And surely the clamour of human malice is not strong enough to drown the words of divine forgiveness: 'Father, forgive them; for they know not what they do.'"³⁸ Besides, if the Jewish people as a whole were cursed, then the apostles (as Jews) would have been under that very curse. Solovyov concludes with pointed implications: "Does it not seem striking that *in the name of Christ* we should condemn all Jewry to which Christ Himself indisputably belongs?"³⁹

II. Christian Inaugurated Eschatology and Ongoing Judaism

It is necessary at the outset to outline my view of the relationship between Christian inaugurated eschatology and ongoing Judaism. This relationship has a large bearing upon my approach in the chapters that follow.

As a Christian, I believe that Jesus Christ has inaugurated the kingdom of God and fulfilled *and reconfigured* Israel's covenants around himself by his cross and resurrection and by pouring out his Spirit.⁴⁰ The fact that Israel's covenants have been fulfilled and transformed means that these covenants are no longer meant to be observed in their original form. Thus, Christ incorporates Gentiles into the messianically transformed people of Abraham,

---

a superabundance of faith eager for its fulfilment, not from the weakness but from the strength and energy of the human spirit which, unafraid of being defiled by matter, purifies it and uses it for its own ends" ("Jews and the Christian Problem," 115).

38. Solovyov, "Jews and the Christian Problem," 107.

39. Solovyov, "Jews and the Christian Problem," 108. He adds, "If we acknowledge Christ as God, we must acknowledge that the Jews are a *God-bearing* race. For the death of Jesus the Romans as well as the Jews are to blame; His birth belongs solely to God and to Israel. It is said that the Jews are always the enemies of Christianity; but the anti-Christian movement of the last few centuries is headed not by Jews, not by Semites, but by Christians of the Aryan race [Solovyov has in view German thinkers]" ("Jews and the Christian Problem," 108).

40. See for example Dunn, *Jesus Remembered*, 890; R. B. Hays, *Moral Vision of the New Testament*, 27. Bruce Chilton and Jacob Neusner rightly comment with regard to Christ and the eschatological outpouring of the Spirit: "the underlying consensus among early Christians, that hearing the gospel of Jesus with faith endowed one with the spirit and its power, is what unified them and put them apart from other groups" (Chilton and Neusner, *Judaism in the New Testament*, 101).

but he does not command his Church to dwell in the land of Canaan.⁴¹ Christ fulfills the Torah (Matt 5:17), but he does not command his Church to observe the Torah's commandments about the Jubilee or about the animal sacrifices in the temple. Instead, Jewish and Gentile believers in Christ live out the covenantal promises and commandments in their new messianic form, that is, as fulfilled and transformed in the inaugurated kingdom of the Messiah, as for instance through the sacraments of the Church.

Yet, such an understanding of inaugurated eschatology seems utterly to devalue the ongoing people of Israel, the Jewish people who do not recognize Jesus as the Messiah. For if the Jewish Messiah has come and has transformed the Jewish people's covenantal promises and commandments, there seems to be no place for an ongoing Jewish people that does not recognize that its Messiah has come and that therefore continues on with the covenantal promises and commandments in their original form. If so, then Christian Israelology would entail that there is no theological space, from a Christian perspective, for ongoing Judaism.

Clearly, that cannot be right. Even in light of Jesus' inauguration of the messianic kingdom, Paul insists that the Jewish people according to the flesh remain God's beloved, elect people (Rom 11:11–12, 28–29). God could never forget or abandon his chosen people, the descendants of Abraham, Isaac, and Jacob.⁴² What else, then, does Christian inaugurated eschatology allow Christians to say theologically about the ongoing Jewish people?

From a Christian perspective, a decisive point is that the covenantal fulfillment and transformation in the Messiah is not a *negation* of the covenants God made with the Jews. Let me explain what I mean by "negation." Theoretically, Christ could have come and, exercising his messianic authority, simply cancelled the Abrahamic and Sinai covenants. In fact, however, in accord with God's promises that his covenants would endure forever, Jesus proclaims his followers to be true children of Abraham (Matt 8:11) and he maintains that not even "an iota" of the law will pass away until the final judgment (Matt 5:18). Christ does not dissolve or negate the covenantal promises and commandments; rather, he fulfills them by inaugurating their

---

41. The land promises in the Old Testament include some that specify clear borders and others that leave the borders ambiguous, potentially spanning the whole world.

42. In preparing this book, I was asked whether "ongoing Jewish people" refers to all ethnic Jews or to believing and practicing Jews. By this phrase, I intend to refer to all people who, by the standards of Rabbinic Judaism, are Jews. This is clearly not limited to believing and practicing Jews, although (just as with respect to Catholics) it is actually believing in God and practicing one's faith that produces spiritual fruit. I concur with Pope Francis who, in his apostolic exhortation *Evangelii Gaudium*, affirms: "God continues to work among the people of the Old Covenant and to bring forth treasures of wisdom which flow from their encounter with his word" (*Evangelii Gaudium*, §249).

eschatological mode of observance. It follows that when reflecting upon the ongoing Jewish people's obedience to the covenants with Abraham and Moses, Christians must begin by acknowledging that such covenants *still exist*. They are fulfilled and transformed, but not negated or cast aside.[43] This is what I mean by a Christian inaugurated eschatology that relies upon fulfillment and transformation. The question, then, is not whether the original covenantal promises and commandments still exist, but rather how (in what mode or modes) they are in force today.

The answer to this question is complicated by the fact that the eschatological kingdom has been inaugurated by Christ, but not consummated. In the consummated kingdom, all will be clear; the perfected eschatological mode of the covenants will be apparent to all. But the inaugurated kingdom is more complex, due to God's providential will to allow it to be still marked by sin and death. On the one hand, the outpouring of the Spirit in the inaugurated kingdom is powerful and fruitful in building up the Church (and all who are interiorly united to the Church through implicit faith) throughout the world. But on the other hand, the Church as the inaugurated kingdom is wounded by continuing sin and division on the part of Christians, who far too often continue to behave in a worldly manner, despite the power of Christ's grace. The inaugurated kingdom, therefore, can be misperceived by others due to the sins of Christians. In God's plan—which never implicates him in sin, but nevertheless permits human sin within the compass of his providential purposes—God permits not only the failure of most Jews to recognize Jesus as the Messiah, but also the failure of most Gentile Christians who "boast[ed] over the branches" (Rom 11:18), that is, over the ongoing Jewish people. The latter failure, bemoaned by Paul, almost immediately scandalized the ongoing Jewish people by standing as a counter-witness of hate-filled abuse rather than Christlike love. God is not to blame for Christians' sins against the ongoing Jewish people, but God has permitted such sins to occur, for reasons that we cannot know but that we can trust are not finally opposed to God's salvific purposes.

As noted above, my view is that Christ's inauguration of his kingdom means that for people who accept Jesus as the Messiah, the Abrahamic covenant of people and land remains in force now solely in its messianic mode, not its original mode.[44] Thus, if there were no legitimate reason today for

---

43. See Francis, *Evangelii Gaudium*, §§247–49. For some of the tensions and possibilities of this perspective, see Soulen, "Priority of the Present."

44. I note that some Christians today propose that Jesus inaugurated the kingdom (or established a covenant) solely for Gentiles. I will discuss this two-covenant position further on in my book (especially in the footnotes), but suffice it to say here that I think this does not make sense—given the New Testament testimony and given that

not recognizing Jesus as the Messiah, then all people would be bound in conscience, on pain of sinning against the Messiah, to observe the Abrahamic covenant in its messianic mode (i.e., in the Church). But as indicated above, and as I will further explain later in this Introduction and in chapters 1 and 6, there are indeed legitimate reasons—from a Christian theological perspective—for why the Jewish people, as a whole (despite the fact of individual conversions), do not recognize Jesus as the Messiah.[45]

These reasons are at least twofold. First, there is the overarching positive "mystery" of God's plan as described in Romans 11, in which God is presented as having a plan and a purpose that serve to explain why "Israel [the Jewish people *as a whole*] failed to obtain what it sought" (Rom 11:7). Christians do not know the inner details of this plan, but we know that "if their rejection means the reconciliation of the world, what will their acceptance mean but life from the dead?" (Rom 11:15). I interpret this verse as indicating that God's plan involves, for positive reasons, the existence of

---

Jesus was the Messiah of Israel. Similarly, other Christians (I am thinking especially of Messianic Jews and of Christian theologians who hold to a Messianic Jewish position or something like it) today propose that Jesus inaugurated the kingdom simply by adding Gentiles onto the unchanged covenants, so that the Jewish Messiah would reign in Jerusalem and the Jewish people would continue to observe Torah and to sacrifice in the temple, while Gentile believers in the Messiah would obey the Noachide commandments and be in certain ways an extension of Israel into the whole world. I will discuss this Messianic Jewish position further on in my book (again especially in the footnotes). Suffice it to say here that in my view, this position fails to measure up to the New Testament testimony (and to the Church's testimony) to Jesus' messianic fulfillment and reconfiguration of Torah and temple around himself.

45. I recognize that, as Terrence Merrigan says, "'dialogue' is perhaps the most ambiguous term in the vocabulary that has developed around the challenge to religions posed by globalization and pluralization"—but as Merrigan goes on to explain, the term should not be abandoned, not least because it indicates "a determination to do justice to the religious other in their particularity" (Merrigan, "Introduction," 2–3). Ellen T. Charry offers a helpful account of the attitude and goals that pertain to Jewish-Christian "dialogue": "Interreligious dialogue seeks a path to mutual theological acceptance rather than theological hegemony. Further, the hope is to understand one's own theological commitments better through engagement with the other. The possibility of conversion is always possible, of course, but that is not the goal. Here, one comes to the table to learn from one's interlocutor, not to defeat her. It is an exchange of gifts, not a war of words" (Charry, "Doctrine of God," 559). For a defense of the continuing place of Jewish-Christian dialogue within interreligious dialogue (rather than over-emphasizing the uniqueness of Jewish-Christian dialogue), see Pawlikowski, "Uniqueness of the Christian-Jewish Dialogue"—although Pawlikowski takes this point in some directions that strike me as troubling, for example in the way he distinguishes (indebted to Peter Phan) between "Christological symbols" and "the religious symbols of Judaism" in "two distinctive paths to an understanding of human salvation" (8). See also Pontifical Council, "Dialogue in Truth and Charity"; as well as the discussion of Judaism in Kärkkäinen, *Doing the Work of Comparative Theology*.

ongoing Judaism until the coming of Christ in glory, that is, until the end of time.⁴⁶

This first reason (God's plan) of itself suffices for why, even after the coming of the Messiah, Christians cannot expect Jesus' messianic status to be recognizable to the Jewish people *as a whole* prior to the eschaton, with the crucial correlative point that Christians should therefore assume that the covenants in their original mode remain legitimately in force for the Jewish people as a whole despite the fact that the Messiah has indeed come and has fulfilled and transformed the covenants. But there is also a second reason, one to which I will appeal relatively often in this book. To use technical theological language, due to Christian "boasting" (cf. Rom 11:18) or persecution of the Jewish people, the ignorance of Jesus' true identity manifested by the ongoing Jewish people (with exceptions of course) is "invincible" because the name of Jesus has been associated indelibly with acts of hatred toward the Jewish people rather than with love.⁴⁷

In sum: the Messiah has come and inaugurated his kingdom in which the covenants are transformed, but because the ongoing Jewish people for legitimate reasons do not recognize Jesus as the Christ, Christians should affirm that the ongoing Jewish people rightly continue to observe their still existing covenants in their original mode. As the Catholic theologian Guy Mansini points out, ongoing Judaism is (from a Christian perspective) not so much a "non-Christian religion" as it is the religion of God's ongoing Jewish people who believe that the Messiah has not come and who obey God's Torah in accordance with this belief. Since this is so, then as Mansini concludes, "Insofar as there is no culpable rejection of the gospel, therefore, we may suppose that God remains faithful to the covenants with Abraham and Moses, and that practicing the Jewish religion is pleasing in his sight and rewarded with grace and blessings."⁴⁸

---

46. See Byrne, *Romans*, 346: "the fact that 'life' follows upon rather than precedes the 'acceptance' of Israel suggests an eschatological reference—the general resurrection as a prelude to the final consummation."

47. This is the case even if, as Jonathan Elukin says, "Jews of early modern Europe could look back on centuries of remembered persecution and expulsion, but they also apparently remembered centuries of residence and attachment to their European homes" (Elukin, *Living Together, Living Apart*, 138). Persecution was not the full story, though in some form and to some degree it was generally present; there were also, in many times and places, Christian "habits of a pragmatic tolerance" (Elukin, *Living Together, Living Apart*, 138). I grant as a matter of course that during the past two millennia there was a significant diversity in the experiences (and self-understandings) of both Jews and Christians.

48. Mansini, *Ecclesiology*, 273.

The above viewpoint can be misunderstood, and so let me say a little more in response to potential misunderstandings. First, it may seem that I am saying that, although subjectively speaking the Jewish people believe the covenants still to be in force, objectively speaking these covenants have in fact been negated and discarded. In other words, the Jewish people may subjectively believe that they have a covenantal obligation to dwell in the land (for example), but in objective fact their covenantal obligation has been *cancelled*, so that what once was the promise of the land is now the promise of no land. But what such a position misses is that, as I have noted, the covenants have not been cancelled by Christ. They are fulfilled and transformed, but they are not cancelled. Objectively speaking, the covenantal promise about the land has been messianically fulfilled and transformed, but, at the same time, the covenantal promise remains—*objectively speaking*—perfectly intact.

Second, it may seem that I am saying that, since the ongoing Jewish people are mistaken about Jesus, Christian triumphalism over the ongoing Jewish people is in fact warranted. In other words, ongoing Judaism is a mere mistake, and when Christ comes in glory, Jews will become Christians. But in fact, the mystery of God's plan for Jews and Gentiles reaches to a much deeper level. Proper Christian understanding of the eschatological consummation involves a reality so glorious that it is presently unfathomable, even if known in part. As 1 John 3:2 puts it, "we are God's children now; it does not yet appear what we shall be, but we know that when he appears we shall be like him, for we shall see him as he is."[49] Equally, Paul says that "our knowledge is imperfect and our prophecy is imperfect. . . . For now we see in a mirror dimly, but then face to face. Now I know in part; then I shall understand fully, even as I have been fully understood" (1 Cor 13:9, 12). The point for my purposes is that it is not adequate to say that in the consummated kingdom "Jews will become Christians." This way of putting it suggests that Christians will be unchanged, while Jews will simply convert. But both Christians and Jews will be radically changed at the consummation of all things, so that neither "Christianity" nor "Judaism" will remain as we know them. Although it is true that Jesus will be recognized by all persons as the Messiah (a significant point indeed!), this does not mean what it would mean if we were dealing simply with an earthly conversion.

Third, it may seem that I am saying that because Christianity embraces the inaugurated kingdom, Christianity is "spiritual" and Judaism is "carnal." But in fact, I hold that Catholic Christianity is an embodied (carnal) religion no less than Judaism is. In Christ, such realities as the exodus, Torah,

---

49. See D. M. Smith, *First, Second, and Third John*, 80.

temple, and land are not simply spiritualized or interiorized, although there is some spiritualization as befits Christ's drawing all peoples into the divine life itself. For example, to say that Christ is the eschatological temple does not mean that Christ is simply a spiritualized temple. After all, his body and his mystical Body are nothing if not bodily, both now and everlastingly! Eucharistic worship is profoundly "carnal" in the sense of being an embodied participation in Christ's embodied sacrifice.

Of course, interior holiness—belief in the divine redeemer, hope in his plan of salvation, and love for God and neighbor—is needed for both Jews and Christians. Christians believe that the promised outpouring of the Spirit has occurred through Jesus Christ. But this does not mean that Jews, awaiting the Messiah in faith (and thus legitimately not recognizing Jesus as the Messiah), lack union with the Spirit. Only a culpable rejection of Jesus would render Jewish life "carnal" in the negative sense. Paul often accuses Christians of being carnal in this negative sense, as when he warns the Corinthians: "For the mind that is set on the flesh is hostile to God; it does not submit to God's law, indeed it cannot; and those who are in the flesh cannot please God" (1 Cor 8:7–8).

Fourth, it may seem that I am saying that since God's plan includes ongoing Judaism—and since Christians should affirm the goodness of ongoing Judaism's efforts to obey its covenantal obligations—it follows that the conversion of Jews to Christianity should be discouraged by Christians.[50] But in fact, I hold that Jesus really is the Messiah. Embracing Jesus as the Messiah is always salutary, for Jewish people as well as for all people. Why would it not be, since it is true? I believe that Jesus, the Jewish Messiah, is the mediator of all salvation and the source of the Holy Spirit who transforms our fallen hearts; and I believe in the salvific power of union with Jesus Christ in his Church, with its holy teaching and holy sacraments. These facts do not, however, negate the truth that God intends there to be both ongoing Judaism and Christianity until the eschatological consummation, that is, until "life from the dead" (Rom 11:15). While I will discuss the significance of "implicit" faith further on in this Introduction—and while I will also later take up the highly charged topic of Christian "mission" and

---

50. On the issue of conversion, see Rabbi Charles David Isbell's remark (in a sermon preached while presiding over the entrance of two Gentiles, Pat and Roger, into the Jewish covenant) that "non-Jewish partners wishing to join us in worshipping the one true God are to be welcomed into the household of faith. Our conversion ceremony highlights the best-known of such stories, introducing us to Ruth, the quintessential 'convert' who marries a nice Jewish boy and becomes the great grandmother of King David himself" (Isbell, *Sermons*, 69).

"proselytizing"—the point here is that I am not discouraging the explicit embrace of Jesus by Jewish persons.

Fifth, it may seem that I am saying that eschatological fulfillment in Christ renders worthless Torah (or temple or land) in its form prior to Christ.[51] I do not think that the eschatological consummation will involve the Messiah literally reigning on the Temple Mount in the city of Jerusalem or teaching Torah observance such as the food laws or the sacrificial cult. How then does this not render Torah, temple, and land everlastingly worthless? Let me offer an example from Christian faith. In the resurrection accounts in the New Testament, Jesus is shown to possess a glorified body. His body is in continuity with his earthly body, but it exists in a radically different, glorified mode. His glorified body is unlike his earthly body in notable ways. Yet, his glorified body does not negate the body that he had in his earthly life, because it truly is that body, now glorified. In other words, again, negation is not the proper way of understanding eschatological fulfillment. Just because Christ has fulfilled Torah and temple (and land), this does not mean that God has negated these elements of the life of his chosen people.

---

51. Christians believe that "through the New Covenant [in Christ] the Abrahamic covenant has obtained that universality for all peoples which was originally intended in the call of Abram (cf. Gen 12:1–3)" (Pontifical Commission, "'Gifts and the Calling of God,'" §33). Another problem, however, is that historical-critical scholars now consider it doubtful that in its original context—as distinct from its Christian canonical context and from its meaning according to earlier Jewish exegetes such as Nahum Sarna and Umberto Cassuto—"the purpose of God's call of Abraham [Genesis 12:1–3] is to bless the nations" (Moberly, *Theology of Genesis*, 148). For Moberly, the likely meaning of Genesis 12:1–3 is that Abraham (and Israel) "will become an object of admiration for others" (*Theology of Genesis*, 151). Moberly here aims to affirm the permanence and intrinsic goodness of God's election of Abraham/Israel, not to contradict the truth of the universalizing interpretation. Still another problem is the concern raised about "exclusionary election" in Rolf P. Knierim's *Task of Old Testament Theology*—against which see also Levenson, "Universal Horizon." In response to this problem, Moberly investigates whether the God of Israel acts justly, with particular attention to the commandments regarding ḥērem warfare: see especially Moberly, *Old Testament Theology*, chapter 2. See also, for study of violent texts in Deuteronomy, Joshua, and the Qur'an (and their history of reception), Jenkins, *Laying Down the Sword*. The justice of Israel's God is rejected by Warrior, "Canaanites, Cowboys, and Indians"; but see Kaminsky, *Yet I Loved Jacob*. For an ambiguous perspective, see Lohr, *Chosen and Unchosen*, especially chapter 6 and Appendix 2: "Ḥerem in the Old Testament: An Overview." Lohr argues that "ḥerem and election are . . . intrinsically linked" (*Chosen and Unchosen*, 225), and he concludes critically that Israel's God is a "God of favorites" without this being ameliorated by a particularly strong reaching out to the nations (*Chosen and Unchosen*, 199).

III. "Invincible Ignorance" and "Implicit Faith"

All the above will need further explication in the chapters that follow, but let me now discuss in more detail what it means to say that Christians over the centuries have scandalized the Jewish people through repeated acts of hatred.[52] Scandal can have powerful consequences, including giving scandalized people the standing that theologians term "invincible ignorance"—with its correlative lack of culpability.

As Gavin D'Costa has noted, the doctrine of invincible ignorance is scripturally grounded. Relevant passages in this regard include Luke 12:47-48, James 4:17, 1 Timothy 1:13, Acts 3:17, Acts 17:30, and Romans 10:14. In Luke 12:47-48, for example, Jesus compares a "servant who knew his master's will" with a servant "who did not know" his master's will. The latter's acting against the will of the master does not result in severe punishment, because he is excused by not knowing the master's will. The notion of "invincible" ignorance adds the element that the servant "who did not know" was not at fault for not knowing—since if he were at fault then he would deserve just as much punishment as the servant who did know. If it is possible to inquire and to find out the truth easily, then one has "vincible" ignorance, for which one is culpable. For example, if I neglect to look at speed limit signs and do not know that the speed limit in a particular residential area is thirty miles per hour, my ignorance does not prevent me from deserving a speeding ticket for going sixty miles per hour.

From a Catholic perspective, there are a wide range of cases of "invincible ignorance." Catholics believe, for instance, that Jesus founded one Church (the inaugurated kingdom) and this Church subsists in the Catholic Church, even if other churches and ecclesiastical communities enjoy an intensive participation in ecclesiality through such things as baptism and Scripture (in the case of Protestants) or are fully Churches though not with the needed element of communion with Rome (in the case of the Orthodox).[53] There are reasons why Protestants are often "invincibly ignorant" of the Catholic Church's identity. The phrase denotes the fact that they legitimately "do not know," which bears upon the standing of such persons

---

52. In this book, I attend to the wrongs done by Catholics to the Jewish people, without denying that Catholics did many wrongs to other people as well (or, for that matter, that non-Catholics wronged Catholics!). Martin K. Hopkins, OP remarks, "It is a fact that all persons deemed heretics or apostates by the medieval Church authorities were treated as enemies of the state, and the treatment was generally harsh" (Hopkins, "Jewish-Catholic Relations," 18). I consider Catholic abuse directed toward Jews to be a uniquely enduring and vicious reality.

53. On this point, see Vatican Council II, *Lumen Gentium* §§13, 15. See also Bullivant, "*Sine Culpa?*."

in God's eyes. James 4:17 states, "Whoever knows what is right and fails to do it, for him it is a sin." It is not a sin for a person not to do "what is right" when he or she, for legitimate reasons, does not know that it is right. On non-culpable (because it is invincible) ignorance, Thomas Aquinas states: "it is not imputed as a sin to man, if he fails to know what he is unable to know. Consequently ignorance of such like things is called *invincible*, because it cannot be overcome by study."[54] Not surprisingly given its presence in Scripture and Aquinas, D'Costa finds that this doctrine also "was applied by many of the early Fathers."[55] Invincible (or non-culpable) ignorance is explicitly applied to the Jewish people in Acts 3:17 ("I know that you acted in ignorance, as did also your rulers") and to the Gentiles in Acts 17:30 ("The times of ignorance God overlooked, but now he commands all men everywhere to repent").

Some Christians, however, worry that the doctrine of invincible ignorance, when applied to knowledge about Jesus Christ, will undermine Christ's identity as the universal Savior. In response to this concern, it is necessary to appreciate the possibility of "implicit" faith in Christ. Instructed by Romans 10:9–10 and many other such passages, Catholics affirm that all who are saved come to salvation through faith in Christ.[56] Yet, this faith may be explicit or implicit. In Hebrews 11, many people prior to Christ are depicted as having saving faith without explicitly knowing Christ. Hebrews 11:6 suggests that the faith that "pleases" God, in other words that draws

---

54. Thomas Aquinas, *Summa theologiae* I-II, q. 76, a. 2.

55. D'Costa, *Vatican II*, 63.

56. See CDF, *Dominus Iesus*. See the helpful defense of this declaration offered (within a volume of generally critical responses) by Robert P. Imbelli, "Reaffirmation of the Christic Center"; as well as Imbelli's *Rekindling the Christic Imagination*. The fact that Christ is the universal Savior means that there is no salvation outside him—that is, outside union with him in some way. Biblical passages cited in this regard (by *Lumen Gentium* and *Ad Gentes* at Vatican II, and throughout the Catholic tradition) include Mark 16:16, John 3:5, and 1 Corinthians 9:16. But the Church's doctrinal development on this matter recognized invincible ignorance and implicit faith: see F. Sullivan, *Salvation outside the Church?*; Louis Capéran, *Salut des infidels*. See the discussion in D'Costa, *Vatican II*, 62–63. See also the remarks of Eugene Korn: "If the universal significance of Jesus is freed from any connotation of conversionary mission 'to' the Jews, this theological point seems a strictly internal matter of Catholic doctrine. Of course, it is acutely interesting for students of rational theology and logic to observe how Catholic thinkers approach the paradox of Jesus' universal significance and the enduring legitimacy of Judaism and Jews who continue to deny Jesus' divinity and salvific character. Is this divine paradox a vicious inconsistency to be eliminated or a virtuous mystery that is cause for humble reflection and celebration? Perhaps the Catholic approach to this mystery can guide Jews in dealing with some of our own dilemmas, such as how we can be God's singular chosen people and yet see gentiles also as God's people" (E. B. Korn, "Jewish Response to 'Theological Questions'," 5).

people into right relationship with God, is possible (or at least has been possible) even for those who solely "believe that he exists and that he rewards those who seek him," so long as they do not (for whatever legitimate reason) have a real opportunity to know Christ explicitly. From the Church Fathers onward, the Church has always held that Christ is the sole Savior but that people can be saved without explicit knowledge of him.

Given that for the Jewish people the identity of Jesus has been obscured by Gentile boasting and by polemics and persecutions (which began almost immediately), there is no sense in holding the Jewish people as a whole culpable for rejecting Christian preaching about Jesus' identity. It follows that, although only God knows hearts, Jews certainly can be united to Christ in the same way that they could prior to his coming, namely by faith in the coming Messiah. As noted above, some people take this claim to imply that Christians should now discourage Jews from becoming Christian, but that is not the point that I am making—no more than my Jewish friends would discourage Christians from renouncing the Trinity and converting to Judaism. Nor am I saying that all individual Jewish people are united to Christ by implicit faith; this of course depends upon whether they sincerely practice Jewish faith. Individual Jewish persons embrace Jesus Christ every year, and I affirm the goodness of such conversions.[57] Coming to know Jesus as Lord and Christ is a wondrous thing, just as Simeon proclaims to God in Luke 2:29–30 when he meets the infant Jesus and recognizes him as Israel's Messiah.

As do I, D'Costa connects the condition of invincible ignorance with the "mystery" of "hardening" described by Paul in Romans 11:25.[58] God

---

57. See the contention of C. David Harley in 1987, which may be exaggerated but may also be true (given the spread of Messianic Jewish communities), that "in the past twenty years tens of thousands of Jewish people have accepted Jesus as their Messiah" (Harley, "Church and the Jewish People," 117–18). On the topic of mission, Gerald H. Anderson has argued that "Christians have no special mission to the Jews, but neither is there any special exemption of the Jews from universal Christian mission" (G. H. Anderson, "Church and the Jewish People," 290). I agree, so long as "universal Christian mission" is contextualized within the history of persecution and thus consists in broad witness, rooted in charity and friendship, rather than pressurized proselytism.

58. See D'Costa, *Catholic Doctrines*, 58–62 and 164–66. Philip Cunningham takes a different approach. He argues, "One can only imagine Paul's reactions if somehow he were to learn the ensuing history of relations between Jews and the later gentile Church. His hope that his gentile converts would live such ethical lives that his Jewish kinsfolk would become 'jealous' of God's obvious presence among them failed miserably as history unfolded; indeed Christian conduct often had the opposite effect on Jews. . . . This leads to the conclusion that Paul's explanation for widespread Jewish rejection of apostolic preaching (God's hardening of Jewish hearts to save gentiles) is inapt today. We Christians must admit that historical Jewish resistance to the Good News reflects less on Jewish hearts than on Christian ones" (Cunningham, "Paul's Letters," 155). *Pace*

permits this "mystery" while also ensuring that his Jewish people have not "stumbled so as to fall" (Rom 11:11). Positing a condition of invincible ignorance helps Christians to perceive how God has continued to care for his beloved Jewish people over the past two millennia. As D'Costa points out, paragraph 840 of the *Catechism of the Catholic Church* "is clearly undergirded by the notion of invincible ignorance in the case of the Jewish people."[59] Recall that Paul grants that his fellow Jews who deny Jesus' messianic identity "have a zeal for God," even if "it is not enlightened" due to their belief that observance of Torah will be the path by which God will bring salvation (Rom 10:2). Paul understands the "hardening" to be God's permission of Jewish rejection of the Messiah of Israel, and so it is; but Paul also connects the "hardening" with God's plan for the Gentiles ("until the full number of the Gentiles come in" [Rom 11:25]). With the benefit of hindsight, I think we can also connect it with the *boasting* of the Gentiles over the Jewish people that, despite Paul's urgent warning, sealed the Jewish people's "invincible ignorance" of Jesus' identity.

Of course this does not mean that Jews are unable to reject Jesus (and reject God) by the sins against charity and by the other mortally sinful vices that also often characterize Christians.[60] Nor, again, does it mean that recog-

---

Cunningham, I do not think that Paul was naïve about the sinfulness of his congregations, and if so, then connecting the ongoing "hardening" with Christian boasting against the Jewish people is plausible. Part of the mystery is that even saintly Christians have often failed terribly vis-à-vis the Jewish people. Ellen Charry states, "What Paul calls the hardening of Israel (Rom. 11:7) has been read by the church as Israel's disobedience to God, but here I will argue that it is in fact obedience to God in service to the redemption of the world" (Charry, "Toward Ending Enmity," 151). This seems a stretch, although the point that ongoing Judaism serves God's plan for the redemption of world is surely correct.

59. D'Costa, *Catholic Doctrines*, 166. For a critique of paragraph 840's phrase "God's People of the Old Covenant and the new People of God," see Signer, "Jews and Judaism." For criticism of *Lumen Gentium*'s presentation of ancient Israel and of the phrase "people of God," see A. K. Harkins, "Biblical and Historical Perspectives."

60. For the view that divine revelation in Christ has been so weak, and human freedom so profoundly limited and impaired, that the sin of "unbelief" (i.e., consciously rejecting God's love in Christ) is either impossible or else, at most, may merit mild punishment in preparation for the final universal restoration, see Hart, *That All Shall Be Saved*. For Hart, it can be metaphysically demonstrated what a good Creator God must do. If God does not do what we know he must, then, according to Hart, the only possible conclusion is that God is not God. Yet, the New Testament does not advocate universal salvation, and in fact points firmly in the opposite direction, especially with regard to Satan. In *New Testament: A Translation*, Hart has to translate some words tendentiously, and he must explain away the fact that Jesus Christ failed to make clear the (supposedly) one thing necessary for worshipping God rather than a demon—with the result that for the past sixteen centuries (and longer) almost all Christians have worshiped a demon as "God." Hart, in *That All Shall Be Saved*, condemns all ecclesial mediations

nizing Jesus Christ and receiving his sacramental grace is not a great boon for every believer, a boon that Christians would wish for Jewish people as for all peoples. However, it does mean that Christians went terribly astray, even if for reasons that were understandable, in assuming that the ongoing Jewish people lost contact with the God who loves them and who elected them for himself.[61] In fact, God has his ways of drawing his beloved people close even during the time of the Pauline "mystery," and this closeness can be seen not least in Jewish commitment to the true God over the centuries despite such horrific suffering.

Classically, Thomas Aquinas argued that implicit faith can efficaciously unite people to Christ even if they do not consciously confess Jesus of Nazareth as Lord and Savior.[62] With regard to the Jewish people after

---

of the gospel (whether Orthodox, Catholic, or Protestant) as corrupt and corrupting. Hart indicates, moreover, that Satan's "redemption" proceeds without need of Christ's Pasch, in the sense that the spark of rational self-reflection and willing cannot be extinguished, and so inevitably, in due time, Satan will move toward his true good. Hart's arguments in *That All Shall Be Saved* largely echo Bulgakov, *Bride of the Lamb*, 454–519, but Bulgakov is more embedded within an Orthodox ecclesiastical context. I agree with Thomas Joseph White, OP's cautionary observation that "theologies of *apokatastasis*" neglect the biblical teaching that "persons (to be justified and eventually saved) must be transformed inwardly in their human hearts by grace to the point of renouncing grave sin and of repenting effectively of their attachment to it" (White, "Universal Mediation of Christ," 194). For Hart, following Bulgakov, it is humanly impossible to sin in any way serious enough to stand as a determinative choice against God, but the New Testament and the Church's tradition teach otherwise.

61. In his "Religion and Election," Bruce D. Marshall argues that in discussing the "virtue of religion," Aquinas has in view the infused virtue, not a humanly acquired justice toward God; and Marshall similarly thinks that proper acts of sacrifice require grace. In this context, and also in the context of the fact that God became incarnate as a Jew, God's election of Israel and his giving Israel the Torah—with its specific cultic life—take on their true (graced) significance. In fact, as Marshall shows, the traditional Christian position that the Jewish rites after Christ are "death-dealing" flows from a high view of the Jewish cult; this cult is now practiced in Christ, so that the "Church's sacramental life simply *is* the worship enjoined upon Israel, enacted and thus fulfilled by Christ" ("Religion and Election," 124). This traditional position, Marshall recognizes, has "gone deeply wrong" in its claim that the Jewish people, despite being forever God's chosen people, have for centuries been damning themselves by their practice of the Torah God gave them. The Church today recognizes that this claim cannot be right; and yet the traditional position is correct that the incarnation and redemption have fulfilled and transformed Israel's covenants (Marshall, "Religion and Election," 125). Marshall considers the problem or paradox to be insoluble, but I think that while his valuation of the Jewish people (and of Christ) is on target, there is a way forward along the lines of inaugurated eschatology, invincible ignorance, and implicit faith.

62. On implicit faith see (among other places) Thomas Aquinas, *Summa theologiae* I-II, q. 103, a. 2; I-II, q. 106, a. 1, ad 3; II-II, q. 2, aa. 7–8. For further background, see Torrell, "Saint Thomas."

the coming of Christ, however, Aquinas supposed that the preaching of the gospel made matters perfectly clear. Indeed he thinks "the gospel truth [is] known universally," other than in rare exceptions such as a boy raised by wolves![63] On this view, no Jew could have an excuse for not believing the gospel. Like the later Council of Florence, then, Aquinas assumed that all Jews are in a sinful condition of "unbelief." He was mistaken on this point, in part because he was blind to the profound damage done by Christian boasting over the Jewish people and therefore failed to realize that they could be in a condition of invincible ignorance regarding Christ.[64]

D'Costa recounts the history of Catholic development of doctrine on this matter. Especially once the New World and its countless unevangelized peoples had been discovered, "theologians recognized the exception for Aquinas might be more of a rule."[65] The most important breakthrough came when sixteenth-century Dominican theologians, including Francisco de Vitoria and Bartolomé de Las Casas, argued that persons (specifically, in this case, Native Americans) "may be invincibly ignorant *even after hearing the gospel*, given the scandalous behaviour of those 'preaching' the gospel. . . . Invincible ignorance was not limited to the wolf-child but could operate even during 'missionary activity' to entire peoples."[66] The Conquistadores opened theologians' eyes to the ability of evangelizers to obscure the gospel by their persecution of the intended recipients of the gospel. Closer to the present, the Second Vatican Council, while affirming clearly that Christ is the universal Savior from whom comes the grace of the Holy Spirit, speaks about the salvation of non-Christians and makes clear that such salvation is possible.[67] Without overlooking Christ's command that Christians proclaim

63. D'Costa, *Vatican II*, 64.

64. See *Summa theologiae* II-II, q. 10, among other places. For further discussion in relation to Galatians, see my "Aquinas and Supersessionism."

65. D'Costa, *Vatican II*, 65.

66. D'Costa, *Vatican II*, 65–66. D'Costa adds a helpful footnote: "See . . .Vitoria, *De Indis recenter inventis* . . . , 76 (q. 2, a. 4), where de Vitoria cites Cardinal Cajetan: 'it is rash and imprudent of anyone to believe something (especially in matters such as these, concerning salvation) unless one knows it to be from a trustworthy source.' Vitoria calls into question Aquinas's distinction between the gospel's fame and its effects in a historical Church. The latter was problematized in a way that Aquinas had not allowed for in his discussion, although of course Aquinas was fully aware of corrupt Christians" (D'Costa, *Vatican II*, 65n16).

67. *Lumen Gentium* remarks that "those cannot be saved who refuse to enter the church or to remain in it, if they are aware that the Catholic Church was founded by God through Jesus Christ as a necessity of salvation" (*Lumen Gentium*, §14, in Tanner, ed., *Trent to Vatican II*, 860). At the same time, the Council's *Gaudium et Spes* (Pastoral Constitution on the Church in the Modern World) teaches, "Since Christ died for everyone, and since the ultimate calling of each of us comes from God and is therefore a

the gospel to the whole world, the Council's *Ad Gentes* teaches that "God, through ways known to himself, can lead people who through no fault of their own are ignorant of the gospel, to that [non-explicit] faith without which it is impossible to please him."[68] The Council and more recent Catholic magisterial documents make clear that the ongoing Jewish people are not cut off from salvation, even though all salvation comes through Christ.[69]

As indicated above, when Christ is proclaimed to the Jewish people, what they often hear is not Jesus Christ—who is self-sacrificial love—but rather is the slander, hatred, threats, and violence that are well documented over the centuries (examples of which I offer below, especially in chapter 6). It is evident that Catholic proclamation of Christ to the Jewish people has regularly been the site of oppressive behaviors on the part of Catholics, as for instance through non-wanted preaching in the Jewish ghettoes, through a requirement that Jewish men attend six or more Catholic sermons per year, and through the persecution of Jews who refused to convert.[70] As noted above, the devastating result is often that, as Ellen Charry says, "[f]or Jews, theological discussion is freighted with the assumption that the Christian interlocutor is convinced that the Jew has no right to exist at all as a Jew."[71] Christians produced this assumption by their willingness to vilify

---

universal one, we are obliged to hold that the Holy Spirit offers everyone the possibility of sharing in his paschal mystery in a manner known to God" (*Gaudium et Spes*, §22, in Tanner, ed., *Trent to Vatican II*, 1082). See also Dulles, "Who Can Be Saved?" Dulles's brief sketch of Aquinas's position, however, is lacking, in part because he deems the notion of "implicit faith" to be "vague and ambiguous" ("Who Can Be Saved?," 30). For the point that believing in Jesus Christ is salvific and so proclamation of the Gospel remains crucial—a point with which I agree though the case of the Jewish people requires profound sensitivity given the scandal caused by Christians—see R. Martin, "*Ad Gentes*"; as well as R. Martin, *Will Many Be Saved?*. See also the reflections by Thomas Joseph White on these matters in "Universal Mediation of Christ," including his discussions of Christ's capital grace and human participation in it, implicit faith, the distinction between operative and cooperative grace, and the real possibility of eternal loss.

68. *Ad Gentes*, §7, in Tanner, ed., *Trent to Vatican II*, 1017. *Ad Gentes* affirms in the same paragraph: "The fundamental reason for this missionary activity is the will of God, who 'desires all people to be saved and to come to the knowledge of the truth. For there is one God, and there is one mediator between God and humankind, the man Christ Jesus, who gave himself as a ransom for all' (1 Tim 2, 4-6); 'and there is salvation in no one else' (Acts 4, 12)" (*Ad Gentes*, §7, in Tanner, ed., *Trent to Vatican II*, 1017).

69. See D'Costa, *Catholic Doctrines*, 162–69.

70. See Stow, *Catholic Thought*, 24.

71. Charry, "Response to Joseph B. Tyson," 263. Charry observes, "Since the seventeenth century, Christians have been learning to handle their theological disagreements with one another without bloodshed, and some would be interested in transferring that experience to tackling theological disagreements with Jews" ("Response to Joseph B. Tyson," 263).

and oppress Jews who had the temerity not to believe in Jesus as proclaimed by Christians.⁷²

The Catholic theologian Philip Cunningham is rightly sensitive to this tragic context, and he concludes that "Christians should not seek to baptize Jews in pre-eschatological historical time. Rather, the Church has a mission alongside Jews, not to Jews."⁷³ As is well known, Karl Barth took essentially the same position, on the grounds that the Jewish people already know the true God, even though paradoxically he also deemed the Jews to be abandoned by God.⁷⁴ A strict rejection of every kind of mission to the Jewish people, however, does not make exegetical or theological sense to me. Mission is about proclaiming the Messiah, and Christians have an undeniable mission to proclaim Jesus Christ, with due sensitivity to context. I hold with D'Costa *both* that "targeted mission" toward the Jewish people is wrong and that Christians necessarily possess a mission to proclaim the gospel to all

---

72. Rather than concealing this history, Catholics must face it without fear and humbly repent. See Pierre-Marie Berthe's instructive "Pourquoi l'Église ne pas avoir peur."

73. Cunningham, "Paul's Letters," 157. See also Cunningham's "Covenant and Conversion." For the same position, see Rutishauser, "'Old Unrevoked Covenant'"; Spillman, "Targeting Jews for Conversion." I agree with Cunningham when he writes, "Naturally, persons who come to share our Christian faith are welcomed, encouraged, and celebrated, but this is not why Christians approach other religions with respect.... Christians must always witness through word and deed to our covenanting with God through Christ. That is our covenantal obligation" ("Covenant and Conversion," 161). Equally, I appreciate his insistence that Christians must "foster among the Christian people attitudes of religious respect especially for the covenanting faith community of the Jewish people," even though I do not think it is the responsibility of Christians to undertake (by refraining from any kind of mission) to preserve the Jewish people's "distinctive relationship with God in the world" (Cunningham, "Covenant and Conversion," 161).

74. See Barth, *Church Dogmatics* IV.3, 876–78. Barth writes movingly but, in my view, in significant part mistakenly: "The Gentile Christian community of every age and land is a guest in the house of Israel. It assumes the election and calling of Israel. It lives in fellowship with the King of Israel. How, then, can we try to hold missions to Israel? It is not the Swiss or the German or the Indian or the Japanese awakened to faith in Jesus Christ, but the Jew, even the unbelieving Jew, so miraculously preserved, as we must say, through the many calamities of his history, who as such is the natural historical monument to the love and faithfulness of God, who in concrete form is the epitome of the man freely chosen and blessed by God, who as a living commentary on the Old Testament is the only convincing proof of God outside the Bible. What have we to teach him that he does not already know, that we have not rather to learn from him?" (Barth, *Church Dogmatics* IV.3, 877). Even so, Barth goes on to depict the synagogue as existing "without consolation" and "dreadfully empty of grace and blessing" (Barth, *Church Dogmatics* IV.3, 877).

people, including the Jewish people, and to welcome converts joyfully in the name of Christ.[75]

If Cunningham simply has in view the delegitimizing, threatening, and insensitive "evangelization" that Christians have often imposed upon the Jewish people, then he and I would agree that such actions are wrong. In the context of dialogue, moreover, the goal is to hear and appreciate where the other person is coming from, not to set a manipulative trap. Due in part to its history, the word *mission* may sound like "trap-setting," but when undertaken with appropriate sensitivity in light of the Christian history of persecuting Jews, it will primarily mean allowing one's deeds to shine with "the comfort with which we ourselves are comforted by God" (2 Cor 1:4) or proclaiming Jesus' name within a personal friendship in an appropriate way. The Jewish scholar David Berger aptly points out that "the history of Christian treatment of Jews is genuinely relevant to this moral calculus. The Jewish community reacts to missionary efforts by Christians through the prism of crusades, Inquisition, blood libels, accusations of host destruction and well poisoning, depictions of Jews as instruments of the devil, and assorted massacres."[76] Christians must exercise the utmost care not to bear witness in a manner that merely confirms this Jewish experience of so-called "missionary efforts."

Given the distinction between bearing witness—which I consider to be "mission" in a broad sense[77]—and targeted missionary efforts, the Pontifical Commission for Religious Relations with the Jews is correct that with regard to targeting the Jewish people, it is appropriate that "the Catholic

---

75. On "targeted mission" see D'Costa, *Catholic Doctrines*, 159n49. See also D'Costa, "Mission to the Jewish People?," especially his conclusion on 613: "Mission cannot be carried out in any way that perpetuates anti-Semitism or suggests supersessionism or abrogation, but must work along the lines of fulfillment. . . . Mission can never take place that fails to respect the dignity and freedom of the individual. But there should be no misunderstanding of the basic principle: mission to the Jews is theologically legitimate. Learning how best to implement that principle is a complex task that still awaits the careful attention of the contemporary Catholic Church in honest dialogue with Jewish groups and individuals"; as well as D'Costa, "Between Doctrine and Discernment," 77–79; D'Costa, "Supersessionism," 104. For critical responses to D'Costa's *Theological Studies* essay, see in the same volume Kessler, "Jewish Response"; Pawlikowski, "Catholic Response."

76. Berger, "Reflections on Conversion," 377. For further background (largely from the 1970s), see also Berger, "Jewish-Christian Relations," 343–49.

77. Irving Greenberg argues that the Jewish people possess a universal mission "to serve as pacesetter for humanity. . . . The mission to testify places an enormous weight on the shoulders of the chosen people. Every day they must witness to infinite value in a world where values are degraded" (I. Greenberg, "Judaism and Christianity: Covenants," 144, 147).

Church neither conducts nor supports any specific institutional mission work directed towards Jews."[78] The meaning of this statement, however, should be carefully delimited. As D'Costa observes, "Sharing the good news about Jesus, his life, death and resurrection, is central to the meaning of the church and entails a personal relationship with Jesus the Saviour."[79] The Church is intrinsically missional and continually proclaims the gospel to all peoples, including the Jewish people, in a wide variety of ways—as for instance in the Pope's *Urbi et Orbi* messages and many other lesser known examples. The Pontifical Commission itself observes that individual Catholics

78. Pontifical Commission, "'Gifts and the Calling of God,'" §40. With regard to Walter Kasper's proposals, D'Costa comments: "Kasper does not explain how Paul's 'missionary journeys' . . . should not be construed as 'targeted and organised'" (D'Costa, *Catholic Doctrines*, 174). My answer is that Paul's missionary work took place prior to the history of persecution, although it (the tragic history) was beginning even then. For D'Costa, "An alternative way of reading Paul would be to say it is permissible for Jewish followers of Jesus to carry out witness to the Jews, especially if the assumption is that conversion does not necessarily mean abandonment of Jewish identity" (*Catholic Doctrines*, 174). D'Costa goes on to suggest: "Mission/witness cannot be carried out in any way that perpetuates anti-Semitism or suggests supersessionism or abrogation. It must work on the lines of fulfilment and the retention of many Jewish practices and beliefs—as was the case with the early church. . . . It may be that Hebrew Catholics form a community of witness that incorporates living testimony to the Jewish people that following Christ and his Church involves no denigration or eradication of Jewish identity" (D'Costa, *Catholic Doctrines*, 187; cf. 189). In my view, Hebrew Catholics—assuming that they do not suppose that Torah observance is required of them as a soteriological imperative in Christ—can witness in this way, but I would emphasize that the witness of all Catholics is a witness to a Jewish life in the mode of messianic fulfillment. D'Costa notes that his position "does not mean the gentile ecclesia has no role in witness, but there might be different ministries emerging within the Catholic Church that is qualitatively made up of the church of the circumcision and the church of the gentiles" (*Catholic Doctrines*, 189). I deny that such a division of the Church into two parts is workable or theologically sound. For reflection on whether Jews who convert to Catholicism should become a distinct community within the Catholic Church (thereby maintaining distinctiveness as Jews, but without making Jewish Torah observance obligatory for Catholic Jews), see also Schoeman, *Salvation Is from the Jews*, 69–72; and Lévy, *Jewish Church*, chapter 3 (Lévy proposes an ordinariate).

79. D'Costa, *Catholic Doctrines*, 147–48. I note that D'Costa is here citing a position identified (and criticized) by Michael McGarry as "papal 'Christocentrism'" (*Catholic Doctrines*, 148n15). For McGarry, it is proper to make an exception for the Jewish people with regard to the Church's mission. In my view (and D'Costa's), however, this would be to deny that Jesus is good news for the Jewish people, which Christians cannot do while remaining convinced that Jesus is the Messiah and universal Savior. See McGarry, "Can Catholics Make an Exception?" David Novak, speaking as one who "has officiated at the conversion of many persons who have greatly enriched the Jewish community—spiritually, intellectually, and politically," argues that "Jewish proselytizing of gentiles, as distinct from welcoming conversion to Judaism, should be discouraged" (Novak, "Covenant and Mission," 55), on the grounds that proselytizing is associated with religious triumphalism. See also Berger, "Reflections on Conversion," 367–77.

necessarily "bear witness to their faith in Jesus Christ also to Jews."[80] The Commission counsels that individual Catholics "should do so in a humble and sensitive manner, acknowledging that Jews are bearers of God's Word, and particularly in view of the great tragedy of the Shoah."[81]

I support appropriate forms of personal and ecclesial witness—or mission in a broad sense—to the Jewish people.[82] In God's plan, some Jewish persons, such as Edith Stein or my friend Lawrence Feingold, embrace Jesus as the Messiah and become Christians. As a convert myself (though not a Jewish convert), I welcome all converts to Jesus, just as my Jewish friends welcome converts to the covenantal community of Israel. For the Christian community, converts are generally a cause of much joy due to their charity-filled witness to Jesus Christ.[83] At the same time, I disagree with Douglas

---

80. Pontifical Commission, "'Gifts and the Calling of God,'" §40.

81. Pontifical Commission, "'Gifts and the Calling of God,'" §40. See the response to "'Gifts and the Calling of God'" offered by Magonet, "Jewish-Catholic Relations Today." After praising the new Catholic commitment to Jewish-Christian dialogue, he focuses attention on §33. He notes that for Jews, while the covenant with Abraham is important, the Sinai covenant is central, since it seals a relationship of enduring love between God and a particular people (Israel) who are obligated to obey the commandments of Torah as interpreted and applied in the community. By contrast, §33 depicts the "covenant" as the Abrahamic covenant and suggests that without the Church, "Israel" would remain overly "particularist." As Magonet points out, this "reflects an old Christian accusation" and neglects the Sinai covenant with its establishment of a people (Magonet, "Jewish-Catholic Relations Today," 111). For further discussion, see Marianne Moyaert, "'Gifts and the Calling'"; Procario-Foley, "Fulfillment and Complementarity." See also Magonet's *Talking to the Other*, especially his reflections beginning on 134.

82. In chapter 5 of *Catholic Doctrines*, D'Costa responds to Jewish concerns about Christian mission, including those set forth by Rosen, "Jewish and Israeli Perspectives"; Novak, "Jewish Mission"; and Di Segni, "Progress and Issues." See also the concerns about Kasper's viewpoint expressed in William B. Goldin's STD dissertation, "St. Thomas Aquinas and Supersessionism"; as well as Philip A. Cunningham's laudatory "Celebrating Judaism." Notably—much like Pontifical Commission, "'Gifts and the Calling of God'"—Kasper distinguishes "Christian witness" from "targeted and organized mission" in Magister, ed., "Oremus Pro Conversione Judaeorum." See also the rejection of mission (but acceptance of "witness") in the ecumenical Christian document "A Sacred Obligation," in Boys, ed., *Seeing Judaism Anew*, xiii–xix; as well as the arguments for mission to the Jewish people in Vanlaningham, "Should the Church Evangelize Israel?" For his part, Hunsinger rules out "any Christian coercion of Jews to convert and any proselytizing efforts that would specifically target them," and Hunsinger suitably proposes instead the witness of love ("After Barth," 65).

83. For a Jewish perspective on Stein (respecting her as a Catholic even though for Judaism she is an apostate), see Novak, "What Does Edith Stein Mean for Jews?"; see also, with preeminently feminist concerns in view, Berkman, "Esther and Mary." For Lawrence Feingold's reflections on Catholicism in light of the people of Israel, see his four-volume set of lectures sponsored by the Association of Hebrew Catholics in St. Louis, Missouri: Feingold, *Mystery of Israel and the Church*. Feingold ranges widely in

Farrow's eschatologically supercharged proposal that Christian mission should be focused anew "on the Jews, in faith and hope that their 'hardening in part' is about to be lifted."[84]

IV. Religious Truth and Religious Persecution

In the chapters that follow, I return more than once to grave sins committed by Christians against the Jewish people and to the notion of "invincible ignorance." Examples of acts of persecution and slanderous attacks could be multiplied and countless pages would be needed to tell this sad tale, which did not prevent the Jewish community from many notable achievements, but which obviously caused tremendous grief and destruction. Even a relatively brief book such as Robert Michael's *A History of Catholic Antisemitism* confronts a reader with more shameful episodes of Christian persecution of the Jewish people than one knows how to deal with.[85]

That said, a solution that rejects tout courts the possibility of discord about whether or not the Messiah has come—by rejecting the possibility of religious truth itself—and cannot be a suitable solution for either Christians or Jews. Nor should Christian guilt carry over into a quest to redefine core Christian doctrines in order to make Jewish-Christian dialogue easier, as for example in the well-intentioned but unacceptable redefinitions of Christianity proposed respectively by the Catholic scholar John Pawlikowski and

---

these books, covering large tracts of theological territory and not limiting himself to the relationship of biblical Israel, ongoing Judaism, and Christianity.

84. Farrow, *Theological Negotiations*, 250; see also Stow, *Catholic Thought*, 225. Citing the eschatologically evocative texts of Luke 21:24 and Romans 11:25–26, Farrow observes: "It is no surprise that these sayings, by Jesus and Paul respectively, are the focus of much attention today. The surprise—the sudden and startling surprise—was the return of Israel to the land and of Jerusalem to Jewish habitation and control. This is seen by many Christians as a sign that the times of the Gentiles have begun to run out, and not only in Jerusalem. Indeed, it is difficult to know how else to see it, for there are no mere accidents of history, not on this scale, where the city of the Great King is concerned" (Farrow, *Theological Negotiations*, 209; cf. 211 for a similar point about seeking "the conversion of the Jews"). Farrow is convinced that the end of the "time of the Gentiles" is quite near, due to the widespread apostasy of the West. He may be correct, but Christians do not possess a clear timetable for Jesus' coming in glory.

85. See for example Michael, *History of Catholic Antisemitism*. See also Schreckenberg, *christliche Adversus-Judaeos-Texte*. For medieval Jewish polemical responses to Christianity, see Chazan, *Fashioning Jewish Identity*; as well as the notable efforts of Rabbi Moses ben Nahman (Nachmanides, also known as the Ramban) chronicled in Chazan's *Barcelona and Beyond*. See also Lasker, *Jewish Philosophical Polemics*; as well as the texts in Maccoby, ed., *Judaism on Trial*.

the Jewish scholar Irving Greenberg.[86] Ellen Charry is correct in this regard that "Christians must ... insist on their right to self-definition," rather than renouncing central Christian truth-claims.[87] In his otherwise instructive book about some of the most shameful Christian slanders of the Jewish people, the Jewish scholar Kenneth Stow argues that the key to Christian "apprehension about Jews" has been, from the very outset of Christianity, "the fear of being compromised and of losing pride of place"; and on this basis Stow proposes that the solution is to accept "the idea perhaps first put forth by the Italian Jew David de Pomis, who wrote, as early as the late sixteenth century, that 'nothing is more a matter of individual will than belief.' By definition, there are no hierarchies, no preferences, no belief that is better than another.... God ... has no preference, but desires only mutual

---

86. Pawlikowski comments: "As a Christian I would at least posit *both* Sinai and the Easter event as equally central, and I would be open to a possible expansion of the list" (Pawlikowski, "Christian Theological Concerns," 49). Pawlikowski's views have developed over the years, and so I do not mean to pin him to these words. Greenberg, affirming that "the Christian experience of election is valid" ("Judaism and Christianity: Covenants," 158), interprets Christianity as a covenantal extension carrying Israel's message to the Gentiles, due to "God seeking to expand the number of covenantal channels to humanity" ("Judaism and Christianity: Covenants," 150): "Christianity is a divinely inspired attempt to bring the covenant of *tikkun olam* to a wider circle of Gentiles. God intended that Judaism and Christianity both work for the perfection of the world (the kingdom of God)" (I. Greenberg, "Judaism and Christianity: Covenants," 155). Greenberg's account of how the disciples came to believe in Christ's resurrection is drawn from Rudolf Bultmann, and his brief summary of how Jesus was mistakenly thought by the Gentiles to be a "God" is the opposite of Paul's letters. Nor is Greenberg's idea that Jews and Christians might agree to describe Jesus as a "failed Messiah" ("Judaism and Christianity: Covenants," 156) acceptable, in part because it does not grasp how Christians understand Christ's work between his inauguration and his consummation of the kingdom. Greenberg concludes by suggesting that if Christians do not drop their understanding of Christ's resurrection, Christianity will be condemned to continue as a religion of abusive arrogance: "Only a modest interpretation of the resurrection could prevent the hegemonic grandiosity of Christian claims and the spiritual arrogance that leads it to mistreat and abuse other religions" ("Judaism and Christianity: Covenants," 157). He adds the hope that Christian doctrine about Jesus' divinity can also be changed, so that "the growing Christian emphasis on Jesus as the path to the Father rather than on Jesus as God incarnate may yet win out" ("I. Greenberg, Judaism and Christianity: Covenants," 157). See R. Kendall Soulen's gentle and helpful response to Greenberg from a Christian perspective, observing that "Christians ... cannot easily yield on the idea that the resurrection of a crucified Messiah, if true at all, has significance for everyone" (Soulen, "Israel and the Church," 169). Lest I be misunderstood, let me emphasize that Greenberg's intentions (like Pawlikowski's) are noble and rooted in an appreciation for Christianity, as can also be seen in I. Greenberg, "Judaism and Christianity: Their Respective Roles."

87. Charry, "Response to Joseph B. Tyson," 263.

human respect."[88] Stow's position would mean that henceforth, Jews (rejecting "hierarchies" and "preferences") must believe against Judaism itself that God has not uniquely elected the Jewish people and that Jewish belief in the God of Israel is not better than belief in the Canaanite god Baal.

Somewhat similarly—although unintentionally so, and without the clear consequences of Stow's viewpoint—the Jewish scholar Peter Ochs proposes that the key to unlocking real dialogue between scriptural traditions (including Judaism and Christianity) is a weakened sense of "reason," along lines that firmly reject "dyadic logic." Such logic, Ochs thinks, necessarily excludes those who do not accept the propositions that one accepts. Instead, he embraces the particularity of traditioned reason, as distinct from a supposed "universal reason." He goes far toward excluding propositional judgments of truth from religious knowledge, or at least toward significantly undermining their importance. For example, he states: "Since this being [God] is relational, our perception is irreducible to the form of discrete propositions and articulated only through the relational processes we have associated with reparative reasoning or with more concrete displays of reparative work."[89] He resists truth-claims insofar as they attempt to impose "strictly monovalent and therefore binarist" readings upon texts.[90] But surely truth-claims—even when they adopt a "binarist" viewpoint (for example,

---

88. Stow, *Jewish Dogs*, xviii, citing David de Pomis, *Enarratio brevis*. Not surprisingly, Stow sharply criticizes *Dominus Iesus* on page 1 of *Jewish Dogs*. Stow's earlier book *Catholic Thought* is largely a study of the Counter-Reformation Catholic Marquardus de Susannis's legal treatise *De Iudaeis et aliis infidelibus* in light of Pope Paul IV's 1555 papal bull *Cum nimis*, which ensured that "Italian Jewry in the latter half of the sixteenth century found itself shut within the walls of ghettoes and shorn of the cultural, economic, and personal privileges it had normally enjoyed" (Stow, *Catholic Thought*, xvii). Stow compares de Pomis with de Susannis: "For de Pomis, then, justice for the Jew consists of the Jews being freed from all repressive restrictions. Otherwise, they cannot be *pares in justitia*. But this is precisely the opposite of de Susannis' concept of justice for the Jew, which consists of the right to the benefits of law but also of the obligation to live as second-class citizens. And de Pomis was undoubtedly aware of this opposition; for there can be no question but that he knew *De Iudaeis* well. . . . Thus, as de Susannis was arguing that it is justice to push the Jew to convert, de Pomis was arguing that justice is the precise opposite. His arguments fell on deaf ears" (Stow, *Catholic Thought*, 223). The thesis of *Catholic Thought* has to do with the pressure upon Jews to convert: "conversion was not only a major part of papal Jewry policy in the later sixteenth century, but it was the core to which all of Jewry policy was united" (Stow, *Catholic Thought*, 5). Reflecting upon Pope Clement VIII's 1593 papal bull *Caeca et obdurata*, Stow demonstrates that the pope "weighed each of the various directions taken by Jewry policy during the preceding forty years in terms of conversionary efficacy" (Stow, *Catholic Thought*, 26). Stow directs attention to Hoffman, *Ursprung und Anfängstatigkeit*; and Browe, *Judenmission in Mittelalter*.

89. Ochs, *Another Reformation*, 10.

90. Ochs, *Religion without Violence*, 183.

the claim that Israel was elected in a way that the Amalekites were not) and even when they describe something that is universally the case—are necessary for both Judaism and Christianity.[91]

Insofar as Stow and Ochs are simply advocating an end to religious pride—an end to the haughty assumption that Christians are ipso facto better than Jews or vice versa—their points are understandable. Even if the Messiah has in fact come, as of course I believe he has, pride is the very opposite of the theocentric humility that both Christianity and Judaism require. As Paul says in Romans: "Therefore you have no excuse, O man, whoever you are, when you judge another; for in passing judgment upon him you condemn yourself, because you, the judge, are doing the very same things" (Rom 2:1). David Novak praises divine humility from a contemporary Jewish perspective. He remarks instructively, "God chooses to practice humility to show humans he is with us when we are most alone in the world. . . . God comes down from his pedestal and involves himself intimately with the most vulnerable, the most lowly, of his people."[92]

As Novak has insisted, it need not be an act of pride to believe, as a Jew or as a Christian, that God has uniquely elected the Jewish people from among all nations to be his beloved people. Nor need it be an act of pride to believe that God gave the Torah to Israel and that the Torah is true and so are God's covenants with Israel. It need not be an act of pride for a Christian to believe that the Messiah has come in Jesus Christ the incarnate Son of God. Likewise the devout Jew who believes that Christians have been misled into worshipping a man—worse, a man who was a false Messiah—has not fallen into pride when he or she argues that the consequences of worshipping Jesus as the Messiah are religiously negative. Nevertheless, believers can deploy truth-claims as a weapon, and this is what has happened

---

91. By contrast, the Presbyterian theologian Rubén Rosario Rodríguez argues that dogmatic truth-claims have no meaning in the absence of orthopraxy. He agrees with the view that "while the Roman Catholic Church—much like Israel—has a distinct dogmatic relationship with God, there is no basis within the scriptural foundations of this covenantal relationship to exclude the possibility that God's relationship to other peoples can take different dogmatic paths. In other words, if God is truly God, then religious pluralism is not a challenge or affront to God but simply revelatory of the myriad ways God has chosen to reveal God's self to all people" (Rodríguez, *Dogmatics after Babel*, 181; cf. 186). For Rodríguez, what makes a doctrine meaningfully "true" is whether or not it is presently inspiring lives of justice and solidarity, through "the work of the Spirit that reveals God's justice and righteousness (*tzedakah*) as summed up in the commandments (*mitzvah*)" (*Dogmatics after Babel*, 182). I agree that orthopraxy is necessary and that right doctrine is no substitute for it; but I do not agree that right doctrine has as little importance (or as little ontological reference) as Rodríguez suggests. For a pluralistic Jewish account of revelation, see Fleischacker, *Divine Teaching*, 408.

92. Novak, "How Jewish Was Barth?," 12.

in Christian persecution of the Jewish people over the centuries.[93] It is clear that Ochs's scriptural-reasoning groups provide an important bulwark against such abuse.

Here we might consider the renewal of Christian faith in the eleventh and twelfth centuries. While Christians prefer to think of saints such as Anselm of Canterbury (himself persecuted by his fellow Christians, who repeatedly forced him into exile), the Jewish scholar Ruth Langer has pointed out that in the same time period, "peasant crusaders decided that they needed to kill off the infidel in their own midst. They massacred the Jewish communities in the Rhineland, even denying the prerogatives of local bishops, as in Mainz, to shelter them in his castle."[94] Langer adds that, liturgically, "even today on the Ninth of Av, while mourning the destruction of the temples, Jews also recite laments for these Rhineland communities."[95] Many more episodes can be recounted of anti-Jewish violence in the midst of epochs that also exhibit sincere Christian piety. This is the case even though from the patristic period onward "a theology developed that granted Jews special, even unique toleration both because they were seen as witnesses to the truth of Christianity and because Romans 11, however one reads it, speaks of their continued separate existence when the fullness of the nations arrives."[96]

At issue, of course, was the meaning of this "separate existence." Because of its ground in the first century in a widespread Jewish rejection of Jesus as the Messiah, Christians long presumed that the "separate existence" entails that the Jewish people are mired in religious darkness and distortion. Yet, as we have seen, Paul emphasizes that the separation involves a "mystery" that cannot be understood in any simple terms. As noted above, Paul insists that the Jewish people have not "stumbled so as to fall" (Rom 11:11).[97]

---

93. Robert Chazan notes that deplorable and dangerous as the polemics were, the polemics at least played a role in some positive developments in the medieval period, as both Christians and Jews sought to respond to each other's barbs. According to Chazan, the result on the Jewish side was that "Jewish biblical exegesis was improved, as it strained to rebut Christian claims; the philosophic foundations of Jewish faith were clarified in the face of Christian pressures; overall assessment of the nature of the religious enterprise was enhanced by the competition of Christian thinking and living" (Chazan, "Medieval Christians and Jews," 144). At times there was even cooperation, both intellectually (especially with regard to scriptural exegesis) and also personally through amicable relationships formed in the midst of business dealings.

94. Langer, "Constructing Memory," 123.

95. Langer, "Constructing Memory," 123.

96. Berger, "Reflections on Conversion," 373.

97. According to Gabriele Boccaccini, Paul considers that three means of salvation are open to humans: Torah observance (for Jews), good works in obedience to natural

INTRODUCTION

He asks rhetorically, "has God rejected his people?," and he responds: "By no means! . . . For the gifts and the call of God are irrevocable" (Rom 11:1, 29).[98] At the same time, as we saw, the "mystery" involves a "hardening"—as part of God's plan of salvation—that "has come upon part of Israel, until the full number of the Gentiles come in" (Rom 11:25). According to Paul the purpose of this "mystery" of separation is not condemnation but mercy: "Just as you were once disobedient to God but now have received mercy because of their disobedience, so they have now been disobedient in order that by the mercy shown to you they also may receive mercy" (Rom 11:18, 28-31).

God's mercy to his Jewish people and to Christians is the heart of the matter, therefore.[99] The plan of God is a plan of mercy for both Jews and Christians; of this we can be sure. Thus Catholics need to ask for mercy from our Jewish brethren, and Catholics should sympathetically interpret ongoing Judaism. In the past, Catholics tended to interpret ongoing Judaism in the harshest way available. Irrationally and blindly, Catholics blamed the Jewish people for everything bad that happened, scapegoating the Jewish people rather than facing up to Catholic culpability. For example, saddened by the secularization of Europe, even Hans Urs von Balthasar

---

law (for Gentiles), and forgiveness of sins in Jesus Christ (for all sinners). I think Boccaccini has downplayed the importance of the third and exaggerated the first two in Paul's vision of salvation. See Boccaccini, *Paul's Three Paths*.

98. I note that "irrevocable" does not mean "incapable of being fulfilled and transformed." It means simply that God's gifts are never negated or lost. Writing about the 2015 document of the Pontifical Commission for Religious Relations with Jews ("'Gifts and the Calling of God'"), Gavin D'Costa states: "If *Gift* is taken at face value, it would imply that the ceremonial law of Israel is still valid, because it is irrevocable" (D'Costa, "Supersessionism," 106). Drawing upon my *Christ's Fulfillment of Torah and Temple*, D'Costa goes on to explain what "still valid" may mean: "the fulfilment of the ceremonial laws, according to some of Thomas' contemporary supporters such as Levering, means that Jewish ceremonial worship does not require practice by Jewish Christians. It is fulfilled in Christ, not superseded. The ceremonial law is intact and valid in a new form of worship, in the worship of Christ. This 'Christic practice' is not true or valid for Jews who in good faith do not know the truth of the gospel, a position that Thomas did not imagine but that Levering does. Most Jews would understandably say that this Christic practice is not recognizably Jewish ceremonial law. Thus from their point of view the ceremonial law has been superseded. Some Catholics concur. In this Thomist move, does fulfilment really bypass economic supersessionism or is it best categorized as mild supersessionism, something that is unavoidable and unnegotiable? It seems unavoidably mild supersessionism, unless all Catholics who are Jews are required by the Church to practise ceremonial Torah" (D'Costa, "Supersessionism," 107).

99. As Heschel puts it: "Israel was taught how to accost Him who is beyond the mystery. Beyond the mind is mystery, but beyond the mystery is mercy. Out of the darkness comes a voice disclosing that the ultimate mystery is not an enigma but the God of mercy" (*God in Search of Man*, 353).

fell somewhat into this embarrassing blame game.¹⁰⁰ Today, one can only hope that the rising surge of *Catholics* who are (unfortunately) embracing secularism will put an end to Catholic scapegoating of the Jewish people. On both coasts of the United States, baptized Catholics often lead the way in secularizing American society; the blame cannot be put upon ongoing Judaism. Moreover, when Catholics come to know the actual religious life of the Jewish people, Catholics discover the spiritual richness of ongoing Judaism, embodied in our time by many great Jewish scholars whose piety and wisdom are clear to all attentive minds.

Undoubtedly, Catholics can see doctrinal deficiencies in ongoing Judaism, most notably the lack of Jesus Christ—which is no small lack. If Jesus were a small matter, then Catholics would convert to Judaism or at least would not reasonably remain Christian. Adam Gregerman says in his study of Walter Kasper's theological writings on Judaism and of the 2015 document "'The Gifts and the Calling of God Are Irrevocable' (Rom 11:29)": "Even though they present the Old Covenant in strongly positive terms,

---

100. Von Balthasar's theology of Judaism is complex but troubling, as can be seen for instance in his *Theo-Drama* III, 391–401. Von Balthasar blames Marxism on a secular Judaism in which the messianic idea has been separated from belief in God, but he does not probe deeper into the roots of Karl Marx's thought in G. W. F. Hegel's secularized Christianity or into eighteenth- and early nineteenth-century Christian utopianism. Citing Henri de Lubac, von Balthasar suggests that Abbot Joachim of Fiore has "offspring . . . as numerous as the sand by the seaside: from the 'spirituals' to the Renaissance, to Münzer, the Enlightenment (Lessing's 'Education of the Human Race', promoted by Nathan the Wise), to freemasonry, Idealism and the many varieties of Messianic, supranational or national socialism" (von Balthasar, *Theo-Drama* III, 400); and he proceeds, on slender evidence, to identify Joachim as a Jew who converted to Catholicism relatively late in life and whose theories about the coming age of the Spirit are rooted in a "judaizing" understanding of the New Covenant. This view that a semi-converted Jew is at the root of everything anti-Christian since the late Middle Ages is dangerous nonsense. The blaming of the Jewish people for Christian secularism has a deadly history. Von Balthasar is somewhat better elsewhere, as in his "Church and Israel," 289–98, in which, while speaking of the "interim state of blindness to which God has destined Israel in her guilt," he makes clear not only that "Israel is not to blame for not having believed God" but also "[n]ever are the elect granted any sort of right over those blinded, no spiritual right either to lord it over them in their humiliation, no right to mockery, revenge, persecution, anti-Semitism. The shadow cast over Israel by God comes from God. It is the shadow of God himself, given solely as a mirror for those entered into the light" (von Balthasar, "Church and Israel," 292). See also Sciglitano, *Marcion and Prometheus*, in which Sciglitano rightly (if a bit too gently) challenges von Balthasar on Joachim and on Judaism (101–5); and P. S. Peterson, *Early von Balthasar*, which identifies von Balthasar's concerns about Jewish influences upon modernity as a form of anti-Semitism commonplace among Catholics prior to 1945. For pre-1945 Catholic culture (treating book reviews and articles published in the 1930s in *Civiltà Cattolica*, including a review of Hilaire Belloc's *Jews*), see Zuccotti, *Under His Very Windows*, 12–15.

they nonetheless compare it unfavorably to the New Covenant. They assess the former as in fundamental ways inferior to the latter."[101] This Christian perspective, in my view, makes sense. How could Christians, believing in Jesus as Messiah and Lord, conclude otherwise? I hasten to add, however, that the comparison between Catholicism and Judaism on the doctrinal level cannot be allowed to become, on either side, a claim to moral superiority in the world. The Pontifical Commission for Religious Relations with the Jews underscores that "the permanence of Israel is accompanied by a continuous spiritual fecundity, in the rabbinical period, in the Middle Ages, and in modern times."[102] Let all say amen to this. Of course there are a number of Catholics and Jews who cause embarrassment to their co-religionists and cause problems in the world, but such "disobedience" cannot overcome "the gifts and the call of God" (Rom 11:29–30).

I note that this affirmation does not compel Christians to affirm the divine inspiration of the Talmud or to make the greatest Jewish scholars into sainted doctors of the Church. Rather it simply speaks the truth about the spiritual gifts that God has given to his ongoing Jewish people. Christians

---

101. Gregerman, "Superiority without Supersessionism," 41. Gregerman adds that they do so in a non-supersessionist manner. He notes that as a Jewish scholar, he disagrees with "their critical judgments of the 'Old Covenant' and their debatable or questionable interpretations of biblical passages or theological concepts. . . . Despite their genuine commitment to improving Jewish-Catholic relations, their views of the Old Covenant, even if not supersessionist, are nonetheless likely to be resisted by Jews as disrespectful and even offensive" ("Superiority without Supersessionism," 41, 43). He appreciates, however, that they are "seek[ing] to reconcile two major claims that are in tension: supersessionism is unacceptable, and the New Covenant fulfills the Old Covenant, having a superior status and achieving superior goals" (Gregerman, "Superiority without Supersessionism," 44). He directs attention in this regard to the various positions offered by Novak, "Covenant in Rabbinic Thought"; Bolton, "Catholic-Jewish Dialogue"; Madges, "Covenant, Universal Mission, and Fulfillment"; and Cunningham, "Gifts and Calling." Gregerman also notes Edward Kessler's view that "fulfillment" language tends toward "replacement" ("Superiority without Supersessionism," 55n54, citing an unpublished conference paper of Kessler's).

102. Pontifical Commission, "Notes," §6. This text is cited as a sign of hope in Stow, *Jewish Dogs*, 170–71. See also "Reflections on Covenant and Mission," published by the Consultation of the National Council of Synagogues and delegates of the [United States] Bishops Committee for Ecumenical and Interreligious Affairs, with separate reflections offered by the Catholic and Jewish participants. In addition, see Boys, *Has God Only One Blessing?*, 41: "in the Late Middle Ages, when many Christians viewed Jews as outsiders and enemies, even as demonic, more positive perceptions existed. Historian Marc Saperstein traces four themes indicative of Christian admiration of Jews in the sermons of some popular preachers: respect for Jewish commitment to the Sabbath, for their standards of decorum (e.g., abhorrence of blasphemous language), for their commitment to education, and for their devotion to the faith — even in the face of suffering." See Saperstein, "Christians and Jews."

do not have to measure this "spiritual fecundity" against that of Christianity as though there were a zero-sum competition or as though Christians were the judge. With Karl Barth, we can appreciate "the supremacy of His free grace towards this people [the Jewish people] as it was revealed and actualised in that One."[103] We do so not as evidence that God runs roughshod over every human "no"—even if in the end God's merciful plan will not be defeated, and even if the eschatological judgment of sin has already taken place in the merciful Christ—but rather with an eye to the truth that God continues to act on behalf of his people Israel, ensuring that his beloved people have never "stumbled so as to fall" (Rom 11:1).[104]

---

103. Barth, *Church Dogmatics* III.3, 216. Barth has much to say about the ongoing Jewish people, emphasizing that after the destruction of Jerusalem and the temple the Jewish people "did not disappear from world history" but "alone of all the great and small nations which once surrounded them continued an inexplicably and unprecedently active and visible life, a life which they are still energetically continuing today.... And from the standpoint of the Christian message the reason for this is that God's decree in His election of this people and covenanting with it is an eternal and unshakeable decree" (*Church Dogmatics* III.3, 217). Certainly, the people of Israel were unfaithful as recorded in the Old Testament itself, but, says Barth, "this could not alter the faithfulness of God, and it has not altered it right up to the present time" (*Church Dogmatics* III.3, 217). Barth holds that the destruction of Jerusalem and of the temple frees Israel to be a people radically and enigmatically unlike any other this-worldly people (a position that cannot account for the State of Israel, despite Barth's strong personal support for the Jewish state). He sees in the Jewish rejection of Christ the spiritual situation of every human being: condemned due to sin, but elect due to God's mercy. For Barth, ongoing Judaism is spiritually empty (having rejected Christ) and yet blessed (because Christ has died for it as God's Yes on behalf of those who resist him). See also Sonderegger, *That Jesus Christ Was Born a Jew*, which offers the twofold conclusion "that Barth's position has demanded a sustained critique of Judaism; and that from his break with Liberalism to his mature period, Barth's anti-Judaism has reflected his unwavering commitment to the doctrine of justification by grace through faith alone" (*That Jesus Christ Was Born a Jew*, 167). See also Marquardt, *Entdeckung des Judentums*; Busch, *Unter dem Bogen des einen Bundes*.

104. Marquardt comments: "Christian theology has sometimes interpreted that unanticipated goodness of the Jewish No as something predestined. According to that position, the Jews had to say No according to God's will and, even against their will, had to serve as a demonstration of the superiority of the divine will and the fact that it alone is efficacious. Their No belonged to the divine necessity in which the sending of Jesus Christ was grounded" ("'Enemies for Our Sake,'" 17–18). Addressing Barth (his own teacher) directly, Marquardt states: "It is a loss of both eschatology and the reality of God, when the *simul iustus—simul peccator* ('justified and sinner at the same time') of the Reformation understanding of justification is not held as something transitory, but is understood as the ultimate and final determination of the relationship between God and humankind. The charge of just such a lack of eschatological content has to be brought against Karl Barth when he teaches that Israel is a continuing witness to God, but only in the negative form of a witness to unbelief and God's anger" ("'Enemies for Our Sake,'" 28).

INTRODUCTION

Paul deeply mourns the fact that his "brethren," his "kinsmen according to the flesh," the people of Israel, have largely not accepted Jesus as the Messiah (Rom 9:3). He knows that Christ is the Savior who is "the end of the law, that every one who has faith may be justified" (Rom 10:3–4). Writing two decades after the events of Christ's death and resurrection, Paul deems the rejection of the Messiah by the majority of his brethren to be a "trespass" and a failure to "obtain what [Israel] sought" (Rom 11:7, 11). As noted above, Christians do not need to deny any of this, and indeed Christians cannot faithfully deny it. But George Hunsinger remarks aptly: "Not even Christian disobedience can *overturn the covenant's fulfillment in Christ. Like Israel's election, it is grounded solely* in the free grace of God."[105] As Paul insists, God is at work in this "mystery" (Rom 11:25) and God is using it not only to accomplish good for the Gentiles, but also so that the people of Israel "may receive mercy" (Rom 11:31). Christians do not need to figure out precisely why God's plan in Christ has unfolded as it has over the centuries, both for good and (vis-à-vis the Jewish people) along lines for which Christians must repent. Bearing witness to the Lord of mercy, we may simply praise God for the gifts he has given, including the manifold spiritual fruits that are vibrantly present in ongoing Judaism, evidence that God has never abandoned his beloved Jewish people and that the love of God still passionately dwells within that people.[106]

105. Hunsinger, "After Barth," 63. Hunsinger continues: "Nor can it be overturned by well-meaning Christians today in their quest for a meaningful repentance. Repentance, yes, but not at the expense of the Word of God. There is only one covenant, and according to apostolic authority, it has been fulfilled in Jesus Christ—for Jews, for Christians, and for the world—by grace alone" ("After Barth," 63). I agree with Hunsinger in this regard, but not when he argues that in some way, even now, Christians and Jews "are all one in Christ, by Christ, despite their being riven into factions" ("After Barth," 64). For Hunsinger, Messianic Jewish groups are a "sign" though "not a model" of Jews and Christians united in Christ in a manner that does not deprive Jews of their Judaism ("After Barth," 68). His suggestion is that Messianic Jews might function as a religious order (or, perhaps, a rite) within the Church, which I think is possible (though rife with practical problems). In my view, the one thing that must not be implied is that observing Torah in accord with ongoing Judaism is necessary for salvation for Jews who are Christians. Hunsinger cites Papademetriou, "Jewish Rite in the Christian Church."

106. Alan Brill, a Jewish theologian, says of his extensive experience reading Christian theological works: "The wisdom contained in these works did not need justification" (*Judaism and Other Religions*, ix). This is how I feel in reading works by contemporary Jewish theologians, philosophers, and exegetes. Brill details his efforts to find a middle way between religious pluralism and religious exclusivism along lines that I identify with. He calls this middle way "inclusivism," in accord with Gavin D'Costa's early work. Although D'Costa uses a different conceptual framework in his more recent work on the topic, his basic position has remained consistent, located between an exclusivist Christian view (according to which only Christians have truth) and a pluralist Christian view (according to which there is no privileged path but rather only

V. A Final Note

In the chapters that follow, my purpose consists of addressing the doctrine of Israel from a Christian theological perspective.[107] I am therefore as likely to be addressing intra-Christian debates as I am to be addressing issues directly pertinent to Jewish-Christian dialogue. As one of my mentors in Jewish-Christian dialogue, Bruce Marshall, has observed, "the perception by Christians of their bond with Judaism can and must grow out of the very heart of the Church's faith."[108] Throughout the book, I seek to value ongoing Judaism as a source of wisdom to which Christians should attend with gratitude. I do so while disagreeing with ongoing Judaism about Jesus and therefore about many important matters of God's plan of salvation.

The Jewish theologian and interfaith theorist Alan Brill offers an important guideline for books such as mine: "One should learn not to seek a position where everything is equal or possesses a common ground syncretism."[109] Equally, as Brill recognizes, minimizing the common ground that exists would be a grave mistake. In 1936, writing against the Nazi sympathizer and Catholic journalist Joseph Eberle, John Oesterreicher articulated the perspective that informs my approach: "[Everyone who knows the] postbiblical religious writings of the Jews knows how much the spirit of faith dwells there, what longing there is for the one true God."[110] This "spirit"

---

various human ways of reaching out toward the ultimate mystery). For his part, Brill defines "inclusivism" as follows: "one acknowledges that many communities possess their own traditions and truths, but maintains the importance of one's comprehension as culminating, or subsuming, other truths. One's own group possesses the truth; other religious groups contain parts of the truth" (*Judaism and Other Religions*, 9). See also Guarino, *Disputed Teachings of Vatican II*, 111.

107. Ephesians 2:13–19 is clear about the eschatological event that has taken place: "But now in Christ Jesus you who once were far off have been brought near in the blood of Christ. For he is our peace, who has made us both one, and has broken down the dividing wall of hostility, by abolishing in his flesh the law of commandments and ordinances, that he might create in himself one new man in place of the two, so making peace, and might reconcile us both to God in one body through the cross, thereby bringing the hostility to an end. And he came and preached peace to you who were far off and you who were near; for through him we both have access in one Spirit to the Father. So then you are no longer strangers and sojourners, but you are fellow citizens with the saints and members of the household of God." For the contrary insistence upon the preservation of ethnic Judaism within the Church, see Willitts, "Jewish Fish."

108. Marshall, "Elder Brothers," 115.

109. Brill, *Judaism and Other Religions*, 10.

110. Oesterreicher, "Dr. Eberle zur Judenfrage," cited in Connelly, *From Enemy to Brother*, 129. See also the heroic writings of Dietrich von Hildebrand, collected in his *Memoiren und Aufsätze*. For von Hildebrand, as Connelly summarizes, "To judge a person by descent was to treat him as an 'animal.' A Christian was bound not only to

or "longing" entails a real relationship with the living covenantal God, for whom the Jewish people are beloved and whom the Jewish people serve. Again, the centrality of Jesus Christ is not compromised when we recognize and value the rich spiritual vitality of ongoing Judaism.

Given that Jesus is the Messiah, Christians must not hide or relativize this fact. But as John Connelly succinctly expresses the Catholic theologian Karl Thieme's seminal insight in the 1950s—the very same point made decades earlier by Solovyov—"Christians ... should condemn the sins of their own people 'which cry out to heaven' before worrying about the 'splinter' in the eye of their brother."[111] Christians should be chastened by what Chris-

---

forsake discrimination but also to show solidarity for discrimination's victims" (*From Enemy to Brother*, 130). Connelly cites *Memoiren und Aufsätze*, 352, where von Hildebrand remarks, "an unprejudiced look at the Jewish literature of the many centuries since Christ shows what a reverent, classically human, deeply religious spirit can still be found there. Whoever has maintained a sense of the world of the religious cannot read selections from postbiblical writings without being moved, whether it is the 'Dudele' or the words of the Talmud about the Just One or the story of the shepherd in the 'Book of the Holy' by Yehuda Hachasid. Everywhere we find traces of the spirit which lives in the Old Testament'" (*From Enemy to Brother*, 132). For the important impact of Jacques Maritain during these years, see for example his "The Mystery of Israel." For criticism of Maritain, however, see Hellman, "Jews in the 'New Middle Ages'"; Crane, "Jacques Maritain"; and Crane, *Passion of Israel*. Early opponents of (Nazi) anti-Semitism—such as Jacques and Raïssa Maritain—were influenced by Leon Bloy, who "had recovered St. Paul's prophetic writings on the Jews while opposing Christian antisemites during the Dreyfus affair of the 1890s" and who "called antisemitism blasphemy because it attacked Christ's family" (Connelly, *From Enemy to Brother*, 129, 132). Yet, "anti-Jewish remarks ... laced his [Bloy's] writings" (Connelly, *From Enemy to Brother*, 183). Pierre Birnbaum castigates Bloy as an anti-Semite in *Antisemitism in France*, 200; by contrast, James Carroll appreciates Bloy's attacks upon the anti-Semitic opponents of Dreyfus, in *Constantine's Sword*, 456. Connelly concludes: "Bloy's epochal achievement was to alert Catholics to untapped meanings in St. Paul's letter to the Romans, chapters 9–11, and it is no exaggeration to say that the path to Vatican II begins with him" (*From Enemy to Brother*, 185)—though Maritain's discovery of E. Peterson's "Church from Jews and Gentiles" with its exegetical reflections on Romans 9–11, was arguably more important with regard to substance.

111. Connelly, *From Enemy to Brother*, 205. By 1950, Thieme—whose work was significant in preparing for *Nostra Aetate*—advocated that not the Jewish people but the (Gentile) Church needs to be converted to Christ (since "all Israel will be saved" [Rom 11:26]), and therefore Christian mission to the Jewish people should cease. I am wary of implying that embracing Jesus as Messiah is not, as such, valuable for the Jewish people—though I think that, for good reasons (rooted in the divinely permitted history of Christian polemic and persecution, and in God's will that the Jewish people remain as a distinctive people in the world), the Jewish people as a whole will not embrace Jesus prior to the eschaton and should not be pressured to do so or condemned for not doing so by Christians. For further background to Thieme's contributions, see Füllenbach, "Shock, Renewal, Crisis." Füllenbach notes that among the signers of Thieme's (and Waldemar Gurian's) 1937 *Memorandum* urging Catholics to "protest against the

tians have done to Jews over the centuries, a boasting that has made the name of Jesus off-putting to the Jewish people as a whole. Without ceasing to proclaim Jesus' name in ways that bespeak charity, Christians should today learn from the ongoing Jewish people against whom so many Christian evangelizers and Christian clergy and laity have sinned.

Thus, Elizabeth Groppe is correct that the "Catholic Church need not articulate its own identity in binary opposition to Judaism as if our status as people of God can only be gained by denying that of the Jews."[112] In the name of Christ, Christian boasting must stop and must be replaced by learning—although the disagreements about Jesus will remain and should

---

antisemitic actions of the National Socialists" were Jacques Maritain, Charles Journet, and Dietrich von Hildebrand. The *Memorandum* condemned "not only racial antisemitism, but also all other forms of modern Judaeophobia, especially a more 'moderate' national-conservative (*völkisch-konservativen*) antisemitism that was often embraced by Christians" (Füllenbach, "Shock, Renewal, Crisis," 204, with reference to the distinction—advocated by *Civiltà Cattolica* and many others—between racial anti-Semitism and religious anti-Judaism).

112. Groppe, "Toward the Future," 78. Groppe goes on to say that "the identity of both the Church and the Jewish people is found in multiple layers of complex historical relationship between the biblical people Israel, the Christian Church, and the rabbinic Judaism of the post-biblical era" ("Toward the Future," 78)—a statement that is accurate in part but leaves out Jesus of Nazareth. Groppe, a Catholic, also goes on to suggest that Jews can and should agree that Christians and Jews are "both part of the one people of God" ("Toward the Future," 79); but I do not see how Jews can affirm this. See also Gordis and Phan, "Catholics and Jews." Along lines that seem to me to be antithetical to Judaism, Gordis and Phan argue, "All of us are 'chosen,' and none of us is exclusively" ("Catholics and Jews," 222). Gordis and Phan are here aiming largely at the Catholic Church, since they go on to say: "The notion of 'one and only true Church' not only precludes genuine interrelationships but strains credulity in view of the Church's human character. . . . We simply note that recent scandals in the Church, from clerical sexual abuse to criminal attempts at concealment and obstruction of justice, even by the higher ecclesiastical echelons, to financial shenanigans in our religious communities make claims about the Church being the only repository of truth and goodness ring hollow" (Gordis and Phan, "Catholics and Jews," 222). But the presence of terrible scandals and wickedness in the Church is already a reality described and anticipated by the New Testament. Gordis and Phan exemplify a common tendency (among Catholics) to employ Jewish-Catholic dialogue as a mode of attacking the doctrines of the Catholic Church. They bemoan the fact that the Catholic Church's "theological language, especially in Christology and ecclesiology, is still wedded to expressions such as *universality, uniqueness, absolute necessity*, and *exclusivity*, which, born in the context of controversies and imperialism, are highly liable to misunderstanding today" ("Catholics and Jews," 220). See also Phan, "Jesus as the Universal Savior." Here Phan proposes, inaccurately in my view: "we might recognize at least two ways of understanding the saving action of God in human history. One is through the christological symbols of the Jesus of the Christian faith, the other through the religious symbols of Judaism, among which is the Jewish Messiah" (Phan, "Jesus as the Universal Savior," 135).

not be suppressed.[113] Theologically speaking, such fruitful learning will be best achieved when Christian engagement with Jewish thinkers takes place within the core of the theological task rather than as a mere sidelight.[114] This is what I have tried to accomplish in engaging the doctrine of Israel, calling upon "the Lord [who] gives wisdom; from his mouth come knowledge and understanding" (Prov 2:6).

---

113. Barth's formulation of what must be learned is striking: "From the existence of this people we have to learn that the elect of God is not a German or a Swiss or a Frenchman, but this Jew. We have to learn that in order to be elect ourselves, for good or evil we must either be Jews or belong to this Jew.... What the history of the Jews tells us is that the divine election is the election of another. Our election can be only in and with this other" (Barth, *Church Dogmatics* III.3, 225–26).

114. The danger in such an approach consists in replicating the polemics of the past, as found for instance in Peter the Venerable, *Against the Inveterate Obduracy of the Jews*. Resnick's "Introduction" (*Against the Inveterate Obduracy of the Jews*, 3–46) sums up the hatred and persecution found in many such works, which focused upon proving the truth of Christian doctrine against Judaism. He concludes that Peter "presents a portrait of medieval Jews that all but strips them of their humanity" (*Against the Inveterate Obduracy of the Jews*, 45). In his *Martin Buber and Christianity*, 13, von Balthasar defends the vigorous theological debate between Christians and Jews that is found in Buber's *Two Types of Faith*.

Chapter 1

Jewish-Christian Dialogue

On the way to the unfathomably glorious eschatological "marriage" of God and humanity, part of the grievous suffering that the Creator God has permitted in his providence is division over the identity and work of Jesus of Nazareth.[1] As a Christian, I affirm that Jesus is the "bridegroom" (Matt 9:15; John 3:29) who has inaugurated the wedding of God and creation, and who has fulfilled Israel's Torah and temple as the messianic Davidic King. Christ now leads his people on the new exodus to the fullness of the new creation, marked by infinite divine mercy and love. I believe that Jesus Christ "fulfils the mission and expectation of Israel in a perfect way," while also, as the incarnate Son and Lord, he "transcends them in an eschatological manner."[2] He enacts the fulfillment of Israel's covenants and expectations, not the mere replacement of them; his purpose is not to discard the people of Israel, but to bring to fulfillment God's promises.[3] In light of this

---

1. Thomas F. Torrance, however, goes much further than I think is accurate: "Schism between Christians and Jews is the deepest schism of all. It is the root cause of all other tragic divisions that have arisen in the one indivisible people of God. Rebellion against God's reconciling purpose, as ordained to take place through Israel, cannot but have dire consequences, no matter where the rebellion may break out. It cannot but generate further fragmentation among the peoples and nations of the earth. . . . Israel will have a basic part in the reunion of the fragmented gentile church. It is not too much to say that the whole future of ecumenism and evangelism depends on the relation of Jews to Jesus Christ as the messianic Savior and King" (Torrance, "Divine Vocation," 119, 122).

2. Pontifical Commission, "'Gifts and the Calling of God,'" §14.

3. See Pontifical Commission, "'Gifts and the Calling of God,'" §23: "The Church does not replace the people of God of Israel, since as the community founded on Christ it represents in him the fulfilment of the promises made to Israel. This does not mean that Israel, not having achieved such a fulfilment, can no longer be considered to be the people of God." I agree with the Pontifical Commission's distinction

transcendent fulfillment, the Pontifical Commission for Religious Relations with the Jews remarks that for Christians "Jesus Christ can be considered as 'the living Torah of God.'"[4]

Whereas Christians reflect upon Torah in light of Christ's work of fulfillment, Jews reflect upon Written Torah in light of Oral Torah and in light of the coming Messiah who will establish God's perfect reign in the eschatological Jerusalem. For Christians, Torah is now central in its fulfilled mode, namely, in the incarnate Word Jesus Christ.[5] It is Christ who stands at the center of all reality, calling all people to union with him in his messianically reconfigured, eschatological Israel (namely, the Church, which in

---

between "fulfillment" and "replacement." For a presentation of Christian theology of the covenants, see Pontifical Commission, "'Gifts and the Calling of God,'" §32. See also the helpful explanation of the difference between fulfillment and replacement in Forte, "Israel and the Church," 90–91; as well as the reflections of Perrier, "Election of Israel Today." By contrast, Peter Phan asks: "But is 'fulfillment' reassuring to those whose covenant we claim to fulfill? What is meant by 'fulfillment' that is so different from replacement that can prevent genocide and pogroms?" (Phan, "Judaism and Christianity," 3). I answer that messianic fulfillment does not entail the covenantal negation presupposed by "replacement," but for Phan this does not go far enough—because fulfillment implies the theological superiority of Christianity.

4. Pontifical Commission, "'Gifts and the Calling of God,'" §26. This does not mean that people who observe Torah are thereby united to Christ: for this mistaken viewpoint, see Henrix, "Son of God." See also Chilton and Neusner's proposal that "the New Testament is rarely understood as its Founder and his disciples conceived it to be, namely, as the Torah, or, in secular language, as Judaism" (Chilton and Neusner, *Judaism in the New Testament*, xv; cf. xviii, 4–10). There is an important insight here, insofar as Jesus and his disciples were Jews who taught Torah and understood themselves to be "Israel" and true Jews, and also insofar as the variety of Second Temple Judaisms is quite striking (Chilton and Neusner, *Judaism in the New Testament*, xiv–xv). But in my view, it is an exaggeration to say that the New Testament simply intends to be "*the statement of Judaism*, that is, from its writers' perspective, the New Testament at every point formed that very same Judaism that the Old Testament had adumbrated.... Christianity did not understand itself as anything other than the natural continuation of the Judaism represented by the Hebrew Scriptures of ancient Israel" (Chilton and Neusner, *Judaism in the New Testament*, xvii–xviii). Christ's eschatological inauguration of the kingdom means that his messianic community is not adequately described as "the very same Judaism" or "the natural continuation" of Judaism.

5. The Jewish scholar Uriel Tal contends that the Jewish rejection of the claim that Jesus is Messiah and Lord "is inherent in the structural-cognitive form of *Torah* hermeneutics. Judaism cannot accept an incarnated mediation between God and Man, between Creator and Creation, because according to the *Torah* God and his manifestations cannot be mediated, only interpreted. Not a Messiah but the *Torah* with its all-embracing earthliness, with its roots in timelessness and its revelation in history interprets the unity of God and Being, of the infinite Absolute and its finite creatures" (Tal, "Future of Jewish-Christian Dialogue," 86). It strikes me that Tal has misunderstood the Christian claim. Jesus, in his human words and deeds, interprets or expresses (perfectly) the divine Word who he is.

Mary and the saints is already present with Christ at the right hand of the Father).[6] By contrast, as the Jewish scholar David Fox Sandmel says, most Jews can appreciate that Christians worship the God of Israel—at least when this worship is not directed toward Jesus—but Christian belief in Israel's God "does not make Christianity part of Israel, *as we understand Israel*, that is, a *people* that has a special *covenant* with God who has given us a specific *land*."[7]

In short, Christians, affirming that Israel's Messiah has embodied and fulfilled Torah, believe that Christ has eschatologically reconfigured "Israel" around himself and has called all people to union with him by pouring out his Spirit.[8] Jews, grounded in belief that the Messiah has not yet come, believe that God's covenants with Israel (the Jewish people) continue unchanged. These differences are not easy ones, for both sides are tempted to deny basic theological legitimacy to the other, and Christians over the centuries have employed political power to persecute and demean the Jewish people.[9]

---

6. See Macaskill, *Union with Christ*, although I have added Mary and the saints: see my *Mary's Bodily Assumption*. Macaskill argues that in the New Testament, "To be united to Jesus, to be in him, is to be in the covenant through his representative headship. Thus, it is to be in a condition of covenantal communion with God, with the covenant-fulfilment of Jesus serving as the grounds for our own communion. In Christ, we keep the covenant.... The new covenant is appropriately described as the covenant of the Spirit (2 Cor 3:6). Across the New Testament, this is reflective of the fact that the Spirit is the gift given within the new covenant, who conforms our being to its terms by writing those terms on our hearts and realizing our conformity to Christ" (Macaskill, *Union with Christ*, 297–98, 300). Macaskill places emphasis upon the sacraments of baptism and the Eucharist, with the latter serving as "a temple meal, in which the Glory itself is present, by which we are transformed" (*Union with Christ*, 302). Especially in Part 1 of his book, he shows that the New Testament offers "a basically apocalyptic conceptuality of union" as indicated by "the widespread motif of revealed wisdom" (*Union with Christ*, 304). Part 1 of his book makes helpful connections with other Second Temple Jewish apocalyptic literature. See also his *Revealed Wisdom*. For further discussion, see the essays in Thate et al. eds., *"In Christ" in Paul*.

7. Sandmel, "Israel, Judaism, and Christianity," 166.

8. See the account of "Israel" according to the Gospels of Matthew and John, in Chilton and Neusner, *Judaism in the New Testament*, 118–20.

9. As Walter Kasper says, even today Christians and Jews exhibit "reciprocal prejudice" and "considerable ignorance on both sides" (Kasper, "Paths Taken," 10). With regard to Christian persecution of the Jewish people over the centuries, I want to be careful not to imply that the Jewish people had no identity other than that of victim, although in this book I will highlight the truth of persistent Christian persecution. On the more positive aspects of the relationship, see Elukin, *Living Together, Living Apart*. Jewish communities developed a strong identity, as described by Leora Batnitzky: "While a local Jewish community's existence depended on the whims of others, premodern Jewish communities also had a tremendous amount of political autonomy.

The last thing that Christians should want to do is to persecute and hate God's beloved people. Even so, there are New Testament passages that may appear to validate denigrating and even persecuting Jews who do not accept Jesus as Lord and Messiah. Some New Testament passages may appear to show that Jews who have rejected Jesus are no longer God's people but have been cut off and replaced by Christians. If Jesus and Paul condemn Pharisees and scribes, and if the crowd in front of Pontius Pilate demands that Jesus be crucified, then why should Christians not denounce the ongoing Jewish people as cursed? Furthermore, does the destruction of the temple mean that God has abandoned the ongoing Jewish people until they confess faith in Jesus at his second coming?

I respond to such questions at length in this chapter. But let me note that other Christians, going to the opposite extreme, take scissors to the New Testament in order to eliminate all polemical verses and truth-claims. This jettisoning of core beliefs leads to a Christianity that does not persuade anyone. It is a form of faith-suicide. It pushes believers into other forms of Christianity, perhaps more anti-Jewish. Judaism itself, of course, has also experienced this kind of scissoring of its beliefs in order to measure up to Enlightenment standards, including the downplaying or rejection of the doctrine of Israel's election. The claim to be God's chosen people may appear to be irrational and offensive. Monotheism or worship of the one true God has come under fire, since it seems exclusivist and prone to violence.[10]

Jewish communities were self-governing, and each community had its own set of bylaws administered by laypersons who, among other things, elected a rabbi for the community, who had jurisdiction over matters of ritual law while also giving credence to the laws of the community as a whole. Each community had its own courts as well as its own educational, health, economic, and social services systems. The community was also responsible for law and order, and had the right to punish its members in various ways, including exacting fines, imprisonment, and corporal punishment. Local Jewish communities often varied greatly from one another. Yet despite local differences, premodern Jews imagined themselves as one united people (as *klal yisrael*, 'the collective people of Israel'). Rabbis and scholars engaged one another on matters of Jewish law, or thought across communities; many economic activities occurred across communities; and perhaps most significantly, Jewish communities frequently came to each other's aid in times of need by, for instance, providing money to help communities rampaged by violent riots. On a theological level, Jews had a common messianic hope that all the Jewish communities dispersed around the world would be reunited in the land of Israel in the days of the Messiah" (Batnitzky, *How Judaism Became a Religion*, 2).

10. For a barrage of arguments and examples making this case, see Kirsch, *God against the Gods*. Kirsch is able to show that Christians have undertaken extensive violent persecutions against non-believers, much to the shame of Christianity. He pays particular attention to the persecutions unleashed against pagan polytheists beginning in the late fourth century. Kirsch romanticizes paganism by failing to perceive that its ancient and modern exponents have generally refused "religious tolerance"

In this opening chapter, I intend to explore the most difficult topics relating to Jewish-Christian dialogue. Among these topics are the character that such dialogue should possess, whether Christian persecution of the Jewish people invalidates Christianity, the controverted figure of Abraham, the meaning of the destruction of Jerusalem and its temple, the polemical (or anti-Jewish) passages of the New Testament, and how to understand the presence of harm-causing rhetorical invective in divinely inspired Scripture. I undertake this task in conversation with a wide spectrum of interlocutors, given that the above themes have been treated by many Christians and Jews from whom I hope to learn.

I. Dialogue and Difference: Finding a Balance

The Catholic theologian Ilaria Morali has set forth the basic stance that, in my view, should characterize healthy Christian-Jewish dialogue for its Christian participants. She states, "for Catholic theologians, the following criteria [for dialogue with non-Christian religions] are not negotiable: (i) faith in the revelation given in Christ, understood as salvific Truth; and (ii) faithfulness to the 'one sacred deposit of the word of God, committed to the Church,' and maintained via 'sacred tradition, sacred Scripture and the teaching authority of the Church.'"[11] As noted above, true dialogue cannot be rooted in a rejection of Christianity by the Christian dialogue partner. Rather, faithfulness to divine revelation is the ultimate ground for the Christian affirmation that the Jewish people remain God's elect people and that God has not covenantally abandoned them.[12]

---

to monotheists. In pagan cultures, the vocal claim that there is only one God (unless merely advanced as a philosophical speculation joined to the worship of the local deities) has generally been taken as an unacceptable attack upon the state and the gods it encourages.

11. Morali, "Catholic Theology," 85.

12. See the alternative readings of Romans 9–11 (by evangelical Baptists) in Compton and Naselli, eds., *Three Views on Israel*. I agree with Michael J. Vlach when he says, "National Israel remains strategic to God's purposes and does not lose its significance with the arrival of Jesus and the church" (Vlach, "Non-Typological Future-Mass-Conversion"). But I also agree with those who, unlike Vlach, "believe national Israel possessed a typological role that found fulfilment in Jesus and the church" (Vlach, "Non-Typological Future-Mass-Conversion," 68). To my mind, Romans 9–11 is ultimately an exploratory text that does not claim to have solved the "mystery," and that therefore contains fruitful internal tensions, including an emphasis on Christ's fulfillment and reconfiguration of Israel; an emphasis that "national Israel" or "ethnic Israel" (and thus ongoing Judaism) retains an important role in God's merciful and salvific plan due to God's irrevocable gifts and call; an emphasis on the "mystery" of "hardening" that in the divine plan has a positive purpose vis-à-vis the Gentiles; and a warning

Yet, does not the history of Christian sins against the Jewish people prove that Christianity must be revised in its core doctrines and its most central texts in order to enter into serious dialogue with the Jewish people? Christians believe that the salvation of the world through the suffering and death of the Messiah is "the purpose of him [God] who accomplishes all things according to the counsel of his will" (Eph 1:11).[13] As part of the same plan, however, God has permitted the scandalizing of the Jewish people over the centuries by a steady drumbeat of Christian persecution. This scandalous behavior is documented in gruesome detail in Dan Cohn-Sherbok's *The Crucified Jew: Twenty Centuries of Christian Anti-Semitism*, as well as in numerous similar books.[14] I have already granted that Christians, despite their faith in incarnate Mercy, have often acted without either mercy or justice toward the ongoing Jewish people—with the result that the good news has been obscured and, for the Jewish people as a whole, looks like its opposite. Nevertheless, the sins of God's people do not mean that their testimonies to divine revelation are false.

Christians must be extremely careful in thinking about the Jewish people, given the disastrous fruits of earlier missteps. Undeniably, some of Jesus' fellow Jews, including his own disciples, tried to derail his mission and, ultimately, encouraged the Romans to arrest and crucify him. But Christians have too often acted as though because Jesus was persecuted by some of his fellow Jews, later Christians can oppress their own Jewish contemporaries. On this view, because there was first-century strife between Jews (some of whom were followers of Christ), later interactions between Christians and the ongoing Jewish people can legitimately follow this same pattern. What this supposition neglects is that the tensions Jesus provoked among his fellow Jews are not the same as the later situations of tension between Christians and Jews. In almost all the later situations, it has been Christians betraying their own Master by their lack of charity toward the ongoing Jewish people.

---

against Gentile Christian boasting over the Jewish people. Paul does not pull all these elements together into a logically neat package, but he provides us with the crucial elements that are needed to understand the centuries that have followed and to chart a course today.

13. Thus as Marquardt says, "the Jewish No served God's own good purpose nonetheless" ("'Enemies for Our Sake,'" 17).

14. See Cohn-Sherbok, *Crucified Jew*. I differ from Cohn-Sherbok's characterization of the New Testament as anti-Semitic, but I accept that the New Testament contributed significantly to centuries of anti-Judaism or anti-Semitism. See Berger, "Anti-Semitism," 4–5. For the pre-Christian background of anti-Judaism, see Feldman, "Anti-Semitism in the Ancient World"; S. J. D. Cohen, "'Anti-Semitism' in Antiquity"; and Gager, *Origins of Anti-Semitism*. See also Gregerman, "Biblical Prophecy," 216–20.

Nor may Christians legitimately follow the all too well-trodden path of blaming the ills that occur in Christian or post-Christian countries (such as the rise of secularization) upon the Jewish people. The tendency has been to blame everything upon Karl Marx or Sigmund Freud as though these are representatives of "Judaism." This path, popular among Catholic intellectuals prior to World War II, overlooks the Christian sources of the same problems as well as the actual political and economic contexts. Christians often pass blame to each other as well, as when Eastern Orthodox thinkers argue that all modern ills flow from the *Filioque* or when Catholic thinkers argue that all modern ills flow from the Reformation. In recent years, the traditionalist Catholic writer E. Michael Jones has self-published a string of books with titles such as *Jewish Fables: Darwinism, Materialism, and Other Jewish Fables*; *The Jews and Moral Subversion*; and *The Jewish Revolutionary Spirit*.[15] These deeply deplorable books have had some influence among fringe Catholic traditionalist groups, to which such anti-Semitic arguments are familiar.[16]

This situation has been exacerbated by the fact that after the Second Vatican Council, some Catholics have taken up the sordid history of Catholic treatment of the Jewish people as a cudgel with which to bash the Catholic Church and to call for change in its core doctrines. The conciliar advances vis-à-vis the Jewish people here become a mere tool for a broadly revisionary intra-Catholic agenda, rather than simply fostering, as intended by the Council, a deeper and more faithful treatment of the ongoing Jewish

---

15. E. M. Jones, *Jewish Revolutionary Spirit*; E. M. Jones, *Jews and Moral Subversion*; E. M. Jones, *Jewish Fables*; E. M. Jones, *Catholics and the Jew Taboo*; and E. M. Jones, *Jewish Privilege*. As was also typical for similar pre-conciliar writings, Jones argues that he can differentiate his anti-Judaism from race-based anti-Semitism (and from the latter's violence). See also the discussion by George G. Higgins of the book Pinay, *Plot Against the Church*, published under a pseudonym in Italian, that was given to each of the more than 2,000 bishops assembled at Vatican II in 1962. As Higgins (writing in 1986) notes, this book remains in print in English and is distributed in "Christian" book clubs. Higgins states with dismay that the book's author(s) and promoters "had convinced themselves and tried desperately to convince the Council Fathers that 'behind Communism, Freemasonry and behind every action which is directed at the destruction of Christian civilization stands Jewry as head of the octopus, which must be destroyed if one wishes to effectively defeat the arms.... For if the head of the octopus is not attacked, the arms can grow again.' This, being translated into basic English, meant that 'Jewry' must be completely destroyed in the name of Christianity" (Higgins, "Twenty Years," 20). See also Lefebvre, *I Accuse the Council!*

16. For background in Father Charles Coughlin's anti-Semitism and his coded language (instead of referring to Jews, he often denounced plutocrats, financiers, bankers, Marxists, and so forth, all the while promoting the *Protocols of the Elders of Zion* and making sure that his audience knew exactly what he meant), see Warren, *Radio Priest*.

people in light of Romans 9–11.¹⁷ When Catholic thinkers justify abandoning core Catholic beliefs in the name of the Jewish people, they undermine real Christian-Jewish dialogue—which is discredited when it is connected in the popular mind with a more or less open abandonment by Christians of Christian faith.

Some Catholic theologians have chosen to avoid the more excessive rhetorical cudgels, but have nevertheless used Jewish-Christian dialogue to justify a profoundly revisionist doctrinal stance. For instance, the Catholic theologian Peter Hünermann remarks: "At this point, it is necessary to ask whether a mere material correction of the dogmatic treatments of topics such as ecclesiology is sufficient to respect the new conception of the relationship between the Church of Christ and the Jewish people. Are there other aspects of dogmatic theology that must be changed or revisited?"¹⁸

17. Gavin D'Costa describes the relationship of Vatican II and Romans 9–11: "Christian attitudes to the Jewish people have been mainly negative, predicated on two claims: that the Jewish people rejected Christ, indeed they killed their own messiah, and have thus forfeited their covenant; and that since that time they have continued in this obstinacy. The Council addressed both of these claims. LG 16 frames the matter of the religions in terms of 'those who have not yet accepted the gospel' and who are 'related [*ordinantur*] to the Church in various ways.' ... The next sentence contains almost verbatim quotes from the Latin Vulgate Bible of Romans 9:4–5 and 11:28–9, highlighting the themes that would most acutely exercise the reception of the Council. It states that the Jewish people are those 'to whom the testaments and promises were given,' ensuring their 'election.' The closing portion of this single Latin sentence affirms: 'God never goes back on his gifts and his calling.' The covenant with the Jews is not revoked by God.... The intense struggle at the Council over the 'deicide' charge and the passage of NA is dramatically and well documented. The final vote was an unambiguous victory against what Jules Isaac, the Jewish historian, had called 'the teaching of contempt.' NA also explicated Romans 11, reiterating LG 16: that the 'Jews still remain very dear to God, whose gift and call are without regret'" (D'Costa, "Between Doctrine and Discernment," 66–67). For further background, see Oesterreicher, "Declaration"; Bea, *Church and the Jewish People*; Tobias, *Jewish Conscience of the Church*; Connelly, *From Enemy to Brother*; and Lamberigts and Declerck, "Vatican II on the Jews." Much of the tension stemmed from the concerns of Eastern Catholic patriarchs. In the end, the omission of the term "deicide" enabled the Syriac, Maronite, Armenian, and Coptic patriarchs to accept the draft. See also Isaac, *Teaching of Contempt*; and Phayer, *Catholic Church and the Holocaust*.

18. Hünermann, "Jewish-Christian Relations," 115. Hünermann retrieves Melchior Cano (and parts of Vatican II) to advocate for a particular notion of "loci theologici," revised in light of "the new determination of the relationship between the church and the Jewish people" (Hünermann, "Jewish-Christian Relations," 118). For Hünermann, "Those who believe and who affirm the eschatological truth of Christ are called to accept a radical openness, a theological ignorance, the radical impossibility of complete self-determination, the impossibility of turning history into a straight line" ("Jewish-Christian Relations," 121). He goes on to insist (with regard to "loci theologici" and the new awareness of "ambiguity in the authority of the Catholic Church") upon "emphasizing the Spirit, and not the letter" (Hünermann, "Jewish-Christian Relations," 123),

Predictably, he answers yes—and proceeds to replace Catholic ecclesiology's emphasis on the constitutive authority of Jesus Christ with a new emphasis on the work of Jesus' followers, specifically on "the evolution of the messianic dynamics that characterizes this people."[19] This focus would turn the Catholic Church on its head, by decentering the true Head.

A better path begins with both sides respectfully acknowledging differences and affirming core beliefs, while taking care from the Christian side not to countenance the old slanders against the ongoing Jewish people.[20] In a 2015 address to persons engaged in Jewish-Christian dialogue, Pope Francis acknowledges differences and affirms core beliefs: "The Christian confessions find their unity in Christ; Judaism finds its unity in the Torah. Christians believe that Jesus Christ is the Word of God made flesh in the world; for Jews the Word of God is present above all in the Torah."[21] Along similar lines, the Catholic theologian Robert Louis Wilken observes that for Christians "the Law is not the key to the Bible; Jesus Christ is.... This is the great debate between Christians and Jews."[22] I note that for Jews, the *living*

---

implying that much solemnly affirmed doctrine is open for reversal. See also Johann Baptist Metz's argument that the Church's new understanding of the Jewish people must involve revising Christian theology itself. See Metz, "Facing the Jews," although Metz is significantly more temperate than Hünermann.

19. Hünermann, "Jewish-Christian Relations," 125. The link to the nineteenth-century liberal theology of Albrecht Ritschl should be evident.

20. For the groundbreaking ten theses put forward by the 1947 meeting of the International Council of Christians and Jews at Seelisberg—ten theses whose main source appears to have been Jules Isaac and that establish the necessary foundations for true Jewish-Christian dialogue and for turning away from centuries of persecution and vilification—see Connelly, *From Enemy to Brother*, 176–78. Connelly notes that the Catholic media (including "liberal" publications) remained almost completely silent on the issue through the 1950s. It was Cardinal Augustin Bea, SJ and Pope John XXIII who ensured that a document engaging the Jewish people would be part of Vatican II, though Cardinal Bea's views were still developing and were in need of correction from John Oesterreicher and Abraham Joshua Heschel in the early 1960s (Connelly, *From Enemy to Brother*, 247–50). See also the summary of Bea's contributions in Bernauer, *Jesuit Kaddish*, 70–78.

21. Pope Francis, "Address to members of the 'International Council of Christians and Jews,'" cited in "'Gifts and the Calling of God,'" §24. See also, for inclusion of Oral Torah, the observation of Pawlikowski, "Can We Speak," 387: "Christians and Jews must make clear the fundamentally different lens that influences the biblical text we share: the centrality of Christ in the Christian tradition and the collected works that constitute oral Torah in Judaism." Pawlikowski is responding to a similar point made in response to *Dabru Emet* by Aitken, "What Does Christianity in Jewish Terms Mean?," 212.

22. Wilken, "Something Greater Than the Temple," 202. Earlier Wilken states, "Christianity is not anti-Jewish, but it is anti-halachic; it does not believe that Christian life is to be ordered by the legislation in the Torah and the institutions associated with the Temple. Christians found in Jesus 'something greater than the Temple [Matt 12:6].'

God is the key to the Bible and to the Torah, and Jews look not only to the Written Torah but also to the Oral Torah. But Pope Francis and Wilken are nevertheless correct to put their finger on the difference between Torah and Christ. Both Judaism and Christianity anticipate a glorious (and universal) eschatological consummation marked by a communion with God far more intimate than that which humans experience now.[23] But for Jews the Torah (Written and Oral) mediates this communion and will in some way everlastingly structure it, whereas for Christians Jesus Christ establishes this communion and, as the divine Son, stands everlastingly at the center of it.[24]

Thus, as Rabbi Giuseppe Laras says, for Jews the encounter with Christianity inevitably "becomes a source of tension and contradiction as soon as the figure of Jesus comes under discussion (how could it be otherwise?)— a figure that, understood as divine and messianic, contrasts with Israel's monotheistic and messianic understanding."[25] For Christians, similarly, the encounter with Judaism has evident tensions, due to Christian belief that

---

Here is the source of conflict between Jews and Christians. It is not that Jews had no place for mercy, justice, or love, or that Christians did not in time develop a body of law to regulate the church's life, but that each started at a different point, subordinating the one to the other. Once Christians dispensed with the authority of the Law, it was inevitable that Jews, who continued to live by the law, would be the object of criticism" ("Something Greater Than the Temple," 187).

23. For discussion of these issues from a Jewish perspective, including reflection on the diversity of commandments (with diverse teleologies) and the role of the Messiah, see Novak, "End of the Law," 40–47. See also Novak's "Law and Eschatology."

24. Tikva Frymer-Kensky argues, along lines that would be rejected by most of the Jewish scholars represented in my book, that "the Torah, and indeed the whole Bible has been marginalized in Judaism. . . . In traditional Judaism, the Torah, regal as it is, is not sovereign. It is yoked to a rabbinic system that it serves. In effect, the Torah was (and is, in most traditional circles) a king or queen in captivity. It is well known that the Christian church was explicitly 'supersessionist.' It showed honor to and interest in the Hebrew Bible and claimed it as its heritage, but it considered the New Testament as its foundational Scripture and drew its behavioral conclusions from there. Judaism was almost equally supersessionist, but it did not make its supersessionism apparent. It behaved ritually as if the Torah was the central facet of Judaism, but it dictated the way that the Torah should be read. In effect, Jewish tradition subordinated and domesticated the Bible" (Frymer-Kensky, "Emergence of Jewish Biblical Theologies," 111). I think it more plausible than does Frymer-Kensky to hold that the Oral Torah keeps the Jewish people close to the Written Torah. It does seem, however, that there are major differences between Written and Oral Torah that make the latter functionally comparable to the New Testament. Frymer-Kensky considers the Hebrew Bible to be a fundamentally ambiguous text that does not have "clear" meanings.

25. Laras, "Jewish Perspectives on Christianity," 24. This is the case even if some strands of Second Temple Jewish thought—for instance Philo—conceived of a divine Logos in some way "alongside" God.

precisely "Israel's monotheistic and messianic understanding" is upheld and fulfilled in the same Jesus whom ongoing Judaism does not accept.[26]

Before 1965, the acknowledgment or discovery of differences was generally the *endpoint* of explicit theological interactions between Christians and Jews, and also served as fuel for Christian persecution of Jews. The fact that Christians actually agree with the Jewish people on so many core beliefs produced enmity when the differences could not be resolved. As a result, the "great debate between Christians and Jews" proceeded for centuries under the distressing shadow of persecution, and indeed was generally no "debate" at all, because Christians heard every "no" to Christianity as a culpable "no" to Jesus Christ.[27] The Jewish scholar Edward Kessler adds that although Jews could not persecute Christians (at least after Constantine), "Judaism also reciprocated the teaching of contempt. . . . Christianity was dismissed as a religion practiced by morally and culturally inferior gentiles, a religion that was based on unbelievable claims, such as God-in-the-flesh."[28] Just as

---

26. As Kaminsky comments from a Jewish perspective, "Both traditions have a strong investment in the notion that humans were created to live forever, both affirm that human sin in some way foiled God's original plan, and both believe that God then created a new way to restore this lost immortality, which will only become fully manifest in the messianic era. At the same time, a serious argument between the two traditions over whether the new path toward immortality was created at Sinai and is accessible through the observance of the commandments, or whether it was made available through the events of Jesus' life, death, and resurrection, still divides Judaism and Christianity" ("Paradise Regained," 41).

27. I agree with Marquardt that "it is necessary to distinguish between historical reasons for the Jewish rejection of the historical Jesus and the No of the Jewish confession of faith"; and I agree too that we should be very cautious when speaking of "the Jews" as an undifferentiated aggregate (Marquardt, "'Enemies for Our Sake,'" 8-9). Marquardt rightly points out that the Jewish people understand their "No" to Christianity (and, through Christianity, to Jesus Christ) to be a "Yes" to the first commandment as well as a "No" to Christian persecution and rejection of Torah. For engagement with Marquardt's broader project, see the essays in Lehming et al., eds., *Wendung nach Jerusalem*; as well as the three essays on Marquardt's theology in Pangritz, *Vergegnungen, Umbrüche und Aufbrüche*.

28. Kessler, "*Dabru Emet*," 197. See also Joel S. Kaminsky's observation that "Jewish scholars, heeding the canons of critical scholarship and intellectual fairness, are beginning to critique widespread Jewish stereotypes of Christianity" ("Paradise Regained," 15). Kaminsky adds, "As long as Jewish people continue to see themselves as the only legitimate biblical tradition, they will view Christianity and its complex of theological ideas as utterly alien to that tradition" ("Paradise Regained," 42). Interestingly, the Talmud applies a principle of invincible ignorance to some Christians: see Laras, "Jewish Perspectives on Christianity," 25-27. By contrast David Meyer, while recognizing that "many rabbis over the centuries taught that Christianity was purely and simply idolatry," contends that whereas Christians taught a deadly contempt for Judaism, "Judaism . . . has nothing to feel guilty about as regards Christianity. The teaching of contempt does not exist in Judaism and never has" ("*Nostra Aetate*," 126-27; along these lines Meyer

there are Christian exclusivists, so are there Jewish exclusivists, for whom "Judaism is the sole path to God" and for whom "those who are not Jews follow a mistaken path and are at best bystanders in the divine scheme, at worst antagonists."[29]

Trying to address and resolve this problem of mutual denigration, John Pawlikowski proposes to affirm that "the distinctive paths followed by Jews and Christians stand on an equal footing."[30] But such a solution can only work in a limited and problematic way, because it cannot apply to the mutually exclusive theological truth-claims of Judaism and Christianity. Again, these truth-claims cannot be dismissed without dismissing the dialogue itself, since Jews and Christians are united at the deepest level by "the horizon to which their gaze is turned: the Truth for whose sake it is worth living."[31]

If by "equal footing" one simply means that Jews and Christians are equal in human dignity, that ongoing Judaism strives to obey the covenants given to the Jewish people by God, and that God has a salvific plan that involves both Jews and Christians, then most believers today will gladly affirm this equality.[32] But no competent Jewish theologian who is not a Christian

---

cites J. Kaplan, *Justice pour la foi juive*, 143).

29. Brill, *Judaism and Other Religions*, 151. Brill's book provides a marvelous survey of key Jewish texts and scholars from the past two millennia on issues pertaining to interfaith dialogue.

30. Pawlikowski, "Christian-Jewish Dialogical Model," 171–72. Pawlikowski affirms, "The Christian path is not inherently superior to the Jewish one" ("Christian-Jewish Dialogical Model," 172). Yet he goes on to say, "With Paul I would want to argue for significant 'newness' in the revelation in Christ. This 'newness', as I have argued in previous writings, relies heavily on an incarnational approach to christology whereby humanity saw with greater transparency than before the intimate link between humanity and divinity" ("Christian-Jewish Dialogical Model," 172). To my mind, this way of describing the incarnation—as simply a manifestation of a truth of human nature—is mistaken; but it does seem that Pawlikowski is claiming for Christianity some kind of "superiority" as least with regard to the new "revelation in Christ." Pawlikowski also directs attention to his earlier writings, in which he advocated a "double covenant" (one for Jews and one for Gentiles)—a viewpoint that he now thinks is inadequate because it separates the first Christians (such as Paul, not to mention Jesus) too firmly from God's covenant with his people Israel. See Pawlikowski, *Jesus and the Theology of Israel*; Pawlikowski, *Christ in the Light*. See also Pawlikowski, "Christology."

31. Forte, "Israel and the Church," 74. For both Jews and Christians, the "Truth has come and has given itself up to the measure of the human possibility to understand it, has spoken the language of humanity, and has inflamed their hearts of flesh with desire" (Forte, "Israel and the Church," 75).

32. I will discuss the issue of salvation later with an eye to "invincible ignorance," but let me note here that I agree with the Pontifical Commission when it states, "From the Christian confession that there can be only one path to salvation, however, it does not in any way follow that the Jews are excluded from God's salvation because they

could grant that the *worship* of Jesus stands theologically or doctrinally on an "equal footing" with ongoing Judaism. Likewise, Christian theologians who worship Jesus as the Son of God and confess that Jesus is the Lord and Messiah of Israel cannot suppose that Judaism is doctrinally equal to Christianity.[33] I concur with the Pontifical Commission for Religious Relations with Jews when it states that "there are not two paths to salvation according to the expression, 'Jews hold to the Torah, Christians hold to Christ'. Christian faith proclaims that Christ's work of salvation is universal and involves all mankind."[34] From a Catholic perspective, Jesus—as the Messiah

---

do not believe in Jesus Christ as the Messiah of Israel and the Son of God. . . . God entrusted Israel with a unique mission, and He does not bring his mysterious plan of salvation for all peoples (cf. 1 Tim 2:4) to fulfilment without drawing into it his 'firstborn son' (Ex 4:22). From this it is self-evident that Paul in the Letter to the Romans definitively negates the question he himself has posed, whether God has repudiated his own people" ("'Gifts and the Calling of God,'" §35).

33. Let me briefly raise here the issue of Messianic Judaism. The key question is whether Torah observance is obligatory, as a matter of salvation, for Jewish Christians. Mark Kinzer suggests that what is at stake is the ongoing survival of the Jewish people as God's distinctive elect people, but it seems to me that God has ensured this survival in another way (namely, ongoing Judaism). See Kinzer, *Postmissionary Messianic Judaism*. The Vatican document "'Gifts and the Calling of God,'" appears to gesture toward Messianic Judaism when it states, "The first Christians were Jews; as a matter of course they gathered as part of the community in the Synagogue, they observed the dietary laws, the Sabbath and the requirement of circumcision, while at the same time confessing Jesus as the Christ, the Messiah sent by God for the salvation of Israel and the entire human race. . . . In the early years of the Church, therefore, there were the so-called Jewish Christians and the Gentile Christians, the *ecclesia ex circumcisione* and the *ecclesia ex gentibus*, one Church originating from Judaism, the other from the Gentiles, who however together constituted the one and only Church of Jesus Christ" (§§15–16). This passage strikes me as both correct and mistaken: correct to note that the first Christians were Jews who continued to observe Torah and worship in the temple and Synagogue, but incorrect in describing a Church "originating" from Gentiles and incorrect in overlooking the intense conflicts described by Paul and Acts that revolved precisely around the point that faith in Christ, not Torah observance, is now what is *required* for salvation. See also, for the perspective I am contesting, Garrigues, "Un seul people"; as well as Hocken, "Jewish People."

34. Pontifical Commission, "'Gifts and the Calling of God,'" §25. The Pontifical Commission goes on to expand upon this point in a helpful manner: "Since God has never revoked his covenant with his people Israel, there cannot be different paths or approaches to God's salvation. The theory that there may be two different paths to salvation, the Jewish path without Christ and the path with the Christ, whom Christians believe is Jesus of Nazareth, would in fact endanger the foundations of Christian faith. Confessing the universal and therefore also exclusive mediation of salvation through Jesus Christ belongs to the core of Christian faith. . . . The Christian faith confesses that God wants to lead all people to salvation, that Jesus Christ is the universal mediator of salvation, and that there is no 'other name under heaven given to the human race by which we are to be saved' (Acts 4:12)" (Pontifical Commission, "'Gifts and the Calling

of Israel—does far more than simply make manifest "the salvation that had long been offered by God to Israel as also for the blessing of the Gentiles."[35]

The above should not be controversial. After all, as Douglas Farrow observes, Christians must affirm "the Church's confession of the glory of Jesus Christ," including the confession "of his deity and of his lordship over all things."[36] Christ has redeemed all peoples, not solely Gentiles, by his cross and resurrection. He has forgiven all sins, so that (in the words of Miroslav Volf) "what is held against transgressors is ultimately not the sins they have committed but the failure to accept their sins as sins—as forgiven sins—and the consequent unwillingness to turn away from them."[37] The ascended Christ reigns even now as Messiah and Lord, possessed of "all authority in heaven and on earth" (Matt 28:18). This is to affirm a superiority, and indeed divinity, of Jesus Christ that ongoing Judaism does not accept and that includes the reconfiguration of Israel's covenants around Christ.[38] With Karl Barth, furthermore, Christians must affirm that those who belong to Christ belong to the inaugurated eschatological Israel: "a man becomes in baptism an active member of the holy people of Israel."[39]

---

of God," §35).

35. C. M. Williamson, "Universal Significance of Christ," 145. See also C. M. Williamson, *Guest in the House of Israel*.

36. Farrow, *Theological Negotiations*, 247.

37. Volf, "Lamb of God," 318.

38. In *Theological Negotiations*, Farrow argues against the Messianic Jewish view that Israel's covenants have not been reconfigured and must be observed by Jewish Christians today. I agree with Farrow's criticisms in this regard. See also N. T. Wright's *Paul*, Book II, 804–911, although Wright's way of phrasing matters has come in for much criticism, to some degree deserved. For a critique, see Kaminsky and Reasoner, "Meaning and Telos of Israel's Election." I agree with them that "some of Wright's arguments suggest that Paul viewed both the Jewish law more negatively and the Jewish people as more expendable than can be sustained on the basis of a close reading of the Pauline letters and the various Hebrew Bible passages upon which Paul built his theology" ("Meaning and Telos of Israel's Election," 422). On the other hand, Kaminsky and Reasoner warn against Wright's "strongly instrumental conception of Israel's election whose telos is only Messiah Jesus" ("Meaning and Telos of Israel's Election," 423). I consider Israel's Messiah and the messianic community ordered around him (the kingdom of God, at present only inaugurated) to be the ultimate "telos" of Israel's election.

39. Barth, *Church Dogmatics* IV.4, 201. See Busch, "Karl Barth and the Jews," 36. In the same place, Busch writes of Barth's concern that the State of Israel would be defeated in the Seven Days War of 1967 and his happiness when it turned out otherwise. In "How Jewish Was Barth?" David Novak notes the presence of anti-Judaism in Barth but attributes it to Barth's not knowing Jewish scholars (with the exception of his philosophy teacher Hermann Cohen). See also Lindsay, *Covenanted Solidarity*; Lindsay, *Barth, Israel and Jesus*; Lindsay, *Reading Auschwitz after Barth*.

Yet, due in part to long-standing Christian replacement theories according to which the ongoing people of Israel are no longer God's people (something that neither Barth nor I hold), as well as due to triumphalistic persecution by Christians of the Jewish people, some Christians argue that Christian understandings of Christ can no longer continue as before. In the words of Mary Boys, "[S]o many Christian teachings have been premised on inadequate notions about Judaism. Once one pulls out the thread of supersessionism, it becomes necessary to reweave the cloth."[40] It should already be clear that many Jewish and Christian scholars today consider that the Christian "denial of doctrinal equality is objectionable, even deeply objectionable, in and of itself."[41] As David Berger has shown, however, this is to impose a standard that contradicts Judaism itself. Berger explains that his Judaism requires him to reject "doctrinal equality" because "the worship of Jesus as God is a serious religious error displeasing to God even if the worshipper is a non-Jew."[42] Although from a Christian perspective the Christian "cloth" may have to be rewoven in certain respects, it cannot be rewoven as regards the core truths that Christians affirm about Jesus, not because of Christian intransigence but simply because these truths—such as that Jesus is the Messiah of Israel, that Jesus rose from the dead, and that Jesus is the incarnate Son of God and Savior of the world—are true. Berger denies that Christians should be required to rend this "cloth," just as Jews must not be expected to rend their own "cloth."

According to Berger, and I fully agree with him, the problem comes when Christians hold explicitly or implicitly that Judaism is "spiritually arid" and is "an expression of narrow, petty legalism pursued in the service of a vengeful God."[43] That such mistaken and destructive caricatures

---

40. Boys, "*Nostra Aetate* Trajectory," 133–34. For Boys, "given how firmly the Church grasped its teaching of contempt and how this grasp so affected fundamentals of our expression of faith, the shift in teaching about Jews and Judaism impinges radically on ecclesial self understanding.... We must reread and reinterpret and rearticulate our tradition, and this process requires generations of thinking and teaching" (Boys, "*Nostra Aetate* Trajectory," 137). Boys is particularly critical of the doctrine that Jesus is the universal Savior, and she interprets Jesus along classically liberal lines as a moral exemplar striving for the coming of a just society. She calls for a "greater humility about our tradition" ("*Nostra Aetate* Trajectory," 141), but humility cannot mean striking at the heart of divine revelation as taught by the New Testament and the tradition of the Church. This would be rationalism rather than humility in the face of what God has given.

41. Berger, "On *Dominus Iesus*," 379. This essay was originally published in *America* magazine.

42. Berger, "On *Dominus Iesus*," 382. For background see also Yuval, *Two Nations in Your Womb*.

43. Berger, "On *Dominus Iesus*," 381. See the important insight of David Novak,

of Judaism exist and have long existed among Christians is all too apparent. Jews too sometimes hold caricatures of Christianity, though without the same historical consequences. As long as caricatures are avoided, it is not a "teaching of contempt" when a Jewish person considers Christian doctrine to be significantly inferior to Judaism, due to Christian worship of the man Jesus. Nor is it a teaching of contempt when a Christian holds that "Judaism errs about religious questions of the most central importance" and that "at the end of days Jews will recognize the divinity of Jesus."[44]

---

assisting (and benefitting from) Christian scholars in this regard: "In his most intense reflection on Judaism in the Letter to the Romans, Paul writes: 'They have zeal for God, but not with proper acknowledgment [*ou kat' epignōsin*]. For they do not acknowledge the righteousness of God.... For Christ is the end of the Law [*telos gar nomou*] so that everyone who believes might become righteous [*eis dikaiōsynēn*]' (Rom. 10:2-4). Note that Paul does not say that the Jews are zealous for the Law for its own sake. He acknowledges they are zealous for God and observe the commandments in the context of their covenantal relationship with God. As such, they are clearly interested in the source of the Law, not just with their own behavior. Moreover, Paul does not say that the Jews are unconcerned with the end of the Law. When he states that Christ is the *telos* of the Law, it is clear that such an assertion presupposes that his hearers—including his Jewish hearers—are vitally concerned with the end of the Law. Thus they certainly do not deny *that* the Law has a true end, that is, it intends a purpose beyond its own observance" (Novak, "End of the Law," 36-37). Novak directs attention here to Sanders, *Paul and Palestinian Judaism*; Luther, *Commentary on Romans*, 130. As Joel Kaminsky observes, the rabbis (like some Jews of Paul's day) believed that "keeping the commandments is a way to hasten the coming of the messianic era. Thus some rabbinic texts speak of Israel's ability to bring on the messianic era by observing Sabbath properly even once, or by fully repenting"; even if other rabbinic texts asserted that "one should not force God to bring the messianic era before its time" (Kaminsky, "Paradise Regained," 38). But even the hastening of the coming of the Messiah derives from the active power of grace, in this case "the original grace that Israel received from encountering God at Sinai" (Kaminsky, "Paradise Regained," 39).

44. Berger, "On *Dominus Iesus*," 382. Berger's alarm at *Dominus Iesus* arises instead from its connection of dialogue with evangelization, or its placement of interreligious dialogue within the framework of mission. But in my view, this is just a Catholic way (no doubt clumsy) of insisting that dialogue not be syncretistic. Insofar as Christians in dialogue with Jews speak of central truths of faith, it is clear that Christians will refer (implicitly or explicitly) to Jesus Christ as Christians understand him. In a broad sense of "mission" (or of "proclaiming the gospel"), any Christian witness to Jesus Christ counts as "mission." I can understand Berger's alarm, since if the purpose of Christian dialogue with Jews were to convert Jews, then such dialogue would be conducted under false pretenses. Citing Ratzinger's *Many Religions—One Covenant*, 104, 109, Berger notes that Ratzinger (who signed *Dominus Iesus*) does not harbor dreams of converting all Jews prior to the coming of Jesus Christ in glory. Berger adds: "if dialogue avoids discussion of core doctrinal issues and focuses on shared moral, social, and political concerns, it may well be justified even with people whose conversionary objectives are much sharper than those of *Dominus Iesus*.... Rabbi Soloveitchik, who did not believe that such objectives had been abandoned by the Catholic Church, endorsed discussion of these matters with full awareness that theological content would play a significant

Importantly, therefore, Berger allows Christians to retain their core doctrinal beliefs and still be involved in dialogue with Jews. He adds that in any true dialogue Jews will not be pressured explicitly or implicitly to accept that Jesus is a prophet for non-Jews or to accept the logic of the incarnation; while Christians likewise will not be pressured "to see the New Testament as an antisemitic work; to demand that it be revised; to question even eschatological confirmation of Christian truth . . . [or] to see Judaism as an absolutely equal religion and to regard as morally abhorrent the denial that it can provide salvation just as effectively as Christianity."[45] These are precisely the things that Christians—often by their fellow Christians—experience pressure to concede, on pain of exclusion from the dialogue. The result is a "dialogue" to which Christians have access only by rejecting central teachings of Christianity. Berger rightly perceives that the Christians involved in such a

---

role" ("On *Dominus Iesus*," 384). See also Michael A. Signer's conclusion that *Dominus Iesus* is not significant for Jewish-Christian dialogue: Signer, "Jewish Response to *Dominus Iesus*"; and the similar perspective of the Catholic scholar Eugene J. Fisher, "What Does *Dominus Iesus* Say about Judaism?"

45. Berger, "*Dabru Emet*," 393. Berger has John Pawlikowski (among many others) in view, as he indicates on 394. He also criticizes David Novak's contention that Jews can affirm that Christians worship the same God as do Jews: while this may be true in one sense, the worship of Jesus is indeed, from the Jewish perspective, the worship of a mere creature. Berger states, "Do Jews and Christians, then, worship the same God? The answer, I think, is yes and no" ("*Dabru Emet*," 395). I am sure that Novak would agree, although Novak focuses on the "yes" by highlighting Christian intentions. Berger agrees with Novak that Christians can be saved, while disagreeing with some of Novak's argument in this regard. Berger also critiques Novak and *Dabru Emet* for suggesting that neither Christians nor Jews should look forward to the eschatological vindication of their respective religious claims. But for Novak, the point is simply that the eschaton will be such a glorious consummation that it will hold surprises for each side. Novak is not suggesting that one of the surprises for Jews will be the revelation that Jesus is Messiah. Novak does not believe that Christians have rightly interpreted Israel's Scriptures, but he wants to leave room for respecting (as an outsider) the revelation that Christians believe they have been given—and, especially, to ask Christians to respect the revelation that Jews think they have been given. For the text of *Dabru Emet*, under the title "A Jewish Statement on Christians and Christianity," see Frymer-Kensky et al., *Christianity in Jewish Terms*, xvii–xx, especially xix: "Jews can respect Christians' faithfulness to their revelation just as we expect Christians to respect our faithfulness to our revelation. Neither Jew nor Christian should be pressed into affirming the teaching of the other community." See also Novak, "Introduction." For (respectively) criticism of *Dabru Emet* and a response, see Levenson, "Jewish-Christian Dialogue"; Frymer-Kensky et al., "Jewish-Christian Dialogue." For an overview of Jewish responses to *Dabru Emet*, see Morgan, "Jewish Perspectives," 13–16. See also, more recently, the 2015 document of the Center for Jewish-Christian Understanding and Cooperation in Israel, signed by twenty-eight Orthodox rabbis and titled "To Do the Will of Our Father in Heaven"; as well as the document of the (Orthodox) Conference of European Rabbis and the Rabbinical Council of America, "Between Jerusalem and Rome."

dialogue will expect Jews to make similar revisions of Judaism.[46] Instead, as he says, Jews should expect Christians to remain Christians, and Christians should expect Jews to remain Jews. Of course, Christians should be willing to hear Jewish thinkers raise "hard questions" for Christians, given the central areas where Christianity has arguably overstepped traditional Jewish bounds.[47]

In addition, Berger denies that Jews should now adopt an understanding of Christianity that parallels the positive shift in contemporary Christian views of Judaism. As an example of what concerns Berger, I note that Ellen Charry argues that the goal of Jewish-Christian dialogue is to establish a spiritual friendship, and she holds that this goal requires "both parties to admit their own insufficiency and that they need the other in order to become their best theological self, that is, to worship God truly, and that, without the other, they falter in that goal."[48] I can understand how Christians may

---

46. Berger makes his case both on theological and practical grounds. Theologically, he notes: "Christians who will not grant Judaism full salvific force are denounced by both Jews and Christians in language appropriate for characterizing moral miscreants. But the reason given for granting Judaism such status has nothing to do with morality at all but rather with the assertion that the first covenant remains in force.... A Christian who rejects this position may or may not be making a theological error from an inner Christian perspective, but he or she is not guilty of a moral defect unless one is prepared to posit a universal moral principle that every religion must be granted full salvific efficacy" (Berger, "*Dabru Emet*," 393). Practically, he observes: "Once Christians are prepared to break the link between a doctrine and its possible anti-Jewish consequences, Jews should refrain from any further interventions" ("*Dabru Emet*," 393; cf. 398).

47. Volf, "Lamb of God," 319. Volf appreciates that there is an important place for seeking to understand the other in the other's terms and highlighting areas of convergence or potential convergence. An excellent example of such work, Volf notes, is Kepnes, "'Turn Us to You.'"

48. Charry, "Toward Ending Enmity," 149-50. Charry's reasoning is as follows: "Unless Judaism makes theological sense of 'the other,' how is it to make sense of the universality of God, of Isaiah's vision that the nations shall stream to the Lord's house in Jerusalem (Isa. 2) and that God is the God of the Ninevites?" ("Toward Ending Enmity," 165). I note that Judaism has accounted theologically for Christianity in various ways over the centuries, and that Judaism has internal resources to understand the ultimate universality of its mission and to avoid implying that "God's embrace applies to Jews only" (Charry, "Toward Ending Enmity," 166). Charry calls upon the Jewish people to affirm that "in Christ God has enabled Jews and Judaism to bring God to the world" ("Toward Ending Enmity," 166). But to my mind, such a recognition would be logically tantamount to accepting Jesus as the Messiah. She goes on to affirm, "Although Jesus of Nazareth remains Judaism's great gift to the world, it is now to be recognized that Jesus Christ is also Christianity's great gift to Judaism ... As redeemer of the world, Christ cuts through Jewish theological insouciance because he is the means that God employs to bring the nations to himself.... Jews will not only celebrate along with Christians but will themselves embrace Christ as their ambassador. Christ is Israel's redeemer in

admit this in a limited sense, so long as Christians do not deny that Jesus is the Messiah of Israel who has fulfilled and reconfigured Israel's covenants around himself. But I cannot see how Jews could grant what Charry requires, any more than Christians could plausibly grant (for example) that it is impossible for Christians "to worship God truly" without the assistance of Islam. Jewish theologians can and do draw insights from Christian thinkers that deepen their articulation of Judaism, but this is not the same thing as confessing "insufficiency" along Charry's lines. Berger warns that this kind of reciprocity must not be a requirement for Jewish-Christian dialogue, and I agree with him.[49]

---

the sense that he enables God's embrace of gentiles, even of Israel's enemies; he fulfills Israel's biblical mandate to bring God to the world on behalf of Judaism itself" (Charry, "Toward Ending Enmity," 167). From a Christian perspective, I find Charry's account of Christ (as not needed by the Jewish people except in the communication of the true God to the Gentiles) to be unacceptable. Novak offers the more limited statement that "the presence of Christianity in the world shows to some Jews that our election into the Covenant has already begun to bless the world and more forcefully anticipate its full and final redemption" (Novak, "End of the Law," 47; see also Novak's engagement with Franz Rosenzweig, whose position is closer to Charry's, in Novak's *Jewish-Christian Dialogue*. See also, along lines congenial to Novak's perspective, Michael A. Signer's view that it is "imperative" that Jews and Christians "become partners in understanding the divine word to be a blessing to the entire world" (Signer, "Searching the Scriptures," 98; cf. Signer's "Rift That Binds.")

49. See Berger, "Revisiting 'Confrontation.'" See also Gregerman, "Jewish Theology." After aptly critiquing the three "reciprocal" requests that Cardinal Koch addresses to the Jewish people, Gregerman observes: "Koch, as a Catholic, speaks of an 'irreducible uniqueness' in the Jewish-Christian relationship. He says he cannot but grapple with this tension between connection (e.g., shared Scripture, fidelity to the one God) and division (e.g., historical separation, disagreement about Christ). Jews, of course, see things differently. For obvious reasons, Jews traditionally have less interest in grappling theologically with Christianity. Jews' willingness to accept proposals for changes therefore differs from Christians' willingness" ("Jewish Theology," 12–13). Gregerman adds, however, a note of openness to "reciprocal" requests (in principle, even if most such requests will be unworkable) insofar as such requests arise from a relationship of friendship: "From numerous Christian colleagues and friends I have movingly heard of the desire to be seen by Jews as more than generic Noahides. Their deep sense of connection to the God of Israel . . . raises important questions about the nature of the Jewish covenant. This request, though almost never put in reciprocal terms, nonetheless appropriately reflects a sense that Christian views of Jews and Judaism have changed dramatically, and that Jews might reconsider their own views. Reciprocity is not a demand (and never a threat), but a reflection of a healthy relationship open to change. It is a dialogue worth continuing" ("Jewish Theology," 13). See also Koch, "Theological Questions"; as well as Eugene Korn's "Jewish Response to 'Theological Questions.'" Korn considers that while Jews and Christians differ sharply with regard to Sinai—and thus Jews cannot see "Christians as partners in that covenant without entailing some form of supersession or cancellation of the Torah of Moses"—it is the case that "[n]ow that Christianity is no longer a threat to Jews and Judaism, Jews must admit

II. Christian Blindness, Christian Charity, and Human Divisions

Given the sins of Christians against Jews over the centuries, Jewish-Christian dialogue sometimes proceeds on the part of the Christian participants as though the Church has been a failure in all areas or as though supernatural charity is a mere myth. In this regard, the Lutheran theologian George Lindbeck criticizes Christian circles in which "self-flagellation has acquired the aura of a virtue. Talk of what is wrong with Christianity is acceptable and praiseworthy, whereas the positive aspects of Christianity are passed over in silence."[50] Despite Christian "blindness" (cf. 2 Cor 4:4, which I am applying now toward Christians) toward the dignity and sometimes even the humanity of the ongoing Jewish people, the real power of Christ's grace to move believers to repentance, love of God, mercy toward others, self-sacrifice out of love, and conversion of life should not be "passed over in silence."[51] When another eminent Protestant theologian, George Hunsinger, states that "when Christianity does not love the Jews, it corrupts its love of Jesus Christ at the very core," I both agree and disagree.[52] I agree because hatred of the Jewish people is anti-Christian; I disagree because of the real

---

that covenantally, both Jews and faithful Christians are children of Abraham" ("Jewish Response to 'Theological Questions,'" 3). This point is disputed by Jon D. Levenson, and I am sympathetic with his concerns even though, as a Christian, I believe that "Jews and faithful Christians are children of Abraham." Moreover, Korn's way of defining the meaning of covenantal "children of Abraham" gets around the key difficulties, in my view: see "Jewish Response to 'Theological Questions,'" 6–7, where Korn outlines points of agreement, including the existence of one loving Creator God who yearns to redeem human beings, the creation of all humans in the image of God, the rejection of violence undertaken in the name of God, the commitment to justice and righteousness, and the possibility of (messianic) redemption. For a similar list of points of agreement, see the 2015 document *To Do the Will of Our Father in Heaven*.

50. Lindbeck, "What of the Future?," 364.

51. For testimonies to grace, see for example Vogt, *Saints and Social Justice*; R. Williams, *Luminaries*.

52. Hunsinger, "After Barth," 60. I largely agree with Hunsinger's further point that "[t]he day is long since past when Christians might hope to alleviate this wound by adopting Saint Paul's strategy of 'making Israel jealous' [Rom 11:11]. Today this strategy, which was scarcely ever adopted, smolders in ruins. After the long and unbearable history of Christian anti-Semitism, and especially after the Shoah—for which Christian history was the dreadful background, if not the direct cause—Christianity would be delusional if it thought it could any longer do anything to make Israel 'jealous'" (Hunsinger, "After Barth," 61). In the sense Paul intends this term—striving to excel in charity, humility, and justice—I do not see anything wrong with striving to implement the "strategy," so long as one's expectations are characterized by repentant humility and are eschatologically grounded (requiring God's coming in glory rather than merely a successful human "strategy").

faith, hope, and charity possessed by the saints and so many other Christian believers over the centuries, despite their sins and significant blind spots, too often with regard to the Jewish people.

As noted above, I hold that Christian antipathy toward ongoing Judaism should be viewed within the "mystery" of "hardening" to which Paul refers in Romans 11—beyond what Paul himself envisioned, although he foresaw Gentile boasting. Christians too have been "hardened." Comprised largely of Gentiles, the Church has "boast[ed] over the branches" (Rom 11:18, 25) with disastrous results. I believe that God has allowed this disobedience—permitted it, not caused it—for purposes known only to God but that must pertain in some way to his plan to "have mercy upon all" (Rom 11:32). Here Hunsinger and I concur that "both Jews and Christians have done something that is contrary to the will of God, each in their own way."[53] Caught up in ingrained misunderstanding and prejudice, Christians frequently did not realize the injustice of what they were doing to the Jewish people. Thus, an aspect of Catholicism's history, in Daniel Jonah Goldhagen's words, is its "betrayal of its own essential and good moral principles" with regard to its treatment of the Jewish people.[54]

---

53. Hunsinger, "After Barth," 66. Hunsinger aptly remarks: "With regard to the rejection of Jesus Christ by the Jews, and then the rejection of the Jews by Christians, which I have contended is tantamount to their own rejection of Jesus Christ, I would take solace in the words of Augustine. 'For in a strange and ineffable way,' he wrote, 'nothing is done without the will of God, even that which is done contrary to it'" (Hunsinger, "After Barth," 66, citing Augustine, *Enchiridion*, 454).

54. Goldhagen, *Moral Reckoning*, 3. Goldhagen adds: "The question for Christians, especially for the Catholic Church, is, What must a religion of love and goodness do to confront its history of hatred and harm, to make amends with its victims, and to right itself so that it is no longer the source of a hatred and harm that, whatever its past, it would no longer endorse?" (*Moral Reckoning*, 3). I think this is a crucial question, even if framed so as to suggest that Catholic history is simply "hatred and harm," which is far from the case overall. For a much more balanced approach to the history—and an explanation for Goldhagen's black-and-white view—see Ruff, *Battle for the Catholic Past*; as well as the paired volumes (one praising Munich priests and Bishop Konrad von Preysing, the other describing in detail the small number of German priests who publicly supported Hitler and the Nazis) by Spicer, *Resisting the Third Reich*; Spicer, *Hitler's Priests*. Ruff points out that "by almost all objective yardsticks, the German Protestant leadership left behind a more troubling record of collaboration than their Catholic counterparts. Between 10 and 20 percent (in some states more than half!) of Protestant clergy . . . formally joined the Nazi Party or ancillary organizations like the SA. . . . By contrast, less than 1 percent of the Catholic clergy joined the Nazi party, and the worst of the 'brown priests' were often reprimanded for their excess zeal" (Ruff, *Battle for the Catholic Past*, 244). For further detailed studies see the essays in Kösters and Ruff, eds., *katholische Kirche im Dritten Reich*. See also Goldhagen's *Devil That Never Dies*, in which it becomes clear that anti-Semitism does not depend upon Christianity for its ongoing sustenance—although Goldhagen does not withdraw his charges against

It is necessary to clarify, however, that the Catholic Church has not definitively taught doctrine about the Jewish people that is now being contradicted by the Church. Of course, in canon law and in papal statements and Councils there are references to the "superstition" and "servitude" of the Jews that assume that their exile is the consequence of deicide. But these statements do not rise to the level of solemn and definitive doctrine, in part because the ongoing existence of the Jewish people was treated as posing practical rather than doctrinal problems. The Church did not attempt to define doctrine about the Jewish people per se, other than assuming that the rejection of Jesus had brought punishment upon them in various forms. Gavin D'Costa has shown that in accord with a standard pattern of doctrinal development, contemporary Church teaching has responded to contemporary events—including the horror of the Holocaust and, beginning much earlier, the end of Christendom—and has begun to understand in an increasingly clear doctrinal manner what justice and charity toward the Jewish people involve.[55] The Church has done so not by rejecting earlier notions of justice and charity, let alone by relativizing Christ the Lord, but by striving anew to live up to Christ's charity.[56]

Christian Scripture and doctrine (see for example *Devil That Never Dies*, 441).

55. See D'Costa, *Vatican II*, chapter 3. For a powerful reflection upon the sins of Christians, including systemic sins of various kinds, see Radner, *Brutal Unity*. The doctrine of the holiness of the Church has never depended upon Christians being sinless or even close to it, as I discuss in *Engaging the Doctrine of the Holy Spirit*, chapter 7. See also D'Costa, "Between Doctrine and Discernment," 69, where he notes that the claim that "the Church" as such is anti-Semitic (as distinct from the anti-Semitism of popes, bishops, clergy, religious, and laity) "would have to show that the formal magisterium (pope or Council) solemnly and formally taught anti-Semitism was a Christian duty or formally taught that the Jews were cursed and the covenant revoked. There is no denial that these teachings existed and were practiced in Catholic culture for nearly two thousand years. But only if it could be shown that the formal magisterium consistently and solemnly taught anti-Judaism would we have a clear case of the Church 'as such' sinning." For criticisms of the doctrine of the holiness of the Church—criticisms that strike me as missing the point—see Bernauer, *Jesuit Kaddish*, 12–13.

56. I disagree with Goldhagen's charge that Christianity "consecrated at its core ... a megatherian hatred of one group of people: the Jews" (*Moral Reckoning*, 3). Goldhagen also describes the Holocaust as an act of "Christians," and I find this to be mistaken, since the Nazis who commanded it were lapsed and anti-Christian. This is so even if Christians participated in various ways in the work of the Holocaust, as Goldhagen shows in *Hitler's Willing Executioners*. For Goldhagen, moral repair requires that the Church renounce Jesus' standing as the universal mediator of salvation and deny that the Christian "Bible's contents are true, are God's word" (*Moral Reckoning*, 262). Goldhagen calls for the latter because, in his view, "[t]he anti-Semitism of the Christian Bible is not incidental to it but constitutive of its story of Jesus' life and death and of its messages about God and humanity" (*Moral Reckoning*, 262). He deems impractical James Carroll's proposal that the Church should proclaim the Christian Bible's anti-Semitic

It is also important to be clear that despite what seems to me to be the evident fact that Christian societies over many centuries deeply wronged the Jewish people, I am not trying to portray the Jewish people as reducible to mere victims. Their achievements—along with the complexity of their interactions with Christians, which on a personal level were often good ones—show that they cannot be understood solely as "victims." Affirming the "value and vitality of the Jewish past," the Jewish scholar Jonathan Elukim has rightly warned against a "Manichean vision of medieval Europe" and a "one-dimensional interest in Jewish suffering."[57] In many times and places, Christians and Jews lived together peacefully and constructively. Nor am I painting the Jewish people over the centuries as free of sin in a way that would further sharpen the contrast with their persecutors. Portraying the Jewish people along these lines would only cause Jews today, who hold worldly power in ways not possible in earlier centuries, to be judged by a standard unbearable for fallen human beings.[58] The fact that

---

texts (which, in Goldhagen's count, number in the hundreds) to be sinful falsehoods that apply not to the Jews but to Christians themselves (*Moral Reckoning*, 269). Instead, Goldhagen proposes that a congress of all Christian leaders, joined by Jewish leaders, should be convened to explore options such as including "in every Christian Bible a detailed, corrective account alongside the text about its many antisemitic passages, and a clear disclaimer explaining that even though these passages were once presented as fact, they are actually false or dubious" (*Moral Reckoning*, 276). Goldhagen considers Christians who defend the New Testament to be bigots, and he makes this case in a manner comparable to how others denounce the Old Testament God as a monster and the doctrine of the election of Israel as a violent fraud. For Carroll's proposal see his *Constantine's Sword*, 566–67.

57. Elukin, *Living Together, Living Apart*, 3, 5. He argues, "Violence against Jews ... was contingent on local conditions and not the result of unchanging hatred or an irrational structure of medieval society.... Moreover, the level of violence against Jews—either oppressive laws, outright attacks, paranoid accusations, or expulsions—were essentially transitory and contingent events that did not fundamentally destroy the modus vivendi between most Christians and Jews of the time" (Elukin, *Living Together, Living Apart*, 5–7). Although he grants (for example) that "Jews were pushed out of most Western European countries (with the exception of Italy and parts of Germany) by the second half of the sixteenth century," and he is well aware of the commonplace undercurrent of discrimination, he holds that a focus on Jewish suffering not only distorts the overall picture but also plays into the patristic Christian trope of Jewish "dispersion and suffering" (Elukin, *Living Together, Living Apart*, 3, 7). His positive thesis is as follows: "Instead of persecution and suffering, it is more important to understand how and why Jews survived in societies whose dominant theology increasingly cast them in the role of deicides" (Elukin, *Living Together, Living Apart*, 6). See also (though still with tragic elements) the interchanges documented in the essays in Signer and Van Engen, eds., *Jews and Christians*; as well as the essays in Coudert and Shoulson, eds., *Hebraica Veritas?*

58. Goldhagen rightly warns against the temptation to "essentialize Jews" (Goldhagen, *Moral Reckoning*, 23), which can be done both in derogatory and in idealizing

the Jewish people were persecuted does not mean that, if the shoe had been on the other foot, they would have necessarily avoided succumbing to the fallen human temptation to persecute those whom one finds threatening or wrongheaded.

Over the centuries, Christians persecuted Jews terribly, and Christians made things even worse by attempting to justify why Jews (supposedly) had to be treated without full human dignity in Christian countries. At best, the result was a cultural denigration of the Jewish people combined with a strict limitation of their opportunities. Regularly, however, there were also pogroms and scapegoating, blood libels, expulsions, vicious slander, and deeply nefarious practices intended to render the Jewish people marginal and powerless—to which the Holocaust adds a dimension of its own.[59] Many Christians today do not know the extent of the injustice prior to the Holocaust, having managed to avoid reading the relevant histories. By contrast, many Jewish people know much more, both from family stories and liturgical remembrance, and from reading works of Jewish history. A Christian Israelology must face what happened without whitewashing it.

In the nineteenth century, the rise of liberal nation-states, often anti-Christian in tone and outlook, allowed Jews to receive full citizenship rights—though generally with the tacit condition that they assimilate rather than continuing to observe Torah. At the same time, matters took a turn for the worse with the rise of racial theory and the negative application of that theory to the Jewish people. Building upon centuries of Christian stereotypes that resonated with a populace whose Christian belief was fading, pagan Nazi "bioracism" served as an excuse for horrifically scapegoating the Jewish people for all the ills of the German nation.[60]

The German theologian Hans Küng aptly remarked three decades after the Holocaust: "Nazi anti-Judaism was the work of godless anti-Christian

---

ways. Regarding the post-Holocaust change for the better, insofar as the Jewish people now possess much more this-worldly power, see the remarks by Novak in Frymer-Kensky et al., "What of the Future?," 367–68.

59. See for example Berger, "From Crusades to Blood Libels," 15–39. See also Stow, *Alienated Minority*. Things were significantly less bad (though not good) in the Muslim world. Berger states, "Pre-modern Jews had flourished and suffered under Islam, but anti-Jewish sentiment rarely reached the heights that it attained in the Christian world. This was partly because Jews were never the only minority in the Muslim orbit, but it was also because Judaism did not play the crucial role in Islam that it did in Christianity" (Berger, "Anti-Semitism," 11). See also M. Cohen, *Under Crescent and Cross*. Berger is aware that "the resurgence of anti-Semitism in the late nineteenth century was part of a general rebellion against the liberalism and modernity that were responsible for emancipating the Jews" ("Anti-Semitism," 9).

60. For the term *bioracism* and a fuller explanation, see Pawlikowski, "Significance of the Christian-Jewish Dialogue," 447.

criminals; but, without the almost two-thousand-year-long pre-history of 'Christian' anti-Judaism which also prevented Christians in Germany from a convinced and energetic resistance on a broad front, it would not have been possible."[61] From a Jewish perspective, David Berger differentiates the tradition of Christian anti-Judaism (and anti-Semitism) from the Nazi variant of the same, by arguing that Nazi ideology stripped away the civilized veneer that had previously served as a check to anti-Jewish passions. He contends, "Nazi anti-Semitism achieved such virulent, unrestrained consequences precisely because it stripped away the semi-civilized rationales that had been given in the past for persecuting Jews and liberated the deepest psychological impulses that had been partly nurtured but partly suppressed by those rationales."[62] Tapping into sheer bloodlust, the Nazis unleashed the full force of what Christians had fomented.

I note that Catholics cannot hide behind the fact that the Nazis also hated Christianity and killed millions of Catholics in the concentration camps. The Holocaust was not a Christian event, but Christianity had a significant role in laying anti-Jewish and anti-Semitic foundations, and many baptized Christians played a part in its implementation or else stood by without any kind of protest.[63] As Peter Hayes has pointed out, it would

61. Küng, "Introduction," 11; see also along the same lines Bernardin, "Anti-Semitism," 6; as well as Steigmann-Gall, "Old Wine in New Bottles?" Steigmann-Gall shows that "racialism was for many Nazis conceived within a Christian frame of reference," insofar as they used Christian anti-Jewish language and categories even while rejecting most Christian doctrinal content ("Old Wine in New Bottles," 305). Küng adds a sobering illustration (not his own): "None of the anti-Jewish measures of the Nazis—distinctive clothing, exclusion from professions, the Nuremberg 'laws' forbidding mixed marriages, expulsions, the concentration camps, massacres, gruesome funeral pires—was new. All that already existed in the so-called Christian Middle Ages . . . and in the period of the 'Christian' Reformation. What was new was the racial grounding of these measures—prepared by the French Count Arthur Gobineau and the Anglo-German Houston Stewart Chamberlain, and then carried through in Nazi Germany with cruelly exact organization, technical perfection and a terrible industrialization of death" (Küng, "Introduction," 11–12). I agree with Küng that "[t]he implicit or explicit excuse that 'The Jews make mistakes as well', 'You have to understand everything in its historical context', 'It wasn't the Church itself', 'You have to choose the lesser evil'—is now obsolete" (Küng, "Introduction," 12). I part ways with him when he moves to attacking "the desuetude of the neo-Platonic, neo-Aristotelian and neo-Scholastic encrustation of Christianity" (Küng, "Introduction," 13) as well as when he celebrates what he perceives to be a salutary movement of young Jews away from the Talmud.

62. Berger, "Jewish-Christian Relations," 354.

63. For further discussion, see Barnett, *Bystanders*. On the one hand, she notes the brutality and speed of the Nazis in dealing with even relatively minor dissent, which raises the point that people under a totalitarian regime have little real choice. But on the other hand, she notes the ways in which, even in February 1933 when the Nazis had only just assumed power, Christians immediately and without external compulsion

be a mistake to uproot the Holocaust from its specific context, inclusive of industrialization, World War I, the Bolshevik Revolution, the Great Depression, and—even more concretely—Nazi totalitarianism and the political and military situation of a populace at war, not only in Germany but in countries under Germany's sway. But part of the context was the presence of "ancient hostilities toward Jews and Judaism, deeply rooted in religious rivalry but updated with the trappings of modern science," which made it plausible for Hitler and others, including many regular citizens, to see "removing Jews from civil society as a magical solution to all social problems."[64]

It follows that Christian Israelology today has, as a practical matter, the task of seeking to repair grave and humanly speaking irreparable wrongs from centuries past.[65] Walter Moberly sums up this duty, which pertains to all Christians: "On the one hand is the need to come to terms with, repent

---

began to treat their Jewish neighbors differently. Moreover, although many leaders and people outside German-controlled areas knew about the ongoing persecution of the Jewish people especially after 1938—and then also knew about the Holocaust after 1942—they generally did little or nothing. See for example Gilbert, *Auschwitz and the Allies*; and the searing indictment of Franklin D. Roosevelt in Medoff, *Jews Should Keep Quiet*. See also Ericksen, "Christian Complicity?" Nonetheless, in my view the point that Barnett makes at 87 needs underlining: "Faced with potential consequences for themselves and their families, they do indeed feel powerless—even when, within the confines of their private lives, they are able to lead 'normal' lives. This powerlessness is linked to a related factor that helps to incapacitate individuals morally—what Bauman terms the phenomenon of 'free-floating responsibility.' Under totalitarian rule, individuals soon find that they have been relieved of any real authority or autonomy, since the state's power is so pervasive that it affects even individual decisions about where to live and what jobs people can have." As she concludes, "the real mystery is what leads the individual, in the decisive moment, to 'embrace' the other" (Barnett, *Bystanders*, 170). See Bauman, *Modernity and the Holocaust*.

64. P. Hayes, *Why?*, xv.

65. See also D'Costa, "Between Doctrine and Discernment," 67–68, regarding Jewish appreciation for Vatican II but also Jewish concern about what Vatican II failed to say: "After the Council this concern settled around three issues: the institutional level of Catholic anti-Semitism such that the Catholic Church itself should acknowledge its guilt and failings and seek repentance as a Church; the level of anti-Semitism in certain popes, particularly Pius XII, should be clarified; and the possibility of New Testament anti-Semitism must be faced." For further background and concerns, see Rosen, "Jewish and Israeli Perspectives"; Rudin, "Dramatic Impact of *Nostra Aetate*"; Tanenbaum, "Jewish Viewpoint on *Nostra Aetate*"; Meyer, "*Nostra Aetate*." Rudin expresses appreciation for "the affirmation of Judaism as an eternal living faith by the Catholic Church" but expresses concern (like Meyer) that "Roman Catholics do not yet fully grasp the profound meaning that the State of Israel has for Jews everywhere" ("Dramatic Impact of *Nostra Aetate*," 17). For Meyer, it is offensive that *Nostra Aetate* does not grant the equality of Catholicism and Judaism. Meyer misinterprets *Nostra Aetate* as saying that God loves the Jewish people only because of the patriarchs (and other biblical heroes) rather than also because the Jews are human beings.

of, and renounce the anti-Jewishness and anti-Judaism of so much Christian tradition. On the other hand is the need to develop an accurate and appreciative understanding of Jewishness and Judaism."[66] Christians should be greatly moved when David Novak and his co-authors, in their 2000 statement *Dabru Emet*, remark that they do not blame Christians today "for the sins committed by their [Christians'] ancestors."[67] It would be understandable if Jewish people today hated Christians for the sins of the past, and it is a sign of grace that Novak and his colleagues renounce such hatred. The least that Christians can do in response is to attempt, in the words of Marc Tanenbaum, to "develop theological conceptions regarding Judaism and the synagogue that reflect in some way the vital reality of the existence of present-day Judaism."[68]

In earthly life, of course, not all divisions can be removed, and even the greatest goods can contribute to generating divisions. In the Gospel of Matthew, Jesus warns that he has "come to set a man against his father, and a daughter against her mother, and a daughter-in-law against her mother-in-law; and a man's foes will be those of his own household" (Matt 10:35–36). Likewise, Jewish doctrines such as election, the one God, and the truthfulness of Torah sometimes cause the division of neighbors from each other, to the point where some contemporary scholars consider monotheism (and/

---

66. Moberly, *Old Testament of the Old Testament*, 148. Moberly goes on to discuss Jewish and Christian receptions of the Tanakh (Hebrew Bible)/Old Testament. The conclusion that Moberly draws is that Christians should retain the terms "Old" and "New" because these terms reflect the Christian belief that "Jesus is the key to understanding God and provides the focal point from which all else should be evaluated and understood" (*Old Testament of the Old Testament*, 158–59). Moberly recognizes the weak spots of his own arguments, including the facts that "both Judaism and Christianity as religious constructs are, arguably, products of late antiquity, particularly the fourth, fifth, and sixth centuries" and that "the obvious biblical precedent for the language of Old and New Testament has clearly pejorative implications about the continuing value of what is represented by Old as opposed to New (Jer. 31:31–34; Hebrews 8; 2 Corinthians 3)" (*Old Testament of the Old Testament*, 168). See also the essays in Brooks and Collins, eds., *Hebrew Bible or Old Testament?*; as well as Christopher R. Seitz's use of the term "Elder Testament" in his *Elder Testament*, especially chapter 1. For discussion of continuity and discontinuity in (and between) Judaism and Christianity, see Brueggemann, "Dialogue between Incommensurate Partners," though I think his insistence upon overcoming "historical discontinuities" between Jews and Christians risks syncretism (398).

67. Novak et al., "*Dabru Emet*," xix. This is especially moving given that, as Berger notes, "[s]ince Jews can understand their faith without reference to Christianity, there is no internal need to engage in theological discussion with Christians" (Berger, "Jewish-Christian Relations," 335). At the same time, it is true that "the case can be made that much Jewish self-understanding can be seen as the Jewish attempt to further distinguish Judaism from Christianity" (Novak, "End of the Law," 35).

68. Tanenbaum, "A Jewish Viewpoint on *Nostra Aetate*," 56.

or the Torah) to be "the originary source of polemic between nations, and therefore ... historically responsible for the exceptionalism that undergirds contemporary conflict."[69] Humans will always find ways of being divisive, so it is foolish to blame religion for every division. It is acceptable that there should remain sharp differences between Judaism and Christianity. The key is to cultivate what Randi Rashkover calls a "lawful knowledge" that carefully "retains the right or freedom to issue truth claims when these claims are justified within the lawful order of the freedom of others to assert alternative claims."[70]

Allowing other people the freedom to assert truth-claims opposed to one's own, even on highly important matters (so long as these truth-claims do not violate "lawful order," a caveat that I understand as pertaining to threats of violent harm or slander), provides an opportunity to hear their insights and to learn from aspects of their thought. While this approach will reduce polemics, it will not stop them altogether. For example, when reading contemporary Jewish thinkers, I often find an implicit or explicit polemic against Christianity. This is what I would expect in the work of believers in Israel's God who consider Christianity to be ultimately false. Again, some Jewish and Christian doctrines are inevitably divisive, just as some secular doctrines are. Faith in "Christ crucified" in fact remains "a stumbling block to Jews and folly to Gentiles" (1 Cor 1:23). I grant also that the proclamation of the gospel of Jesus Christ, both in its rhetorically intense original context and in its often equally intense later contexts (when

---

69. Rashkover, *Freedom and Law*, 2. These scholars include Jacob Taubes, Giorgio Agamben, Alain Badiou, Regina Schwartz, Jan Assmann, and many others.

70. Rashkover, *Freedom and Law*, 5. Rashkover and I disagree somewhat about the details. Rashkover summarizes her argument: "As recipients of divine revelation, persons are epistemologically justified in their religious assertions to the extent that they may admit the *possibility* of the truth of exterior positions. ... If the condition of the possibility of my claim is the reality of divine freedom, such freedom also justifies the possibility of another's claim. Consequently, the condition of the possibility of my claim is the possibility of the truth-value of another's claim and to defend my tradition means to recognize the possibility of truths exterior to my own. ... Apologetics is rerouted from a tug-of-war over competing truths into the exercise of exposure to the range of other possible claims, and Jewish-Christian relations acquire a basis for a curriculum of free earning within the law" (Rashkover, *Freedom and Law*, 6). I affirm that we should be open to other perspectives and possibilities that arise from learning more and from seeing things from new angles. But I do not hold to an eschatological deferral of truth or certitude. Rashkover is indebted to Karl Barth's eschatological deferral of dogmatic truth in light of divine freedom. Yet, I agree with her when she insists (with basic humility in view) that the Christian must hold with Barth: "My articulation of the gospel is always justified only within the order of the difference between God's own Revelation and Speaking of the Word and my reception of this Word through God's lawful love" (Rashkover, *Freedom and Law*, 271).

Christians often fought against their fellow Christians), has caused harm in addition to good.

Here I think of Lauren Winner's discouraging but realistic statement, put forward in light of the history of Christian divisions. She remarks rather shockingly, "Eucharist, prayer, baptism: These things are blighted."[71] She immediately adds, however, that for Christians these practices, despite the blight, are very much worth continuing "because they are gifts from the Lord."[72] Inevitably, human sinfulness damages gifts that "are perfect in kind" and "are given by a flawless giver."[73] In the wilderness, the people of Israel on exodus already experienced this fact.

It is the Christian task to learn to proclaim the inevitably divisive gospel of Jesus Christ in a manner least obscured by our sin and most reflective of the charity of Christ. It is not our responsibility to smooth over all divisiveness or to remove the "sword" that Jesus brings by bringing his peace (Matt 10:34).[74] Jesus faced opposition and his followers will face the same, in part because his words and deeds are immensely challenging. But it is our responsibility to act with humility and care, taking up our cross and following Jesus, rather than placing other people upon the cross by persecuting them.[75]

III. "Our Father Abraham" (Rom 4:12): A Figure of Unity or Division?

Sometimes it is hoped that many of the remaining divisions between Jews and Christians (and Muslims) can be overcome by appealing to the figure who can be said to stand at the root of all three faiths: Abraham. Let me

---

71. Winner, *Dangers of Christian Practice*, 137.

72. Winner, *Dangers of Christian Practice*, 137.

73. Winner, *Dangers of Christian Practice*, 154.

74. Rudolf Schnackenburg comments on this verse: "to prevent a misinterpretation of his mission Jesus speaks of the struggle that breaks out in families because of his coming. He is to bring not 'peace,' but the 'sword' (in Luke 12:51, 'division'). This sounds like a correction of his message of peace (see 5:9), but it actually stands in a different context of meaning. The gospel has dividing power as well, surrendering none of its acuity 'for the sake of dear peace'" (Schnackenburg, *Gospel of Matthew*, 101).

75. For Rashkover, the ideal is when "I may freely present my claim without polemically defending it against another's" (Rashkover, *Freedom and Law*, 271). I think truth-claims often have a polemic embedded within them, however; and when we hand on truth-claims, we inevitably do so against other possible truth-claims or against other possible ways of handing on truth-claims. Indeed, Rashkover's book offers a sustained implicit polemic against certain ways of handing on truth-claims. See also Rashkover, *Revelation and Theopolitics*.

therefore briefly attend to the figure of Abraham from a Christian perspective, but with attention to Jewish exegesis as well.

Christians and Jews both celebrate Abraham and his covenant, yet in decidedly different ways.[76] Recall that according to Genesis, Abraham is from Ur of the Chaldeans and descends from Noah's son Shem. God gave Abraham a command and a promise: "Go from your country and your kindred and your father's house to the land that I will show you. And I will make of you a great nation, and I will bless you. . . . I will bless those who bless you, and him who curses you I will curse; and by you all the families of the earth shall bless themselves" (Gen 12:1-3). Although the precise meaning of this promise is contested, it is clear that Abraham's descendants will stand at the center of humanity and will be a blessing to all peoples.[77]

Abraham's response to God's command is one of humble obedience: "So Abram went, as the Lord had told him" (Gen 12:4). As Bill Arnold remarks, "the simplicity of 'so Abram went' portrays a picture of bold and radical dependence on God's word, the diametric opposite of Adam's and Eve's rationalization (3:1-7), which makes Abram's obedience a model of faith

---

76. Norbert Lohfink addresses the issues that arise if one accepts the historical-critical conclusion that "covenant" is a rather late concept in Israel's history. Approaching the issues canonically, he notes that "[t]he term that occurs in the Tanakh itself to signify the unity of the canon is . . . not 'covenant' but 'torah'" (Lohfink, "Concept of 'Covenant,'" 23). For Lohfink, as he makes clear in a further essay, the motivating question is whether all nations are expected to "come to God on Mt. Zion" and "observe the torah and become part of God's covenant with Israel" (Lohfink, "Covenant and Torah," 35). Lohfink and Zenger conclude, "Jews and Christians believe that they live in and from the 'covenant with God.' These are not two different covenants. It is one and the same covenant, in whose dynamic reality they, of course, share in different ways. The covenant at Sinai was established with Israel alone. Into *this* event between God and Israel no third party can be 'included' in such a way that thereby Israel's special relationship to its God is retroactively changed. But insofar as the Sinai covenant establishes not a static but a dynamic and historically open reality, there is legitimacy to the Christian position that says: in and through Jesus, the Christ, the covenant of God with Israel *has* been opened to the nations or to all people" (Lohfink and Zenger, "Theological Relevance," 193). Lohfink and Zenger defend the proposals of the Rhineland Synod of the Evangelical [Lutheran] Church (1980), which were criticized by Wolfhart Pannenberg in his *Systematic Theology* III, 472-74, and also by Gunneweg, *Biblische Theologie*, 73-74. I agree with the critics, because it seems to me that Lohfink and Zenger have not given enough attention to how the Messiah fulfills and reconfigures Israel's covenants around himself. Lohfink and Zenger direct appreciative notice to van Buren, *People of Israel*.

77. David Novak interprets it to mean that Abraham will imitate the divine justice, which "is proactive: it is meant to transform the world into something infinitely better than it had been before"—from which it follows that Abraham will be a blessing to all nations because Abraham's imitation of the divine justice will transform the world (Novak, "How Jewish Was Barth?," 11).

for the rest of the Bible."[78] Jonathan Sacks argues that Abraham uniquely accepted the challenge of personal responsibility (by freely undergoing exile at God's command), moral responsibility (by rescuing Lot), collective responsibility (by interceding for Sodom and Gomorrah), and ontological responsibility (by standing as a creature before God). Sacks proposes: "With Abraham a new faith is born: the faith of responsibility, in which the divine command and the human act meet and give birth to a new and blessed order, built on the principles of righteousness and justice."[79]

In this light, it is not surprising that the book of Genesis presents Abraham's life as tremendously arduous. He sojourned in such fear that without daring to say anything, he twice allowed a ruler in whose lands he was dwelling to add his wife Sarah to the royal concubines (see Gen 12:15; 20:2–18). At other times, he engaged in battle against powerful opponents in order to defend his family. According to Genesis 14, he and his servants battled against the combined armies of four kings (the kings of Elam, Goiim, Shinar, and Ellasar), and he was victorious in rescuing his nephew Lot.[80] According to Genesis 18, he boldly interceded with God on behalf of the cities of Sodom and Gomorrah, but the cities were destroyed nonetheless, due to the wickedness of the inhabitants.[81]

Genesis tells us that Abraham endured painful strife in his domestic life because his wife Sarah was barren. He was caught in a conflict between Sarah and her slave Hagar with whom (at Sarah's command) Abraham had a son, Ishmael. Moreover, even when Sarah herself had a son, Isaac, God

---

78. Arnold, *Genesis*, 133.

79. Sacks, "Long Walk to Freedom," 68. Joel Kaminsky points out that the rabbis gave Sinai, not Abraham, the highest place, arguing that "the rift created by Adam's fall was indeed healed by the giving of the Torah. While a new fall was created when Israel worshiped the golden calf, any future redemption is now focused on Israel as a corporate body, rather than on Adam and Eve. . . . The observance of the commandments issued at Sinai provide a previously unavailable remedy to Adam's sin" (Kaminsky, "Paradise Regained," 37). See also the valuable study—covering both Testaments—by Enrique Nardoni, *Rise Up, O Judge*.

80. Arnold explains that "Abram and Lot become embroiled in international politics, as a war between opposing coalitions, 'four kings against five' (v. 9), results in a battle in their area, the Siddim Valley"—but "[a]ttempts have failed to identify positively any of the nine kings of vv. 1–2 with historical figures, in spite of enormous scholarly effort" (Arnold, *Genesis*, 145).

81. See L. E. Goodman, "Judaism and the Problem of Evil," 193: "Discovery of the tension between God's justice and human suffering does not await the drama of the book of Job. Abraham, learning of the impending destruction of Sodom and Gomorrah, did not retire resigned. . . . The prayers and pleas and the hard words were all elements of his brief for the Cities of the Plain. But the case rested on Abraham's grasp of the logic of God: universal sovereignty demands universal justice."

tested Abraham by requesting this son in sacrifice—only to provide a sacrificial ram once it was clear that Abraham would obey. Abraham had to show that he depended solely upon God for the fulfillment of the covenantal promise.[82] Although Abraham had extensive herds, he never had extensive lands of his own; when Sarah died, he had to ask permission of the Hittites to purchase a burial place for her.

Jewish and Christian scholars, within and outside of the context of Jewish-Christian dialogue, have raised the question of whether Abraham actually existed or did any of these things. If Christians or Jews believe solely in a typologically rich literary figure of Abraham (as sufficient for God's purposes), does this affect Jewish-Christian dialogue about the status of Abraham and his covenant? Of course, the tools of archaeology and historical research cannot answer the question of whether Abraham actually existed, although scholars can offer reasons for favoring positive or negative answers.[83] Jon Levenson considers it highly unlikely that Abraham actually lived, but he does not think this is important. In his view, what is important is the divinely guided depiction of the figure of Abraham in Written Torah and Oral Torah. He argues that God instructs his people through the figure of Abraham without needing the biblical Abraham actually to have lived, let alone the Abraham of the Oral Torah who differs significantly from the Abraham of Genesis.[84]

Some Christians suppose that the lack of a historical referent would invalidate the Abrahamic covenant and all that we find in the New Testament about Abraham. I do not think it would. By God's will, the Abrahamic covenant was truly in effect in the people into which Christ was born; and,

---

82. For discussion of this episode in Genesis 22, see for example Moberly, *Bible, Theology, and Faith*, chapters 3–5.

83. For background see Bergsma and Pitre, *Old Testament*, 131–65, especially 148–52. Bergsma and Pitre point out that certain elements of the Abraham narratives are unlikely to have been invented at a late date. See also the similar summary in Provan et al., *Biblical History of Israel*, 111–21; as well as Levenson, *Inheriting Abraham*, 3. Levenson, however, concludes that "the very idea that he [Abraham] had a connection with those subsequent traditions—even those of biblical Israel—is open to doubt in the minds of most historians who seek to be intellectually honest.... In the case of the Abrahamic narratives in Genesis, the current consensus among historians is that the material dates to the first millennium BCE (some of it even to the second half) and is thus centuries removed from the supposedly historical figure it renders" (Levenson, *Inheriting Abraham*, 13–14). See also the conclusion of Ronald S. Hendel that the Abrahamic narratives combine legend and invention with some elements of ancient historical memory: Hendel, *Remembering Abraham*. Bill T. Arnold argues that at least "the Genesis traditions about the religion of Israel's ancestors are genuinely ancient and pre-Yahwistic" (Arnold, "Genesis Narratives," 42).

84. See also the reflections of Signer, "Abraham."

for Christians, Christ is the one who brings the covenant to fulfillment, as asserted by Christ in the Gospel of John: "Abraham rejoiced that he was to see my day; he saw it and was glad.... Before Abraham was, I am" (John 8:56, 58).[85] Given Christ's priority, a typological or symbolic figure of Abraham could theoretically have been a sufficient ground for God's purposes, since the *covenant* existed and was always ordered toward Christ. In accord with Paul's claim that Abraham became "the father of many nations" (Rom 4:18), Abraham undeniably became the father of countless believers—either as a historical man or a typological figure. This assumes that Paul's retelling of the Genesis story does not make a definitive judgment about the story's genre or about details such as Abraham's age (Rom 4:19).

However, without insisting upon it as a theological necessity, I disagree with Levenson. In my view, Abraham was a real historical person. There is little reason to deny the historicity of Abraham until those who doubt his historicity can show us more—especially in light of the clues that other biblical scholars bring forward that seem to indicate a historical core to the Abraham narratives. There is no way of knowing that Abraham is not historical, and so I do not feel compelled to skepticism.

Either way, Christians and Jews should agree with Rabbi Sacks's statement in praise of the Abrahamic covenant and its fruits: "There has never been anyone like Abraham."[86] Stephen Williams speaks for all Christians

---

85. I discuss the Gospel of John in the context of Jewish-Christian dialogue further on, but here see Paddison, "Christology and Jewish-Christian Understanding"; Culpepper, "Gospel of John"; J. C. Beker, "New Testament View of Judaism"; Kysar, "Anti-Semitism in John"; and the essays (notably those by James D. G. Dunn and R. A. Culpepper) in Bieringer et al., eds., *Anti-Judaism and the Fourth Gospel*. Although I disagree with Kysar's rejection of the "universal authority" of the Gospel of John, it seems that what he mainly has in view is the necessity of distinguishing between polemical language that pertains to the first-century time and place, on the one hand, and the core revelatory contents of the Gospel, on the other. I think some distinction like this is indeed necessary. Paddison remarks, "The perennial risk of thinking about Christology in the context of inter-faith communication is that grip is lost on the stumbling stone of God's revelation in Christ, the astounding way in which God has fulfilled his covenant promises. Reading John, and its Christological claims, in company with Jews should not be an exercise in supersessionism. Neither, however, should it be an exercise in glibly shifting a set of disagreements or in ironing out the creases of necessary particularities" ("Christology and Jewish-Christian Understanding," 56). Paddison makes clear that Christians must learn how to read John's Gospel without supposing that the ongoing Jewish people are no longer God's covenantal people. As a model of willingness to face divergent truth-claims, Paddison directs attention to Neusner, *Telling Tales*. See also Scot McKnight's call, with the Gospel of Matthew in view, to "distinguish between the *nature* of the disagreement (Jesus as Messiah, sociological factors, etc.) and the *means* of the disagreement (polemical tones)": McKnight, "Loyal Critic," 78.

86. Sacks, "New Kind of Hero," 73.

when he rejoices in "father Abraham, into whose covenant family I am adopted in the election of grace."[87]

In the Gospel of Matthew, when Jesus foretells the inclusion of the Gentiles in the eschatological Israel, he depicts this consummation in terms of "sit[ting] at table with Abraham, Isaac, and Jacob in the kingdom of heaven" (Matt 8:11). Jesus notes that Abraham, Isaac, and Jacob—here standing in for all the founders of the people of Israel—are still alive (presumably as disembodied souls), awaiting the resurrection of the dead (Matt 22:32). In the Gospel of Luke, Jesus tells a parable in which a blessed poor man, after his death, dwells in "Abraham's bosom" with the angels of God (Luke 16:22). Perhaps most important for the Christian understanding of Abraham, however, are Paul's references to him, especially in Romans and Galatians.[88] Paul considers Abraham to be an exemplar of the righteousness that comes through faith rather than through Torah observance. He makes much of Genesis 15:6, "And he [Abraham] believed the Lord; and he [the Lord] reckoned it to him as righteousness." Since this verse comes before God institutes circumcision in Genesis 17:10, Paul holds that Abraham is deemed righteous because of his obedient faith.

For Paul, then, Abraham stands as evidence that observance of the Mosaic law is not the decisive path of salvation for Israel and the nations. Abraham is "the father of all who believe without being circumcised and who thus have righteousness reckoned to them, and likewise the father of the circumcised who are not merely circumcised but also follow the example of the faith which our father Abraham had before he was circumcised" (Rom 4:11-12).[89] Faith and baptism in Christ make believers into

---

87. S. N. Williams, *Election of Grace*, 177.

88. In footnotes and occasionally in the body of the text, I will take note of the debates currently ongoing between exegetes who read Paul as requiring Torah observance of Jewish Christians (including Paul himself) as a matter of salvation, and exegetes who argue that Paul did not strictly observe Torah himself and did not require it of Jewish Christians as a matter of salvation. My view is that the exegetical debate is, like many such debates, insoluble, due to the pliability and relative paucity of the evidence. Nevertheless, I consider that the latter group of exegetes have the better exegetical case and that, theologically speaking, it is necessary for Christians to hold that Torah observance in its "original" mode (as distinct from Torah observance in its messianically reconfigured mode) is not necessary or required for salvation in Christ for any believer, Jewish or Gentile. For the most influential statement of the exegetical position that I oppose (while granting the many insights of this viewpoint), see the essays collected in Nanos, *Reading Romans within Judaism*.

89. Here see also James 2:17-24: "So faith by itself, if it has no works, is dead. But some will say, 'You have faith and I have works.' Show me your faith apart from your works, and I by my works will show you my faith. You believe that God is one; you do well. Even the demons believe—and shudder. Do you want to be shown, you foolish

children of Abraham. As Bruce Chilton and Jacob Neusner sum up: "By means of baptism, [believers] realize the promise of Abraham, and become his descendants (Romans 4:13–25). At the same moment, each person who is baptized overcomes the consequences of Adam's fault, in the grace and righteousness which is thereby released (Romans 5:17)."[90]

In Galatians, Paul makes an extended argument that the Mosaic law cannot accomplish the righteousness to which it points. Recalling an argument that he had with Peter, Paul states: "We ourselves, who are Jews by birth and not Gentile sinners, yet who know that a man is not justified by works of the law but through faith in Jesus Christ, even we have believed in Christ Jesus, in order to be justified by faith in Christ, and not by works of the law, because by works of the law shall no flesh be justified" (Gal 2:15–16).[91] Lest this is unclear, Paul reiterates his point in a more succinct

---

fellow, that faith apart from works is barren? Was not Abraham our father justified by works, when he offered his son Isaac upon the altar? You see that faith was active along with his works, and faith was completed by works, and the Scripture was fulfilled which says, 'Abraham believed God, and it was reckoned to him as righteousness'; and he was called the friend of God. You see that a man is justified by works and not by faith alone." William F. Brosend II argues persuasively, *"James and Paul simply do not mean the same thing when they write of 'works,' and interpreters who write as if they did distort the thought of both"* (Brosend, *James and Jude*, 81, his italics). By contrast, Chilton and Neusner argue (with Galatians in view) that "Paul's presentation of Abraham is designed to deny the strictures of James" (Chilton and Neusner, *Judaism in the New Testament*, 103).

90. Chilton and Neusner, *Judaism in the New Testament*, 81. Chilton and Neusner go on to compare "the two Judaisms, Paul's and the sages'. The difference between the situation of Adam and the situation of Israel finds its definition in the Torah. . . . Christ on the cross concludes the old Adam and in his resurrection commences the new. Here we find the Judaic counterpart to that enormous conception. It is the Torah that forms the antidote to Adam's sin. But then Israel has to regain the Land, that is, Eden, by that act of reconciliation with God that takes place through voluntary obedience to the covenant, the Torah, the commandments" (Chilton and Neusner, *Judaism in the New Testament*, 93).

91. Chilton and Neusner comment: "The radical quality of Paul's position needs to be appreciated, before his characteristic interpretation of Scripture may be understood. He was isolated from *every other Christian Jew* by his own account in Galatians 2:11–13: James, Peter, Barnabas, and 'the rest of the Jews'" (Chilton and Neusner, *Judaism in the New Testament*, 100). I note that this "isolation," if it is the correct word, did not last long and was resolved by a council in Jerusalem, although Chilton and Neusner think that Acts 15 romanticizes this council and turns a set of meetings into one meeting. According to Chilton and Neusner, James and Paul remain sharply at odds in their understanding of the Church: "James' perspective here [Acts 15] is not that all who believe are Israel (the Pauline definition), but that *in addition* to Israel God has established a people in his name" (*Judaism in the New Testament*, 105). See also Chilton, *Temple of Jesus*, especially the summary on 154–59. Chilton's view requires assumptions about Jesus that I do not share—indeed, Chilton's Jesus strikes me as a

form: "if justification were through the law, then Christ died to no purpose" (Gal 2:21). Justification comes through faith in the Messiah and his saving sacrifice on the cross. Such faith brings with it the transformative Spirit by which the human heart is transformed by charity.

Dismayed that his (Gentile) Galatian congregation now supposes that observing Torah is necessary for salvation, Paul pushes further. He first asks rhetorically, "Does he who supplies the Spirit to you and works miracles among you do so by works of the law, or by hearing with faith?" (Gal 3:5). Citing Deuteronomy 27:26, he then urges that the Mosaic law bears within it a curse aimed at all who are unable to obey it fully.[92] Christ redeemed us from this curse by perfectly fulfilling the Mosaic law on the cross while at the same time taking on the punishment (or curse: Paul here cites Deuteronomy 21:23) owed by those under the curse. Paul explains the interim purpose of the Mosaic law: "Why then the law? It was added because of transgressions, till the offspring should come to whom the promise had been made" (Gal 3:19). He compares the law to a guardian who cares for a person until the person comes of age. Through faith in Christ, the division between Jews and Gentiles—based upon election and Torah observance—has come to an end in the messianic community. We are now all Israelites, all children of Abraham in the Messiah: "you are all one in Christ Jesus. And if you are Christ's, then you are Abraham's offspring, heirs according to promise" (Gal 3:28–29).[93]

Paul goes on to offer an allegorical reading of Sarah and Hagar that paints a vivid portrait of his understanding of the covenants. Hagar, a slave,

---

rather negligible figure—although I am intrigued by Chilton's emphasis on Peter as a mediating figure between Paul and James.

92. See Watson, *Paul and the Hermeneutics of Faith*, 427–34.

93. Chilton and Neusner observe that Paul's argument does not depend upon the contextual meaning, because Paul begins with Christ and reads Israel's Scriptures in light of Christ: "'Scripture' for Paul is what the documents finally mean, the ultimate significance in the light of which the interpretation of individual documents and passages unfolds. That is why it is natural for Paul to proceed from Christ to the passages at issue: the point of departure was the point at which one had arrived by means of baptism" (Chilton and Neusner, *Judaism in the New Testament*, 104). In *Echoes of Scripture* Richard B. Hays calls Paul's exegesis "ecclesiocentric"—not because Hays denies the centrality of Christ, but because he thinks Paul places the emphasis on how Scripture points forward toward the messianic community of Jews and Gentiles in Christ. Paul's exegesis might also be called "pneumatocentric" because, as Hays says, Paul insists upon "the hermeneutical priority of Spirit-experience" (*Echoes of Scripture*, 108). Hays concludes that Paul's "eschatologically privileged hermeneutical perspective ... allows him to acknowledge the truth of God's revelation to Israel while at the same time discovering new dimensions of meaning in that revelation that were necessarily concealed from readers in all prior generations" (*Echoes of Scripture*, 109).

was the mother of Abraham's son Ishmael, through whom the covenantal promise did not descend. By contrast, Sarah was a free woman, the wife of Abraham, and she was the mother of his son Isaac, through whom the covenantal promise descended—even though Isaac was born after Ishmael. Hagar conceived a son in the regular way; whereas Sarah conceived a son only after having received a divine promise that she would do so, a promise that seemed unbelievable due to her advanced age and barrenness (see Gen 18, 21). Paul explains: "the son of the slave was born according to the flesh, the son of the free woman through promise. Now this is an allegory: these women are two covenants. One is from Mount Sinai, bearing children for slavery; she is Hagar . . . ; she corresponds to the present Jerusalem. . . . But the Jerusalem above [Sarah] is free, and she is our mother" (Gal 4:23–26).[94] In other words, Paul holds that believers, who are freed from a state of sin by Christ's fulfillment of Torah on the cross on behalf of all people and who are united to Christ the Savior by his Spirit, are born into God's Abrahamic family and received into the "Jerusalem above" through faith and baptism.[95]

Jon Levenson is aware of all this, and he also points out the connection made by Hebrews 11:17–19 between Genesis 22 and Jesus, the incarnate Son who "endured the cross, despising the shame, and is seated at the right hand of the throne of God" (Heb 12:2).[96] For Levenson the fundamental

---

94. For the imagery employed here by Paul, see Niehaus, *God at Sinai*, 341. Niehaus links this to Hebrews 12's contrast between Mount Sinai and the heavenly Jerusalem (see *God at Sinai*, 342–44).

95. For discussion see Pitre et al., *Paul, a New Covenant Jew*, 48–52. Stephen Chester is quite right when he comments: "Despite Paul's assertion that law and promise ultimately complement one another in God's purposes (3:21), his arguments will have been shocking to those who revered the law" (S. Chester, "Paul and the Galatian Believers," 72). Scott W. Hahn comments similarly, "Paul wants his readers to link the 'Judaized' Gentiles with Ishmael and his sorry fate. . . . On the other hand, Gentile late-comers are meant to be associated with the late-in-coming Abrahamic son of the promise: Isaac/Christ. . . . In light of the expulsion and disinheritance of Ishmael (Abraham's firstborn son 'after the flesh,' and his first son to be circumcised), it is an inescapable conclusion that circumcision is no guarantee of the Abrahamic inheritance of the promised blessing. Indeed, circumcision may have been necessary at one time, but even then it was not sufficient for what mattered most. Indeed, even Abrahamic sonship is no guarantee of the inheritance, because not all sons are heirs" (Hahn, *Kinship by Covenant*, 273). Certainly, as Hahn says, "Christ's death has exhausted the curses of the Old Covenant [i.e. the curses attached to disobedience] and released the blessings of the New. As a result, Jews and Gentiles are offered a new way of sharing the Abrahamic blessing and inheritance of divine sonship: by faith in Christ" (*Kinship by Covenant*, 274). When Hahn states that "Christ's death has effected the termination of the Deuteronomic covenant" (*Kinship by Covenant*, 274), Hahn has in view the covenant at Horeb after the golden calf, which he differentiates sharply from the Sinai covenant.

96. See Levenson, *Inheriting Abraham*, chapter 3; as well as Levenson, *Death and Resurrection*. See also Kessler, *Bound by the Bible*, which argues that the rabbis and

problem with the New Testament's interpretation of Abraham—in addition to its mistake about Jesus—is that it seeks "to detach Abraham from the Jewish people."[97] It does this by incorporating Gentiles fully into the family of Abraham's descendants, without requiring Gentiles (or Jews) to observe the Mosaic law. In Levenson's view, this separates Abraham from Moses and cuts against the Jewish tradition according to which "Abraham is known as *'Avraham 'Avinu*, 'Our Father Abraham'" and is not only the "biological progenitor" of all Jews (including converts) but also "the founder of Judaism itself."[98]

Levenson notes that for Paul in Romans 4, "the key thing is not birth but faith, and Gentiles and Jews—the uncircumcised and the circumcised—qualify equally for 'descent' from Abraham if they have faith."[99] Paul says as much when he writes in Romans 2:28-29, "For he is not a real Jew who is one outwardly, nor is true circumcision something external and physical. He is a Jew who is one inwardly, and real circumcision is a matter of

---

the church fathers made a number of similar moves in interpreting Genesis 22, and they display evidence of knowing each others' characteristic viewpoints. See also the relationships (and contrasts) between rabbinic and patristic exegesis found in G. A. Anderson, *Genesis of Perfection*. For further discussion of (implicit and explicit) talmudic references to Christianity—as well as for the broader exchange and polemic—see Schäfer, *Jesus in the Talmud*; Schäfer, *Jewish Jesus*; Maier, *Jesus von Nazareth*; Hirshman, *Rivalry of Genius*; Jaffé, *Judaïsme et l'avènement du christianisme*; Schremer, *Brothers Estranged*; Kalmin, *Jewish Babylonia*; Kalmin, "Christians and Heretics"; Naeh, "Freedom and Celibacy"; Zellentin, *Rabbinic Parodies*; Boyarin, *Socrates and the Fat Rabbis*; A. M. Gray, "People, Not the Peoples"; and Siegal, *Early Christian Monastic Literature*.

97. Levenson, *Inheriting Abraham*, 11; cf. 9.

98. Levenson, *Inheriting Abraham*, 3.

99. Levenson, *Inheriting Abraham*, 6. Levenson goes on to observe, "That Abraham lived before Moses' reception of the Torah and, according to Genesis, was pronounced righteous by God because of his faith proved to Paul, himself once a practicing Jew, that the commandments of the Torah were not necessary for a right relationship with God. . . . The faith of Abraham the Gentile made him righteous in God's eyes even before circumcision made him into Abraham the first Jew. In Paul's theology, the community for which Abraham served as a paradigm was thus a mixed group of Gentiles and Jews, a community created by God and founded upon faith in the gospel of Christ crucified and risen from the dead" (*Inheriting Abraham*, 6-7). For a contrasting viewpoint see Thiessen, *Contesting Conversion*. According to Thiessen, Luke conceived of Jewishness genealogically and held that Jewish Christians (but not Gentile Christians) should continue the practice of circumcision on the eighth day. In my view, whether or not this is correct for Luke-Acts, it does not get at the Pauline redefinition of Israel as reconfigured by the Messiah. For an analysis of this redefinition (focusing on Romans 9–11), see Chilton and Neusner, *Judaism in the New Testament*, chapter 4. See also Concannon, "When You Were Gentiles," 35, for the argument (which strikes me as highly eccentric) that Paul offers the dream of a "polyethnic body." More broadly, for Jewish perspectives on Gentile salvation, see Donaldson, *Judaism and the Gentiles*.

the heart, spiritual and not literal." Later in Romans, Paul argues further along the same lines: "For not all who are descended from Israel belong to Israel, and not all are children of Abraham because they are his descendants, but 'Through Isaac shall your descendants be named.' This means that it is not the children of the flesh who are the children of God, but the children of the promise are reckoned as descendants" (Rom 9:6–8). This reasoning about the promise is the basis for Paul's claim in Galatians that the Church (Jews and Gentiles) is "the Israel of God" (Gal 6:16).[100] As he remarks in this context, "neither circumcision counts for anything, nor uncircumcision, but a new creation" in Jesus Christ crucified and risen (Gal 6:15). He also makes this point in 1 Corinthians 7:19, "For neither circumcision counts for anything nor uncircumcision, but keeping the commandments of God."[101] With this verse in view, Matthew Thiessen observes that God, through the Spirit of Christ, has "rewritten gentile genealogies in order to bring them into Abraham's lineage. . . . In Christ and through the reception of Christ's

---

100. Stephen Chester states, "By 'Israel' some understand Paul here to be asking a blessing upon the Jewish nation despite the rejection of Christ by a majority. Others take him to speak of the Gentile Galatian believers alone, indicating the replacement of the people of Israel in God's purposes by the church. Yet that the reference to Israel comes in the context of Paul's discussion of the irrelevance of circumcision makes it more likely that by Israel he now refers to all Jewish and Gentile believers together" (S. Chester, "Paul and the Galatian Believers," 77–78). See also Dunn, *Theology of Paul the Apostle*, 504–9, where Dunn reflects upon Paul's use of "Israel" in Romans 9–11 and concludes: "Now he [Paul] makes clear what was only implicit before—implicit in the 'in Christ' (etc.) motif, and in the use of Israel terms to describe Christian converts—that Christian identity is unavoidably corporate and bound up with the identity of Israel. But the identity of Israel itself is now in question, precisely because Israel too is caught up in the overlap of the ages, caught between the times. It is no accident, then, that 'Israel' appears in both parts of the basic assertion: 'not all from Israel are Israel' (9.6). . . . [Israel] is divided between the Israel of the old covenant, and, or so we might say, the Israel of the new covenant, consisting of believing Jew and Gentile" (Dunn, *Theology of Paul the Apostle*, 508; see also the discussion in Dunn, *Theology of Paul's Letter*, 344–46. For Paul, the Gentiles have been grafted into "Israel" in Christ (who reconfigured Israel around himself). I agree with Dunn's contention: "A Christianity which does not understand itself in some proper sense as 'Israel' forfeits its claim to the scriptures of Israel" (*Theology of Paul the Apostle*, 508). By contrast, William S. Campbell argues, "The ending of Galatians chapter 6 clearly speaks of two entities, and not one, as indicated by the connecting καί, 'Peace and mercy be upon all who walk by this rule, and upon the Israel of God' (v. 16)" (Campbell, "Covenantal Theology and Participation," 51). I disagree with Campbell that the καί indicates "two entities," and thus I also differ from the perspective articulated in Campbell's *Paul and the Creation of Christian Identity*, including 61–64 on Abraham, where he insists that Paul throughout his letters intends "to substantiate abiding differences" (*Paul and the Creation of Christian Identity*, 64) between Jews and Gentiles in the Church of Christ. For praise of Campbell's work, see Ehrensperger, "Trajectories."

101. For discussion see Fitzmyer, *First Corinthians*, 308.

pneuma, gentiles have become Abrahamic seed and sons and now stand to inherit all the promises that God made to Abraham's seed."[102]

The interpretation of these verses has been debated in recent scholarship, and I differ from Thiessen with regard to what is here required for the salvation of Jewish followers of Christ. But the centrality of faith is not disputed. It will not surprise, then, that for Christians (especially Catholics and Orthodox) the greatest daughter of Abraham is Mary, who in her faith—her obedient "let it be to me according to your word" (Luke 1:38)—became the temple in whom dwelt the incarnate Son.[103] Thus, introducing Pope John Paul II's encyclical on Mary, *Redemptoris Mater*, Joseph Ratzinger remarks: "The central attitude by which Mary is defined in the encyclical is faith.... The Pope sees Mary's attitude in relation to Abraham: just as Abraham's faith stands at the beginning of the Old Covenant, so Mary's faith at the Annunciation opens the New Covenant."[104]

By now, it should be clear why Jews and Christians are in certain ways more divided than united by the figure of Abraham. This is so not only because the figure of Abraham differs when read in light of Oral Torah or the New Testament, but also because in Judaism and Christianity, "Abraham for

---

102. Thiessen, *Paul and the Gentile Problem*, 163. According to Thiessen, Paul continued to require Jewish believers to circumcise their children *as a matter of salvation*: otherwise they would no longer be "Jews" and no longer inheritors of the promise. I note, however, that in Christ there is another way to inherit the Abrahamic promise, namely through Christ and his Spirit; and this new way, according to Paul, is the divinely intended path of salvation for both Jews and Gentiles. Thiessen's position that Paul continued to insist upon (as a requisite for salvation) Torah observance for Jewish believers in Christ cuts against a number of Paul's own statements and deeds, and it also runs up against Acts 13:38–39, where Paul (according to Luke) proclaims in the synagogue at Antioch, "Let it be known to you therefore, brethren, that through this man [Jesus Christ] forgiveness of sins is proclaimed to you, and by him every one that believes is freed from everything from which you could not be freed by the law of Moses." For Thiessen, Acts 21:24–26 and 24:14–18 demonstrate that Paul observed Torah and required Jewish believers to do so as a matter of salvation. I think that Paul is willing to observe Torah and does not oppose Jewish Christians doing so—*unless* it is understood to be required for salvation. As Philip A. Cunningham says with regard to Romans 14, "There were Jews and gentiles in Christ who no longer felt bound by kosher laws (and hence could eat meat offered to idols without hesitation), and there were Jews and gentiles in Christ who felt obligated not to consume idol-meat" (Cunningham, "Paul's Letters," 149). See also Thiessen's "Paul, the Animal Apocalypse."

103. See G. A. Anderson, *Christian Doctrine and the Old Testament*, chapter 7; as well as Joseph Ratzinger, *Daughter Zion*, 44: "The second image—'the power of the Most High will overshadow you' [Lk 1:35]—belongs to the theology of Israel's cult; it refers to the cloud which overshadows the temple and thereby indicates the presence of God. Mary appears as the sacred tent over whom God's hidden presence becomes effective."

104. Ratzinger, "Sign of the Woman," 24–25.

the most part is seen as the father of the chosen community alone."[105] Even if Christians were to reject what Paul teaches about Abraham—a rejection that would call into question the entirety of Paul's gospel—Christians would still differ from the Oral Torah's teachings about Abraham. According to the Oral Torah, Abraham observed the Mosaic law and union with Abraham requires observing the Mosaic law. The point is that there is no "neutral Abraham" who can enable us to avoid "the question of who Abraham's heirs are and how they inherit his legacy."[106]

IV. POLEMICS: THE DESTRUCTION OF JERUSALEM AND THE CRUCIFIXION OF JESUS

Just as tensions between Jews and Christians arise over the figure of Abraham, so also the New Testament deems Jewish rejection of Jesus as the Messiah to be a disaster. While contemporary Christian authors sometimes try to minimize this tension, there is a limit to what can be done. In his "great sorrow and unceasing anguish" about the rejection of Jesus' messianic status by many of his fellow Jews, Paul goes so far as to say: "I could wish that I myself were accursed and cut off from Christ for the sake of my brethren, my kinsmen according to the flesh" (Rom 9:2–3). Some scholars suggest that Paul considered Torah observance to be the path of salvation for the Jewish people—or at least still strictly requisite—even while Paul *also* wished that Jews would accept Jesus as the Messiah.[107] In my view, the

---

105. Levenson, *Inheriting Abraham*, 213. In response to Louis Massignon (1883–1962)—the Catholic scholar of Islam who did much to coin the notion of three "Abrahamic" religions—Levenson observes that "Islam has historically believed that all three religions can be faithful to Abraham provided they do not contaminate his message of *islām* (submission to God) with the later and divisive distortions that they [Jews and Christians, possessed of distorted Scriptures] falsely regard as normative" (*Inheriting Abraham*, 211). See also the appreciative study of Massignon offered by Krokus, *Theology of Louis Massignon*, even if, like Levenson, I disagree with Massignon's approach to both Judaism and Islam. For medieval Jewish efforts to respond to, and to blunt the sometimes dire consequences of, medieval Christians' responses to the Talmud's negative remarks about Christianity and Gentiles, see Berger, "Christians, Gentiles, and the Talmud," 158–76.

106. Levenson, *Inheriting Abraham*, 214.

107. See for example Fredriksen, *Paul*. Fredriksen argues that for Paul (who in her view remained completely Torah observant), "Israel must remain Israel, that family group, God's 'sons' and Paul's blood brothers, united by the covenants, the Law, the temple cult, the promises, the patriarchs, and—again the family, 'flesh' connection—by the Christ, the son of David (Rom 9.4–5; cf. 1.3, 15.9).... The Law was a curse *for gentiles*. The Law only revealed sin *for gentiles*. The Law was a service of death *for gentiles*. But for Israel the Law, God-given, was a defining privilege. The vast majority of his

tension that motivates Paul's anguished cry is clearly far more intense than this exegetical position admits. Paul fervently disagrees with his fellow Jews who do not accept Jesus as the Messiah. I agree with Donald Hagner that Paul's polemical critique includes "his rejection of the Law as central to human salvation, and his insistence upon the necessity of faith in Jesus Christ"; and Paul considers his fellow Jews who do not accept the gospel to be in a condition of "slavery, blindness, and disobedience."[108]

To bring out the depth of the situation and the urgency of the matter, Paul and the entire New Testament use very sharp language—even if, in the context of the first century, such language is hardly abnormal. In fact, if the Messiah has indeed come, then sharp language is needed for alerting people to what has happened. Had the New Testament authors suggested by their language that a mistake in this regard did not matter much, this would have been evidence of the unseriousness of their testimony to Jesus as the Messiah.[109] In addition, hard as it may be to believe today, Luke Timothy

---

kinsmen, Paul was nevertheless convinced, misunderstood the Law when they heard it. Its *telos* was the returning Christ (Rom 10.4), but most of Israel did not understand this: 'for to this day, when they read the ancient covenant, that same veil remains unlifted because only through Christ is it taken away. Yes, to this day, whenever Moses is read a veil lies over their minds, but turning to the Lord takes away the veil' (2 Cor 3.14–15). Israel would so turn—that is, they would indeed recognize Jesus as the son of David, the eschatological Lord Messiah—only when God enabled them. And God would do so soon, once 'the fullness of the nations' was brought in (Rom 11.25)" (Fredriksen, *Paul*, 165–66). By "soon," Fredriksen means within Paul's lifetime or shortly thereafter, since this is what she holds Paul erroneously believed.

108. Hagner, "Paul's Quarrel with Judaism," 149. Hagner grants that Paul's position is an instance of "anti-Judaism," but Hagner carefully differentiates this from "anti-Semitism," which he defines as "racial *hatred* of the Jews" ("Paul's Quarrel with Judaism," 128). In his essay on the letters of Paul that are considered "deutero-Pauline," James D. G. Dunn remarks: "A surprising feature of the deutero-Pauline literature is its *lack* of anti-Semitism, or, more precisely, the absence of passages that have given scope to the anti-Judaism of later years. The surprise is occasioned by the fact that the deutero-Paulines are in effect surrounded by just such material. The earlier Pauline writings include the fierceness of 1 Thess 2:14–16 and Galatians. The contemporary Christian writings include Matthew, Acts, and John" (Dunn, "Anti-Semitism," 151). For the view that Paul is more appreciative of Judaism than is "deutero-Paul," see Zaas, "Guide to Reading [Colossians]."

109. Thus, I disagree with Amy-Jill Levine's conclusion that the Gospel of Matthew's Christocentrism (combined with other factors) makes it "anti-Jewish" (Levine, "Anti-Judaism," 36). Levine grants, of course, that "[w]hether Matthew is 'anti-Jewish' depends on how one defines that term" ("Anti-Judaism," 13). Levine explains her definition: "Douglas R. A. Hare proposes three categories of varying intensity: prophetic anti-Judaism, an internal critique that resembles biblical prophecy in its hopes the salvation of the Jewish people; Jewish-Christian anti-Judaism, also an internal critique, but one that replaces central Jewish symbols such as Torah and temple with christology; and Gentilizing anti-Judaism, an external polemic that removes Jews from the hope

Johnson points out that "Paul saves his best shots not for his fellow Jews but for gentiles and those who want gentiles to act like Jews. When Paul says of actual Jews that they are blinded (2 Cor 4:4), or veiled and have their hearts hardened (2 Cor 3:14–15), or are ignorant (Rom 10:3) and enemies of God (Rom 11:28) who have stumbled (Rom 11:11), his rhetoric is mild by the standards of the day."[110] There is no doubt in my mind—or in Johnson's—that for Paul, the truth that Jesus is the crucified and risen Messiah changes things radically, though by way of fulfillment rather than negation (Rom 11:28–29). Jesus Christ has inaugurated the new creation, and Paul is an apostle and prophet of the new covenant in Christ. Johnson remarks that "for Paul, the Jesus who interpreted his blood that he shared with his followers as the blood of a new covenant (1 Cor 11:25) cannot be compared to Moses."[111]

There is good reason to believe that Jesus foretold the destruction of the Jerusalem temple and connected this event with the rejection of himself (including by his own disciples) and, correspondingly, with his eschatological

---

of salvation and replaces Judaism with the 'new' or 'true' Israel of the church. Because the first two categories presuppose a monolithic system called 'Judaism' and the third suggests that only (ethnic) Gentiles would condemn those who keep Jewish practice, George Smiga refines the categories under the rubrics 'prophetic polemic,' 'subordinating polemic,' and 'abrogating anti-Judaism.' I [Levine] locate particular passages in Matthew's Gospel as subordinating polemic, but I find the text as a whole conforms more closely to abrogating anti-Judaism" (Levine, "Anti-Judaism," 14; citing Hare, "Rejection of the Jews"; and Smiga, *Pain and Polemic*, 12–23; with reference also to M. S. Taylor, *Anti-Judaism*). In my view, it cannot be "anti-Jewish" for a first-century text to argue that Israel's Messiah, and the people gathered around him, is as soteriologically central as Jews of that time would expect the Messiah and his people to be. Philip A. Cunningham has noted, "On the basis of history, one has to wonder if a somewhat benign 'christocentric supersessionism' can really exist for any length of time without becoming anti-Jewish" (Cunningham, "Paul's Letters," 144n13). For this concern, see Ruether, "Anti-Judaism"; Ruether, "Anti-Semitism and Christian Theology"; Ruether, *Faith and Fratricide*. See also the discussion of Ruether's position, including a response by Ruether, in the essays in A. Davies, ed., *Anti-Semitism and the Foundations of Christianity*. In "Are the Gospels Anti-Semitic?," Eugene J. Fisher argues that the doctrine of biblical inspiration allows for distinguishing the timebound polemical edge from the enduring truth-claims.

110. L. T. Johnson, *Constructing Paul*, 134. Johnson goes on to add that such Pauline rhetoric is "positively anemic compared to the full-blooded curses by the Jews of Qumran leveled against all Jews not members of their community. Such evidence of internal rivalry never leads us to question whether the members of the new covenant at Qumran were truly Jews! Nor should it in the case of Paul. His hope for the salvation of all Israel, furthermore, represents an embrace of the people as a whole that is the exact opposite of Qumran's ready assignment to the everlasting pit of those not among its members" (L. T. Johnson, *Constructing Paul*, 134).

111. L. T. Johnson, *Constructing Paul*, 144.

inauguration of the kingdom on the cross. Certainly, as Joseph Blenkinsopp says, "[e]arly Christian apologists interpreted the destruction of the temple in A.D. 70 as the fulfillment of a prophecy of Jesus, as punishment for the failure of most contemporary Jews to accept Jesus as their Messiah, and as a sign that the old order had come to an end."[112] As "early Christian apologists," the evangelists who know of the temple's destruction present it as part of the eschatological tribulation or judgment upon all sin, including the sin of his disciples and opponents. Jesus himself is the eschatological temple who, by freely enduring his crucifixion out of love for all sinners, bears the eschatological judgment.

In the Gospel of Luke, shortly after he had been acclaimed by his disciples on the Mount of Olives as the "King who comes in the name of the Lord" (Luke 19:38), Jesus proclaims with deep sorrow about Jerusalem: "Would that even today you knew the things that make for peace! But now they are hidden from your eyes. For the days shall come upon you, when your enemies will cast up a bank about you and surround you . . . and they will not leave one stone upon another in you; because you did not know the time of your visitation" (Luke 19:42-44).[113] The Gospel of Matthew portrays a similar occurrence. After lamenting over Jerusalem and proclaiming that its "house is forsaken and desolate" now that Jerusalem has rejected his efforts to "[gather its] children together" (Matt 23:37-38), Jesus leaves the

112. Blenkinsopp, *Ezekiel*, 197.

113. See Chanikuzhy, *Jesus, the Eschatological Temple*, 116-24. For various perspectives regarding Luke-Acts and Judaism, see Schmidt, "Anti-Judaism and Luke"; in the same volume, Balch, "Response to Daryl D. Schmidt," and McNicol, "Response to Daryl D. Schmidt"; and the essays in Tyson, ed., *Luke-Acts and the Jewish People*. McNicol sums up what seems to me to be the key point: "according to Luke, . . . there would be consequences for the leadership of Israel in their rejection of Jesus as the Messiah. Those consequences revolved around the destruction of the temple and its replacement by another house: the restored community of the children of Abraham who obtained salvation in Jesus. As Stephen's speech in Acts 7:2-53 makes abundantly clear, the place (cf. Acts 7:7) of the fulfillment of the promise of 2 Sam. 7:10-14 was not a temple of masonry in Jerusalem, but a spiritual fellowship: the church founded in Jerusalem" (McNicol, "Response to Daryl D. Schmidt," 118). McNicol concludes with regard to the issue of anti-Judaism: "Luke considered the early Christian movement to be a legitimate form of Judaism. Therefore, by definition, Luke did not consider Judaism to be debased and the object of divine rejection. Consequently, Luke is not an expression of anti-Judaism. However, the question of perspective is critical. To orthodox Christians, Mormonism, which appropriates most of the symbols central to Christianity and yet sees its own emergence and its central belief system as bringing Christianity to its purest form, is unacceptable. In the view of orthodox Christians, too many vital doctrines would have to be set aside. To Mormons, however, it is a very different matter. They view their faith as the true fulfillment of Christianity. . . . This is similar to the way certain Jews and Christians would have appropriated the point of view expressed in Luke-Acts at the end of the first century" (McNicol, "Response to Daryl D. Schmidt," 119).

temple and, in response to his disciples' praise for the temple's buildings, tells them that "there will not be left here one stone upon another, that will not be thrown down" (Matt 24:2).[114]

I agree with scholars who favor the historical authenticity of the Gospels' testimony to Jesus' prophecy about the temple. John Meier observes that "the historical Jesus . . . regularly went up to the temple, joined in the temple feasts, and used the temple as a solemn auditorium for addressing large numbers of his fellow Jews. . . . Jesus clearly accepted the Jerusalem temple *as part of the present order of things.*"[115] The words italicized by Meier

---

114. I note that this is prophetic discourse, even though, as Levine says, "The Gospel as genre is . . . distinct from the prophetic corpus" (Levine, "Anti-Judaism," 17). Regarding the question of whether Jesus in Matthew's Gospel (and the Gospel as a whole) functions in the mode of prophetic critique of Judaism, Warren Carter argues against Levine that the Gospel is "internal prophetic critique" in which "some forms of Judaism are strongly denounced (Pharisees and Sadducees, often not distinguished from each other)" while "[a]nother form of Judaism, namely, disciples who follow the Jew Jesus, is highly commended" (W. Carter, "Response to Amy-Jill Levine," 49–50; cf. 54). Carter is on target when he asks regarding Matthew's Gospel: "If its soteriology is christocentric and exclusive, and if that system is available to Jews (as Levine thinks it is), does that christocentric exclusivity necessarily render the Gospel anti-Judaic (any more than it would be anti-Gentilic if other Gentile salvific systems are not legitimated)?" (W. Carter, "Response to Amy-Jill Levine," 50). Likewise, the original context of the Gospel is significant, as Carter insists: "If one posits, as some have argued, a Gentile community, independent of a synagogue or Jewish community, that no longer engages in Jewish mission on the theological premise that Jews have been rejected from salvation history . . . , the rhetoric sounds much more hateful, final, and much less familial than if one posits a (largely) Jewish group recently separated or separating from, or in conflict with, a synagogue or Jewish community" (W. Carter, "Response to Amy-Jill Levine," 55). Carter affirms that when he reads the Gospel, he is disturbed by what (no longer in the original context) he hears as "anti-Judaic passages," whereas other people whom he knows, who read the Gospel as accurately depicting Jesus' words and deeds, hear the same passages as "an internal family feud" in which everyone is "capable of noble and faithful as well as faithless actions" (W. Carter, "Response to Amy-Jill Levine," 58–59). Similarly, Philip L. Shuler, in his "Response to Amy-Jill Levine," denies that the Gospel of Matthew is anti-Jewish. He adds the observation that both Christian Scripture and Jewish Scripture may be read in abusive ways. Carter directs attention to the sharp critique of the New Testament in Beck, *Mature Christianity*, as well as to the quite different perspective of A. K. M. Adam, "Matthew's Readers." Adam sees Matthew's Gospel as a polemical text *within* Judaism (advancing a particular kind of Judaism, one in which the Messiah has come in Jesus) rather than as anti-Jewish.

115. Meier, *Companions and Competitors*, 500. Meier diverges from my own viewpoint, however, when he argues that the idea that Jesus' community of followers "within Israel would slowly undergo a process of separation from Israel as it pursued a mission to the Gentiles in this present world—the long-term result being that his community would become predominantly Gentile itself—finds no place in Jesus' message or practice" (Meier, *Companions and Competitors*, 251). Much depends here upon the interpretation of the parables, as well as how one understands Jesus' other words and deeds (assuming one grants the authenticity of the Gospel narratives in this regard)

turn out to be crucial. He goes on to argue that Jesus believed that the present order of things was about to come to an end. Jesus' cleansing of the temple was "most likely... a symbolic, prophetic action by which Jesus foretells and, in a sense, unleashes the imminent end of the present temple."[116] In light of this prophetic action, Meier deems the Gospels' testimony that Jesus predicted the destruction of the temple to be historically accurate.[117] Additionally, commenting on Luke 19:44, Meier notes that God's "visitation" in the LXX usually has reference to divine judgment.[118]

I think Jesus prophesied the destruction of the temple (and of Jerusalem) as an eschatological sign of God's judgment upon all sin, both Israel's and the whole world's, as part of the eschatological tribulation that was anticipated, in some form at least, by many Second Temple Jews—a judgment that Jesus himself bore on the cross for all sinners in inaugurating the eschatological temple.[119] N. T. Wright underscores that Jesus understood

---

related to his rejection by the leaders of his people. More broadly, the issue has to do with whether Jesus envisioned a significant time period between his inauguration of the kingdom and the eschatological consummation. For a response to anti-Judaic readings of the parables, see Levine, *Short Stories by Jesus*.

116. Meier, *Companions and Competitors*, 501.

117. Meier states: "in addition to an argument from multiple attestation of sources and forms, we have here as well an argument from coherence: the sayings about the temple explain the otherwise puzzling prophetic action of Jesus in the temple" (*Companions and Competitors*, 501). He then offers his conclusion: "For Qumran, the present temple is not to be entered or used because it is defiled; only after a future purification and renewal will a utopian or an eschatological temple be used by the Qumranites to offer fitting worship. For Jesus, the present temple, whatever its failings, is the temple willed by God for the supreme acts of worship by all Jews. It is, however, an institution that belongs to and is doomed to disappear with this present age. Apparently the full coming of the kingdom of God in power would do away with the temple Jesus and his contemporaries used. Whether Jesus expected some new or better temple to be built after the present one disappeared is unclear. Different versions of a saying witnessed in both Mark and John (Mark 14:58; John 2:19) indicate that some sort of a new temple would be built after the present one was destroyed. It is difficult to say, though, whether we should interpret this prophecy symbolically—e.g., of the restored Israel of the end time or of Jesus' disciples—or literally of some future temple building" (Meier, *Companions and Competitors*, 501). I think that the symbolic reading is correct.

118. See Meier, *Mentor, Message, and Miracles*, 851n62.

119. For background see Pitre, *Jesus, the Tribulation, and the End*, especially chapters 2 and 4. McKnight comments that in the Gospel of Matthew, "the visible demonstration of this rejection by God of the Jewish people as the people of God is the destruction of Jerusalem. The sacking of Jerusalem is a sign of God's judgment" ("A Loyal Critic," 75). I agree with McKnight that "for Matthew, the church is the salvation-historical climax of the Jewish nation, both in continuity (true Israel) and discontinuity (new Israel)" (McKnight, "A Loyal Critic," 75). But I do not think God has rejected "the Jewish people as the people of God"; Paul makes clear that the ongoing Jewish people remain God's elect people. Ongoing Judaism is still Israel, although, from another angle, Jesus

the temple's destruction not as merely a negative judgment but also as a sign of Israel's and the world's blessing, insofar as what the destruction signifies is the inauguration of the new order in the Messiah, who embodies the eschatological temple.[120] While agreeing that Jesus foretold the destruction of the temple, Richard Bauckham offers a further clarification of the meaning of this prophecy, at least according to the Gospel of Luke: "Luke has left the future of Israel relatively open."[121] Above all, Jesus' prophecy would be profoundly misunderstood if taken to imply "God's ultimate rejection of Israel."[122] In interpreting the prophecy, as Brant Pitre suggests, Christians should focus on the fact that Jesus has inaugurated the eschatological temple by atoning "for the sins of Israel" (and of the whole world) and taking "the sufferings of the eschatological tribulation upon himself."[123] On the cross, God himself becomes the atoning temple. Christ brings absolute forgiveness for all sinners when he dies on the cross as "a ransom for many" (Mark

---

as the Messiah has eschatologically fulfilled and reconfigured Israel around himself. McKnight expands upon his position: "Matthew's stiff and persistent warning given to disobedient (nonmessianic) Judaism is not, however, to be taken to indicate that he sees only judgment and damnation for nonmessianic Judaism. That most that can be said is that this judgment is reserved by Matthew for only the leaders and their followers among the nation as a special, privileged body, not for individual Jews" (McKnight, "A Loyal Critic," 74-75).

120. See N. T. Wright, *Day the Revolution Began*, 216-17. See also (among other writings) N. T. Wright, *History and Eschatology*, chapter 4. Wright argues that the eschatological discourse of Mark 13 "is primarily about the fall of the temple, and second, that, since the temple was the heaven-and-earth place, the *microcosmos*, its imminent destruction was bound to mean more than the mere failure of national hope. It was, from the Jewish point of view, *the collapse of the space-time order itself*—not in the sense that the literal space, time and matter would suddenly cease to exist, but that the created order of 'heaven and earth' had lost the linchpin which held it together. This line of thought goes back to Jeremiah, for whom the destruction of the temple meant the return of creation itself to primal chaos. As with Jeremiah, this was the event that Jesus predicted would happen within a generation" (*History and Eschatology*, 149-50).

121. Bauckham, *Jewish World around the New Testament*, 369.

122. On this point see Chanikuzhy, *Jesus, the Eschatological Temple*, 123. In making the point that Jesus' prophecy, like Jeremiah's earlier prophecy of the destruction of the temple by the Babylonians, was "never intended to convey an ultimate rejection," Chanikuzhy draws upon Kinman, *Jesus' Entry into Jerusalem*, 132-44.

123. Pitre, *Jesus, the Tribulation, and the End*, 448, 451. Marius Reiser remarks (though without reference to the destruction of the temple): "judgment is not merely *one* element of early Jewish eschatology among others, but the most important element in that eschatology, and therefore the principal theme of many early Jewish writings in which prophetic preaching of judgment, especially the announcement of the day of YHWH, was taken up and developed. . . . For that very reason, Jesus could not preach the reign of God without speaking of judgment. And that Jesus, who spoke with absolute certainty about the reign of God, also spoke with utter seriousness about judgment is something that . . . can no longer be doubted" (Reiser, *Jesus and Judgment*, 302).

10:45), and all who participate in the events leading to Christ's crucifixion are forgiven (Luke 23:34; Acts 3:17; 1 Cor 2:8).¹²⁴

As George Hunsinger remarks, Christians have "said far too much about Israel's disobedience and far too little about its ongoing obedience, even after its rejection of Jesus Christ"—and Christians have "said far too much about the church's obedience and far too little about its disobedience, most especially its historic disobedience in the form of anti-Semitism, mass persecution of Jews, and the teaching of contempt."¹²⁵ For centuries, Christians interpreted as a *still ongoing curse* the cry of the Jewish people before Pontius Pilate, "His blood be on us and on our children!" (Matt 27:25).¹²⁶ Origen, for example, argued that this verse means that the guilt for the blood of Jesus falls upon "all generations of Jews in the following generations even to the consummation of all things."¹²⁷ Thomas Aquinas, too, fell into this error in his *Commentary on the Gospel of Matthew*. Aquinas comments on Matthew 27:25, "And in this way it came about that Christ's blood is demanded of them even to this day."¹²⁸ Many more commentators in the same vein could be mentioned.¹²⁹

124. This point was rightly noted by medieval Jews in responding to Christian persecutors: see Berger, *Jewish-Christian Debate*, 198: "Furthermore, one can respond to those heretics [i.e. Christians] who say that we are in exile because we sinned in connection with Jesus' death not only by pointing out that we had been in exile before his birth but also by citing the statement in their books that at the time of his death he asked his father, 'Father, forgive them, for they know not what they do' [Luke 23:34]. I may conclude, then, that if the father and son are one entity and possess a single will, this sin must have been entirely forgiven."

125. Hunsinger, "After Barth," 63.

126. Edward Kessler points out: "one of the achievements of Jewish-Christian dialogue has been the realisation that texts have a history; and a compromised history at that. It is impossible to read the Passion narratives of the Gospels without recognising the antisemitic uses to which past readings of them have been put.... Jews, Christians and Muslims can choose to prioritise and act on more inclusive or more exclusive readings.... It is often an exclusive reading of selected texts that has marginalised the other. Examples abound in Jewish and Christian texts, notably violent passages such as Deuteronomy 20" (Kessler, *Introduction to Jewish-Christian Dialogue*, 207).

127. Origen, *Commentary on Matthew*, ser. 124, cited in Wilken, "Something Greater Than the Temple," 187.

128. Thomas Aquinas, *Commentary on Matthew*, §2343. Like Augustine, Aquinas connects the situation of the Jewish people to that of Cain. For further discussion, see Hood, *Aquinas and the Jews*.

129. Hans Urs von Balthasar adopts this error but then largely (though not entirely) neutralizes it. In *Theo-Drama* III, 388, he states: "It is impossible to escape the fact that, in Matthew, Israel (explicitly the holy people, *laos*, the ethnic collective it was from the beginning) takes guilt for the death of Jesus upon itself and succeeding generations: 'His blood be on us and on our children!' (Mt 27:25). The Evangelist is deliberately pronouncing a 'dogmatic theologoumenon' here. It is absolutely clear that no guilt attaches

Fortunately, some commentators did better. John Chrysostom describes the people's statement in Matthew 27:25 as "madness," and he devotes his commentary on the passage to warning Christians against giving way to the "wicked passions" that are present in *Christians*. About the Jewish people Chrysostom says only this: "Nevertheless, the lover of man [Jesus], . . . so far from confirming their sentence upon their children, confirmed it not even on them, but from the one and from the other received those that repented, and counts them worthy of good things beyond number. For indeed even Paul was of them, and the thousands that believed in Jerusalem [Acts 21:20]."[130] Elsewhere, however, Chrysostom unleashes some despicably anti-Jewish rhetoric, in the context of addressing Christians in Antioch who had begun to observe and participate in Jewish ritual feasts.[131] Emil Fackenheim, who studied and appreciated Aquinas and Augustine at the University of Toronto's Pontifical Institute for Medieval Studies, remarks: "[Chrysostom] preached about holiness 'with a golden mouth.' But about Jews, I once was forced to add, the preacher of the golden mouth was a preacher of the filthy mouth."[132]

---

to individual Jews, either at that time or since, on the basis of this passage or others. (Ezekiel 18 would rule this out in any case.) What we are dealing with here is only Israel as an ethnic personality or macro-I. And, as we shall see, it only applies in part, for when Jesus steps forth onto the stage, he causes Israel to split into a 'falling' and a 'rising' Israel (Lk 2:34). All the same, as Jesus' ministry draws to a close, there are more and more signs and prophecies of Israel's 'fall' and its consequences," as for instance the parable of the Vineyard (Matt 21:33–46), the parable of the Wedding Feast (Matt 22:1–10), the seven woes against the Pharisees and Scribes (Matt 23), and the prophecy of the collapse of Jerusalem and the temple (Matt 23–24).

130. Chrysostom, *Homilies on Matthew*, Homily 86, p. 513.

131. Chrysostom sought to respond to Christians who were "attracted to the faith and ceremonial practices of their Jewish fellow-citizens" (Kelly, *Golden Mouth*, 63). J. N. D. Kelly describes Chrysostom's rhetoric against these Christians: "These tirades reveal John as a master of unscrupulous, often coarse invective. His object, of course, is to convince his hearers of the folly, the sheer apostasy, of taking any part whatever in Jewish rituals. But to achieve this pastoral aim he paints the Jews themselves, their religion and their social habits in repulsive colours. Through rejecting the Saviour foretold in their own scriptures they have forfeited the status of children and been reduced to that of dogs, to which, ironically, Jesus had once assigned the Gentiles (Matt. 15.26). . . . The Jews' souls have become the dwelling-places of demons: not surprisingly, since they are the 'Christ-killers' (*Christoktonoi*) who did not shrink from slaying the Lord" (Kelly, *Golden Mouth*, 63–64). Kelly is summarizing Chrysostom's *Discourses Against Judaizing Christians*. See also Wilken's *John Chrysostom and the Jews*, especially chapter 4. As Wilken shows, Chrysostom understood himself to be responding to a real threat and he employed classical rhetorical invective to do it (along with theological arguments). Wilken highlights the impact that Emperor Julian (361–363) and his plan to rebuild the Jewish temple had upon Christians of Chrysostom's generation.

132. Fackenheim, "Jewish-Christian Relations," 24.

Thankfully, today Christian commentators stick closer to the text of Matthew 27:25. Toward the end of the Second Vatican Council, the Catholic biblical scholar Joseph Fitzmyer published an instructive article addressing anti-Jewish and anti-Semitic readings of Matthew 27:25.[133] In their 1971 Anchor Bible commentary on Matthew, similarly, William F. Albright and C. S. Mann remark that the people's words were not meant either by the tradents or by the evangelist as "a condemnation of generations unborn and ought never so to be used."[134] Scholars have also interpreted Matthew 27:25 within the full context of the Bible, where the formulation is a standard "expression of responsibility for the shedding of blood," as in Joshua 2:19–20, 2 Samuel 1:16, 1 Kings 2:33, and Jeremiah 26:15.[135] In their recent contribution to the Catholic Commentary on Sacred Scripture series, Curtis Mitch and Edward Sri state that Matthew has in view at most two generations ("us" and "our children"), with a view to "the judgment that will soon fall on Jerusalem, which in Matthew is expected to take place within a generation."[136]

The Jewish exegete Aaron Gale makes a similar point in *The Jewish Annotated New Testament*. While aware that Christians over the centuries tragically used Matthew 27:25 as a justification for holding all Jewish people uniquely guilty for Jesus' death, Gale comments that "Matthew's first readers

---

133. Fitzmyer, "Antisemitism." See also Kosmala, "'His Blood on Us.'"

134. Albright and Mann, *Matthew*, 345.

135. Senior, *Matthew*, 324. Senior states, "Matthew probably interpreted the destruction of Jerusalem and the temple as God's judgment for the rejection of Jesus and therefore considered that generation as absorbing the terrible consequences (see above, 21:41; 22:7). Even if Matthew did not envisage such a temporal limit to the people's words in 27:25, it is highly unlikely that he was thinking of a blanket condemnation of all Israel for all time" (Senior, *Matthew*, 325). See also Ian Boxall's remarks on this topic: "The invisibility of the Pharisees aside [i.e. they do not receive blame], Matthew's passion story has heightened Jewish responsibility for Jesus' death in a manner that historians would consider to skew the historical balance between Jewish politico-religious leaders and the Roman authorities led by Pilate. The tragic consequences of this in the reception of Matthew's Gospel are only too evident.... Most disturbing in terms of its negative effects is the saying attributed to 'all the people' (*pas ho laos*) at 27.25" (Boxall, *Discovering Matthew*, 157). But as Boxall goes on to say, "If 'all the people' are the Jewish people rejecting their Messiah at the instigation of their leaders, their 'children' are the generation of Jerusalem's fall at the hands of the Romans in 70 CE. Following prophetic precedent (e.g. Jer. 12.7), the evangelist interprets these events witnessed by the children as divine judgement on the city for its rejection of the Messiah—see the echo here of 23.35: 'so that upon you may come all the righteous blood shed on earth'. Thus from the temporal perspective of the evangelist and his readers, the judgement is now past" (Boxall, *Discovering Matthew*, 158).

136. Mitch and Sri, *Gospel of Matthew*, 355. For an alternative interpretation of Matthew 27:25 as meaning that Jesus' Jewish opponents receive the saving power of his blood, see D. Sullivan, "New Insights into Matthew."

likely related the verse to the Jerusalem population, devastated in 70 C.E."[137] Likewise, the Jewish exegete Amy-Jill Levine observes that "'the people as a whole' did not shout for Jesus' death: among the 'Jews' are such faithful followers as the women from Galilee and Joseph of Arimathea.... Matthew 27:25 is neither historical recollection nor a condemnation of all Jews. Rather, it is a very specific reflection by the evangelist on the fate of Jerusalem."[138]

The point is that the eschatological judgment on Jerusalem and the T\temple known to the New Testament does not extend beyond the events of 70 AD, understood as confirming that Jesus has inaugurated the eschatological temple by bearing on the cross the judgment upon *all sin*. In his study of patristic Christian and Rabbinic responses to the destruction of the temple, Adam Gregerman notes, "The Christians, like the rabbis, are intent on demonstrating how a historical event confirms (or does not disconfirm) their claims to be the true people of God, even as rabbinic contemporaries denied this claim explicitly or implicitly."[139] The patristic Christian interpre-

---

137. Gale, "Introduction and Annotations" to the Gospel of Matthew, in the *Jewish Annotated New Testament*, 52. In his brief Introduction to the Gospel, Gale comments that "the phrase reflects Matthew's interpretation of the tragic events of 70 CE, when Rome destroyed Jerusalem and burned the Temple: the 'children' of the Jerusalem crowd were the ones to witness that destruction. Following this tragic event, in which thousands of Jews were killed or exiled, the survival of Judaism was in doubt.... The conflict inherent in Matthew's Gospel may reflect this competition for survival, thereby explaining the harsh attitudes exhibited toward the Pharisees, who were the forerunners of the rabbis" (Gale, "Introduction and Annotations," 2). I think that Matthew's Gospel is more reflective of Jesus' own words, and the context of his lifetime, than Gale supposes.

138. Levine, "Matthew, Mark, and Luke," 92. For Levine, Jesus' prophecy of the destruction of the temple is an invention of the evangelist that has exacted a terrible cost: "Christian Europe witnessed centuries of pogroms promulgated by church members.... While the violence has mostly subsided, the charge remains. I have been accused of being a 'Christ-killer'; so have my children" ("Matthew, Mark, and Luke," 91). In her "Anti-Judaism," Levine concludes: "Historically, Matthew 27 may be the evangelist's reflection on the tragedies of the war against Rome in 66–70 and the resulting destruction of the temple in light of the cross. If so, Matthew does not blame all Jews in all locations at all times for the death of Jesus; the condemnation was a local matter internal to Jerusalem" (34).

139. Gregerman, *Building on the Ruins*, 230–31. Specifically, Gregerman examines Justin Martyr's *Dialogue with Trypho*, Origen's *Contra Celsum*, Eusebius's *Proof of the Gospel*, and the *Midrash on Lamentations*. For 4 Ezra and 2 Baruch on the destruction of the temple—and thus for early Jewish responses that can be compared to early Christian responses found in the New Testament—see Chanikuzhy, *Jesus, the Eschatological Temple*, 44–63. For further background (covering rabbinic and patristic sources) see Wilken, *John Chrysostom and the Jews*, 134–38; Wilken, "Something Greater Than the Temple," 187–96.

tation of the destruction of the temple along apologetic lines is understandable but too often reflects anti-Jewish bias.

In this regard, consider also Augustine's remarks in his Sermon 10—remarks that are related to his concerns about intra-Christian divisions in North Africa, but that he frames in terms of a critique of ongoing Judaism. Preaching on 1 Kings 3:16–27, Augustine proposes that the two women who seek a judgment from King Solomon allegorically represent the Synagogue and the Church. He then states that "the Synagogue is convicted of having killed Christ her son."[140] Of course, the Romans killed Christ, and Christ was handed over by one of his own disciples—although the Jewish crowd in Matthew's Gospel also called for his death. In fact, the Catechism of the Council of Trent underscores that every Christian sinner is far guiltier of killing Christ than is any Jewish person.[141] Augustine's accusation is therefore misleading on multiple levels. Similarly, in his *Contra Faustum Manichaeum*,

---

140. Augustine, "Sermon 10," 283. See also Oort, "Jews and Judaism in Augustine's *Sermones*." Wilken notes that the term "Christ-killers" came "into the Christian vocabulary in the fourth century, originally to refer to the Jews who lived in Jesus' time. The *Apostolic Constitutions*, a work that ... was produced in a community where there was rivalry between Jews and Christians, urges Christians to avoid the 'house of demons or the synagogue of "Christ Killers"' (*Const. app.* 2.61.1)" (*John Chrysostom and the Jews*, 125). On the symbolism of Synagoga and Ecclesia, see Boys, *Has God Only One Blessing?*, 31–35.

141. See *Roman Catechism* 1, 5, 11, cited in the *Catechism*, §598. *Nostra Aetate* makes the same point: "Although the Jewish authorities with their followers pressed for the death of Christ, still those things which were perpetrated during his passion cannot be ascribed indiscriminately to all the Jews living at the time nor to the Jews of today. Although the church is the new people of God, the Jews should not be represented as rejected by God or accursed, as if that follows from holy scripture. All should therefore take care that in holding religious instruction and preaching the word of God, they teach nothing which is not in keeping with the truth of the gospel and the spirit of Christ" (*Nostra Aetate*, §4, 970–71). Sadly, however, David Berger is correct when he writes: "the Catholic teaching that all sinners are responsible for the crucifixion was once seen as perfectly consistent with the doctrine that the Jewish collective, and the Jewish collective alone, suffered specific, grave, and ongoing punishment for its role" (Berger, "Jews, Christians, and *The Passion*," 413). Berger's comments come in the context of a nuanced critique of Mel Gibson's movie *The Passion*, a critique with which I agree, especially since Berger recognizes that "the fervent embrace of the film by traditionalist Christian audiences is not necessarily a sign of hostility" but rather "emerges out of positive religious emotions as well as understandable resentments flowing from the demonization of the religious Right by influential sectors of American public opinion" ("Jews, Christians, and *The Passion*," 416); see also, for the constructive response to Gibson offered by Fisher, *Life in Dialogue*, 73–80). Berger concludes by identifying a paradox: "many religious liberals" oppose the movie's anti-Semitism while also denouncing all "efforts by Israel, no matter how manifestly necessary, to defend its citizens against mass murder at the hands of terrorists" ("Jews, Christians, and *The Passion*," 415).

while insisting that Christians must not kill "[t]he impious people of the fleshly Jews," Augustine states that as a penalty for killing Christ and for refusing his grace, the Jewish people (those who did not become Christian) received a divine punishment of endless subjugation.[142] As Augustine puts it, "the Christian faithful see well enough the subjection that the Jews merited when they killed the Lord for their proud kingdom."[143] This claim—which involves misapplying Hosea 9:17—is historically and theologically erroneous as a statement about "the Jews."

What about other sharply negative words that one finds in the New Testament itself? In part, the genres of prophetic condemnation and classical invective explain some of these words.[144] In *Among the Gentiles: Greco-Roman Religion and Christianity*, Luke Timothy Johnson bemoans the sharpness of Jewish and Christian invective against pagan religion. Johnson observes that in the New Testament, the process of Christian "identity formation" included "a sustained polemic against the Jews who failed to see in Jesus either a Lord or a Messiah."[145] As noted above, he concludes that this polemic is actually mild relative to the New Testament's anti-pagan polemic. He states, "What contemporary readers, both Christian and Jewish, seldom notice is how much more sustained and savage the polemic of the New Testament is with respect to the Gentile world than with respect to Judaism."[146] The polemic against pagan religion as de-

142. Augustine, *Answer to Faustus*, XII.12, p. 133.

143. Augustine, *Answer to Faustus*, XII.12, p. 133. For further discussion see J. Cohen, "'Slay Them Not'"; Massie, *Peuple prophétique et nation témoin*; Unterseher, *Mark of Cain and the Jews*; Fredriksen, "*Secundum Carnem*"; Fredriksen, *Augustine and the Jews*. In *Augustine and the Jews*, Fredriksen argues that Augustine's witness doctrine served to protect the Jewish people from being killed by Christians—and she adds that in his later works, Augustine ties this protection not so much to Genesis 4 (Cain) as to Psalm 59:11, "Slay them not, lest my people forget." Fredriksen also argues that Augustine in *City of God* realizes that Christians, and not solely Jews, are wanderers and pilgrims on the earth, lacking a homeland: thus wandering is no longer simply seen as a curse. For detailed and often critical responses to Fredriksen's proposals, see G. W. Lee, "Israel between the Two Cities"; Boustan, "Augustine as Revolutionary?"; and J. Cohen, "Revisiting Augustine's Doctrine." On the "wandering Jew" trope, see also Matter, "Wandering to the End."

144. Levine holds that the denunciations put forward by Matthew's Jesus cannot be located within the accepted rhetorical practice of the day, because the words spoken by Matthew's Jesus are considered unacceptable by his hearers (see Levine, "Anti-Judaism," 18). But in my view, this is because his hearers understood him to be uttering "blasphemy" (as Matt 26:65 suggests), as indeed would be the case unless Jesus really were divine.

145. L. T. Johnson, *Among the Gentiles*, 2.

146. L. T. Johnson, *Among the Gentiles*, 2; see also L. T. Johnson, "New Testament's Anti-Jewish Slander." E. P. Sanders likewise comments upon the severity of the polemic

mon worship is found already in the prophetic tradition and throughout Second Temple Judaism.¹⁴⁷ Somewhat similarly, the prophets polemicized against their fellow Jews for failures to obey Torah, including such sins as idolatry and economic injustice.

Jesus employs polemical language frequently, not only against his opponents such as various scribes and Pharisees (see the seven woes of Matthew 23), but also against his generation (which he calls a "brood of vipers" among other things [Matt 12:34]) and against his own disciples, whose foolishness and lack of faith he often denounces and whose leader (Peter) he once connects with "Satan" (Matt 16:23). In his seven "woes," Jesus presents his opponents among the scribes and Pharisees as having all sorts of faults, especially hypocrisy, pride, vainglory, blindness about spiritual matters, and murderous impulses against the righteous.¹⁴⁸ Jesus' disciples do not come off much better. Even after his Resurrection, they remain an argumentative lot, as when Paul "opposed [Peter] to his face, because he stood condemned" of hypocrisy (Gal 2:11).

The New Testament does not depict the first generation of Christians as above sin. According to his own self-description, Paul as a Christian

---

against paganism: "The book of Revelation . . . heaps invective on Rome, using 'Babylon' as a code word for the imperial city. Babylon 'made all nations drink of the wine of the wrath of her fornication' (Rev. 14:8); she is 'mother of whores and of earth's abominations' (Rev. 17:5); Babylon is 'a dwelling place of demons, a haunt of every foul and hateful bird, a haunt of every foul and hateful beast' (Rev. 18:2); 'the kings of the earth, who committed fornication and lived in luxury with her, will weep and wail over her when they see the smoke of her burning' (Rev. 18:9); 'Babylon the great city will be thrown down, and will be found no more' (Rev. 18:21)" (Sanders, "Reflections on Anti-Judaism," 280).

147. Johnson does recognize "how different Judaism was" from Greco-Roman religion (L. T. Johnson, *Among the Gentiles*, 129).

148. Sanders argues with respect to the seven woes: "If Jesus spoke the entire chapter, the criticism would actually be less severe than that cited in the *Psalms of Solomon* and the *Dead Sea Scrolls*. Matthew 23, after all, includes the statement that followers of Jesus should do what the scribes and Pharisees say, even though the performance of those authorities is flawed (Matt. 23:2). This verse gives the scribes and Pharisees more credit than the authors of the *Psalms of Solomon* and the *Dead Sea Scrolls* gave their opponents. Put another way, if Jesus spoke a 'woe' over Jerusalem (Matt. 23:37-39; Luke 13:34-35), so did other prophets (e.g., Jeremiah 7)" (Sanders, "Reflections on Anti-Judaism," 270). See also the reconstruction offered by Keith, *Jesus against the Scribal Elite*, 57-59. Keith's overall thesis is as follows: "After a possible initial stage of genuine curiosity or inquiry, the conflict grew into a more hostile interchange between Jesus and the scribal-literate authorities. Concerned that Jesus was treading too closely upon their carefully guarded and scribal-literacy-undergirded social positions, they attempted to demonstrate publicly that Jesus was not a scribal-literate authority. . . . The conflict between Jesus and scribal-literate authorities eventually grew into issues much larger than Jesus's scribal-literate status" (Keith, *Jesus against the Scribal Elite*, 151).

strove mightily not to fall into sinful actions, and he knows that he may fall into sin without knowing that he has done so (see 1 Cor 9:27). Paul similarly bemoans the sins of many members of the churches, including the Galatians who have been "bewitched" (Gal 3:1) and the Corinthians to whom he fears he must make "another painful visit" (2 Cor 2:1). In the book of Revelation, the glorified Jesus condemns the church at Sardis as "dead" (Rev 3:1), and he threatens the church at Laodicea: "I will spew you out of my mouth. For you say, I am rich, I have prospered, and I need nothing; not knowing that you are wretched, pitiable, poor, blind, and naked" (Rev 3:16–17). The same Jesus makes reference to a "synagogue of Satan" whose members "say that they are Jews and are not" in Smyrna and in Philadelphia (Rev 2:9; 3:9).[149] This language, which claims that the true Jews are believers in Jesus, hearkens back to Jesus' condemnation in the Gospel of John of some of his Jewish auditors who "had believed in him" (John 8:31) but who have now rejected him: "You are of your father the devil, and your will is to do your father's desires. He was a murderer from the beginning, and has nothing to do with the truth, because there is no truth in him" (John 8:44).[150] Shortly before this encounter, Jesus had made a similar point about one of his disciples, Judas: "Did I not choose you, the Twelve, and one of you is a devil?" (John 6:70).

As noted above, such polemical language, commonplace in first-century Judaisms, functions in part to indicate that the stakes are high. It matters whether Jesus is the Messiah, and it matters whether he is understood

---

149. See Borgen, "Polemic in Revelation." Borgen suggests that the polemic was likely mutual, with each side claiming to be the true Jews: "each group [Christians and Jews] made an exclusive claim to be the legitimate owner of the Jewish traditions. When the redemptive death of Jesus Christ is understood to be the constitutive foundation of the true Israel and the true Jews, then from the viewpoint of John the other Jews say that they are Jews, but are not. . . . Correspondingly, the Jews in the synagogue would make an exclusive claim on the basis of their understanding of the constitutive elements of the people of Israel, and as a result they would be inclined to persecute members of the *ekklēsia*" (Borgen, "Polemic in Revelation," 211). See also Ian Boxall's comments on Revelation 2:9: "Many would see this as an attack on hostile members of the non-Christian Jewish synagogue, who have rejected rival claims of Christians to be 'true Jews', possibly expelling them from the synagogue community (a similar situation is envisaged at Jn 9:22) and reporting them to local magistrates. . . . A second possibility is that they are Jewish Christians, perhaps of a rival 'synagogue' or 'congregation' in this sprawling city, who are understood to be too closely accommodated to the 'satanic' culture of the province and the empire. . . . Alternatively, the rival group could be Christians from a Gentile background who had Judaised in order to escape hostility from the authorities" (Boxall, *Revelation of Saint John*, 54).

150. For discussion, see (in addition to texts cited above) Rensberger, "Anti-Judaism and John"; Freyne, "Vilifying the Other." For a defense of the passion account in John's Gospel, see Kaufman, *Beloved Disciple*.

properly. In the New Testament, such language may also indicate an experience of persecution, since Christians then were a persecuted minority among the Jewish people in Judea and the diaspora. It is not for nothing that Paul speaks of his "former life in Judaism," in which he "persecuted the Church of God violently and tried to destroy it" (Gal 1:13). Paul boasts of the persecution he has endured as an apostle of Christ. He states, "Five times I have received at the hands of the Jews the forty lashes less one. Three times I have been beaten with rods; once I was stoned" (2 Cor 11: 24–25). Not only was Saul (the future Paul) involved in the stoning of Stephen, but also Saul "laid waste the Church, and entering house after house, he dragged off men and women and committed them to prison" (Acts 8:3). The book of Acts describes Paul being beaten by an enraged crowd of his Jewish brethren for daring to enter the temple (Acts 21). It depicts a conspiracy in which "more than forty" of Paul's fellow Jews "bound themselves by an oath neither to eat nor drink till they had killed Paul" (Acts 23:12).[151] These stories expose the intensity of the tensions unleashed by the proclamation of Jesus as the Messiah. It is little wonder that, in a culture in which polemical rhetoric was standard fare, we find such rhetoric in the New Testament.

As indicated above, New Testament authors not only condemned Jews who did not accept Jesus as the Messiah, but also condemned fellow followers of Jesus. Most notably, John 8:44—"You are of your father the devil, and your will is to do your father's desires"—attacks "putative [Christian] believers, perhaps representing people in the Johannine environment who not only hoped to remain in the synagogue, but who regarded Jesus only as an authentic teacher, not as the incarnate *Logos* who brought the ultimate

---

151. See Keener, *Acts* III, 3300–309. In Acts 28, the imprisoned Paul (in Rome) is disappointed by the tepid response to his preaching given by the Roman Jewish community. Rather understandably, they leave his presence after he pronounces a prophetic judgment upon them: "The Holy Spirit was right in saying to your fathers through Isaiah the prophet: 'Go to this people, and say, You shall indeed hear but never understand, and you shall indeed see but never perceive. For this people's heart has grown dull, and their ears are heavy of hearing, and their eyes they have closed; lest they should perceive with their eyes, and hear with their ears, and understand with their heart, and turn for me to heal them.' Let it be known to you then that this salvation of God has been sent to the Gentiles; they will listen" (Acts 28:25–28; cf. Isa 6:9–10; Ps 67:2). On this striking passage, see Sandt, "Acts 28, 28." Van de Sandt argues against the common view that "after Paul's last statement in Acts the people of Israel no longer have the opportunity to be saved. Acts 28.28 marks the end of God speaking to his people, a conclusive verdict for Israel" (Sandt, "Acts 28, 28," 343). As van de Sandt concludes, "The statement in v. 28 . . . does not imply God's abandonment of Israel as a people. In keeping with the prophetic heritage the severe indictment represents a summons to add force to Israel's responsibility" (Sandt, "Acts 28, 28," 358).

revelation of God."[152] Consider Paul's furious condemnation of the members of the Galatian congregation: "I am astonished that you are so quickly deserting him who called you in the grace of Christ and turning to a different gospel—not that there is another gospel, but there are some who trouble you and want to pervert the gospel of Christ" (Gal 1:6–7). Paul places a curse upon the Christians who have persuaded the Gentile Galatians that they need to observe Torah (see Gal 1:9), and in fact Paul does not hesitate to use a graphic image: "I wish those who unsettle you would mutilate themselves [or more literally: cut the whole thing off]!" (Gal 5:12).[153]

The Jewish scholar Kenneth Stow finds throughout the Christian tradition a "metaphor of the Jewish dog,"[154] although Jesus actually uses the

152. Rensberger, "Anti-Judaism and John," 149. See also, more broadly, Reinhartz, "Gospel of John"; Reinhartz, *Cast Out of the Covenant*. In her book, Reinhartz focuses on John's rhetorical invective against "the Jews," that is, Jesus' Jewish enemies (as distinct from his Jewish friends). She points out, "The relentless focus on the *Ioudaioi*'s intentions to kill Jesus identifies them as the enemies of Jesus and all believers. The same point is made through the pervasive rhetoric of binary opposition.... This rhetoric is expressed in the Gospel's use of contrasting metaphors. One set of metaphors describes opposing states of being, such as light/darkness, life/death, above/below, from God/not from God. Another set describes opposing activities, such as believing/disbelieving, accepting/rejecting, doing good/doing evil, loving/hating. The positive element of each pair is associated with Jesus.... In the Gospel, it is the *Ioudaioi*, the Jews, who exemplify and concretize the negative pole of these binaries" (*Cast Out of the Covenant*, 76–77). Although I read John's text as indicating the divergent responses Jesus received among his own people (just as the proclamation of Jesus receives divergent responses among Gentile peoples)—and indicating the high stakes involved therein—I agree with Reinhartz that this rhetoric was bound to be devastating for the ongoing Jewish people. In my view, the Gospel of John must be read in light of the commandment of love that Christ proclaims as normative in the Gospel of John. It is not surprising that, as the work of a human author, the text's rhetoric has caused problems, without thereby negating its divine inspiration and truth. Insofar as the Gospel of John has led or leads believers to hate or persecute the ongoing Jewish people, it is the Church's task to call such believers back to the cruciform love commanded by Christ.

153. The translation in brackets comes from Sanders, "Reflections on Anti-Judaism," 270.

154. Stow, *Jewish Dogs*, 5. Stow shows that in John Chrysostom and later commentators, the Gentile dogs of Matthew 15:26 were turned into Jewish dogs. The image became a common trope, appearing in connection with the blood libel and with injunctions to avoid polluting oneself by associating with Jews. A few of the examples Stow gives are mistaken; for example, he cites Thomas Aquinas's *Summa theologiae* II-II q. 10 to the effect "[n]on-Christians must be irrational and inhuman" (*Jewish Dogs*, 9), whereas in fact Aquinas clearly upholds the rationality and humanity of the Jewish people, despite his view that the Jewish people are in a sinful state of unbelief. But in general Stow's wide-ranging presentation is accurate (and appalling). Stow notes that in Martin Luther's early *That Jesus Christ Was Born a Jew*, Luther deems that Catholics, not Jews, are the true dogs. Stow turns with understandable zest to medieval Jewish mockery of Catholics, including linkages of Gentiles (Christians) with dogs by the *Nizzahon*

image of dogs to describe Gentiles (Matt 15:26) while Paul uses the image to describe Christians (Phil 3:2), specifically his Christian opponents. In 2 Corinthians, Paul complains bitterly about the influence upon the Corinthian Christians had by "false apostles, deceitful workmen, disguising themselves as apostles of Christ" (2 Cor 11:13). Paul ends by comparing these false Christian apostles to Satan himself, whose servants they are: "And no wonder, for even Satan disguises himself as an angel of light. So it is not strange if his servants also disguise themselves as servants of righteousness" (2 Cor 11:14-15).[155]

How should we evaluate this frequent and wide-ranging use of rhetorical invective? In its context, it does not demonstrate that the persons who used it lacked charity. Anger, including clearly voiced anger, is not necessarily sinful. Moreover, as Ian Boxall writes with Revelation 2:9 in view, "This sort of name-calling has a powerful place in religious and political rhetoric, and is regularly found in the biblical tradition. Biblical writers suffered fewer scruples than some of their modern critics about negative stereotyping of those with whom they disagreed."[156] This was because the traditions of prophetic discourse and classical rhetoric involved precisely such negative stereotyping. The first point to make, therefore, is that rhetorical invective does not necessarily mean that its author or speaker is sinning.

Secondly, however, awareness that invective can be dangerous is not solely a modern discovery. The practice of "name-calling" does not proceed without challenge in the New Testament. The Apostle James, for example, offers a clear warning. He remarks that "no human being can tame the tongue—a restless evil, full of deadly poison. With it we bless the Lord and Father, and with it we curse men, who are made in the likeness of God. From the same mouth come blessing and cursing. My brethren, this ought not to be so" (Jas 3:8-10). Paul himself says something similar, though

---

Yashan and by the thirteenth-century Jewish scholars Moshe of Coucy and Eleazar the Rokeah. He also suggests that the third-century *Midrash Tannaim to Deuteronomy* 12:31, which subtly links Gentiles and dogs, may be a response to Matthew 15:26. As Stow demonstrates, medieval "Jews saw Christianity and Christians—the goyim—as earthly, if not brutal, their nature worldly and spiritually wanting, and their ritual akin to the worst kind of paganism. Jewish commentaries, including the commentary of the all-important eleventh-century Rashi on Deuteronomy 18:9, which also forbids sacrificing children to pagan gods, say that the human sacrifice this verse forbids is the way of the *nokhrim*, the Christians. To which, Rashi adds: 'learn not to do' these things. For Rashi, Christians sacrifice and eat their (idolatrous) God" (Stow, *Jewish Dogs*, 142-43). See also Shachar, *Judensau*.

155. For medieval Christian demonization of the Jewish people, see Trachtenberg, *Devil and the Jews*.

156. Boxall, *Revelation of Saint John*, 54.

without direct reference to speech: "Love is patient and kind; love is not jealous or boastful; it is not arrogant or rude. . . . Love bears all things" (1 Cor 13:4–5, 7).

The doctrine of biblical inspiration and truth does not require of Christians that we embrace the New Testament's passionate invective in all its dimensions. We can recognize it for the ancient genre that it is, and we can also allow for the expression of personal emotion that is not the intended truth inspired by the divine author. Just because Paul says that it is "true" that "Cretans are always liars, evil beasts, lazy gluttons" (Titus 1:12–13), we do not need to take this as true literally; it is a hyperbolic expression of Paul's concerns about the situation of the Christian community in Crete. We can test Paul's language by his own standard of love, and we can grant that he sometimes falls short, without thereby requiring us to doubt the truth of his gospel. For instance, he rejoices over the coming of "God's wrath" upon "the Jews, who killed both the Lord Jesus and the prophets, and drove us out, and displease God and oppose all men by hindering us from speaking to the Gentiles" (1 Thess 2:14–16).[157] The truth content of this statement is that some of Paul's Jewish brethren have indeed persecuted him; and also that a small number of Jews (including, of course, some of Jesus' own disciples) were influential in the events that led to Jesus' death. But it is obviously untrue that "the Jews" "killed . . . the Lord Jesus," since the Romans killed him; and we do not need to canonize Paul's emotions in this letter against his fellow Jews for whom he elsewhere expresses deep love. Room must be given for human authors to speak in the rhetorical genres of their day and with the emotion that humans feel in the heat of controversy. To allow for such room upholds, rather than undermines, biblical truth.

---

157. For discussion see Eubank, *First and Second Thessalonians*, 66–69. Eubank proposes, "These verses are best read as an outburst of righteous indignation at the opposition that the earliest Christians received from some fellow Jews. But such expressions of judgment do not have the last word in Scripture. The Old Testament prophets, whom Paul imitates here, charge the people with killing the prophets and bringing wrath down on themselves, but they always offer the hope of restoration (e.g., compare Jer 2:30 with 31:1–40). Similarly, Paul did not rest with this word of condemnation [see Rom 9–11]" (Eubank, *First and Second Thessalonians*, 68–69). See also Sanders, "Reflections on Anti-Judaism," 274–76. For Sanders, these verses are indeed "anti-Jewish." He explains, "What is anti-Jewish about this is the contrast between 'the Jews' and 'us' in connection with a list of exaggerated or erroneous accusations. . . . One might argue against this conclusion by noting the similar language in Neh. 9:26: 'They were disobedient and rebelled against you [God] and cast your law behind their backs and killed your prophets'" ("Reflections on Anti-Judaism," 276). Sanders goes on to say that, especially in light of Romans 9–11, he does not think that Paul was anti-Jewish. I read Paul's statement as hyperbole indicating the mortal threat under which important prophets operated and expressing his anger at treatment he has received. See also Schlueter, *Filling Up the Measure*.

The same point holds with respect to Johannine rhetorical invective, as in John 8:44 and Revelation 2:9.[158] In certain ways I agree with David Rensberger that John's "use of such violent language is, in the long view, difficult to defend," because of all the harm it has caused to innocent Jewish persons.[159] But God willed to communicate his Word through human authors, and God made clear the truth by which all such language—and all later Christian language—is to be measured: "Beloved, let us love one another; for love is of God" (1 John 4:7).[160] Importantly, the evangelist John and the book of Revelation have not misjudged the identity of Jesus or misunderstood the radical call to embrace him as Lord and Messiah. Jesus' words possess authority, as does the Gospel of John. I am simply pointing out that rhetorical invective is timebound and we need to strive to perceive the enduring truth that God and Jesus Christ intend to communicate.

Admittedly, given that people *can* join forces with demonic powers in one way or another (or so Christians believe), it will not be possible

---

158. Rensberger, "Anti-Judaism and John," 152.

159. Rensberger, "Anti-Judaism and John," 152. Hans Urs von Balthasar does not seem to perceive the dangerous consequences, and in fact he employs further incendiary language when he writes: "In John, Jesus himself uncovers the hidden evil when he unveils the diabolical nature of the Jews' lingering in the preliminary and their refusal to cross the threshold of faith" (von Balthasar, *Theo-Logic* II, 331). In the same deeply troubling vein, von Balthasar goes on to deplore (this time speaking for Paul) "the fancied sufficiency of rigid clinging to the law" (*Theo-Logic* II, 331). Even worse, von Balthasar adds: "One can cling to the preliminary only in bad conscience, and it is just this know-it-all attitude that is the true sin of unbelief" (*Theo-Logic* II, 331). The trope of the (ongoing) Jewish people concealing a "hidden evil" of a "diabolical nature" due to their legalistic "refusal" to have faith, so that the post-biblical practice of Judaism becomes equated with having a "bad conscience," is precisely the root of anti-Semitism; and it paints a false portrait of ongoing Judaism. Continuing his account of John and Paul, von Balthasar describes "the incapacity of the Jews" and their "self-absolutizing life according to the law" that constitutes "an impotence" and a rejection of "God and his providence" (*Theo-Logic* II, 332, 334). In all this, von Balthasar, in a work originally published in 1985, reads the New Testament along the harshest lines of Christian anti-Judaism.

160. As Augustine says—and as I think can be applied to rhetorical invective without undermining the actual teaching that God wills to communicate—"[w]hoever . . . thinks that he understands the divine Scriptures or any part of them so that it does not build the double love of God and of neighbor does not understand it at all" (Augustine, *On Christian Doctrine*, I.xxxvi.40, p. 30). Similarly, though now with historical-critical scholarship (and thus knowledge of ancient genres and rhetorical practices) in view, Pope Benedict XVI insists with regard to "passages of Scripture that strike us as problematic": "correct interpretation of these passages requires a degree of expertise, acquired through a training that interprets the texts in their historical-literary context and within the Christian perspective, which has as its ultimate hermeneutical key 'the Gospel and the new commandment of Jesus Christ brought about in the paschal mystery'" (Benedict XVI, *Verbum Domini*, §42).

for interpreters to determine in every case whether a particular use of demonizing language is meant to be taken as a literal accusation of demonic possession. In general, though, it is evident that we are often dealing with rhetorical exaggeration through the genre of invective. The coming of the Messiah required culturally accessible language that was sufficiently charged to convey the gospel's world-changing importance and also to convey the actual intensity of the intra-Jewish conflict over the identity of Jesus. Not only the evangelists and apostles, but also Jesus uses polemical rhetoric as a way of alerting people (including complacent believers today) to the radical challenge that he brings. To the degree that the authors of the Gospels communicate his precise words, I am certainly not accusing him of sin in his dealings with his opponents.[161]

V. Conclusion

Jewish-Christian dialogue must not require either Christians or Jews to reject their core beliefs. Differences will endure, including painful differences over Abraham, Jesus, the meaning of the temple's destruction, and so on. The New Testament fully reflects these painful differences. It could not have been otherwise.

Yet, Christians involved in Jewish-Christian dialogue must recognize that the New Testament's polemical language had a profoundly deleterious effect upon later people toward whom it was not directed. Philip Cunningham states, "Paul expects gentile believers to respect even Jews not in the Church. He gives many reasons why gentiles in Christ have no grounds for boasting."[162] Christians—mainly Gentiles—took the New Testament's language and condemned the ongoing Jewish people over the centuries as a

---

161. Thus, I disagree with the arguments put forward by Branick, "Sinful Flesh."

162. Cunningham, "Paul's Letters," 149. Cunningham goes on to emphasize—and, in my view, over-emphasize—Paul's imminent eschatology as decisive for Paul's understanding of Jews and Gentiles. He then contrasts this eschatology sharply with that of people today: "most Christians today have consciously or unconsciously postponed the eschaton into the indefinite future. Similarly, very few modern Jews anticipate the dawn of the messianic age very soon" (Cunningham, "Paul's Letters," 153). I don't think Cunningham is correct here. Many Christians today do not know the day or the hour of his coming and the consummation of all things, but we live in his presence, anticipate his imminent coming, and pray "Come, Lord Jesus!" (Rev 22:20). When Christianity is "alive" rather than merely nominal, people do not put eschatology to the side, though this doesn't mean claiming to know "that day or that hour." I see more continuity between our situation and Paul's than does Cunningham. Paul had a sense that Gentile boasting over the Jewish people was going to be destructive; we have a clear-eyed recognition that Paul was correct.

rejected and spiritually dead people whose subjugation is justified until the end of time. For Christians, a crucial purpose of Jewish-Christian dialogue is to heal and mend such distortions in Christianity itself.

I have emphasized that believers who value scriptural truth need not embrace the passionate polemical edge found in biblical language. We can distinguish the truth-claims of inspired Scripture from its timebound rhetorical devices, just as these truth-claims are distinguishable from "the urgent emotion" felt at the time.[163] We can insist upon the new commandment of love, upon Paul's description of love, and upon James's rules for charitable speech. Christians are not under obligation always to defend the anger that can be present in prophetic or Greco-Roman rhetorical invective, understood as a commonplace communicative genre. Furthermore, even when Jesus or New Testament authors were justified in employing polemical language, it cannot be easily applied to later situations but must instead be carefully interpreted so as to understand what is actually being taught by the Word of God. Here it is necessary to appreciate the truth of James' warning that "we all make many mistakes" in our use of words (Jas 3:2). At the heart of Christian-Jewish dialogue is humility—and charity.

Now that Christians and Jews have developed friendships, the antagonisms of past generations can be overcome, even if no generation will lack in blind spots. Augustine had it right in *On Christian Doctrine*, although he did not know how to apply it to the Jewish people. Namely, charity is the hermeneutical key to all Scripture and any reading that posits a meaning of Scripture that runs counter to real charity cannot be correct. Jewish-Christian dialogue will not be able to iron out all differences and disagreements; charity does not require that no difficulties remain. But we can heed the counsel Paul gave to the Romans: "love one another with brotherly affection; outdo one another in showing honor" (Rom 12:10).

---

163. Cunningham, "Paul's Letters," 145.

Chapter 2

CREATION AND SCRIPTURE

I. INTRODUCTION

In the Revised Standard Version of the Bible, the first verse of Genesis reads: "In the beginning God created the heavens and the earth" (Gen 1:1). This majestic opening frames the entirety of the biblical story. Theologically speaking, everything depends upon the revelation that we are creatures of the Creator God. To recognize ourselves as creatures—freely loved into being by a Creator who is in no way creaturely—changes everything in terms of human purposes and hopes. The reality of the transcendent, personal, and active Creator God, and the fact that all things depend upon this God for existence, is a central component of divine revelation. David Novak remarks, "in the Hebraic tradition, God's superiority to both the human and the non-human world is pure transcendence. God is the Creator of the universe 'out of nothing' (*ex nihilo*), which among other things means that the creation of everything and everybody . . . is the result or product of God's totally free, truly autonomous will."[1] In metaphysical terms, says Novak, the relationship of God and the universe is clear from a Jewish perspective: "The universe is necessarily dependent upon God for its being, while God is not necessarily dependent on the created universe for anything. . . . Hence the ontological contingency of the universe is more radical than the logical dependence of a conclusion on its premise."[2]

Yet, an equally plausible and perhaps more accurate translation of the Hebrew of Genesis 1:1–2 is offered by the Jewish Study Bible: "When God began to create heaven and earth—the earth being unformed and void, with

---

1. Novak, *Athens and Jerusalem*, 56.
2. Novak, *Athens and Jerusalem*, 56.

darkness over the surface of the deep and a wind from God sweeping over the water."[3] This way of translating the first two verses of Genesis implies that the Creator God worked with some kind of "unformed" preexisting substrate. If so, the question becomes whether God really is the transcendent source of all finite being. If the answer were no, then God would not be infinite plenitude and the source of all finite being, but rather God would merely be a powerful finite being. If there is a preexisting substrate that does not depend for its existence upon God, then God is not infinitely "to be": God's being stops where the uncreated preexisting substrate's being begins. If God were a finite being, God would be creaturely.

One can easily see how high the stakes are. Why then does Israel's God allow the language of Genesis 1 to leave ambiguous something as important as whether or not God created *ex nihilo*?[4] One answer is that God worked through real historical authors and a real historical people, with the result that we should expect the Bible's texts to reflect in certain ways the limitations of their original contexts, even while conveying a divine revelation that transcends its cultural contexts. I agree with this answer, but I wish to press further. In providentially arranging the modes of his revelation, God was not constrained to permit any major ambiguity in the final form of Genesis 1. Yet God chose to permit this. A Christian Israelology, for which the doctrine of creation and the nature of Scripture are crucial, should seek understanding of the path taken by God.

Pope Benedict XVI observes in his apostolic exhortation on Scripture, *Verbum Domini*: "Creation is the setting in which the entire history

---

3. See the Jewish Publication Society, *Jewish Study Bible*. In his "Ancient Near Eastern Context," Bernard F. Batto articulates the widely held view that "[s]imilar to *Enuma Elish* (and some Egyptian creation accounts), Genesis 1 opens at a time prior to creation when there was as yet only the divine spirit and a chaotic watery primeval substance" (51).

4. On biblical language, see such works as Caird, *Language and Imagery of the Bible*; Childs, *Myth and Reality*; B. W. Anderson, *Creation versus Chaos*. See also Frymer-Kensky, "Emergence of Jewish Biblical Theologies," 115-16. Frymer-Kensky observes that the Hebrew literally says, "At the beginning of—he created," but it mirrors an Akkadian grammatical construction that renders likely (but not certain) the translation offered by the Jewish Study Bible. Frymer-Kensky concludes, "The composers of the first chapter of Genesis knew Hebrew at least as well as I do. They could say something clearly when they wanted to. Moreover, the beautiful litany is carefully, poetically constructed.... The ambiguity of the phrase must be purposeful" ("Emergence of Jewish Biblical Theologies," 116). In my view, this does not exclude the value of a later certainty, whether philosophical or canonical or both. For Frymer-Kensky, however, every claim to certainty of any kind is undermined by the Hebrew Bible itself, in one or another of its texts.

of the love between God and his creation develops."⁵ The medieval Jewish theologian Moses Maimonides makes a similar point but with even more force: "the foundation of the whole Law is the view that God has brought the world into being out of nothing."⁶ Even the "pure privation" that according to Maimonides is present at the outset depends entirely "on God for its 'existence.'"⁷ Yet, the Anglican biblical scholar Markus Bockmuehl has recently asked about creation *ex nihilo* (whose truth he affirms), "how did this idea arise out of a biblical tradition that prima facie appears not to support it?"⁸ If one has to ask this question in this way, then there is evidently a problem.

Unsurprisingly, the Church Fathers had an answer for scriptural-hermeneutical problems of this kind. Origen states that "the Word of God has arranged for certain stumbling-blocks" to be included Scripture, so that we readers do not fail to raise our minds to mysteries that inevitably exceed the *letter* or literal meaning of the text.⁹ Similarly, Augustine argues that it is often best for readers of Scripture to "labor in hunger" rather than, by easily

---

5. Benedict XVI, *Verbum Domini*, §9. Discussing the Second Vatican Council's Dogmatic Constitution on Divine Revelation, *Dei Verbum*, Benedict XVI states that in addition to "the study of literary genres and historical context as basic elements for understanding the meaning intended by the sacred author," interpreters must read biblical texts in the context of Scripture's canonical unity, the living tradition of the Church, and the analogy of faith (Benedict XVI, *Verbum Domini*, §34). His explanation of ambiguous or troubling biblical passages is that God worked through history (*Verbum Domini*, §12).

6. Maimonides, *Guide of the Perplexed*, Part II, ch. 30, p. 349. For discussion, see D. Davies, "Reason, Will, and Purpose." As Davies observes, Maimonides "insists that a genuinely *ex nihilo* creation must be entirely different from any sort of generation that humans can experience" (D. Davies, "Reason, Will, and Purpose," 229).

7. See Ivy, "Maimonides on Creation," 191; cf. 202-3, 209 for more explanation. See also, in the same volume, Staub, "Gersonides and Contemporary Theories," where Staub argues that Gersonides occupies a middle ground: "Gersonides frames the problem as a choice between creation out of something, a position he attributes to Plato, and creation out of nothing, Maimonides' position. He dismissed the Platonic hypothesis that, prior to creation, there had existed a preexistent matter with chaotic motion because, applying the laws of Aristotelian physics, he shows that such chaotic matter presumes the causation of forms, which themselves would have had to be created. He rejects the Maimonidean hypothesis of creation out of absolutely nothing on the grounds that the creative causation of forms can have had no effect unless there is a material receptacle disposed to receive their causation" (247).

8. Bockmuehl, "Introduction," 2. See also Bockmuehl, "Idea of Creation out of Nothing." For New Testament understandings of creation, see Pennington and McDonough, eds., *Cosmology and New Testament Theology*; and McDonough, *Christ as Creator*.

9. Origen, *On First Principles*, IV.2.9, p. 285 (Greek).

receiving knowledge, becoming "indolent in disdain."[10] Augustine assures us that "the Holy Spirit has magnificently and wholesomely modulated the Holy Scriptures so that the more open places present themselves to hunger and the more obscure places may deter a disdainful attitude"—and furthermore that little (and nothing of significance) is "found in these obscure places which is not found plainly said elsewhere."[11]

Neither Origen nor Augustine, however, had any doubt that Genesis 1 plainly teaches creation *ex nihilo*. Working with the Septuagint text, Origen reads Genesis 1 in light of John 1. He argues that "the beginning" (Gen 1:1 and John 1:1) is the Word, Jesus Christ. It is in the Word, who is the Savior, that God creates (*ex nihilo*) "heaven and earth" (Gen 1:1).[12] When Origen arrives at "darkness" and "the deep" (Gen 1:2), he argues that since these are mentioned prior to God's creation of the visible realm (with its light, firmament, and waters), "the deep" must refer to the angelic realm, to which belong the immaterial and invisible angels and demons.[13] Somewhat similarly, Augustine conceives of "heaven and earth" as formless matter, from which it follows that Genesis 1:2's reference to darkness and the deep simply expresses the formlessness of the original creation.[14]

Jewish theologians echo this approach. Nachmanides contends that what Genesis 1:1-2 shows is that God "created all things from absolute non-existence"—but did so by creating a substrate of "primary matter" to which God then gave form.[15] Similarly, after affirming strongly that "Judaism affirms the principle of creation out of absolute nothingness," Joseph B. Soloveitchik reasons that it must be the case that "the chaos and the void, the deep, the darkness" of Genesis 1:2 were "fashioned by the Almighty before the creation of the orderly, majestic, beautiful world."[16] These primal realities are not evil in themselves, but they became disordered, because "the forces of relative nothingness at times exceed their bounds. They wish to burst forth out of the chains of obedience that the Almighty imposed

---

10. Augustine, *On Christian Doctrine*, II.9, p. 38.

11. Augustine, *On Christian Doctrine*, II.9, p. 38. For further discussion see Sheridan, *Language for God in Patristic Tradition*; and Graves, *Inspiration and Interpretation of Scripture*.

12. Origen, *Homilies on Genesis and Exodus*, Homily 1, p. 47.

13. Origen, *Homilies on Genesis and Exodus*, Homily 1, pp. 47-48.

14. For further discussion see Blowers, *Drama of the Divine Economy*; and Bouteneff, *Beginnings*.

15. Ramban (Nachmanides), *Commentary on the Torah*, 23. See also Gaon, *Book of Beliefs and Opinions*, 81, 106.

16. Soloveitchik, *Halakhic Man*, 102.

upon them and seek to plunge the earth back into chaos and the void."[17] For Soloveitchik, what prevents this chaos from winning out is God's Torah.[18]

These interpretations of Genesis 1:1–2 show that theological readers have long been aware of its difficulties. Modern biblical scholarship has simply intensified the ambiguity. Gary Anderson describes the problem that modern scholars have identified: "The consensus among scholars... is that the first three verses depict God forming the world out of preexistent matter. On this view the first two verses constitute a set of subordinate clauses that set up the main clause in verse 3: [1] 'When God set out to create the heavens and the earth, [2] and when the earth was a formless void.'"[19] Anderson affirms the doctrine of creation *ex nihilo* on other grounds, but he goes on to remark that "reading Genesis 1:1 in light of *Enuma Elish* suggests that God [in Gen 1] is both confronted with and limited by the state of the universe prior to creation."[20]

---

17. Soloveitchik, *Halakhic Man*, 102–3. By contrast, the Jewish biblical scholar and theologian Jon D. Levenson argues that Israel's Scriptures do not hold that God created all things out of "nothing" in the sense of utter nonbeing, with God as the creative source and origin of all finite being. Rather, God the Creator worked upon "a primordial, uncreated chaos" that, as chaos, was not a privation of being but rather was "a real, active force, except that its charge was entirely negative." See Levenson, *Creation*, xx–xxi.

18. Soloveitchik, *Halakhic Man*, 103. The Torah "carves out a boundary, sets up markers, establishes special domains, all for the purpose of separating existence from 'nothingness,' the ordered cosmos from the void, and creation from the naught" (Soloveitchik, *Halakhic Man*, 103). Rather similarly, but without the explicit affirmation of creation *ex nihilo*, Richard J. Clifford, SJ, argues that Genesis 1:1–3 is trying to describe the character of divine action: see Clifford, "*Creatio ex nihilo*," 65. Clifford directs attention to his *Creation Accounts*. John H. Walton argues that the Hebrew verb *bārāʾ* ("create") has to do not with bringing something into existence, but with establishing a functional *order*. At the outset, there is a formless void, a darkness without order; God then creates a "very good" (Gen 1:31) functional order: see Walton, *Lost World of Genesis One*, 92.

19. G. A. Anderson, "*Creatio ex nihilo*," 16. By contrast, Nathan Chambers argues that "Gen 1:1 is an independent clause" (Chambers, *Reconsidering Creation*, 239; cf. 133–77).

20. G. A. Anderson, "*Creatio ex nihilo*," 22. Anderson points out, "One way out of this impasse is to appeal to the Greek translation of the Hebrew original. The Septuagint renders Genesis 1:1 as an independent sentence and thus portrays the making of the heavens and the earth as the first act of creation and the subsequent description of the chaotic nature of the earth, heaven, and waters as a description of how they appeared after this first creative act. Indeed, as Menahem Kister has shown, it is a short step from the LXX to an early Jewish exegetical tradition that understood all the items listed in Genesis 1:2 as items created by God. The adoption of the LXX translation in the prologue of the Gospel of John lends considerable authority to this particular translation for the Christian reader of the Bible" (G. A. Anderson, "*Creatio ex nihilo*," 17). For Anderson, Genesis 1's purpose is to deny that there is any competitor to God:

Believers who seek to know the truth about God the Creator (and about his creation) therefore seem to be in a quandary, a quandary of God's own making through his people Israel and their Scriptures.[21] In this light, the present chapter inquires into the fittingness of ambiguous biblical language with respect to creation *ex nihilo*. In a manner that I find particularly helpful, Walter Brueggemann suggests that if we wish to understand Genesis on creation, we need to appreciate the importance of language. He reminds us: "By God's speech that which did not exist comes into being. The way of God with his world is the way of language."[22] The Catholic theologian Bruno Forte remarks that this insight belongs to Judaism as much as it belongs (later) to Christianity. He states, "For the faith of Israel, the Word of God is inseparably the Word that speaks, creates, and saves."[23] It would be more accurate to lowercase this "Word" in its Old Testament contexts, but otherwise Forte is correct.

God creates in an uncontested way (by contrast to pagan creation myths). In his view, later Greco-Roman thinkers pressed a new question: is matter itself a competitor or constraint upon God's creative work? In accord with the logic of Genesis 1, the answer is no; God has no competitor or constraint of any kind in creating (creation *ex nihilo*). Anderson is sensitive to Gerhard May's argument that creation *ex nihilo* is a patristic development rather than a biblical doctrine: see May, *Creatio ex Nihilo*. For Anderson, it is to be expected that the reception history of the biblical text should inform our understanding of the meaning of the biblical text, even when the original author had a different meaning in view. See also Arnold, *Genesis*, 27–52; Kister, "*Tohu wa-Bohu*"; and Chambers, *Reconsidering Creation*.

21. Walter Brueggemann insists that the quandary can be a fruitful one: "The very ambiguity of *creation from nothing* and *creation from chaos* is a rich expository possibility. We need not choose between them, even as the text does not.... The former asserts the majestic and exclusive power of God. The latter lets us affirm that even the way life is can be claimed by God" (Brueggemann, *Genesis*, 30).

22. Brueggemann, *Genesis*, 24. Brueggemann points out that in Genesis 1, "God's characteristic action is *to speak* (vv. 3, 5, 6, 8, 9, 10, 11, 14, 20, 22, 24, 26, 28, 29)" (Brueggemann, *Genesis*, 24). Likewise, the contemporary Jewish theologian Jonathan Sacks offers an interpretation of Genesis 1 that highlights divine language. Sacks remarks that "[w]hat is truly creative is not science or technology per se, but the word. This is what forms all beings.... Creation begins with the creative word, the idea, the vision, the dream" (Sacks, *Genesis*, 25). See also Ian McFarland's appeal to John 1 in his *From Nothing*.

23. Forte, "Israel and the Church," 76. Forte adds, "Even from a simple approach to the texts, it is evident that the term 'dabar' refers not only to the noetic content, but also to the operative efficacy of the Word, which does what it says, exerting a profound impact on the transformation of the heart and on the events of history. The 'informative' character is added to the 'performative' character: it is in virtue of this density that one can understand how profound the link between words and events in the economy of salvation is" ("Israel and the Church," 76).

Thomas Aquinas, too, gives a privileged position to divine speech in his theology of creation. Aquinas considers that the Father, in speaking his Word, speaks the fullness of the divine knowledge. The Word contains all creaturely ways in which the Godhead can be participated. As Aquinas puts it, "the Word is expressive of creatures."[24] Gilles Emery sums up the relation between the procession of the Word and creation *ex nihilo* as follows: "From one side, the Word is the perfect expression of the Father. From another, the Word is the expression of creatures contained in the Father's knowledge, and, because this is creative knowledge, the Word is also the creative cause of all that the Father does."[25] Although we cannot express God's mode of creation, we can affirm that reflection upon language gives us some insight. We can at least make a step "toward characterizing what free creation amounts to by allusion to its eternal model: the procession of the Word within God."[26] These insights are rooted first and foremost in God's speaking a word at the outset of his work of creation: "And God said, 'Let there be light'; and there was light" (Gen 1:3).[27]

---

24. Thomas Aquinas, *Summa theologiae* I, q. 34, a. 3, ad 3. See also Thomas Aquinas, *Commentary on John*, ch. 1, lect. 2, §77, p. 34.

25. Emery, *Trinitarian Theology of Aquinas*, 196. See also the reflections on divine "intellectual procession" in Lonergan, *Verbum*; as well as Goris, "Theology and Theory." Note that I am not here intending to downplay love. On the contrary, as Gaven Kerr says, "In Aquinas's metaphysical thought we can . . . think of creation as an act of love, an unconditional act of love from the creator to the creature. This idea should cause us to stop and think, since whilst it does not deny the sheer power implicit in the act of creation, if one were to think of it solely in terms of power, one would belittle creation as nothing more than an awesome magic trick. But to think about creation as an act of sheer unconditional love is to render the act of creation meaningful on an entirely new level; for once creation takes on the significance of a loving act, rational creatures, who are themselves capable of love, must realize that in their love they are elevated to the nobility of the special mark of the creator as loving" (G. Kerr, *Aquinas and the Metaphysics of Creation*, 237).

26. Burrell, "Creation in St. Thomas," 124. For further discussion, see Wawrykow, "Aquinas and Bonaventure on Creation." Regarding the question of whether Aquinas thought that a doctrine of creation could be attained without divine revelation, John Wippel and Mark Johnson have shown that the answer is yes (as Wawrykow notes): see Wippel, "Aquinas on Creation"; and M. Johnson, "Did Aquinas Attribute a Doctrine of Creation to Aristotle?"

27. John 1:1–3 is grounded in the personified wisdom of Proverbs 8 and Wisdom of Solomon 7. According to Wisdom of Solomon, "wisdom" is "the fashioner of all things" and is "a reflection of eternal light" (7:22, 26). Mention should also be made of the apparent link between the divine word and creation *ex nihilo* made by Hebrews 11:3: "By faith we understand that the world was created by the word of God, so that what is seen was made out of things which do not appear." Similarly, Paul writes about God speaking or calling things into existence from nonexistence. Paul praises God as the one who "calls into existence the things that do not exist" (Rom 4:17). Reinhard Feldmeier and

The first task of this chapter, therefore, is to lay some theological foundations regarding creation and language. I do so by surveying the insights of the Jewish philosopher Franz Rosenzweig and the Catholic biblical scholar Olivier-Thomas Venard. They propose that creation and creatures reflect the divine speech and thus a divine language. Creatures are themselves an embodied or enacted "language" reflecting their Creator.[28] For Venard, this means attending to the creation of all creatures in the Word and to the metaphysical depths of language.

If language has a special connection to the act of creation in light of language's metaphysical density, it may also be the case that anthropomorphic or ambiguous language regarding the act of creation has value. Drawing upon the work of the Jewish theologian Abraham Joshua Heschel, the chapter's second section seeks to show that anthropomorphisms and ambiguous language have a twofold impact upon readers: stimulating mystical participation and prompting metaphysical clarification.[29] Guided by Heschel, I explore the debate between Rabbi Akiva (and his school) and Rabbi Ishmael (and his school) about the nature and interpretation of the Torah. Rabbi Akiva is metaphorical and mystical; Rabbi Ishmael is precise and metaphysical. Arguably, for appreciating God's act of creation, we need both approaches.[30]

As a third and final step, I benefit from the work of the Reformed theologian Kevin Vanhoozer on the relationship of biblical language and

---

Hermann Spieckermann argue that the root of such claims is in fact Genesis 1. They maintain, "The connection of God's speech with his creative activity—a concept well attested in Egyptian religion—is already extremely significant in the priestly (document's) creation account. It became the model for later reflection, already attested in the Old Testament, concerning the relationship of God's word and creation" (Feldmeier and Spieckermann, *God of the Living*, 252). For Feldmeier and Spieckermann, Genesis 1, and not simply later canonical texts such as John 1 and Hebrews 11, contains a strong insistence upon the importance of divine speech—and thus of the divine word—for God's act of creation. For both appreciation and serious concerns about Feldmeier and Spieckermann's broader project, see Elliott, "Character of the Biblical God," 51–54.

28. For further discussion, see Leithart, *Traces of the Trinity*; as well as my discussion of the divine ideas in chapter 1 of *Engaging the Doctrine of Creation*.

29. See also E. J. Fisher, "Heschel's Impact."

30. Aviya Kushner remarks, "Genesis 1:1 is a microcosm of biblical Hebrew; it is ambiguous, rich, lyrical, evocative" (Kushner, *Grammar of God*, 26). Kushner comments: "I've often walked into the dining room . . . just when my brother brings up the first line of Genesis, the opening of the world. 'It's a problem,' my younger brother Davi says. 'Every commentator knows it's a problem.' 'It all comes down to how you read that one word,' my mother says. 'Do you read the verb in the first line as *bara*, in the past tense, so that it means "In the beginning God *created*," or do you read it as *bro*, a form of the infinitive, so that it reads "In the beginning of God's *creating*"?'" (Kushner, *Grammar of God*, 7).

doctrinal formulation.³¹ Vanhoozer responds especially to those who think the Bible's purpose is simply to function as a deposit of propositional truths. Influenced by Hans Urs von Balthasar's understanding of "theo-drama," Vanhoozer highlights the theo-dramatic framework in which biblical speech, including speech about and by God, instructs the people of God. Applied to Israel's doctrine of creation, the point is that Genesis 1 invites *participation* in the creative Word rather than functioning solely as a catechetical text.

Each of these scholars contributes to appreciating why God allows for ambiguity in Genesis 1 with respect to creation *ex nihilo*. Rosenzweig and Venard emphasize that language, including biblical language, is never *just* language. On this basis, the mystical and metaphysical labor encouraged by ambiguities in biblical language about God—as found in Heschel's contrast between Rabbi Akiva and Rabbi Ishmael—has a purpose: to allow us to proceed further into the mystery of *divine* speech. Indeed, we discover that the scriptural-hermeneutical process itself belongs, as Vanhoozer suggests, to the theo-drama through which God enables us to encounter him as the loving Creator and to learn how to wrestle with, or participate in, his Word. The language of creation, the language of Torah, and the language of self-surrendering love fit together.

II. Creation and Language: Franz Rosenzweig and Olivier-Thomas Venard

Franz Rosenzweig

In *The Star of Redemption*, Franz Rosenzweig includes reflections on language under the broader rubric of creation.³² I will focus on only a few

---

31. Vanhoozer and I have different understandings of the Church. In his view, (Roman) Catholic ecclesiology is an impediment to catholicity because, for Catholic ecclesiology, a *full* sharing in the unity and communion of Christ's Church requires being in communion with the Church of Rome, though a (full) sharing in the salvific benefits of Christ is open to Christians who are not in communion with the Church of Rome. In response, Vanhoozer turns the tables and holds that catholicity requires affirming the Reformed view that the communion of Christ's Church is present wherever the gospel is preached and the sacraments celebrated. He makes clear that no *full* sharing in the unity and communion of Christ's Church is possible for those who do not accept this basic tenet of Reformed ecclesiology, though such persons can still share in the salvific benefits of Christ. See his *Biblical Authority after Babel*. See also Vatican II's Decree on Ecumenism, *Unitatis Redintegratio*; as well as paragraph 15 of Vatican II's Dogmatic Constitution on the Church, *Lumen Gentium*.

32. For helpful background to, and succinct analysis of, Rosenzweig's masterwork,

aspects of his proposal. He begins with the "work of art," which has a "linguistic value" even simply as a "thing said."[33] It has not yet been converted into language; it has not yet been interpreted in "the spoken word."[34] Yet, in a certain real sense, it speaks. Rosenzweig states that art, as such, "is only the language of the inexpressible, it is language as long as there is not yet language, it is the language of the primordial world."[35] Art bears witness to the creation of things from nothing, in the sense that art expresses the primordial world in which the forms of things come forth and speak their distinct essences.

Rosenzweig has in view here the relationship of creation to revelation. He argues that the latter expresses what is silently spoken in creation. Language, therefore, is a deep reality, intimately bound up with the creation. Rosenzweig says of language that it is "the truly 'higher' mathematics, which reveals to us . . . the entire course of the believed miracle," namely, the whole order and end (or goal) of creation.[36] He examines the union of inner word and outer word that occurs in language: "when it comes to us from the 'outside,' nothing other than it echoes from our 'inside' toward the 'outside.'"[37] Pressing further, he proposes that our interior language is "the word that has come from the mouth of God."[38]

He then turns to Genesis 1, with its divine speech. He finds "[t]he word of Creation which resounds in us and expresses itself outside of us" to be rooted in "the silence of the original word."[39] Creation, revelation, and language are united. The fact of language is not something merely added on to reality or extrinsic to reality, let alone to human personhood. Rather, speech—divine speech—is already present in creation, even before this speech expresses itself in human language. Creation is itself an expressive word, even before this is put into words. The latter step begins revelation.[40]

---

see Michael Wyschogrod, "Franz Rosenzweig's *The Star of Redemption*." David Novak frequently adverts to Rosenzweig in his various writings. See for example his chapter on "Franz Rosenzweig's Theology." See also Batnitzky, "Dialogue as Judgment."

33. Rosenzweig, *Star of Redemption*, 159–60. For background to Rosenzweig's aesthetics—emphasizing that for Rosenzweig "art shares with Judaism the quality of uncanniness" (and exploring Rosenzweig's debt to Friedrich Schelling)—see Batnitzky, *Idolatry and Representation*, chapter 4 (quotation from 84).

34. Rosenzweig, *Star of Redemption*, 159.

35. Rosenzweig, *Star of Redemption*, 159.

36. Rosenzweig, *Star of Redemption*, 163.

37. Rosenzweig, *Star of Redemption*, 163.

38. Rosenzweig, *Star of Redemption*, 163.

39. Rosenzweig, *Star of Redemption*, 163.

40. For further context, see Mosès, *System and Revelation*.

Rosenzweig describes what he calls "the treasury of verbal forms in Creation."[41] By this image, he means all the diverse essences or created things, each of which expresses itself in the sense of being intelligible and distinct. These "verbal forms" are rooted in the reality that "[i]n the beginning," "God created" (Gen 1:1). The coming forth of things from this ongoing (yet past) act of creation is the coming forth, by divine acts of speech, of creatures—and therefore of creaturely speech rooted in God's creative act. God expresses the intrinsic speech of each creature when he calls each creature "good." First and foremost, language is expressive of the goodness intrinsic to things as particular essences.

For Rosenzweig, each element of creation is filled with not-yet-expressed revelation. Coming forth from divine speech, creation brims with unspoken language. For this reason, "at least in the beginning, Creation was inwardly vaster than Revelation; there is much prediction in it that is a long way from being revealed; no one knows how long it will be until the day when every creature will have opened its mouth and will be understood as prediction of the miracle."[42] If the first moment of creation is silent ("God created"), we find that "at the second moment, the word that creates the whole of Creation irrupts, as the first action word of Creation, the 'God said.'"[43] Yet in this divine speech, which bursts forth in its creative power and presence, we still perceive so much depth of speech that has not yet come to be. On this view, the whole plan and goal of the created entity is *present* in its coming to be but is not yet spoken, not yet revealed.

Rosenzweig also considers that God's "word [in creating] is like a prediction of his future word; but he does not yet speak himself, not yet as Self."[44] God only speaks as "Self" when he speaks dialogically in revelatory communication with human beings. The Creator thereby becomes what, in a certain sense, he has been from the outset, namely the Revealer. In revelation, the miracle that we come to know is that God, in love, has a plan for creation, a goal that spans and overcomes the death of his creatures. This is the revelation that Israel receives, a revelation whose language is foreshadowed in the language of creation.

---

41. Rosenzweig, *Star of Redemption*, 166.
42. Rosenzweig, *Star of Redemption*, 166.
43. Rosenzweig, *Star of Redemption*, 166.
44. Rosenzweig, *Star of Redemption*, 166.

Olivier-Thomas Venard, OP

In *La Langue de l'ineffable*, Olivier-Thomas Venard reflects upon the question of language and Scripture from an angle related to that of Rosenzweig.[45] Venard is familiar with Rosenzweig's work, although he does not cite him in the selections I discuss here. For Venard, the relationship between human words and the divine Word (the Son, incarnate as Jesus Christ) is the central mystery. The revelation of the divine Word enables us to discern, in our interior generation of a mental word, an analogy between human words and the Word that assures us of the "realism" of language. Thus, Venard argues that the problem of language has a theological grounding. This theological grounding ultimately flows from the revelation of the Word, but even prior to that is found in "faith in the Creator of both language and the real."[46] Language is not simply a system of human signs; language is already rooted in reality, in the divine speech of creation. Venard emphasizes that "the major presuppositions of every realist theory of language are not linguistic but theological."[47] As in Rosenzweig, divine speech is inescapably present, even before God reveals himself in a personal way.

Engaging the work of the nineteenth-century biblical scholar Ernest Renan, Venard explores "the unity of thought and language portrayed in the Bible in the form of God's gift of language to Adam."[48] According to Renan, this portrait was simply a Jewish way of expressing the fact that language is revelatory and is always present in thought, and that therefore language must be "divine" (and a "divine" gift). "Revelation" here does not involve the transcendent God; rather, for Renan human beings easily ascribe "divine" qualities to something so exalted as language. Renan holds that so long as one perceives that one is dealing with a metaphor, understanding the gift of language as a divine revelation shows a fitting appreciation for language's exalted characteristics. Although for Renan language is a human invention, it is one that arises at the same time as thought. Language's coming forth in consciousness is so amazing that it is rightly (though solely metaphorically) to be called "divine."

As Venard shows, Renan was writing in response to Louis de Bonald, who *identified* human language with the divine Word.[49] De Bonald argued

---

45. See Venard, *Langue de l'ineffable*. I employ here the English translation of parts of this volume: see Venard, *Poetic Christ*.

46. Venard, *Poetic Christ*, 303. Venard is drawing upon Renan's *De l'origine du langage*.

47. Venard, *Poetic Christ*, 304.

48. Venard, *Poetic Christ*, 305.

49. See Venard, *Poetic Christ*, 308, discussing de Bonald, "De l'origine du langage."

that language cannot be invented; it must be present wherever thought is. It follows that language is a gift, and de Bonald proposes that Adam and Eve must have been the recipients. He holds that just as divine speech brought the cosmos into existence *ex nihilo*, so also the Creator, by enlightening minds, must be responsible for giving human intellects language.

De Bonald's position was so thoroughly theological, Venard notes, that "in 1866 the Linguistic Society of Paris forbad public discussion on the origin of languages."[50] Although the origin of languages remains a popular topic today, it is now a strictly secular discussion: the possible role of God is not considered. Many modern scholars consider "human nature," as such, first to have arisen without the gift of language; only later did humans develop linguistic abilities. Venard observes that many modern scholars fail to see what an extraordinary reality language is, given "the incommensurability of the signified to any signifier, of conceptualization and sensation."[51] Indeed, Venard argues that without God as its ultimate source and ground, language cannot really be the bearer of true (realist) signification in the way that rationality requires it to be. Signification transcends what is possible for a strictly material organ.[52] Since this is so, we should expect God to be able to speak to humans, and we should expect humans to be able to speak to God. From the outset, God seeks "to communicate himself in order to create a *convivium* with humanity."[53] In God's creative plan, "language ... is not an element *superadded* to the human-divine conviviality but lies at the very heart of the relationship between God and humanity."[54]

In this light, Venard retrieves the patristic and medieval insight that creatures express the "divine ideas," the divine knowledge of all the ways in which God's being can be finitely participated.[55] Creatures are already an expressive language, rooted in God's own knowledge of himself. Given that human language has the ability to express truth about reality, human language expresses the truth of creatures and thereby connects with the fact that creatures themselves are expressive of God's knowledge of creatures.

---

50. Venard, *Poetic Christ*, 309.

51. Venard, *Poetic Christ*, 311. For an example of this kind of scholarship—though aware that language is a wonder—see the popular survey by Christine Kenneally, *First Word*. For non-theist arguments that only humans can possess language, see Terrace, *Why Chimpanzees Can't Learn Language*; and Berwick and Chomsky, *Why Only Us*.

52. See for example Hart, *Experience of God*.

53. Venard, *Poetic Christ*, 314.

54. Venard, *Poetic Christ*, 325.

55. For discussion of Aquinas on the divine ideas, see Doolan, "Aquinas on the Divine Ideas"; Doolan, *Aquinas on the Divine Ideas as Exemplar Causes*; and Davison, "'He Fathers-Forth.'" See also chapter 1 of my *Engaging the Doctrine of Creation*.

Thus, the first link between human language and God's speech is found in the doctrine of creation. The divine Word is the Creator, and creatures are created in the Word.

For Venard, the key point is that a "realist" creaturely knowledge of things, a knowledge that is expressed in words, would be impossible if it were not grounded by divine knowledge of things—and thus grounded ultimately in God creating through speaking his Word. Venard reasons that Israel's doctrine of creation is tightly tied to language, to God's speech and human (scriptural) speech, because of what creatures in fact are. As Venard observes, "creation is a language."[56] The divine language expressed in creatures is reflected in human language about creatures; there is an analogous relationship between human speech and divine speech. The speech that we find in Genesis 1–2 describes the God-human relationship in a manner that is rooted in the actual reality of that relationship, namely, God's creative speaking and God's dialogic relationship to his rational human images. The theology of creation is inseparable from inquiry into revelation, Scripture, and language. As Venard (much like Rosenzweig) concludes, "In reality, creation and redemption, creation and revelation are inseparable."[57]

Turning his attention to Scripture, Venard notes that without the "book of nature" or creation, the "book of Scripture" would be unintelligible.[58] What then does Scripture add to the "book of nature"? In Venard's view, the answer cannot be that Scripture adds to our knowledge by contradicting in some fundamental way the meaning or *language* inscribed in creatures. Scripture reveals that all things have a relation to God's creative speech and that God, in revealing himself to Israel, does not come as an alien voice. God comes as the one who spoke all things into existence, establishing humans in an original dialogic communion with him and with each other. In Genesis 1, the overflowing power and meaning of divine speech awaits further

56. Venard, *Poetic Christ*, 328.

57. Venard, *Poetic Christ*, 331.

58. Venard, *Poetic Christ*, 332. As he points out elsewhere, "The world which surrounds us *signifies* as realistically as any language does: it grasps humanity just as humanity grasps it. Or to put it more simply, *being, thinking* or *speaking* are always just as much to be grasped as to grasp; humanity does not create but discovers meaning" (Venard, *Poetic Christ*, 425). In arguing that God's language and the language of creatures (not only the ontological language of creatures but also human language) are not alien or opposed to each other, he cites von Balthasar, *Theo-Logic* II, 82–84. He also regularly cites Ellul, *Humiliation of the Word*. Von Balthasar articulates the fundamental point in *Theo-Logic* II, 84: "the incarnate Word comes into 'his own property' (Jn 1:11). Hence, he does not travel merely into a foreign land (as Karl Barth says) but into a country whose language he knows; not only the Galilean variety of Aramaic that he learns as a child in Nazareth, but, more profoundly, the ontological language of creatureliness as such." For Venard's debt to von Balthasar, see O'Regan, "Thomism in Ecstasy."

revelation, even though from the outset it is apparent that divine speech expresses a transcendent goodness, generosity, and love whose heights go far beyond our imagining. Already in Genesis 1 God's speech establishes the divine-human communion that is God's purpose in creating.[59]

Recall that for Rosenzweig, God creates in silence (Gen 1:1), and then God speaks ("Let there be" [Gen 1:3]) as these creatures burst forth with expressive language, thereby initiating revelation. Rosenzweig holds that human language is rooted in the resounding of God's creative speech in us. For his part, as already noted, Venard argues that there is an analogous relationship between human and divine speech. He emphasizes that creatures, as such (in their very being), express the divine language, so that "creation is a language." It follows that God's creative *speaking* in Genesis 1 provides a crucial insight into the Creator-creature relationship: creation is not only *ex nihilo*, but also it expresses the divine ideas, the primal divine language by which God eternally knows creatures and of which creatures are the temporal expression. The truth of human words is rooted in the creative speaking of the divine Word. As Hans Urs von Balthasar puts it, "The logic of the creature is not foreign to the logic of God; it could be likened to a dialect of the standard language spoken in pure form by God."[60]

III. Abraham Heschel's Heavenly Torah: Rabbis Ishmael and Akiva

Creation, then, is not simply *ex nihilo*; it is also rooted in God's speaking, and thus in his Word. Creatures are a language even before human language about creatures; and scriptural language conveys this fact. Creation must be understood not only metaphysically, but also as divine speech expressing itself in finite words and thereby establishing a dialogic communion. Thus Israel's doctrine of creation maps onto a doctrine of Scripture as well, since Scripture records the communion of God and his creatures, especially the *"imago dei"* which he speaks into being and with whom he converses directly (Gen 1:27-30). Genesis 1-2 captures this union of creation, language, and communion, in which God has priority as Speaker.

Even so, Genesis 1-2 contains anthropomorphisms that seem to cut against the priority of the word of God. Not only can Genesis 1:1-3 be read as God's action upon preexistent matter, but also God's speech (Gen 1:3 and onward) might be understood in light of the anthropomorphic portrait

---

59. Venard is here reflecting on Genesis 1 itself, rather than on the relation of Genesis 1 in its composition history to other biblical texts.
60. Von Balthasar, *Theo-Logic* II, 84.

of God making man from clay, planting a garden, and walking in the garden (Gen 2–3). Such speech would be creaturely in nature, locking Israel's (scriptural) doctrine of creation into a firmly creaturely mode. Even if we grant that Rosenzweig and Venard have seen deeply into the connection of divine speech (the divine Word) and the nature of all finite beings (divine words or ideas), our original question regarding Genesis 1's language has only begun to be addressed. What are these ambiguities doing in Genesis 1, and how do they befit Israel's doctrine of creation?

Abraham Joshua Heschel has set forth two contrasting yet complementary ways of understanding why God allowed Scripture to contain potentially confusing texts about central matters such as the doctrine of creation. In *Heavenly Torah*, Heschel compares the positions of Rabbi Ishmael and Rabbi Akiva, along with their schools.[61] These two decisive rabbinic figures—or, more accurately, their two schools—exhibit approaches to scriptural language that tease out the value of ambiguous language in stimulating doctrinal engagement. This is especially so given that doctrine, even when philosophically clarified, remains transcendent mystery.

---

61. See Heschel, *Heavenly Torah*. For Heschel, as Azzan Yadin-Israel says, Rabbi Akiva is "the paramount Jewish interpreter" (Yadin-Israel, *Scripture and Tradition*, 103). Much more than Heschel's *Heavenly Torah*, Yadin-Israel's work is the place to go for historical analysis of the schools of Rabbi Ishmael and Rabbi Akiva. According to Yadin-Israel, "the image of Rabbi Akiva reflected in the tannaitic sources differs from that found in later strata of rabbinic literature. Briefly stated, the earlier material portrays Rabbi Akiva as deeply committed to extra-scriptural traditions and regularly adducing midrashic arguments intended to buttress these traditions. And though Rabbi Akiva's contemporaries criticize him on several occasions for derashot that do not sufficiently hew to the line of acceptable midrash, his hermeneutics are, on the whole, less speculative and more congruent with those of his contemporaries than is often supposed. In short, the familiar image of Rabbi Akiva as an inspired midrashist who derives meaning from every word and letter of the Torah owes more to later rabbinic sources. . . . Rabbi Akiva emerges as a relatively sober interpreter: attentive to hermeneutic markers, committed to intertextual elucidation, consistent in his use of midrashic terminology (*ha-katuv*, *din*, 'what is the instruction,' and so on). Even prima facie problematic derashot based on *ish' ish'*, or *hu'*, or an opening *vav*, are shown, upon further analysis, to be plausible and rule-bound. Within the tannaitic sources, Rabbi Akiva turns out to be much closer to Rabbi Ishmael" (Yadin-Israel, *Scripture and Tradition*, 103, 138). Yadin-Israel grants that "there remains a profound difference between the two with regard to the status of midrash vis-à-vis extra-scriptural tradition. For Rabbi Ishmael midrashim, interpretation enjoys primacy, almost exclusively, as a source of legal authority. Rabbi Akiva, in contrast, privileges extra-scriptural tradition and, where the two overlap, relegates midrash to an ancillary role" (Yadin-Israel, *Scripture and Tradition*, 138). See also Yadin-Israel, "Concepts of Scripture." He suggests that "the Sifra is an ex post facto engagement of Scripture, a sustained attempt at finding biblical 'hooks' on which to hang already existing extrascriptural traditions" (Yadin-Israel, "Concepts of Scripture," 58). For further discussion of the approach of Rabbi Ishmael and his school, see Yadin-Israel, *Scripture as Logos*.

According to Heschel, Rabbi Ishmael interprets metaphorically all passages about God that are not philosophically plausible. For example, he denies that God the Creator has spatial location or physical organs, and he finds to be metaphorical the descriptions of God as a warrior or as preeminent among the gods. For Rabbi Ishmael, the existence of a primordial "earth" that is "without form" and is a "void"—and thus the existence of "waters" (Gen 1:2)—cannot be taken literally. By contrast, some members of the school of Rabbi Akiva delight in stating that "from chaos and emptiness God made the world, and so there was primal matter prior to the creation of the world."[62] With Maimonides and others, I consider these members of the school of Rabbi Akiva to be wrong on this point, especially if they mean to say that the primal matter was not created by God in the sense of not depending absolutely upon God's radical and primal gift of being. But their point is less about creation than it is about allowing biblical speech to challenge preconceived expectations about God and the world.

For Rabbi Ishmael, the scriptural speech about the Creator God among the gods (even if God is preeminent over them) cannot be taken literally, because Rabbi Ishmael rightly knows that there are no other gods: nothing is divine but the transcendent God. He therefore favors the scriptural passages that support this claim over against the scriptural passages that speak about Israel's God among the gods. For the school of Rabbi Akiva, by contrast, what separates God from the gods is simply God's ability (in some mystically knowable way that exceeds our rational grasp) to see, hear, touch, smell, and sing; the gods cannot measure up to God in these respects, and therefore cannot be present and active in the world as Israel's God is. God alone is truly able to be in real communion with humans. Therefore God alone is not a god. Communion, described mystically in embodied terms, is the mystical mark of true Godhead.

Heschel describes Rabbi Akiva as a proponent of "Merkavah mysticism," according to which we must "search for the place where heaven and earth embrace."[63] Earthly images about God offer an opportunity for envi-

---

62. Heschel, *Heavenly Torah*, 236.

63. Heschel, *Heavenly Torah*, 234. Reuven Hammer comments (relying upon the contrast found in the later rabbinic literature and in Heschel's work): "It could be said that whereas Ishmael appealed to the mind, Akiva appealed to the heart. It is fortunate for Judaism that emerging Rabbinic Judaism did not find it necessary to choose between the two. . . . Nevertheless, Akiva's approach answered a need of that time more convincingly than Ishmael's. In contrast to Ishmael's rational interpretations of Torah, it was Akiva's more mystical approach that basically prevailed over time in the popular mind as being the authentic Jewish approach" (R. Hammer, *Akiva*, 76). With regard to Rabbi Akiva's mysticism, Hammer writes that "Akiva, the mystic, had no difficulty imagining that Moses could have ascended to heaven to receive the Torah.

CREATION AND SCRIPTURE

sioning such an embrace. Regarding the philosophical tradition of divine "attributes," Heschel asks rhetorically, "Is it not evident that even those expressions which seem fitting to describe the divine attributes, in reality are utterly futile in relation to God's essence? . . . Do we imagine that God's essence can be reduced to our definitions?"[64] Philosophical language is in a certain sense equally finite and inadequate, by comparison to the greatness of God, as is anthropomorphic language. We cannot suppose that by refining our language philosophically, we are getting ever closer to grasping the infinite Creator God. The reality of God stands utterly beyond our philosophical language.

Thus, Rabbi Akiva rejoices in the language about the Creator God that is earthly or anthropomorphic. It is not that he necessarily takes such language literally, but rather that he sees all human scriptural speech about God to be a prompting to make a mystical ascent. Scripture's speech about God is earthly and limited because it offers an affirmation of communion between the earthly realm and the heavenly realm. The school of Rabbi Akiva urges that we need to probe into the earthly images (as for example the anthropomorphisms of Genesis 1–2) in order to gain the fruit intended by God. Heschel underscores that Rabbi Akiva sees the images as a divinely ordained symbolic language that we should not philosophically cast aside in the quest for the "true" meaning. Heschel states, "The source of Rabbi Akiva's power lay in his soaring imagination, far beyond the field of critical thought, in a place where the cutting edge of the intellect cannot reach."[65]

According to Heschel, the basic idea behind Rabbi Akiva's boldness is the point that in scriptural speech, we find words about God that force us

---

Had not Akiva attempted to reach the seventh heaven—and perhaps felt that he had done so—when engaging in the mysticism of the heavenly chariot, 'entering paradise'? Akiva states clearly that the Torah Israel was given was the preexisting instrument with which the world was created. It was not like any other written work; it existed before the world existed. Nor did God dictate it to Moses. Rather Moses received it complete and entire while he was literally in heaven" (R. Hammer, *Akiva*, 69). For further background (examining the whole tradition of Jewish "mysticism," biblical and post-biblical), see Sweeney, *Jewish Mysticism*, including his discussion of Rabbi Akiva at 214–16 and elsewhere.

64. Heschel, *Heavenly Torah*, 235.

65. Heschel, *Heavenly Torah*, 235. James Kugel comments (in an imagined dialogue with a student): "what Rabbi Akiva said nonetheless seems to me to be quite clear. Because what, after all, is the difference between swirls of marble and 'Water! Water!'? It is really all about seeing. When you see the pure marble, you are standing inside somewhere, a palace, as I said; but seeing a great marble floor with the light twinkling on its surface, you suddenly think you are seeing the outside, the waves of a lake, perhaps, or a stream. So too with the things you have mentioned, it is really just a matter of perspective, and of not mistaking the inside for the outside" (Kugel, *Kingly Sanctuary*, 22).

out of any comfortable modes of thought, wherein we might be tempted to imagine the sufficiency of our language. We must confront the actual words of Scripture in their real strangeness. Indeed, we should even accentuate that strangeness and boldness. Heschel observes that Rabbi Akiva is willing, even with regard to the divine Presence, to offer interpretations that contain "exaggerations to the point of irreverence for the divine and distortion of basic doctrines."[66] If we immediately interpret the difficulty away, we lose an opportunity to enter into a deeper understanding. At issue is Rabbi Akiva's attempt to identify the link of "the lower realm to the higher, by finding in the words of the lower realm references to the higher."[67]

Heschel suggests that the rabbinic sages as a whole were agreed that the Bible should not be treated simply as a matter of historical record or historical concern. Nor should any biblical text be treated as mere poetry. Some rabbis denied that even the book of Chronicles was "literal history."[68] Their purpose was not to deny the significance of the history of the Jewish people, or the truth of God's creative and covenantal deeds. Rather, their point was to underscore that the Bible is not a mere book, because scriptural language has greater power for communication than we suppose.[69] Scriptural metaphors should not be discarded as "mere" metaphors. Instead, we should follow the metaphorical tracks further into the mystery of divine language and divine creation, a mystery that ultimately exceeds human grasp. Heschel sums up, "Basic to the study of Torah (in this view) is not our

---

66. Heschel, *Heavenly Torah*, 232.

67. Heschel, *Heavenly Torah*, 238.

68. Heschel, *Heavenly Torah*, 243.

69. Addressing the question of whether a real divine revelation has actually occurred, James Kugel points out that historical tools are powerless to determine whether a text is divinely inspired or not. He warns against "confusing God's having given us the Torah with the particular circumstances in which this is said to have happened" (*Kingly Sanctuary*, 62). In Kugel's view, Judaism does not depend upon a historical Sinai or a historical Moses, since Judaism's testimony is simply that God gave Israel the Torah, not where or when God did it. For Kugel, obeying the Torah in continuity with the Jewish people over the centuries is the way to serve God and to experience his presence; and the Torah's narratives are not meant to be simple "historical recitation" but rather (as when the Torah describes God's "finger") something far greater. Kugel states, "We could not do without the Torah, and the fact of its divine origin is crucial; it shows us, in the most basic way, how God has allowed us to come before Him as His servants. But by the same token, we cannot be literalists with the Torah or act as if it stands alone. The volumes that follow—Mishnah, Talmud, and so forth—are vital to its understanding and carry further its trajectory. So it is simply wrong to think that Bible criticism and Judaism share any common ground; at bottom, they do not even agree on the very idea of what Scripture is or how it is to be understood" (Kugel, *Kingly Sanctuary*, 75–76).

intellectual grasp but our awareness of the holiness of Torah."[70] Every text of the Torah, no matter how obscure, contains tremendous riches of meaning, even if the literal meaning seems impossible.

Heschel notes that for Maimonides and Saadia Gaon, the meaning of biblical texts that contradict reason—or that are contradictory in another way to what the people of Israel know to be true—must be purely metaphorical, comprehensible solely through philosophical clarification. Thus, God is not a "fire," no matter what Deuteronomy 4:24 says. According to Heschel, however, the rabbis understood such scriptural texts to contain "substantive meanings and symbolic significance," going beyond the realm of metaphor into a dimension of divine reality that exceeds our apprehension.[71] The mystics or kabbalists shared this view. Certain rabbis of a mystical bent even argued that "the Torah speaks primarily of heavenly things and only secondarily of things on earth. The hidden meaning of a scriptural text is actually its literal meaning."[72] If a reader finds that the scriptural speech contains unwarranted exaggerations, many rabbinic teachers would respond that the problem comes not from the text of the Torah but from the limited mind of the reader whose mind is unable to penetrate the divine language. On this view, the Torah's words are true (literally), even when they appear not to be true—since they can be literally true in a heavenly sense known to God, given the kind of reality that scriptural language is.

The school of Rabbi Ishmael, while granting that the Torah's texts allows for many interpretations, held that the Torah almost always must be read in the "plain sense."[73] By contrast, the school of Rabbi Akiva warned against relying strictly on literal interpretation. Even rabbis not connected to the school of Rabbi Akiva were willing to go well beyond the "plain sense," given that the perfection of the Torah ensures that every single letter has a profound purpose. As divine language, scriptural texts are able to have more than one meaning.

As Heschel shows, Rabbi Ishmael was willing to propose allegorical meanings when the alternative was "an interpretation unacceptable to common sense."[74] For instance, faced with Exodus 24:10's affirmation that Moses and Aaron (and Nadab and Abihu) and seventy elders "saw the God of Israel," the school of Rabbi Ishmael "divorced this text from its literal

---

70. Heschel, *Heavenly Torah*, 246.
71. Heschel, *Heavenly Torah*, 249.
72. Heschel, *Heavenly Torah*, 250.
73. Heschel, *Heavenly Torah*, 252.
74. Heschel, *Heavenly Torah*, 254.

sense" on the grounds that humans cannot see God.[75] In certain cases—as for instance Exodus 16:20, which says of the leftover manna that "it became infested with maggots and stank"—the school of Rabbi Ishmael argued that the literal sense permissibly requires reversing the order of the text: food first spoils and stinks, and then produces maggots. For its part, the school of Rabbi Akiva "derived mounds and mounds of *halakhot* from each tittle on the letters."[76] But the school of Rabbi Akiva gladly interpreted Exodus 24:10 in a literal way, arguing that the elders in fact saw the divine Presence. This "literal" sense goes beyond the presumed limits of human apprehension of the divine, and thereby serves the school of Rabbi Akiva in opening up the mysteries of scriptural language.

Regarding Exodus 19:20, "The Lord came down upon Mount Sinai," Rabbi Ishmael considers that God allowed the people to hear a heavenly voice but God did not come down—despite the text saying that God did so. Other biblical texts such as Exodus 20:19 and Deuteronomy 4:36 support Rabbi Ishmael in this view. Rabbi Akiva likewise reads all three of these verses together, but he concludes that actually God bent down the heavens and touched them to the top of Mount Sinai, so that God spoke from the very point where heaven and earth miraculously met.[77] This solution shows the freedom that Rabbi Akiva takes in insisting upon divine-human communion, a freedom that allows for "literal" readings (in a manner refused by Rabbi Ishmael) but that does not arrive at what most readers would deem to be a possible literal meaning. Rabbi Akiva often preserves the plain sense by arriving at a mystical meaning.

The reason that Rabbi Ishmael takes the position that he does on Exodus 19:20 is that he is looking for a way to preserve the transcendence and omnipresence of God rather than localizing God in an anthropomorphic way. The Second Temple Hellenistic Jewish philosopher Aristobulus, with similar goals in view, accepts that God "came down" but argues that this divine action was accomplished, not by any spatial movement, but by an act of revealing "God's powers to the whole world, outside the normal course of nature."[78] Heschel considers that the fundamental issue is whether God, who encompasses the cosmos rather than vice versa, can make himself small and local (in accord with the later doctrine of *tzimtzum*). Even more, Heschel proposes that at bottom the issue is the nature of divine revelation: "Is it verbal communication? Is it the revelation of God's will alone? Or is it

---

75. Heschel, *Heavenly Torah*, 313.
76. Heschel, *Heavenly Torah*, 255.
77. See R. Hammer, *Akiva*, 70.
78. Heschel, *Heavenly Torah*, 361.

an event that affects the Divine Essence?"[79] For Heschel, it must affect the divine essence; otherwise it would be a language that does not involve true communion. Heschel mentions the later rabbinic viewpoint that, whatever the descent on Mount Sinai was, it was not a corporeal descent. He cites Rabbi Judah Loew of Prague who argues that Scripture's human speech about divine action gives the human perspective, but the human perspective should not lead us to anthropomorphize God. Rabbi Akiva opens up a richer sense of the depths of scriptural speech, in which anthropomorphisms do not merely bring God to earth but rather enable us to expand our understanding of the potential meanings of language itself.

Heschel devotes a chapter to the phrase "Thus says the Lord." According to Rabbi Ishmael, the use of the phrase "Thus says the Lord" intends to convey God's will, rather than God's exact words. On this view, "Moses was able to alter God's language and to convey the intent alone."[80] According to Rabbi Akiva, by contrast, the very words spoken by God (and heard by Moses) were the words that Moses wrote down. Rabbi Akiva took this view not in order to demand a literalistic reading; rather, for Rabbi Akiva what is at stake is whether Moses "spoke in the language of the Holy and Blessed One."[81] God's own language allows for mystical connection with the heavenly realm, through the words themselves.[82] Language is at the very heart of the matter, especially when it seems ambiguous.

While for Rabbi Akiva the words given by Moses were precisely the ones spoken by God to Moses, for Rabbi Ishmael we have to reckon with the fact that human capacities are limited and vary from person to person. Thus, according to Rabbi Ishmael, "a person is addressed as befits his ability, and even Moses our master heard only according to his ability."[83] For

79. Heschel, *Heavenly Torah*, 361.
80. Heschel, *Heavenly Torah*, 424.
81. Heschel, *Heavenly Torah*, 426.
82. Heschel's sympathies here for Rabbi Akiva can be tempered by the defense of Rabbi Ishmael's interpretations offered by R. Hammer, *Akiva*, 72–73. As an example, Hammer points out that "when 'defiled' is written three times regarding a woman suspected of adultery (Num. 5:13–14), Akiva took it to mean that she is defiled for three things: her husband, her paramour, and eating the priestly portion. Ishmael responded that the verses simply teach that unless there is doubt, we never make her undergo the ordeal described in Numbers 5:16–31" (R. Hammer, *Akiva*, 72). I should note that Heschel's own view of Scripture's provenance (like Rosenzweig's) involves accepting the claims of historical criticism regarding the complex human origins of the biblical texts, but doing so with the certitude that God guides the formation of Israel's Scriptures. Heschel's appreciation for Rabbi Akiva's mysticism is joined to an appreciation for Rabbi Ishmael's understanding of the partnership of God and humans with regard to the language of the Torah.
83. Heschel, *Heavenly Torah*, 481.

Rabbi Ishmael, Moses heard God speaking in Moses' own voice. Scriptural language is inspired human language, but it is still just human language. Moses could not have borne (or understood) God speaking in God's own voice, and so God condescended to speak his words in Moses' own interior voice, so that Moses could understand. By contrast, against Rabbi Ishmael's view, Rabbi Akiva insists that what was heard was the divine voice, a voice that all Israel heard through Moses. It was truly divine language that made itself heard. Heschel sums up the difference: "Rabbi Akiva believed that Moses spoke with the voice of the Shekhinah. And Rabbi Ishmael believed that the Shekhinah spoke with Moses' voice."[84] The latter view grounds the principle that "the Torah speaks in human language."[85]

Heschel emphasizes that the latter view means that even Moses understood God's words in accord with Moses' own (limited) abilities, just as the prophets' hearing of God's words depended upon their own limited abilities. The result was that Moses and the prophets contributed something to God's revelation, if only because God had to speak his word to them in strict accord with their particular intellectual and spiritual abilities.[86] One rabbi even claimed that God spoke at Mount Sinai in the Egyptian language, since it seems likely that after centuries of slavery in Egypt, the people were more fluent in the Egyptian language. By contrast, as Heschel points out, Rabbi

---

84. Heschel, *Heavenly Torah*, 481–82.

85. Heschel, *Heavenly Torah*, 482.

86. David Novak comments in a related way, though with a different topic in mind, that "humans who make themselves God's partners are condemned like idolaters are condemned; yet humans whom God has chosen to be his partners are included in the greatest activity of God that we could conceive: the creation of the cosmos from nothing to everything" (Novak, "How Jewish Was Barth?," 19). On the topic of God's speaking, see also Seitz, *Elder Testament*, 66–67; and Sommer, *Revelation and Authority*. Sommer treats Heschel (and Rosenzweig) extensively, though generally in passing. He notes that "Heschel's approach to revelation in particular and to religion in general emphasizes simultaneously God's movement toward humanity and humanity's movement toward God" (Sommer, *Revelation and Authority*, 110). Regarding Heschel's view of God's *pathos* and God's responsiveness to Jewish religious observance, Sommer comments that Heschel emphasizes "the idea of partnership between heaven and earth" and that when this idea "expresses itself in relationship to the issue of revelation, Heschel links it with the older Jewish notion that there is a human factor in prophecy: revelation is dialogue, in which each side influences and is influenced" (Sommer, *Revelation and Authority*, 112). Sommer argues that the distinction between earthly Torah and heavenly Torah has "roots in Exodus's Sinai narrative," according to which "the original tablets containing the Decalogue written with the finger of God (Exodus 31.18, 32.16) were shattered by Moses (32.19), and consequently the Israelites never received the original, heavenly tablets in a readable, intact form. The whole and readable tablets placed into the ark resulted from a collaboration between heaven and earth" (Sommer, *Revelation and Authority*, 115–16).

Akiva suggests that "at the assembly at Mount Sinai, Israel was addressed beyond its ability."[87] Rabbi Akiva thinks that God ensured that his Torah elevated the souls of his hearers, so that they were spiritually capable of understanding the deep meanings of the divine words. Scripture's ambiguities reveal to us that we are dealing not with mere human language but with the divine language itself.

According to Rabbi Ishmael, when God spoke to Moses in accord with Moses' own abilities, the Torah was not thereby diluted from what it should have been. On the contrary, the fact of Moses' cooperation in divine revelation was approved by God. As Heschel puts it, "Moses did things on his own, and the Holy and Blessed One agreed with his actions. The prophet participates in the act of prophecy, and thus may even alter the language of the Holy and Blessed One."[88] For Rabbi Ishmael, therefore, the truth of the Torah is not harmed even when Moses, as a particularly active prophet, persuades God to change his mind (see Numbers 14:20). Rabbi Ishmael insists that part of divine revelation stems from the contributions of mere human speech. As Rabbi Ishmael argues, "Moses had the power to do something below and have the Holy and Blessed One agree from above."[89]

Quite differently, Rabbi Akiva thinks that God raises the human mind to the Torah that "always existed and was written down in heaven even before it was given to Moses."[90] Not only the Torah's reportage of divine speech, but even the human speech of Moses is enabled by God to be divine speech. Rabbi Akiva also suggests that absolutely everything that can be known from the divinely revealed words of the Torah was already perceived, through God's power, by the Israelites at Sinai. Thus the whole Torah—including the Oral Torah—was already present and divinely given in full at Sinai.[91] By comparison, the school of Rabbi Ishmael held that at Sinai "[t]here

---

87. Heschel, *Heavenly Torah*, 484.

88. Heschel, *Heavenly Torah*, 484.

89. Heschel, *Heavenly Torah*, 492.

90. Heschel, *Heavenly Torah*, 485. Along these lines, Jonathan Sacks observes that "as an Orthodox Jew I believe that the Torah is beyond history, but there is certainly a history of interpretation which can be traced from rabbinic midrash to the medieval commentators to now" (Sacks, "Interview," 108–9).

91. See Sommer, *Revelation and Authority*, chapters 2 and 3. Sommer suggests that certain biblical texts "raise the possibility that the people heard no words at the lawgiving [at Sinai]," and he notes that Heschel and Rosenzweig "build on an implication of nonverbal revelation by proposing that the specific words found in scripture are a human response to God's commanding but nonverbal self-disclosure" (Sommer, *Revelation and Authority*, 95). On this view, the whole Torah could be revealed at Sinai without it being revealed in words. In my view, the propositional character of divine revelation cannot be ruled out so completely. For further discussion, see Mansini,

was a partnership based in reason, for as they heard the words, they would explicate them on their own."[92] On this view, human reasoning, not mystical exaltation, characterized the people's cooperation with God at Sinai, in the interaction of divine speech and human speech.

Heschel devotes a number of chapters to various rabbinic theories of the revelation of the Torah, and it is clear that many rabbinic sages took a maximalist view, even to the point of holding that "not only the commandments but also how they are to be observed, their derivative rules, minutiae, and interpretations were all given to Moses at Sinai."[93] Some rabbis held that Moses received a divine book; others, that Moses ascended to heaven and copied the divine Torah. Scriptural language is divine language, which is why the Torah reveals the very roots of all things. Nonetheless, the position of the school of Rabbi Ishmael always had adherents in advocating a "minimalist" position. The most well known proponent of this view is Maimonides. Heschel remarks that for the school of Rabbi Ishmael, "many laws and rules were not given to Moses by the Holy and Blessed One, but rather the Sages themselves extracted them from the text by means of the modes of exegesis applicable to the Torah."[94] Here human language is seen as making a distinct contribution, rather than becoming divine language per se in Scripture.

What have we learned from the above canvassing of rabbinic thought (especially Rabbi Ishmael and Rabbi Akiva) as set forth by Heschel?[95] The

---

Fundamental Theology.

92. Heschel, *Heavenly Torah*, 486. Similarly, see Rabbi Charles David Isbell's observation that "[n]o matter how great God is, lacking human partners who will respond with their own efforts, the work of salvation comes to a grinding halt" (Isbell, *Sermons*, 76).

93. Heschel, *Heavenly Torah*, 563.

94. Heschel, *Heavenly Torah*, 560.

95. The Protestant theologian Friedrich-Wilhelm Marquardt praises the Talmud for its anthropomorphic portrait of God, suggesting that God may be more human in the Talmud than he is (in Christ) in the New Testament or at least in the writings of Christian theologians: "In the Talmud God can cry from pain and anguish, roar like a lion, make self-accusations, admit to being wrong, and give human beings credit for being right; God can rejoice over being bested in debate, and ask for blessing from human beings. There is a treatise in the Talmud about the laughter of God (b. *Avoda zara* 3b). God even prays that divine love might overcome divine justice. God can and wants to be saved, redeemed along with Israel from the power of the *goyim*, and therefore he is a God who needs salvation. Christians often smirk at such *haggadot*. However, I am always moved that *we* speak about God taking on human form, yet in the Talmud God appears much more human than we can possibly imagine theologically.... [T]he Talmud interests me because it makes me consider what corresponds more to God—our Christian language about God taking on human form or the Jewish knowledge about the humanity of God" (Marquardt, "Why the Talmud Interests Me," 83–84). Marquardt

rabbinic interpreters do not ignore difficulties in the inspired biblical text such as the ones confronted by the theology of creation. The textual difficulties are seen by many rabbis as doorways into direct mystical experience of God, opening up the divine language. Of course, the rabbis did not conceive of the Torah as human speech of the kind that historical-critical scholars envision today. Many rabbis considered that human scriptural speech was simply dictated by God (and thus was nothing other than divine speech) or was copied directly from the heavenly Torah. Other rabbis granted that human prophets had a cooperative role in divine revelation, even to the point of correcting God. All were agreed, however, about the perfection of the Torah. Scriptural language is a true medium of the divine language.

Agreeing with each other about the Torah's perfection, Rabbi Ishmael and Rabbi Akiva ask whether the Torah is a "heavenly language" or whether God accommodated his language to the limited capacities and culture of Moses and the prophets. Rabbi Ishmael and his school hasten to interpret non-literally any biblical statements about God that do not comport with God's transcendence. Rabbi Akiva and his school mystically affirm this transcendence while accentuating God's choice to draw close to creatures and therefore also refusing to interpret away the anthropomorphisms in the scriptural text.

Arguably, then, Genesis 1's complex and ambiguous language is richly suited to the purposes of teaching the creation. If we follow Heschel's path and read Scripture both with Rabbi Ishmael and Rabbi Akiva, we can see that Genesis 1 gives support to both the mystical and the philosophical approaches to God's creative act. Genesis 1 offers room both for Scripture as God's own language, and for Scripture as a human construction that shows the impact of the culture in which it was written. By allowing for divergent ways of parsing the grammar of Genesis 1:1–3, the biblical text allows both for a philosophical insistence upon creation *ex nihilo* and for a mystical appreciation of God's engagement with formlessness. Genesis 1 does not evacuate God's creative act of deep mystery, but it reveals that the expressive creaturely forms that come forth from the Creator are rooted in the divine knowing and speaking, in the divine "language." Heschel's insights into the mystical and the rational modes of understanding Torah, therefore, can lead

---

would come down firmly on the side of Rabbi Akiva. For discussion of Marquardt's engagement with the Talmud, see Pangritz, "Wendung nach Jerusalem," 181–86.

us further into the value of the language of Scripture for speaking the divine creation.

IV. Kevin Vanhoozer: Theo-Dramatic and Dialogical Speech-Acts

Thus far, I have proposed, with Rosenzweig and Venard, that the preeminence of divine speaking in Genesis 1 illuminates creation as a language rooted in the divine word, and, with Heschel, that the combination of mystical and rational modes of Torah interpretation helps to shed light on the fittingness of the ambiguous words of Genesis 1 for appreciating the depths of the mystery proclaimed by Scripture. As a final step, let me turn to the work of Kevin Vanhoozer, who attends primarily to the theo-dramatic and dialogical contexts in which Scripture (and thus Genesis 1) should be interpreted. Rather than being mere abstract reasoning, scripturally grounded doctrine flows from and informs the lived interaction of God and his people. Again, this will help us to see why it is fitting that Genesis 1:1 does not simply say, "In the beginning God created the heavens and the earth *ex nihilo*."

In *The Drama of Doctrine*, Vanhoozer distances himself from a single-minded focus upon propositional truth with regard to scriptural speech. He refers to the evangelical context in which he is writing: "Partly in response to the mid-twentieth-century tendency to deny the verbal and cognitive dimensions of revelation, Carl F. H. Henry and others argued that God's word should be equated with the revealed propositions of the Bible, objective truths stated in conceptual and verbal form."[96] For this previous generation of evangelicals, who were reacting to liberal Protestantism's rejection of enduring propositional revelation, the task of theology was "to systematize the information conveyed through biblical propositions."[97]

In Vanhoozer's view, while this reaction was understandable and helpful in important ways, the theological task is inevitably more complicated. With Karl Barth, he holds that God efficaciously communicates his own self to his people, rather than merely giving his people information about himself. Vanhoozer fears, however, that Barth tends to "deverbalize the word of God," to dissociate it too sharply from the written words of Scripture. For Vanhoozer (and for me as well), Barth is correct about the personal character of divine revelation but he separates this personal dimension too

---

96. Vanhoozer, *Drama of Doctrine*, 45.
97. Vanhoozer, *Drama of Doctrine*, 45.

sharply from scriptural words.[98] After all, *language* communicates personal presence.[99]

What then is the relationship, according to Vanhoozer, between the active and living Word of God and scriptural words? Vanhoozer appeals here to the notion of speech-acts.[100] Scriptural words belong to God's acting in the economy of salvation. Vanhoozer also mentions Hans Urs von Balthasar's similar characterization (indebted to Goethe): "deed-words."[101] Scripture, therefore, should be understood as "a collection of diverse kinds of divine communicative acts (divine discourse)."[102] In all the human words of Scripture—and not solely in Scripture's divine speech—God is communicating or speaking to his people.[103] The fact that Scripture is comprised of speech-acts means that divine revelation can be personal and propositional at the same time, especially since propositions are not simply assertions or judgments of truth but include other kinds of communication.

Vanhoozer follows von Balthasar in distinguishing between a dramatic and a metaphysical approach to Scripture's content. The dramatic approach looks to Scripture not so much for clear and distinct ideas, but for divine

---

98. For further reflection, see Vanhoozer, "Person of the Book?" For Jewish theological discussion of Karl Barth's theology, see especially Novak, "Before Revelation" and Novak, "Karl Barth on Divine Command"; and Wyschogrod, "Why Was and Is the Theology of Barth of Interest." Novak also points out that Barth influenced Joseph B. Soloveitchik's *Halakhic Man*, particularly with regard to Soloveitchik's distinction between "*halakhic* man" and "*homo religiosus*."

99. See Wahlberg, *Revelation as Testimony*.

100. Here Vanhoozer is indebted to Barth and also to twentieth-century philosophy of language, notably the Wittgenstein-influenced work of J. L. Austin, *How to Do Things with Words*. See also John R. Searle, *Speech Acts*.

101. Vanhoozer, *Drama of Doctrine*, 47. Vanhoozer does not provide a bibliographical reference here.

102. Vanhoozer, *Drama of Doctrine*, 47.

103. See also the development of this point, in conversation with Augustine and Calvin and instructed especially by the Letter to the Hebrews, in G. W. Lee, *Today When You Hear His Voice*. Lee employs Barth's approach, but in a form slightly "corrected" by John Webster: "Canon names the textual expression of God's self-commitment to his Word, but the Word continues to reveal himself through the church's ongoing proclamation of Christ. . . . Yet God's activity in revelation has a particularly textual character. . . . It is therefore possible to locate Scriptural authority in God's present address while affirming the essential relation between fresh events of revelation and their original locutions. The divine address is continuous with yet extends the literal sense; it abides fixity of written form, but imposes the text on new situations with fresh power and meaning. . . . Our understanding of divine address can thus affirm Barth's basic conviction that Scripture speaks with God's authority as God makes himself vitally and actively present in the contemporary moment" (G. W. Lee, *Today When You Hear His Voice*, 202–3). See also Webster, *Holy Scripture*, 30–39.

action in time, manifesting God's love for his wayward human creatures. Vanhoozer states, "The prophets were neither philosophers nor moralists but speech agents and symbolic actors concerned with what God was doing in history and with how the people ought to respond."[104] Yet, the metaphysical dimension is not forgotten when it is sublated within the dramatic approach. God is unique among the biblical "actors" because "[o]nly his speaking sets the stage: 'Then God said, "Let there be light"; and there was light' (Gen. 1:3)."[105] Beyond what is needed for setting forth the dramatic "stage," however, the biblical words do not seek metaphysical precision—as for instance with regard to the nature of the void or the waters. Vanhoozer remarks, "The Christian faith is not a system of ideas or moral values but a five-act theo-drama in which God's speech and action play the decisive parts."[106]

Rather than expecting each scriptural passage to get all the philosophical judgments of truth exactly right, therefore, we can perceive human scriptural speech about divine speech-acts within a broader framework. This framework is God's effort to communicate himself to human beings from within an ongoing drama. Vanhoozer explains, "Our theo-dramatically revised Scripture principle views the Bible not simply as a deposit of revealed truths but as the result of God's multifaceted communicative action."[107] The triune God communicates the truth about himself through a dramatic work of salvation, in which he reveals more about himself as the dramatic action unfolds.

In *Remythologizing Theology*, Vanhoozer points out that the Bible "demythologizes" ancient Near Eastern sources in Genesis 1. These sources, or myths, depicted the "waters" (Gen 1:2) as symbols of "the chaos with which the deities had to struggle in order to bring order into the world."[108] Vanhoozer takes note also of Jon Levenson's view that the "waters" are uncreated and that God struggles to control chaos. Vanhoozer freely admits, "Nowhere in the seven-day creation scheme of Genesis does it explicitly say . . . that God created the waters."[109] As he recognizes, therefore, Genesis 1 and other similar texts raise "issues in three distinct, though overlapping

---

104. Vanhoozer, *Drama of Doctrine*, 51.
105. Vanhoozer, *Drama of Doctrine*, 44.
106. Vanhoozer, *Drama of Doctrine*, 57.
107. Vanhoozer, *Drama of Doctrine*, 67.
108. Vanhoozer, *Remythologizing Theology*, 36.
109. Vanhoozer, *Remythologizing Theology*, 36.

areas: (1) the nature of God; (2) the God/world relation; (3) the theological interpretation of the Bible."[110]

For Vanhoozer, these issues require a thorough investigation of the God who speaks. Somewhat like Rabbi Akiva, he holds that "[t]hinking biblically is a matter of reading Scripture *along the grain of* the text. . . . [R]easoning about God on the basis of Scripture involves marshaling and looking along the grain of metaphors."[111] It is a mistake to seek to leave behind the anthropomorphic language about God, or at least to do so too quickly. Scripture attributes to God hands, arms, ears, and other body parts; and, likewise, Scripture attributes to God such human acts as repenting, remembering, forgetting, and sleeping (as well as speaking). Vanhoozer cautions that if we philosophize away these anthropomorphisms too quickly, we risk failing "to explain what *is* being said about God by means of these figures."[112]

Like Rabbi Ishmael, however, Vanhoozer holds that the path of attending to the anthropomorphic language should lead to philosophical or metaphysical clarification. He rejects Ludwig Feuerbach's view that we must choose between metaphysical clarifications and anthropomorphic images. After all, metaphors can be instructive in their effort "to describe the less familiar in terms of the more familiar . . . all the while maintaining a dynamic tension between 'is' and 'is not.'"[113] For Vanhoozer, then, Scripture itself calls forth metaphysical reasoning. He insists, "Behind the metaphors and anthropomorphisms in Scripture lurks a subterranean metaphysic: 'Metaphor . . . raises questions that only analogy . . . can answer.'"[114] By "metaphysics," he means the use of analogy to apprehend God's utter transcendence of all finite beings, as well as God's possession of, in an infinite and unfathomable mode, every perfection of being.[115]

Vanhoozer holds that God accommodates his speech to human capacities. Although he briefly mentions Scripture's use of the phrase "Thus says the Lord," he does not emulate the rabbinic reflection upon whether the prophet sums up God's intention in human words or repeats verbatim the heavenly words of God. But much like Rabbi Ishmael's side of the rabbinic discussion, he proposes that God's speech in and through Scripture generally

---

110. Vanhoozer, *Remythologizing Theology*, 57.
111. Vanhoozer, *Remythologizing Theology*, 189.
112. Vanhoozer, *Remythologizing Theology*, 61.
113. Vanhoozer, *Remythologizing Theology*, 61.
114. Vanhoozer, *Remythologizing Theology*, 190, citing Wicker, *Story-Shaped World*, 27.
115. See Wittman, *God and Creation*.

occurs through "'indirect' divine authorship."[116] This is how we should read the anthropomorphisms that we find in human scriptural speech, including the traces of the Near Eastern creation myths that we find in Genesis 1. God is accommodating his speech to the capacities of his human hearers, and in this way "*God* is using language to make himself known."[117] Given that God takes human speech to himself and makes it his own language, we find an echo of the school of Rabbi Akiva. But Vanhoozer also speaks about the biblical authors' "poetic license," emphasizing their human contributions to scriptural revelation.[118]

Vanhoozer does not hesitate to affirm along metaphysical lines that God is "the eternal one, the Creator who speaks worlds into existence."[119] In other words, creation *ex nihilo* is what Genesis 1 is in fact describing, even though Genesis 1 includes some anthropomorphic or mythological traces. For Vanhoozer, reasoning with the grain of Scripture leads to the affirmation that "YHWH is the one God who created the heavens and the earth, and hence in some respects is *not* like us."[120] At the same time, the Bible's portrait of God engaging dialogically, through divine speech, with particular human beings is not mere anthropomorphism. God can act upon humans through the highest human instrument, namely language. As Vanhoozer says, "Scripture both depicts instances of divine dialogue and is itself a mode of divine communication, sometimes direct and sometimes indirect."[121]

On biblical and philosophical grounds, he contends that the anthropomorphisms in Genesis 1 can be perceived and metaphysically corrected

---

116. Vanhoozer, *Remythologizing Theology*, 192.
117. Vanhoozer, *Remythologizing Theology*, 193.
118. Vanhoozer, *Remythologizing Theology*, 63.
119. Vanhoozer, *Remythologizing Theology*, 193.
120. Vanhoozer, *Remythologizing Theology*, 193.
121. Vanhoozer, *Remythologizing Theology*, 193. See also Wolterstorff, *Divine Discourse*. Wolterstorff gets to the root of the matter when he describes the "strange but riveting declaration, both unsettling and consoling if true, introduced most emphatically into our human odyssey by Judaism, that God speaks to us on our way, and that, accordingly, our calling as human beings is to listen to that speech from beyond and 'hear'" (*Divine Discourse*, ix). He goes on to say, "Central in the philosophical thought of our century has been the topic of language. Might it be that in addition to *homo linguisticus*, on which we have focused our attention, there is *deus loquens*? The ultimate possibility for our language-preoccupied century to consider: might it be that God is a member of the community of speakers?" (*Divine Discourse*, ix). Wolterstorff advocates a position that accords with Vanhoozer's: "we must suppose that God's book requires and rewards close attention to what its human authors wrote. For it is by way of that, that God discourses" (*Divine Discourse*, 202).

in light of other scriptural texts.[122] He cites Genesis 14:19's affirmation that "God Most High" is "maker of heaven and earth" and Romans 4:17's statement that God "calls into existence the things that do not exist." These passages, in the context of the whole of Scripture, lead him to reject Jon Levenson's view that God "creates" simply by ordering a chaotic substrate. Such a view of God would undermine the cosmos's ontological dependence upon God. God is the Creator of all that is, the transcendent source and sustainer of all finite being. Vanhoozer adds, however, that God meets his people primarily in terms of covenant—ethics and eschatology—rather than primarily in terms of ontology.

Let me mention a final element of Vanhoozer's approach. Namely, in his emphasis on communicative speech-acts, he privileges the relationship of dialogue in exploring what it means for humans to live in the presence of God. Indeed, he argues that the Trinity itself is a "being-in-communicative-action."[123] Faced with thorny problems such as the entrance of the eternal God into time or God's providential governance of all things, he proposes that we take instruction from Mikhail Bakhtin's "dialogical conception of authorship."[124] After all, the biblical theo-drama is intrinsically dialogic. Without describing all the elements of Bakhtin's position, which explores

---

122. Vanhoozer states that "the metaphysics that derives from biblical reasoning examines not being-in-general but *being-through-Christ*" (*Remythologizing Theology*, 197). I agree that the context of creation is always the reality that undergirds metaphysics, and that Christ (as Word) is Creator. But I do not think that Christian revelation has to be known in order for valuable metaphysical reasoning to take place. For further discussion see my *Engaging the Doctrine of Revelation*, chapter 8.

123. Vanhoozer, *Remythologizing Theology*, 320. I note that we need to be sure that "communicative action" here is understood analogously, with regard for the incomprehensible mystery of the divine Trinitarian life. Pierce Taylor Hibbs argues, "It is *expected* that God would create through speech, through communion behavior, because God is a communicating being who eternally communes with himself in three persons" (*Speaking Trinity*, 32). Hibbs defines divine "communion behavior" as "an interpersonal, trinitarian divine behavior amongst the Father, Son, and Holy Spirit, whereby they express mutual and intimate love and glory to one another" (*Speaking Trinity*, 15). Language is at the heart of this "communion behavior": "The Word—both as a divine person and as some high form of divine interpersonal discourse—was in the beginning. . . . The Word as eternal Son and as divine discourse, eternally communicated by the Father in the hearing and power of the Spirit, indicates that language is not a human invention; it is a divine disposition, a disposition to express, in the highest sense, mutual love and glory among the persons of the Godhead" (*Speaking Trinity*, 4). I fear, however, that the analogous character of our knowledge of the divine Trinity is underappreciated here. The revelation of the Father, Son, and Spirit in the economy does not give us warrant for describing them as united by a behavior or disposition, since this would construe their unity along the lines of the unity of three distinct gods.

124. Vanhoozer, *Remythologizing Theology*, 324. See Bahktin, *Problems of Dostoevsky's Poetics*.

the relationship between an author and his or her characters, I note that for Vanhoozer (seeking not least to get around the conundrum of predestination) "dialogical authorship represents a new way of conceiving the relation of divine authorship and sovereignty on the one hand and human freedom and responsibility on the other."[125]

Vanhoozer connects this Bakhtinian understanding of authorship with the interpretation of difficult biblical passages such as the repeated statement in Exodus that God hardened Pharaoh's heart. He argues that God did this in a dialogical fashion, by means of "communicative overtures" that hardened Pharaoh's heart precisely in and through Pharaoh's refusal to say yes to God.[126] For Vanhoozer, as for me, it is necessary to affirm that "God does not author evil."[127] Sin and evil come about when rational creatures freely repulse God's speech-acts, God's dialogically framed communication of himself and his goodness.

In sum, Vanhoozer grants the mythic and anthropomorphic elements of Genesis's creation accounts, including the fact that (as Levenson emphasizes) Genesis 1 does not say—or at least does not clearly say—that God created the "waters." For Vanhoozer, as for Rabbi Akiva, the answer is not to deny the anthropomorphisms but rather to value them. Vanhoozer argues that metaphysics is not opposed to metaphor; and, in this regard, his view of the Creator God includes the insights of Rabbi Ishmael. God accommodates his speech to the human capacities and culture of the prophets, including Moses. Yet, for Vanhoozer, this speech—indeed the whole of Scripture—is divine speech. Arguably, his emphasis on a theo-dramatic dialogue fits with the rabbinic emphasis on dialogue both as constitutive of the Oral Torah

---

125. Vanhoozer, *Remythologizing Theology*, 334. Once predestination is understood strictly as God's eternal will to elevate a creature by grace to union with God—and once it is admitted that it is *possible* for God to overcome human resistance by a further work of grace or by an infusion of grace so powerful as to ensure the sinlessness of the person (as for instance in the case of the humanity of Jesus Christ)—then the issue of predestination cannot be resolved even through an eminently dialogical account, in my view. Eastern Orthodox theologians, along with some Catholics and Protestants, tend to solve the problem by asserting God's universal efficacious salvation of all rational creatures (see most recently the writings of David Bentley Hart). For the argument that two seemingly contradictory truths about predestination (namely, God's superabundant love for each and every rational creature, on the one hand, and God's absolute priority, power to save, and permission of some to be damned, on the other) need to be held by Christians—resisting all attempts to resolve the tension in this life, since God has reserved to himself the revelation of the resolution at the eschatological judgment—see my *Predestination*. See also the essays and responses in Louth et al., *Five Views*.

126. Vanhoozer, *Remythologizing Theology*, 341.

127. Vanhoozer, *Remythologizing Theology*, 342.

and as constantly present in Scripture's depictions of God's covenantal interaction with his people.[128]

Vanhoozer's placing of the truth of biblical language within a dialogic theo-dramatic framework is appropriate for exhibiting how the doctrinal truth (creation *ex nihilo*) arises not simply from a scriptural proof-text (whether Genesis 1:1 or elsewhere) but from within the theo-dramatic dialogue, whose roots are the divine creative speech and God's decisions to "make man in his own image" and to speak to man and woman (Gen 1:27–30). Language is important for understanding creation, precisely as *ex nihilo*—but the divine discourse in Scripture can reveal this without foregrounding philosophical logic and while retaining metaphorical and anthropomorphic modes of speech. We do not need "In the beginning God created the heavens and the earth *ex nihilo*"; it suffices to perceive the pattern of the divine speaking. We perceive this pattern best from within the theo-drama, in Spirit-enabled dialogue with the divine Speaker, the divine Word. This happens when, as members of God's people, we enter into the scriptural words (speech-acts or word-deeds) through which God speaks, interacts, and acts today with his people, who are spoken into being through God's creative and redemptive Word.

V. Conclusion

Comparing the philosophical view of creation with the biblical one—and admittedly painting with a rather broad brush—the Jewish theologian Michael Wyschogrod states, "If Hashem [God] does not find his dignity impaired by being known as the creator of the world, the elector of Abraham, and the redeemer of Abraham's seed from the land of Egypt, then it is not the task of man to protect Hashem's dignity more than he wishes it protected."[129] Wyschogrod is concerned to refute the "depersonalization

---

128. See also Buber, *I and Thou*. Buber and Rosenzweig worked quite closely with each other, although Rosenzweig's understanding of Judaism (especially with regard to Torah observance) differed from Buber's. For von Balthasar's assessment of Buber and Rosenzweig, see his discussion of their writings in *Theo-Drama* I, 632–39. Von Balthasar focuses strictly upon the working out of the "I-Thou" dimension. As von Balthasar says, for Rosenzweig (indebted to Schelling) "there is the God-world relationship that thought includes in the system and the other God-world relationship in which 'the free personality' resists being absorbed into the system" (*Theo-Drama* I, 637). See also von Balthasar's *Martin Buber and Christianity*.

129. Wyschogrod, *Body of Faith*, 95.

of God" and the "dehistoricization of Judaism" that he finds to have been "completed in philosophical Judaism of the Maimonidean variety."[130]

I do not share this rejection of (Greek) metaphysics for understanding the testimony of scriptural words. It seems to me that Rabbi Ishmael provides a necessary complement to Rabbi Akiva.[131] But I do think that the biblical doctrine of the Creator God and creation cannot be summed up solely by elucidating the metaphysical necessity and implications of creation *ex nihilo*. There is more to be said, and it must be said by attending to the depths of language: to God speaking, to the expressiveness or intrinsic "language" of creatures, to the dialogic communion God establishes with his rational creatures, and to the Word of God who is both Creator and, in a relationship of love with his creatures, Redeemer.

Rosenzweig and Venard helped us to see that creation itself bursts forth with divine language, fulfilled in God's self-revelation and in the promise of the perfection of creation. Heschel (and Rabbi Akiva) helped us to see that the anthropomorphisms of the Torah prompt mystical ascent along the paths of language that leads to a deeper understanding of the Creator who also "comes down" to his people in intimate covenantal love. Insofar as anthropomorphisms are present in Genesis 1, this is how it should be. Heschel (and Rabbi Ishmael) helped us to see that Scripture

---

130. Wyschogrod, *Body of Faith*, 92. For discussion of Wyschogrod's theology, see Batnitzky, "Jesus in Modern Jewish Thought." Batnitzky's critique is sharp: "Just as Kant understands Christ as the combination of phenomenal and noumenal natures, and Levinas describes 'incarnation' as the combination of the self and the Other, Wyschogrod also maintains that the body of faith combines the human and the divine. For Wyschogrod, divine revelation, by way of God's erotic love for Abraham, enters into the biological order and begets the body of faith. . . . For Wyschogrod, not only is the body of faith the combination of divine and human nature, but the body of faith itself is also the source of salvation. Wyschogrod states, 'Separated from the Jewish people, nothing is Judaism. If anything, it is the Jewish people that is Judaism.' He maintains that Judaism is not the Torah (understood as knowledge, law, ritual, or anything else) but only the Jewish people. . . . [F]or Wyschogrod, the body of faith believes in itself. Jewish faith is the Jewish people's belief in the very being of the Jewish people. . . . The Bible, on Wyschogrod's reading, allows only one meaning: a personal God with human qualities and human emotions falls in love with Abraham who (literally) fathers the body of faith. . . . Ironically, by making the Jewish people the meaning of Judaism, Wyschogrod's theology, whose sole purpose is to not shy away from God's scandalous love for the people of Israel, ends up removing God from the conversation. Wyschogrod's incarnational theology, like Levinas' incarnational philosophy, cannot but affirm the very position it seeks to reject: belief in the human at the cost of the divine" (Batnitzky, "Jesus in Modern Jewish Thought," 168–69). I agree with Batnitzky's concern about Wyschogrod's rejection of the medieval Jewish philosophical tradition, and I am intrigued by the connection that Batnitzky draws to the influence of liberal Protestantism.

131. See my *Scripture and Metaphysics*, by contrast to such works as Hector, *Theology without Metaphysics*.

is a divine language accommodated to human abilities, with God speaking through human authors (with their human limitations) from the outset, so that God's speaking can here be said to be a divine-human collaboration. This prompts philosophical clarification to distinguish divine speech from human speech, given that God is not in any way a creature. At the same time, scriptural language is also, as Rabbi Akiva says, a heavenly language come to earth: it is truly the divine word (or, for Christians, the language of the Word who takes on flesh). Vanhoozer helped us to see that what we need to look for in Genesis 1 is not necessarily a philosophically clear propositional judgment, but rather is the theo-dramatic dialogical framework in which God inspires and employs for his own purposes the human (limited) speech of his people. It is here that we find the Creator who is known in relation to his creatures. As when Jacob received his new name "Israel," we encounter the Creator only when we wrestle with him "until the breaking of the day," seeking the "blessing" of knowing the Creator's "name" (Gen 32:24, 29). Creation *ex nihilo* is true, but not as a descriptor of the work of an aloof, depersonalized Creator. Rather our knowing of creation *ex nihilo* is the fruit of theo-dramatic wrestling with the Word of God who speaks to us through his scriptural words.

As a philosopher, Rosenzweig remarks that "rabbinic theology formulates our concept of the creative power of God by asking the question whether God created the world out of justice or rather out of love."[132] In response, he fills out the portrait of the theo-drama in which creation *ex nihilo* is apprehended. By scripturally *revealing* that he has created, God ties his act of creation to his covenantal election of a people and to the consummation of creation through this people—the eschatological marriage of God and creation. As I have emphasized, creation fits within a theo-drama of intimate (marital) love. Rosenzweig states, "the relationship we are seeking between the world and the Creator was not, for the world, the fact of having been created once and for all, but its continuous Revelation as creature."[133] He therefore insists that the person "who has not yet been reached by the voice of Revelation has no right to accept the idea of Creation."[134] Creation, revelation, and redemption are intelligible together, because God the Creator does not create in an arbitrary moment and then (lacking love) turn away. Rather, God speaks personally, bringing about a true dialogue, rooted in his divine word.

---

132. Rosenzweig, *Star of Redemption*, 128.
133. Rosenzweig, *Star of Redemption*, 131.
134. Rosenzweig, *Star of Redemption*, 146.

Rosenzweig takes this argument in his own philosophical direction, which I do not need to follow here. The conclusion that I wish to draw is simple: Genesis 1 points outward toward the whole of the Scriptures, toward the whole dramatic and dialogic story of God and his people, a story that still awaits its final consummation, even though the shape of this consummation has been revealed. This is (in part) what Ludwig Feuerbach has missed when he asserts, "the creation out of nothing, i.e., the creation as a purely imperious act, had its origin only in the unfathomable depth of Hebrew egotism."[135] Divine speech and divine language are not "a purely imperious act." Creation *ex nihilo* is not an impersonal coming forth, a sheer display of brute power, but rather the wondrous language of the divine Word who speaks forth the inner language of all beings and who is the "true light that enlightens every man" (John 1:9). Scripture is a dramatic, dialogic, analogical, anthropomorphic, heavenly, and mystical language that enables us to hear the divine speech and to apprehend divine mysteries, including creation *ex nihilo* as a mystery of expressive love calling forth the responsive love of creatures.

In Genesis 1:1–3, when "[i]n the beginning God created the heavens and the earth" and when "God said, 'Let there be light,'" we discover God the Creator. God freely speaks all things *ex nihilo* as "the Alpha and the Omega, the first and the last, the beginning and the end" (Rev 22:13). This same God "used to speak to Moses face to face, as a man speaks to his friend" (Exod 33:11), and this same God "spoke of old to our fathers by the prophets" (Heb 1:1). Still more, the Speaker and ultimately the language spoken is none other than the divine Word, who grounds the truth of all language. It is he who "reflects the glory of God and bears the very stamp of his nature, upholding the universe by his word of power" (Heb 1:3).

---

135. Feuerbach, *Essence of Christianity*, 117.

Chapter 3

Exodus

I. Introduction

The first step of my Christian Israelology had to do with the Creator God who gave Jacob his name "Israel." The second step involves God the Redeemer who proclaims to Moses: "I have seen the affliction of my people who are in Egypt, and have heard their cry because of their taskmasters; I know their sufferings, and I have come down to deliver them out of the hand of the Egyptians" (Exod 3:7-8). This chapter is about the exodus, both as a reality central to the self-understanding of the Jewish people and as a reality central to Christian self-understanding. Some Second Temple Jews hoped for a "new exodus" that would inaugurate the eschatological kingdom of God. In the light of his crucifixion and Resurrection, Jesus' followers believed that he had set this new exodus in motion.

Commenting upon Jesus' words at the Last Supper, Brant Pitre argues that they "flowed directly out of a deeply Jewish understanding of the covenant at Mount Sinai and the hope for a new exodus."[1] Pitre draws upon the work of N. T. Wright, who proposes that in Romans 5-8 Paul makes the new exodus "an all-embracing theme" and who finds that Jesus does the same in the Lord's Prayer and elsewhere.[2] Wright sums up what is perhaps Paul's most important statement of Christ's atoning work: "Romans 3:21-26 is in fact a compressed statement about the 'redemption which is found in the Messiah, Jesus,' and this compressed statement is designed not as a full statement of 'atonement theology,' but rather as a summary, with

---

1. Pitre, *Jesus and the Last Supper*, 514.

2. N. T. Wright, *Paul* II, 1013; N. T. Wright, "Lord's Prayer as a Paradigm." See also Pitre, *Jesus, the Tribulation, and the End*, 137-53.

particular reference to God's covenant faithfulness, of the 'new Exodus' that was achieved on the cross."[3] Wright goes on to observe that the task of Romans 5–8 consists in unpacking "this 'new Exodus' more fully, taking his time to explain how it all 'works.'"[4]

The result is that, as Bruno Forte says, "the Church views itself as a people living in a condition of exodus, assembled in the twelve tribes" through Jesus' symbolic choosing of the Twelve, and sustained by the blood of the new Passover lamb.[5] Similarly, for Jewish reflection, the original exodus and the participation in it of every generation of Jews are utterly central. After citing numerous biblical scholars who deny the historicity of the exodus, the Jewish biblical scholar Richard Elliott Friedman argues at length that a small group of Levites came out of Egyptian slavery around 3,300 years ago.[6] He contends that the actual historical occurrence of the exodus matters greatly, since "[w]e have evidence that without the historical anchor of the exodus, we would not have had the rise of the idea of monotheism. And without the experience of that returning group from Egypt, we might not have had the ethic of caring for the stranger."[7] Another Jewish biblical scholar, Benjamin Sommer, puts the matter perhaps even more strongly. He observes that "there are no archaeological or historical reasons to doubt the core elements of the Bible's presentation of Israel's history," including that "at least some Israelites were enslaved to Egyptians and were surprisingly rescued from Egyptian bondage" and that "they experienced a revelation

---

3. N. T. Wright, *Day the Revolution Began*, 271.

4. N. T. Wright, *Day the Revolution Began*, 271; cf. 270–94, 324–41, and elsewhere. For discussion, see Estelle, *Echoes of Exodus*, 280–81. See also such works as Keesmaat, "Exodus and Romans 8:14–30"; Wilder, *Echoes of the Exodus Narrative*; Nixon, *Exodus in the New Testament*. For further discussion, see D. L. Smith, "Uses of 'New Exodus.'"

5. Forte, "Israel and the Church," 83. To my mind, this point cannot be squared with the general perspective in Pollefeyt, ed., *Jews and Christians*. The key consists in distinguishing fulfillment (and its implications vis-à-vis the ongoing Jewish people) from replacement or substitution (with its implication of a negation of the Jewish people's covenantal status).

6. Friedman, *Exodus*.

7. Friedman, *Exodus*, 5. See also the defense of the historicity of the exodus, and specifically of the revelation of the Torah at Sinai, by Bartholomew, *God Who Acts in History*; as well as Thomas Joseph White, OP's twofold conclusion: "First, I presume that what is recounted in Exodus has some basis in real events of ancient history. Second, I assume that there are sources in the text and that the text has been heavily redacted so as to show how the ancient event is symbolic of the later historical and spiritual life of the people of Israel" (White, *Exodus*, 14). See also Levenson, "Review of *Exodus*," 477–78.

that played a crucial role in the formation of their national, religious, and ethnic identity."[8]

The exodus motif is central to the Old Testament. Jon Levenson observes that the Torah presents "the Sinaitic experience as disclosing the essential, normative relationship of YHWH to his people Israel. Sinai was a kind of archetype, a mold into which new experiences could be fit."[9] Thus, I hardly need to defend the importance of the exodus for both Jews and Christians. It is "[t]he foundational story of the Jewish people" and it is almost equally important in Christianity, since Jesus is "a second Moses, leading forth his people a second time."[10]

In this chapter, I focus on the meaning of the exodus and thus also the meaning of the new exodus. My first section examines the book of Exodus. I highlight the revelation of the life-giving God, who hears the cries of his suffering people and who redeems them from Egyptian slavery. Rabbi Shai Held remarks, "Everyone thinks they know the story of the Exodus: No longer able to bear their oppression and enslavement, the Israelites cry out to God, who remembers the covenant and redeems them."[11] This is indeed the story of the exodus—although Held emphasizes that the story should *also* be understood as contrasting "gratitude and ingratitude."[12] The main point

---

8. Sommer, *Revelation and Authority*, 17. Sommer notes that archaeological and historical-critical evidence does not and cannot suffice to prove or disprove anything about the biblical account, and therefore it is not historically irresponsible to hold in faith that there was an exodus (and a divine revelation) of some kind. See also Rabbi Tony Bayfield's *Being Jewish Today*, 9, where he remarks with regard to the exodus: "Fundamentalist Jews insist on its absolute historicity; at another extreme—but also for ideological reasons—are those who insist it's all invention." Bayfield goes on to affirm: "God made a covenant with the Jewish people at Sinai—with their descendants and with those who choose to join. From that moment on, a journey of meaning and purpose towards the Prophetic vision of the End of Days has continued, challenged both from within and without, often battered and sometimes severely damaged but never entirely halted" (*Being Jewish Today*, 131–32).

9. Levenson, *Sinai and Zion*, 18. See also Fishbane, "'Exodus' Motif"; Zakovitch, *"And You Shall Tell Your Son"*; Stock, *Way in the Wilderness*; Daube, *Exodus Pattern*; Isbell, *Function of Exodus Motifs*; and Ninow, *Indicators of Typology*.

10. Held, *Heart of Torah* I, 134; Daube, *Exodus Pattern*, 11. See also Carmen Joy Imes's observation, pertinent to both the exodus and the new exodus, that "the wilderness journey from Egypt to Canaan is liminal space. Far more than just a place to pass *through*, it is the workshop of Israel's *becoming*. The wilderness is the temporary destination that makes them who they are" (Imes, *Bearing God's Name*, 18).

11. Held, *Heart of Torah* I, 128.

12. Held, *Heart of Torah* I, 128. He suggests, "The liberation of the Israelites from Egypt is a liberation from a mode of seeing the world and living in it at least as much as it is an escape from concrete political circumstances" (Held, *Heart of Torah* I, 133). His ground for this claim is that Moses embodies gratitude (acknowledging indebtedness

is that God does indeed rescue his beloved people from their oppression and enslavement.

Nevertheless, even after the people of Israel escape the Egyptians, they still find themselves subject to grievous suffering. Their *new* suffering comes about both because of the rigors of the journey through desert terrain and because of their sins. In fact, on the exodus, the people of Israel are able to sin in a new way because they are now in a more direct relationship to God. They have moved "from being slaves to the Egyptians" to being "slaves to God."[13] What being "slaves to God" means is already apparent in the representative figures of Moses and Pharaoh. Moses accepts God's sovereignty whereas Pharaoh rejects it.[14] As "slaves to God," the Israelites are liberated while the Egyptians are tormented by the ten plagues and by their final defeat in the crossing of the Sea. David Daube observes that God is presented as a just sovereign or master of his slaves, ensuring their "protection from human domination."[15] But if so, how is it that the people of Israel suffer so much under God's protection?

In my chapter's first section, I ask whether anything has really changed for the better. The people of Israel suffered grievously in Egypt and, despite being redeemed, they still suffer grievously on the exodus.[16] I argue that

---

and dependency) to God and others, whereas Pharaoh embodies ingratitude: "Unbridled self-assertion and a refusal to acknowledge indebtedness to anyone or anything else are what underlie Pharaoh's rule, and his way of being in the world. Acknowledgment of others and a willingness to face his own indebtedness, on the other hand, are what underlie Moses' leadership, and his way of being in the world" (Held, *Heart of Torah* I, 133).

13. Daube, *Exodus Pattern*, 44.

14. See Davis, *Opening Israel's Scriptures*, 44: "Moses and Pharaoh are the two most vividly drawn human characters in Exodus, and together they illumine the central theme of knowing God. Each of these mighty opponents is subject to YHWH's self-revelation, to which the two respond in drastically different ways." See also Davis, *Getting Involved with God*; Davis, "Losing a Friend."

15. Daube, *Exodus Pattern*, 46.

16. See Hannah Arendt's remarks in her March 27, 1942 column in *Jewish World*, titled "Moses or Washington": "It is a dreadfully long time now since Moses led the children of Israel up out of the land of Egypt, out of the house of bondage. Even the renowned memory of the Jews, the memory of an ancient people that holds to this myth of its foundation, is beginning to deteriorate. Even ancient peoples forget the deeds of their patriarchs when they can no longer make sense of the deeds of their grandfathers, fathers, and sons. When Reform rabbis took control of our national feasts a hundred years ago and let them vanish into a religion that no one believed in any longer, they did not in fact succeed in dissolving the Jewish people into a 'Mosaic confession.' But they did achieve one thing: they destroyed the legends of its founding. Ever since, we are no longer an ancient people but a very modern one, simply burdened or blessed with an especially long national history" (Arendt, "Moses or Washington," 149).

there is an important difference between the two situations, because on the exodus they receive the gifts of God's law and of God's life-giving power and presence. Their suffering now belongs to their journey *with* God the redeemer who has constituted them as his people.[17]

Christians too, grow spiritually while "groan[ing] inwardly" (Rom 8:23) on the new exodus in Christ toward "the glory that is to be revealed" (Rom 8:18), in a hope shaped by God's redemptive presence in the midst of suffering. Paul remarks: "we rejoice in our sufferings, knowing that suffering produces endurance, and endurance produces character, and character produces hope, and hope does not disappoint us, because God's love has been poured out into our hearts through the Holy Spirit who has been given to us" (Rom 5:3–5). It is not a coincidence that Paul's statements here are found in a section of the Letter to the Romans where, according to N. T. Wright, the "Passover sequence" of the exodus "is . . . recapitulated majestically."[18]

Next, in the second section of my chapter, I clarify that we should not view the exodus narrative solely in terms of redemption from oppressive suffering. Instead, we need to value what God does at Mount Sinai. Put simply, a central purpose of the exodus is to establish Israel as a *nation* under God's sovereignty. In this vein, Carmen Joy Imes remarks about the laws that constitute Israel as a nation: "Israel's laws are the fences within which life can flourish. They make possible a distinctive way of life so that other nations can see what Yahweh is like and what he expects." [19]

From this perspective, my second section concentrates upon expositing the approach taken by Rabbi Jonathan Sacks. Sacks argues that the main purpose of the exodus was to establish Israel's political life as a nation under the just sovereign, God. The politics of nationhood under God is central to the book of Exodus. The establishment of the nation of Israel by means of the exodus makes of Israel (in the words of Stanley Hauerwas, describing the

---

17. Rabbi Held, recognizing that the Torah itself (the Pentateuch) ends prior to Israel entering into the land, comments that what we have in the Torah involves "a promise, followed by a journey, and finally . . . a promise left often painfully unfulfilled. This is the stuff of deep spiritual growth, but it can also cause great pain and suffering" (Held, *Heart of Torah* I, 137–38).

18. N. T. Wright, *Paul* II, 1014. Estelle observes, "How the Passover was celebrated by the first generation of Israelites fleeing out of Egypt differed from how it was practiced in Jesus' day when the preparation of the sacrifice was made at the temple, which in turn differed from the Passover celebrated by Jews outside Jerusalem after the destruction of the temple in 70 CE when there is an absence of the sacrificial animal. . . . In contrast to rabbinic Judaism, the Passover was understood as a kind of atonement offering making the redemption from Egypt possible" (Estelle, *Echoes of Exodus*, 290). For further background, see Prosic, *Development and Symbolism*.

19. Imes, *Bearing God's Name*, 35. Regarding the purposes of Israel's legal code, she draws attention to LeFebvre, *Collections, Codes, and Torah*.

Church) "a political alternative to the politics of nations and empires."[20] Jon Levenson puts this point more concretely, with an emphasis on democratic freedom under God. He considers that the terrain of the exodus functions as "a symbol of freedom, which stands in opposition to the massive and burdensome regime of Egypt, where state and cult are presented as colluding in the perpetuation of slavery and degradation. The mountain of God is a beacon to the slaves of Egypt, a symbol of a new kind of master and a radically different relationship of people to state."[21]

It is all too easy for Christians to minimize the importance of the Jewish people's nationhood. Describing a recent Jewish-Christian dialogue, Rabbi Tony Bayfield notes that "the Jews had varying degrees of trouble getting their heads round incarnation while the Christians struggled most of all with accepting that Israel is as important to Judaism as it is to Jews."[22] Christians often do not grasp how strongly Judaism is bound to land-based nationhood rooted in the Abrahamic covenantal promises. Yet, Christians too understand themselves to be "a holy nation" (1 Pet 2:9).[23] Hauerwas

---

20. Hauerwas, *Against the Nations*, 123.

21. Levenson, *Sinai and Zion*, 23. In chapter 12 of his *In God's Shadow*, Michael Walzer likewise argues that the laws and political practices of the Jewish people in the Torah have significant proto-democratic elements, though he finds the figure of God to be despotic. See also, for early modern approaches that read "the Old Testament as a political work," Neuman, "Political Hebraism," 59.

22. Bayfield, *Being Jewish Today*, 106. Bayfield goes on to describe both the "triumph" of the state of Israel (as a democratic state and as "the one place where, for better and for worse, we Jews can be wholly/holy ourselves") and the "tragedy" of Israel through its failure to be "fully a state for all its people" or "to live peaceably and collaboratively with its Palestinian neighbors," with the result that it has become "an occupying power, a situation from which its government, indefensibly, no longer wishes to escape" (*Being Jewish Today*, 127–28). Bayfield sets forth at some length "five inalienable rights" that bind the Jewish people to the land of Israel and that fully legitimize the Jewish state of Israel: a historic right, a pragmatic right, a moral right, a legal right, and a theological or covenantal right. He affirms that "two peoples—Jews and Palestinians—now have valid claims to the Land" (*Being Jewish Today*, 128), and the only solution is explicit compromise—willingly and mutually giving up part of the land, without intention to reconquer it—on the part of both Jews and Palestinians. Drawing upon Dow Marmur's *Star of Return*—which in part is a critique of Heschel's *Sabbath*—Bayfield underscores that "Jewish covenant is rooted not solely in Jewish time [the Sabbath] but in Jewish place as well.... For Marmur, as for me, the physical, earthly Jerusalem ... grounds the spiritual, heavenly Jerusalem" (Bayfield, *Being Jewish Today*, 131). Bayfield has the rise of British anti-Semitism in view, including in the Labour Party, with its "collective denial that Israel is part of Jewish theology," a denial that "paves the way for the new lie: Israel is about Jews, not Judaism, and is, therefore, at best an unnecessary enterprise and, at worst, a racist one" (*Being Jewish Today*, 133).

23. 1 Peter's language here is a deliberate reference to the exodus (specifically Exodus 19): see Green, *1 Peter*, 62. See also Estelle, *Echoes of Exodus*, chapter 10; as well as

prefers to describe the Church as a "polis," to distinguish it from the political forms of life that characterize modern nation-states.²⁴ Ephraim Radner likewise gives a distinctive stamp to the Church's "nationhood." He contends, "The Church is that nation which *gathers* other nations within the being and rule of God in Christ."²⁵

Without denying the truth of 1 Peter 2:9, I think that "nation" or "polis" is not the best image for the Church. The Church goes beyond the land-based particularity of a nation or polis, and a world-embracing "nation" does not make sense in earthly politics. Nevertheless, as the fulfillment and reconfiguration of the covenantal promises, Christ's inaugurated kingdom does indeed embrace the nations and point forward not merely to the restoration of the nation of Israel but to its eschatological perfecting in the marriage of God and creation. For the first Christians, not only had Jesus provided a "radical redefinition of what the kingdom would actually mean," but also "the kingdom had indeed come with power in the events which

---

the insightful summary of 1 Peter 2:9-10 by J. B. Wells, *God's Holy People*, 222: "All the terms and associations of Israel's election, which were initially attributed to Christ, are now applied to the body of believers in their relationship to Christ."

24. See Hauerwas, *In Good Company*.

25. Radner, *Church*, 102. Radner explains further, "To gather the nations is to communicate the whole Scriptures of Christ to the nations," by employing the languages/cultures of the nations and without flattening the diversity of the nations (*Church*, 102). He holds that the Church is the way that Israel fulfills its mandate to be a blessing to all nations: "As Israel relates to the Nations, so does the Church, insofar as it is continuous with Israel's popular vocation. . . . Israel is a nation 'for the nations,' and the Church is how Israel is just that" (Radner, *Church*, 98–99). After reflecting critically upon the phrase "people of God" popular in post-Word War II Protestant and Catholic ecclesiology—arguing that the phrase pushed Israel's nationhood into the background, making Israel into a pre-nation or pre-political collective and setting "people" in opposition to "institution"—he challenges "communion ecclesiology" on similar grounds, as being aimed at weakening any emphasis on political or institutional elements and therefore as "politically flaccid, incapable of application and traction" (Radner, *Church*, 121). The solution, he suggests, is to return to a figural understanding of the Church as Israel, but now in a non-supersessionist way and with deep repentance (for ecclesiastical failures, above all the failure to be one people and thus the failure "to engage and reconcile the peoplehood of the nations" [Radner, *Church*, 126]). A properly repentant Church will figurally identify with "the actual life of Israel, scripturally described" (Radner, *Church*, 124). But what about the ongoing Jewish people? He argues that Christians should conceive of the Church as "Israel" by recognizing that "Israel" (though in actuality one) has been divided for centuries, just as the two kingdoms (Judah and Israel) were divided. He suggests that a solution might be "to speak of the Church as Israel under a certain aspect. She is 'Israel-on-the-way'—the way by which the nations, beginning with the Jews, are gathered into Christ. This aspect is distinct from other aspects of Israel, in particular from her Jewish self-ordering in the world" (Radner, *Church*, 130; as an example of this kind an approach, he cites Jocz, *Theology of Election*).

followed Jesus' death."²⁶ Thus the new exodus is about the establishment of the eschatological kingdom inclusive of the Gentiles, just as the exodus is about the establishment of the nation of Israel.

After the second section concentrating upon the contributions made by Jonathan Sacks's political reading of the exodus, my third and final section returns to Scripture, specifically the New Testament. I argue that in the New Testament, the themes identified in my first two sections—redemption from suffering and the political constitution of the people of God—are uniquely joined together. Of course, just as did the Israelites on the exodus, Christ's followers still suffer and die: we are journeying with and toward Christ our King, being configured to him by the Spirit in the midst of the trials. The purpose of the new exodus led by Christ, however, is to attain the new Jerusalem, the perfection of the Spirit-filled kingdom which will be cosmic in scope (see Rom 8:18–23) and in which "death shall be no more, neither shall there be mourning nor crying nor pain any more" (Rev 21:4).

Throughout the chapter, I inquire into what kind of deliverance the exodus journey provides. What should be expected from God's redemption of the Israelites from Egypt, his establishment of the nation of Israel, and his sending of Christ as the royal Redeemer and the Head of the new exodus of God's people? I affirm that, as Daniel Keating remarks, Christians "have attained a truly kingly and priestly status not as separate individuals but *as a people*, the Church."²⁷ But why is there still so much sin and suffering among the people being redeemed and on the journey as servants of the loving covenantal God? Why is it that, as Rabbi Held puts it, "[t]he perpetual elusiveness of our destination can enliven our hearts, but sometimes it can also break them"?²⁸

---

26. N. T. Wright, *History and Eschatology*, 144, 146. The inaugurated kingdom accords with the eschatological prophecies of Isaiah 19:19–25, which proclaim that the Gentile nations (represented by Egypt) will, like the Israelites of the exodus, "cry to the Lord because of oppressors" and "he will send them a savior, and will defend and deliver them" so that they worship him alone (Isa 19:20; cf. Isa 2:3). See Fishbane, "'Exodus' Motif," 128–30; as well as Simkovich, *Making of Jewish Universalism*, which treats the prophecies about the nations coming to worship the God of Israel (for example, Isa 2:2–4), about the nations being absorbed into Israel (Jer 12:14–17; Zech 2:10–17), and about Jerusalem becoming the center of worship for all individuals and nations with the exception of those that will be punished (for example, Isa 56:1–8; Isa 66:18–24; Zech 14:16–19; Dan 4:34–37; Ps 96:7–13).

27. Keating, *First and Second Peter, Jude*, 55.

28. Held, *Heart of Torah* I, 138. Hannah Arendt summed up what she perceived to be Catholic theology of the Jewish people in a brief essay written in April 1942: "For the Catholic Church, Jews are both God's chosen and, after the crucifixion of Christ, cursed people. According to their plan of salvation—as one can read in the Epistle to the Romans, chapter 2—God and suffering humanity are waiting for the promised return of

II. The God of Life and His Suffering People

The book of Exodus begins by recalling the end of the book of Genesis, by means of a brief overview of the twelve sons of Jacob and of the favor enjoyed by Joseph under Pharaoh. Almost immediately, however, the book of Exodus descends into a pit of suffering and misery. Thomas Joseph White sets the scene: "The book of Exodus begins with the Israelites in the darkness of slavery, as prisoners to a society of efficiency, cruelty, and idolatry."[29]

According to Exodus 2, by the time of Moses' birth, Pharaoh has ordered that the Israelites' male children be killed at birth, in a bid to stem the Israelites' population growth. For this reason Moses' mother places her infant son in a basket in the reeds on the bank of the river Nile, where Pharaoh's daughter finds and adopts him. The same chapter of Exodus reports that when Moses grows up, he tries to resolve his people's plight by means of his own power: he kills an Egyptian who is abusing a Hebrew. This action results in Moses being compelled to flee to the land of Midian, where he becomes a shepherd.[30]

At this moment of seeming defeat, the God of Israel (re-)introduces himself. On Mount Horeb, he manifests himself to the shepherd Moses as a fire that does not consume its fuel—that is, as unquenchable energy. God names himself by means of the verb "to be," indicating that he transcends temporal change and finite modes of being.[31] He proclaims that he is the

---

the Lord upon the conversion of the Jews. Until that happens, the Jews must remain true to their Law, while preserved from destruction by the *ordo christianus*, and live as meek and indigent witnesses to the truth of the salvation history revealed in the crucified and resurrected Christ. If the Jews were to be untrue to their own Law, without becoming Christians, or if—as Zionism demands—they were to become a people like all the peoples, the plan of salvation is undone" (Arendt, "Cui Bono?," 151). Her point is that Catholics envision Jews not as real people but as figures whose role must always be pitiable and despised, but who must play the role until they finally see the light at the end of time.

29. White, *Exodus*, 6. For White, the ending of the book of Exodus suggests that its fundamental theme is the formation of a people able to know and rightly worship the true God; for the same viewpoint see Ratzinger, *Spirit of the Liturgy*, 17. White is also attentive to the establishment of the nation. He comments, "The book of Exodus seeks to portray how the people of Israel became God's own chosen people through their deliverance from Egypt and by a divinely instituted covenant articulated to them through a prophet" (*Exodus*, 25).

30. See the reflections on Moses' character (and God's), including the significance of Moses being a shepherd, in Held, *Heart of Torah* I, 124–25.

31. See the valuable discussion of this topic in White, *Exodus*, 35–44, 292–304. Many commentators go the route followed by Göran Larsson, who states: "'I AM' is not a philosophical concept, but rather a historical one. It does not deal primarily with the essence of the supreme being. It testifies of one who is active in history, constantly

God of Abraham, Isaac, and Jacob and that he will redeem Israel from Egyptian slavery. God says to Moses about the Israelites: "I know their sufferings, and I have come down to deliver them out of the hand of the Egyptians, and to bring them up out of that land to a good and broad land, a land flowing with milk and honey" (Exod 3:7–8).

When Moses asks for a sign that he can show to the people in order to persuade them that God truly has commissioned him, God responds with three signs that display his power—as the Creator—over life and death. Göran Larsson notes that these signs emphasize "God's power over humans and the earth," and the signs show that the Israelites' "time of healing has drawn near."[32] First, God turns Moses' staff into a deadly serpent and then turns it back again; second, he turns Moses himself leprous and then heals him; third, he claims the power to turn water from the river Nile into blood. In all three ways, God makes clear that he has power to cause death and to preserve life. Shortly afterward, when God threatens to kill Moses—relenting only when Moses' son receives circumcision—we see again that God wields power over life and death.[33] When Moses and Aaron perform the signs in the people's sight, the people believe Moses and Aaron. But when the immediate result of their intervention with Pharaoh is to cause Pharaoh to make the people's burdens even heavier, the people reject Moses and Aaron and remove their trust from God (Exod 5:21).

Fortunately, God does not stop there. He reaffirms his promise to redeem Israel. They will be his people and he will be their God, and they will live in the land that he promised to Abraham, Isaac, and Jacob. To bring this about, God undertakes a series of plagues aimed against Pharaoh and the Egyptians, demonstrating his power over life and death. God turns Aaron's staff into a serpent and Aaron's staff swallows the serpent-staffs of Egypt's magicians. God turns the Nile into blood, and sends hail, locusts, and thick darkness. All these plagues forebode the death that is coming to the people

---

intervening to realize a plan with the world in general and with a particular instrument, the people of Israel" (Larsson, *Bound for Freedom*, 33). This sharp opposition between the metaphysical and the historical fails to appreciate that metaphysical transcendence is precisely what allows for God's radical freedom and governance vis-à-vis history.

32. Larsson, *Bound for Freedom*, 36.

33. For discussion, see Dozeman, *Exodus*, 154–56. Dozeman points out, "Twice in Exodus Yahweh is presented as a destroyer. God seeks to kill Moses or Gershom [Moses' son] in 4:24–26, and 'the destroyer' kills the Egyptian firstborn in chapter 12. The two stories are related. Both explore Yahweh's claim on firstborn, introduced in 4:22. The historical and religious background of the divine claim on firstborn is not clear from the biblical text, especially whether the claim required the sacrifice of the firstborn" (Dozeman, *Exodus*, 156). See also Levenson, *Death and Resurrection*.

of Egypt. Finally, God sends the tenth plague: the killing of all the firstborn males of Egypt, just as Pharaoh had commanded be done to the Hebrews.[34]

In the tenth plague, God shows that toward the Egyptians he wills death whereas toward the Israelites he wills life. Prior to the execution of this final plague, God requires that the Israelites trust him and do what he commands. What he commands is an act of worship, expressed through a sacrificial lamb.[35] Each Hebrew family must kill a lamb and smear some of its blood on their doorposts and lintel. The lamb's blood, as a sign of dependence upon God, will protect each family from the slaughter. Through the death of the sacrificial lamb, God's people will have life, while the Egyptians, unmarked by the lamb's blood, will experience death.

Although sacrificial animals had appeared regularly in the book Genesis in covenant-making and in worship, the command regarding the Passover lamb may seem strange. After all, if God has absolute power over life and death—as, throughout the plagues, God has been demonstrating to both the Israelites and the Egyptians—then why would the blood of a slain lamb be needed in order for the Israelites to survive? Why could not God simply kill the Egyptian firstborn, as a punishment for the Egyptians' oppression of the Hebrew slaves, and let the Israelites go free? Surely the God who is in charge of life and death does not need the blood of a lamb to identify the dwellings of his people!

In fact, what is revealed here is God's will to give the people of Israel the fullness of life. Larsson states, "Blood as such does not possess any magical power. God does not need it.... Only through relationship with the Lord can blood come to symbolize salvation."[36] The question, then, is what kind

---

34. White comments: "In their teaching regarding the death of the Egyptian firstborn, the scriptures indicate an ironic form of divine justice. The Egyptians sought to subjugate the Hebrews by means of a strategically planned genocide, but instead they are punished and obliged to liberate the Hebrews due to the death of their own firstborn" (White, *Exodus*, 90). See also White's reflections on divine justice: *Exodus*, 90–94, although I hold that the death of all the Egyptian firstborn can be interpreted in some other way than literally God taking away the lives of infants. I think that this part of the book of Exodus, while rooted in historical realities and cognizant of divine action, does not intend to offer a historically literal rendition of events and causes. For the literary richness of the story of the ten plagues, see Sarna, *Exploring Exodus*, 75–77. Sarna affirms, "The entire account has a didactic and theological purpose, not a historiographic one. In order to underline and emphasize these points, the narrator has devised a literary structure of impressive artistry" (*Exploring Exodus*, 75, 77).

35. See the theological reflections offered by White, *Exodus*, 94–102. White observes of the Passover lamb that "this typological sign is arguably the most significant given in all of scripture—a symbol that stands at the center of the divine economy and gives unity to the whole" (White, *Exodus*, 100).

36. Larsson, *Bound for Freedom*, 82.

of relationship with God does the blood enact? According to Carol Meyers, it may be that the blood simply signifies divine protection or "God's guardianship of Israel."[37] In my view, the Israelites' obedience to God's command regarding the blood of the lamb denotes their willingness to place their lives entirely into God's hands. In response, God redeems them from death and leads them toward the promised land. In the annual Passover ritual, with its sacrificial lamb and its feast of unleavened bread, they commemorate their trust that their Redeemer has power over life and death and that he will redeem his chosen people from death.[38]

When Pharaoh finally accedes to Moses and Aaron's request to let the people go, God commands that all the firstborn of Israel must be consecrated to God, since they belong to God (Exod 13:11–12).[39] Again, the people must recognize God's power over life and death. Along these lines, White remarks that the consecration of the firstborn helps "the Israelite to recognize that God is the author of existence and life and to give thanks to God for the gifts of being and human flourishing."[40] As soon as they embark from Egypt, God goes "before them by day in a pillar of cloud to lead them along the way, and by night in a pillar of fire to give them light, that they might travel by day and by night" (Exod 13:21). At this stage of their journey, God's presence never leaves them. God's presence secures their salvation from death, when "the Lord in the pillar of fire and of cloud looked down upon the host of the Egyptians, clogging their chariot wheels" (Exod

---

37. Meyers, *Exodus*, 97. The full sentence reads, "The powerful apotropaic function of blood to protect against evil demons is incorporated into the symbolic power of the narrative to demonstrate God's guardianship of Israel."

38. Larsson emphasizes the political or communal unity established by the Passover ritual: "The ordinance that the consumption of the lambs must take place during one and same night and in one and the same house (12:8, 22, 46) stresses the relationship character of the meal. All the participants had to eat the lamb together at the same time. The table fellowship could not be broken. If anything was left until the morning it could not be eaten but had to be burned (v. 10; 34:25). The very preparation of the lambs dynamically manifests the call to the new all-embracing relationship of the oppressed and disunited people at their first Passover. The lambs must not be cut up but should be roasted whole (12:9), nor should their bones be broken (12:46; cf. John 19:32–36). The bones symbolize a wholeness; the Hebrew word *'etsem* means 'bone,' 'substance,' and 'person.' Through this ordinance the lamb as a symbol of relationship and unity is emphasized. In this respect the theme of the paschal lamb in the New Testament is highly appropriate: It was slaughtered 'to gather into one the dispersed children of God' (John 11:52)" (Larsson, *Exodus*, 83).

39. Although child sacrifice is certainly not commanded here, Dozeman connects these verses with the probability that "[t]he sacrifice of the firstborn was likely practiced by the Israelites" at least at some point in their history (Dozeman, *Exodus*, 297).

40. White, *Exodus*, 109.

14:24–25). The Egyptian soldiers die while crossing the sea, whereas the Israelites pass over it on dry land.

Yet, during this crisis the Israelites lose their trust in God. Despite all that happened during the plagues, the Israelites see the Egyptian soldiers from afar and fall into despair. Moses calms them by telling them that in order to live, they need only trust in God's power: "Fear not, stand firm, and see the salvation of the Lord, which he will work for you today; for the Egyptians whom you see today, you shall never see again. The Lord will fight for you, and you have only to be still" (Exod 14:13–14).[41] The point is that God's power suffices to quell the most powerful human empire. Once the people of Israel see the Egyptian soldiers dying in the sea, the people's trust in God is renewed and they sing a song of triumphant joy.

Extending his promise to giving his people life, God makes himself powerfully present at Mount Sinai and bestows upon his people a just law, grounded in the ten commandments. For a people to live well, a just law that guides communal life is necessary. God also gives the leaders of his people an unimaginably glorious access to his own life. After Moses renews the covenant through sacrificial offerings and the people proclaim their obedience to God's commandments (Exod 24:7), God invites Moses and Aaron, joined by seventy-two elders, to ascend Mount Sinai, where "they saw the God of Israel" and "they beheld God, and ate and drank" (Exod 24:10–11). Furthermore, on top of Mount Sinai, Moses enters into God's glory and dwells in God's wondrous presence for "forty days and forty nights" (Exod 24:18).[42]

During the exodus journey, God provides his starving people with a miraculous bread-like food, manna (Exod 16:4).[43] He requires the people to

---

41. Dozeman describes Moses' words as a "war oracle": "Moses responds with a word of assurance in the form of a war oracle. E. W. Conrad separates the war oracle into the following parts: a word of assurance, 'Do not be afraid!'; a directive that the people 'Stand firm!'; a prediction that they will see the salvation of Yahweh; and the clarification that Yahweh will fight for the people requiring that they 'Keep still!' The war oracle indicates both victory over an enemy (2 Chr 20:17–20) and the revelation of God in the event (1 Sam 12:16–18)" (Dozeman, *Exodus*, 314). Because of the presence of the living God who is redeeming his people from Egyptian slavery, however, there is much more going on in Exodus 14:13–14 than one finds in a standard ancient Near Eastern "war oracle."

42. For discussion of Moses' exalted role, see L. M. Morales, *Who Shall Ascend*, 87–93. For historical-critical and canonical (theological) background to Exodus 24, see Childs, *Book of Exodus*, 487–511. Childs finds that "the all-encompassing focus of the chapter falls on God's mercy and gracious condescension" (*Book of Exodus*, 508).

43. For discussion see Moberly, *Old Testament Theology*, chapter 3. Moberly addresses efforts to explain the miracle of the manna in terms of natural science, cautioning that much is lost in such approaches; and he similarly addresses those who seek

depend upon his provision, since the manna rots within twenty-four hours; each morning new manna is required. But in preparation for the seventh day, the Sabbath, God takes care to provide two days worth of manna and it does not rot when stored. God also repeatedly gives the people water, as befits a desert journey. Lastly, God ensures that the Israelites will not be conquered by the peoples whom they encounter. The people of Amalek fight a battle with the Israelites at Rephidim, before the Israelites have even reached Mount Sinai. The Israelites do not win this battle by their own strength. Rather, when Moses raises the "rod of God," the Israelites conquer, and when Moses allows the rod to fall, the Israelites lose ground (Exod 17:9).

When they reach Mount Sinai, God sums up the revelation of his life-giving power to the Israelites: "You have seen what I did to the Egyptians, and how I bore you on eagles' wings and brought you to myself" (Exod 19:4). To be brought to God by God—to have left one's mortal enemies in the dust and now to be in communion with God—is surely a marker of the fullness of life!⁴⁴ When the young Moses took things into his own hands and killed the Egyptian, he was driven into exile in Midian. But when Moses and the people do hardly anything other than offer a sacrificial lamb in obedience to God, Moses and the people receive everything. The key is to trust in God who reveals himself to be the all-powerful source of life.

It would seem, then, that the book of Exodus is a story of great triumph, moving from suffering in Egypt to the fullness of life, through the power of the divine life-giver. But, as noted above, there is a tension in the book that calls this plotline into question. Namely, the people continue to suffer and die. Their suffering is mainly attributed to their lack of trust in God and to their sins, preeminently their idolatry. They are constantly distrusting God. We regularly read that the people "murmured against" Moses, Aaron, and God (Exod 16:2). The people blame Moses and Aaron—and God—for taking them "out into this wilderness to kill this whole assembly

---

to explain away the tension between the Israelites' apparent grave hunger and their possession of extensive livestock (which would die without grazing grounds). As he points out, much depends upon "one's judgment as to the narrative's likely genre. For a judgment about genre entails a sense of which questions a text will, and will not, fruitfully sustain" (*Old Testament Theology*, 91). Rightly in my view, Moberly distinguishes between "Historie" and "Geschichte" (indebted to various sources, most recently Jasper, *Short Introduction to Hermeneutics*, 93), and he suggests that the genre of Exodus 16 is that of "Geschichte" or a legend handed down over the generations as part of culture-forming identity. See also his "Miracles."

44. With an eye both to Exodus 19:4–6 and to the cultic system of Exodus, Leviticus, and Numbers, Morales comments: "it was God's will that *all* Israel become holy. Having conveyed Israel from the status of unclean, among the nations, to that of clean in relationship with himself, God purposed to sanctify his people to be his own treasured possession" (L. M. Morales, *Who Shall Ascend*, 164).

with hunger" (Exod 16:3). The people exclaim, "Why did you bring us up out of Egypt, to kill us and our children and our cattle with thirst?" (Exod 17:3). The people, tired of waiting for Moses to come down from Mount Sinai, have Aaron make a golden calf for them. All the people rejoice upon seeing the golden calf: "These are your gods, O Israel, who brought you up out of the land of Egypt!" (Exod 32:4). They celebrate a feast, followed by an orgy, having completely forgotten the true God.

For their lack of faith, the people are punished. But we should sympathetically recognize that their words and deeds arise out of intense sufferings. For example, if the people had not been starving to death and thirsting to death in the middle of the desert, they might not have murmured against God so bitterly. If the people had not been awaiting a leader who had been gone too long, they might not have feasted and danced around the golden calf. Having been chased by Egyptian soldiers and having wandered in the desert, they presumably were in a condition of stress. Indeed, God had been performing glorious miracles for them. But the actual condition of their lives still involved a great deal of suffering, just as their lives had involved a great deal of suffering while in Egypt.

Their rebellious actions, of course, produce even more suffering and dying. In the book of Exodus, the most notable instance of this bitter fruit comes after Moses descends from the mountain and discovers them partying around the golden calf.[45] The result is a civil war. The Levites gather themselves to Moses' side, and Moses commands them in God's name: "Put every man his sword on his side, and go back and forth from gate to gate throughout the camp, and slay every man his brother, and every man his companion, and every man his neighbor" (Exod 32:27). What a grim enterprise! It leads to the death of "about three thousand men" (Exod 32:28). After these men died, to cap matters off "the Lord sent a plague upon the people" (Exod 32:35). A lot of dying takes place, and a lot of suffering. In terms of the scope of the suffering and dying, it sounds very similar to—and in certain ways even worse than—the experience of the Israelites in Egypt.

Arguably, Moses has the best time of it, even though he too suffers, especially from the murmuring of the people against him. The people's murmurings are real threats rather than gentle complaining. Moses cries out

45. For historical-critical reconstruction, see Dozeman, *Exodus*, 679–712. Dozeman argues that the story of the golden calf is non-historical, so that, in the story, "the construction of the golden calf in the wilderness is meant to be an interpretation of the story of Jeroboam .... The Non-P historian, unlike the author of Nehemiah, is willing to sacrifice grammar and narrative context to insure that monarchy looms in the background of any interpretation of the golden calf in Exodus 32" (Dozeman, *Exodus*, 687). I have doubts about this reconstruction, but even if true it would not affect my argument here.

to God in the midst of one crisis, "What shall I do with this people? They are almost ready to stone me" (Exod 17:4). But Moses enters into God's presence regularly, and, overall, Moses enjoys profound communion with God: "the Lord used to speak to Moses face to face, as a man speaks to his friend" (Exod 33:11). Moses sees God pass before him and proclaim his divine glory, although Moses does not see God's "face" (Exod 33:20). Moses' own face shines with the reflection of God (Exod 34:29).[46]

On the other hand, the portrait painted in the book of Numbers makes clear that Moses suffered grievously. Dennis Olson comments, "In Numbers 11–25, death, disorder, and rebellion suddenly overwhelm the pages of Numbers with dead bodies of a whole generation of Israelites strewn along

---

46. Paul refers to Moses' shining face when he compares the Mosaic law with the outpouring of the Holy Spirit, arguing that the Mosaic law was great but the Spirit's outpouring is far greater—because ultimately the law brings condemnation but the Spirit brings life. Paul asks rhetorically, "Now if the dispensation of death, carved in letters on stone, came with such splendor that the Israelites could not look at Moses' face because of its brightness, fading as this was, will not the dispensation of the Spirit be attended with greater splendor?" (2 Cor 3:7-8). For historical-critical exegetical discussion of 2 Corinthians 3:7-18, see Matera, *II Corinthians*, 85-97, indebted to Stockhausen, *Moses' Veil*. Matera's central point is that "it is not Paul's purpose to denigrate the ministry of Moses, even though he uses the language of death and condemnation to describe it [in light of Ezekiel 36-37]. Rather the primary purpose of his argument is to show that if there was glory attached to the ministry of death and condemnation, then there is all the more reason for confidence about the ministry of the Spirit and of righteousness that he exercises. . . . Paul can call the Mosaic ministry a ministry of death because, even though its prescriptions embodied God's will, they were frustrated by the power of sin, which used them to bring people to death. Although this is true, it should be noted that Paul is not making a comparison between the law and the Spirit here but between two ministries, *both* of which ultimately have God's law in view. The difference between them is that Paul's new covenant ministry brings life, because it is vivified by the Spirit, who writes the law on the hearts of God's people, whereas the Mosaic ministry of the old covenant cannot bring life, because the law it announces is written in letters on tablets of stone" (Matera, *II Corinthians*, 86, 88). Paul is aware that many Israelites of the past, including Moses, were blessed and beloved of God, and also that many members of the Corinthian church are unrepentant sinners. See also the approaches to 2 Corinthians 3-4 found in R. B. Hays, *Echoes of Scripture*, 125-55; Watson, *Paul and the Hermeneutics of Faith*, 281-313; and Blackwell, *Christosis*, chapter 6. Hays argues that Paul's meaning is that the person "who turns to the Lord [Christ] and finds the veil taken away will return to the reading of Moses [i.e. the Torah] to discover that all of Scripture is a vast metaphorical witness to the lived reality of the new community in Christ" (*Echoes of Scripture*, 151). Comparing Paul's reading of Exodus to that of his Jewish near-contemporaries Josephus and (especially) Philo, Watson notes that from the Pauline perspective, "readings of Exodus that celebrate the advent of the law will be characterized by a certain evasiveness. They will tend to conceal the darker side of the event [visible in the golden calf episode of Exodus 32], in which the reception of the gift turns a blessing into a curse" (*Paul and the Hermeneutics of Faith*, 299).

the desert road of Israel's forty-year sojourn."[47] The book of Numbers tells of terrible insurrections against Moses' leadership. His own brother and sister, Aaron and Miriam, rise up against him (Num 12). A rebellion led by Korah, Dathan, and Abiram takes place and is put down with severe loss of life (Num 16). The whole congregation, lacking trust in God's power, fears to enter the promised land due to the strength of the inhabitants of the land. Eventually the whole congregation, living in Moabite and Midianite territory, comes to worship the Baal of Peor, the Moabite god (Num 25). God sends terrible plagues and deadly sicknesses, killing thousands, upon the people as punishment for their various sins. Furthermore, in performing a miracle of causing water to pour forth from a rock, Moses fails to give credit to God. God punishes him by telling him that neither Moses nor Aaron will enter the promised land (Num 20:12), a severe punishment for a man whose sole mission had been to lead the people of Israel into the promised land.[48]

Why does all this suffering and death take place after the people's liberation from Egyptian slavery and persecution? Given that the book of Exodus shows that Israel's God has absolute power over life and death and wishes to give his covenantal people the fullness of life, why are the ensuing years so miserable? It may easily appear that it would have been better for that generation of Israelites to remain slaves in Egypt, where they might have suffered less.[49] Were the people essentially correct when they com-

---

47. Olson, *Numbers*, 8. In Olson's view, "much of the book of Numbers was written in light of the experience of exile from Babylon and perhaps was written early in the return to the promised land of Judah" (Olson, *Numbers*, 8).

48. For various ways of reading Numbers, see the chapters devoted to Numbers 10–12, Numbers 15–16, and Numbers 25 in Briggs, *Theological Hermeneutics*. See also the observations regarding Numbers in Sonderegger, *Doctrine of God*, 281: "Such compressed misery; such jealousy and envy; such hunger and thirst; such emptiness. The book of Numbers of has placed us solidly within a world of suffering and hardship, a landscape stretched over with pain." Sonderegger recognizes that this world is the real world: "The harsh environment of Numbers resembles, in its very disorder, repetition, and larger order, human life itself" (*Doctrine of God*, 276).

49. See also the exchange between Jon D. Levenson and Jorge V. Pixley in Bellis and Kaminsky, eds., *Jews, Christians*; Levenson, "Liberation Theology"; Pixley, "History and Particularity"; and Levenson, "Perils of Engaged Scholarship." Levenson emphasizes, "If the exodus were an expression of only 'the preferential option for the poor,' the story would be rather different from the one we know from the Bible. First, *all* the slaves and oppressed of Egypt, indeed of the entire world, would be released, and not just the Israelites. Second, the newly freed would remain in the countries in which they had been enslaved, only under a new social and political system" ("Liberation Theology," 223). Instead, says Levenson, we should look to "the chosenness of Israel" and the fulfillment of the promise about the land ("Liberation Theology," 223). He explains, "That from which God liberates Israel is the condition of exile in Egypt and the dehumanizing enslavement to Pharaoh. That *for* which he liberates them is life in the promised land and

plained bitterly to Moses at the very outset of the exodus, "Is it because there are no graves in Egypt that you have taken us away to die in the wilderness? What have you done to us, in bringing us out of Egypt? Is not this what we said to you in Egypt, 'Let us alone and let us serve the Egyptians'?" (Exod 14:11–12).[50]

In response, I note that during Israel's exodus journey, God gives his people three revelations that change the character of their sufferings. First, he shows them the full extent of his power over life and death, power that flows from his nature as "I am"—the Creator God. He displays this power in redeeming the Israelites from Egyptian slavery despite Pharaoh's earthly preeminence. Second, God reveals a life-giving law, with its core of ten commandments by which all aspects of Israel's life are measured. Third, God reveals to them a new possibility of intimate covenantal friendship with God, as when the elders of Israel eat and drink in his presence.

Yet, as shown above, the people on the exodus frequently do not trust God, obey his law, or desire his friendship. The people continue to endure the consequences of fallenness, just as all peoples before them. Still in their sins, they still suffer and die. The book of Exodus presents their sufferings as divine punishments (imposed by God), and in a sense their sufferings are such—since the people turn away from the giver of life. But of course

---

the ennobling and sanctifying service of himself that is its precondition. The people Israel perform that service by obeying the commandments that God has given them.... [The exodus] is a movement from one form of servitude to another, from the service of a brutal, self-interested tyrant to the service of a kind, loving, and generous monarch, YHWH, God of Israel" ("Liberation Theology," 226–27). Given the fact that this God cares for his whole creation, Levenson recognizes that there are also universal implications to the exodus. A longer version of "Liberation Theology" appears as "Exodus and Liberation," in Levenson's *Hebrew Bible*, 127–59. Levenson is responding to Pixley, *On Exodus*. Bellis and Kaminsky, eds., *Jews, Christians* also includes a further exchange: see Collins, "Exodus and Biblical Theology"; Levenson, "Exodus and Biblical Theology." See also Walzer, *Exodus and Revolution*. For background to the ongoing discussion, see Gregerman, "Old Wine in New Bottles."

50. Rabbi Held comments on this passage: "Overcome with fear, the Israelites turn on Moses with a vengeance, insisting that continued slavery in Egypt would have been better than being slaughtered in the wilderness. We feel the pathos of the moment. Oppression in Egypt was horrific, but at least it was familiar" (Held, *Heart of Torah* I, 155). In Held's view, the problem is that the Israelites still have a passive slave mentality. When Moses responds to their accusation by telling them that they need only trust God, Held suggests that God corrects Moses sharply by saying, "Why do you cry to me? Tell the sons of Israel to go forward" (Exod 14:15). Held argues: "God says in effect, 'don't tell them to be passive.... You can't leave Egypt—not really—until you discover that you can take responsibility for your life and affect your own fate'" (Held, *Heart of Torah* I, 157). Held grants, of course, that in Exodus the people's fate really does hinge solely or almost solely upon God's powerful action. Since this is so, I read Moses' counsel to the people more positively than does Held.

their sufferings are easily recognizable and, as history shows, are intrinsic to the fallen human condition in the midst of trials. Within their all-too-familiar sufferings, they receive God's demonstration of his power over life and death in redeeming them from Egyptian slavery, God's gift of his law, and God's invitation to enter into intimate friendship with him. These revelations constitute them as a nation in the world, under God's rule.

But do these revelations really *matter*, given the continuance of such terrible suffering and death? Does it matter that the Israelites on the exodus (as Pope Benedict XVI says of Christians) "belong to a new society which is the goal of their common pilgrimage and which is anticipated in the course of that pilgrimage"?[51] Let me now turn to this "political" question, aided by Jonathan Sacks.[52] But let me anticipate my own answer: the redemption from slavery to suffering and death must ultimately be tied to God's work of nation-building—specifically, God's building up of his eschatological kingdom.

III. Rabbi Jonathan Sacks: The Establishment of the Nation of Israel

Sacks takes as his starting point the fact that in the book of Genesis, God relates to individuals and to families; whereas in the book of Exodus, the Israelites become a *nation* that shares, however imperfectly, in "a covenant of love" with the living God.[53] On Mount Sinai, Sacks says, "the Israelites

---

51. Benedict XVI, *Spe Salvi*, §4, p. 15. In this perspective, even though the coming of Jesus Christ and the outpouring the Spirit open up a new dimension of Israel's life, now reconfigured around the Messiah, Walter Brueggemann is surely onto something when he says: "If Christians are to think with theological seriousness about the church as the partner of the sovereign, faithful God, then it seems clear that the same thematics pertain to that relationship as pertain to Israel as Yahweh's partner: the same assurances, the same demands, the same costs, and the same surprises. It strikes me that for all the polemics that sustain supersessionism, the truth is that these two communities, because they face the same God, share the same reassuring, demanding life. It is perhaps with such realization that Franz Rosenzweig could dare to imagine that were both communities honest, they would recognize that they live parallel histories, with the same hopes to hope and the same obediences to obey" (Brueggemann, *Theology of the Old Testament*, 449). I think that the word "same" is an exaggeration but nonetheless the basic point is correct.

52. Brueggemann, *Theology of the Old Testament*, 446. See also Levenson, *Resurrection*.

53. Sacks, *Letter in the Scroll*, 86. Sacks adds, "Judaism has often been seen—notoriously by Christianity—as a religion of law and justice rather than of love and compassion. This is quite untrue. To be sure, Judaism is a religion of law and justice between human beings, because only where there is law can there be a just society, and Judaism

became an *edah*, a body politic, as opposed to an *am*, a people with shared ancestry and history. Their assent to the covenant turned them into a nation under the sovereignty of God whose written constitution was the Torah."[54]

In this section, I will focus upon Sacks's *Exodus: The Book of Redemption*, a volume that collects his brief commentaries on the weekly Torah portions from the book of Exodus in the Jewish liturgy. At the outset of his book, Sacks examines the inspiration that the book of Exodus has given to the oppressed over the centuries, and he also underscores the liberative power of "the message of monotheism" in its biblical form.[55] He ties Moses to later figures such as Martin Luther King Jr. The living God is on the side of the powerless.

Sacks does not comment much upon the suffering and humiliation of the Israelites on the exodus journey. Instead, the main point of his book is that through the gift of the law and through the divinely commissioned leadership of Moses, "the Jewish project takes on substance and form" as it moves from the individuals and families of Genesis to the fully constituted nation of Israel.[56] In his view, the "Jewish project" is not about individuals or families; it is about a nation, about political life together, about the right use of power. The book of Exodus critiques the politics of Egypt and introduces, instead, the covenantal politics of a nation that stands under God's judgment and rule, and that must therefore defend the powerless and uphold the equal dignity of each member of the nation.

In my view, this political emphasis is only part of the story, but it certainly reflects a central dimension of the book of Exodus.[57] Recalling God's

---

is nothing if not a religion of society. But between God and man there is a bond of love.... It is no accident that the Bible takes marriage as its central metaphor for the relationship between man and God" (Sacks, *Letter in the Scroll*, 86, 88). On self-sacrificial love in Judaism, see also Shatz, "Ego, Love, and Self-Sacrifice." For Sacks's discussion of this theme, see *To Heal a Fractured World*, 30–56. See also David Berger's comment, "For centuries, even millennia, Christian authors depicted Judaism as a legalistic religion indifferent to considerations of loving-kindness and grace. As Paul succinctly puts it, 'The letter kills, but the spirit gives life' (2 Cor. 3:6)" (Berger, "Texts, Values, and Historical Change," 202). This is a misunderstanding of Paul, but I recognize with deep regret that Christian authors did indeed regularly describe Judaism in this way.

54. Sacks, *To Heal a Fractured World*, 87.
55. Sacks, *Exodus*, 1.
56. Sacks, *Exodus*, 2. On the history and theory of political life, linked with reflections on Judaism, see Sacks, *Politics of Hope*.
57. See also Sacks's polemical point, oft repeated in his corpus, that "Christianity and Islam both insisted that theirs was the only true path of worship—that one God is to be served in one way. Judaism is structurally unique—the only world religion ever to believe in a universal God, the God of all peoples, times and places, and at the same time to believe in a particular way of life that not all people have to follow, because just

promise in Genesis 15 to make of (childless) Abraham a great nation, Sacks shows how the book of Exodus exhibits the fulfillment of this promise. He emphasizes the revelation of the one God whose sovereignty is not locally limited.[58] Interpreting the Sinai event in political terms, he considers the covenant at Mount Sinai to be "nothing less than *the first-ever statement of a free society*."[59] The people freely bind themselves to God's law. God

---

as there is more than one way to be a leader, so there is more than one way to find God" (Sacks, *Letter in the Scroll*, 90; see also Sacks, *Future Tense*, 74). Of course, Judaism nonetheless traditionally found Christianity and Islam to be false paths, even if perhaps acceptable paths for the gentiles. Sacks grants that "Israel's message is a universal one" and that all nations are called to hear it (Sacks, *Future Tense*, 76). Asking why Israel did not attempt to convert the nations, Sacks argues that the answer is that *"humans* [e.g., Christians and Muslims] *impose uniformity; God makes space for difference*" (*Future Tense*, 79). This strikes me as an exaggeration of the actual message of the Hebrew Bible, in which the nations are generally presented as idolatrous, not "different" in a positive way. But I can agree with Sacks's broader point: "Any attempt to impose a single vision on the world, or even on a single society, is fundamentally untrue to the human condition and leads to massive and unacceptable loss of liberty" (*To Heal a Fractured World*, 107). To think of Christianity as a monochrome "single vision," or as something to be "imposed," is to misunderstand Christianity; on this point see von Balthasar, *Truth Is Symphonic*.

58. In *Future Tense*, Sacks makes a conceptual distinction between God and YHWH. He describes "God" or "*Elokim*" as "the totality of forces operative in the universe" (*Future Tense*, 218). To me, that sounds like a creature (the worship of the universe's cosmic energies), not God. Sacks comments, "The heroes of the Hebrew Bible do not encounter God merely as Dylan Thomas's 'force that through the green fuse drives the flower', or as Matthew Arnold's 'the eternal not ourselves that makes for righteousness'. They meet him as personal presence, the One who hears our cry, notes our deeds, who calls to us and who listens when we call to him. That is *Hashem*, the God of revelation and particularity, the God of the priests who summons Israel to become a holy nation, and of the prophets who charges them with the work of righteousness and justice, love and compassion.... The God of creation, *Elokim*, is universal. The God of revelation, *Hashem*, is particular" (Sacks, *Future Tense*, 218–19). As defined by Sacks, however, the "God of creation" would not be worth knowing or encountering, because he is merely the totality of universal energies—not the free, personal, transcendent, and immanent God.

59. Sacks, *Exodus*, 11. Sacks recognizes that eventually the Israelites received a priestly (Levitical) and royal (Davidic) hierarchy. He argues, however, that the early rabbinic sages go beyond this: "In a vaulting leap of imagination . . . the sages saw that the political threat to Israel under Roman rule could be countered, spiritually and educationally, by a full implementation of the biblical ideal, a society of equals. Even if there should come a time when there would be no more kings or (functioning) priests, still the 'crown of Torah' would remain" (Sacks, *Exodus*, 212). According to Sacks, the key was universal education. He explains, "It was, of course, not the production of intellectuals that motivated the Judaic love of learning, but rather the idea that a society structured around divine law should be one in which everyone had equal access to knowledge and therefore equal dignity as citizens in the republic of faith" (Sacks, *Exodus*, 214–15). The mention of "faith" here is significant for Sacks: as he comments

rules them not to enslave them, but to enable all of them to become kings and priests of God, in the dignity of full partnership.⁶⁰ At Sinai, political order is grounded not in a human hierarchy but in free consent to God's law. The ten commandments show that this politics oppresses no one; instead, Israel receives the fundaments of human decency. The covenant is not merely an external political order but also extends to the people's interior lives as a "moral and spiritual code."⁶¹ Rooted in justice and free consent, the covenant provides a real alternative to hierarchical societies and organic societies.

For Sacks, the lessons of the book of Exodus, especially with regard to the covenantal partnership of the people with God,⁶² were not fully retained by either Christianity or Islam. He does not think that Christianity and Islam allow for God really to have a partner. Likewise, in his view, Christianity and Islam do not fully retain human freedom vis-à-vis God.⁶³

---

in *Future Tense*, 69, "Judaism is not an ethnicity, a culture, a set of folkways, a defiance of antisemitism or political correctness plus a *yarmulkah* (cap) and Jewish jokes. It is a faith, and the people who are in a state of denial about this are Jews. It was as a faith that Jews were born as a people, and it is as a faith that Jews will survive as a people."

60. See Sacks's comments in *To Heal a Fractured World*, 154–60. He argues, "Insofar . . . as we can speak of an overarching theme for the Hebrew Bible, it is the story of the transfer of initiative from heaven to earth, from God to humankind, from caring father to wayward but slowly maturing child. . . . The implication is simple: passive dependence on God inhibits religious maturity. Just as, in Jewish law, a child is bound by the command to honour its parents only when he or she is no longer a child (12 for a girl, 13 for a boy), so Israel only learned to honour God when it accepted responsibility" (Sacks, *To Heal a Fractured World*, 155). On this reading, the sins committed by Israel in biblical times belong to Israel's rebellious adolescence, which Israel, now a mature adult, has outgrown (aided by God's unbreakable covenantal love). Sacks understands Jeremiah 31's prophecy of a new covenant to have been fulfilled by the study of Torah and by the formation of Oral Torah. Yet, even in maturity, humans are never autonomous: "The existence of a covenant with God means that all human sovereignty is delegated, conditional and constitutional" (Sacks, *To Heal a Fractured World*, 167). See also Jacob Schacter, "Halakhic Authority," 168.

61. Sacks, *Exodus*, 11. In response to the 1994 terrorist attack by a religious Jew against Muslims in Hebron, Sacks urges his fellow Jews, "You experienced injustice, therefore practise justice. You know what it is like to be a slave, therefore do not enslave others. You have been victims, therefore you may not be oppressors. . . . We did not survive Pharaoh so that we could become like Pharaoh" (Sacks, *Faith in the Future*, 102).

62. Sacks gives a central place to this theme of partnership in *Exodus*, 330.

63. For further analysis of human freedom as defended by Judaism against any kind of determinism, see Sacks, *Tradition in an Untraditional Age*, 203–18. See also Sacks, *To Heal a Fractured World*, 189–201. Sacks emphasizes, "Judaism is a faith suffused with love, but infinitely transcending man's love of God is *God's love of humankind*. . . . [Out of love] he suffers every time human beings wrong one another, yet he is prepared to suffer rather than take back from humankind the gift of freedom he bestowed on us" (*To Heal a Fractured World*, 199).

The Jewish people alone witness to both God's fidelity to a real partnership and to God's transcendence.

I do not agree with Sacks's view of Christianity,[64] but he is onto something important when he identifies the "subtext" of the book of Exodus as a combination of theocentrism and covenantal partnership. He notes that Exodus contains numerous paired narratives, in which "*the first is the work of God alone, while the second involves a human contribution.*"[65] Without the latter (human participation), the work of God cannot be sustained; without the former (God's work), humans remain in a state of enslavement that paralyzes them.[66] A covenantal politics involves both God's liberative action and the necessary partnership of the people with God in sustaining freedom and justice.

Sacks approvingly notes that the book of Exodus recognizes the human flaws of the Israelites. The Jewish authors who wrote the book of Exodus were not triumphalistic about the achievements of their people or rulers. Instead, the book of Exodus sets forth a mission, a journey toward an ideal covenantal politics that will take many generations to be perfected. Nevertheless, the people are able to share in the perfected goal each Sabbath, which is why Sabbath-keeping is central in the book of Exodus. Sacks observes, "*On Shabbat we rehearse utopia*, or what Judaism came later to call the messianic age."[67] In this utopia, there are no masters, no work, no

---

64. Sacks also mistakenly claims that Christianity believes in a divine revelation made not to a people but to one man, the divine Son. Sacks is generally not an accurate interpreter of Christianity; see for example the misleading antinomies between Judaism and "Christianity" that he presents in *Great Partnership*, 62–66.

65. Sacks, *Exodus*, 15. Sacks clarifies this point: "To occupy holy space or time is to renounce human creativity so as to be existentially open to divine creativity," because "nothing in holiness is the result of human initiative" (*Exodus*, 141). Theologically, he states, "*Holiness is the space we make for God.* In the simplest and most elegant way, holiness is to humanity what *tzimtzum* is to God. Just as God effaces Himself to make space for mankind, so we renounce ourselves to make space for God" (Sacks, *Exodus*, 141). Indebted to the rabbinic sages, he adds that "it is precisely when we renounce our will in favour of the will of God, as we do on Shabbat, that we become God's partners in creation" (Sacks, *Exodus*, 205).

66. See also Sacks's meditation "Awakening from Above." He goes on to argue that the Written Torah is divine communication, whereas the Oral Torah is a divine-human partnership (see Sacks, *Exodus*, 275; see also Sacks, *To Heal a Fractured World*, 157–59).

67. Sacks, *Exodus*, 17. Sacks makes clear that "Tanakh, the Hebrew Bible, is not a code for Utopia. That is a prophetic dream, not a present-tense reality. In the here-and-now, however, the Torah tells us something not without moral grandeur: that small gestures of mutual assistance can in the long run transform the human situation" (Sacks, *Exodus*, 165). But he adds in a later meditation, titled "The Sabbath: First Day or Last?": "The Sabbath is not simply a day of rest. It is an anticipation of 'the end of history,' the messianic age. On it, we recover the lost harmonies of the Garden of Eden.... The

hierarchy, and no strife; "all are equal and all are free."[68] God will bring about this perfect politics, but each generation of Israelites must take up the work of advancing toward it, by instantiating as perfect a politics as possible and by boldly "travelling the long road to freedom" in response to "the call of God."[69]

Having offered this overview of the book of Exodus and its significance, Sacks in the remainder of his book offers short meditations that follow the narrative of Exodus. He begins with the refusal of the midwives to obey Pharaoh's command to kill the Israelite male babies. He points out that in Egypt such disobedience was practically unthinkable, because Pharaoh ruled as a god, or at least a designate of god. He praises the opening of Exodus for calling slavery into question, beginning the long path toward its abolition. In the nation of Israel, such civil disobedience continued: the kings were regularly denounced by the prophets for their injustice.

Other meditations address the call of Moses. Sacks suggests that Moses burned with a zeal for justice and a desire to know why the innocent suffer. After his first attempt at persuasion causes Pharaoh to worsen the condition of the Israelites, Moses accuses God: "O Lord, why have you done evil to this people? Why did you ever send me? For since I came to Pharaoh to speak in your name, he has done evil to this people, and you have not delivered your people at all" (Exod 5:22–23). Sacks points out that this quest for justice cannot intrinsically be part of paganism or modern secularism, since the latter two worldviews assume that the powerful will win. If there is no just God, it is foolish to expect that justice will be done to the powerless.

Sabbath is a full dress rehearsal for an ideal society that has not yet come to pass, but will do, because we know what we are aiming for—because we experienced it at the beginning" (*Exodus*, 281–82). See also Sacks, *Faith in the Future*, 132–37, where he argues that the Sabbath is "a day dedicated to thinking about the purpose of what we do" and therefore to contemplating and praising the Creator (132; cf. 137). He again adds a mystical note: "For those who observe it Shabbat becomes a way back into Eden, paradise temporarily regained. Peace in the home is where world peace begins, so that for Jewish mystics the seventh day was a kind of cosmic wedding and the Sabbath itself was the bride" (*Faith in the Future*, 133). He goes on to reflect upon the Sabbath's ecological and political meanings, remarking that "no one who observes the Sabbath can ever forget what it is to be free" (*Faith in the Future*, 136).

68. Sacks, *Exodus*, 17. I agree with Ellen Davis when she comments, "it should be noted that Exodus enjoins Sabbath observance on theological, not pastoral, grounds. The reason to keep Sabbath is that we should not go more than a few days in a row without stopping to consider what it is to be the creatures of God, living among other creatures in a world that God has made. We are not our own, and we are not in charge" (*Opening Israel's Scriptures*, 56). In her discussion of "Becoming God's People—Exodus 16–40," she recognizes that Israel moves from being a family to being a people, but she does not attend to nation-building (though she does see Israel as the antitype to Egypt).

69. Sacks, *Exodus*, 17.

In God's plan, pain and suffering may have a good purpose, but our task is to denounce unjust pain and suffering in this world and to beg God to remedy it. We must "fight slavery, tyranny, poverty and disease" and thereby "become God's partners in the work of redemption."[70]

Another set of meditations concentrates upon the Passover, beginning with the four cups of wine at the Seder. Everyone, no matter how poor, must be enabled by the community to drink these four cups, which represent stages of redemption. There is also a fifth cup, which stands for the possession of the land, but that is optional to drink. After the exile of the Jewish people by the Romans, having lost "freedom, a land, a home," how could the Jewish people continue to celebrate the Passover and the entrance into the promised land?[71] In raising this question, Sacks addresses the post-biblical sufferings of the Jewish people. He answers, "Memory was transfigured into hope," namely, a hope that God would liberate his people once again and restore them to the land.[72]

Addressing the question of why Pharaoh's heart was hardened, Sacks reasons that Pharaoh fell into evildoing and was enslaved by it. We can sin so deeply that we essentially, even if not entirely, lose our freedom to do otherwise. Not the Israelites but Pharaoh "was the real slave."[73] Sacks draws the moral that those who are being persecuted do not have to accept the oppressor's claim that they have no freedom.[74]

Sacks defends the tenth plague, in which God commands the killing of the Egyptian firstborn. Sacks argues that this is a display of retributive

---

70. Sacks, *Exodus*, 40. Sacks makes clear that he considers Jews to have made important achievements in this regard. He states, "Numerically we are small, but in terms of our contributions to civilization and humankind, we are vast. . . . But it is, of course, the Jewish contribution to the life of the spirit that is not only unique but has shaped the entire course of Western civilization. Somehow this tiny people produced an unceasing flow of patriarchs, priests, poets and prophets, masters of halakha and *aggada*, codifiers and commentators, philosophers and mystics, sages and saints, in a way that almost defies comprehension" (Sacks, *Exodus*, 267–268).

71. Sacks, *Exodus*, 45.

72. Sacks, *Exodus*, 46.

73. Sacks, *Exodus*, 50.

74. See also Sacks's comments on Passover in *Faith in the Future*. He describes Passover as "the Jewish festival of freedom," and he emphasizes, "The redemption brought about by Moses was not something that happened in the privacy of the soul. It was a political revolution, an event that changed the history of a people. They had been slaves in Egypt. Now they were free human beings, travelling through the desert on the way to their own land. A free God wants the free worship of free human beings" (*Faith in the Future*, 138–39). He adds a political implication: "every time we help the poor to escape from poverty, or give the homeless a home or cause the unheeded to be heard we bring God's kingdom one step closer" (Sacks, *Faith in the Future*, 140).

justice, a display that is necessary for evildoers to hear. The tenth plague is linked with the earlier plagues in which God showed that, due to Pharaoh's evildoing, the life-giving land and the life-giving Nile were producing the signs of death. Sacks draws the lesson: "reality has an ethical structure. . . . If used for evil ends, the powers of nature will turn against man, so that what he does will be done to him in turn. There is justice in history."[75] The problem was a political one: the profound injustice of Pharaoh, building his empire upon slaves and commanding the death of the Israelite firstborn. God has the power to overturn and repay such evil empires. Sacks comments, "The best test of a civilization is to see how it treats children, its own and others."[76]

Commenting on Exodus 12–13, Sacks notes that Moses' speech on the eve of the exodus directs attention to the future, to the coming generations who are to be taught about this event (the Passover). He gives a political interpretation of Moses' speech: what Moses is teaching is that freedom requires education, forming our intellect and will by recalling history.[77] He recognizes that people—including Jews—can feel as though the law is a burden. But a proper understanding of freedom will recognize that a just law makes true freedom possible.[78]

For Sacks, as we have seen, the book of Exodus describes a deeply contemporary political reality: the nation of Israel. It does not primarily describe a spiritual journey or offer a topography of human alienation from

---

75. Sacks, *Exodus*, 74.

76. Sacks, *Exodus*, 75.

77. Politically, Sacks thinks that the result is a democratized society in which everyone has access to knowledge. See also, for similar points, Sacks, *Letter in the Scroll*, 163–69; Sacks, *Dignity of Difference*, 125–41.

78. Sacks knows that in a certain sense "Judaism emphasizes the work of God," but, again, he wants to suggest that actually Judaism's fundamental emphasis consists in "God's call to us to accept responsibility and become, with him, co-authors of the script of history, his partners in the work of creation" (Sacks, *To Heal a Fractured World*, 134–35). Sacks goes so far as to describe "responsibility" as the Torah's "greatest overarching theme" (Sacks, *To Heal a Fractured World*, 135). In making this case, he offers an interpretation of Genesis 2–4 as the discovery and unfolding of freedom and moral responsibility; and he reads the story of Noah as revealing the fact that one cannot "survive" morally without coming to the aid of one's neighbors. He shows, too, that the meaning of the Babel story is the impossibility of "construct[ing] a self-sufficient universe . . . in which man is accountable only to himself" (Sacks, *To Heal a Fractured World*, 144). He goes on to observe that the Torah "ends as it began, with choice, freedom and responsibility. In the beginning it was the choice of individuals—Adam and Eve, then Cain—now it is the choice of the nation as a whole [Deut 30]" (Sacks, *To Heal a Fractured World*, 178).

the God who seeks out his people in order to overcome their alienation.[79] Highlighting two "arcs" in the book of Exodus—the first one more political (from Egypt to Sinai) and the second one more spiritual (the construction of the tabernacle and the regulations for the Sabbath)—Sacks considers even the "second arc" to be fundamentally political, having to do with "the place of God in society."[80] In the conclusion of his book, Sacks identifies a third "arc," whose presence is only discernable at the end of Exodus: namely, the unity of the books of Genesis and Exodus as a single story, in which the construction of the tabernacle mirrors the creation of the universe, the journey of Abraham mirrors the journey of Moses, and God's forgiveness of Adam and Eve mirrors God's forgiveness of Israel.[81] This third "arc" is "a way back from sin to harmony, exile to return."[82] But for Sacks the key element even of this third "arc" is political, since the movement is from the created order, to the chaos of sin, to the restored order of an "ideal society" or nation built upon "*ordered liberty*, brought about by the rule of law."[83]

In treating the tabernacle (Exod 25), Sacks makes clear that "the Divine Presence lives not in a building but in its builders; not in a physical place but in the human heart."[84] He adds that this is the answer—or at least the "fragment of the answer"—to the haunting question of "where was God at Auschwitz?"[85] Oppressors can control human bodies but not the human

---

79. For an interpretation that coheres with Sacks's, see J. A. Berman, *Created Equal*. See also Yoram Hazony's argument that the Bible "presents the covenant of Abraham, and later on the Mosaic law, as a response to the nature of political states and their rulers *in general*" (Hazony, *Philosophy of Hebrew Scripture*, 140–41).

80. Sacks, *Exodus*, 332. Sacks appreciates that the Sanctuary is "a visible symbol of the presence of God in the midst of the people," but he emphasizes the way in which the joint project of building the sanctuary solidified the unity of the new nation of Israel (Sacks, *Exodus*, 332).

81. See Sacks, *Exodus*, 334–36. For further background, focused on the tabernacle, see L. M. Morales, *Tabernacle Prefigured*.

82. Sacks, *Exodus*, 336.

83. Sacks, *Exodus*, 337. Sacks concludes, "Genesis-Exodus is a single literary unit, in which the meaning of the universe and our place within it is explored through a series of dramas, some personal, others political, yet adding up to a momentous proposition: that just as God created order in the universe, so we are called on to create order in our personal lives and in society as a whole" (Sacks, *Exodus*, 337).

84. Sacks, *Exodus*, 192. Sacks goes on to offer a strong critique of the temple, arguing that the way in which Solomon conscripted laborers and levied taxes to build the temple caused profound resentment among the Israelites, represented something like a return to Egypt, and led to the division of Israel into two kingdoms. See also Sacks's meditation "Home We Make for God," where he notes (indebted to numerous commentators) that God's making of the universe in Genesis 1:1–2:3 is paralleled by God's commands regarding the making of the tabernacle in Exodus 25, 39–40.

85. Sacks, *Faith in the Future*, 143. Earlier he states that "the greatest pain is to seek

spirit.⁸⁶ Thus, even while Sacks emphasizes the nation's political life, he does not draw an opposition between nation-building and God's saving presence. On the contrary, he understands the purpose of the nation—including the contemporary State of Israel⁸⁷—to be the establishment of a place for God's presence, in partnership with God. He states, "Judaism is a religion of ritual, of repeated daily deeds. It is a religion of holiness whose focus is the house of worship."⁸⁸ Individuals, by themselves, cannot embody God's presence as God wishes it to be embodied. Thus the *nation's* purpose is "to build a home for the Divine Presence."⁸⁹ For this reason, Israel was even able to remain a nation after losing its sovereignty and its land. Indeed, despite its communal and individual failures, Israel "will always refuse to worship anything less than God Himself."⁹⁰

God and not to be able to find Him"; and in this context he poses similarly haunting questions to God: "When the Temple was destroyed, where were You? When Your sages and saints were put to death as martyrs, where were You? When Your people were dispersed and scattered and exiled and forced to wander homeless across the earth, where were You? When they were tortured and murdered for their faith, where were You? Almighty God, when Your people cried out to You from Auschwitz and Bergen-Belsen and Sohibor and Maidanek, where were You? When one million Jewish children were gassed, burned or buried alive, where were You?" (Sacks, *Faith in the Future*, 93–94).

86. Hitler wanted to destroy Judaism, but Hitler's power failed and, indeed, the State of Israel rose from the ashes. Sacks contends that the return of the Jewish people to the land of Israel and the establishment of the State of Israel have a profound religious significance. Citing Joseph B. Soloveitchik, he suggests an eschatological meaning for the establishment of the State of Israel: "God had re-entered history. It was the beginning of the end of exile. This century [the twentieth century], one after another of the prophecies of Moses and Isaiah has come true. All except one. The Jewish people always knew that this would be the last of the promises to come true. Therefore, in our prayers it was always the last: 'Lord who blesses His people Israel with peace'" (*Faith in the Future*, 95).

87. With respect to Israeli political, economic, and military decisions, Sacks comments in a 2012 interview: "The prophet cannot be an armchair philosopher or a critic from the sidelines. Since I do not live in the State of Israel, I've been profoundly reluctant to tell Israelis how Israel should be structured" (Sacks, "Interview," 121). See also Sacks, *Not in God's Name*, 260–61.

88. Sacks, *Exodus*, 223.

89. Sacks, *Exodus*, 291.

90. Sacks, *Exodus*, 146. See also Sacks's meditation on "A Stiff-Necked People," in which he cites rabbinic sayings (and historical examples) that appreciatively emphasize the obstinacy of the people of Israel in refusing to cease being Jews, despite the pressure put on them by their persecutors over the centuries (see *Exodus*, 251–58). At the same time, Sacks repeatedly warns against "the belief that those who do not share my faith—or my race or my ideology—do not share my humanity. At best they are second-class citizens. At worst they forfeit the sanctity of life itself. They are the unsaved, the unbelievers, the infidel, the unredeemed; they stand outside the circle of salvation. If faith is what makes us human, then those who do not share my faith are less than fully human. From this equation flowed the Crusades, the Inquisitions, the jihads, the

Sacks contends that in receiving the Mosaic law and attempting to follow it, Judaism has undertaken a unique and uniquely valuable "act of sacrifice," one involving obedience to a set of concrete laws.[91] This mission has begun but only *just* begun. The exodus journey of the nation of Israel continues. Commenting upon Exodus 40, Sacks observes, "In Jewish history, even an encampment is called a journey. So long as we have not yet reached our destination, even a place of rest is merely temporary. There is a way still to go."[92] Today as in the ancient past, Jews understand that their only security in this world consists in journeying in faith with the God who has made covenant with them and to whom the Torah testifies.[93]

Since journeying *with God* is the center of Jewish life, it should be clear that Sacks does not reduce the book of Exodus or Judaism itself merely to human politics or economics. In *The Great Partnership*, he states: "Politics, in the Abrahamic vision, is not the highest good. It is not where we meet God, not where we construct our deepest relationships, not where we exercise our highest virtues."[94] In *To Heal a Fractured World*, he celebrates *hesed* ("covenant love") for "its power to bathe the world in the light of the divine presence" and he writes movingly about God's transcendent love for each and every person and about the necessity of sanctifying God's name

---

pogroms, the blood of human sacrifice through the ages" (Sacks, *Letter in the Scroll*, 91). In *Not in God's Name*, Sacks argues, "*Religion acquires influence when it relinquishes power*. . . . Religion—as understood by Abraham and those who followed him—is at its best when it resists the temptation of politics and opts instead for influence" (235). I agree that "religion" is all this, but what about the Jewish State of Israel? Sacks tries to clarify his meaning: "The real clash of the twenty-first century will not be *between* civilisations or religions, but *within* them. It will be between those who accept and those who reject the separation of religion and power. Those who believe that political problems have religious solutions are deluding themselves as well as failing to understand who Abraham was and what he represented" (Sacks, *Not in God's Name*, 262; cf. Sacks, *Home We Build Together*, 217–27).

91. Sacks, *Exodus*, 205. In a later meditation, Sacks observes that in view of the book of Exodus (in accord with the perspective of the whole Hebrew Bible), "God creates order. Human beings create chaos. It is only when human beings create their own symbolic order—the ark, the Tabernacle—by precise and exacting obedience to God's command, that there is a chance for humanity to survive" (Sacks, *Exodus*, 313). He is indebted to Kugel, *On Being a Jew*.

92. Sacks, *Exodus*, 323. Sacks directs attention to M. Berman, *Wandering God*.

93. See Sacks, *Exodus*, 326, referring to Hasan-Rokem and Dundes, *Wandering Jew*.

94. Sacks, *Great Partnership*, 135. At the same time, Sacks is concerned about the political ramifications of widespread cultural atheism: "I fear for the future of the West if it loses its faith. You cannot defend Western freedom on the basis of moral relativism, the only morality left when we lose our mooring in a sacred ontology or a divine-human covenant" (*Great Partnership*, 109).

by acts of goodness.⁹⁵ Likewise, in *The Dignity of Difference*, he underscores that status before God has nothing to do with economic status: we are "beings of ultimate, non-transactional value" because God has "called us into existence and summoned us to be a blessing."⁹⁶ When he writes about the exodus, however, his focus is God's nation-building, in which the people of Israel participate. The exodus is ultimately about the (gradual) upbuilding of God's kingdom, grounded in God's law, and exhibiting freedom, justice, care for the oppressed, and right worship.

IV. A New Exodus in Christ

As a Christian, I think that the exodus points toward its eschatological completion in a new exodus in Christ, who inaugurates the kingdom of God and who, in his person, is the inbreaking of the kingdom. Like the Jewish people on the exodus, Christians are on a journey to the promised land, not merely as individuals but as the inaugurated kingdom under the headship of Christ. The promised land is none other than the consummated kingdom, the full dwelling of God with creation.

The letter to the Hebrews conveys this point when it connects Christians to Abraham, who "sojourned in the land of promise" while looking "forward to the city which has foundations, whose builder and maker is God" (Heb 11:9–10).⁹⁷ According to Hebrews, Christians are "strangers and exiles on the earth" who are "seeking a homeland" (Heb 11:13–14). This homeland cannot be established by humans but rather will come down from above, as the fruit of God's grace, at Jesus' coming in glory (Rev 21:2).⁹⁸ But, although we still sin, suffer, and die, we have a foretaste of our homeland even now, because Jesus has inaugurated his kingdom by his paschal

---

95. See Sacks, *To Heal a Fractured World*, 45, 56, 57–70, 133, 267–73. See also a remark of Rabbi Abraham Isaac Kook, quoted by Sacks in *To Heal a Fractured World*, 113: "The love for people must be alive in the heart and soul, a love for all people and a love for all nations, expressing itself in a desire for their spiritual and material advancement" (Kook, *Lights of Penitence*, 136).

96. Sacks, *Dignity of Difference*, 158.

97. See Healy, *Hebrews*, 236: "For Abraham's descendants, the summit of the promised land was the holy city, Jerusalem. But even that city was only a shadow and anticipation of the glorious city prepared by God."

98. See Leithart, *Revelation 12–22*, 345: "heaven and earth are united in the bride city who is one Spirit with the Lamb." Leithart underscores the uniting of Jews and Gentiles, as well as the reality of the marriage of God and humankind. Leithart also notes the (graced) cooperation of humans in the coming of the kingdom (see Leithart, *Revelation 12–22*, 347).

mystery. The purpose of our actions in faith and charity, moved by the indwelling Holy Spirit, is to build up the kingdom of God.

Having poured out his Spirit, Jesus is constantly gathering a people who undertake the new exodus journey, guided by the Spirit and nourished by the new manna (the Eucharist) and the living water (baptism). This is what it means to say, as Joseph Ratzinger does in response to Jacob Neusner, that "the community of his disciples is the new Israel."[99] But can Christians discuss the new exodus in Jesus Christ without cutting it off from the exodus as understood by Jonathan Sacks and thus without rejecting ongoing Judaism? As I will discuss further on in this book, I think an important part of the answer consists in Christians appreciating that "for Jews the *land* of Israel and life in this land are matters of faith."[100]

My understanding of the new exodus builds upon Sacks's understanding of the exodus. Christians must grasp the crucial importance of nationhood—and thus kingdom. With respect to the new exodus, Brant Pitre argues that, at his Last Supper, "Jesus revealed to the twelve disciples that he saw himself as the eschatological Passover lamb whose death would inaugurate the eschatological exodus spoken of by the prophets."[101] Similarly, Nicholas Perrin makes the case that Jesus and his disciples understood themselves to be undertaking "a new exodus" whose culmination would be the perfected "land," which would be the perfection of "the communal life" of believers and which would instantiate "the long-awaited final temple" in its eschatological form.[102] In distinct ways, both Pitre and Perrin suggest that the new exodus is marked by believers' sharing in Christ's tribulation (his cross), as "the birth canal through which renewed Israel and renewed creation would emerge."[103]

---

99. Ratzinger, *Jesus of Nazareth* I, 111.

100. M. Barth, *Jesus the Jew*, 93. Markus Barth tries to separate Jewish "life in this land"—which he affirms—from the question of the existence of the State of Israel. Although at one point he affirms that "after Auschwitz, the Jews have a rational and moral right to a state of their own, in which they cannot only defend themselves but also live in the way they choose," he goes on to make clear that the State of Israel's "right to exist" is not unconditional but rather is qualified by whether or not the people of Israel act justly in the land toward the Jewish and non-Jewish peoples of the land—a point that strikes me as erroneous regarding the State of Israel's right to exist. For background to Markus Barth's perspective, see Lindsay, "Jewish-Christian Dialogue." Lindsay shows that Markus Barth's friendships with Jewish scholars were doomed by his intense anger about the State of Israel's actions toward the Palestinians beginning in the late 1960s, as well as by other political disagreements and by his dismay over what were (in his view) attacks on Christianity by Jewish scholars in the light of Auschwitz.

101. Pitre, *Jesus and the Last Supper*, 482.

102. Perrin, *Jesus the Priest*, 108.

103. Perrin, *Jesus the Priest*, 286. See also Pitre, *Jesus, the Tribulation, and the End*,

The Christian new exodus is predicated upon the book of Exodus's narrative of suffering and redemption. According to the book of Acts, the first Christian preachers brought out this connection. Prior to his death by stoning, Stephen spends much of his speech describing Moses and the exodus.[104] As Stephen points out in a prophetic mode of discourse, the people of Israel failed to trust God during the exodus journey but instead made themselves a golden calf, with the result that God punished them. Both Stephen and Peter (Acts 3:22–23; Acts 7:37) quote God's words to Moses, "I will raise up for them [the people of Israel] a prophet like you from among their brethren; and I will put my words in his mouth" (Deut 18:18).[105] Jesus is this prophet, the new Moses.

Over and over again, the God who has power over life and death—the God who reveals himself in the book of Exodus and who leads the Israelites on the exodus journey—reveals himself in the book of Acts. Not only has God raised Christ from the dead, but also the miracles performed by Christ and his followers reveal God's power over life and death and God's will to give life. Susan Garrett links Acts 7 (Stephen's speech) with Luke 4:16–20, in which Christ reads from the Scriptures at his home-synagogue of Nazareth and reveals himself to be the anointed one who will "proclaim liberty to the captives, and the opening of the prison to those who are bound" (Isa 61:1).[106] For Luke-Acts, Christ leads a new exodus for all who are in slavery to the threat of death: "Like Pharaoh, the devil was an arrogant and relentless tyrant. He had oppressed even Jesus, bringing about the death on the cross (Luke 22:3, 53), but death and Hades had been unable to hold Jesus (Acts 2:24, 27, 31–32)."[107] By faith, Christians are united to Christ's new exodus, which fulfills Moses' exodus by truly freeing people from slavery to death. Yet on this new exodus journey, Christians still continue to suffer and die, even if now with hope grounded in Christ's resurrection. On the new exodus, believers are configured to Christ's cross, which is the path of embodied charity and humility in a world marked by grasping and pride.[108]

506–7.

104. See Estelle, *Echoes of Exodus*, 247: "Moses and the exodus actually occupy about 60 percent of Stephen's speech."

105. See Chalmers, *Interpreting the Prophets*, 84.

106. See Garrett, "Meaning of Jesus' Death"; Garrett, "Exodus from Bondage." Both essays are cited in Estelle, *Echoes of Exodus*, 248.

107. Garrett, "Exodus from Bondage," 659. See also Pao, *Acts and the Isaianic New Exodus*.

108. See Blackwell, *Christosis*, where (commenting on Romans 5) he describes "believers' embodiment of the path of Christ. That is, they must experience this death in themselves; otherwise, it will remain external to them. Therefore, the objective

Believers share sacramentally in Christ's death and Resurrection by which the new exodus is inaugurated. Paul remarks about baptism: "We were buried therefore with him by baptism into death, so that as Christ was raised from the dead by the glory of the Father, we too might walk in newness of life. For if we have been united with him in a death like his, we shall certainly be united with him in a resurrection like his" (Rom 6:4–5).[109] In Christ, we can even "rejoice in our sufferings" (Rom 5:3), because the indwelling Holy Spirit gives us a strong hope of sharing forever in "the glory of God" (Rom 5:2, 5). Through the Spirit, we are "heirs of God and fellow heirs with Christ, provided we suffer with him in order that we may also be glorified with him" (Rom 8:17). Alastair Roberts and Andrew Wilson point out that "Paul's gospel is an exodus," because Paul holds that God has rescued us from slavery to sin and death (and Satan) through the blood of Christ and the waters of baptism. God leads us by the Spirit to the true promised land (resurrection life).[110] Thus Paul rejoices in "Christ, our paschal Lamb" (1 Cor 5:7) and compares Christians to the Israelites who "all were baptized into Moses in the cloud and in the sea, and all ate the same supernatural food and all drank the same supernatural drink [the Eucharist]" (1 Cor 10:2–4).

On the new exodus, just as on the exodus, it is possible to fail to enter the promised land. After enumerating the sins of some of the Corinthian Christians, Paul warns: "Do you not know that the unrighteous will not inherit the kingdom of God?" (1 Cor 6:9). There will be some who will be "overthrown in the wilderness" just as happened to the murmuring Israelites on the exodus (1 Cor 10:5).[111] Paul urges, "We must not indulge in immorality as some of them did," and we must "shun the worship of idols" (1 Cor 10:8, 14). Yet we should take heart because, even in the midst of our temptations and sufferings, we already share in resurrection life insofar as we are truly united with the risen Christ by the Spirit. As Paul tells his flock,

---

accomplishment of salvation in Christ's death meets the subjective experience of believers as they follow him in death" (220–21). For further discussion see Newman, "Bodily Suffering"; as well as my *Dying and the Virtues*, especially chapters 6 and 7.

109. Discussing New Testament use of Hosea 6:2, Michael Morales offers an intriguing suggestion: "Jesus' third-day resurrection, then, does not fulfil the prophecy of Hosea 6:2 *apart from* the Spirit's uniting Israel to Jesus (and his third-day resurrection), resurrecting God's people from the dead in and with him—this fulfills the third-day resurrection of Jesus. . . . Jesus' resurrection was the resurrection of the corporate people of God, the new and *living* Israel" (L. M. Morales, *Who Shall Ascend*, 280). See also Phythian-Adams, *People and the Presence*.

110. Roberts and Wilson, *Echoes of Exodus*, 143.

111. For further background to the "exodus motif" in Paul, see Estelle, *Echoes of Exodus*, chapter 9. See also W. D. Davies, "Paul and the New Exodus."

"For all things are yours, whether Paul or Apollos or Cephas or the world or life or death or the present or the future, all are yours; and you are Christ's; and Christ is God's" (1 Cor 3:21–22). In this sense, as Michael Morales says, it is already true that the "church has experienced the resurrection, the new exodus out of bondage to sin and death," a "new exodus from the depths of Sheol to the heights of the heavenly Mount Zion."[112]

The Gospel of Matthew presents Jesus, who earlier had acted as the new Moses at the Sermon on the Mount, now as the triumphant "ruler of all" and "exalted Lord," calling all nations to come to him: "All authority in heaven and on earth has been given to me. Go therefore and make disciples of all nations, baptizing them in the name of the Father and of the Son and of the Holy Spirit, teaching them to observe all that I have commanded you; and behold, I am with you always, to the close of the age" (Matt 28:18–20).[113] The risen Jesus in the Gospel of Luke opens up the full meaning of the Scriptures to his disciples (Luke 24:44–46). He then sends his disciples to preach the gospel to all nations, spreading the inaugurated kingdom. Pentecost makes manifest the new covenant community or inaugurated kingdom that Christ has established.[114] Roberts and Wilson compare Acts 1–2 to Sinai and the exodus: "The anointed leader has gone up, and the divine presence comes down.... The gift that defines God's people—first the law and then the Spirit—is given. The people are commissioned as kings and priests, and the tabernacle/temple is established."[115]

All of this depends, of course, upon the authority of Christ as the new Moses (and new Adam, new Isaac, new Joshua, and so on) able to lead the new exodus through "his glory, authority, revelation, life, death, resurrection, and ascension."[116] In his commentary on the Gospel of John, Craig Keener remarks: "As in the exodus tradition, divine signs attest the identity of the true Lord."[117] God shows his life-giving power in Christ, just as God

---

112. L. M. Morales, *Who Shall Ascend*, 281.

113. Davies and Allison, *Commentary on Matthew XIX–XXVIII*, 682, 686; cf. the whole of 682–89.

114. See Watts, "New Exodus." See also Watts, *Isaiah's New Exodus*.

115. Roberts and Wilson, *Echoes of Exodus*, 138. They add that "it is tragic, if predictable, to read that just as the victories of Israel were marred by the greed of Achan, so the progress of the church was marred by the greed of Ananias and Sapphira (Josh. 7:1–26; Acts 5:1–10)" (*Echoes of Exodus*, 139).

116. Roberts and Wilson, *Echoes of Exodus*, 133.

117. Keener, *Gospel of John* II, 945. See also L. Michael Morales's chapter on "New Exodus." For John, "Jesus is God's Passover Lamb of the New Exodus (John 1:29, 36), and the Son who will baptize God's people with the Spirit of the New Creation (John 1:30–34)" ("New Exodus," 159). Morales's chapter on "The Spirit of the New Exodus" also draws heavily on the Gospel of John, as well as on the book of Revelation.

did for the Israelites on the exodus from Egypt. Christ tells his disciples, "Believe me that I am in the Father and the Father is in me; or else believe me for the sake of the works themselves" (John 14:11). His life-giving works include raising his friend Lazarus from the dead. His works also include raising himself from the dead, as the Son of the Father: "I lay down my life, that I may take it again. No one takes it from me, but I lay it down of my own accord. I have power to lay it down, and I have power to take it again" (John 10:17–18).[118]

Jesus' resurrection and ascension are followed by the descent of the Spirit at Pentecost and by the life-giving miracles performed by the apostles. According to Acts 3, immediately after Peter heals a lame man who daily begged for alms at the temple gate, Peter tells him: "'I have no silver and gold, but I give you what I have; in the name of Jesus Christ of Nazareth, rise and walk.' And he took him by the right hand and raised him up; and immediately his feet and ankles were made strong. And leaping up he stood and walked and entered the temple with them, walking and leaping and praising God" (Acts 3:6–8).[119] It should be clear that God the life-giver is at the center of the Christian proclamation of the new exodus.

But what about the exodus's nation-building dimension, highlighted by Sacks? Recall that Sacks describes the nation of Israel journeying toward the eschatological kingdom which will be marked by perfect peace and justice. He understands the Sabbath as a way of entering into this perfected realm even in the midst of the earthly journey. Although Sacks considers the Sabbath to be an enjoyment of the Divine Presence, he sees it most typically in political and economic terms: the difference between rich and poor is taken away; wealth provides no advantage. The Sabbath, like the Jubilee (Lev 25), is a foretaste of the perfected "body politic."[120]

---

118. Jesus says this in the context of his discourse on the Good Shepherd. Keener emphasizes Christ's status as the life-giver: "The contrast between the shepherd who cares for and brings life to the sheep and the thieves who come to destroy the sheep (10:10) leads into a discussion of how fully the good shepherd loves his sheep" (Keener, *Gospel of John* I, 813). Raymond S. Brown, SS comments on John 10:17–18: "We note that in both vss. 17 and 18 it is Jesus himself who takes up his life again. The normal NT phraseology is not that Jesus rose form the dead but that *the Father* raised him up.... But since in Johannine thought the Father and the Son possess the same power (x 28–30), it really makes little difference whether the resurrection is attributed to the action of the Father or of the Son. This is a profound theological insight on which later Trinitarian theology would capitalize" (R. S. Brown, *Gospel According to John*, 399).

119. For background see Keener, *Acts* II, 1063–72. See also the descriptions of miraculous healings following upon prayer (including the healings of people unable to walk) in Keener's *Miracles*.

120. Norman C. Habel takes a more negative view of Leviticus 25–27: "The controlling power in this land economy lies with the priests, who are responsible for upholding

Among Christians, however, it may seem as though that the kingdom is merely or mainly an interior reality. In the Gospel of Luke, Jesus teaches, "The kingdom of God is not coming with signs to be observed; nor will they say, 'Behold, here it is!' or 'There!' for behold, the kingdom of God is in your midst" (Luke 17:20–21). There is an evident risk of concluding that the "kingdom" is a solely interior reality rather than a "body politic" (in Sacks's phrase).[121]

Some help in this regard comes from Brant Pitre. He notes that there is "an unbreakable bond between three realities: the Last Supper, the new Passover, and the eschatological kingdom of God. This connection both presumes and implies that the banquet of the kingdom will bring to fruition in an ultimate way the 'transition from bondage to freedom' and the exodus of the people of God signified by the Jewish Passover."[122] The sinfulness that plagued the Israelites on their exodus journey has been borne by Christ, the Passover Lamb, on behalf of the whole people.[123] Note, however, that "Paul does not conceptualize the two covenants in strictly chronological terms."[124] By faith, people could belong to the new covenant prior to Christ's coming. Moreover, Christians remain plagued by sin, as we observed above with

---

the sabbath principle; ultimately the priests are the only social group that can progressively accumulate land. The social model implied in this land economy means political power for priests, security for peasants, and dependency for slaves, hired laborers, and immigrant aliens" (Habel, *Land Is Mine*, 114).

121. Sacks, *To Heal a Fractured World*, 87. See L. T. Johnson, *Gospel of Luke*, 266–67: "The kingdom announced by Jesus is real. It is not merely a matter of 'internal awareness.' It is expressed in the healings and exorcisms, and indeed by the conversion of the people. Thus Luke can have Jesus speak of the kingdom of God 'reaching' them (11:20) and 'being given to them' (12:32). We shall see, shortly, that Jesus is proclaimed as a king (19:38), and disposes of rule within the kingdom (22:29); he dies as a king (23:38) and provides a place in his kingdom (23:42–43). He continues to instruct his followers about the kingdom of God after his resurrection (Acts 1:3), and his resurrection is an enthronement by God (Acts 2:34); people can in fact 'enter the kingdom' (Acts 14:21). But this kingdom is not to be equated absolutely with the end-time when the rule of God will be established, and the Son of Man will serve as 'judge of the living and the dead' (Acts 17:31). For Luke's readers, that is still in the future. There is continuity between the two moments, but also a critical distinction." Johnson concludes that "the kingdom of God is not a place, but a rule"—a rule that has been inaugurated in believers but that has not yet been consummated and universalized (*Gospel of Luke*, 267). See also Schnackenburg, *God's Rule and Kingdom*, 350–51.

122. Pitre, *Jesus and the Last Supper*, 492.

123. See L. M. Morales, *Exodus Old and New*, especially 141–47 on the Suffering Servant of Isaiah 52–53.

124. Pitre et al., *Paul, a New Covenant Jew*, 49. In Paul's view, however (as Galatians 4 shows), the Mosaic covenant is a covenant of "slavery" (to the law, in a manner required by the sins of the people) in a way that the Abrahamic covenant was not.

regard to 1 Corinthians 10. But while Christians remain sinners, we have a redeemer who, in his new Passover, enables us to make the new exodus journey. Christians participate in this new Passover by faith and by the sacraments—preeminently the Eucharist, which is both the "inauguration" and "a foretaste" of "the messianic banquet."[125]

Among other things, the Eucharist helps us to recognize that the inaugurated eschatological kingdom and the "messianic banquet" involve a tangible body politic, not merely a spiritual condition. Drawing upon the work of Mary Douglas, Pitre (joined by his co-authors Michael Barber and John Kincaid) comments: "This sacrificial bread (and wine) of the presence was celebrated as a constant reminder of God's everlasting covenant with Israel (Lev 24:1–9).... Paul's account of the Last Supper suggests that the Lord's Supper serves a similar role in relation to the new covenant."[126] As a sacrament that builds up the Church in love through participation in Jesus' kingdom-inaugurating act on the cross, the Eucharist unites the people of God in the new exodus on the way to the fullness of the eschatological kingdom of God, a fullness that is already present in the risen and ascended Christ—and which is certainly not a merely interior or individualistic reality.[127]

Now that Christ our head has passed over, we who are joined to him experience kingdom life with him. The letter to the Colossians urges believers, "If then you have been raised with Christ, seek the things that are above, where Christ is, seated at the right hand of God.... For you have died, and your life is hidden with Christ in God" (Col 3:1–2). In the Gospel of John, similarly, Jesus promises his disciples that he is not abandoning them. On their journey—their new exodus—they are to expect suffering and death, but Jesus bestows upon them his own "peace" (John 14:27). This peace flows from the gift of "the Counselor, the Holy Spirit, whom the Father will send

---

125. Pitre, *Jesus and the Last Supper*, 498. He sums up his argument: "Just as the first exodus was set in motion by the Passover sacrifice, so too the new exodus, which will usher in the kingdom, is set in motion by a new Passover—an eschatological Passover—that is accomplished by means of his own suffering, death, and restoration to life 'in the kingdom.'... [T]he Last Supper is not only an anticipation of the messianic banquet, it is also a foretaste of the power of the kingdom of God. In particular, it gives the disciples a share in the redemptive power of the kingdom, which will be unleashed in Jesus' death on the cross and fulfilled by Jesus' restoration to life and entry into the joyful banquet of the heavenly kingdom" (Pitre, *Jesus and the Last Supper*, 511–12).

126. Pitre et al., *Paul, a New Covenant Jew*, 235, with reference to Douglas, "Eucharist."

127. See my *Did Jesus Rise from the Dead?*, chapter 7; and my *Jesus and the Demise of Death*, chapter 4.

in my name" (John 14:26).[128] The Holy Spirit abides in Christ's followers on the new exodus. Paul affirms that Christians have hope even in the midst of severe sufferings, "because God's love has been poured into our hearts through the Holy Spirit who has been given to us" (Rom 5:5).[129] Again, the Holy Spirit is given to us not simply to transform us individually but to ensure that "we, though many, are one body in Christ, and individually members of one another" (Rom 12:5). Like the people of Israel on the exodus, who were delivered from Egyptian slavery and promised the inheritance of the land of Canaan (see Exod 23:30; Gen 17:8), God in Christ "has delivered us from the dominion of darkness and transferred us to the kingdom of his beloved Son, in whom we have redemption, the forgiveness of sins" (Col 1:13–14).[130]

In view of this inaugurated "kingdom," Christ gave concrete structure to the community of his followers. He spent a night in prayer and then "called his disciples, and chose from them twelve, whom he named apostles" (Luke 6:13).[131] In accord with the twelve tribes of the exodus, Christ appointed twelve apostles in founding his Church, the eschatological Israel. The first letter of Peter speaks of "the flock of God" tended by the elders and led by "the chief Shepherd" Jesus Christ (1 Pet 5:2, 4). Similarly, the letter to the Ephesians announces the establishment, by "the blood of Christ," of the messianic community of Jews and Gentiles. Christ "came and preached peace to you who were far off and peace to those who were near. . . . So then you are no longer strangers and sojourners, but you are fellow citizens with the saints and members of the household of God, built upon the foundation of the apostles and prophets, Christ Jesus himself being the cornerstone" (Eph 2:17–20).[132] Far from being merely individuals grateful for personal salvation, believers are visibly "a holy temple in the Lord" (Eph 2:21). Believers

---

128. See the extensive discussion offered by Keener, including his observation that "this ministry of the Spirit cannot be limited to the apostolic witness nor to the Fourth Gospel itself (cf. 1 John 2:20–27). The presence of the Spirit with them 'forever' indicates that this exposition is expected to continue in the community, not to end with the death of the apostles; the Paraclete would equip the community to confront ever new situations" (Keener, *Gospel of John* II, 981).

129. For interpretations of Romans 5:5 (interpreting the "love of God" as "God's love for us" or "our love for God"—or both), see Wilken, "*Fides Caritate Formata.*"

130. For an account of what forgiveness involves, see Rabbi Charles David Isbell's story of a powerful reconciliation between erstwhile friends that took place in the context of Yom Kippur: Isbell, *Sermons*, 99–100.

131. For background, see L. T. Johnson, *Gospel of Luke*, 102–3.

132. See also Pao, *Acts and the Isaianic New Exodus*, 250: "the New Exodus in Acts provides a striking vision of the soteriological equality of the Jews and the Gentiles."

have been "baptized into one body" and have become "the body of Christ" (1 Cor 12:13, 27).[133]

In a visionary mode, the book of Revelation describes the fullness of the Church as it exists in "seven churches," led by the risen and glorified Christ "who loves us and has freed us from our sins by his blood and made us a kingdom, priests to his God and Father" (Rev 1:4-6).[134] Speaking to the seer John, Christ commands that John write to each of the seven churches, laying out their strengths and weaknesses. The new exodus journey is not going to be an easy one. Christ warns the first church (in Ephesus) that unless it repents and regains "the love [it] had at first" (Rev 2:4), it will not continue. Christ praises the second church (in Smyrna) and encourages its members not to fear their coming imprisonment. He urges them, "Be faithful unto death" and assures them that he is the divine life-giver: "I will give you the crown of life.... He who conquers shall not be hurt by the second death" (Rev 2:10-11). In the visions that follow, the Lord makes clear that these churches are embarked on the new exodus. Referring to God's declaration (Exod 19:6) that the people of Israel "shall be to me a kingdom of priests and a holy nation," the "new song" sung by the twenty-four elders (the Church) praises Christ the paschal Lamb: "[B]y your blood you ransomed men for God from every tribe and tongue and people and nation, and have made them a kingdom and priests to our God, and they shall reign on earth" (Rev 5:9-10).[135] The nation-building or corporate dimension is clear in this depiction of the Church's new exodus.

---

133. See I. A. Morales, "Baptism and Union with Christ." See also studies such as M. V. Lee, *Paul*; Macaskill, *Living in Union with Christ*; Thompson, *Church according to Paul*. Thompson is correct to affirm, "God calls communities rather than individuals, who live faithfully only in community. The election traditions, to which Paul frequently appeals, remind us that we enter a community with those whom we did not choose, but whom God has chosen.... To live in continuity with Israel is to recognize that the believing community is a community of memory that continually repeats its founding narrative, which it reenacts through rituals" (*Church according to Paul*, 244-45). Macaskill adds the point that Christ's unity (and God's) is the ground of believers' corporate unity, so that divisions among believers do not destroy this unity (see *Living in Union with Christ*, 69). As he says, "baptism always carries with it an affirmation of our collective identification with Christ" (Macaskill, *Living in Union with Christ*, 72). I discuss these realities further, including Catholic ecclesiological affirmation of the unity and holiness of the Church, in my *Engaging the Doctrine of the Holy Spirit*.

134. See P. S. Williamson, *Revelation*, 47, 50. Williamson notes, "From early on, Christian interpreters of Revelation have pointed out that 'seven' symbolizes completeness, suggesting that the book was intended by the Holy Spirit for the whole Church, not only in Asia but also in the whole world" (*Revelation*, 50).

135. For further discussion of the book of Revelation and the exodus/new exodus, see Estelle, *Echoes of Exodus*, chapter 11.

Likewise employing exodus motifs, as we have seen, Hebrews states that believers, worshipping Christ, have "come to Mount Zion and to the city of the living God, the heavenly Jerusalem, and to innumerable angels in festal gathering, and to the assembly of the first-born who are enrolled in heaven" (Heb 12:22–23).[136] The new exodus, in a sense, has already reached its goal; the kingdom is inaugurated and Christians can already experience it. The exodus was plagued by unresolved sin; whereas now the problem of alienation from God has been resolved in and through Christ. N. T. Wright comments, "It is, to be sure, a deep mystery that on the cross God 'condemned sin' in the flesh of the Messiah. But this stands at the heart of Christianity, offering the way forward through the Red Sea, leaving behind the Egypt of sin and death, and pointing onward to the land of promise."[137]

In Christ, a participatory path to ideal political life—centered around the Divine Presence—opens up.[138] We must emulate Christ who, in humble love, is the life-giver. Hebrews urges, "let us run with perseverance the race that is set before us, looking to Jesus the pioneer and perfecter of our faith, who for the joy that was set before him endured the cross, despising the shame, and is seated at the right hand of the throne of God" (Heb 12:2). On the new exodus, we both have far to go and have (in Christ) already arrived. In the midst of our "hard struggle with sufferings" (Heb 10:32), we can already "be grateful for receiving a kingdom that cannot be shaken" (Heb 12:28).

Admittedly, it remains possible for individual believers, though not the whole Church, to fail on the new exodus. The Letter to the Hebrews warns against this possibility, with the failure of the exodus generation in view: "Take care, brethren, lest there be in any of you an evil, unbelieving heart, leading you to fall away from the living God" (Heb 3:12).[139] But we

---

136. For a comparison between Mount Sinai and Mount Zion, see Healy, *Hebrews*, 276.

137. N. T. Wright, "Romans," 588. I explore the saving power of the cross in *Engaging the Doctrine of Creation*, chapter 7.

138. See Grant Macaskill's reflections on the Eucharist as (for Paul) the new exodus/new Passover meal, uniting believers in deliverance from sin and death: "Jesus's action is itself understood in relation to the paradigmatic covenant memory of the exodus, in which the distinctive relationship of Israel to God and to the world is manifest. This is now reconfigured in relation to his act of representation [on the cross], by which we are delivered from iniquity and its consequences" (*Living in Union with Christ*, 86). Macaskill recognizes, of course, that Christians remain burdened by sin despite the powerful presence of the Spirit. Thus he also urges, with Romans 6–7 in view, that "we have not taught Christians to distrust themselves properly, to recognize that their flesh will take those commandments and make them serve our self-exaltation against God" (*Living in Union with Christ*, 104).

139. See Roberts and Wilson, *Echoes of Exodus*, 145.

are secure so long as we rely upon Christ, "the mediator of a new covenant" (Heb 12:24). Christ's self-offering truly suffices for our salvation; we must be united to him as our Passover Lamb. Joined with Christ at "Mount Zion," Christians on the new exodus "offer to God acceptable worship, with reverence and awe; for our God is a consuming fire" (Heb 12:28-29; cf. Deut 4:24).[140]

The concrete unity of believers on the new exodus is such that, as Paul says, "[i]f one member suffers, all suffer together; if one member is honored, all rejoice together" (1 Cor 12:26). The unifying agent is the Spirit of Christ. Christians operate under "the law of Christ" (Gal 6:2) when the Spirit fills believers with "love, joy, peace, patience, kindness, goodness, faithfulness, gentleness, self-control" (Gal 5:22-23).[141] It should not surprise us that this does not happen automatically. Christ himself suggests that many professed Christians will lack charity (see Matt 25:31-46)—and the history of the Church bears this out. Such Christians face judgment and ultimate separation from the community (see Acts 5; 1 Cor 5).[142]

If the Church is united corporately, however, should it not strive to occupy a distinctive land in the world? Hans Urs von Balthasar comments in this regard: "The *Catholica* is in fact a region whose middle point is everywhere (where the Eucharist is celebrated); and (structurally) she can theoretically be everywhere: geographically, her periphery extends to 'the very ends of the earth' (Rev 1:8), a periphery that in any case can never be far from the midpoint."[143] Von Balthasar rejects the notion that the Church's center is localizable in Rome or anywhere else. The kingdom is inaugurated in the Church gathered in faith around Christ in the Eucharist. But the kingdom will not be triumphantly evident prior to the eschaton. A certain hiddenness fits with the self-surrendering love that characterizes Jesus Christ.[144] Recall Christ's words, "If they persecuted me, they will persecute you; if they kept my word, they will keep yours also" (John 15:20).

---

140. For Hebrews 12's connections with the original exodus, see Healy, *Hebrews*, 272-82.

141. For background, see R. J. Morales, *Spirit and the Restoration of Israel*.

142. See Reiser, *Jesus and Judgment*.

143. Von Balthasar, "Claim to Catholicity," 65-66.

144. Von Balthasar puts this sharply in discussing Origen's commentary on Ezekiel 16: "Here as elsewhere (for example, in the magnificent seventh homily on Leviticus), he [Origen] presents himself as the unworthiest of all and takes all the guilt on himself. The force and sincerity of this gesture help him convince other believers that the gravest, the most momentous guilt is to be found in Jerusalem, in the members of the Church. And the more pharisaically proud they are of their ecclesiastical purity and *gnosis*, the guiltier they are" (von Balthasar, "Casta Meretrix," 257).

At the same time, the body of Christ is not nowhere. Christ's bridal Church, of which he is bridegroom and head, is already established and consummated in Mary, who is joined by all the saints.[145] In the present earthly world, too, Christ's Church has a visible form: "God has appointed in the Church first apostles, second prophets, third teachers, then workers of miracles, then healers, helpers, administrators, speakers in various kinds of tongues" (1 Cor 12:27-28). The new exodus is always a nation- or Church-building enterprise. Redemption from slavery to suffering and death takes place in individuals but not as *solitary* individuals. Scot McKnight is correct when he states: "Kingdom is—almost always, with varying degrees of emphasis—a complex of king, rule, people, land, and law. Church is also a complex: a king (Christ), a rule (Christ rules over the body of Christ), a people (the church), a land (expanding Israel into the diaspora), and a law (the law of Christ, life in the Spirit)."[146] Ultimately, of course, the "land" that is the goal of the new exodus is where the glorified Christ is, the new creation or messianic banquet or consummated kingdom, which will exceed anything that we can imagine. But we have a foretaste of it now, even in the midst of our suffering and dying—in union with the suffering and dying of Christ for the salvation of the world.

V. Conclusion

For the Jewish theologian Joshua Berman, as for Sacks, the story of the exodus is primarily though not exclusively the story of how "Moses leaves the palace to cast his lot with his slave-kin, and to found for them an order where all are equal citizens under the sovereignty of the King of Kings."[147]

---

145. See my *Mary's Bodily Assumption*.

146. McKnight, *Kingdom Conspiracy*, 205.

147. J. A. Berman, *Created Equal*, 166. For Yoram Hazony, the message of the exodus narrative is also primarily political: namely, "God loves those who resist the injustice of the state. It is to those that he reveals himself, and those whom he is willing to help" (Hazony, *Philosophy of Hebrew Scripture*, 144). Hazony adds that in the constitution of the kingdom of Israel (at the time of Saul), we see that the state is a conditional contract between the people and God, and "the fact of God's reluctance hangs over the established state, whose rulers must take into account the possibility that if they go too far in the pursuit of evil, God's agreement to the continued existence of their kingdom will be withdrawn" (*Philosophy of Hebrew Scripture*, 152). Hazony concludes that the vision of the state supported by the Torah is that of a limited state, limited both in the power of its rulers and in its territorial boundaries. In his view, the Israelites are delivered twice, "once in Exodus, and once again in Samuel. Their first deliverer is Moses, who redeems them from the tyranny of the state; their second deliverer is David, who redeems them from anarchy" (Hazony, *Philosophy of Hebrew Scripture*, 160). The crucial

This political-ethical reading of the exodus fits with classical liberal Protestant interpretations of Jesus' mission in one respect while turning such interpretations on their head in another. Classical liberal Protestant interpretations of Jesus focused on an ethical breakthrough. They did so, however, along individualistic lines. Joseph Ratzinger points out that Adolf von Harnack, and early twentieth-century liberal theology in general, "saw Jesus' message about the Kingdom of God as a double revolution against the Judaism of Jesus' time. Whereas Judaism focused entirely on the collective, on the chosen people . . . Jesus' addressed the individual, whose infinite value he recognized and made the foundation of his teaching."[148] In addition to this supposedly salutary individualism, von Harnack argued that Jesus advanced a second revolution by rejecting the ritual life and priesthood of Judaism and focusing "strictly on morality."[149] By contrast, Sacks and Berman emphasize the value of the ritual and communal life of Judaism within the framework of the more democratic political life brought about by the exodus.[150]

Sacks argues that Judaism's focus on nationhood and appreciation for the ritual mediation of the Divine Presence reveal the goodness of God's work for the redemption of the (still suffering) world. Ratzinger agrees, though with Christ in view. As he notes, in post-Christian Western societies, Christ's teaching about the kingdom tends to be interpreted as, at best, a vision for "a world governed by peace, justice, and the conservation of

---

thing, therefore, is to find the middle ground politically between tyranny and anarchy.

148. Ratzinger, *Jesus of Nazareth* I, 51.

149. Ratzinger, *Jesus of Nazareth* I, 51. See also Marquardt's study of the Jewish scholar Leo Baeck's critical responses to Harnack, in which Marquardt identifies various other significant Jewish responses: Marquardt, "Elements Unresolved." Marquardt remarks, "Baeck traces Harnack's method back to an *inherited error* of the theological school from which Harnack had descended: the teachings of the Protestant theologian Albrecht Ritschl, for whom theological statements, including faith statements, were *expressions of value judgments*. In Ritschl's school the correctness and even truth of an expression of faith was derived from its value for a person or a group of persons. Something of a Feuerbachian projection of the thought onto the heavenly screen was in play, and Baeck pointed this out. . . . Baeck draws the consequences from this: Harnack portrays 'my' Christianity, the Christianity of his value judgments, he does not portray 'the' essence of 'the' Christianity and not at all the essence of *historically* original Christianity. . . . Baeck sees precisely that with such a method everything Jewish is *a priori* declared irrelevant for Jesus" (Marquardt, "Elements Unresolved," 37–38, 40).

150. Berman does this by arguing that "[i]n Deuteronomy, a new emphasis is ascribed to the priesthood: the priests emerge as the guardians of the law, the constitution" and furthermore that "[i]n archaic states [such as ancient Israel] that practice a collective power strategy, ritual sanctifies and culturally reinforces an egalitarian spirit through numinous experience" (J. A. Berman, *Created Equal*, 65).

creation."[151] In this contemporary vision of the kingdom, the Church as a distinctive "body politic" is stripped away as divisive, along with both "Christ" and "God," who are also seen as divisive. As Ratzinger puts it, the result is that "God has disappeared; man is the only actor left on the stage.... Only the organization of the world counts."[152] Against this distortion, Ratzinger insists that Christ's proclamation of the kingdom involves the extension of God's Lordship over the whole world, but not a Lordship recognizable in worldly terms of power, since Christ reigns as self-sacrificial love.

Like the New Testament as a whole, Ratzinger does not shy away from the contention that "the community of his [Jesus'] disciples is the new Israel."[153] He recognizes that there are two claimants to the Scriptures of Israel and to the covenantal promises. He explains that "there are two responses in history to the destruction of the temple and the radical exile of Israel: Judaism and Christianity.... [T]he two ways were by no means clearly separated from one another at the beginning, and thus they each developed again and again through debate with the other."[154] For Christians to stop claiming to be the messianically reconfigured Israel would simply lead to a Marcionism in which the Old Testament would be rejected as unnecessary or irrelevant to Christians.

If the exodus and the nation of Israel have now been fulfilled and reconfigured in a new exodus in Christ, however, can this really be said while truly valuing ongoing Judaism and its perspective? Paul van Buren raises a crucial concern: "A major difficulty for the attempt to speak positively among ourselves [i.e. among Christians] of the Jewish people is that there are almost no precedents in our conversation over the past eighteen centuries for doing so."[155] Tragically, in previous centuries, affirming the

---

151. Ratzinger, *Jesus of Nazareth* I, 53–54.

152. Ratzinger, *Jesus of Nazareth* I, 54. See also the similar critique of the contemporary "anthropocentric methodology" found in von Balthasar, "Claim to Catholicity," 84–86; as well as the anthropocentrism classically articulated by Troeltsch, "On the Possibility of a Liberal Christianity."

153. Ratzinger, *Jesus of Nazareth* I, 111. This point is also made in Thompson, *Church according to Paul*.

154. Benedict XVI, "Grace and Vocation," 164. See for example Siegal, *Jewish-Christian Dialogues*.

155. Van Buren, *People of Israel*, 9. Throughout his book, van Buren speaks of "the Gentile church" as distinct from "the Jewish people" (van Buren, *People of Israel*, 262). I think the phrase "the Gentile Church" is deeply misleading. The Church in time and space is composed not only of Gentiles but also of Jews, and the Church is the body of Christ (a Jew) as well as the reconfigured eschatological Israel of the Messiah. Such a reality, whatever else it might be, is not "Gentile." I understand, of course, that — in distinction from ongoing Judaism — there are a great majority of Gentiles in the Church, but this does not establish something that is rightly called "the Gentile Church." Van

importance of the exodus and the new exodus hardly led to valuing ongoing Judaism. Appreciation for the Jewish people was limited to Old Testament Israel and did not extend much beyond it, even though Maimonides and some other Jewish thinkers might receive a place at the table with regard to certain topics.

In my view, the shared dynamic of struggle and of yearning for a transcendent fulfillment is what allows a Christian theology of the exodus and new exodus to learn from and appreciate Jewish theology of the exodus (which includes the same dynamic of struggle and yearning) without exacerbating pain and rivalry between Jews and Christians.[156] After all, even

---

Buren argues more fully: "God's light for the Gentiles has taken the form of Israel represented in the Jew Jesus Christ. The church has Israel in the person of Jesus. It does not follow, however, that the church has therefore no need of the Jewish people themselves, for Jesus is Israel for the church in the reality of his own identity with his people. Jesus is Israel for the church as a Jew and so as one of and one with his people. To this day, the church needs that people in order to have Jesus as he is, as a Jew, not a Gentile. Jesus is Israel by the will of the Father, but he bears this calling always as one who stands with his people in their covenant with God" (van Buren, *People of Israel*, 263). I agree that the Church needs the people of Israel, the Jewish people. Jesus is one of the Jewish people, sharing in their covenant. Jesus is not less than this for the Church. Yet he also is more than this: he is the One who eschatologically fulfills and reconfigures the covenant around himself. His identity therefore enables him to call all people to union in him, rather than simply being "Israel for the church in the reality of his own identity with his people."

156. Somewhat ambiguously, Pope Emeritus Benedict XVI denies that "the Jewish people have been totally cut off from the promise" ("Grace and Vocation," 169). He defends a strong distinction between the Mosaic covenant and the Abrahamic covenant. He thinks that while God will always be faithful, the Mosaic covenant—like the Davidic covenant—can be broken from the side of human beings, as happened in the event of the golden calf and also prior to the Babylonian exile. Moreover, the Mosaic covenant itself does not abrogate the universal purposes of the Abrahamic covenant. The notion of a new covenant appears already in the prophets, including Jeremiah 31 and Ezekiel 16, among others. From God's side, then, "the covenant between God and Israel is indestructible because of the continuity of God's election" (Benedict XVI, "Grace and Vocation," 182). But from the human side, it can be broken and therefore can be open to a new covenant, as in fact Jesus Christ instituted at the Last Supper. God does not "revoke" his covenantal love for his people Israel, but neither does God commit to stopping the unfolding of his covenantal promises at a particular stage. God permits Israel to break the Mosaic covenant and this has consequences that lead to the new covenant. God seals his relationship to the whole human race by overcoming sin and death (not least that of his people Israel) in and through the paschal mystery of Christ: the Sinai covenant is fulfilled, and reconstituted through the establishment of the new Israel, by Christ's "love that vanquishes death" (Benedict XVI, "Grace and Vocation," 184). For a critical response to Pope Emeritus Benedict XVI's essay, see Striet, "Christliche Theologie," 113–21. In addressing issues of Jewish-Christian dialogue, Striet (a Roman Catholic theologian) makes clear that his understanding of God and salvation are profoundly eccentric. See also the exchange between Pope Emeritus Benedict XVI

though Christians believe that the kingdom has been inaugurated—so that kingdom-building has replaced nation-building in the strict sense—Christians and Jews agree that the full consummation has not yet happened. The new exodus in Christ involves a liberation *but not yet a consummation*, just as was the case for the exodus of Israel from Egypt. Despite our significant disagreements about Jesus, therefore, Christians and Jews can recognize in the other a shared commitment to journeying toward the eschaton.[157] Rabbi Held emphasizes the exodus's status as a journey in which the final destination (the eschaton) remains outside our grasp. Christians can appreciate this perspective while also appreciating ongoing Judaism's emphasis that God's redemptive work is even now building up a nation (or kingdom).

Of course, it is not possible to exclude tension altogether.[158] The new exodus in Christ clearly differs from ongoing Judaism's understanding of the exodus. But from the perspective of a Christian theology of Israel, Jewish thinkers' emphasis on the constitution of the nation of Israel, under the sovereignty of the God of Israel, is a crucial contribution. Christian faith in the new exodus in Christ does not mean negating the value of the exodus or denying that ongoing Judaism has much to teach Christians through its corporate journeying in this world in hope of the coming messianic consummation.

As will be clear by now, Christians reframe the meaning of Israel's nation-building in terms of the new exodus and the inaugurated kingdom, reconfiguring Israel around the Messiah who gives the new law through the eschatological outpouring of the Spirit made possible by his redemptive Passover sacrifice. Christians adopt a different understanding of the promised land, now conceived as the eschatological new creation of the whole world toward which we are journeying in and with Christ, a new creation that has been inaugurated not only in Christ's glorified flesh but also in the Virgin Mary's glorified flesh, by the power of Christ's cross. In Christ, suffering and death have been turned into the path marked out by God the life-giver to give eternal life. This new exodus is corporate and ecclesial; and it is given form by the "law of Christ" (Gal 6:2). It is the exodus of all who

---

and Rabbi Arie Folger, "Briefwechsel."

157. See also my discussion of such matters in the book's Introduction and chapter 1.

158. See for example Bayfield, *Being Jewish Today*, 49, where he describes going to see his granddaughter sing "*St Matthew's Passion* with the Bach Choir at the Royal Festival Hall—in English. It's the most exquisite music, a pinnacle of our Western musical tradition, and yet the text, Matthew's Gospel, is arguably the most polemic with regard to Jewish complicity in the death of Jesus. At the end I exploded to my family: 'Why is it that at the very heart of Western culture we're portrayed as the personification of evil?'"

are united in the "body of Christ" and who in a certain sense are already sharing in the heavenly life of Christ, not least through the Eucharist as the new manna and as the saving sacrifice of the new Passover lamb.

Of course, it is evident that the deepest problems that led to the Israelites' exodus from Egypt are still the ones that plague human beings, including Christians, today. Specifically, we still are profoundly burdened by sin, suffering, and death. Finding ourselves bound to suffering and vulnerable to death, we murmur against each other and against God. We strive against each other and are caught up in patterns of oppression, domination, and misery, reflecting what Hebrews 2:15 describes as a "lifelong bondage" to death. What we need is redemption, which God has given us through the paschal Lamb. Yet we find ourselves still to be sinners, tempted to return to "Egypt" and ever in need of the renewal of the grace of the Holy Spirit and the consolation of Christ.

This would not have surprised the One who inaugurated the new exodus. Recall that at the Last Supper itself, "a dispute . . . arose among them [the disciples], which of them was to be regarded as the greatest" (Luke 22:24). When Christians find that our new exodus murmuring and sinfulness parallels that of the people of Israel on the exodus, we should not lose heart by any means. Like the Israelites, we know that the Lord goes before us (cf. Exod 13:21) and, even more, indwells us in restoring us to the image of his self-surrendering love. In repentance, we should rededicate ourselves to Christ and to the humble obedience to God that characterizes a kingdom under Christ's sovereignty.

On the new exodus, then, Christians have sinned against God and neighbor—even though many Christians have displayed powerful self-surrendering love. Clearly, the new exodus has not yet attained its glorious destination, which only Christ's coming in glory can bring about. Christ calls to all people in mercy. He has come to redeem sinners, and he runs to embrace them, to free them from slavery to sin and death, and to unite them in love within his inaugurated kingdom. The new exodus does not depend upon our greatness, any more than the exodus from Egypt depended upon the Israelites' greatness. Nourished by the sacraments of Christ our head, journeying with him and in him toward the new creation that he will bring, let us strive anew to "fulfil the law of Christ. For if any one thinks he is something, when he is nothing, he deceives himself" (Gal 6:2–3).

Chapter 4

Torah

I. Introduction

In his *Summa theologiae*, Thomas Aquinas carefully examines many of the laws contained in the Torah, dividing them into moral precepts, ceremonial precepts, and judicial precepts, and interpreting them literally and spiritually.[1] He engages the Torah as a Christian biblical reality, contextualized by the prophets and by the New Testament. In the present chapter, I seek to engage the Torah as a Christian biblical reality, and to do so in a manner instructed as much as possible by ongoing Judaism.

Aquinas's theology differs from many modern Christian engagements with Israel's Torah, in that he cares about the individual laws and seeks to explain their wisdom and goodness.[2] Understandably, however, he does not read the Torah in light of the Oral Torah; nor does he read it with much interest in ongoing Judaism, although he finds Maimonides to be of help in giving a reasonable meaning to otherwise obscure precepts.[3] For Aquinas,

---

1. Thomas Aquinas, *Summa theologiae* I-II, qq. 98–105.
2. See my "Aristotle and the Mosaic Law."
3. I note that some contemporary biblical exegetes reject the view of Aquinas and of ongoing Judaism that the Torah aims to deliver law. In *Lost World of the Torah*, John H. Walton and J. Harvey Walton argue that "the Torah provides Israel wisdom for establishing order that upholds the reputation of Yahweh, their king and their God, and thereby secures his favor in the form of continuing presence and blessing. This is far different from the idea that it provides principles or rules for morality.... Yahweh's revelation to Israel was not to provide legislation, an ideal social system, or a moral system" (214). Walton and Walton are correct that the genre of the Torah is not that of a mere legal collection or a comprehensive one, but they exaggerate the implications of this. They dismiss (and misunderstand) the texts of ongoing Judaism by stating that these texts "are highly speculative and represent significant distortions of the original

Rabbinic Judaism was a grave mistake and the Oral Torah is a sad declension from the Torah of biblical Israel.

As a Christian, I believe that the Oral Torah does not possess the divinely inspired authority and standing of the written Torah. In my view, the way to obey Torah today is to obey it in the Messiah and his messianically reconfigured community, so that, as Matthew Thomas says, "Christ's law and teachings necessarily take precedence over the old."[4] I am aware, likewise, of the sharp criticisms of Christianity in the Talmud. Yet, I deny that Christian theologians should steer clear of Rabbinic Jewish teaching. The Catholic theologian Louis Bouyer rightly defends ongoing Judaism against all too common Christian misunderstandings: "It is not true that the *halakah* . . . is limited to accumulating ritual prohibitions. . . . It attaches to these prohibitions (as the word 'hedge' shows) only the value of a safeguard [of Torah]. And if it is deeply concerned with the material details of obedience to the Torah, it is because of a profoundly thought-out conviction that one does not reach the interior of man except through the exterior."[5] Bouyer's point is not only to defend Rabbinic Judaism but also to indicate its affinity with Catholicism—given Catholicism's "exterior" sacraments and canon law. The practice of Rabbinic Judaism, Bouyer perceives, aims to ensure that "each action of the day, each object or being he [the Jewish believer] meets, becomes an occasion for celebrating the revealed God as the Master and Creator of everything, and the Savior of those who believe in the Word [Torah]."[6]

---

material" (Walton and Walton, *Lost World of the Torah*, 217). Yet, after stating that "[j]ust as he [God] was carrying out his plans and purposes through Israel, he is now carrying them out through the church," they add in a footnote that "[i]t is possible that he also continues to carry them out through Israel. Paul seems to think so in Romans 9–11" (Walton and Walton, *Lost World of the Torah*, 121 and 121n4). See also Walton, *Old Testament Theology for Christians*.

4. Thomas, *Paul's 'Works of the Law'*, 226. Investigating what Paul means by "works of the law" in Romans and Galatians, Thomas examines the interpretations offered by the first- and second-century church fathers and compares these interpretations to those of the Reformers and contemporary advocates of the Reformers' position (the "old perspective on Paul") and to the interpretations of E. P. Sanders, James D. G. Dunn, and N. T. Wright ("the new perspective on Paul"). Thomas's conclusion about "Christ's law and teachings" strikes me as similar to Bruce Chilton and Jacob Neusner's observation that "the Gospels show how Jesus proposes to mediate between the Torah of Sinai and his own instruction, presented not in the name of Sinai's Torah but his own. . . . God Incarnate affirms the Torah—but at the same time brings the Torah to fulfillment. . . . [K]nowledge of God Incarnate bears Torah that surpasses Sinai's" (Chilton and Neusner, *Judaism in the New Testament*, 130–31; cf. 135).

5. Bouyer, *Church of God*, 224.

6. Bouyer, *Church of God*, 225. Bouyer adds that he is not suggesting that Rabbinic Jewish spirituality substitutes a "lay, secularized 'prophetic faith' for the 'priestly

Bouyer, with his deep knowledge of the Jewish and Christian liturgies and worldviews, has seen to the heart of the matter. It follows that Christians, especially sacramentally oriented Christians, can benefit from studying Rabbinic Jewish understandings of Torah. This is especially the case in light of recent studies of biblical Israel's law that show "the *complementariness* of the different codes as they are *reread, reinterpreted*, and *reapplied* to one another according to the changing circumstances of Israel's history."[7] Such a rereading is done eschatologically by Jesus and Paul, in a manner further demonstrating that "biblical law, based on common values and a common story, explains *who Israel is* and not just *what Israel does*."[8] This rereading of Israel's law does not negate the prior code or change its fundamental purpose of calling God's people to holiness, though its content is now shaped by Christ.

In seeking to develop a Christian doctrine of Torah, I approach the theme first from the perspective of Rabbinic Judaism, and specifically through the work of Rabbi Joseph B. Soloveitchik. In taking this approach, I do not intend to fall into what the Jewish theologian Michael Wyschogrod, in an essay on Jewish-Christian dialogue, calls "[t]he obvious temptation... to stress the continuities and to ignore the discontinuities."[9] The discontinuities are well described by Wyschogrod when he offers a thought experiment asking where an extraterrestrial visitor today would find the laws of the Torah adhered to most closely. As Wyschogrod says, such an extraterrestrial visitor "would have to conclude that it is Orthodox Jews who follow the way of life of the Pentateuch most closely. They obey the festivals of the Pentateuch, the dietary laws, the menstrual laws, the law forbidding the mixing of wool and linen in clothing, and many other commandments."[10] Orthodox Jews also obey the commandment to love one's neighbor as oneself and the commandment to love God above all things.

---

religion', the religion of the sacrifices. The imaginary opposition is a historical misunderstanding, since prophetism originated in the priestly milieus and achieved its major expression only in the work of two priests, Jeremiah and Ezekiel. Rather, it is a question, in the line expressed by the theme of the *kavanah*, of the last meaning given to sacrificial religion by the religion of the Word. Sacrifice, like all ritual prescriptions of the Torah, is in no way discredited there, but is seen as the expression and acceptance in faith of a consecration of the whole existence of the People to the God who spoke to them" (Bouyer, *Church of God*, 227).

7. Schembri, "On the Unity of the Two Testaments," 1327–28. See also B. Wells, "What Is Biblical Law?"; J. Berman, "History of Legal Theory."

8. Schembri, "On the Unity of the Two Testaments," 1328. In my view, Schembri's approach solves some of the more difficult problems regarding Paul and the Law.

9. Wyschogrod, "Impact of Dialogue," 226.

10. Wyschogrod, "Impact of Dialogue," 227.

I consider Wyschogrod to be correct that "the Judaism of the rabbis is not fundamentally discontinuous with biblical Judaism."[11] At least, it is clear that the Judaism practiced by the Pharisees in Jesus' day is broadly consonant with Rabbinic Judaism, even given the fact that the Pharisees were able in their time to carry out the animal sacrifices at the temple.[12] Although distortions could arise in their devotion to Torah (as distortions can afflict other forms of religious observance), it is clear that neither the Pharisees nor Rabbinic Jews held that the coming of the kingdom of God depends more fundamentally on human action than it does on the action of God. Even so, the path of salvation in Rabbinic Judaism is built upon the keeping of *mitsvot*, grounded inasmuch as possible in the commandments of the Torah (as interpreted by the Oral Torah).[13] Although Christianity requires works of love in union with Christ, the path of salvation is Jesus Christ and his fulfillment of Torah on the cross, as well as his eschatological outpouring of his Spirit so that we might live out our "identity-forming covenant commitment with Jesus Christ embodied in the call to holiness."[14]

Lest the above tension be exaggerated, David Novak makes the helpful point that "*both* Christianity and Rabbinic Judaism come out of, and thereby supersede, a religion based on the Hebrew Bible, plus some developments

11. Wyschogrod, "Impact of Dialogue," 227.

12. See the discussion of the Pharisees in Dunn, *Jesus Remembered*, 266-70; as well as Roland Deines's survey of scholarship about the Pharisees in Deines, *Die Pharisäer*. Dunn highlights a debate between E. P. Sanders and Jacob Neusner regarding the Pharisees. Neusner emphasizes the Pharisees' concern for ritual purity and connections to later rabbinic sages, whereas Sanders downplays these elements. With regard to the Pharisees' concern for ritual purity, Dunn agrees with Neusner. Dunn adds, "Where the Pharisees stood most clearly among their contemporaries, however, was in their concern to keep the law with scrupulous accuracy and exactness (*akribeia*), and in their development of a distinctive halakhic interpretation of Torah, 'the traditions of their fathers', the so-called 'oral law'. Here it is important to recall that the Pharisees were not a uniform, far less monolithic, party. Most famous at the time of Jesus were the many disputes on points of halakhic detail between the 'schools' of Hillel and Shammai, remembered respectively for the mildness and the severity of their rulings. To acknowledge this is to make no concession to the old accusation of Pharisaic 'legalism', since Pharisees were characteristically more flexible in their rulings than Qumran, and the Hillelites more lenient in their rulings on divorce than Jesus" (Dunn, *Jesus Remembered*, 260-70). See also Sanders, *Judaism: Practice and Belief*, chapter 3; Neusner, *Judaism*; Neusner, *From Politics to Piety*; Neusner, "Mr Maccoby's Red Cow." Note, too, Neusner's critique (in a work co-authored with Bruce Chilton) of Sanders's description of a single "Judaism" that spans the period 63 BCE—66 CE: see Chilton and Neusner, *Judaism in the New Testament*, 10-18, 48-51. See also C. Hayes, *What's Divine about Divine Law?*, 294-98 for a discussion of Hillel's halakhic reasoning and its reception.

13. See Novak, "*Mitsvah*," 116-17.

14. Schembri, "On the Unity of the Two Testaments," 1325 (I have removed the italics from this quotation).

coming from the elaborative interpretations of Second Temple Jewish theology."[15] Christianity was never a rejection of Rabbinic Judaism per se. The same point is made by the Lutheran theologian Robert Jenson, who accords a central role to the destruction of the Temple and the expulsion of Jews from the land. He states, "When land and temple were gone, two denominations survived that could if need be do without land and temple, and it is vital to remember that both were indeed denominations *within* what is often called late second-temple Judaism."[16] I consider the term *denomination* to be unhelpful here, and it also seems to me that Christianity was not merely "within" Second Temple Judaism, because the resurrection

---

15. Novak, "Supersessionism Hard and Soft," 30. For the same point, see Novak, "From Supersessionism to Parallelism," 20. For discussion of central issues at the heart of the development of Rabbinic Judaism, see Yadin-Israel, *Scripture and Tradition*, 201–3 and elsewhere. See also James L. Kugel's argument that Rabbinic Jews and Christians share a great deal of common heritage: Kugel, *Bible as It Was*. Kugel sums up the conclusions of his book: "What I wish to show is that, the history of Jewish-Christian polemics aside (and along with it the sad story of church-supported anti-Semitism), rabbinic Judaism and Christianity emerged out of a common mentality including, prominently, a common set of beliefs about the Bible. In other words, it is not only Scripture itself, the written word, that Jews and Christians share. Both groups received, along with the written texts that make up the Hebrew Bible, the same set of attitudes about how the Bible ought to be read and explained, what it was meant for and how it was to be used. Moreover . . . both carried forward a substantial body of common explanations of individual words, verses, incident, stories, songs, prayers, laws, and prophecies in Scripture" (*Bible as It Was*, 47). See also the somewhat similar—though more focused on contemporary application—project of Jacob Neusner in his *Christian Faith*.

16. Jenson, "Toward a Christian Theology of Judaism," 3. Jenson aims to grant Rabbinic Judaism a very high status indeed: "My final—and perhaps most radical—suggestion to Christian theology (*not*, let me say again, to Jewish self-understanding) is that, so long as the time of detour lasts, the embodiment of the risen Christ is whole only in the form of the church *and* an identifiable community of Abraham and Sarah's descendants. The church and the synagogue are together and only together the present availability to the world of the risen Jesus Christ" ("Toward a Christian Theology of Judaism," 13). I consider this to be a mistaken suggestion, but one rooted in the goodness of the fact that God's Jewish people continue to exist in a distinctive form—even if the acceptance of Jesus as the Messiah by the whole Jewish people would be a great good (see Rom 11:12). I agree with Jenson that "the church should acknowledge that God, in the time between the times . . . wants a community that studies and obeys Torah as Judaism does" ("Toward a Christian Theology of Judaism," 11). God allowed the great majority of Jews in the mid-first century to reject the claim that Jesus is the Messiah, and God has continued to permit this. A Christian can see here not only a negative rejection, but also positive goods that God has providentially willed. Although in this essay Jenson does not advocate Messianic Judaism, he does raise the key Messianic Jewish concern: "The church is essentially an *ekklesia* of Jews and gentiles, but the Jews within it constantly tend to vanish from sight as Jews" ("Toward a Christian Theology of Judaism," 10). By contrast, it seems to me that to be "in Christ" is to be Jewish in a messianically reconfigured way.

of Jesus Christ makes a break with any existing context (despite the presence of crucial continuity as well). But I agree with Jenson and Novak that neither Christianity nor Rabbinic Judaism is *merely* the continuation of Second Temple Judaism. Christianity and Rabbinic Judaism differ on a central point—the identity of the Messiah and all else that follows directly from this—but neither should claim to have originated as the negation of the other.[17]

Nevertheless, as discussed above, Christians and Jews differ sharply over how to understand and obey the Torah. Jews read the (Written) Torah through the lens of Oral Torah, while Christians consider the Torah to be embodied and fulfilled in Jesus Christ.[18] The biblical scholar Richard Hays points out that in Romans 10:8-9, by quoting Deuteronomy 30:14, Paul equates the Torah with Jesus. In fact, this equation has roots in Second Temple Jewish texts, even if something new is being asserted. Hays states, "Echoing Job, Baruch, and Sirach, Paul hints at the notion that the word of God spoken in the Law is identical with the Wisdom of God, who 'appeared upon earth and lived among men' (Bar. 3:37)—not as Torah, as Israel's sages affirmed, but in the person of Jesus Messiah."[19] For his part, Jenson notes

---

17. See Jenson, "Toward a Christian Theology of Judaism," 6. Yet, in "When Jews Are Christians," Novak remarks that "[f]rom the fact that the first generation of Christians were mostly Jewish ('according to the flesh,' as Paul put it in Romans 4:1), one could argue that Christianity was *at that time* a form of Judaism, perhaps even a heterodox form of pharisaic Judaism [in light of Acts 15:5]" ("When Jews Are Christians," 224).

18. I agree with Mark J. Boda that "the NT makes clear that the Scriptures have as their goal the redemption of all creation through the Son, Jesus the Christ (2 Tim. 3:14-17; Luke 24). Interpretation of these Scriptures must then be christotelic in character; what has been revealed is by definition part of a larger story that has the revelation of and redemption through the Son as its goal.... To read the OT (and the NT) as if Jesus did not show up at the turn of the ages and change the course of history would not be Christian" (Boda, *Heartbeat of Old Testament Theology*, 173). At the same time, I share the concern expressed by Christopher Seitz in this regard: "It has been held by some that there is only a *Vetus Testamentum in Novo receptum*.... But crucial in all this is just what it means to focus on the use of the OT in the NT and how this affects in turn our handling of the Scriptures of Israel as an abiding witness in their own right" (Seitz, *Character of Christian Scripture*, 21-22). Each "phase" of redemptive history is present in the next "phase"—rather than being cancelled or discarded.

19. R. B. Hays, *Echoes of Scripture*, 82. I agree with Andrew Chester that there is diversity in the New Testament portraits of the Torah in relation to Christ, but I disagree with his view of Hebrews (and I agree only with his second way of interpreting Matthew). Discussing "the variety of attitudes to Torah in the messianic or final age, as those are manifested in a wide range of early Jewish and Christian sources," Chester identifies "four main strands: first, in at least some Jewish traditions, and in Matthew and James (and Paul and the Didache to an extent), Torah is seen as continuing in force with *intensified* demands. Second, in Paul (on one reading of him at least) and Justin, as well as Hermas, the Kerygma Petrou and Irenaeus (reflecting Jewish tradition), Torah is

that according to John 6—as also of course according to Paul and to Christianity as a whole—"the Word that became flesh as Jesus . . . is the Word called 'Torah.'"[20] Indeed, Jenson puts the matter even more strongly: "If the church's faith is true, Jesus Christ *is* the *torah*."[21]

Given this sharp difference, how can there be a relationship between the way in which Rabbinic Jews observe Torah and the pattern of Christian life "in Christ" which is also somehow life "in Torah"? How could Christians have anything to learn about Christ or life in Christ by reading Jewish masters of Halakhah such as Soloveitchik? I argue in this chapter that by following the law of Christ, Christians share in a Torah-ordered life much more than may be at first imagined—even by some Christians.[22] The worldview set forth by Soloveitchik's *Halakhic Man* will help us see how this is so, because the Christian worldview is similar in notable ways, even while being reconfigured around Jesus Christ, the embodiment of Torah.

How Much Shared Ground Is Possible?

Before proceeding, however, let me address the question of how much shared ground is possible for Jews and Christians who agree that the Torah is authoritative divine revelation but disagree about whether Jesus is the Messiah and also, therefore, about what proper interpretation and embodiment of Torah entails. Novak explains part of the difference: "The difference between Jewish exegesis and Christian exegesis arises over analysis of *which* of the Torah's norms were taken to be perpetually binding, and *which* of the Torah's norms were only binding in the past and no longer apply in the present."[23] Christians generally accept the moral teachings, but not

---

seen as having its true *fulfilment* in Christ. Third, the understanding that Christ brings a *new law* is evident in Justin, Irenaeus and the Didascalia. It is possible to see Matthew as representing this position, and if it incorporates the idea that Christ brings the true, perfect and final Torah, then the Johannine letters, Fourth Gospel and Paul can all be included as well. Finally, we find the idea that Torah has been *rejected*, or at least superseded, completely. Despite what is sometimes claimed, this has no basis in Jewish tradition. It is, however, starkly portrayed by Barnabas and, almost as strongly, by Hebrews as well" (A. Chester, *Messiah and Exaltation*, 8).

20. Jenson, "Toward a Christian Theology of Judaism," 12.

21. Jenson, *Triune Story*, 107.

22. Novak states, "When Christians stop seeing Judaism as legalism, they will be in a much better position to realize the importance of law in Christianity. And when Jews stop seeing Christianity as antinomianism, as against the law, they will be in a much better position to realize the importance of grace in Judaism" ("*Mitsvah*," 116).

23. Novak, "Supersessionism Hard and Soft," 31. See also Neusner, "Israel as Kingdom of Priests." Neusner highlights the role of the Torah for Rabbinic Judaism: "Israel

the laws about food, ritual purity, or about doing no work on the Sabbath (for example), since Christians believe that these laws (and their purposes) have been fulfilled and reconfigured by the Messiah, so that we now observe them "in Christ."

No doubt, this is a significant difference. From a Jewish perspective, it makes little sense when Christians claim they observe the Torah's ritual laws by means of union with the Messiah in his supreme fulfillment of these laws on the cross. Wyschogrod argues that "there is no Judaism without law.... If I must determine whether I am dealing with a Jew whose Judaism is in relatively good shape, I observe his or her behavior. If he or she observes the sabbath, eats kosher, attends a synagogue fairly often, refrains from eating leavened bread during Passover, etc., I come away feeling fairly secure about that person's Judaism."[24] I believe that Christians should not practice Judaism in this way, as though Christ had not transformed Torah observance—although behavior is quite important for Christianity too. It therefore does not surprise me when Wyschogrod states, "Christianity, ever since Paul, represents an extremely sustained and fundamental critique of Jewish law."[25] In my view, of course, Christianity is not so much a critique but rather is a messianic fulfillment and reconfiguration.

Wyschogrod is acquainted with the passage in Acts 21 where Paul, meeting with James and the other elders of the Jerusalem church, learns about the many Jews there who have believed in Jesus and "are all zealous for the law, and they have been told about you that you teach all the Jews who are among the Gentiles to forsake Moses, telling them not to circumcise their children or observe the customs" (Acts 21:20-21).[26] Paul agrees

---

is Israel by virtue of the Torah" ("Israel as Kingdom of Priests," 48).

24. Wyschogrod, "Impact of Dialogue," 230.

25. Wyschogrod, "Impact of Dialogue," 231.

26. For discussion, see Keener, *Acts* III, 3123-43. Keener suggests that in Acts 21, "The question ... is whether law observance is acceptable for Jews, a practice Paul explicitly approves in his letters (1 Cor 7:19; Gal 5:6; 6:15)" (*Acts* III, 3142). Keener recognizes that some scholars interpret Galatians 5:3 and other texts to imply that Paul considers Torah observance to be mandatory for Jews who believe in Christ. Although Keener does not rule out such a view, he considers it better to say simply that "Paul affirms the right of Jews (including himself) to observe the law" (*Acts* III, 3141). Keener holds that Paul "allowed setting aside such customs (albeit not the moral heart of the law) for Gentile converts and perhaps for himself for strategic missiological purposes (cf. Acts 16:34) but did not personally reject law practice (1 Cor 9:20-21)" (*Acts* III, 3130). In my view, Keener is right that Paul continued to observe Torah, but I would stress much more than does Keener the importance of the fact that Paul was willing to make exceptions and, in addition, that Paul's theology rejects Torah observance as the path of salvific justification before God. The latter point needs more attention in Novak, "*Mitsvah*," 116.

to purify himself ritually and to pay the cost of the ritual offering that four other Jewish Jesus-followers intend to make. Paul follows through on this promise, as we would expect from his statement in 1 Corinthians 9:20, "To the Jews I became as a Jew, in order to win Jews; to those under the law I became as one under the law—though not being myself under the law—that I might win those under the law." The question is whether Paul is "zealous for the law" in the manner that the Jerusalem elders are. Does he think that Jews who follow Jesus must, in order to be saved, continue to obey Torah as they did prior to Jesus' death and resurrection?

In answer, the biblical scholar Joseph Fitzmyer points out that "to be justified Paul feels no obligation to observe the Mosaic law and all its precepts."[27] Paul holds that he is "not ... without law toward God but under the law of Christ" (1 Cor 9:21; cf. Gal 6:2; Rom 8:2). Because Christ has fulfilled the Torah, Christians now participate, as members of Christ's body (1 Cor 12:12-27), in the "law of Christ"—namely in Christ's own love and salvific action on the cross by which he fulfilled and reconfigured Torah as the Messiah.[28] For Paul, this does not mean that Christian Jews may no longer observe Torah, as is clear from 1 Corinthians 9:20 and elsewhere. But it means that the Jewish salvific *obligation* to observe all the laws of the Torah—as distinct from observing Torah as fulfilled and reconfigured in the "law of Christ"—is no longer in force, even for Christians who are Jews.

Wyschogrod recognizes that, in the opinion of some biblical scholars, Paul intends to teach only that *Gentile* Christians do not need to observe all the laws of the Torah.[29] Although Wyschogrod wishes he could share this perspective and tries hard to share it, he cannot convince himself that it is true. As he comments, "When Paul says (Gal. 3:19) that the law was a temporary measure promulgated through angels, it is difficult to maintain

---

27. Fitzmyer, *First Corinthians*, 370.

28. I recognize that, for some Jews, the words of Jesper Svartvik will ring true: "there is no Christian symbol that makes Jews feel as uneasy as the cross, especially if it is a crucifix" (Svartvik, "What If There Is Life?," 8). This is because of the many centuries of unjust Christian taunts against Jews as Christ-killers, and it is also because the crucifix is a visible reminder of the nodal point of disagreement between Jews and Christians—a point of disagreement that goes back to the very earliest days of Christian belief, when the controversy was solely between Jews. At the same time, perhaps due to generational shifts, Edward Kessler points out: "A survey of attitudes in 2009 showed that 75% of Israeli Jews do not see Christians as missionaries and are not bothered by encountering a Christian wearing a cross" (Kessler, "'I Am Joseph,'" 67-68).

29. See especially the work of Christian New Testament scholars associated with Messianic Jewish movements: for example, Nanos, *Collected Essays*; and Fredriksen, *When Christians Were Jews*. See the review of Fredriksen's book by Anthony Giambrone, OP, in *Nova et Vetera*.

that this is true for gentiles but not for Jews."³⁰ In my view, as will already be clear, Wyschogrod is correct about this. As the biblical scholar John Barclay notes, Galatians contains a "sustained polemic . . . against the works of the law, justification by the law and submission to the law"; and Paul makes "emphatic, repeated and unambiguous attempts to limit the significance of the law, to drive a wedge between the law and the Abrahamic promises and to contrast the law with faith in Christ."³¹ Paul argues that faith in Christ and sacramental membership in his body—rather than an observance of Torah distinct from Torah's fulfillment in Christ (through which Christ bore the penalty of the law for our sake [Gal 3:10–14])—are what is required of God's people. Now that the messianic kingdom has been inaugurated, Paul insists that "no man is justified before God by the law" (Gal 3:11) and that "in Christ Jesus neither circumcision nor uncircumcision is of any avail, but faith working through love" (Gal 5:6).³²

Jesus and the Torah

An attempt can be made to argue that Jesus himself would not have countenanced Galatians' view of the Torah. For example, Jesus teaches in the Gospel of Matthew: "Do not think that I have come to abolish the law and the prophets; I have come not to abolish them but to fulfil them. . . . Whoever then relaxes one of the least of these commandments and teaches men so, shall be called least in the kingdom of heaven" (Matt 5:17, 19). In the very same Gospel, however, Jesus causes deep offense to the Pharisees when he teaches regarding the food laws:

---

30. Wyschogrod, "Impact of Dialogue," 233.

31. Barclay, *Obeying the Truth*, 63. See also Barclay's *Paul and the Gift*, as well as Isaac Augustine Morales, OP's response to Barclay's book: "Paul and the Gift of Sonship," praising Barclay's book and suggesting that his argument would be enhanced by highlighting adoptive sonship.

32. For further discussion, see Pitre et al., *Paul, a New Covenant Jew*. For an alternative viewpoint, see Wilson, "Supersession and Superfluity." According to Wilson, "in Galatians the apostle Paul advocates neither for the supersession of the law with the coming of Christ, nor for its superfluity in shaping the behavior of Christ-followers with the dawning of the Spirit; instead, Paul's chief burden in Galatians is to convince his largely Gentile hearers of the *suspension of the curse of the law* for those who by faith in Messiah Jesus walk by the Spirit and thus fulfill the law of Moses, which by implication still persists into the *post Christum* era" ("Supersession and Superfluity," 236). There is nothing in this statement with which I need disagree, so long as Wilson is not claiming that Paul thinks that Jews who are Christians must still observe Torah (outside of participating in its fulfillment in Christ) on pain of incurring the curse of the law. If I understand Wilson correctly, he is unsure what the answer is to this latter question, whereas my answer would certainly be no.

"Hear and understand: not what goes into the mouth defiles a man, but what comes out of the mouth, this defiles a man" (Matt 15:10–11). In this context, he calls the Pharisees of his day "blind guides" (Matt 15:14).[33] In the Gospel of Mark, the evangelist interprets Jesus' statement that "whatever goes into a man from outside cannot defile him" to mean that Jesus thereby "declared all foods clean" (Mark 7:18–19).[34]

33. In his *Halakhah*, Chaim N. Saiman notes that "Jesus scoffed at the Pharisees' legal obsessions, arguing that their edifice of technicalities inevitably distracts the believer from the 'weightier matters of the law' [Matt 23:23]. From the rabbinic perspective, however, what this fails to understand is that those same technicalities are the prism through which the weightier matters obtain religious significance. . . . A modest response to Jesus's challenge would acknowledge that all legal systems—halakhah included—have the potential to become overrun by technical minutiae that can drown out the law's overarching goals and principles. The rabbis' idea of halakhah, however, suggests that the opposite may also be true. Whether by design, effect, or by some combination thereof, halakhah became the forum to explore and develop the most weighty matters of the law" (Saiman, *Halakhah*, 125–26). I note that Catholic moral theology, at least in the past, has had similarities with halakhic reasoning and has often come under the same kinds of attack, both for being obsessed with minutiae and for the hypocrisy and narrowness of its practitioners. In my view, Jesus' criticisms aim at excesses that one finds in every epoch, and he is also signaling the newness of what he brings as the Messiah. He does not reject halakhic reasoning as such.

34. Chilton and Neusner argue that the Gospel of Mark "manifest[s] an overt concern to distance itself from Judaism" and exemplifies a "program of distinction from Judaism" (*Judaism in the New Testament*, 117). According to Chilton and Neusner, however, Jesus himself did not deviate from the purity laws—though Jesus did hold that Israelites should be assumed to be ritually pure unless their actions showed otherwise. According to their reconstruction, "James insisted upon the leadership of the movement from Jerusalem, the continuation of sacrifice in the Temple, the purity of all those (Jews and non-Jews) associated with him, and the separation of Jews and non-Jews at meals" (*Judaism in the New Testament*, 127). I am persuaded by Matthew Thiessen's argument, in *Jesus and the Forces of Death*, that for Matthew, Mark, and Luke, Jesus is "a mobile power who removes the most stubborn sources of the impurities he encounters. Jesus not only removes the sources of ritual impurity, but he also removes moral impurities or sins. . . . [R]itual impurity remained of fundamental importance for the Gospel writers, but they were convinced that God had introduced something *new* into the world to deal with the sources of these impurities: Jesus. By inserting a new, mobile, and powerfully contagious force of holiness into the world in the person of Jesus, Israel's God has signaled the very coming of the kingdom" (178–79). If so, then the Jewish impurity laws are relativized for Jesus' followers, despite Thiessen's emphasis that Jesus and his followers are not "lax" toward or unconcerned with ritual impurity. For Thiessen, Jesus' affirmation of God's law in Mark 7:8–13 makes it unlikely that in Mark 7:14–23 he rejects the food laws. Instead, Thiessen proposes that Jesus (or Mark) is "address[ing] the question of whether one can defile kosher food with one's ritually impure hands and then introduce that ritual impurity into one's body by the consumption of that defiled food" (*Jesus and the Forces of Death*, 192). In my view, this interpretation does not do justice to what we find in 7:14–23. I propose that just as Jesus (as a kingdom-establishing "mobile power") deals with ritual impurities in a new way,

Jesus also overturned the Torah's explicit teaching on divorce.³⁵

As we have seen above, the meaning of Jesus' extensive criticisms of the Pharisees and their approach to Torah observance is contested. Commenting on Matthew 15:11, the biblical scholars W. D. Davies and Dale Allison point out that "if Jesus did in fact dispense with Scriptural food laws, the heated debates in the early church on that very issue just do not make sense."³⁶ In their view (unlike my own), Mark 7:15 does not derive from Jesus, but rather was composed to persuade "people perceived as preoccupied with the literal observance of Torah and tradition to the neglect of the weightier matters of the law."³⁷ From a somewhat similar perspective, James Dunn affirms that Jesus "did not set himself antithetically over against the law," by contrast to portraits of Jesus' debates with the Pharisees that interpret Jesus as being opposed to the Torah itself.³⁸ But Dunn thinks that Jesus did separate himself from the Pharisees' emphasis on observing Torah as the test "of obedience and loyalty to the covenant," and so for Dunn it is not surprising that "the fundamental concerns Jesus enunciated and defended gave stimulus and scope to his subsequent followers to press still further at various points into a rationale for conduct which no longer remained within the boundaries clearly marked out by the law."³⁹ Going a step further, N.

---

so also Jesus' followers are enabled to deal with unclean foods in a new way, namely, by consuming them within the body of Christ—though not if this will cause offense to the weak brother in Christ. Thiessen directs attention to Furstenberg, "Defilement Penetrating the Body"; VanMaaren, "Does Mark's Jesus Abrogate Torah?" See also, more broadly, Guelich, "Anti-Semitism."

35. See Meier, *Law and Love*, 126: "Jesus absolutely forbade divorce and branded divorce and remarriage as the sin of adultery." Meier raises the question, "How can the Law-abiding Jesus claim that a fellow Jew who dutifully follows the Law in divorcing and remarrying commits a sin against one of the commandments of the Decalogue?" (*Law and Love*, 127). In answer, he rightly points to Jesus' eschatological conception of his prophetic task.

36. Davies and Allison, *Commentary on Matthew VIII–XVIII*, 528.

37. Davies and Allison, *Commentary on Matthew VIII–XVIII*, 529; cf. 531. See also the very similar approach of Dunn, *Jesus Remembered*, 574-77. Dunn sums up his position: "Jesus' teaching was heard differently. Some heard Jesus as not content to debate issues of ritual purity solely at the level of ritual but pressing home the concerns behind such law and halakhoth to the more fundamental level of purity of motive and intention. Others heard Jesus, when the teaching was rehearsed within wider circles of discipleship, as validating or commending a more radical conclusion, to the effect that Israel's purity law no longer applied to the followers of Jesus.... Either way, it is again evident that Jesus had no interest in making ritual purity a test case of covenant loyalty" (Dunn, *Jesus Remembered*, 576-77).

38. Dunn, *Jesus Remembered*, 582.

39. Dunn, *Jesus Remembered*, 583. He adds the point that "Jesus was remembered as giving particular prominence to the Torah injunction to 'love your neighbour as

T. Wright thinks that Jesus himself *was* in fact "cryptically subverting the Jewish food laws."[40]

To my mind, no matter whether Mark 7:15 and Matthew 15:11 derive from Jesus himself (as in fact they do in their canonical force, guided by the Spirit of the risen Christ[41]), it is clearly the case that the Pharisees were offended by Jesus' general approach to the Torah. Moreover, they were rightly offended. They saw that the logical implication of his position was a grave weakening of Torah observance as they understood it. Even if Jesus merely opposed (more generally) a focus on ritual purity, he never placed Torah observance at the center of his teaching in the manner that the Pharisees did. The Jewish scholar Jacob Neusner tells Jesus in an imagined dialogue, "I really don't see how your teachings and the Torah's teachings come together. That isn't because things you say don't appeal to the Torah; some of them do. It's because most of what you say and most of what the Torah says scarcely intersect."[42] Neusner recognizes that Torah observance as understood by first-century Jews is not central to Jesus' vision of the inaugurated kingdom. Speaking as a Rabbinic Jew, Neusner says to Jesus, "You talk about the kingdom of heaven. To me, that means living under the rule of God. The Torah gives us the rules that form the rule of God. And about most of these rules

---

yourself' and as pressing home its full implications" (Dunn, *Jesus Remembered*, 583). By contrast, John P. Meier argues that "the historical Jesus never directly connects his individual halakhic pronouncements to some basic or organizing principle of love" (*Law and Love*, 655). Meier considers that "Jesus' legal commands express the proper eschatological implementation of God's will as expressed in Torah—an eschatological implementation that is meant not just for the short, sui generis interval but for the whole future of Israel as God's people, restored in the end time" (*Law and Love*, 658).

40. N. T. Wright, *Jesus and the Victory*, 284. Wright notes that Jesus' words are connected with his eschatological "belief that a new day is dawning in which new things can be expected" (*Jesus and the Victory*, 284). See also Wright's engagement with Sanders on Jesus' relation to the Pharisees, in *Jesus and the Victory*, 376-98. In my view, Wright errs when he reduces (or comes close to reducing) the Pharisees' efforts to observe Torah to a political program focused on enhancing and upholding Israel's national identity. But I agree with Wright that Jesus undermined the food laws, within the context of inaugurating the eschatological kingdom. Although as a matter of historical reconstruction it may be possible that Jesus did not speak the words that Mark 7 and Matthew 15 attribute to him—Meier's arguments against authenticity in *Law and Love*, 384-97 are at least plausible—it seems clear that Jesus stood out against the program of Torah observance outlined by the Pharisees. On Jesus' relation to the Pharisees, see also Meier, *Companions and Competitors*, 289-388.

41. Craig A. Carter is correct that "[t]he nature of interpretation depends upon the inspired nature of the Bible," which in turn depends upon the activity in human history of God the Father, Son, and Spirit. See C. A. Carter, *Interpreting Scripture*, 25. See also the critical (and also at times appreciative) insights regarding historical-critical study of Jesus, in von Balthasar, *Glory of the Lord* I, 174, 209, 466-67, 533, 618.

42. Neusner, *Rabbi Talks with Jesus*, 134.

you have very little to say."[43] In the Gospels, Jesus does a lot of teaching, but observance of the Torah's laws—while present here and there—is certainly not at the center of it.

In light of Neusner's work, Joseph Ratzinger has helpfully proposed that both Galatians and the Gospel of Matthew's Sermon on the Mount sketch a "Torah of the Messiah" that is distinct from Israel's Torah in its form prior to Christ.[44] Just as God (through Moses) gave the Torah at Mount Sinai, so

---

43. Neusner, *Rabbi Talks with Jesus*, 134.

44. Ratzinger, *Jesus of Nazareth* I, 100. See also, with reference to Matthew 11, Joslyn-Siemiatkoski, *More Torah, More Life*, 164–65: "Matthew presents Jesus as the teacher of wisdom who guides his disciples to knowledge of the God of Israel. Indeed, Jesus is the Son of God, the special agent of revelation for Israel, according to this pericope. Implicit is that other teachers, the 'wise,' are ineffective teachers. In keeping with the rhetoric of Matthew, this critique of the wise is aimed at the Pharisees and scribes, of whom the rabbis of Avot can be considered heirs.... Both Avot and Matthew [11:30] utilize the yoke as an image of following the commandments of God, employing the image of taking on the yoke offered by Wisdom in the book of Sirach: 'Put your neck under her yoke, and let your souls receive instruction; it is to be found close by' (Sir. 51:26). We see then that in offering his yoke, Jesus speaks not only as a personification of Wisdom but as an incarnation of it. While the rabbis offer the yoke of Torah instruction, the yoke represents what Torah teaches, not what a rabbi might teach. But in Matthew, Jesus is both the teacher and the yoke." Joslyn-Siemiatkoski is here drawing upon Meier, *Matthew*, 128. As Joslyn-Siemiatkoski goes on to say with Galatians 5:1 in view as well as in light of Matthew's teaching that Jesus opens the way to the definitive observance of Torah: Jewish "commentaries on Avot... insist that obedience to Torah is not a limitation but a practice that actually liberates one spiritually. By taking on the rabbinic path of the yoke of Torah, one is free from the demands of the world that take one away from true service to God. This message of spiritual liberation is not far from the one the Gospel of Matthew offers concerning Jesus.... Once again, we have encountered a moment in which Christians and Jews possess a shared spiritual insight yet remain divided by the path by which to attain this insight—between Jesus and Torah" (*More Torah, More Life*, 166). No doubt, then, as Joslyn-Siemiatkoski sums up the two perspectives, "Torah occupies a similar place for Jews that the person of Jesus Christ does for Christians. Both represent modes of mediation with the divine and access to blessedness and redemption. And yet we also see that Torah consistently operates as a means for expressing covenantal relationship with the God of Israel whereas Jesus Christ operates as the means of approaching the God of Israel because he is also substantially, according to Christian doctrine, the incarnation of God. Thus, there exists an ontological distinction between the path of studying Torah and the path of following Jesus. Despite the shared symbols and imagery stemming out of a shared world of the first century CE, there is an irreducible difference of meaning that Torah and Jesus convey" (*More Torah, More Life*, 168). Yet, Joslyn-Siemiatkoski concludes that in order to avoid the consequences of "a long heritage of supersessionist thought," Christians need to affirm that "despite the universalizing claims made for Jesus Christ in Christian theology, an alternative path exists for Jews" (*More Torah, More Life*, 168). This way of putting it risks undermining Christian claims about Jesus' messianic lordship over the entire creation. There are better ways of saying what he is trying to say, namely, that God has not abandoned the Jewish people to whom he gave the gift of Torah and that

Jesus gives the new Torah in his Sermon on the Mount. Jesus thereby sets forth the pattern of life for those united to him in the "great new family of God drawn from Israel and the Gentiles."[45] In Matthew 5:17–19, Jesus makes clear that this new Torah is not an abolition of the Mosaic Torah, but rather is its new-covenant fulfillment. As Catherine of Siena maintains in her *Dialogue* (with God as the speaker), "The law of love is the New Law given by the Word, my only-begotten Son. It is built on love. The Old Law was not dissolved by the New, but fulfilled."[46]

Ratzinger takes particular note of the reason why Neusner finds Jesus' teachings to be ultimately *incompatible* with Torah observance of the kind practiced by the Pharisees (and advanced by the Oral Torah). Neusner perceives Jesus to be placing himself at the center and making human perfection a matter not of observing Torah but rather of following Jesus. In Ratzinger's view, with which I agree, Neusner has here identified the most fundamental difference. In fact, Jesus' way of speaking about human perfection in the Gospel of Matthew shows that "Jesus understands himself as the Torah—as the word of God in person."[47] The Gospel of Matthew accords with the prologue of the Gospel of John.

If Jesus *is* the Torah, and if the Sabbath commandment and the other commandments find their fulfillment in Jesus, then humans become like God not by Torah observance per se (nor by Torah observance in accord with the Oral Torah) but by configuration to Jesus Christ in his eschatological fulfillment of Torah. Thus, it is the obedience of faith in Jesus Christ that unites believers to the divine will and instantiates "the obedience intended by the Torah."[48] The precepts that bind the Jewish people together in ritual purity and in a distinctive community are fulfilled and transformed by Jesus, the Messiah who embodies supreme love of God and love of neighbor (see Matt 22:36–40). Following Jesus in love for God and neighbor binds

---

the Jewish people as a whole are not culpable for rejecting Jesus as Messiah.

45. Ratzinger, *Jesus of Nazareth* I, 101; cf. 117.

46. Catherine of Siena, *Dialogue*, 112.

47. Ratzinger, *Jesus of Nazareth* I, 110–11. By contrast—differing both from Neusner and from Ratzinger (though writing prior to them)—Friedrich-Wilhelm Marquardt comments, "The Jesus of the Sermon on the Mount is not teaching anything originally Jesus-like, rather he teaches as a good rabbi" ("Why the Talmud Interests Me," 79).

48. Ratzinger, *Jesus of Nazareth* I, 117. Ratzinger adds, "This universalization of Israel's faith and hope, and the concomitant liberation from the letter of the Law for the new communion with Jesus, is tied to Jesus' authority and his claim to Sonship.... If Jesus does not speak with the full authority of the Son, if his interpretation is not the beginning of a new communion in a new, free obedience, then there is only one alternative: Jesus is enticing us to disobedience against God's commandment" (*Jesus of Nazareth* I, 119–20).

together God's messianic people. Ratzinger concludes that for Christianity, "The Torah of the Messiah is the Messiah, Jesus, himself.... In this Torah, which is Jesus himself, the abiding essence of what was inscribed on the stone tablets at Sinai is now written in living flesh, namely, the twofold commandment of love."[49]

It is no wonder, then, that for David Novak, as for almost all Jewish thinkers, the dividing point between Christianity and Judaism is the affirmation that Jesus is the Messiah.[50] Warning against syncretism (likely with Messianic Judaism in view), Novak emphasizes that Jews and Christians "must respect the essentially different existential decisions we make as to *who* Jesus of Nazareth *is* and *what* he means for the covenant between God and His people, Israel."[51] These decisions, says Novak, lead to paths

---

49. Ratzinger, *Many Religions—One Covenant*, 70. Hans Urs von Balthasar describes this in more eschatologically charged terms, emphasizing the violation of the Torah (producing the Babylonian exile) and the desolation it wreaked: see von Balthasar, *Glory of the Lord* VII, 34–37. Instead of describing Jesus as Torah in person, von Balthasar presents a Jesus who refuses a "wholesale rejection of Judaism" because he "knows how to take hold of what is genuine among the debris . . . and how to purify it and give new wholeness to the fragments in his person" (*Glory of the Lord* VII, 37). For von Balthasar, the "failure" ultimately helps to reveal the kenotic form of Jesus Christ (see *Glory of the Lord* VII, 39); see also von Balthasar, *Theo-Drama* II, 28). For further discussion, see von Balthasar, "Church and Israel," 289–98, in which he states that (for Paul in Romans 9–11) not only is Israel "not to blame for not having believed God," but also Israel, as "rejected and cut off" by God, enters into "a unique relationship to the Messiah who for the world's redemption was 'made sin' by God: as we Christians cannot look on him without seeing the wounds caused by our sins—since, innocent, he bore them for us—so guilty Israel, according to Paul, suffers for the world's redemption.... And so anyone who strikes Israel strikes the Messiah, who, as God's suffering Servant, gathers up in himself all the afflictions of God's servant Israel" (292–93).

50. Failure to accomplish the expected deeds of the Messiah is among the reasons that Dan Cohn-Sherbok offers for rejecting the veracity of the proclamation of Jesus' resurrection: see Cohn-Sherbok, "Resurrection of Jesus." Cohn-Sherbok develops this point, among others, in his *Jewish Messiah*, chapter 4. Cohn-Sherbok concludes that Jews today should repudiate the notion of a coming Messiah. See also Neusner and Chilton, *Jewish-Christian Debates*, chapter 5, where Neusner explains that for the Rabbis, "The Messiah will be a sage, coming when Israel fully accepts, in all humility, God's sole rule" (*Jewish-Christian Debates*, 164); and the Messiah will usher in "the age of Israel" understood as "the family, the children of Abraham, Isaac, and Jacob" (*Jewish-Christian Debates*, 164). Neusner takes as a given that "[i]f Jesus is the Christ, then history has come to its fulfillment and Israel is no longer God's people" (*Jewish-Christian Debates*, 164); whereas in my Christian view, Israel is still God's people.

51. Novak, "Supersessionism Hard and Soft," 30. James Kugel, too, warns against "the wrongheaded efforts of those who, even as these lines are being written, have announced their renewed intention to bring about the 'conversion of the Jews' by creating some strange hybrid of Christian teaching and traditional Jewish practices" (Kugel, *Bible as It Was*, 47).

that cannot be joined, despite the commonalities that exist between Jews and Christians. Theologically, he finds, it is impossible to be both Jewish and Christian, because "either the Jewish people or the Christian Church is the fullest, most complete location for that ultimate relationship, the final purpose for humans created in the image and likeness (*tselem u-demut*) of God."⁵²

Novak hastens to point out that this does not mean that the path *not* chosen is thereby worthless. Jews should not dismiss Christians as having retrogressed and returned to pagan idolatry, and Christians should not dismiss Jews as having fallen into talmudic "legalism."⁵³ But as Novak also says, "A complete denial of supersessionism leaves Christians unable to affirm Christianity as having brought something new and fuller to the ancient covenant between God and Israel," just as a complete Jewish denial of supersessionism (that is, Judaism's supersession of pagan myth through its unique election) would, in Novak's view, make it difficult for Jews to explain internally why they should not become Christians.⁵⁴

---

52. Novak, "Supersessionism Hard and Soft," 31.

53. Employing a technical language of his own in which "person" is firmly linked in a Trinitarian key with "mission" and specifically with the sending of the divine Son, von Balthasar arrives at a misleading conclusion: "Judaism hovers in an openness that is unfulfilled. In what sense is the Jew a person? Certainly, the great ones, chosen from among the people to be its prophets and leaders, are persons. But what of the individuals of the nation? They are not persons in the New Testament sense" (*Theo-Drama* II, 427). I think a reading of the various figures of the Old Testament (including minor figures) shows the opposite, even in the technical sense employed by von Balthasar. To say that Jews are "not persons in the New Testament sense" is unacceptable in light of centuries of Christian denials of the full humanity of the Jewish people, culminating in the Holocaust. Similarly, I question the claim that "Israel's whole meaning is to be found exclusively in the Messiah who fulfills," since this deprives the Jewish people and ongoing Judaism of any "meaning" at present, beyond unintelligible fragments (von Balthasar, *Theo-Logic* III, 281). I affirm the centrality of Christ as providing the fullness of meaning (cf. von Balthasar, *Theo-Logic* III, 285), rather than as a principle for denying meaning.

54. Novak, "Supersessionism Hard and Soft," 28. Novak comments, "A soft Jewish supersessionism, unlike hard Jewish supersessionism, does not equate Christianity with the idolatrous past superseded by the Torah. Instead, it somewhat grudgingly accepts Christianity (and Islam) as monotheistic and not polytheistic, though demoting Christianity (and Islam) to the status, in effect, of a watered down version of Judaism for the Gentiles" ("Supersessionism Hard and Soft," 29). As indicated above, Novak thinks that we can get beyond some aspects of even "soft" supersessionism by recognizing that both Rabbinic Judaism and Christianity "supersede" biblical Judaism.

The Approach of This Chapter

In light of Christ and the New Testament, we cannot expect Christians and Jews to agree about Torah, let alone about Oral Torah. But Novak is correct to say that "Christians can very well recognize in good faith that the central Jewish concern with keeping the *mitsvot*, including the very legally oriented tradition (*halakhah*) that so carefully structures the practice, is not legalism but, rather, a genuinely theological enterprise from beginning to end."[55] In fact, as I will attempt to show in the two sections that follow, when Christians understand why Rabbinic Judaism values Halakhah, Christians will be better able to perceive the implications of our affirmation that Christ *is* "Torah." Christians should be able to love Torah and to appreciate Oral Torah, while remaining Christians. Walter Moberly insightfully observes that "it is fully possible for Christians, once faith in Christ is established, to read torah more positively than is possible in a polemical context and thus, within an appropriate re-framing, to re-engage torah's enduring value."[56] Christians can do this not solely by reading the first five books of the Bible or by

---

55. Novak, "Avoiding Charges of Legalism," 32. See also the remarks of E. P. Sanders: "we should note that *no one has ever been a legalist* (except, perhaps, a few modern existentialists). The ancient world, like the modern, knew hypocrites, and I assume that they could be found in all groups, as they are now; the ancient world knew about self-righteousness, triviality, and the like. But the crucial first item on our list of legalism's components was entirely absent. No first-century Jew thought that he or she stood alone before God, with the obligation of doing enough good deeds to earn God's favor. No first-century Jew believed that there was no prior grace. . . . The charge of legalism, to be true, requires that Jewish individuals be engaged in the anxious or arrogant effort to save themselves by their own personal achievements. In fact, Judaism is the antithesis of this extremely individualistic way of thinking" (Sanders, "Reflections on Anti-Judaism," 285).

56. Moberly, *Old Testament Theology*, 100–101. It is worth quoting the full passage, in which Moberly is reflecting upon John 6: "Even if in a first-century context there was a polemic between Jews and Christians as to the respective roles of torah and Jesus as the definitive locus of God's self-revelation—a matter about which Jews and Christians still differ—and even if a reading of Jesus as divine bread was meant in that context to carry a strong implied negative to the Jewish tradition in which torah is divine bread, it does not follow that Christians need simply to replicate that negative today. For although faith in Christ undoubtedly relativizes Torah [I would say: enables Christians to obey Torah as fulfilled and reconfigured by Christ], it is fully possible for Christians, once faith in Christ is established, to read torah more positively than is possible in a polemical context and thus within an appropriate re-framing, to re-engage torah's enduring value." See also, on this point, the Jewish-Christian dialogue undertaken by Jacob Neusner and Bruce D. Chilton, *Revelation*, although Chilton does not recognize Jesus as embodied Torah.

studying each biblical precept, but also by exploring why a master of Rabbinic Halakhah finds the path of Torah (Written and Oral) so enriching.[57]

Rabbi Joseph B. Soloveitchik is well known as "the outstanding figure of modern Orthodox Judaism in 20th-century America."[58] He was well versed not only in the Torah and in the Rabbinic Jewish tradition (especially Maimonides and his school), but also in modern German philosophy.[59] His grandfather, Rabbi Ḥayyim Soloveitchik, was "the originator of the Brisker method" (named for his hometown of Brisk, in present-day Belarus) of halakhic reasoning.[60] Chaim Saiman observes, "Brisk's core ideas resonate with a broad cross-section of rabbinic thinkers. Even while the range of that thought is more diverse than the Brisker conception allows, the method exerts a strong pull on the entire field of halakhic theology."[61] Whereas Ḥayyim Soloveitchik focused solely on Talmud, his grandson combined the "Brisker method" of halakhic reasoning with a "philosophical and secular education, to the point of earning a doctorate in philosophy from the University of Berlin."[62]

This philosophical training enabled his approach to Halakhah to reach a wide contemporary audience, not only among Jewish scholars but also among Christian theologians. Although he criticizes Christianity for what he deems to be "its flight from the concrete world . . . , its negation of the body, its focus on a single emotion (love), and its rejection of the law," he also appropriates Christian themes.[63] In accord with the viewpoint of many contemporary Christian scholars who have valued Soloveitchik's work, R. R. Reno praises *Halakhic Man* for providing "a pro-nomian antidote to our [modern Christian] antinomian diseases."[64]

---

57. My chapter thus affirms the belief, in R. Kendall Soulen's words, that "God's choice of the Jewish people, and the distinction between Jew and Gentile that it entails, are an abiding part of God's positive purpose in the world, irrespective of the posture that Jews may take toward the church's claims on behalf of Jesus of Nazareth": see Soulen, "Israel and the Church," 173.

58. Plen, "Rabbi Soloveitchik."

59. See for example Ozar, "Emergence of Max Scheler"; Kolbrener, *Last Rabbi*. For appreciative introductions to Soloveitchik's life and thought, see Sokolow, *Reading the Rav*; and the essays in Kanarfogel and Schwartz, eds., *Scholarly Man of Faith*.

60. Saiman, *Halakhah*, 205. Saiman gives some helpful historical background to the "Brisker method" on 195–98.

61. Saiman, *Halakhah*, 212.

62. Saiman, *Halakhah*, 198.

63. Shatz, "Contemporary Scholarship on Soloveitchik's Thought," 143–45. On Soloveitchik's appropriation (and modification) of Christian theology, including aspects of the work of Karl Barth, see Brill, "Elements of Dialectical Theology."

64. Reno, "Loving the Law." See also Rutishauser, *Human Condition*. For Jewish

After surveying Soloveitchik's *Halakhic Man* in the first section of this chapter, I will draw out fifteen points that characterize his vision. In the chapter's second section, I will then propose that each of these points connects with the New Testament's understanding of Christian life as centered upon Christ. Of course, these connections involve a greater difference, given that the place that Soloveitchik gives to Torah is given by the New Testament to Jesus Christ. I am not suggesting that when a Jewish theologian "speaks of the 'supernal Torah' he means the same thing as what Thomas Aquinas [or the New Testament] means by the eternal Logos."[65] Nevertheless, as I hope to show, engaging Israel's Torah in light of Soloveitchik's approach to "halakhic man" will enrich Christian understanding of life in Christ. A Christian doctrine of Torah recognizes Torah's openness to messianic fulfillment (in Jesus Christ). Saiman points out that something similar is the case for Rabbinic Judaism: "According to traditional theology, halakhah,

---

criticism of *Halakhic Man*, see Dorff, "Halakhic Man." For both appreciation and critique, see Sacks, "Joseph Soloveitchik: Conflict and Creation," Sacks, "Rabbi Soloveitchik: Halakhic Man," and Sacks, "Rabbi Soloveitchik's Early Epistemology." Sacks notes that "what gives Soloveitchik's thought its particular power" is "its ability to move from highly individualised experiences to ideal types, and then to discover those types in the Biblical narrative, rabbinic homily and halakhic detail" (*Tradition in an Untraditional Age*, 40). For the differences between Soloveitchick, *Halakhic Man* and Soloveitchick, *Lonely Man of Faith*, see also Borowitz, *Choices in Modern Jewish Thought*, 222–23; as well as Singer and Sokol, "Joseph Soloveitchik"; L. Kaplan, "Religious Philosophy of Soloveitchik"; Ravitzky, "Rabbi J. B. Soloveitchik." Sacks thinks that Ravitzky's reading is best: "*Halakhic Man* and *U-vikashtem Mi-sham* are complementary studies. The former is an *analytical* treatment of the halakhic personality, splitting it into its component parts (cognitive man and *homo religiosus*). The latter is a *synthetic* treatment of the same personality, moving in Hegelian dialectic through freedom (active speculation and the search for religious experience) and submission (to the revealed Divine command) to the ultimate union of the Divine and human will" (Sacks, "Rabbi Soloveitchik's Early Epistemology," 290).

65. Groppe, "Tri-Unity of God," 173. Groppe herself rejects this claim as ahistorical, but she nonetheless describes Jesus as the one "in whom the supernal Torah of God took flesh" ("Tri-Unity of God," 175) and she sees the incarnation as parallel to the supernal Torah dwelling in Israel and in Israel's Scriptures. Though he certainly does not grant that Jesus is the divine Torah incarnate, see Michael Wyschogrod's suggestion that an analogy can be drawn between the Christian doctrine of the incarnation and a Jewish understanding of God's dwelling in the Jewish people: Wyschogrod, "Jewish Perspective on the Incarnation," in light of Wyschogrod, *Body of Faith*. Groppe's narrative of salvation history leaves out the central New Testament teaching that Christ, on the cross, redeems Israel and the Gentiles by bearing the consequences of sin. Aware of this omission, she states that "the narrative of salvation history that I have briefly sketched above does not directly address the overarching question of the Christ Jesus and the Jewish People Today Project: How might we Christians in our time affirm both the people Israel's covenantal life with God and our faith claim that Jesus Christ is the Savior of all humanity?" (Groppe, "Tri-Unity of God," 178).

like the Jewish people, will only reach its ultimate fulfillment in the messianic age."⁶⁶ While Christians do not think this "ultimate fulfillment" has been fully reached, we believe that Jesus, the Messiah, has inaugurated the kingdom of God—which on earth shares in Jesus' sufferings and awaits the final consummation when "the creation itself will be set free from its bondage to decay and obtain the glorious liberty of the children of God" (Rom 8:21), in the marriage of God and creation.

One last preparatory question: In holding that Christ has come and redeemed the whole human race, are Christians committed "to approach[ing] Jews with presuppositions of the inadequacy of Jewish covenantal life"?⁶⁷ Here we do well to recall Hans Urs von Balthasar's observation, which accords with Aquinas's perspective as well: "The condition of fallen nature cannot simply be equated with 'the Gentiles', nor can nature on its way toward restoration be equated with Judaism, nor can nature restored be equated with Christianity: each condition participates in all the others."⁶⁸ Christians do not need to denigrate or negate ongoing Rabbinic Jewish covenantal life in order to extol the gospel; in fact, especially given the history of Christian lack of charity vis-à-vis the Jewish people, the opposite is true. Christians can extol Christ, who is the fulfillment of Israel's Torah, while also admiring the goodness of Halakhah in ongoing Judaism.⁶⁹

66. Saiman, *Halakhah*, 247. Jacob Neusner argues that, even now, "by Torah study we are changed in our very being, not alone as to knowledge or even as to virtue and basic status, but as to what we are. . . . Through learning in the Torah we become something different from, better and more holy than, what we were. Through that learning we meet God, God's mind and our mind coming together in shared rationality" (Neusner, "How We Meet God," 50). Neusner defends the view that "Torah study changes us . . . in our relationship to heaven, endowing us with supernatural power" ("How We Meet God," 74).

67. Groppe, "Tri-Unity of God," 179–80. Groppe suggests that from this perspective of Christian "condescension" toward Jews, Christians would have to ask: "Should it not have been the Jews—far more so than the Gentiles—who saw in Christ the fulfillment of the promises they themselves had carried? Is not their lack of faith in Christ culpable in a way that the disbelief of the Hindu or Muslim or Buddhist is not?" (Groppe, "Tri-Unity of God," 180). I note that Paul addresses this issue in Romans 11, and he makes clear that we must leave it as a divinely governed "mystery" (Rom 11:25) whose ultimate purpose is grounded in divine mercy.

68. Von Balthasar, *Theo-Drama* II, 13.

69. Groppe comments, "The world would be spiritually poorer, not richer, were all Jews to stop hallowing the Sabbath, to cease grappling with the meaning of Torah, and to abandon their commitment toward *tikkun olam* (the repairing of the world) in anticipation of the inauguration of the messianic era" ("Tri-Unity of God," 180). Surely this is true, but not with respect to the eschaton, for which we must ardently hope: see Romans 11:12, 15. See also Richard Sklba's remark that, although Christians are necessarily missional (and therefore glad to receive converts), "Formal mission to the Jewish

Soloveitchik and the New Testament agree that perfect wisdom is the Divine Presence measuring and judging all reality. According to both—though certainly with a different understanding of Jesus and of Torah—the Divine Presence is available to those who await the coming of the Messiah while (by God's grace) living in accordance with divine wisdom.[70] What does it mean to live in accordance with the word (or Word) of God? By surveying Soloveitchik's *Halakhic Man* and identifying fifteen principles central to its worldview—and by reading the New Testament in light of these principles—the remainder of my chapter will attempt to shed light upon the meaning of Torah, the meaningfulness of describing Christ as Torah in person, and the characteristics of Christian discipleship to incarnate Torah.

II. The Halakhic Man of Joseph B. Soloveitchik

In *Halakhic Man*, Soloveitchik begins by contrasting "*homo religiosus*" and "cognitive man," two types popular in the scholarly world of 1944, when Soloveitchik's work was first published. "Cognitive man," according to Soloveitchik, is a rationalist who seeks to explain all things in terms of

---

nation as such, cannot be held by Christians if such a conviction would presume the historical termination of Judaism" (Sklba, "Covenant Renewed," 79).

70. See Cunningham and Pollefeyt, "Triune One," 193. Cunningham and Pollefeyt state that "from a Christian point of view it might be said that God's covenantal sharing-in-life, dwelling within the flesh of the people of Israel, became even more focused, more intimate with the incarnation of the Logos in Jesus, the 'authentic son of Israel.' From a Christian perspective, then, the glorified Christ covenantally abides both within the church and within the community of Israel because the triune God abides with both peoples. . . . [T]he incarnation of the Logos and the life, death, and glorification of the Jew Jesus were absolutely necessary for history's eventual culmination in the eschatological Reign of God" (Cunningham and Pollefeyt, "Triune One," 198–99). In my view, this perspective underestimates the radical newness of the incarnation, and it is also not enough to say (as do Cunningham and Pollefeyt) that the Jewish people are united to Christians by "covenanting with God in their distinctive Torah-shaped interactions with the inviting and revealing Logos and the empowering and inspiring Spirit" ("Triune One," 201). Faith in the redemptive Messiah is necessary, even if such faith is only implicitly faith in Jesus. For Christians involved in Jewish-Christian dialogue, it is clear that dilution of Christian soteriology—and thus a form of syncretistic reductionism—is a danger. Avery Dulles, SJ sought to underline this danger in his "Covenant with Israel." Dulles cautions that Christians cannot simply dismiss Hebrews 8 as irrelevant today. Cunningham finds that Dulles thereby minimizes "the full significance of *Nostra Aetate*, chapter 4" and "uncritically read[s] Romans 9–11 through the lenses of the non-Pauline Letter to the Hebrews, whose very different circumstances and genre are left unexplored" (Cunningham, "Paul's Letters," 161)—but I do not think that this does justice to the christological point that Dulles was trying to make, namely, Christ has truly fulfilled the covenants.

necessary laws and rational, universal principles; he thereby remains on the surface of reality. By contrast, *homo religiosus* plunges into the depths of reality and stands in awe of the mysteries and obscurities of existence; even the lawfulness or orderliness of the cosmos points to an obscure mystery (God himself, the freedom of the Creator). Cognitive man sticks serenely to empirical reality alone; *homo religiosus* strives for transcendence of earthly limitations.[71]

However, "halakhic man" is neither of the above. For halakhic man, reality cannot be reduced to the empirical or explained by reason; but halakhic man does not yearn to transcend the world. Instead, halakhic man is focused upon his ideal, drawn from "his Torah, given to him from Sinai"; and halakhic man orients himself always by means of this ideal, with its "fixed statutes and firm principles."[72] The Torah does not need to be warranted in terms of empirical existence, as though the latter were the governing framework. Rather, the task of halakhic man is "to superimpose his a priori ideal system upon the realm of concrete empirical existence," though without worrying about achieving an exact correlation.[73]

All reality can be judged in terms of whether it fits with "the requirements of the ideal Halakhah."[74] In one way or another, halakhic principles and precepts can be brought to bear upon any empirical reality or situation, in order to measure the empirical reality by the ideal Halakhah. Soloveitchik offers the example of the setting of the sun. It must be measured, ultimately, by its relation to the laws for when the Sabbath begins and for when certain

71. To avoid misunderstanding Soloveitchik's perspective here, see Soloveitchik's *And From There*. Commenting on the Song of Songs, Soloveitchik states: "The lover/Creator loves His beloved/creation. The Creator has captured the heart of His creation; the Eternal has captivated the spirit of every living thing. The Creator has promised the creation that He will never abandon her. The creation has drawn the Creator's heart with one of her eyes that gaze upon the face of eternity. . . . The Creator loves His creation, yet He nevertheless rests in a hidden place, in the shade. The creation craves her Creator, yet she nevertheless refuses to open the doors of her dwelling" (*And From There*, 5). Citing Maimonides, Soloveitchik adds: "The religious sensibility does not offer decisive proofs, draw inferences, or make deductions, It 'senses' and experiences God in its innermost ontological consciousness. Without Him, there is no reality" (*And From There*, 13). In his view, the human search for God is rooted in intuitive knowledge and in love—namely, in God's love for us and our yearning for God. See also Soloveitchik's "Exaltation of God," especially 61–62, 65; as well as Sztuden, "Identity of Love."

72. Soloveitchik, *Halakhic Man*, 19.

73. Soloveitchik, *Halakhic Man*, 18.

74. Soloveitchik, *Halakhic Man*, 20. See also Saiman's *Halakhah*, especially his survey of the "Brisker method" (noted above). In the opening pages of his book, Saiman explores the resurgence of halakhic study as a popular practice in modern Judaism, though he notes that "less than twenty percent of world Jewry now adheres to the classical halakhic constitution" (*Halakhah*, 215).

prayers must be said. A similar thing can be said for astronomical phenomena, mountains, the stages of fruit, colors, the care of trees and plants, the bodily functions of the human being, illness, the state and society, economics, family life, judicial systems, and so on. The metaphysical priority of the Halakhah vis-à-vis empirical realities means that "Halakhah has a fixed a priori relationship to the whole of reality in all of its fine and detailed particulars."[75]

Given that Halakhah is always an "a priori" system—given by God, rather than produced by empirical reflection—it may often happen that the real world does not correspond with Halakhah. For example, many laws pertain to the temple sacrifices; but for various reasons, most notably the destruction of the temple, animal sacrifices no longer are performed in the temple in Jerusalem. Halakhic man nonetheless proceeds to make halakhic judgments about the proper animal sacrifices. Every portion of the Halakhah, even if it seems unlikely ever to be empirically real ever again, must be studied intensively by the halakhist. Soloveitchik notes that Maimonides "codified all of the laws of the Torah from the first mishnah in Berakhot to the last mishnah in Uktzin"; and as codified, the Torah includes all the precepts revealed to Israel at Sinai and their authentic interpretation.[76] When all this is studied and mastered by the halakhist, then that halakhist can be said to have a true (though not exhaustive) comprehension of the divine knowledge and will. The entire world will eschatologically be brought into conformity with the Halakhah, but the purpose of the halakhic man is not to accomplish this. Rather, the halakhic man simply studies Halakhah and makes normative determinations, whether for practical purposes or not. It is the study of Torah (understood in this sense) that is the purpose of life, because the Torah opens up God's wisdom and will.[77]

Soloveitchik emphasizes that the halakhic man does not seek another world than the one that we have. It is in this world, after all, that Halakhah can be studied and obeyed. Death, therefore, stands as an opponent of the halakhic man because it involves the cessation of such meritorious study and obedience. The halakhic man does not look beyond the "clamorous,

---

75. Soloveitchik, *Halakhic Man*, 23.

76. Soloveitchik, *Halakhic Man*, 25.

77. Lest this be misunderstood, let me underscore once again Soloveitchik's spirituality. In "Exaltation of God," 67, Soloveitchik comments that to experience "the infinite goodness of God as beautiful means to encounter Him, not as mystery, defying all rules of orderliness, eluding the grasp of the necessary and lawful and harmonious. He is no longer the strange, alien, numinous God who makes the worshipper shudder, wonderstruck in the presence-absence of the unknown and mysterious. On the contrary, *caritas Dei* inspires, ennobles, and befriends man. God is known to and intimate with him."

tumultuous life, pulsating with exuberance and strength" that is the present life, because the present life involves the labor of studying and performing God's commandments, which suffices for the halakhic man.[78] There is no need to seek the transcendent realm in order to serve God, since God's Torah has come to earth.

Soloveitchik notes that it is permitted to fail to observe a commandment, if what is at stake is someone's life—for example if by performing some work on the Sabbath one may thereby enable the person whose life is saved to observe Torah for many more years. In this sense, he emphasizes that "[t]he teachings of the Torah do not oppose the laws of life and reality."[79] The priority of Halakhah does not amount to an anti-empirical fanaticism or delusion. Even fear of death is well known to the halakhic man, because death brings to an end the glorious but finite experience of studying and performing Torah in God's world. This does not mean that Soloveitchik denies the world-to-come. Rather, having insisted upon the priority of Halakhah over anything empirical, he also and equally strongly insists that it is the "empirical world" and "the problems of earthly life in all its details and particulars" that stand at the center for the halakhic man, because God has willed it so by giving Israel the Torah.[80]

Soloveitchik gladly grants that "God's Torah has implanted in halakhic man's consciousness both the idea of everlasting life and the desire for eternity."[81] By performing and obeying Torah, the halakhic man reaches out in yearning for God and seeks to do God's will forever. By contrast to *homo religiosus*, however, the halakhic man does not start from a strictly earthly position; instead, the halakhic man starts from the everlasting Torah, which belongs to the divine realm. The longing of the halakhic man is therefore "to bring transcendence down into this valley of the shadow of death—i.e., into our world—and transform it into a land of the living."[82] Because of the gift of the divine Torah, the halakhic man does not need to try to escape from this world in a flight upward to the spiritual realm. Instead, armed with

78. Soloveitchik, *Halakhic Man*, 33.
79. Soloveitchik, *Halakhic Man*, 34.
80. Soloveitchik, *Halakhic Man*, 39.
81. Soloveitchik, *Halakhic Man*, 40.
82. Soloveitchik, *Halakhic Man*, 40. Soloveitchik explains somewhat further on: "Halakhic man vanquishes even the fear of death . . . by means of the law and the Halakhah, and he transforms the phenomenon, which so terrifies him, into an object of man's observation and cognition. For when death becomes an object of man's cognition, the fright accompanying death dissipates. Death is frightening, death is menacing, death is dreadful only so long as it appears as a subject confronting man. However, when man succeeds in transforming death-subject into death-object, the horror is gone" (*Halakhic Man*, 73).

the Torah, the task of the halakhic man is to sanctify this world by studying and obeying Torah. Every time the halakhic man succeeds in studying and obeying Torah, divine wisdom (the divine ideal) takes concrete earthly shape. God has descended by giving Israel the Torah, which is a transcendent ideal that, through its performance, transforms earthly existence.

Soloveitchik emphasizes that the path of Torah observance is open to and required of every Jew. It is not merely for an esoteric elite, focused on their hidden lore. He holds that authentic Jewish obedience to Torah wards off any esotericism. The life that God wills is an earthly, concrete life of obedience. Soloveitchik states with regard to the halakhic man, "When his soul yearns for God, he immerses himself in reality, plunges, with his entire being, into the very midst of concrete existence, and petitions God to descend upon the mountain and to dwell within our reality, with all its laws and principles."[83] Real transformation thereby takes place. Through the gift of the transcendent Torah, God brings "holiness into a world situated within the realms of concrete reality, the Absolute into the relative and conditional. Transcendence becomes embodied in man's deeds, deeds that are shaped by the lawful physical order of which man is a part."[84]

On this view, holiness does not consist primarily in the human actualization of an ethical ideal, as though humans were the definition of holiness. Rather, holiness is the awe-inspiring descent of God through his Torah. Soloveitchik describes "the 'descent' of God, whom no thought can grasp, onto Mount Sinai, the bending down of a hidden and concealed world and lowering it onto the face of reality."[85] This "hidden" world consists in the Torah, which takes embodied shape on earth through Israel's study and performance of Torah. The source of this holy descent is God; the goal is the world-to-come, in which the Torah will govern all things. Thus the people of Israel are holy not by a mystical union with God, but rather are holy in an earthly way "through actualizing the Halakhah in the empirical world."[86]

83. Soloveitchik, *Halakhic Man*, 73.

84. Soloveitchik, *Halakhic Man*, 73.

85. Soloveitchik, *Halakhic Man*, 46. At the same time, divine absence and judgment are a repeated theme in Soloveitchik's writings, since he considers that the encounter with the descending God is also a fearful thing for the finite, unworthy creature. For further discussion see his "Absence of God," 73–86.

86. Soloveitchik, *Halakhic Man*, 46. In his "Intention in Reading Shema," 92–93, Soloveitchik emphasizes that "[t]he Halakhah has its own standards and laws and cannot always align itself with mystical craving and longing. In addition, the Halakhah, as an exoteric discipline, must make its norm accessible and realizable to all, philosopher and simpleton, mystical and pragmatic mind alike. Of course, halakhic premises may serve, from time to time, as Archimedean fulcra, from which a God-intoxicated and lovesick soul makes the great leap from finitude into infinity. Nonetheless, the Halakhah

It might seem that the people of Israel cannot today really obey Torah, given that there is no high priest, no temple, and no sacrificial offerings. Soloveitchik responds to this problem by remarking that God commanded Moses to make God a sanctuary. God himself did not make the sanctuary; the people of Israel made it. Since this is so, it follows that "[i]t is man who sanctifies space and makes a sanctuary for his Creator."[87] The destruction of the temple, therefore, cannot bring an end to sacred space, because the people can still make a sanctuary. When they pray in obedience to Torah as interpreted by the halakhic man, they can perform the sacrificial offerings. Soloveitchik explains, "Through the power of our mouths, through verbal sanctification alone, we can create holy offerings for the Temple treasury and holy offerings for the altar."[88] Influenced by Kabbalah, he calls this truth "the secret of *tzimtzum*, of 'contraction.'"[89] Even the act of creation is already a "descent" or "contraction" of God, who "contracts" to allow something other than himself to exist, while at the same time indwelling every holy entity.[90]

---

cannot and should not put up requirements such that only a select few are able to fulfill them.... Not all halakhically adequate performances extend into the transforming experience of spiritual attachment."

87. Soloveitchik, *Halakhic Man*, 47.

88. Soloveitchik, *Halakhic Man*, 47. See also his "Reflections on the Amidah," 131: "The Temple cult, the offering of sacrifices, is a fundamental ingredient in Halakhah. To bring a sacrifice is to come close to God. The Torah desired that man be intimate with God.... The Talmudic dictum 'the prayers were established by the Patriarchs' does not contradict a second statement of the Sages, 'the prayers were established to correspond to the fixed daily sacrificial offerings, the *temidim*.'" In the same essay, Soloveitchik goes on to say that in a certain sense "[n]othing has changed with the destruction of the Temple and the cessation of literal sacrifice. Now too we sacrifice to God—that great and awesome offering in which man overcomes his being by ascending to the transcendent metaphysical altar" ("Reflections on the Amidah," 178–79).

89. Soloveitchik, *Halakhic Man*, 48. For background to the development of the doctrine of *tzimtzum* by Rabbi Isaac ben Solomon Luria (1534–72)—influenced by, and contributing to, Kabbalah—see Sacks, *To Heal a Fractured World*, 74–77.

90. In his *Abraham's Journey*, 198, Soloveitchik says, "How beautiful is the doctrine of *tzimtzum*, contraction. What is creation if not withdrawal by God in order to make it possible for a world to emerge in space and time?" At the same time, Soloveitchik observes in *And From There*, 26, "If not for sin, man would be able to reveal the Creator in the creation without any disappointment. Then he would see God's glory filling the universe and would sense that the regal splendor and majesty of the surrounding world emanate from the Infinite; then he would be aware of the presence of the *Shekinah* in every growing blade of grass and every flowing stream." On *tzimtzum* as "self-limitation," see Soloveitchik's essay "Torah and Humility," 220.

In his critique of the perspective of "mystical doctrine,"[91] Soloveitchik has in view Hasidic Judaism, as well as Kabbalah and Christianity. As noted above, he considers that the mystics aim to liberate humanity from the constraints of the earthly realm. The halakhic man, immersed in earthly life since the heavenly Torah has come to earth, has the opposite intention—insofar as the "halakhic man declares that the true home of the Divine Presence is in this world," rather than in "the hidden and awesome transcendental realm."[92] The Divine Presence enters this world insofar as "[t]he Halakhah fixes firmly established and clearly delimited laws, statutes, and measures for each and every commandment—what constitutes eating and what are its measurements, what constitutes drinking and what are its standards," and so on.[93] For example, the Halakhah commands tithing and, for those who seek perfection in this commandment, sets the maximum at twenty percent of one's income. Soloveitchik notes that such quantification is a mark of *tzimtzum* or "contraction."[94] For every act commanded by God, the Halakhah sets a firm quantity or measure, thereby bringing the ideal Halakhah to the concrete world. Thus, the halakhic man approves and upholds "a sensuous religion," "which a man of flesh and blood can feel with all of his senses, sinews, and organs, with his entire being."[95]

---

91. Soloveitchik, *Halakhic Man*, 50; cf. 67. See also his "Reflections on Amidah," 173–74. If I understand Soloveitchik correctly, I share his general concerns about Kabbalah (without, for my part, rejecting practices of spiritual ascent). For discussion of Lurianic Kabbalah—which along broadly Gnostic lines teaches that "the performance of positive commandments [mitzvoth] motivates the coupling of the Abba and the Imma that together prompt the emanation of the following seven sefirot to complete the creation, i.e., to bring about Tikkun (Repair) of the world"; and which encourages the worshiper to engage "in *devequt*, cleaving to the Shekinah by throwing oneself down to the deepest depths of the created world to retrieve the sparks of the divine presence in one's soul, thereby enabling them to rise from their encasement in the *qelippot* or husks of material form to be reunited in a process of Tikkun"— see Sweeney, *Jewish Mysticism*, 349, 351. For a heartbreaking critique of Lurianic Kabbalah in the context of the messianic claims of Shabbetai Zevi in the seventeenth century, see Singer, *Satan in Goray*; and also Scholem, *Sabbatai Sevi*.

92. Soloveitchik, *Halakhic Man*, 53. In *And From There*, 20–21, Soloveitchik comments along these lines: "The Halakhah approves of this confrontation between God and man within the world. We are commanded by the Halakhah to utter a benediction over every cosmic phenomenon. . . . For the Jew there is no such thing as routine. Everything is a wondrous miracle. He is excited by everything, from the novel and unknown to the everyday and the ordinary. In everything he sees the glory of God; over everything he utters a benediction."

93. Soloveitchik, *Halakhic Man*, 55.

94. Soloveitchik, *Halakhic Man*, 56.

95. Soloveitchik, *Halakhic Man*, 58.

Yet, does this mean that Soloveitchik is proposing a Judaism without exalted religious experience, a Torah that governs daily life but that ensures that everything is mundane and no one feels an exalted yearning for God? On the contrary—and against the halakhic ruling of Maimonides—Soloveitchik approves singing hymns on High Holidays, hymns that express Israel's passionate yearning for God. He insists upon the experience of "divine mercy and grace" and upon "times of spiritual ecstasy and exaltation, when our entire existence thirsts for the living God."[96]

Nevertheless, he argues that such experience is not the center of observant Jewish life. Ecstasy and yearning have a place in the life of the halakhic man who sings hymns on the High Holidays, but these emotionally charged spiritual states are not the heart of the matter. The heart of the matter is the Halakhah and its implementation. He explains that "the Halakhah declares that any religiosity which does not lead to determinate actions, firm and clear-cut measures, chiseled and delimited laws and statutes will prove sterile."[97] Here, he compares the objectivity of the Halakhah

---

96. Soloveitchik, *Halakhic Man*, 58. See also Soloveitchik's *And From There*, in which he states (for example), "In man's yearning and frustration, God is revealed. The ontological consciousness, which is all yearning and upward striving, becomes identified with the transcendental consciousness. The world is nothing but the glory emanating from the Infinite" (*And From There*, 15). In his essay "Religious Styles," 199, he states, "Only by being in touch with impressive religious living, by observing the ecstasy of man coming close to the Almighty and the despair of that man when he is exiled from his Maker—only that type of observation leads to the acquisition of style in religious living." In the same essay, he provides ample leeway for individual religious styles. He goes on to comment sadly that "the great conflict which divided the Jewish people into *Hasidim* and *Mitnagdim* at the end of the eighteenth century never revolved about the way of doing things.... Their conflict revolved about *style*, not about *way*. Hasidic performance was ecstatic, in a more democratic and popular manner. They acted not only with their hands, but with their hearts as well. On the other hand, the Gaon and Lithuanian Jewry [from which Soloveitchik himself descends] knew very little of ecstasy. Their motto was not ecstasy but discipline and surrender. No wonder they produced great scholars; intellectual accomplishments are always the result of a disciplined mind" (*Halakhic Morality*, 199). For the point that in addition to his Brisk father and grandfather, Soloveitchik had a Lubavitch Hasid as his childhood tutor, see Sokolow, *Reading the Rav*, 93.

97. Soloveitchik, *Halakhic Man*, 59. Later he comments further: "Is it possible for halakhic man to achieve such emotional exaltation that all his thoughts and senses ache and pine for the living God? Halakhic man is worthy and fit to devote himself to a majestic religious experience in all its uniqueness, with all its delicate shades and hues. However, for him such a powerful, exalted experience only follows upon cognition, only occurs after he has acquired knowledge of the a priori, ideal Halakhah and its reflected image in the real world" (Soloveitchik, *Halakhic Man*, 83). He compares this to a physicist's delight in the order that he has perceived, through mathematical equations, in the cosmos. See also Rynhold, "Science or Hermeneutics?"; L. Kaplan, "Rabbi Soloveitchik's Philosophy"; Shatz, "Contemporary Scholarship on Soloveitchik's

with the objectivity of physics and mathematics.[98] The purpose of the Halakhah's objectivity is to bring order to religious subjectivity. Otherwise, religious subjectivity will dissipate itself and ultimately burn itself out, due to its constant waxing and waning. Thus, the Halakhah serves the Jewish people not only by governing external actions, but also by giving structure to inner spiritual currents, including currents of spiritual dryness. It follows that for many halakhic authorities, even if one does not feel like performing a commandment, the simple *intention* to perform it is meritorious. Even for the authorities who teach the opposite, there is never any requirement to be mystically supercharged, but only a requirement that there be a "clear, plain thought to fulfill via this particular act such and such a commandment."[99]

Although the halakhic man remains firmly in this world, the activities of the halakhic man do not thereby leave the empirical world unchallenged or unchanged. For one thing, the world's priorities are challenged by the halakhic man, in the sense that while the world goes about its own business, the halakhic man knows that the world exists so that the ideal Halakhah can be actualized within it. Soloveitchik observes that the "[h]alakhic man cognizes the world in order to subordinate it to religious performances."[100] The observance of Torah therefore has a "normative" aspect, as the people of Israel actualize the commandments of the Torah in the world.[101] Even if the norm commanded by Torah cannot be realized, the halakhic man will still study it and rejoice in it. It is the ideal realm of the laws that has priority, even though the laws are meant to be applied wherever and whenever possible. For the halakhic man, the actual doing of the commandments is delightful, since human beings were created for the commandments.

Thought," 179–82; D. Schwartz, *Religion and Halakha*, chapters 5 and 8.

98. Jonathan Sacks suggests that *Halakhic Man*, "with its comparison between the halakhist and the modern theoretical mathematician, is set in counterpoint to Heschel's romantic-nostalgic portrayal of Eastern European Jewry in *Earth Is the Lord's*" (Sacks, "Joseph Soloveitchik: Conflict and Creation," 53fn33). This point is amplified by a personal story told by Sacks in "Rabbi Soloveitchik: Halakhic Man," 270: in conversation with Sacks in 1967, Soloveitchik "said—in a reference to A. J. Heschel—it was possible to construct a philosophy of Shabbat as a 'sanctuary in time'. This might be a beautiful idea; but it was a misleading one. Shabbat for the halakhah was the thirty-nine *avot melakhot* (parent-categories of forbidden work) and their derivatives. Any philosophising must begin and end with this point."

99. Soloveitchik, *Halakhic Man*, 60.

100. Soloveitchik, *Halakhic Man*, 63. David Shatz points out that Soloveitchik is here going beyond the rabbinic text to which he is obliquely referring: see Shatz, "Contemporary Scholarship on Soloveitchik's Thought," 165.

101. Soloveitchik, *Halakhic Man*, 63.

In addition, the relationship of the Jewish people to God continues even when the Jewish people sin, even if the damage done in the world by sin must not be minimized. In obedience to Halakhah, the people of Israel can sorrowfully confess their sins to God (above all on the Day of Atonement) while at the very same time joyfully acknowledging their ongoing privileged relationship to God.[102] Soloveitchik sees here the sign of God's great mercy upon his people, by giving them such a relationship and providing a way for their sins to be addressed. Through the gift of the Torah, "the man who knows his duty, his task as a partner in the creation of worlds through constructing a halakhic world and actualizing it in reality has been elected by God at the very inception and has been recognized as worthy of standing before Him."[103] Similarly, Soloveitchik notes that the Torah enables people to refrain from both constant self-analysis and from the fear or despair promoted by such self-analysis. The halakhic man may sin; but the halakhic man knows how to deal with that sin, in accord with the norms of the Halakhah. Spiritual health comes from focusing not on self but on the study of, and obedience to, the Torah. Here Soloveitchik cautions

---

102. For discussion of "The Halakhic Theology of Atonement," see chapter 4 of Neusner, *Performing Israel's Faith*. Neusner's third chapter is devoted to "The Aggadic Theology of Sin, Repentance, and Atonement." As Neusner comments, "In Judaism as set forth by the Rabbinic sages in the Mishnah and the Talmuds, the Day of Atonement, which the Torah lays out as principally a Temple occasion, overspreads the world.... What mattered to the compilers of Leviticus and the Mishnah alike was the timeless performance of atonement through the bloody rites of the Temple. What captured the attention of the framers of the Tosefta's amplification, by contrast, was the personal discipline of atonement through repentance on the Day of Atonement and a life of virtue and Torah-learning on the rest of the days of the year. They took out of the Holy of Holies and brought into the homes and streets of the holy people that very mysterious rite of atonement that the Day of Atonement called forth" (Neusner, *Performing Israel's Faith*, 162–63).

103. Soloveitchik, *Halakhic Man*, 71. There is no individualism here, of course. In his *Kol Dodi Dofek* Soloveitchik remarks: "A Jew who participates in the suffering of his nation and its fate, but does not join in its destiny, which is expressed in a life of Torah and mitzvoth, destroys the essence of Judaism and injures his own uniqueness. By the same token, a Jew who is observant but does not feel the hurt of the nation, and who attempts to distance himself from Jewish fate, desecrates his Jewishness" (*Kol Dodi Dofek*, 73). He rejects secular Zionism's claim that the Jewish people can become an "ordinary" nation as the State of Israel, or that the Jewish citizens of the State of Israel have no intrinsic connection to the Jews in other nations around the world. In "Transcendent Pharisee," 185, William Kolbrener shows that Soloveitchik's position fits with that of David Novak: "Soloveitchik finds himself between those embracing the immanence of a messianic present, claiming the State of Israel represents the beginnings of the fulfilment of a messianic ideal, and those rejectionists refusing to accord any meaning to contingent historical processes." See also Chaim Saiman's reflections on the impact of the establishment of the State of Israel upon halakhic thinking, in Saiman, *Halakhah*, 215–41.

against the notion that spiritual maturity means the near-disappearance of one's own will, since in fact the self is "part of that concrete reality which Halakhah purified and hallowed."[104]

Soloveitchik may seem to go a bit far when he proclaims that the "[h]alakhic man is a mighty ruler in the kingdom of spirit and intellect. Nothing can lead him astray; everything is subject to him.... Even the Holy One, blessed be He, has, as it were, handed over His imprimatur, His official seal in Torah matters, to man."[105] Here, however, Soloveitchik is describing the participation of the people of Israel in God's creative work, a participation in the *perfecting* of creation.[106] Halakhic judgments belong to the power of interpretation that God grants to Israel,[107] so that Israel can place guards and fences around the Torah. Soloveitchik makes clear that the wisdom of the Torah—and thus of the Halakhah—is "rooted in the will of the Holy One, blessed be He, the revealer of the Law."[108] Furthermore, he believes that when the student of Torah strives to study Halakhah, the Divine Presence rests upon the student. The authority of human halakhic judgment is

---

104. Soloveitchik, *Halakhic Man*, 78.

105. Soloveitchik, *Halakhic Man*, 80.

106. See also Soloveitchik, *Halakhic Man*, 101: "When God created the world, He provided an opportunity for the work of His hands—man—to participate in His creation. The Creator, as it were, impaired reality in order that mortal man could repair its flaws and perfect it. God gave the Book of Creation—that repository of the mysteries of creation—to man, not simply for the sake of theoretical study but in order that man might continue the act of creation." Soloveitchik expands upon this theme in extensive detail, beginning on pp. 105–6, where he writes: "When man, the crowing glory of the cosmos, approaches the world, he finds his task at hand—the task of creation. He must stand guard over the pure, clear existence, repair the defects in the cosmos, and replenish the 'privation' in being. Man, the creature, is commanded to become a partner with the Creator in the renewal of the cosmos; complete and ultimate creation—this is the deepest desire of the Jewish people."

107. For a description of "halakhic flexibility" that allows for "halakhic re-evaluation . . . in response to new economic, humanitarian, and religious concerns," see Berger, "Texts, Values, and Historical Change." After showing that "rabbinic decisors [have] allowed their rulings to be affected by economic and communal needs, by ideological commitments, and by humanitarian concerns," Berger concludes: "There are no magic formulas for the balancing of humanitarian and ideological concerns, on the one hand, and the straightforward meaning of texts on the other. For this task to be accomplished with integrity from the perspective of Orthodox Judaism, the decisor must genuinely believe in the authority of the Torah, in its divine origin, and in its eternal validity. In other words, what is nowadays described as 'the halakhic process' rests upon a foundation consisting of theology as well as legal analysis" ("Texts, Values, and Historical Change," 214, 216).

108. Soloveitchik, *Halakhic Man*, 85–86.

therefore not separated, for Soloveitchik, from the power of the *Shekinah* or Divine Presence.[109]

Moreover, because the student of Halakhah has confidence in sharing in the work of God, the student of Halakhah will stand up boldly against "the oppression of the helpless, the defrauding of the poor, the plight of the orphan."[110] Soloveitchik emphasizes that the core of Halakhah consists in "the ideals of justice and righteousness."[111] It is by implementing these ideals that the halakhic man participates in God's creative work most properly—even if it is the halakhic implementation, not any practical or empirical result, that obliges the halakhic man (given the priority of Halakhah). Soloveitchik goes so far as to say that the worship of God, with the exception of study of the Torah, takes place primarily not in the synagogue but in the actualization of the ideals of justice and righteousness in the world. He asserts that "halakhic men, par excellence" are always "champions of truth and justice," risking their own position to defend the poor.[112]

109. Again, Soloveitchik is aware of the concealment or hiddenness of the Divine Presence. He remarks in *And From There*, 22: "God reveals Himself to His creation, but also eludes it.... The Halakhah knows of the *Shekinah* revealed, but also of the *Shekinah* removed." The distinction that Jonathan Sacks makes between *Halakhic Man* and other writings by Soloveitchik is helpful to keep in mind. Sacks observes that "halakhah might mean either of two things: a *process* or a *product*, the process of studying Jewish law or the product of that study, the law itself. In Rabbi Soloveitchik's later work—the lectures on *Teshuvah*, for example—the latter comes into play.... But in *Halakhic Man* we are in different territory. Here the subject is halakhah as process—the act, the life, of studying halakhah" (Sacks, "Rabbi Soloveitchik: Halakhic Man," 471).

110. Soloveitchik, *Halakhic Man*, 91.

111. Soloveitchik, *Halakhic Man*, 91. Citing Maimonides, Soloveitchik notes that "[i]f a person sinned against his fellow man, repentance and the Day of Atonement cannot grant him atonement until he has appeased his fellow.... That dualism, so prevalent in other religions, which distinguishes between the man who stands before the Lord in an atmosphere suffused with heavenly solemnity and the man driving a hard bargain with his fellow in the marketplace, is totally foreign to the Halakhah" (Soloveitchik, *Halakhic Man*, 92). He compares this approach rather harshly to Christianity: "How many noblemen bowed down before the cross in a spirit of abject submission and self-denial, confessed their sins with scalding tears and bitter cries and in the very same breath, as soon as they left the dim precincts of the cathedral, ordered that innocent people be cruelly slain" (Soloveitchik, *Halakhic Man*, 93).

112. Soloveitchik, *Halakhic Man*, 95. In his essay "The Community," Soloveitchik remarks, "It is not enough for the charitable person to extend help to the needy. He must do more than that: he must try to restore to the dependent person a sense of dignity and worth. That is why Jews have developed special sensitivity regarding orphans and widows, since these persons are extremely sensitive and lose their self-confidence at the slightest provocation" ("The Community," 13). He goes on to emphasize the importance of praying for others and of being "a prayerful, compassionate community" ("The Community," 20). Elsewhere, he notes that "[t]he unique character of the community of Israel and its standing apart from others find expression in the message of

Jonathan Sacks points out that Soloveitchik expects that study of Torah to have a transformative personal impact, as the halakhic student becomes configured to the Halakhah. It is not that all students of Halakhah already possess the characteristics with which Soloveitchik endows the mature halakhic man; indeed, only a few may presently measure up to this standard. But the study of Halakhah makes it possible increasingly to become such a "halakhic man." To be configured to Torah by rendering halakhic judgments is to become fully a partner of God, a sharer in God's plan for the perfecting of the world. For Soloveitchik, this is what God intends his Jewish people to be.[113]

III. A Christian "Halakhic" Man?

Without seeking to be comprehensive, I propose that the following fifteen points have a central place in Soloveitchik's portrait of "halakhic man":

1. Halakhic man orients himself by the divine ideal, Torah.
2. All this-worldly reality must be judged and measured by the Torah.
3. Halakhic man focuses upon studying and obeying Torah in this world, rather than upon seeking the afterlife or upon rising to an otherworldly realm.

---

tzedakah that it introduced to the world and its fashioning of a life of charity and aid" ("Tzedakah," 125; in this essay Soloveitchik draws heavily upon Maimonides). Sadly, Soloveitchik does not expect Orthodox Jews to receive love from non-Jews: "Love has not yet pierced the darkness of prejudice and instinctual hatred that confronts a Jew who wants to maintain his distinctiveness and singularity. Whether we like it or not, we must rely on our Jewish brethren and not on others" ("Tzedakah," 139).

113. Somewhat critically, Sacks describes Soloveitchik's halakhic man as "[a]n intellectual aristocrat who carries a world within his head" and who undertakes "study magnified to epic proportions as the crucible in which a new selfhood is forged" ("Rabbi Soloveitchik: Halakhic Man," 276); and Sacks points out that "a sense of loneliness permeates his work. . . . There is little in *Halakhic Man*, where there could have been so much, about the delights of intellectual companionship, *chevrutah*. This is in strange contrast to Talmudic Judaism itself, which has nothing positive to say about isolation. . . . Modern halakhic man has friends: but they are people of the mind" ("Rabbi Soloveitchik: Halakhic Man," 278). Sacks also notes that Soloveitchik wrote *Halakhic Man* in 1944, precisely when "[t]he world of the Lithuanian yeshivot, to which it is a tribute, was . . . being reduced to ashes" ("Rabbi Soloveitchik: Halakhic Man," 280)—though the context of the Holocaust goes unmentioned. For a helpful explanation of Soloveitchik's approach to religious knowledge in *Halakhic Mind*—connecting it with that of Samson Raphael Hirsch and probing critically into Soloveitchik's account of "cognition" and "pluralism"—see Sacks, "Rabbi Soloveitchik's Early Epistemology," 293–99.

4. Torah is not for an esoteric spiritual elite, but rather is for all Jews.
5. Halakhic man seeks to instantiate, in the empirical world, the transcendent ideal (Torah) that has descended to earth.
6. The eschatological world-to-come will reflect Torah in a perfectly full way.
7. The Divine Presence "contracts" to dwell in a small space (*tzimtzum*): this happens in creation and in the giving of Torah to Israel.
8. The this-worldliness of Halakhah produces a "sensuous religion," preoccupied with embodied actions.
9. Judaism is not a religion built upon the quest for exalted spiritual experience, although such experience takes place.
10. Performing the commandments is delightful, rather than being a spiritual struggle.
11. Halakhah teaches the people of Israel how, at the same time, to abase themselves for their sins and to recognize their privileged relationship with God.
12. Halakhic man focuses on Torah rather than on the self's subjective condition, but does not encourage the compete disappearance of our own will.
13. By making authoritative halakhic judgments, halakhic man participates in God's work of perfecting the creation.
14. Halakhic man stands up for justice and righteousness.
15. True worship primarily occurs in the actualization of Halakhah's justice and righteousness in the world.

In the present section, I seek to show that the New Testament's account of Christ and of believers' life in Christ is in notable ways similar to Soloveitchik's account of Torah and the people of Israel's Torah-observant life, as summed up by the above fifteen points. Again, I am well aware of the many differences, not least the fact that the Oral Torah, the halakhic tradition of legal reasoning, and many of the laws of the Written Torah do not have an easy analogue in Christianity—although Christian moral teachings are certainly shaped by the Torah (well beyond solely the Decalogue) and include a Christian form of "halakhic" or legal reasoning.[114]

---

114. See Bockmuehl, *Jewish Law in Gentile Churches*, as well as numerous works of Christian moral theology and canon law.

For each of the fifteen points that I have drawn from Soloveitchik's understanding of Torah observance, I offer a brief response drawn from New Testament texts in order to draw out connections with Soloveitchik's perspective. Again, for the New Testament, "[t]he Torah of the Messiah is the Messiah, Jesus, himself."[115] It would be a shame to produce a false syncretism of the kind that Soloveitchik rightly abhorred.[116] Instead, I seek Christian Israelological insight into the reality of life in Christ by listening to Rabbinic Judaism's love of Torah and by reading the New Testament from this angle.

1. Halakhic man orients himself by the divine ideal, Torah.

The Apostle Paul makes clear that Christians must orient ourselves by the divine ideal, Christ. Christ comes from heaven, from the Father. Christ is the center of the Father's "plan for the fullness of time, to unite all things in him [Christ], things in heaven and things on earth" (Eph 1:10). Christ "is the image of the invisible God, the first-born of all creation; for in him all things were created" (Col 1:15–16).[117] A heavenly ideal—or image of the Fa-

---

115. Ratzinger, *Many Religions—One Covenant*, 70.

116. See his 1964 essay "Confrontation." In light of the growing impulse toward interreligious dialogue (of a kind that he feared might lead to syncretistic pressure), Soloveitchik cautions: "The individuality of a faith community expresses itself in a threefold way. First, the divine imperatives and commandments to which a faith community is unreservedly committed must not be equated with the ritual and ethos of another community. Each faith community is engaged in a singular normative gesture reflecting the numinous nature of the act of faith itself, and it is futile to try to find common denominators. Particularly when we speak of the Jewish faith community, whose very essence is expressed in the Halachic performance which is a most individuating factor, any attempt to equate our identity with another is sheer absurdity. Second, the axiological awareness of each faith community is an exclusive one, for it believes—and this belief is indispensable to the survival of the community—that its system of dogmas, doctrines and values is best fitted for the attainment of the ultimate good. Third, each faith community is unyielding in its eschatological expectations.... Standardization of practices, equalization of dogmatic certitudes, and the waiving of eschatological claims spell the end of the vibrant and great faith experience of any religious community" ("Confrontation," 102). For critical and appreciative discussion of this essay, with an eye to whether Soloveitchik would change or nuance it today, see E. B. Korn, "Man of Faith"; Shatz, "Morality, Liberalism, and Interfaith Dialogue"; and I. Greenberg, *For the Sake of Heaven*, 13–14. Above, I have already discussed the responses to Soloveitchik offered by David Berger (who is responding to Korn's essay as well) and David Novak.

117. In this book, I do not attempt to distinguish authentically Pauline letters from non-Pauline letters attributed to Paul, in part because I engage the letters as canonical works in Christian Scripture. For contrasting views on whether Paul wrote Colossians, see N. T. Wright, *Colossians and Philemon*; McDonald, *Colossians and Ephesians*.

ther—has been given to us by the Father; and indeed this ideal is the one in whom "all things were created." Christ, the incarnate Word (John 1:1–14), is the one "who descended from heaven" and "who comes from above" (John 3:13, 31). God the Father "sent his Son into the world, not to condemn the world, but that the world might be saved through him" (John 3:17).

Christians must orient ourselves by this creative and redemptive Word. Paul exhorts believers, "As therefore you received Christ Jesus the Lord, so live in him, rooted and built up in him and established in the faith" (Col 2:6–7). Similarly, Paul instructs Christians: "Have this mind among yourselves, which was in Christ Jesus, who, though he was in the form of God, did not count equality with God a thing to be grasped, but emptied himself, taking the form of a servant" (Phil 2:5–7). We should orient ourselves by the humble self-giving love that Christ embodies. Christ "humbled himself and became obedient unto death, even death on a cross" (Phil 2:8).

Oriented by Christ, the Christian must "take [up] his cross and follow" Christ (Matt 10:38). Jesus commands that believers follow him in self-sacrificial love: "If any man would come after me, let him deny himself and take up his cross and follow me. For whoever would save his life will lose it, and whoever loses his life for my sake will find it" (Matt 16:24–25). The same point appears in the Gospel of John. Jesus gives his disciples the commandment to orient themselves entirely by his embodied love: "This is my commandment, that you love one another as I have loved you. Greater love has no man than this, that a man lay down his life for his friends" (John 15:12–13).

2. All this-worldly reality must be judged and measured by the Torah.

When the Apostle Paul came to the Corinthians and proclaimed the gospel, he "decided to know nothing amonxg [the Corinthians] except Jesus Christ and him crucified" (1 Cor 2:2). This knowledge suffices to enable Paul to judge and measure all this-worldly realities. Craig Keener comments, "For Pauline Christians, the world's values are no longer determinative; we live instead in light of the cross, which shames the world's evaluation and proclaims the absolute superiority of the divine, eternal evaluation."[118]

It may seem, however, that there is a broader wisdom than Christ. For example, Paul refers to the "wisdom of this world" and "wisdom of this age" (1 Cor 1:20 and 2:6). But in defense of his reliance solely upon his knowledge of Christ, he urges that "Christ crucified" is none other than "Christ

---

118. Keener, *Mind of the Spirit*, 261.

the power of God and the wisdom of God" (1 Cor 1:23-24). Since this is so, it is in light of Christ, and by Christ's measure, that all human works will be judged. Paul cautions that "no other foundation can any one lay than that which is laid, which is Jesus Christ" (1 Cor 3:11). Only works done on this foundation of Christ's love will survive the judgment.

In light of Christ, Paul makes judgments about whatever topics the Corinthians bring to his attention, including lawsuits, marriage, and food (1 Cor 6-8). In the book of Revelation, similarly, everything pertaining to human existence is judged by the measure of Christ, including the true value of merchants' "cargo of gold, silver, jewels and pearls, fine linen, purple, silk and scarlet, all kinds of scented wood, all articles of ivory, all articles of costly wood, bronze, iron and marble, cinnamon, spice, incense, myrrh, frankincense, wine, oil, fine flour and wheat, cattle and sheep, horses and chariots, and slaves, that is, human souls" (Rev 21:12-13). By the light of Christ, we are to judge the basic human needs of food, clothing, and life; all these have value, but only as secondary to God's "kingdom and his righteousness" (Matt 6:33).

Paul holds that he has "the mind of Christ" because he has received the Spirit, and the person who has the mind of Christ "judges all things" (1 Cor 2:15-16). The measure of judgment is Christ, whose servant Paul is (see 1 Cor 4:1). Paul tells the Corinthians that he is their father and guide "in Christ" (1 Cor 4:15), and he thereby has authority to judge and measure their actions. In the Letter to the Hebrews, we find the specification that God has placed "everything in subjection to him [Christ]," and has "left nothing outside his control" (Heb 2:8). From eternity, God's purpose has been to draw all things into subjection to Christ (and Christ's measure). Ephesians 1:9-10 praises God's eternal "purpose which he set forth in Christ as a plan for the fullness of time, to unite all things in him" (Eph 1:9-10). Christ is the preexistent Word (John 1:1), and from eternity God has created us "in Christ Jesus for good works, which God prepared beforehand, that we should walk in them" (Eph 2:10).[119] Christ is the "first-born among many brethren" and all humans must be "conformed" to Christ's image (Rom 8:29). Paul teaches

---

119. Stephen Fowl comments: "In 2.1-10 readers learn that the Ephesians were dead through their sin and their captivity to powers hostile to God. God transforms this death into new life in Christ. This perspective on the Ephesians' salvation reflects the cosmic drama of salvation laid out in Ephesians 1. In 2.11-22 Paul reflects on the Ephesians' salvation in terms of their relationship to Israel. . . . From the perspective of being in Christ, and as part of their remembering, Romans, Greeks, Scythians, or any other inhabitant of Ephesus, need to learn that they are Gentiles. . . . Being a Gentile does not begin with understanding oneself in relation to Jews, but in relation to Christ, the Messiah of Israel. Being a Gentile is not primarily about circumcision, but about alienation from the Messiah" (Fowl, "Learning to Be a Gentile," 23-25).

that even now, "God has put all things in subjection under his [Christ's] feet" (1 Cor 15:27), although things are also still in the process of being subjected to Christ.[120] The point is that Christ is the measure and judge by which Christians evaluate all this-worldly reality.

3. Halakhic man focuses upon studying and obeying Torah in this world, rather than upon seeking the afterlife or upon connecting with an otherworldly realm.

This point may at first seem quite distant from Christianity. Indeed, Paul urges: "seek the things that are above, where Christ is, seated at the right hand of God. Set your minds on things that are above, not on things that are on earth" (Col 3:1–2). In the Gospel of John, similarly, Christ tells his disciples, "when I go and prepare a place for you, I will come again and will take you to myself, that where I am you may be also" (John 14:3). Yves Congar rightly states that the Church is "a fellowship in heavenly things, in Christ, through the sacraments, preaching, acts of the visible ministry and of the authority that derive from the Apostles."[121]

Yet, in the Gospel of Matthew, the risen Christ gives his disciples firmly this-worldly commands regarding what they should now do: "Go therefore and make disciples of all nations, baptizing them in the name of the Father and of the Son and of the Holy Spirit, teaching them to observe all that I have commanded you" (Matt 28:19–20). The risen Christ here emphasizes that the disciples should be focused upon spreading the gospel on earth, which involves the earthly tasks of baptizing and teaching. In the book of Acts, the risen Christ likewise tells his disciples to be his "witnesses in Jerusalem and in all Judea and Samaria and to the end of the earth" (Acts 1:8). When Christ ascends "out of their sight," the disciples gawk after him, "gazing into heaven" (Acts 1:10). While doing so, they receive a rebuke from two angelic figures. Rather than "gazing into heaven," therefore, the first

---

120. See Nardoni, *Rise Up, O Judge*, 322–23: "The Christian community ... believes that it lives between the beginning of the establishment of God's kingdom on earth and its final consummation. It received the commandment to love and to serve from Jesus' teaching in the washing of his disciples' feet. It is committed to care for any person in need, following the lesson of the good Samaritan. It works, exhorts, and prays that Zacchaeus may have many followers so that the impoverished Lazarus may sit at the rich man's table.... In the face of the elusive character of justice, the Christian community does not lose hope because it trusts deeply in the power of the Spirit, who dwells in the community and is acting in the world."

121. Congar, *Lay People in the Church*, 110. Congar is commenting on patristic ecclesiology, but he has in view Catholic ecclesiology as such.

Christians devote themselves "to the apostles' teaching and fellowship, to the breaking of bread and the prayers" (Acts 2:42). This life of fellowship also involves sharing possessions with each other. To ensure that no one in the community lacks basic necessities, the first Christians appoint deacons to oversee the distribution of food and clothing to widows and orphans.

Far from isolating himself in an otherworldly flight, Paul endures "hardships, calamities, beatings, imprisonments, tumults, labors, watching, hunger" (2 Cor 6:4–5). Admittedly, Paul describes a mystical experience of being "caught up to the third heaven" and of hearing "things that cannot be told, which man may not utter" (2 Cor 12:2–4). But rather than supposing that such exalted experience is at the center of his life, Paul adds that God gave him a "thorn" in order to prevent him "from being too elated by the abundance of revelations" (2 Cor 12:7). He "boasts" not about his exalted experiences, but about his this-worldly labors to spread the gospel. Among the "varieties of gifts" given by the Holy Spirit (1 Cor 12:4), Paul argues that the highest and most necessary gift is this-worldly love: "Love does not insist on its own way; it is not irritable or resentful; it does not rejoice at wrong, but rejoices in the right" (1 Cor 13:5–6).

To embody Christ in the world, therefore, the true path is not that of a focus upon spiritual exaltation—by understanding "all mysteries and all knowledge" (1 Cor 13:2)—but rather is a focus upon embodying the self-surrendering love that Christ reveals. Paul sums up his path of configuration and obedience to Christ in this world: "Owe no one anything, except to love one another; for he who loves his neighbor has fulfilled the law. . . . Love does no wrong to a neighbor; therefore love is the fulfilling of the law" (Rom 13:8, 10). Indeed, Paul insists that all the commandments of the Torah "are summed up in this sentence, 'You shall love your neighbor as yourself'" (Rom 13:9; cf. Lev 19:18). Christ teaches the same, as we saw in the Gospel of John's description of the commandment of love and as also appears in Christ's statement that the greatest two commandments are love of God and love of neighbor (see Matt 22:36–40).

The Christian must learn to emulate Christ in the obedience of love *in this world* for the sake of others, even to the point of death. In the book of Revelation, Babylon (the symbolic city of idolatry) is filled "with the blood of the saints and the blood of the martyrs of Jesus" (Rev 17:6). While otherworldly mysticism is not ruled out, it does not stand at the center of Christian life.[122]

---

122. See the recognition of this point, against some Rabbinic Jewish misperceptions, in Goshen-Gottstein, "Judaisms and Incarnational Theologies."

4. Torah is not for an esoteric spiritual elite, but rather is for all Jews.

Christ is for all people, not for an elite (esoteric or otherwise). In his public ministry, Christ ate with "tax collectors [Jews who grew wealthy serving the oppressive Roman regime] and sinners [Jews who did not obey Torah]" (Matt 11:19). In the Gospel of Luke, Christ finds his disciples having "an argument ... as to which of them was the greatest"; in response, Christ "took a child and put him by his side, and said to them, 'Whoever receives this child in my name receives me, and whoever receives me receives him who sent me; for he who is least among you all is the one who is great'" (Luke 9:47–48). Christ warns sharply against seeking to become a member of any powerful elite, since a true attitude of love is incompatible with ambitions to dominate over others. He instructs his disciples, "You know that the rulers of the Gentiles lord it over them, and their great men exercise authority over them. It shall not be so among you; but whoever would be great among you must be your servant, and whoever would be first among you must be your slave" (Matt 20:25–27). Preaching Christ requires becoming the servant of all, rather than striving to belong to the privileged few.

All Christians can imitate Christ, who "came not to be served but to serve" (Matt 20:28). In this regard, Christ tells a parable that warns against presumption and that directs Christians toward service in this world. In the parable, Christ tells people who profess not to have recognized him: "I was hungry and you gave me food, I was thirsty and you gave me drink, I was a stranger and you welcomed me, I was naked and you clothed me, I was sick and you visited me, I was in prison and you came to see me" (Matt 25:35–36). To people who do such acts of love, Christ will give the kingdom prepared "from the foundation of the world" (Matt 25:34). He tells them, "Truly, I say to you, as you did it to one of the least of these my brethren, you did it to me" (Matt 25:40). By contrast, people who do not do such acts of love will not inherit the kingdom. There will be people who say to him "[w]e ate and drank in your presence" but to whom he will reply, "I do not know where you come from," because in fact they have been "workers of iniquity" (Luke 13:26–27).

When Christ asks to wash Peter's feet, Peter thinks that this menial task is below Christ's dignity. Not understanding the humility that makes imitating Christ possible for all people, Peter attempts to correct Christ. In response Christ tells him, "If I do not wash you, you have no part in me" (John 13:8). After performing this task for all his twelve disciples, Christ explains what he has done: "You call me Teacher and Lord; and you are right, for so I am. If I then, your Lord and Teacher, have washed your feet, you also ought to wash one another's feet. For I have given you an example, that you also should do as I have done to you" (John 13:13–15). Every Christian can serve others and every Christian can be served. Christ is for everyone.

Christ warns his followers against using his teaching to constitute an elite subgroup: "Neither be called masters, for you have one master, the Christ" (Matt 23:10). But how is it that the apostles themselves do not constitute an elite? Paul faces this question directly. He describes the Church as Christ's body, and he points out that all the members of the body are important: "And if the ear should say, 'Because I am not an eye, I do not belong to the body,' that would not make it any less a part of the body. If the whole body were an eye, where would be the hearing? If the whole body were an ear, where would be the sense of smell?" (1 Cor 12:16–17). All members have need of all the other members. If this analogy does not make it clear that Christ is for everyone (rather than being for an elite such as the apostles or leaders), Paul adds that all humans are called to the vocation of love. Union with Christ is meant to place all people on the "still more excellent way" (1 Cor 12:31). The seeming elite in the Church may "speak in the tongues of men and of angels" and "have prophetic powers, and understand all mysteries and all knowledge," but without love, this seeming elite is "nothing" (1 Cor 13:1–2). Love is open to all persons. No one, then, lacks the invitation to follow Christ. Paul seeks to give Christ to all people, no matter what their status in this world, because Christ is for all. As Paul remarks, "For consider your call, brethren; not many of you were wise according to the flesh, not many were powerful, not many were of noble birth; but God chose what is foolish in the world to shame the wise, God chose what is weak in the world to shame the strong, God chose what is low and despised in the world" (1 Cor 1:26–28).

5. Halakhic man seeks to instantiate, in the empirical world, the transcendent ideal (Torah) that has descended to earth.

The Christian seeks to instantiate Christ in the world, to make people into "other Christs" and to make the world into a realm reflective of Christ. Having "descended" to earth (Eph 4:9–10) from God the Father, Christ seeks to configure his people to his image "until we all attain to the unity of the faith and of the knowledge of the Son of God, to mature manhood, to the measure of the stature of the fullness of Christ" (Eph 4:13).[123] Paul goes so far as to teach the Galatians, "I have been crucified with Christ; it is no

---

123. For further discussion in light of temple theology, see Macaskill, *Union with Christ*, 153.

longer I who live, but Christ who lives in me; and the life I now live in the flesh I live by faith in the Son of God, who loved me and gave himself for me" (Gal 2:20). The point is that by faith and charity, Paul instantiates Christ in the world. Paul makes the same point in his Letter to the Romans. He exhorts, "Do not be conformed to this world but be transformed by the renewal of your mind, that you may prove what is the will of God, what is good and acceptable and perfect" (Rom 12:2).[124] This (ongoing) transformation configures the Christian to Christ. Earlier in the Letter to the Romans, Paul describes God's saving purpose, which is to ensure that Christians "be conformed to the image of his Son, in order that he might be the first-born of many brethren" (Rom 8:29).

Yet, what about the instantiation of Christ in the entire world, not simply in individual persons? Admittedly, Jesus was not sanguine about the possibility of fully configuring the world to himself prior to the eschaton. He foretold that in the years to come, due to "false prophets" and the increase of wickedness, "most men's love will grow cold" (Matt 24:12). In *this* sense of "world," Christ requires that his followers not be "of the world" (John 15:19). His followers must live by self-sacrificial love rather than by the world's ambition, greed, lust, pride, and so forth.

Even so, Christ's followers are called to attempt to instantiate Christ in the entire world. Christ refers to this task when he states that before the final consummation of all things, "the gospel of the kingdom will be preached throughout the whole world, as a testimony to all nations" (Matt 24:14). Christ sends his followers into the world just as the Father sent Christ into the world (John 17:18). Through the Spirit, Christ empowers his followers to embody his self-sacrificial love throughout the world. The resulting transformation of the world will be real, even if not always perceivable. Due to the power of the transformative Spirit, there will be people "who keep the commandments of God and bear testimony to Jesus" (Rev 12:17), some of whom will be persecuted even unto death (Rev 7:14). As Christians go into the world, their presence—or their failure—will be known by the following test: "If any one says, 'I love God,' and hates his brother, he is a liar; for he who does not love his brother whom he has seen, cannot love God whom he has not seen. And this commandment we have from him, that he who loves God should love his brother also" (1 John 4:20–21). The world will be changed for the better by persons imbued with real love. The Letter to the Hebrews teaches, "Strive for peace with all men, and for the holiness without which no one will see the Lord" (Heb 12:14). This holiness is not

---

124. Miroslav Volf and Matthew Croasmun comment upon the collective dimension of this call, while recognizing that Paul is speaking to each individual. See Volf and Croasmun, *For the Life of the World*, 126.

an otherworldly matter but rather is a concrete instantiation in this world of the self-sacrificial love of Christ, the eternal Word who "became flesh and dwelt among us" (John 1:14).

6. The eschatological world-to-come will reflect Torah in a perfectly full way.

The book of Revelation describes the eschatological world-to-come as fully illumined by Christ. As the seer of Revelation says, "its lamp is the Lamb" (Rev 21:23). Christ illumines the world-to-come because Christ, as the incarnate Son, shares fully in "the glory of God" (Rev 21:23), and God's glory illumines the world-to-come. Because Christ perfectly illumines the world-to-come, "there shall be no night there," and nothing evil will be there (Rev 21:25). The world-to-come will perfectly reflect Christ. Christ's illumination of the world-to-come is inseparable from Christ's sharing in the divine glory of God the Father.

The seer of the book of Revelation also uses the image of God's throne. Christ ("the Lamb") shares in this throne. A constitutive part of the world-to-come consists in the worship that everyone there will offer to Christ, just as they worship God the Father. Christ will be the judge of all things, and he will establish the relationship of all things to himself in the world-to-come. Paul remarks that "we must all appear before the judgment seat of Christ, so that each one may receive good or evil, according to what he has done in the body" (2 Cor 5:10). Even now, the perfect reflection of Christ in the blessed is being prepared. Paul argues that Christians, gazing upon Christ's glory, are now "being changed into his likeness from one degree of glory to another" (2 Cor 3:18). Christians already possess "treasure in earthen vessels" (2 Cor 4:7). Although Christians are subject to death, they already share in the "life of Jesus" (2 Cor 4:11) as a principle of glory. Thus, Paul looks forward to experiencing "an eternal weight of glory beyond all comparison" (2 Cor 4:17).

In the world-to-come, says Paul, the blessed will "understand fully" and know God "face to face" (1 Cor 13:12). Even now, no one can separate the Christian "from the love of God in Christ Jesus our Lord" (Rom 8:39), although a person can freely turn away from Christ. In a certain sense, it is already true that "Christ is all, and in all" (Col 3:11). This will be perfectly the case in the world-to-come, in which everything will reflect Christ. The Elder John remarks that "we are God's children now; it does not yet appear what we shall be, but we know that when he appears we shall be like him, for we shall see him as he is" (1 John 3:2). If we are now sons in the Son, in the world-to-come we will supremely reflect the Son, Christ Jesus.

Furthermore, the whole creation—as the eschatological new creation—will share in the victory of Christ. Paul states that "the creation itself will be set free from its bondage to decay and obtain the glorious liberty of the children of God" (Rom 8:21). Whatever this "glorious liberty" means precisely, it surely entails that the world-to-come will fully reflect Christ, since the final state of the blessed will consist in being "children of God, and if children, then heirs, heirs of God and fellow heirs with Christ, provided we suffer with him in order that we may also be glorified with him" (Rom 8:16–17).

According to Paul, too, God the Father "has put all things under his [Christ's] feet and has made him the head over all things for the Church"—and God has exalted Christ in this manner "not only in this age but also in that which is to come" (Eph 1:21–22). Christ will judge the world by his love. As Jesus says in the Gospel of John, "He who rejects me and does not receive my sayings has a judge; the word that I have spoken will be his judge on the last day" (John 12:48). The word that Christ has spoken is the perfect love of the "Word" who "became flesh and dwelt among us, full of grace and truth" (John 1:14). In the world-to-come, the blessed will reflect Christ so perfectly that they will share in his act of judgment, because they will fully share in his love. Paul asks, "Do you not know that the saints will judge the world?" (1 Cor 6:2).

The First Letter of Peter affirms that the purpose of redemption is "that in everything God may be glorified through Jesus Christ. To him belong glory and dominion for ever and ever" (1 Pet 4:11). In the world-to-come, God will be utterly glorified, in everything, through Christ. Fully ordered to and governed by Christ, the blessed and the whole redeemed creation will give perfect glory to God. The "glory of God" and "the Lamb" will give light to the "nations," and the "kings of the earth" will be ordered by this light (Rev 21:24). The world-to-come will perfectly reflect the light and love of Christ.

7. The Divine Presence "contracts" to dwell in a small space (*tzimtzum*): this happens in creation and in the giving of Torah to Israel.

The "contraction" of the Divine Presence should not be taken as a literal (bodily) contraction but rather as the mystery of God's "contracting" in order to give room to finite entities to exist. According to Christianity, the

Divine Presence can also indwell finite human beings, and can even take on flesh so that a particular man *is* God. In a certain sense, both the incarnation and the divine indwelling in believers can be described as divine "contraction."[125]

Christians believe that "the Word became flesh and dwelt among us" (John 1:14). When the Divine Presence comes fully into the world in the womb of Mary, "The true light that enlightens every man was coming into the world. He was in the world, and the world was made through him, yet the world knew him not" (John 1:9–10). The Apostle Paul tells us that Christ Jesus "was in the form of God" but nonetheless "emptied himself, taking the form of a servant, being born in the likeness of men" (Phil 2:6–7). Christ existed as God (the divine "Son") prior—though the priority is not one of time—to "taking the form of a servant." By emptying himself to take on the humble form of a man, Christ shows how greatly God desires intimacy with his people and to what lengths God will go in order to achieve it.

In the letter to the Colossians, we read that Christ, who is the Father's "beloved Son," is the one in whom "all things were created, in heaven and on earth, visible and invisible, whether thrones or dominions or principalities or authorities—all things were created through him and for him" (Col 1:16). Paul professes that "for us there is one God, the Father, from whom are all things and for whom we exist, and one Lord, Jesus Christ, through whom are all things and through whom we exist" (1 Cor 8:6).[126] There are not two Creator Gods; but there is a distinction between the Father and Christ. As "Lord" (the Septuagint translation for YHWH), Christ is on the side of the Creator, not the creature—even though in his humanity Christ is obviously a creature. The divine Son has become "flesh and dwelt among us"; he has "emptied himself, taking the form of a servant."

According to the Gospel of Matthew, Christ is the one who fulfills the prophecy regarding "'Emmanuel' (which means, God with us)" (Matt 1:23). Christ is also the one who fulfills "the law and the prophets" and who gives the law in his own name with the freedom of the divine lawgiver: "It was also said, 'Whoever divorces his wife, let him give her a certificate of divorce.' But I say to you that every one who divorces his wife, except on

---

125. See Weinandy, *Does God Change?*

126. For discussion of 1 Corinthians 8:6 in the context of Deuteronomy 6:4–9 (and more generally of Deuteronomy's role in Paul's letters and in other Second Temple Jewish writings), see Lincicum, *Paul*, 138–40. Lincicum describes Paul's "particular dynamic of fidelity and radicalism" (*Paul*, 199), a dynamic that is certainly on display in 1 Corinthians 8:6; and he points in this regard to the "*traditio legis* motif," which "shows Christ delivering the law to his apostles, sometimes with the inscription written on the open scroll, *Dominus legem dat*" (*Paul*, 200). See also Watson, *Paul and the Hermeneutics of Faith*, especially 417.

the ground of unchastity, makes her an adulteress; and whoever marries a divorced woman commits adultery" (Matt 5:31–32). Furthermore, in the Gospel of Matthew, Christ lays claim to an extraordinary intimacy with God the Father—not only by distinctively calling God "Father," but also by stating that he alone knows the Father: "All things have been delivered to me by my Father; and no one knows the Son except the Father, and no one knows the Father except the Son and any one to whom the Son chooses to reveal him" (Matt 11:27).

The Divine Presence manifests itself supremely through Christ's love and mercy on the cross. Christ calls upon the Father to "glorify your Son that the Son may glorify you" (John 17:1), and this happens through Christ's cross and resurrection. The glorification of the Father takes place through Christ's redemptive love for sinners, since the Father is glorified most perfectly by the obedience of supreme love. Through Christ's humility, God makes room for us to participate in his work of redemption by love.

The "contraction" of the Divine Presence is such that when we see Christ crucified, we see the Father, in his supreme love and mercy for his people. Christ truly is God rather than simply being a human receptacle of God. His disciple Philip says to him, "Lord, show us the Father, and we shall be satisfied" (John 14:8). He expresses disappointment in Philip, given that Philip has not yet recognized him. He replies to Philip, "Have I been with you so long, and yet you do not know me, Philip? He who has seen me has seen the Father" (John 14:9).[127]

From the above, it is clear that in the New Testament we find a distinction between Father and Son (and Spirit). The Son is not the Father; but the Son is God. Thus Christ applies the divine name "I am" to himself, as in John 8:58. The opening verse of the Gospel of John describes a distinction between God (the Father) and the Son (or Word) that does not divide the unity of God: "the Word was with God, and the Word was God" (John 1:1). We saw this point as well in Paul's affirmation of "one God," the Father, and "one Lord," Christ—both of whom are affirmed as the one Creator.[128] The "contraction" of the Divine Presence in the coming of Christ thus not only reveals the Divine Presence as radical love for all people, but also reveals that the mystery of divine unity is not monadic. In a sense, God makes room for the Other even in himself.

It is not only as Christ that God empties himself or makes himself "small" so as to dwell in the world. In creation, God has made a "home" for himself (John 1:11), even though God is often not recognized in that

---

127. See Humphrey, *And I Turned to See the Voice*, 16–18.
128. See Tilling, *Paul's Divine Christology*.

"home." The Father and the Son may also be said to "contract" so as to dwell in believers. Christ promises in the Gospel of John: "If a man loves me, he will keep my word, and my Father will love him, and we will come to him and make our home with him" (John 14:23).

8. The this-worldliness of Halakhah produces a "sensuous religion," preoccupied with embodied actions.

Catholic Christianity is a "sensuous religion," preoccupied with embodied actions. The very fact that "the Word became flesh and dwelt among us" (John 1:14) already makes this so. Christ's preeminent act of worship, by which he gives supreme glory to God the Father, is his suffering and dying on the cross for the salvation of sinners. One could not find a more embodied divine action at the heart of any other religion.

During his earthly ministry, Christ showed that Christianity would be a "sensuous religion." For example, in healing a man afflicted with leprosy, Christ "stretched out his hand and touched him" (Mark 1:41). In healing a blind man, Christ first "spit on his eyes and laid his hands upon him" and then "laid his hands upon his eyes" (Mark 8:23, 25). Likewise, he instituted sacraments, preeminently baptism and the Eucharist.[129] In the sacrament of the Eucharist, Christ's body and blood are present in a sacramental mode under the signs of bread and wine. In the sacrament of baptism, which is a washing by water, Christ unites us to himself by the baptismal water, through which we receive the saving power of his cross and resurrection.

The sensuous action of consuming "the Lord's supper" (1 Cor 11:20) stands at the center of Christian life. As Paul says, "The cup of blessing which we bless, is it not a participation in the blood of Christ? The bread which we break, is it not a participation in the body of Christ? Because there is one bread we who are many are one body, for we all partake of the one bread" (1 Cor 10:16–17).[130] Believers become "one body" with Christ and with each other through sharing in this sacramental meal.

Paul emphasizes the significance of bodily actions for all aspects of Christian life. In union with Christ through faith and charity, Christians partake in the outpouring of the Spirit. Paul explains what this means for Christian embodiment: "Do you not know that you are God's temple and

---

129. See Weinandy, "Human Acts of Christ." Weinandy argues that "the sacraments are founded upon Jesus' historic, priestly, human actions, which he now, as its [the Church's] risen Head, actively makes sacramentally present within his Body" ("Human Acts of Christ," 151).

130. See Lincicum, "Sacraments in the Pauline Epistles."

that God's Spirit dwells in you? If any one destroys God's temple, God will destroy him. For God's temple is holy, and that temple you are" (1 Cor 3:16–17).[131] For Christians, actions done in the body are actions done in (and as) God's temple. This means that every embodied action has an extraordinary moral significance. Prior to becoming Christian, the Gentile Corinthians thought little of having sexual intercourse with a prostitute; but as Christians they learned that "[t]he body is not meant for immorality, but for the Lord, and the Lord for the body" (1 Cor 6:13). Paul commands each Christian to "glorify God in your body" (1 Cor 6:20).

Christianity is a "sensuous religion" because Christians are "in Christ" and are "members of Christ" (1 Cor 6:15).[132] The Church is "the body of Christ" (1 Cor 12:27). To receive the Eucharist without caring for the poor members of the Church is to "be guilty of profaning the body and blood of the Lord" (1 Cor 11:27). Elsewhere, Paul describes the "works of the flesh" (Gal 5:19) that typify what Christians must avoid on pain of failing to attain to the kingdom of Christ. These works include such things as "immorality, impurity, licentiousness, idolatry, sorcery, enmity, strife, jealousy, anger, selfishness, dissension, party spirit, envy, drunkenness, carousing, and the like" (Gal 5:19–21). In this sense, Christians "have crucified the flesh with its passions and desires" (Gal 5:24). Certain embodied actions cannot be done without renouncing the love that Christ exhibited in the flesh. Paul exhorts Christians to "not grow weary in well-doing" (Gal 6:9) and to "[b]ear one another's burdens, and so fulfill the law of Christ" (Gal 6:2).[133]

9. Judaism is not a religion built upon the quest for exalted spiritual experience, although such experience takes place.

Above, I have already addressed this point somewhat, in describing Paul's relativizing of his own exalted spiritual experiences. In the Gospels, Christ experiences spiritual exaltation on the Mount of Transfiguration. Jeffrey Niehaus compares this to Moses' experience on Mount Sinai: "Like Moses, Jesus reflects the glory of God's presence, his face shining like the sun and his clothes as white as the light."[134] Having been taken by Jesus up the mountain, Peter, James, and John see Jesus transfigured with light and speaking with Moses and Elijah. Peter's response, however, shows his firm earthliness. Misunderstanding what is happening, he proposes to "make three booths

---

131. See Macaskill, *Union with Christ*, 154–57.
132. See the essays in Thate et al., eds., *"In Christ" in Paul*.
133. See Barclay, *Obeying the Truth*.
134. Niehaus, *God at Sinai*, 337.

here, one for you and one for Moses and one for Elijah" (Matt 17:4). Peter's proposal is ignored; instead God, manifesting himself in a bright cloud and a heavenly voice, proclaims, "This is my beloved Son, with whom I am well pleased; listen to him" (Matt 17:5).

Throughout the Gospels, the disciples are consistently caught by surprise, and their experience, while it often issues in awe, is not presented as spiritual exaltation. Even when the disciples see the risen Christ, we find no encouragement of a quest for spiritual exaltation. In the Gospel of Matthew, the eleven disciples see and worship the risen Lord. Rather than entering into an exalted spiritual trance or something similar, they receive a workmanlike mission to preach and baptize (see Matt 28:19-20). At Christ's ascension, any sense of exalted spiritual experience is deflated by the angels' warning against gazing up to heaven (Acts 1:11). The life of the first Christians appears to have been one in which their feet were firmly planted on the ground: "And day by day, attending the temple together and breaking bread in their homes, they partook of food with glad and generous hearts" (Acts 2:46).

In the Gospel of John, the risen Christ asks Peter three times whether Peter loves him; and each time, after Peter responds, Christ commands Peter to feed (or tend) Christ's flock (John 21:15-17). When Peter asks about the future path of the beloved disciple, Christ tells Peter to focus instead on what Peter needs to do, namely, to follow Christ. This path will be one of suffering, not spiritual exaltation. Foreshadowing Peter's death on a cross at the hands of Roman soldiers, Christ explains to Peter: "when you are old, you will stretch out your hands, and another will fasten your belt for you and carry you where you do not wish to go" (John 21:18).

This simple command to follow Christ in a mission that will entail suffering is in accord with the simplicity of Christ's instructions about how to pray. Christ warns against "heap[ing] up empty phrases" and against praying in a manner that attracts the notice of others (Matt 6:7). He tells his disciples to "go into your room and shut the door and pray to your Father," and to pray with simple petitions, including "forgive us our trespasses as we forgive those who trespass against us" (Matt 6:6, 12).

A seeming exception to this general rule about exalted spiritual experience takes place at Pentecost, when the apostles receive "tongues as of fire, distributed and resting on each one of them. And they were all filled with the Holy Spirit" (Acts 2:3-4). Yet, this exception in fact proves the rule, because the "tongues . . . of fire" enable the apostles to preach the gospel to the assembled throng, composed of Jews from various nations who speak various languages. The book of Acts focuses not upon the nature of this experience, let alone upon seeking to replicate it, but rather upon the apostolic labor of preaching the gospel. In sum, Christianity is a religion built upon the mundane tasks of worshiping, proclaiming, and obeying Christ, even though exalted spiritual experiences can and do take place.

10. Performing the commandments is delightful, rather than being a spiritual struggle.

For the virtuous follower of Christ, the performance of an action configured to Christ should be delightful rather than being a spiritual struggle.[135] Christ urges, "Take my yoke upon you, and learn from me; for I am gentle and lowly in heart, and you will find rest for your souls. For my yoke is easy, and my burden is light" (Matt 11:29-30). Christ's claim does not mean that performing his commandments (including his command against divorce and remarriage, his command to turn the other cheek, his command to love one's enemies, his command to love one another as he has loved us, and so on) will be without difficulty.[136] In fact, elsewhere in the Gospel of Matthew he observes that "the gate is narrow and the way is hard, that leads to life" (Matt 7:14). Similarly, he says that the person "who does not take his cross and follow me is not worthy of me" (Matt 10:38). Interiorly, however, when we have love, obeying Christ's commandments will be delightful.

Christ expresses this joy in a parable: "The kingdom of heaven is like treasure hidden in a field, which a man found and covered up; then in his joy he goes and sells all that he has and buys that field" (Matt 13:44). The joy of the kingdom of heaven is the discovery of the love and mercy of Christ. Christ observes in the Gospel of John, "As the Father has loved me, so have I loved you; abide in my love. If you keep my commandments, you will abide in my love, just as I have kept my Father's commandments and abide in his love. These things I have spoken to you, that my joy may be in you, and that your joy may be full" (John 15:9-11).

In light of Christ's victory over sin and death, Paul urges that the "kingdom of God" means "righteousness and peace and joy in the Holy Spirit," and Paul adds that the person "who thus serves Christ is acceptable to God and approved by men" (Rom 14:17-18). Paul expects that those who follow

---

135. See for example Thomas Aquinas, *Summa theologiae* II-II, q. 155; as well as Aquinas's deployment of Aristotle's understanding of a virtuous habit.

136. Sometimes Catholic ethics is accused of being too focused on prohibitions, and the same accusation is made against traditional Jewish ethics. Rabbi Charles David Isbell comments, "The rabbis taught that there were 613 commandments in the Torah. 365 of them were negative, but 248 were positive. So never let it be assumed that Judaism is only about the *don'ts* of life. It is equally about the *do's*: walking humbly with God, loving Him with all our being, loving others" (Isbell, *Sermons*, 103).

Christ's commandments will not be burdened but will in fact "rejoice in the Lord always" (Phil 4:4). Each Christian will learn that (as Paul says) "I can do all things in him [Christ] who strengthens me" (Phil 4:13). Paul makes this statement not during an easy time in his life, but during his imprisonment by the Romans (Phil 1:13).

Admittedly, in a passage from the letter to the Romans that has inspired divergent schools of interpretation, Paul states that "I do not understand my own actions. For I do not do what I want, but I do the very thing I hate. . . . I can will what is right, but I cannot do it. For I do not do the good I want, but the evil I do not want is what I do" (Rom 7:15–16, 19). Some commentators argue that Paul is describing his present condition as a redeemed sinner, while other commentators argue that Paul is describing his condition prior to his reception of the grace of the Holy Spirit in Christ. Still others say that Paul is describing both of these conditions, since he truly has been freed from sin but continues to have to fight against sinful impulses.[137] Ephesians 2:3 describes the condition of the unredeemed person: "we all once lived in the passions of our flesh, following the desires of body and mind, and so we were by nature children of wrath, like the rest of mankind." In such a condition, people have to struggle desperately in order even to have a chance of doing the right thing. Elements of this struggle do indeed persist for the Christian. As Grant Macaskill remarks, "Sin continues to squat in our minds after its tenure has been ended. It always seeks to turn us in on ourselves."[138]

Yet, the life weighed down by the passions of the flesh is not the life for which Christ has freed us. Paul calls upon Christ's followers "to grow up in every way into him who is the head, into Christ" (Eph 4:15). We are to "be imitators of God" and to "walk in love, as Christ loved us and gave himself up for us" (Eph 5:1–2); and we are "to be strengthened with might through his Spirit in the inner man" so that we are "rooted and grounded in love" (Eph 3:16–17). These descriptions of spiritual maturity in Christ indicate that performing acts of love and of the other virtues will be delightful for the mature Christian. Such maturity is the only way that Paul's description of Christian life in Romans 12:9–14 could be a reality: "Let love be genuine; hate what is evil, hold fast to what is good; outdo one another in showing honor. Never flag in zeal, be aglow with the Spirit, serve the Lord. Rejoice in your hope, be patient in tribulation, be constant in prayer. Contribute to the needs of the saints, practice hospitality. Bless those who persecute you."

---

137. See Macaskill, *Union with Christ*, 105–10; Keener, *Mind of the Spirit*, 55–112. I agree with Macaskill that Paul is describing both conditions at the same time.

138. Macaskill, *Union with Christ*, 111.

Imagine truly blessing one's persecutor without having a transformed heart! One could not grit one's teeth and do such a thing; one would fail. The truly loving person whom Paul has in view is someone for whom acting according to Christ's love has become delightful.

Even now, real sanctity can be ours. We do not need to undertake years of practice in order to be able to delight in doing the good, because Christ has truly freed us.[139] Paul encourages believers: "just as you once yielded your members to impurity and to greater and greater iniquity, so now yield your members to righteousness for sanctification" (Rom 6:19). Christians must "cast off the works of darkness and put on the armor of light" (Rom 13:12). Only in this way will we truly "serve our Lord Jesus Christ" rather than our "own appetites" (Rom 16:18).[140] Obeying Christ's commandment of love may at times be a struggle—and believers may fail due to the weakness of the "flesh," requiring a process of ongoing repentance and conversion—but God in Christ has already given believers the strength, by the grace of the Spirit, to do Christ's works of love with delight. As Keener comments: "Our thinking does not create the new reality, subjecting the genuineness of our identity in Christ to the starts and bumps of the renewing of our minds; instead, it recognizes the new reality already inaugurated in Christ, the actual beginning of the new creation."[141]

---

139. See Craig Keener's position that we should "challenge the expectation, sometimes implicitly connected to new believers in Christ, that they must struggle with temptation and sometimes fail. This script truncates Paul's gospel and refuses to accept its teaching of the new identity in Christ. Struggle, of course, sometimes occurs; but for the believer, the battle must be one of faith (i.e. recognizing the truth of what God has accomplished in Christ).... For Paul, one overcomes the character of the flesh not by addressing it on its own terms but by recognizing the greater reality of what God has done for us in Christ" (*Mind of the Spirit*, 258–59). Keener explains further: "This does not mean that we should deny that temptations confront us and are sometimes rooted in past choices or our biology; rather, it means that we are called to share God's perspective on our justification. We must stand firm in defining our *core* identity in terms of Christ rather than in terms of those past choices, experiences, or genetics. Yes, the temptations may be deeply rooted in our past and even in our present neurochemistry, but believers in Christ are defined first and foremost by our identity and destiny in Christ" (Keener, *Mind of the Spirit*, 262).

140. See Sandnes, *Belly and Body in the Pauline Epistles*.

141. Keener, *Mind of the Spirit*, 264. Keener's additional remarks may help avoid misunderstanding (and even despair): "Our negative choices also wire our brains for particular neurochemical responses, so that we become accustomed to respond to stimuli in such detrimental ways automatically. In such cases, walking by the Spirit rather than by the flesh requires a continuous, deliberate rethinking and retuning, with many determined decisions to believe God's truth about our identity.... Even so, the old memories and patterns may resurface, especially under stress, whether in dreams or while awake, and therefore continued vigilance is important. Naturally, this will be harder for some people in some areas than for others" (Keener, *Mind of the Spirit*, 263).

11. Halakhah teaches the people of Israel how, at the same time, to abase themselves for their sins and to recognize their privileged relationship with God.

Christ teaches Christians how to abase ourselves for our sins, while at the same time giving thanks for our privileged relationship to God through Christ. Peter is emblematic of this situation. He abandoned Christ in Christ's hour of greatest need. Yet, Christ never disowned Peter; on the contrary, the risen Christ forgave the repentant Peter. On the cross, Christ bears the sins of all humanity. All people are abased before God, because all are sinners. Yet, in Christ, God shows his love for all people. Despite their sins, God calls all people to this privileged relationship of love.

Some passages of Paul's letters are particularly helpful for illumining this combination of abasement (including our ongoing need to ask for forgiveness) and God's establishment in Christ of a renewed relationship. As Paul remarks, "one will hardly die for a righteous man—though perhaps for a good man one will dare even to die. But God shows his love for us in that while we were yet sinners Christ died for us" (Rom 5:7-8). As sinners, Christians are responsible for causing Christ's death. Yet Paul rejoices that "Christ died for us" and that we have been "reconciled to God by the death of his Son" (Rom 5:10).[142] God calls us in Christ into a wondrously privileged relationship of intimacy and friendship with God.

Through his perfect love that is "the fulfilling of the law" (Rom 13:10), Christ makes believers into adopted sons and daughters of God (Rom 8:14-19).[143] Paul tells the Gentiles, "So then you are no longer strangers and sojourners, but you are fellow citizens with the saints and members of the household of God" (Eph 2:19). In this privileged relationship, however, Christians must not become "puffed up," because pride is the opposite of Christ's humility and indeed pride destroys one's union with Christ. Cautioning the Corinthians, Paul asks rhetorically: "What have you that you did

---

Keener goes on to say, "We may therefore fight this battle by embracing Christ's accomplished victory, rather than approaching it with an expectation of defeat. In fact, it is a battle that can be fought at the point of temptation, which is not itself sin: that is, in principle a believer need not succumb to deliberate sin.... When we do fail, it feels easy (at least for me) to become discouraged and succumb to the repeated cycle of expected further failure; but that is why we must ground our identity in Christ's finished work and in the vision of our eschatological destiny in him, not in our past performance.... Of course, we recognize that this power is Christ's and not our own, and God's forgiveness in him means that we have no reason to fear confessing sin" (Keener, *Mind of the Spirit*, 264).

142. See Cousar, *Theology of the Cross*.
143. See Burke, *Adopted into God's Family*.

not receive? If then you received it, why do you boast as if it were not a gift?" (1 Cor 4:6–7). Believers' privileged relationship with God comes through God's action, not by reason of our own goodness.

In his Farewell Discourse at his Last Supper, Jesus tells his disciples: "You did not choose me, but I chose you and appointed you that you should go and bear fruit and that your fruit should abide" (John 15:16). In the First Letter of Peter, the same emphasis appears when Peter tells the Christian Gentiles, "You are a chosen race, a royal priesthood, a holy nation, God's own people, that you may declare the wonderful deeds of him who called you out of darkness into his marvelous light" (1 Pet 2:9). The focus of Christianity is always on the glory of Christ, rather than the glory of Christians. In the liturgical, sacramental, and prayerful rhythm of the Christian life, there is regular confession of sin as well as ever-present glorification of God for what he has done in Christ.

In portraying this combination of repentance and privileged relationship with God, the First Letter of John reminds Christians that "the blood of Jesus his Son cleanses us from all sin. If we say we have no sin, we deceive ourselves, and the truth is not in us. If we confess our sins, he is faithful and just, and will forgive our sins and cleanse us from all unrighteousness" (1 John 1:7–9). Even more clearly, the letter of James plants repentance firmly within the Christian rhythm of life: "Therefore confess your sins to one another, and pray for one another, that you may be healed" (Jas 5:16). At the same time, James joyfully praises the intimate relationship with God found in "our Lord Jesus Christ, the Lord of glory" (Jas 2:1). The Christian life moves from Good Friday to Easter Sunday, from Advent to Lent, and so on, encompassing both ongoing repentance and ongoing praise of God for his merciful election of his people in Christ.[144]

---

144. For an effort to celebrate "the death and resurrection of Jesus" and to rediscover "the cross of Jesus amid the crosses of history" while keeping in view the ways in which New Testament texts about the cross have been used to persecute the Jewish people, see Boys, *Redeeming Our Sacred Story*, quotations from 270. While continuing to believe in the cross's redemptive power, Boys argues that "Christians need more frank acknowledgment of how the cross also became a symbol of our violence toward the 'other,' particularly Jews" (*Redeeming Our Sacred Story*, 261). I agree with this; Christians, as sinners, have misused and abused the most sacred realities. Of course, we should avoid painting Christians solely as sinners, since grace and charity have also been real—indeed marvelously so—even if this has generally not been evident in Christians' relationships with the Jewish people. Boys continues: "Do we not have an obligation after the Holocaust to rethink how the passion narratives are proclaimed? If we were truly to face Auschwitz, would we not alter the liturgy of Good Friday? Pay more attention to the lyrics of our hymns? In too many other liturgical and educational settings, we hear the 'same old, same old' canards about Pharisees, Jewish failures to recognize the messiah, and Jewish responsibility for the death of Jesus" (Boys, *Redeeming Our Sacred*

12. Halakhic man focuses on Torah rather than on the self's subjective condition, but does not encourage the complete disappearance of our own will.

Christians focus on Christ rather than on the self's subjective condition. Exemplifying this focus, Paul says that "it is no longer I who live, but Christ who lives in me" (Gal 2:20), and he adds that "I have been crucified with Christ" (Gal 2:20). Given that Christ is at the center of his life, Paul holds that "the life I now live in the flesh I live by faith in the Son of God, who loved me and gave himself for me" (Gal 2:20).[145]

Note that Paul does not annihilate his "I" in Galatians 2:20, but rather he insists that for each of us, our center is no longer the "I" but rather Christ. Had Paul meant to annihilate the "I" through the disappearance of the Christian's own will, he could hardly have urged the Philippians to "work out your own salvation with fear and trembling" (Phil 2:12). Paul assumes in faith that God's Spirit is at work in us, to unite us ever more deeply with the love of Christ. Thus Paul immediately adds that "God is at work in you, both to will and to work for his good pleasure" (Phil 2:13).

Instead of suppressing his own "I," Paul seeks the configuration of his "I" to that of Christ, so that he may "[d]o nothing from selfishness or conceit" but may act always in humility and love, seeking "the interests of others" (Phil 2:3-4).[146] Praising "the surpassing worth of knowing Christ Jesus my Lord," he seeks "the righteousness from God that depends on faith, that I may know him and the power of his resurrection, and may share his sufferings, becoming like him in his death, that if possible I may attain the resurrection from the dead" (Phil 3:8-11). With Christ at the center, Paul turns his attention outward in love, spending himself in the service of others. He constantly preaches "not ourselves, but Jesus Christ as Lord, with

---

Story, 262). I agree that even if Jesus dealt with particular Pharisees whom he rightly corrected, Christians today need to avoid generalizations about the Pharisees, recognizing the polemical impulses present in the New Testament. But in my view, the way that the Passion Narratives are proclaimed in the Catholic Church today makes it clear that *all of us* are equally responsible for Jesus' death. I find the liturgy of Good Friday to be extremely powerful and important.

145. See Gorman, *Inhabiting the Cruciform God*, 63–72.

146. See Abraham Joshua Heschel's insight: "Religious thinking, believing, feeling are among the most deceptive activities of the human spirit. We often assume it is God we believe in, but in reality it may be a symbol of personal interests that we dwell upon. We may assume that we feel drawn to God, but in reality it may be a power within the world that is the object of our adoration. We may assume it is God we care for, but it may be our own ego we are concerned with. To examine our religious existence is, therefore, a task to be performed constantly" (*God in Search of Man*, 9). Yet, this attention to interiority does not mean that Heschel devalues external actions.

ourselves as your servants for Jesus' sake" (2 Cor 4:5). Indeed, having been called by the risen Christ to be an apostle, he finds that "necessity is laid upon me. Woe to me if I do not preach the gospel!" (1 Cor 9:16).[147]

When misunderstood, Paul's emphasis on faith may seem to point the Christian's attention inward. But Paul has in view "faith working through love" (Gal 5:6). Paul urges the Galatians, "through love be servants of one another. For the whole law is fulfilled in one word, 'You shall love your neighbor as yourself'" (Gal 5:13-14). To be a Christian is none other than to "walk by the Spirit" and to "[b]ear one another's burdens, and so fulfill the law of Christ" (Gal 5:25; 6:2). Christian life means looking outward, in light of Christ's commands, toward God and one's neighbor. In all this, Christ remains firmly at the center: Paul refuses to boast or glory in anything "except in the cross of our Lord Jesus Christ, by which the world has been crucified to me, and I to the world" (Gal 6:14). A navel-gazing faith would be worse than useless, since such a faith would not be "faith working through love," nor would it be obedient to Christ. As James says, "Show me your faith apart from your works, and I by my works will show you my faith. . . . For as the body apart from the spirit is dead, so faith apart from works is dead" (Jas 2:18, 26). The outward-orientation of Christ-centered Christianity is well summed up by the Letter to the Hebrews: "Jesus also suffered outside the gate in order to sanctify the people through his own blood. Therefore let us go forth to him outside the camp, bearing abuse for him" (Heb 13:12-13).

Because Christ stands always at the center and we must always focus upon Christ, Paul remarks: "I do not even judge myself. I am not aware of anything against myself, but I am not thereby acquitted. It is the Lord who judges me. Therefore do not pronounce judgment before the time, before the Lord comes" (1 Cor 4:3-5). Yet Christians are not passive or deprived of personal volition. Rather, Paul emphasizes, "I press on to make it [resurrection life with Christ] my own, because Christ Jesus has made me his own. Brethren, I do not consider that I have made it my own; but one thing I do, forgetting what lies behind and straining forward to what lies ahead, I press on toward the goal for the prize of the upward call of God in Christ Jesus" (Phil 3:12-14). Paul's attention is focused upon Christ, but Paul recognizes

---

147. Heschel remarks along lines that seem apt here: "A pious man is usually pictured as a sort of bookworm, a person who thrives among the pages of ancient tomes, and to whom life with its longing, sadness, and tensions, is but a footnote in a scholarly commentary on the Bible. The truth is that a religious man is like a salamander, that legendary animal that originates from a fire of myrtlewood kept burning for seven years. Religion is born of fire, of a flame, in which the dross of the mind and soul is melted away" (Heschel, *God in Search of Man*, 317).

the significant cooperative action of his own will in bringing about Christ's will for him.

Already during his earthly ministry, according to the Gospel of Luke, Christ sent out his followers to proclaim that "the kingdom of God has come near" (Luke 10:11). Christ tells his disciples, "He who hears you hears me" (Luke 10:16). The focus of the Christian will be on witnessing to Christ. In Acts 4:19, Peter and John insist that "we cannot but speak of what we have seen and heard." In this witness, the test of success is "enduring patiently" without flagging in love for Christ (Rev 2:3).

13. By making authoritative halakhic judgments, halakhic man participates in God's work of perfecting his creation.

By sharing in Christ's superabundant fulfillment of Torah on the cross, Christians participate in God's work of perfecting his creation. In a certain sense, the perfection of creation comes about through God's work alone: only God can accomplish the perfecting of all things. This is why, in the book of Revelation, the seer perceives the new Jerusalem coming down from heaven (Rev 21:2). God alone has the power to consummate his kingdom, and no one can oppose him. When in the book of Revelation Christ goes out to eschatological battle, the battle turns out to involve the immediate collapse of his enemy, since no one can stand before God. Mere human agency cannot bring about the kingdom of God by any stretch of the imagination.

God, however, calls forth the participation of his people in the perfecting of creation. Hebrews 12:2 states that Christians are to "run with perseverance the race that is set before us, looking to Jesus the pioneer and perfecter of our faith, who for the joy that was set before him endured the cross, despising the shame, and is seated at the right hand of the throne of God." As Christians "run . . . the race" of life, we look to Christ (the incarnate Word) and seek to apply Christ's cruciform law of love to every earthly situation. Paul describes the application of Christ to daily life: "Bear one another's burdens and so fulfill the law of Christ" (Gal 6:2). This may sound rather simple, but actually obeying Christ's law requires discipline.

In this regard, Paul takes up specific questions with regard to sexual morality, and he issues authoritative judgments on these disputed questions. He applies Christ's cruciform law of love. His guiding principle is that "[t]he body is not meant for immorality, but for the Lord, and the Lord for the body" (1 Cor 6:13).[148] Applying Christ's law of love to concrete daily life

---

148. For discussion, see my *Aquinas's Eschatological Ethics*.

is also done by Christians in light of the Decalogue. Paul concludes in this light that no "idolater, reviler, drunkard, or robber" (1 Cor 5:11) will inherit the kingdom of God.

The paradigmatic act of Christ's "law" is his willingness to endure affliction out of love for others, in order to lead others to salvation. This kind of freely chosen suffering, out of love and in service to another person's true spiritual good, is the fundamental way in which Christians apply the law of Christ to daily life. Such acts of loving compassion ("suffering-with") enable the Christian to participate in God's work of perfecting his creation. An example is the affliction that Paul endures in Christ. Paul goes so far as to "boast" in the afflictions that he has experienced in undertaking his ministry, including his "hardships, calamities, beatings, imprisonments, tumults, labors, watching, hunger" (2 Cor 7:4–5). With regard to suffering out of love for the sake of the kingdom of God, Paul even states: "I rejoice in my sufferings for your sake, and in my flesh I complete what is lacking in Christ's afflictions for the sake of his body, that is, the Church" (Col 1:24). Christ's cross is superabundant atonement for sin, and so in this sense nothing is lacking. But had Paul not suffered in order to spread the gospel, Christianity might have fizzled out. In this sense, there is something "lacking," and the sufferings by which we cooperate with Christ contribute to the perfecting of creation.

The work of forgiveness also applies Christ's law of love to daily living and thereby participates in the perfecting of creation. When a Christian sins, he or she wounds the entire Christian community as the "body of Christ" (1 Cor 12:27). Paul reminds the Corinthians, "If one member suffers, all suffer together" (1 Cor 12:26). Although the sinner must be corrected, the sinner who repents must be fully forgiven. About such an individual, Paul commands the Corinthians "to forgive and comfort him, or he may be overwhelmed by excessive sorrow" (2 Cor 2:7). Accomplishing the work of forgiveness participates in perfecting Christ's kingdom by strengthening the Church as a community of Christ's mercy. Paul assures the Corinthians that the work of mercy stands at the very heart of their life together, not merely as individuals but as members of Christ's body. This work derives not from human resources but from Christ, so that believers are able to comfort each other "with the comfort with which we ourselves are comforted by God" (2 Cor 1:4).

Reflecting upon the way in which our sufferings out of love for others participate in Christ's redemptive perfecting of creation, Paul says of himself that "we are always being given up to death for Jesus' sake, so that the life of Jesus may be manifested in our mortal flesh" (2 Cor 4:11). In Paul's case, this was literally true, since in preaching the gospel he experienced deadly "peril" (2 Cor 1:10). Paul's broader point, however, is that the task of "building upon" the "foundation" that is "Jesus Christ" (1 Cor 3:10–11)—the task of participating in the perfecting of creation—will always require "walk[ing] in a manner worthy of God, who calls you into his own kingdom and glory" (1 Thess 2:12). And such walking means applying the "law of Christ" (Gal 6:2) by being willing to suffer out of love for others in service to God's plan of salvation in Christ.

In the Gospel of John, Christ explains that the Father "takes away" (John 15:2) or prunes each branch that bears no or little fruit, with the result that the fruitful tree—the kingdom of God—emerges more and more clearly. The perfecting of creation begins to take shape wherever people abide in the love of Christ: "By this my Father is glorified, that you bear much fruit, and so prove to be my disciples. As the Father has loved me, so I have loved you; abide in my love" (John 15:8–9). Abiding in Christ's love, as manifested by suffering out of love, by forgiveness, by almsgiving, and so on, is our participation in the perfecting of creation. Ultimately, the goal is that "we are to grow up in every way into him who is the head, into Christ, from whom the whole body, joined and knit together by every joint with which it is supplied, when each part is working properly, makes bodily growth and upbuilds itself in love" (Eph 4:15–16; cf. Eph 1:9–10).

14. Halakhic man stands up fearlessly for justice.

The Christian stands up fearlessly for justice. In Christ's parables and teachings, one of the central themes is the willingness to stand up for justice even at great personal cost. Christ teaches, "Blessed are those who are persecuted for righteousness' sake, for theirs is the kingdom of heaven" (Matt 5:10). Standing up for justice can mean simply "speaking the truth in love" (Eph 4:15), which can often lead to dire earthly consequences for the person who dares to speak. In general, the poor and oppressed in society are in need of people willing to stand up for justice on their behalf. In the parable of the Rich Man and Lazarus, the poor man (Lazarus) was "full of sores" and he "desired to be fed with what fell from the rich man's table" (Luke 16:20–21), but the rich man paid him no attention. The tables are turned, however, when the rich man and Lazarus both die; and one of the points of the parable is to show the central requirement of justice toward the poor.

In the deacon Stephen's speech prior to his martyrdom, he commends Moses as an example because Moses "defended the oppressed man and avenged him by striking the Egyptian" (Acts 7:24). When Christ teaches in the Sermon on the Mount "if any one strikes you on the right cheek, turn to him the other also" (Matt 5:39), he is warning against resorting to violence for the purpose of defending one's private interests. He also rejects Peter's efforts to defend him by violence. As Christ says in this context, "Put your sword back into its place; for all who take the sword will perish by the sword" (Matt 26:52).

Christ emphasizes care for the poor to such a degree that he urges his hearers, "When you give a dinner or a banquet, do not invite your friends or your brothers or your kinsmen or rich neighbors, lest they also invite you in return, and you be repaid. But when you give a feast, invite the poor, the maimed, the lame, the blind, and you will be blessed, because they cannot repay you" (Luke 15:12–14). God will repay deeds that show care for those who do not have earthly means. Such deeds involve a deeper justice than is normally involved in the giving of banquets, to which the host generally invites friends or associates. The justice that Christ has in view has the needs of the poor at its heart. As Christ puts it elsewhere, "as you did it to one of the least of these my brethren [the hungry, the thirsty, the stranger, the naked, the sick, the imprisoned], you did it to me" (Matt 25:40).

Likewise, Paul urges justice and righteousness, often in terms of care for the poor. Regarding almsgiving, Paul teaches that "he who sows sparingly will also reap sparingly, and he who sows bountifully will also reap bountifully" (2 Cor 9:6). Paul does not require giving alms to a degree that would impoverish the givers (2 Cor 8:13), but within these bounds he encourages bountiful almsgiving: "as a matter of equality your abundance at the present time should supply their want, so that their abundance may supply your want, that there may be equality" (2 Cor 8:14). Similarly, James urges Christians to "be doers of the word, and not hearers only, deceiving yourselves" (Jas 1:22). James goes so far as to identify the reality of Christian faith with a commitment to doing acts of justice and righteousness: "Religion that is pure and undefiled before God and the Father is this: to visit orphans and widows in their affliction, and to keep oneself unstained from the world" (Jas 1:27).

In scathing terms, James condemns Christians who, in the liturgical assembly, show preference for the rich over the poor. He comments with biting irony, "If a brother or sister is poorly clothed and in lack of daily food, and one of you says to them, 'Go in peace, be warmed and filled,' without giving them the things needed for the body, what does it profit?" (Jas 2:15–16). He warns the unjust rich about the coming judgment, and he instructs them to do justice before it is too late: "Behold, the wages of the laborers who mowed your fields, which you kept back by fraud, cry out; and the cries of the harvesters have reached the ears of the Lord of hosts. You have lived on the earth in luxury and in pleasure; you have fattened your hearts in a day of slaughter. You have condemned, you have killed the righteous man; he does not resist you" (Jas 5:4–6).

According to the book of Revelation, the consummated kingdom will be a place in which the blessed, through the saving power of Christ and by his Spirit, will be completely freed from sin and injustice. At the center of the heavenly liturgy is "the Lamb who was slain" (Rev 5:12); and the Lamb alone is able to "open the scroll" that reveals the meaning and purpose of human history (Rev 5:3). When the Lamb (the risen and ascended Christ) conquers unjust Babylon, "the kings of the earth, who committed fornication and were wanton with her, will weep and wail over her when they see the smoke of her burning" (Rev 18:9). Joining these unjust kings will be the unjust "merchants of the earth" who dealt in rich cargo, including the cargo of "slaves, that is, human souls" (Rev 18:13).

Prior to the final consummation of the kingdom, unjust rulers and merchants will continue to hold sway over the earth, causing devastation. Therefore, at present the souls of the righteous dead continue to cry out to God for justice, as they did during their earthly lives (Rev 6:9–10). In accord with the prayers of the just, Christians will fearlessly come to the aid of the victims of injustice.

15. True worship primarily occurs in the actualization of Halakhah's justice and righteousness in the world.

True worship occurs in the actualization of Christ's justice and righteousness in the world. Along these lines, Paul says, "I appeal to you therefore, brethren, by the mercies of God, to present your bodies as a living sacrifice, holy and acceptable to God, which is your spiritual worship" (Rom 12:1). Such worship occurs when believers obey the will of God in Christ. At the same time, this spiritual worship should not, for Paul, be separated from the celebration of the Eucharist, which Paul describes as a "participation" or "communion" in the body and blood of Christ (1 Cor 10:16), and whose ethical dimension Paul accentuates. Paul observes that because the Eucharist is a communion in Christ's body and blood—offered on the cross for our salvation—it follows that Christians must not participate in eucharistic worship in "an unworthy manner" (1 Cor 11:27). To do so would be to fail to recognize the intrinsic relationship between eucharistic worship and the "spiritual worship" that we offer through our acts of justice and righteousness. In offering our whole selves to the Father in Christ, we need to take care to "examine" ourselves so as not to "be guilty of profaning the body and blood of the Lord" (1 Cor 11:27–28). Such a profanation of Christ takes place when we share in the eucharistic worship while acting unjustly vis-à-vis our neighbor.[149]

In this light, Paul bemoans the fact that among the Corinthians the eucharistic table itself has become a place of separation between the wealthy and the poor, so that "each one goes ahead with his own meal, and one is hungry and another is drunk" (1 Cor 11:21). To proceed in such a fashion, says Paul, is to receive a judgment unto spiritual death, because such an approach to eucharistic worship serves to "despise the Church of God and humiliate those who have nothing" (1 Cor 11:22). In the eucharistic worship, the same attention to the needs of our impoverished neighbor must be present as is found in the offering of our "bodies as a living sacrifice, holy and acceptable to God" through deeds of justice and righteousness.

Liturgical worship stands at the center of Christian life because it is a participation in Christ's salvific self-offering in love, but it never stands at the center as though it were separated from Christians' acts of justice and care for the poor. In 1 Timothy 6:18–19, Paul instructs Timothy to ensure that the rich members of Timothy's congregation enact justice and righteousness: "They are to do good, to be rich in good deeds, liberal and generous, thus laying up for themselves a good foundation for the future, so that they may take hold of the life which is life indeed." In his leadership of the congregation, Timothy too must act with justice, rebuking those who "persist in sin" and being sure to do nothing "from partiality," as well as refusing to "participate in another man's sins" (1 Tim 5:20–22). In everything, Christians must act in the world with "righteousness, godliness, faith, love, steadfastness, gentleness," thereby keeping "the commandment unstained and free from reproach" in a manner that bears witness to the love of Christ in the Church and in the world (1 Tim 6:11, 14).

IV. Conclusion

Let me recall the paths traversed in this chapter. After an extensive introductory discussion of differences between Jews and Christians regarding Torah and of the roots of these differences in the New Testament and Rabbinic Judaism, the chapter's first section appreciatively sketched Soloveitchik's portrayal of the "halakhic man." In the second section, then, I compared fifteen aspects of his portrayal of the "halakhic man" to the New Testament's presentation of the ideal Christian. In the New Testament, the place that Soloveitchik accords to Torah (Written and Oral) is given to Jesus as the incarnate Son and the perfect embodiment of Torah.

---

149. See R. B. Hays, *First Corinthians*, 203.

Undoubtedly, it can seem that we are dealing with a difference so radical as to disallow any connection. In this vein, Jonah Chanan Steinberg argues that Christians carried to an extreme the book of Wisdom's movement toward a personified Wisdom distinct from Israel's Torah. As Steinberg describes it, "union with the Word came to mean a merging of oneself with the person of the Christ, very much in opposition to absorption with 'works of the law.'"[150] Steinberg insists there is little space for connecting the two approaches. He notes that the "early rabbis energetically resuscitated the equation of the mediating figure with the religion of Israel—that is, they ubiquitously equated Wisdom and Torah," and the rabbis believed that identification with Torah through performing its commandments could enable a person to "achieve companionship with God and divine nature."[151] In

---

150. Steinberg, "Theosis through Works of the Law," 69. See also Schäfer, *Two Gods in Heaven*, emphasizing the development of personified divine Wisdom or Word in Second Temple Jewish sources such as Wisdom of Solomon and Philo (a point that has been well known to Christians from the outset). For Schäfer, the point is that "the idea of a triumphant monotheism cannot be maintained for postexilic Judaism after Daniel, let alone for post-New Testament Judaism. Late antique Judaism was itself susceptible to binitarian thought, regardless of all efforts to separate it from Christianity.... Despite the usurpation of binitarian ideas by New Testament Christology and early Christian authors, rabbinic Judaism and the Judaism of the early mystics held firm to those ideas. By reviving the idea of two Gods in the Jewish heaven, late antique Judaism was also responding to Christianity's claims, but this response was in essence genuinely Jewish, and as such, not only defensive and delimiting, but affirmative as well. To this extent, early Christianity and rabbinic Judaism were also competing for the second God beside God the Creator" (Schäfer, *Two Gods in Heaven*, 14-15; cf. 135). As Schäfer knows, the notion that the Word is a "second God beside God the Creator" is anathema both to ongoing Judaism and Christianity, but his argument is that the Son of Man texts in Daniel (for example) drove both Judaism and Christianity in this direction—and did so in a context in which Jewish and Christian exegetes were in "dialogue" in the sense that they were drawing upon and critiquing each other.

151. Steinberg, "Theosis through Works of the Law," 69-70. Steinberg observes, "Jews tend to resist the idea of divinization because it sounds too Christian. The notion that God might assume a human face, might become manifest to a redemptive end in a human life, simply smacks too much of 'that man,' as rabbinic parlance warily calls Jesus" ("Theosis through Works of the Law," 72). Yet, he provides examples of early rabbinic midrashim that endorse a "concept of *earthly* divinization through righteous action" ("Theosis through Works of the Law," 72). I assume that this is the kind of thing that Paul polemicizes against when he states that "Israel who pursued the righteousness which is based on law did not succeed in fulfilling that law. Why? Because they did not pursue it through faith, but as if it were based on works" (Rom 9:31–32). In my view, this is far from meaning that the Jewish people "cherished the illusion that they could so adequately fulfill its commandments as to put God in their debt" (Cranfield, "Light from Saint Paul," 131). But some Jewish groups sought to stimulate God's sending of the Messiah by meticulous Torah observance—which no doubt could be distorted into an effort to establish one's own righteousness (Rom 10:3) rather than receiving righteousness as a sheer gift from the Messiah.

his own way, Soloveitchik advocates this rabbinic approach, though not in these specific terms.

From my perspective, union with Christ (Torah in Person) is not nearly so lawless as might be supposed, although Christians obey Torah as fulfilled and reconfigured around the Messiah. I hope to have shown some connections, however broad, between Soloveitchik's teachings about the halakhic man and the New Testament's teachings on the Christian and life in Christ. I focused on the New Testament in order to show connections specifically between ongoing Judaism as conceived by Soloveitchik and Christianity as articulated in its founding texts. I identified many family resemblances between Soloveitchik's vision of Jewish Torah observance and the New Testament's vision of Christ and life in Christ.

Of course, I am not saying that these two perspectives can both be right in the same way. After all, either the Messiah has come and reconfigured the Torah around himself, or the Messiah has not come.[152] For most Jews—not expecting the inauguration of the kingdom to involve a yet further delay in setting the world to rights, and certainly not expecting the inauguration of the kingdom to be congruent with a world in which the Temple is destroyed and the Jewish people expelled from the land for centuries—it seems clear that Jesus, crucified by the Romans, cannot have been the Messiah. By contrast, Christians hold that Jesus, when properly understood as having inaugurated God's kingdom of mercy and love, has indeed brought about the

152. I note that not all Second Temple Jewish eschatology envisioned a Messiah; as Michael F. Bird states about the Second Temple period, "messianism remained only one way of telling the story of Israel's hope for the future.... While messianism could figure prominently in eschatological hopes for the future, not all eschatology necessarily required a Messiah (e.g., 2 Macc. 2:18; 14:15; Tob. 13:11–17; 14:47; Bar. 2:27–35; 4:36–37; 5:5–9; Sir. 36:11–17; Jub. 23.27–31)" (Bird, *Are You the One?*, 32–33). Bird similarly grants that there was not "a uniform hope for the coming Davidic king in common Judaism. What messianic aspirations did exist displayed a variety of beliefs about a coming deliverer. One obvious distinction is that some conceived of the Messiah as an earthly warrior (1QM; Pss. Sol. 17–18), while there were others who conceived of him as a preexisting and transcendent figure (1 Enoch; 4 Ezra). Or there again, some, like those at Qumran, could conceive of two Messiahs, one of Aaron and one of Israel.... These figures could be variously related to one or more of the offices of prophet, priest, and king. Such idealized figures could fit a number of patterns or different types of savior/deliverer models from Israel's sacred traditions. Various expectations were projected onto them in order to line up with known and celebrated concepts of liberation" (Bird, *Are You the One?*, 33). See also the wide spectrum of thought indicated by Novenson, *Grammar of Messianism*. For further background, see A. Chester, *Messiah and Exaltation*, especially chapters 4–7; as well as the valuable survey offered by Jipp, *Messianic Theology*. I note that the Jewish scholar Geza Vermès flatly denies that the New Testament teaches that Jesus is the Messiah; rather, on his view (which I find mistaken), the New Testament presents Jesus simply as a healer and prophet. See Vermès, *Changing Faces of Jesus*; and see also, in a similar vein, Levine, *Misunderstood Jew*.

fulfillment of such prophecies as Isaiah 9:2, 6-7: "The people who walked in darkness have seen a great light. . . . For to us a child is born, to us a son is given; and the government will be upon his shoulder, and his name will be called, 'Wonderful Counselor, Mighty God, Everlasting Father, Prince of Peace.' Of the increase of his government and peace there will be no end, upon the throne of David." Christians deem Jesus to be the fulfillment of Isaiah 11:1's prophecy that "there shall come forth a shoot from the stump of Jesse" and Isaiah 53:5-6's prophecy about the Servant who "was wounded for our transgressions" because "the Lord has laid on him the iniquity of us all." Christians find in Jesus the fulfillment of Jeremiah 23:5-6, Ezekiel 34:22-24, Daniel 9:24-27, and so on. No doubt, these texts and others like them generally do not speak literally of a Messiah, but they do speak of "a figure with royal qualities who is sent by God" to redeem his people.[153]

Although the King is already present, Christians await the full restoration of Israel and consummation of the kingdom. The path that God has chosen is the path of the cross (self-giving love and humility) rather than the path of power. God has chosen the path of vulnerability rather than the path of visible triumph. The victory is a victory of love rather than a victory in the world's eyes, and therefore the victory is hidden—though manifested by the risen Christ and his Spirit. The victory has been obscured by the ongoing sinfulness of Christ's followers. Even so, the victory of Christ is present and is powerful in human lives, transformed by Spirit-filled faith, hope, and love. Of course the eschatological promises regarding the Davidic King have not yet fully come to realization: it is not yet true that "[t]he wolf shall dwell with the lamb" and that "[t]hey shall not hurt or destroy in all my holy mountain; for the earth shall be full of the knowledge of the Lord" (Isa 11:6, 9). In a full and complete sense, it is not yet the case that "[i]n that day the root of Jesse shall stand as an ensign to the peoples; him shall the nations seek, and his dwellings shall be glorious" (Isa 11:10).

Christianity and Judaism will not be able to come to an agreement on the identity of Jesus or even on the warrants that would justify hailing Jesus as the Messiah. Yet, both Jews and Christians seek to live from a Torah-shaped perspective. How we do this involves the differences between the Oral Torah (as interpreted and carried forward in ongoing Judaism) and the

---

153. Bird, *Are You the One?*, 46. See also the definition of a messiah given in A. Chester, *Messiah and Exaltation*, 4: "a messiah should be understood, in the most concise form of the definition, as 'the agent of final divine deliverance.'" As Chester says, "it is divine deliverance itself that is the more important and underlying point of focus for Jewish hope. That is, the figure of the messiah is potentially important, but it is not all-important. . . . [I]t is the role of the agent of final divine deliverance that the early Christians see Jesus as fulfilling" (*Messiah and Exaltation*, 5-6). For Ezekiel's messianic hope or "messianic allusions," see Block, *Beyond the River Chebar*, chapter 4.

New Testament (as handed down in the life of the Church). George Lindbeck comments with regard to the first few centuries after Christ: "What the rabbis did to make the Jews in diaspora an interconnected people, the catholics did for the gentile Christians. Both went far beyond their common scripture, and they did so in different directions, one by means of the oral Torah, and the other through the New Testament. Yet each group lived in the world of Israel's story and of Israel's God."[154] Living "in the world of Israel's story," Christians must live in the world of the Torah; the Church must learn to see itself "in the mirror of Israel," as Lindbeck puts it.[155]

While seeking to appropriate the Torah in Christ, therefore, a Christian Israelology can appreciate the characteristics that Soloveitchik sketches with respect to the "halakhic man." Although Soloveitchik mentions few biblical texts, his understanding of the halakhic man accords with the love of Torah sketched in many biblical texts, among them Psalm 119 and Proverbs 8–9. I value these texts both as testimony to the wisdom and goodness of the divinely given Torah and as prefiguring Christ who is the incarnate Word and wisdom of God.[156]

Soloveitchik affirms that sin will ultimately be dealt with by the Messiah, who will establish the eschatological age. Before the coming of the Davidic Messiah, however, Soloveitchik argues that the path of the halakhic man, implementing Torah, is the path of the forgiveness of sins and the perfecting of the world. Such wisdom does not simply exist in the head; it regulates daily and hourly action, and is adaptable to whatever circumstances that may arise. Studying Torah aims to enable the Jewish believer to judge and measure all reality in accord with the ideal Halakhah. It

---

154. Lindbeck, "Church as Israel," 87.

155. Lindbeck, "Church as Israel," 94. Lindbeck adds that the Church must do this "while, in contrast to the past, fully acknowledging that the covenant with the Jews has not been revoked" ("Church as Israel," 94). He adds, too, that this "mirror" is by no means a triumphalistic one, since biblical Israel often acknowledged its sinfulness. He states, "Only by gazing at itself in the mirror of Israel can the church as a whole learn how to lament biblically for its intramural and extramural divisiveness and lovelessness" (Lindbeck, "Church as Israel," 94). See also Lindbeck, "Postmodern Hermeneutics," 109: "Losing the image of the church as Israel destroys the self-image of the church as a community chosen by God"; as well as Lindbeck's similar reflections in "What of the Future?" See also Radner, *Profound Ignorance*, 242–52, where Radner argues that Jesus' suffering body and Israel's suffering body parallel each other, including in the experience of divine presence. He concludes that "Israel, tout court, is of the Spirit, wherever this may lead and even though it may lead in different directions" (Radner, *Profound Ignorance*, 252). Radner makes this argument as part of rejecting Christian triumphalism both vis-à-vis the Jewish people and vis-à-vis suffering.

156. See Witherington, *Jesus the Sage*; Thorsteinsson, *Jesus as Philosopher*, 108–9 and elsewhere.

instantiates what Soloveitchik calls "the Torah way of life" and "the Torah style of living."[157]

Likewise, for Christians who believe that the perfect embodiment of Torah has been manifested in Christ Jesus, every situation is open to the impress of divine Wisdom.[158] Christ is a living person who reigns at the right hand of the Father and who, even when spiritual darkness and confusion descend upon our lives, does not cease to be the One who is with us "always, to the close of the age" (Matt 28:20). Christ calls us to take up our own cross and to follow him. We are to live according to his Spirit-filled self-sacrificial love in the world. Just as in Torah (understood via Oral Torah) the Jewish people find "guidelines for living in the presence of a holy God,"[159] so also Christians find in Christ (incarnate Torah) the path for dwelling with God.

Christians should approach each day in the knowledge that we are not "without law toward God but under the law of Christ" (1 Cor 9:21). With Soloveitchik, let us proclaim in the words of the Psalmist: "I long for your salvation, O Lord, and your law is my delight. Let my soul live, that I may praise you, and let your ordinances help me. I have gone astray like a lost sheep; seek your servant, for I do not forget your commandments" (Ps 119:174–76).

---

157. Soloveitchik, "Religious Styles," 199.

158. See also what Yves R. Simon has to say about the moral virtue of prudence: Y. R. Simon, *Definition of Moral Virtue*, 96–98.

159. Walton, *Old Testament Theology for Christians*, 157. In Walton's view, this means that "the Torah was contingent on the temple, not the other way around. It was designed for the temple venue and cannot be extrapolated to a universal context outside the temple" (*Old Testament Theology for Christians*, 157). I agree that Torah and temple cannot be separated—indeed Christ fulfills both at once. From a Jewish perspective, too, ongoing Torah observance continues to have the temple in view, even if not the literal performance of the precepts relevant to the temple. Walton adds, "The Torah was incumbent on each Israelite because, in theory, any individual's neglect or violation of the Torah could potentially result in the removal of God's presence from his people" (Walton, *Old Testament Theology for Christians*, 157).

Chapter 5

TEMPLE

I. INTRODUCTION

In discussing the Temple and its cult in this chapter, I have in view what Jon Levenson describes as "the enthronement and glorification of YHWH in his cosmic abode.... Between the Temple and ordinary reality lies a barrier of *holiness*."[1] But, more simply, I have in view all the cultic sacrifices and rituals that pertain to Israel's worship of God. A Christian theology of such rites inevitably faces the problem of "supersessionism." On the one hand,

---

1. Levenson, *Sinai and Zion*, 126–27. Let me make mention here of the writings of Margaret Barker, including, among many other works, her *Temple Mysticism* and *King of the Jews*. I agree with Barker that "[t]he writings of John are the primary New Testament witness to the mind of Christ and to the Temple he came to restore," so long as "primary" allows the other New Testament texts to witness as well (*King of the Jews*, 606). But I do not agree with—indeed I would strongly contest—Barker's reconstruction according to which "there are two streams in the Old Testament. One is the Moses and exodus stream which became the story of the people in the promised land under kings who were mostly failures. The other is the story of the temple and its priest-kings who entered heaven but ceased to function when their temple cult was destroyed. 'The Jews' [of John's Gospel] were the disciples of Moses who built the second temple. They were very influential in creating the present form of the Hebrew Scriptures, and their work has long dominated the way the Hebrew Scriptures have been read. The 'others' were those who remembered the temple and the anointed priest-kings, the people the Third-Isaiah called the rejected servants of the Lord, his chosen ones who would be called by a new name (Isa. 65.15)" (Barker, *King of the Jews*, 32). To my mind, this historical reconstruction is not only unwarranted historically but also fosters enmity between followers of Jesus (here conceived as the exemplar of the priest-kings of the first temple) and the ongoing Jewish people (here conceived as Second Temple Jews forgetful of the original purity). In *Temple Mysticism*, Barker compares the doomed priest-kings with the blinded Jews who took control of the cult and who deliberately damaged Israel's original Scriptures.

this is because animal sacrifices have been superseded among both Jews and Christians by non-bloody forms of worship ever since the destruction of the Second Temple in 70 AD. On the other hand, supersessionism comes to the fore because Christians, including Jewish converts to Christianity, have long been forbidden on pain of mortal sin to practice Jewish rites as though salvation depended upon their practice.

The Council of Florence included among its documents Pope Eugenius IV's Bull *Cantate Domino*, promulgated in 1442. This papal bull teaches solemnly that the Catholic Church "firmly believes, professes and teaches that the legal prescriptions of the Old Testament or the Mosaic law, which are divided into ceremonies, holy sacrifices and sacraments, because they were instituted to signify something in the future . . . came to an end" with the coming of Jesus Christ.[2] To this statement, *Cantate Domino* adds the warning that "[w]hoever, after the passion [of Christ], places his hope in the legal prescriptions and submits himself to them as necessary for salvation and as if faith in Christ without them could not save, sins mortally. . . . [A]fter the promulgation of the gospel they cannot be observed without loss of eternal salvation."[3] It may seem that this statement places all non-Christian Jewish people, committed to observing the "legal prescriptions" and to praying for the temple's rebuilding, in a situation of permanent mortal sin.

Does *Cantate Domino* commit Catholics, on pain of solemn doctrinal rupture, to a harsh supersessionism according to which the ongoing Jewish people are damned? Must Catholics suppose—as for centuries many did suppose—that Jews who religiously observe the Torah's ritual commandments and who daily pray for the restoration of the temple and its cult are cutting themselves off from salvation? The answer is no. For one thing, although *Cantate Domino* assumes that Jews who observe Torah are culpable for denying that Jesus is the Messiah (a view held by Augustine and Aquinas, among many others), *Cantate Domino* addresses its solemn teaching not to Jews but to *Christians* who were religiously observing "circumcision, the sabbath, and other legal prescriptions."[4] Moreover, *Cantate Domino* does

2. Eugenius IV, *Cantate Domino*, 575–76.
3. Eugenius IV, *Cantate Domino*, 576.
4. Eugenius IV, *Cantate Domino*, 576. Gavin D'Costa explains the context: "The Egyptian Copts were represented by Abbot Andrew, who himself represented the Patriarch John of the Copts, who lived in Cairo. Andrew was interrogated by Cardinals Cesarini, Le Jeune and Torquemada regarding the beliefs of the Copts. The main problems they found related to 'certain practices' such as circumcising male children, the practice of Sabbath on Saturday, and the enforcement of certain food regulations. These practices were regarded as following the old ceremonial law that was now invalid, dead and deadening. Unity could thus be attained, but only if these practices ceased. Andrew expressed agreement with this solution" (D'Costa, *Catholic Doctrines*, 37).

not account for "invincible ignorance." Jesus is the Messiah, but, as Gavin D'Costa says, "those who do not accept this truth *may* be acting in good faith (or in more traditional terms be seen as not culpable of knowingly 'rejecting' truth and salvation)"—which, indeed, is what the *Catechism of the Catholic Church* teaches about the Jewish people.[5]

It follows, as D'Costa shows in more detail, that Catholics are not doctrinally committed to a harsh supersessionism vis-à-vis the ritual life that characterizes the ongoing Jewish people.[6] On the contrary, Catholics can and should have deep appreciation for Jewish rituals on multiple levels. Admittedly, Catholics cannot agree with Rabbi Leibel Reznick when he contends, "As long as the Temple stood, man's ideals and goals were obtainable. When the Temple was destroyed, the Temple-Man [enjoying "ultimate oneness" with God] was destroyed. For two thousand years the Jewish people have prayed for the return of the Temple-Man so that mankind's hopes and ambitions can be realized and fulfilled."[7] Yet, Christians can recognize that this account of the "Temple-Man" squares in large part with Christian understanding of the life that has been made possible for the whole world by the coming of Jesus Christ and that will be consummated by his return in glory. Furthermore, Christians can be appreciative of the temple sacrifices commanded by God, not only on the grounds that these animal sacrifices belonged to God's people Israel, but also on the grounds that "a sacrifice is

---

5. D'Costa, *Catholic Doctrines*, 39, citing *Catechism*, §840.

6. I agree with Norbert Lohfink, SJ and Erich Zenger that the Church's "'new' thinking" about Rabbinic Judaism, beginning at the Second Vatican Council, stands as "a 'change,' 'rethinking,' 'reversal' that, indeed, brings to expression the reality that on this issue a rupture needs to take place in the history of Christianity—a paradigm shift" (Lohfink and Zenger, "Theological Context," 4). But I distinguish this from a rupture in definitive doctrine, which Lohfink and Zenger seem to embrace as part of the Church's "vitality" ("Theological Context," 4). With D'Costa, I think that such a rupture has not taken place. See also, on this theologically crucial point, D'Costa's *Vatican II*, especially 1–2, 113–59, as well as the reflections on *Nostra Aetate* in Guarino, *Disputed Teachings of Vatican II*, 109–18. Guarino responds to Gerald O'Collins, SJ's contention that *Nostra Aetate* represents a reversal of definitive doctrine: see O'Collins, *Second Vatican Council on Other Religions*, 203–4. For a similar attribution to the Council of a Spirit-willed rupture (first and foremost with the teachings of the New Testament), see Baum, "Catholic Dogma after Auschwitz." See also F. Sullivan, *Creative Fidelity*, 78, 115–16; and F. Sullivan, *Salvation outside the Church?*, 68–69. As Edward H. Flannery remarks in his *Anguish of the Jews*, 274: "[Anti-Semitism] never became a universal dogmatic tradition, let alone a formal definition, of the Church; even though individual bishops, regional councils, and certain popes dealing in *ad hoc* applications of principle were disseminators of it."

7. Reznick, *Holy Temple Revisited*, xv–xvi.

both noble and socially valuable because it is both simultaneously a relinquishment and a gift."[8]

In this chapter, therefore, I explore the meaning of the temple as part of my Christian Israelology. In some detail, I first examine the place of the temple and its cult according to the Bible. I treat not only the Old Testament's portraits and prophecies regarding Solomon's temple, the Second Temple, and the eschatological temple, but also the New Testament's depictions of Jesus Christ as the eschatological temple and of the Eucharist as a sharing in Christ's perfect sacrifice on the cross. I discuss the New Testament evidence in dialogue especially with the Jewish biblical scholar Eyal Regev, for whom the fact that Jesus' followers continued to frequent the Jerusalem temple after Jesus' resurrection indicates that they did not perceive Jesus to be the replacement of the temple in any sense. Although I disagree with Regev and argue that Jesus is indeed the eschatological temple, I agree that the New Testament should not be read as an anti-temple work. I pay particular attention to the ways in which the prophets point forward to an eschatological temple and to how the New Testament understands the fulfillment of these prophecies in Christ along lines that do not denigrate the Jerusalem temple.

The chapter's second section addresses Jewish and Christian critics of the temple and its sacrifices. I briefly sketch the critical distancing from the temple's animal sacrifices that one finds in many contemporary Jewish and Christian scholars, among them Jonathan Sacks and René Girard. For my part, I am glad that Christian worship does not involve animal sacrifice and I sympathize with Jews who are likewise glad that Jewish worship continues today without animal sacrifices. But I disagree with many common criticisms of the temple sacrifices, because they lack appreciation for cultic sacrificial offering as a positive spiritual work in its own right, one which God willed for the good of the Jewish people and in preparation for the coming of Christ.[9]

---

8. Heyman, *Power of Sacrifice*, 221.

9. For reflection on whether (after the destruction of the temple by the Romans) animal sacrifices continued to be offered privately—and if so why sacrifices ended up ceasing entirely, especially given that animal sacrifices had continued without the temple in previous epochs—see Chanikuzhy, *Jesus, the Eschatological Temple*, 68–70, which relies upon Guttmann, "End of the Jewish Sacrificial Cult." Guttmann speculates that the *Nasi* of the Jewish people after 70, Yohanan ben Zakkai, opposed the Sadducean priests and therefore may not have wished to strengthen the priests by encouraging private animal sacrifices. Guttman also notes that even had Yohanan ben Zakkai or later rabbis wished to revive private animal sacrifices, the Romans refused to appoint a new high priest. According to Chanikuzhy, "Gamaliel II was the only Nasi who seems to have made a paschal sacrifice after the destruction of the temple" (*Jesus, the Eschatological Temple*, 69n246).

Third, I examine the Jewish biblical scholar Jonathan Klawans's *Purity, Sacrifice, and the Temple: Symbolism and Supersessionism in the Study of Ancient Judaism*. The first two sections come together in this third and final section. In the process of surveying Klawans's argument in detail, I contest his conclusions at important points even while generally agreeing with his concerns about criticisms of cultic sacrifice.[10] The key question is whether the Christian view of the supersession of the animal sacrifices by Christ's supreme self-sacrifice in love (the eschatological temple) is negative toward the temple. In part, the answer to this question depends upon whether Hebrews is an anti-temple text.

My conclusion is that Christians must be supersessionists of a kind, but not supersessionists who despise the temple cult or the ongoing Jewish people. Catholics do not desire the rebuilding of the temple in Jerusalem, because the eschatological temple—Jesus Christ—is now present and open for the purposes of atonement and communion. But the Church should "recognise the bonds that intimately unite it to the history of Jerusalem and its Temple, as well as to the prayer and cult of the Jewish people."[11]

II. Biblical Reflections on the Temple

The Jerusalem Temple

In 1 Maccabees, we read that King Antiochus, after defeating Egypt in battle, led his army to Jerusalem. At this time, some Jews were seeking to give up their distinctive practices and to become indistinguishable from the other

---

10. Klawans does not address feminist concerns. Katherine Sonderegger points out, "Delores Williams galvanized a generation of womanist theologians with her searing indictment of sacrifice, a condition she termed 'surrogacy.' . . . For the oppressed—for oppressed Black women, especially—the very notion and piety of sacrifice, Williams argues, can only deepen the inner emigration that is sacral life within the Christian church. Williams argues that the biblical figure of Hagar expresses, in compressed form, the constricted life Black women are forced to bear. They are assigned the role of substitute: the 'surrogate'" (Sonderegger, *Doctrine of the Holy Trinity*, 402). Sonderegger defends Temple sacrifice against Williams's concerns, arguing that "sacrifice—the Heavenly and earthly sacrifice engraved into the heart of ancient Israel—is not *recommendation* or *preference*. It is rather the molten core of the chosen people before the Holy God. It is realism in the life and worship of Israel. *This* exchange is ordered and wild, lawful and beyond any code or plan, deeply enmeshed in life and food and liberty, but saturated with bloody death too" (Sonderegger, *Doctrine of the Holy Trinity*, 406). In my view, Williams's concerns—while understandable especially when it comes to the theology of redemptive suffering, a reality I have explored in my *Dying and the Virtues*—do not apply to temple sacrifice. See D. Williams, *Sisters in the Wilderness*.

11. D'Costa, *Catholic Doctrines*, 102.

nations.[12] When King Antiochus ordered them to "observe the ordinances of the Gentiles" (1 Macc 1:13), they were delighted to obey him. They proceeded to build a gymnasium and to abandon the covenant with God. They no longer observed Torah and they renounced any further practice of circumcision. They allowed King Antiochus to plunder the temple: "He went up against Israel and took the golden altar, the lampstand for the light, and all its utensils. He took also the table for the bread of the Presence, the cups for drink offerings, the bowls, the golden censers, the curtain, the crowns, and the gold decoration on the front of the temple; he stripped it all off" (1 Macc 1:21–22).[13]

Going further, King Antiochus wrote letters forbidding worship of YHWH in the temple. In these letters, Antiochus "directed them . . . to forbid burnt offerings and sacrifices and drink offerings in the sanctuary, to profane Sabbaths and feasts, to defile the sanctuary and the priests, to build altars and sacred precincts and shrines for idols, to sacrifice swine and unclean animals, and to leave their sons uncircumcised" (1 Macc 1:44–48). In sum, he launched an all-out attack upon the temple cult commanded in the Torah. Banning all copies of the Torah and burning any copies that they found, the agents appointed by Antiochus went so far as to "[erect] a desolating sacrilege upon the altar of burnt offering" in the temple itself (1 Macc 1:54).

In response, Mattathias the priest, surnamed Maccabeus, and his five sons rebelled. They refused to obey the Jews who had capitulated to Antiochus.[14] Instead, they killed a Jew who was offering sacrifice to a god other

---

12. Shaye J. D. Cohen explains, "During the reign of Antiochus Epiphanes, a group of Jews known to modern scholarship as 'the extreme Hellenizers' tried to remove the distinctive characteristics of Judaism in order to make it indistinguishable from other forms of Semitic-Hellenistic polytheism" (*From the Maccabees to the Mishnah*, 33). In Cohen's view, which seems a stretch to me, "it is likely that these Jews, who included many priests, high priests, and aristocrats, were attempting not to destroy Judaism but to reform it" (*From the Maccabees to the Mishnah*, 33).

13. For a brief discussion of these events, see S. J. D. Cohen, *From the Maccabees to the Mishnah*, 22–23. Cohen observes, "In antiquity, religious persecutions were something of a rarity. . . . What provoked the persecution by Epiphanes remains an enigma in spite of intense study by many scholars, but a persecution there was, and the war that it sparked is history's first recorded struggle for religious liberty" (S. J. D. Cohen, *From the Maccabees to the Mishnah*, 22).

14. Cohen gives a bit of background to this rebellion: "Mattathias, the patriarch of the clan, and his son Judah the Maccabee were country priests who drew the bulk of their support from the countryside and fought against the well-to-do priests of Jerusalem. The Maccabees expelled or killed many of the 'old guard' and advanced 'new men' like themselves to become a new aristocracy" (S. J. D. Cohen, *From the Maccabees to the Mishnah*, 23).

than YHWH. Retreating to hideouts in the wilderness, they established a guerrilla force determined to restore Torah observance centered around the temple cult.

King Antiochus eventually died, and order was restored in the temple, but this did not end the difficulties. Instead, a new king, Demetrius, tricked the Jewish people with offers of peace. Arriving at the temple, Demetrius's agent Nicanor was treated well by the priests in the temple. They came out of the temple "to greet him peaceably and to show him the burnt offering that was being offered for the king" (1 Macc 7:33). But Nicanor delivered a terrible threat: "Unless Judas [Maccabeus] and his army are delivered into my hands this time, then if I return safely I will burn up this house [the temple]" (1 Macc 7:35). The temple priests prostrated themselves in prayer, begging God to protect his temple.[15] In fact, Nicanor did not return safely; instead he was killed and his army was defeated by the army of Judas Maccabeus.

Both 1 and 2 Maccabees have in view the Second Temple, built by the Jews who returned to Jerusalem from Babylonian exile in the late sixth century BC.[16] The original temple was built by King Solomon at the height of his reign. It required much labor and expense to build the temple and to construct its stands of bronze, its molten sea, its pillars of bronze and capitals, and so on. According to 1 Kings, when King Solomon dedicated it, God approved it by a miraculous sign: "when the priests came out of the holy place, a cloud filled the house of the Lord, so that the priests could not stand to minister because of the cloud; for the glory of the Lord filled the house of the Lord" (1 Kgs 8:10-11).[17] God promised to place his "name" upon the temple, and God fulfilled his promise (1 Kgs 8:15-21). Scott Hahn comments, "Heaven remains the dwelling place of God, but in a mysterious way he will dwell with his people on earth in the sanctuary where he will cause his name or divine presence to be."[18]

---

15. Daniel J. Harrington, SJ notes, "The prayer offered by the priests in 7:37-38 echoes that of Solomon in 1 Kings 8 by identifying the Jerusalem temple as God's dwelling place on earth and in asking God to punish the enemies of Israel" (Harrington, *First and Second Maccabees*, 51).

16. For discussion see Regev, *Temple in Early Christianity*, 12; and Goldstein, *II Maccabees*.

17. For Jesus Christ as the "new Solomon" who establishes the new (eschatological) temple, see Kreitzer, "Messianic Man of Peace."

18. Hahn, *Kingdom of God*, 111. For background regarding ancient Near Eastern temple theology, see Pitkänen, "From Tent of Meeting to Temple"; cf. Pitkänen, *Central Sanctuary*. For the symbolism of the Solomonic temple's design and ornamentation (in light of debates about the historicity of Solomon's temple, which the author views as essentially historical), see the detailed study by Hurowitz, "Yhwh's Exalted House." Hurowitz shows that "the principle of gradation found in the Tabernacle characterized the

Between 1 Kings 6, which describes the commencement of the building of the temple, and 1 Kings 8, which describes the solemn dedication of the temple, there is a short pause in 1 Kings 7 in which the author describes the other buildings that Solomon built, including his own palace and also a house "for Pharaoh's daughter whom he had taken in marriage" (1 Kgs 7:8). A mention of Pharaoh in the Bible is always a warning sign, and especially so in this case because Solomon later fell into idolatry due the influence of his many wives, who "turned away his heart after other gods," notably "Ashtoreth the goddess of the Sidonians, and . . . Milcom the abomination of the Ammonites" (1 Kgs 11:4-5).

When Solomon had begun building the temple, God had exhorted Solomon: "Concerning this house which you are building, if you will walk in my statutes and obey my ordinances and keep all my commandments and walk in them, then I will establish my word with you. . . . And I will dwell among the children of Israel" (1 Kgs 6:12-13). Jerome Walsh interprets this statement as an indication that the building of the temple "is not of first importance to Yahweh. Yahweh's desire is obedience."[19] Surely this is true, and it is also true, as Daniel Hays remarks, that "Solomon is a mixed bag of obedience and disobedience, and the narrative in 1 Kings about building the temple has numerous peculiar texts suggesting that something is not quite right."[20]

Nevertheless, the goodness of Solomon's temple is strongly affirmed. For the Jewish biblical scholar and theologian Jon Levenson, as for many other Jewish thinkers, theologically speaking it is even true that "the creation of the world and the construction of the Temple are parallel events."[21] Along similar lines, Ephrem the Syrian repeatedly uses temple imagery in depicting Eden, which—says Ephrem—contained "the Glory of the Holy of Holies" and whose "outer Tabernacle" (where Adam served as priest) was separated from its "innermost Tabernacle."[22] In the eighth century, the Christian monk and scholar Bede praised the "size and beauty" of Solomon's

---

design of the Solomonic Temple as well. The purpose of the material and technological gradation was certainly to inspire a feeling of increasing holiness and grandeur while approaching the most sacred spot," the Holy of Holies where YHWH was enthroned ("Yhwh's Exalted House," 89).

19. Walsh, *1 Kings*, 105. See also Bodner, *Theology of the Book of Kings*, 67.

20. J. D. Hays, *Temple and the Tabernacle*, 12; for the same point see Bodner, *Theology of the Book of Kings*, 68.

21. Levenson, *Sinai and Zion*, 143. For an extensive discussion of this point, drawing upon numerous biblical texts as well as Second Temple and rabbinic texts, see Beale, *Temple and the Church's Mission*, 29-80.

22. Ephrem the Syrian, *Hymns on Paradise*, III.7, p. 93; III.16, p. 96.

temple.²³ The biblical scholar Daniel Block identifies the key reason for praising Solomon's temple when he remarks that "the temple in Jerusalem was a divine project."²⁴

After Solomon's death, however, the temple is essentially ignored in most of 1 and 2 Kings, with the exception of some references to the plundering or, less frequently, the refurbishing of the temple. The temple reappears briefly in the acts of King Hezekiah—as well as in the apostasies of father Ahaz and son Manasseh—and then appears again, near the very end of 2 Kings, in the reforming work of King Josiah. Robert Fyall comments that 2 Kings depicts Josiah as "not only the new David, but the new Moses. Torah is to govern and be the standard for everything, including the Temple."²⁵ Fyall argues that Solomon's temple, therefore, takes second place to the Torah. He considers that in the Bible, "Faithfulness to Yahweh is possible without Temple but not without Torah."²⁶ This may be so, but not in the deepest sense that Levenson identifies in Scripture as read by the rabbis: "the world, 'heaven and earth,' are not complete until the Jerusalem Temple has gone up."²⁷ The rabbis here saw deeply into the Torah's creation account, in which God rests on the seventh day in his cosmic temple. Genesis 1 describes "the creation of the cosmic temple with all of its functions and with God dwelling in its midst," and Solomon's Temple contains much "imagery from the Garden of Eden."²⁸

Like Eden, Solomon's temple came to a bad end. It was burned down by the Babylonians in 586 BC. The Babylonian ruler Nebuchadnezzar besieged Jerusalem, and the city could not hold out. Nebuchadnezzar's captain of the guard, a man named Nebuzaradan, entered the city with orders to burn down its main buildings, and "he burned the house of the Lord" (2 Kgs 25:9). He and his soldiers pillaged all that was materially valuable in

---

23. Bede, *On Ezra and Nehemiah*, 66.

24. Block, *For the Glory of God*, 306. He includes a detailed comparison of the building of the tabernacle (see Exodus 25–40) with the building of the temple (see parts of 2 Samuel, 1 Kings, and 1 Chronicles). He concludes, "The temple in Jerusalem was a remarkable achievement. Although built at tremendous cost, its magnificence matched that of any known temple structure in the ancient Near East at this time.... For worshipers this building symbolized YHWH's presence on earth" (*For the Glory of God*, 309–10). See also the lengthy analysis of Solomon's temple in light of the Mosaic tabernacle in J. D. Hays, *Temple and the Tabernacle*, chapter 4.

25. Fyall, "Curious Silence," 54.

26. Fyall, "Curious Silence," 57.

27. Levenson, *Creation*, 99.

28. Walton, *Lost World of Genesis One*, 82, 84. Walton directs attention to Hurowitz, *I Have Built You an Exalted House*; and Weinfeld, "Sabbath, Temple, and Enthronement."

the temple—all the precious metals—and the ark of the covenant was never seen again.

Daniel Hays draws the moral: "The story in 1–2 Kings is painfully clear. Worship of God in the spectacular temple that Solomon builds is corrupted very early, and true worship of God in this temple is the rare exception rather than the rule."[29] Nonetheless, the psalmists offer abundant praise of God and his temple. For example, the author of Psalm 84 bursts forth, "My soul longs, yes, faints for the courts of the Lord; my heart and flesh sing for joy to the living God. . . . Blessed are those who dwell in your house, ever singing your praise!" (Ps 84:2, 4). There is hardly a greater testimony anywhere to the desire for God's presence—intimately associated with the temple—than Psalm 27:4: "One thing have I asked of the Lord, that will I seek after; that I may dwell in the house of the Lord all the days of my life, to behold the beauty of the Lord, and to inquire in his temple." Psalm 27 has a place in the Jewish liturgy within "the Jewish penitential month of Elul"; the psalm is "recited in the synagogue during each of the ten holy days."[30]

The Prophets and the Temple

Not surprisingly, the prophets of Israel devoted much attention to the destruction of Solomon's temple and how to understand such an event. Jeremiah received the mission of preaching to the people just prior to the catastrophe and of trying unsuccessfully to stave off the disaster. Through Jeremiah, God warns the people that their disobedience to his law—their injustice toward both God and neighbor—will mean that the kingdom of Judah will be cut off. God underscores the priority of justice: "For in the day that I [God] brought them out of the land of Egypt, I did not speak to your fathers or command them concerning burnt offerings or sacrifices. But this

---

29. J. D. Hays, *Temple and the Tabernacle*, 103.

30. Charry, *Psalms 1–50*, 137; Craigie and Tate, *Psalms 1–50*, 231. As Charry observes, the psalmist "models piety for everyone: he asks to dwell in God's house and to envision the loveliness of the Lord all his life by remaining in God's temple. A similar thought appears in Pss. 15:1; 23:6; and 24:3; it will recur in Pss. 61:4 and 92:13" (Charry, *Psalms 1–50*, 138). For historical-critical reconstruction of Psalm 27's background, see Craigie and Tate, *Psalms 1–50*, 230–35, which suggests (in accord with numerous other scholars) that "the background to this liturgical psalm is to be found in a royal event such as the anniversary of a coronation" (Craigie and Tate, *Psalms 1–50*, 234). Note that the request to "dwell in the house of the Lord," according to Craigie and Tate, "should not be taken literally, as if referring to a temple servant who would actually live perpetually within the temple precincts. It refers rather to living permanently in God's presence; such a life was regularly punctuated by actual visits to the temple, such as that in which the psalmist was engaged" (*Psalms 1–50*, 232).

command I gave them, 'Obey my voice, and I will be your God, and you shall be my people, and walk in all the ways that I command you, that it may be well with you'" (Jer 7:22–23). Since the people have not obeyed, Jerusalem will be destroyed and the temple along with it. Jeremiah proclaims the urgent word of the Lord, a final opportunity for repentance: "Thus says the Lord of hosts, the God of Israel, Amend your ways and your doings, and I will let you dwell in this place. Do not trust in those deceptive words: 'This is the temple of the Lord, the temple of the Lord, the temple of the Lord'" (Jer 7:3–4).

Commenting on this passage, Thomas Aquinas emphasizes that the temple is to be revered: "'The temple of the Lord,' is holy, 'the temple of the Lord,' is precious, 'the temple of the Lord,' is revered by all."[31] The problem is not the temple, upon which God has placed his name, nor the temple's sacrificial worship, which God commanded in the Torah. Rather the problem is the sinful people who imagined that "because of the sanctity of the temple, they would be able to avoid all punishment without an emendation of life."[32]

Ezekiel, too, describes the scene just prior to the destruction of the temple. He focuses in particular on false worship, a theme of Jeremiah's as well, but presented with special power by Ezekiel. God tells the prophet to prophesy doom: "An end! The end has come upon the four corners of the land" (Ezek 7:2). The injustice of the people requires punishment. As Daniel Hays comments, "the central theme of Ezekiel 1–24 is the loss of God's presence in the temple and the associated judgment on Jerusalem."[33]

Ezekiel receives a vision of what is happening inside the temple.[34] Even if the images are symbolic or exaggerated for rhetorical effect, it is hard to deny that Ezekiel, a priest who was exiled from Jerusalem to Babylon around

---

31. Thomas Aquinas, *Exposition of Jeremiah*, chap. 7, lect. 1. See also Hammele, *Bild der Juden*, 390: "it should be noted that Thomas, in all assertions and ascriptions that he makes, abstains from any polemics against the Jews. In addition, the following applies to his scriptural commentaries: as he consistently starts from the scriptural text, his interpretations always refer to the biblical Jews and are therefore not directly related to the Jews of the thirteenth century."

32. Thomas Aquinas, *Exposition of Jeremiah*, chap. 7, lect. 1. Walter Brueggemann likewise points out, "The prophet is not rejecting liturgy or temple claims in principle" (*Commentary on Jeremiah*, 78).

33. J. D. Hays, *Temple and the Tabernacle*, 104.

34. For the interpretation of this vision, see J. B. Taylor, "Temple in Ezekiel," 64: "It is not impossible that the four examples of idolatry described in Ezekiel 8 (the image of jealousy alongside the altar; the portrayal of unclean creatures in the darkened recesses of the Temple; the women weeping for Tammuz; and the twenty-five sun worshippers) were purely imaginary or at best typical of the Temple's wrongdoings." Ezekiel shows the thoroughgoing nature of idolatry by "condemning the priests, the elders, the women and lay worshippers in turn" (J. B. Taylor, "Temple in Ezekiel," 65).

598 BC (twelve years before the final Babylonian conquest of the city), knew something of what was taking place.[35] In a vision, Ezekiel is shown a door into the court of the temple; and when he enters, he sees painted upon the wall "all kinds of creeping things, and loathsome beasts, and all the idols of the house of Israel" (Ezek 8:10). Even worse, seventy elders of Israel (a symbolic number indicating the fullness of Israel's leadership) are present, and they are worshipping the idols. At the entrance of the temple's north gate, Ezekiel sees women weeping for the goddess Tammuz; and "between the porch and the altar" of the temple, Ezekiel sees twenty-five men worshipping the sun god (Ezek 8:16). Ezekiel eventually sees the "glory of the God of Israel" abandoning the temple (and the city), thereby undoing what the glory cloud of 1 Kings 8 had brought about.[36]

Yet, this is not the end of the story. God promises through Jeremiah that the whole city of Jerusalem, including the temple, "shall be rebuilt for the Lord" (Jer 31:38). God promises that not only will the Davidic monarchy be restored, but also "the Levitical priests shall never lack a man in my presence to offer burnt offerings, to burn cereal offerings, and to make sacrifices for ever" (Jer 33:18). These sacrifices, so it seems, will take place at the rebuilt temple. God promises that the nations round about, and especially Babylon, will be punished for their pride and idolatry; while the tribes of Israel (the northern kingdom, exiled in 722 by the Assyrians) and the tribes of Judah will return to Zion with repentance and gladness, joined "to the Lord in an everlasting covenant which will never be forgotten" (Jer 50:5).[37]

Ezekiel makes clear that the temple will be laid low and the city besieged and utterly ruined (see Ezek 21:27), but he does not portray this event explicitly. God promises through Ezekiel not only that the temple will be

---

35. For brief discussion of Ezekiel's career, see Blenkinsopp, *Ezekiel*, 8–9. On the question of whether Ezekiel would have heard of Jeremiah's prophecies (given that Ezekiel was already in exile during the central events prophesied and endured by Jeremiah), see J. B. Taylor, "Temple in Ezekiel," 61–62.

36. See J. D. Hays, *Tabernacle and the Temple*, 111, for the view that God's "presence—that is, the very glory of God—does not return to the temple in the postexilic time. In fact, the presence of God does not return to the temple until Jesus enters in through the gates in the New Testament." On the topic of the divine presence and the abandonment of the temple by God, see Kutsko, *Between Heaven and Earth*. The imagery that Ezekiel uses to describe God's chariot (in Ezekiel 1 and 10–11) is shared by other ancient Near Eastern cultures, as Hays shows.

37. Brueggemann comments, "It is precisely at the end of the Exile that the renewed, restored relation with God is celebrated as everlasting and beyond disruption. That is, at the very moment of discontinuity deep continuity is asserted. The rhetoric of return clearly intends that the Exile is not one of many disruptions, but is the only one of its kind" (*Commentary on Jeremiah*, 465). If so, then it is not surprising that the resolution of the Babylonian Exile would require the coming of the Messiah.

reestablished, but also that the people of Israel will never be anything other than God's covenantal people. They will never be assimilated to the Gentile nations (see Ezek 20:32). In large part, they will not become like the nations because they will have the rebuilt temple, and God will dwell among them. Regarding his people Israel, God promises: "I will make a covenant of peace with them; it shall be an everlasting covenant with them; and I will bless them and multiply them, and will set my sanctuary in the midst of them for evermore. My dwelling place shall be with them" (Ezek 37:26-27). Ezekiel's promises echo the covenantal blessings of Leviticus 26:2-13. Moshe Greenberg observes that Ezekiel "locates God's presence . . . in a temple" and Ezekiel uses "*miškan* in a new sense . . . approaching post-biblical Shekinah," insofar as "God's *miškan* is no longer 'amidst' the people" but "is now a protective tent 'over them.'"[38]

When Ezekiel describes the new temple, he does not describe it along the lines of the original temple—or, for that matter, along the lines of the actual dimensions of the Second Temple. He depicts utterly distinct dimensions, and he also sees (in the vision) an extraordinary stream of life-giving water flowing from the new temple. Joseph Blenkinsopp suggests that just as Ezekiel receives a vision of a "heavenly temple" or divine throne in chapter 1, so it is significant that in chapters 47-48 the new temple follows "heavenly specifications" reflecting "a symbolic structure of meaning."[39] Similarly, Paul Joyce concludes that "Ezekiel 40-48 combine both dream and reality. The interweaving of the richly visionary and the precisely mathematical in these chapters is striking."[40]

---

38. M. Greenberg, *Ezekiel 21-37*, 758, 760.

39. Blenkinsopp, *Ezekiel*, 193, 199. On the other hand, Blenkinsopp grants that "[u]nlike the dimensions of the new Jerusalem in Revelation, which is about 1,500 miles in length, breadth, and height, the measurements recorded by the seer's guide are in themselves quite feasible" (Blenkinsopp, *Ezekiel*, 198). But he argues that "[t]here are enough allusions in chapters 40-48 of a mythic-symbolic and idealistic kind to rule out the suggestion that a literal program or blueprint for the future was intended" by Ezekiel (Blenkinsopp, *Ezekiel*, 197). In general, the book of Revelation's "description of the new Jerusalem . . . draws heavily on Ezekiel's vision" (Blenkinsopp, *Ezekiel*, 196). Paul M. Joyce points out: "Treatments of Ezekiel 40-48 cover the range from the realistic . . . through to the eschatological . . . and the utopian" (Joyce, "Temple and Worship," 147).

40. Joyce, "Temple and Worship," 147. As an example, he notes that Ezekiel 40:2, in which the prophet describes being taken to a high mountain (perhaps intended to be Sinai?) north of Jerusalem. The new temple seen by the prophet is on this mountain. The new temple is also so perfectly filled with God's glory (Ezek 43:5) that "the divine presence renders the ark of the Covenant and other cultic paraphernalia redundant," which explains why the ark is not described as being present (Joyce, "Temple and Worship," 147).

In Ezekiel's vision of the rebuilt temple, he is taken by a man "whose appearance was like bronze" (Ezek 40:3) and who leads him around the new temple. He sees the thick wall around the temple area, and he sees the gateway and the gate. He sees much more, including "the glory of the God of Israel [coming] from the east; and the sound of his coming was like the sound of many waters; and the earth shone with his glory" (Ezek 43:2). Ezekiel explicitly links this coming of God's glory with God's earlier departure. In Ezekiel's vision, God enters the new temple and "the glory of the Lord filled the Temple" (Ezek 43:5).[41] Not only this, but God proclaims to Ezekiel: "Son of man, this is the place of my throne and the place of the soles of my feet, where I will dwell in the midst of the sons of Israel for ever. And the house of Israel shall no more defile my holy name, neither they, nor their kings" (Ezek 43:7).[42]

In this eschatological temple, according to Ezekiel, there will still be animal sacrifices. Blenkinsopp remarks that "for Ezekiel and the priestly tradition which he represents there is no access to the deity and no way to remove sin and thus be acceptable other than the priesthood and the sacrificial system."[43] The altar will be rebuilt "for offering burnt offerings upon it

---

41. As Peter H. Rice comments, in the Gospel of Luke "Jesus's arrival [to the temple in Luke 19] may recall and reverse Ezekiel's vision of God's departure from the Temple" (Rice, *Behold, Your House*, 150).

42. Blenkinsopp notes that Ezekiel envisions a new exodus, with the new temple as its completion (see *Ezekiel*, 194). As he points out, there is "a remarkably close parallelism with the Priestly version of the Sinai event, according to which Moses saw a vision of the divine effulgence and received detailed specifications for the construction of the tent (tabernacle) and ark together with their furnishings (Exod. 24:15b-18a; 25—31). Everything had to be made according to the pattern or model (*tabnit* in Hebrew) revealed to him (Exod. 25:9, 40)" (Blenkinsopp, *Ezekiel*, 194). At the same time, Blenkinsopp also makes clear: "This motif of temple or city built according to a celestial prototype is by no means confined to the biblical writings. Gudea, ruler of the Sumerian city of Lagash, was shown in a dream the model according to which the temple of Ningirsu was to be built" (Blenkinsopp, *Ezekiel*, 195).

43. Blenkinsopp, *Ezekiel*, 213. He adds: "It is not surprising, therefore, that the first act of the repatriates from the Babylonian diaspora was to set up the altar and resume the daily offering (the *tamid*) even before the temple was rebuilt (Ezra 3:1–3). In doing so, they acted in accordance with the Deuteronomic law which required the setting up of an altar immediately upon entering the land (Deut. 27:6–7), following the example of David, who built the first altar in Jerusalem to avert disaster from the land (I Chron. 21:18–22:1)" (Blenkinsopp, *Ezekiel*, 213). See also Joyce, "Temple and Worship," 152. Blenkinsopp remarks about the prophets' views of temple sacrifice: "Like all religious institutions, sacrifice can get detached from its original purposes, degenerating into the routine performance of socially sanctioned acts devoid of inner meaning. The prophetic polemic against this practice, which was the central expression of the religious life of their contemporaries, focused on the disjunction between external act and internal disposition. (It did not, however, amount to advocacy of a *purely spiritual* religion,

and for throwing blood against it" (Ezek 43:18). God provides Ezekiel with a plan for sanctifying the new altar, beginning with offering "a bull for a sin offering," and then offering many other animals for a sin-offering, including seven days worth of goats, bulls, and rams (Ezek 43:19). After seven days, the altar will be purified and ready for continuous use with respect to burnt offerings and peace offerings. God also states that no foreigner—no uncircumcised person or Gentile—will be permitted to enter the new temple. Only the "sons of Zadok" (Ezek 44:15) will be allowed to minister at the new altar, because the other Levitical families proved themselves to be idolaters.[44]

Prophesying during the period of the return of the Babylonian exiles to the land of Judah, Zechariah proclaims God's words that "I have returned to Jerusalem with compassion; my house shall be built in it" (Zech 1:16).[45] God promises that once again he will "dwell in the midst" of his people Israel; he "will inherit Judah as his portion in the holy land, and will again choose Jerusalem" (Zech 2:11–12).[46] Zechariah connects the rebuilding of the temple with the restoration of the Davidic kingship. God promises that the one who will rebuild the temple will also reign upon the throne of David (Zech 6:13).[47] Moreover, Zechariah's prophecy declares that when the tem-

---

whatever that might be)" (Blenkinsopp, *Ezekiel*, 214).

44. Blenkinsopp points out that in Ezekiel 40:45–46 there is a distinction between altar priests and priests responsible for maintaining the temple, but not the sharp division found in Ezekiel 44. Following the position taken by numerous other commentators, he holds that Ezekiel 44:10–16 was added by a later editor. He states, "The history of the Israelite priesthood is notoriously obscure, but it looks as if, as a result of internecine strife among priestly clans, one group claiming descent from Zadok emerged victorious and fortified their claim by providing Zadok with a fictitious pedigree as descending from Levi through his third son, Eleazar (I Chron. 6:1–15)" (Blenkinsopp, *Ezekiel*, 219). Whatever one makes of this reconstruction, not only strife but also idolatry or syncretism was (and is) a constant temptation for priestly leadership—and it is also the case that conflict is sometimes necessary in defense of right worship against an unacceptable syncretism.

45. For basic historical background, connecting Zechariah with Haggai and Nehemiah, see Baldwin, *Haggai, Zechariah, Malachi*, 100. Baldwin reads Zechariah from an explicitly Christian perspective. See also Chalmers, *Interpreting the Prophets*, 59. For a succinct historical-critical survey of the book of Zechariah, see Fuhr and Yates, *Message of the Twelve*, chapter 15.

46. According to Beale, "Zechariah 2:11 has come full circle back to the introductory note about the temple in 1:16. God will construct his future temple on a huge scale, and his tabernacling presence will reside with both Jews and Gentiles who trust him" (*Temple and the Church's Mission*, 143).

47. Interpreters debate how Joshua (the high priest) and Zerubbabel (descended from David) relate in this passage. For background to this and similar issues, see Meyers and Meyers, *Haggai, Zechariah 1–8*.

ple is rebuilt and the king reigns anew in Jerusalem, the nations will come to worship the God of Israel, and the people of Israel will be set at the head of all nations (Zech 8:20–23). The prophet proclaims that on the day in which these promises are consummated—the eschatological day of the Lord—"the Lord will put a shield about the inhabitants of Jerusalem so that the feeblest among them on that day shall be like David, and the house of David shall be like God, like the angel of the Lord, at their head" (Zech 12:8).[48] Every nation that does not recognize the rule of David, and that seeks to fight against the Davidic king, will be destroyed by God. The Israelites will mourn for all the sins they have committed, and "there shall be a fountain opened up for the house of David and the inhabitants of Jerusalem to cleanse them from sin and uncleanness" (Zech 13:1).

According to Zechariah, when the throne of David is restored and the rebellious nations conquered by the Lord, the result will be that "the Lord will become king over all the earth; on that day the Lord will be one and his name one" (Zech 14:9). Here we see a vision of the temple cult becoming universal. All of Israel's previous enemies will now annually make pilgrimage to the temple in Jerusalem "to worship the King, the Lord of hosts, and to keep the feast of booths" (Zech 14:16). The whole of Jerusalem and Judah will be so holy, in relation to the world, that all Jerusalem will be the temple. As G. K. Beale describes this eschatological prophecy: "the Shekinah presence of God, formerly sequestered in the old holy of holies, will burst forth from the heavenly sanctuary and encompass the entire future new Jerusalem."[49]

---

48. Note that, as Fuhr and Yates remark, "Contemporary scholarship has generally attributed the material in chapters 9–14 to a 'Second Zechariah' who comes after the original prophet responsible for chapters 1–8. The reference to 'Greece' in 9:13 and some highly speculative reconstructions of how the messages in chapters 9–14 might relate to specific political conflicts in the postexilic community have led to dating this material to the time of Alexander the Great, or even as late as the Maccabean era" (*Message of the Twelve*, 273). Against supposing a date of authorship later than 445, Fuhr and Yates cite Boda, *Haggai, Zechariah*. But they grant that "[t]he attribution of this book to Zechariah does not preclude the possibility of inspired prophetic activity or later updating of the text that expanded on or provided further clarification of Zechariah's earlier messages. Even scholars not affirming single authorship of the book have recognized the book's essential theological unity" (*Message of the Twelve*, 273). Against resistance to reading prophetic books as the work of multiple authors over a relatively wide period of time, see Walton and Sandy, *Lost World of Scripture*, 224–32, cited by Fuhr and Yates.

49. Beale, *Temple and the Church's Mission*, 143. Fuhr and Yates put the matter in less fulsome terms, but with similar implications: "The Feast of Booths (or Tabernacles) was one of Israel's three major pilgrimages but would now be for all peoples. . . . The presence of the Lord and his glory would cover the city to the extent that even common objects like the bells on horses and cooking pots would be as holy as items used at the altar. . . . Israel and the nations would give their allegiance and worship to the Lord

Much more could be added, including Isaiah's prophecy of a "new heavens and a new earth" (Isa 65:17) and Isaiah's conclusion—noted above—that the Israelites will bring people to Jerusalem "from all the nations as an offering to the Lord" and that some of these Gentiles will be chosen to serve as priests and Levites (Isa 66:20–21).[50] By now, however, it should be clear how important the temple in Jerusalem was for the biblical people of Israel.[51] The rebuilt Second Temple, even if originally unimpressive, had become by Jesus' time—thanks in part to Herod the Great's extensive refurbishing and expansion of the temple—a large and impressive complex. Martin Goodman notes that the Second Temple "had a vast piazza for worshippers to gather" and was decorated with "outstanding works of art, such as the golden vine" and "the huge purple, blue and scarlet embroidered tapestries."[52] Goodman pictures the crowd that thronged the temple

---

alone" (Fuhr and Yates, *Message of the Twelve*, 298–99). For Fuhr and Yates, Jesus Christ holds the key to the fulfillment of these prophecies.

50. Indeed, Beale considers that "the future-oriented redemptive-historical 'new Exodus' context of Isaiah 63–66 (indeed, of chs. 40–66) points strongly to Isaiah 66:1 not being merely a reference to the fact that the *entire present* cosmos is God's temple in which he dwells... but that there will be a future new cosmos and temple that God will create and in which he will dwell for ever, and which will be an extension of the present *heavenly* temple" (*Temple and the Church's Mission*, 135). See also Tobit 14:5, which depicts Tobit as prophesying: "Our brethren will be scattered over the earth from the good land, and Jerusalem will be desolate. The house of God in it will be burned down and will be in ruins for a time. But God will again have mercy on them, and bring them back into their land; and they will rebuild the house of God, though it will not be like the former one until the times of the age are completed. After this they will return from the places of their captivity, and will rebuild Jerusalem in splendor. And the house of God will be rebuilt there with a glorious building for all generations for ever, just as the prophets said of it." The point is that the Second Temple was not the eschatological temple foretold by many prophets.

51. I pass over the non-biblical Second Temple material, such as the Qumran documents and other such texts. This material also shows the importance of the temple. See for example Gärtner, *Temple and the Community in Qumran*; Regev, "Community as Temple"; Regev, "Temple and Righteousness"; Church, *Hebrews and the Temple*; and Hoskins, *Jesus as the Fulfillment*, 89–102. Regev highlights crucial differences between Paul and Qumran, including the fact that "[t]he authors of the Community Rule do not call themselves a Temple or bestow upon their community explicit Temple titles" (Regev, *Temple in Early Christianity*, 63).

52. M. Goodman, "Temple in First Century," 460. Goodman provides a stirring description of Jewish horror and protest when in 40 AD Emperor Caligula commanded that an image of himself be installed in the temple and worshipped. In the end, Caligula was assassinated before this order could take effect. As Goodman notes, an important part of the mystique of the Jerusalem temple was that its sacrificial cult was (in the Torah) "laid out by the divine recipient of the offerings" rather than being decided upon by the worshippers who then "judged their success by what they saw as signs of divine pleasure or displeasure" ("Temple in First Century," 461).

during festivals such as Passover, and he conveys a sense of what arriving there might have been like, with "the building towering high above [the pilgrim], the precious metals and stones glinting in the sun . . . giving rise in descriptions of the building to recurrent imagery of intense light."[53]

Luke-Acts on the Temple

According to Luke-Acts, the Second Temple was important for the first followers of Jesus Christ. Steve Smith rightly comments that "Luke is positive about the Temple in many places," even though Luke's Jesus holds that "the Jerusalem leaders did not allow the temple to take [the] eschatological role that belonged to it," resulting in "the divine abandonment of the temple (Lk. 23.45)."[54] In Luke 19, Jesus proclaims that the temple will be destroyed in an eschatological judgment. According to John 2:19 and (in a slightly different way) Mark 14:58 and Matthew 26:61, Jesus promises that he himself will rebuild the temple in three days; and John 2:21-22 makes clear that this new temple will be his "body." As Christopher Rowland remarks, the eschatological judgment of the temple is connected in the Synoptic Gospels with

---

53. M. Goodman, "Temple in First Century," 462, with reference to Hayward, *Jewish Temple*, 15-16. Raising the question of why, if the temple was so beloved, the Jewish people did not quickly rebuild it (after its destruction in 70 AD), Goodman answers that the Romans refused to allow it, for reasons first related to Emperor Vespasian's uncertain grip on power and then, later, upon the claim to fame of the future Emperor Trajan's family (related to the Jewish War) and finally upon Emperor Hadrian's response to a Jewish rebellion in the diaspora in 115-17 AD. Goodman adds along somewhat speculative but plausible lines: "According to Josephus (*War* 6.238-66) Titus (and presumably also Vespasian) had not intended that the Temple should be burned. Since previous emperors had valued highly the Jews' practice of offering sacrifices in the Temple for the wellbeing of the emperors themselves, it is not at all unlikely that original Roman war aims involved the re-establishment of the Temple cult under the leadership of pro-Roman high priests such as had cooperated with the Roman state since direct Roman rule was first imposed on Judaea in 6 CE. But once the Temple was destroyed, neither Vespasian nor Titus could safely apologize, since, if the destruction was not portrayed as deliberate, it had to be the product of an incompetent failure of discipline by the commanders on the ground, and would constitute an act of the greatest impiety which would besmirch the record of the new regime" (M. Goodman, "Temple in First Century," 464).

54. S. Smith, *Fate of the Jerusalem Temple*, 194. See also Head, "Temple in Luke's Gospel." Head concludes, "Luke affirms the role of the Temple in many ways, as a place of prayer and revelation, as in some respects central to God's dealings with the cosmos. At the same time the Temple, like the city in which it resides, stands under the threat of judgement inasmuch as it partakes in the rejection of God's beloved Son" ("Temple in Luke's Gospel," 119). For emphasis on the New Testament's ambiguous attitude toward the Temple and its sacrifices, see Joseph, *Jesus and the Temple*.

the detail that "[a]t the death of Jesus the veil, which hides the innermost part of the Temple, is torn asunder. This portends doom for the institution and its ideology."[55] In all the Gospels, the divine presence is now found in Jesus rather than preeminently in the temple. As Rowland rightly says, "The respect for the institutions of Law and Temple cannot mask the underlying thrust of the Gospel and Acts which moves away from allocating a special role for the Temple as the locus of the divine presence."[56]

Nevertheless, Luke states that after witnessing Jesus' ascension, Jesus' followers "worshiped him, and returned to Jerusalem with great joy, and were continually in the temple blessing God" (Luke 24:52). One reason that they continued to frequent the temple, as Goodman points out, was that "the Temple was the main area for public meetings of all kinds in Jerusalem," and so the apostles could hardly have chosen any other place to proclaim the good news of the Messiah.[57] The book of Acts reports that the first Christians not only regularly preached the gospel in the temple; they also spent their time "attending the temple together and breaking bread in their homes" (Acts 2:46).[58] This observation suggests—as does much other

---

55. Rowland, "Temple in the New Testament," 471. Historically speaking, Rowland considers it plausible to hold that "[i]n the final days of his life, possibly in the light of the hostility he encountered, he [Jesus] may have uttered prophecies of doom on the Temple and Jerusalem after initially entertaining hopes of reform. There are hints that he might also have begun to contemplate a separate sectarian existence for his followers, with distinctive rites and institutions in the words he uttered at the Last Supper" ("Temple in the New Testament," 472). To my mind, there are more than "hints" and Jesus was not simply winging it. For the Gospel of Matthew as a Jewish "sectarian" text—a moniker that I find inadequate but that has the advantage of making clear that Jesus and his followers had competitors in proclaiming the divinely ordained path for the salvation of Israel and the world—see Kampen, *Matthew within Sectarian Judaism*.

56. Rowland, "Temple in the New Testament," 472. See also, for the same point though from a different direction, Huizenga, *New Isaac*, 273–91. Huizenga argues persuasively that "[s]ince the Akedah was the patriarchal grounding of the temple and its sacrifices, particularly the 'whole-offering,' the presentation of Jesus as a new Isaac in the Gospel of Matthew functions in service of the Matthean theme of Jesus as the replacement for the temple" (*New Isaac*, 291).

57. M. Goodman, "Temple in First Century," 461.

58. Regev argues that we should not "assume that Luke's gospel and the book of Acts reflect the same approach to the Temple. . . . [E]ven if they do exhibit certain similarities, they differ in both genre and sources: Luke is based on Mark and Q, continuing the gospel biographical genre, while Acts is based on various unknown sources, employing a historiographical genre which requires differences in how it deals with the Temple and the cult" (Regev, *Temple in Early Christianity*, 153). Luke-Acts mentions the temple around 120 times, and Regev shows that Luke-Acts is generally positive about the temple. Regev states, "Throughout the gospel the reader is shown that the Temple is the origin and basis of Jesus, supporting a key mode of piety and devotion. The reader is supposed to feel devastated when he reads about the coming destruction,

New Testament evidence—that the members of the Christian community in Jerusalem continued to observe Torah, including the temple rituals. When Paul meets the Jerusalem elders in the book of Acts, they commend his work among the Gentiles but express the fear that Jewish believers, who continue to be "zealous for the law" (Acts 21:20), will misunderstand Paul. As we saw in chapter 4, they urge Paul to correct the supposed misunderstanding that Paul "teach[es] all the Jews who are among the Gentiles to forsake Moses, telling them not to circumcise their children or observe the customs" (Acts 21:21). Paul is glad to participate in the temple ritual of purification that his co-believers request of him.

In my view, Peter Rice correctly argues that Acts here suggests that the temple now holds "specifically (and only) cultural significance," since Paul's participation has to do with "Jewish custom" rather than with the rites of sacrificial atonement for the purpose of reconciliation with God.[59] Rowland similarly observes that we need to attend to the way in which, in the narrative of Acts, God's presence moves from Jerusalem to Rome.[60] Indeed, before completing the temple ritual, Paul is attacked by "Jews from Asia" (Acts 21:27) who loudly complain about what Paul has been doing in his ministry.[61] After this event, the temple is essentially left behind.

---

not to think about the dawn of a new age. Even when Jesus ascends, the apostles remain in the Temple as if nothing has changed" (*Temple in Early Christianity*, 171). In my view, it is possible both to be devastated (due to the greatness of the temple) and to rejoice in the "dawn of a new age." The importance of the temple in Jerusalem can be strongly affirmed even while holding that Jesus, as the Messiah, reconfigures the temple and its cult around himself.

59. Rice, *Behold, Your House*, 161.

60. See Rowland, "Temple in the New Testament," 473. Rowland comments on Stephen's speech in Acts 7: "In three ways Stephen's speech challenges the divine approbation of the Temple: by making the command to Moses about the tabernacle the result of angelic revelation only; by referring to the implicit disobedience of Solomon; and the suggestion that the Temple was little better than the idolatrous places of the nations" ("Temple in the New Testament," 473).

61. Rowland comments: "Parallel to Jesus in the Gospel, Paul in Acts goes up to Jerusalem, explicitly driven by a divine impulse, like Jesus according to Lk. 9.51, and with prophetic warning of the impending rejection (Acts 21.11). In the case of both Jesus and Paul the reception in Jerusalem and the Temple is hostle. The chance is offered and rejected and the message goes to the ends of the earth leaving Jerusalem and its Temple behind" ("Temple in the New Testament," 475). For a more positive interpretation of Acts 21 vis-à-vis the temple cult, see Regev, *Temple in Early Christianity*, 181–84. Regev suggests that our choice must be between the temple as "a negative entity deserving condemnation and rejection" (due to the malfeasance of the chief priests) and the temple as the center of early Christian life in the sense that nothing significant changed with regard to the temple (*Temple in Early Christianity*, 183). As indicated above, I think there is a third option: the temple is willed by God and a place of great value, but Jesus reconfigures all aspects of Jewish life, including the temple, around

Paul, Jesus, and the Temple

In his letters, Paul is insistent that no one, whether Jew or Gentile, can be "justified by works of the law" (Gal 2:16), that is, by observing the precepts of Torah; the reason being that our sinfulness makes it impossible to succeed in obeying the whole Torah, and so the Torah is not a sufficient path to right relationship with God. Instead, for Paul the key is that Jesus has come as the Messiah of Israel and, having supremely fulfilled the Torah on the cross, has reconfigured Israel around himself. In order to make all believers into his own "body" (1 Cor 12:27), Christ has poured out the eschatological Spirit upon all who have faith. For Paul, the community of believers is "the temple of the living God" (2 Cor 6:16). Just as worshippers in the temple must be pure, so believers must be pure: "For God's temple is holy, and that temple you are" (1 Cor 3:17).

Paul thinks it is fine for Jews who believe in Jesus to observe certain Jewish rituals, but not if they thereby intend to claim that observance of Torah is required for them in order to be justified or to attain eternal life. The latter elements come through faith in Christ. Nijay Gupta is correct that "Paul is arguing in Galatians that the coming of the Messiah led to a new era, one where the conduit of Torah (works) is no longer valid," given the "*relational* and participatory dynamics of πίστις [in Christ]."[62] As a Jew, Paul observes Torah or does not observe Torah in accord with the needs of his gospel mission. As noted above, he tells the Corinthians, "To the Jews I became as a Jew, in order to win Jews; to those under the law I became as one under the law—though not being myself under the law—that I might win those under the law" (1 Cor 9:20).[63] Joseph Fitzmyer explains that by

---

himself. Regev grants that although "Luke is more occupied than the other gospels with the notion of repentance and forgiveness of sins," Luke "never relates atonement to the Temple" despite the temple cult being in itself directed toward atonement (*Temple in Early Christianity*, 194). For the argument that in Luke's Gospel, Jesus brings the temple's sacrificial function to an end, see Rice, *Behold, Your House*, 150. See also N. H. Taylor, "Luke-Acts and the Temple," 709–21. On Mark 15:37–39's account of the tearing of the temple curtain, see Catalano, "Matter of Perspective." Drawing critically upon R. S. Brown, *Death of the Messiah* II, 1097–140, Catalano argues (implausibly in my view) that the tearing of the temple curtain signifies divine mourning.

62. Gupta, *Paul and the Language of Faith*, 143, 146. Gupta directs attention to Oakes, "Πίστις as Relational Way of Life."

63. For Regev, if Paul sought to "transform the concept of holiness and the worship of God from the Jewish sacrificial system to the belief in Christ and the life of the Christian community," then this would mean that Paul is "denying the relevance of the Temple" (Regev, *Temple in Early Christianity*, 55). But in my view, the temple remains relevant for Paul because Jesus, as the Messiah, fulfills and reconfigures it around himself without negating it as though it had no value. Regev makes much of the fact that

claiming that he is not in fact "under the law," Paul is saying the same thing as he says "in Gal 2:15–16, where Paul speaks of himself and Cephas, 'We ourselves, who are Jews by birth and not Gentile sinners, know that a human being is not justified by works of the law, but through faith in Jesus Christ.' . . . [T]o be justified Paul feels no obligation to observe the Mosaic law and all its precepts."[64]

According to the Gospel of Matthew, when Jesus' disciples praised the temple buildings, he tells them: "You see all these, do you not? Truly, I say to you, there will not be left here one stone upon another, that will not be thrown down" (Matt 24:2). Earlier in the same Gospel, he tells his disciples that he has not come "to abolish the law and the prophets"; he has come to "fulfill them" (Matt 5:17). He warns against relaxing the commandments of the Torah and he promises that "till heaven and earth pass away, not an iota, not a dot, will pass from the law until all is accomplished" (Matt 5:18).

How does Jesus intend to "fulfill" the entirety of "the law and the prophets"? This question becomes more difficult in the face of his repeated suggestion that he himself, in his body, will serve as the new (eschatological) temple. As already indicated, this suggestion is especially prominent in the

---

Paul does not state "that the Eucharist is a sacrifice" (*Temple in Early Christianity*, 73; cf. 81), but I think this neglects what Paul does say. As Regev recognizes but minimizes, Paul teaches that Christ's self-offering on the cross is a sacrifice (see Rom 3:23–25; Rom 8:3; 1 Cor 5:7; 2 Cor 5:21). Ultimately, Regev's goal is to show that "Paul can view Jesus as a sin-sacrifice and kaporet but nevertheless continue to offer sacrifices at the Temple and consider the Temple cult to be atoning," although Regev grants that "when the Temple is not the sole place of God's dwelling place and the animal sacrifices are not the only way to achieve cultic atonement, they are no longer the same" (*Temple in Early Christianity*, 88–89). On the issue of Paul and the Torah, Regev holds that Paul's "belief that the Law does not lead to justification—but only to Christ—does not mean that Paul thinks Jews should no longer observe it" (*Temple in Early Christianity*, 94). I accept this, but I note that Paul does not think that Jews should observe it as a necessary path for justification and atonement.

64. Fitzmyer, *First Corinthians*, 370. The Messianic Jewish New Testament scholar Mark Nanos disagrees with Fitzmyer's interpretation here: see Nanos, "Paul's Relationship to Torah." Nanos sums up his position, which I find insufficiently attuned to Paul's statements about the new covenant in Christ: "1 Cor. 9.19–23 can be understood very differently, with a working hypothesis that Paul was Torah-observant as a matter of covenant fidelity, and known to be halakhically faithful by the audience to which he addressed this text. When approached from this perspective, there is no reason to suppose that his addressees would imagine Paul's language signified lifestyle adaptability. Rather, it would immediately be recognized that Paul was explaining his evangelistic tactic of adapting rhetorically, a discursive strategy they had witnessed themselves, and one that is also evident in his pastoral approach to them in this letter" (Nanos, "Paul's Relationship to Torah," 139). The position advocated by Nanos is critically engaged by Pitre et al., *Paul, a New Covenant Jew*. See also Bird "Salvation in Paul's Judaism?," which (among other things) responds to Nanos, "Paul and Judaism."

Gospel of John.⁶⁵ God indwelt the temple; the Word of God tabernacles in Jesus (see John 1:14). Early in the Gospel, Jesus symbolically drives out the money-changers and those who are selling sacrificial animals from the temple precincts. When the leaders of the people ask what "sign" of his authority he can offer to justify such radical actions, he compares the temple with his own body. He replies to them, "Destroy this temple, and in three days I will raise it up" (John 2:19).⁶⁶ Naturally, when he uses the word *temple*, his listeners assume that he is speaking about destroying and rebuilding the temple in Jerusalem.

In John 6, Jesus compares himself to a perfect temple (or Passover) sacrifice, which, when consumed, gives eternal life: "Truly, truly, I say to you, unless you eat the flesh of the Son of man and drink his blood, you have no life in you; he who eats my flesh and drinks my blood has eternal life, and I will raise him up at the last day" (John 6:53–54).⁶⁷ In John 7, he

---

65. See Hoskins, *Jesus as the Fulfillment*; Coloe, *God Dwells with Us*; A. R. Kerr, *Temple of Jesus' Body*; Regev, *Temple in Early Christianity*, chapter 6; and Salier, "Temple in John." Salier sums up the view (which I share, although I think that the word "replacement" is misleading if it is taken as a negation) that Jesus fulfills and reconfigures the temple around himself: "The Temple is integral to both the narrative and theological interests of the Fourth Gospel. The focus throughout the Gospel is clearly upon Jesus as the one who will bring about the gracious replacement and fulfilment of the hopes of Israel and therefore the world. One of the ways in which this theme is expressed is through an extended refection on the relationship of Jesus to the Temple. The Temple forms the physical setting for the revelation of the Son of God in his teaching ministry and is the place where he is also rejected. It is clear that Jesus comes to represent all that the Temple meant for the people of Israel. He is the locus of divine revelation, worship and presence. And he will be that for the world. While there is criticism of practices associated with the Temple, it is not subject to criticism as an institution" ("Temple in John," 134).

66. See the extensive discussion of John 2:13-22 in Chanikuzhy, *Jesus, the Eschatological Temple*, 233-329, which demonstrates that "the temple action proclaims the arrival of the eschatological temple through the death and resurrection of Jesus" (*Jesus, the Eschatological Temple*, 328-29). Regev comments that most interpreters hold that in John 2:19-22, "the moral or figurative destruction of the Temple parallels the destruction of the body of Jesus, and the building of the new Temple takes place via the resurrection of Jesus—perhaps 'the Temple of the new age is Christ.' This may be a simple replacement, so that believers enter into a living communion with the Father through Jesus—the new heavenly Temple or the eschatological temple. But in what sense is Jesus's body a Temple? The simplest explanation seems to be that the flesh/body of Jesus reveals the divine glory, just as the Temple reveals the glory of God for Israel (cf. Isa 6:1-5)" (*Temple in Early Christianity*, 201). I think that Jesus in the flesh, by his self-offering on the cross, perfectly fulfills the purposes of the temple and thereby functions, in his risen and glorified body, as the eschatological temple. But it is important also to include the element of incorporation into Christ through faith and the sacraments.

67. Hoskins states, "The reference to Jesus' flesh and blood in 6:53-56 is ... an anticipation of his death on the cross. As was the case in 2:13-25, the second Passover

depicts himself as the source of "living water" (John 7:38), that is, the Spirit that God has promised to pour forth.[68] This image of living water, coming as it does on the Feast of Tabernacles, reflects the water that flowed forth from the temple precincts during that feast—an event that received an eschatological inflection in the prophecy of Ezekiel. Paul Hoskins has shown that for John, "Jesus is the true Temple and the fulfillment of the Old Testament feasts," in the sense that "the Temple and Old Testament feasts anticipate and reach their fullness through the blessings that Jesus brings."[69]

Hoskins suggests that although the emphasis in John 19 is on Jesus as the Passover lamb and as "the fulfillment of Passover," we can also perceive that "his fulfillment of the Temple lies close at hand (2:19-22). If the proper place to sacrifice and eat the Passover lamb is the Temple (Deut 16:2-7), then the sacrifice of Jesus as the Passover lamb could indicate that

---

in the Fourth Gospel is linked with Jesus' death, but it adds to the impression created by 1:29 that Jesus will fulfill the Passover as a sacrificial victim. As is the case with the flesh and blood of the Passover lamb, the flesh and blood of Jesus are both essential elements for participating in this new Passover" (Hoskins, *Jesus as the Fulfillment*, 177).

68. For discussion see Chanikuzhy, *Jesus, the Eschatological Temple*, 332-71. As Chanikuzhy notes, "The rituals of the feast of Tabernacles are well attested to and interpreted in the Mishnah.... The Tosephta (*t. Sukk.* 3,3-9) interprets the water ceremony of Tabernacles as a symbolic anticipation of the eschatological outpouring of living water. It also explains why the south gate is named the Water Gate: because the eschatological outpouring of water from underneath the temple will flow through the south gate. Besides, it identifies the eschatological outpouring of water in Ex 47, 2.5.9.12 with the eschatological rivers of living water in Zch 14,8" (Chanikuzhy, *Jesus, the Eschatological Temple*, 335-36). Addressing the question of whether in John 7:38 Jesus is the source of the living water, Chanikuzhy concludes: "Both the ideas of Jesus and the believer becoming a source seem to be present in the FG [Fourth Gospel]. However, since the living waters are identified with the Holy Spirit, Jesus is the giver of the Holy Spirit (15,26; 16,7; 19,30; 20,22) and since water flows from the side of Jesus (19,34) and from the throne of the Lamb (Ap 22,1), we have to agree that in 7,38 Jesus is to be understood as the source of the living water" (Chanikuzhy, *Jesus, the Eschatological Temple*, 354).

69. Hoskins, *Jesus as the Fulfillment*, 203. Hoskins sums up his perspective: "According to the Fourth Gospel, Christ is the true Temple, the dwelling place of God in the midst of his people. Those who are with him during his ministry witness God dwelling among them (John 1:14). His death/resurrection/exaltation makes it possible for his disciples to continue to experience God dwelling among them, because it results in the gift of the Spirit. The Spirit enables his disciples to experience union with Jesus and the Father. This union will come to fruition when they eventually go to dwell with Jesus where he is (14:3). These points anticipate the Temple typology found in Paul and Revelation. When Paul calls the church the Temple of God, he is focusing upon the church as the current, already abundant realization of God's promise to dwell among his people. God dwells in this Temple through the Spirit. The entire Temple is 'in Christ,' that is, in union with Christ. Then, in the book of Revelation, one finds the consummation of God's promise to dwell among his people" (Hoskins, *Jesus as the Fulfillment*, 201).

he is also the true Temple, the designated place of sacrifice."⁷⁰ In accord with Jesus' status as the perfect Passover sacrifice in whom the work of the temple is fulfilled, John the Baptist twice speaks of him as "the Lamb of God, who takes away the sins of the world" (John 1:29). Even the flowing forth of blood and water from the pierced side of Jesus on the cross is a temple image. Mary Coloe points out in this regard: "In Jesus' death, the 'inner chamber' of his body/Temple is opened, releasing the waters of the Spirit. One Temple [Jesus' body] is in the process of being destroyed, even as a new Temple [Jesus' body] is being raised."⁷¹ The enduring Spirit-filled body of Christ will, as the new Temple, "be an ongoing source within the world of life-giving waters (John 4:14, 7:38) and cleansing from sin (John 20:23)."⁷²

Focusing on the Gospel of Mark, Timothy Gray has argued that "the Last Supper and the trial narrative take up the theme of temple replacement. By paralleling the preparations for Jesus' entry into the temple and the preparations for the Last Supper, Mark puts forward Jesus' offering of his body and blood—the elements of the Passover meal—as an alternative to the temple cult."⁷³ Scholars debate whether Mark wrote his Gospel before or immediately after the destruction of the Temple in 70 AD, with most scholars holding that it was written in the midst of the crisis but before the destruction of the temple.⁷⁴ Unlike Gray, Regev maintains that Jesus' reference in the Gospel of Mark to "the desolating sacrilege set up where it ought not to be" (Mark 13:14; cf. Dan 11:31) indicates a high view of the temple and leaves open the future of the temple. According to Regev, Jesus in Mark 13 intends to describe the destruction of Jerusalem and the desecration of the temple, rather than the destruction of the temple. Asking whether Mark's Jesus has in view the eschatological "beginning of a new Temple-less age, in which the community replaces the destroyed Temple," Regev answers that the Danielic context of the "desolating sacrilege" should

---

70. Hoskins, *Jesus as the Fulfillment*, 178–79.

71. Coloe, *God Dwells with Us*, 207.

72. Coloe, *God Dwells with Us*, 207. With regard to the pierced side, she adds: "Ezekiel's description of the altar in the Temple also refers to a gutter cavity around the altar in which the water and blood flow down to be drained. The term for this gutter is קיח (Ezek 43:13). This is an unusual architectural term and seems to have developed from an analogy with the human body where it usually means 'lap' or 'bosom.' A writer familiar with the Jerusalem Temple and its altar, who has already brought together architecture and anatomy, in speaking of Jesus' body as the Temple (2:21), may here be further exploiting the rich symbolism of Jewish sacrifice. Christians need no longer look to the blood and water in the קיח (cavity) of a pierced altar, for the blood and water have now been released from the side (πλευρά) of Jesus" (*God Dwells with Us*, 207).

73. T. C. Gray, *Temple in Mark*, 197.

74. See Regev, *Temple in Early Christianity*, 116–17.

help us to recognize that "Mark protests the desecration of the Temple and shows concern for the sacredness of the cult."[75]

I think it is unnecessary to suppose that showing concern for the temple's sacredness stands in opposition to envisioning the temple as fulfilled by Jesus or as Messianically reconfigured so that Jesus Christ is now the true temple, just as Gray holds. In my view, for Mark as for John, Jesus fulfills the temple and the animal sacrifices by embodying perfect sacrificial worship, manifesting the divine glory (supreme love), and establishing the divine justice and mercy. Joel Marcus puts it well when he states that for Mark, Christ's resurrection constitutes "the creation of a new Temple composed of the resurrected Lord in union with his eschatological community of 'others.'"[76]

Regev presses further, asking why, if Mark "wishes to promote the idea of the Christian community as the new Temple," Mark pays so much attention to Jesus' careful observance of the Jewish rite of Passover.[77] It would seem that if Jesus had wanted to replace the Passover ritual, he should have just come out and done it at the Last Supper. In my view, however, to understand the Last Supper we must differentiate between a replacement that is a negation and a replacement that is a fulfillment. The temple and its cult are not negated, because they are oriented toward the reality that fulfills them—Jesus Christ and the community's eucharistic sharing in Christ's perfect sacrifice.[78] Although Christ and his community (as his "body") are indeed the new temple—and in this sense are a "replacement"—the new temple worship that Christ establishes is one that fulfills rather than negates

---

75. Regev, *Temple in Early Christianity*, 120. For the same position see Duran, "'Not One Stone.'" She holds that "the gospel does not see the temple's destruction as paving the way for Jesus's own brand of salvation, but grieves the event, even as it grieves the crucifixion" (Duran, "'Not One Stone,'" 311). In my view, it grieves the temple's destruction (as does Jesus), but this need not be set in opposition with the messianic fulfillment and reconfiguration of the temple in Jesus Christ. Duran goes on to report "the more troubling idea, expressed by N. T. Wright and others, that the historical Jesus sought to lessen people's hold on the physical temple, so as to replace it with a spiritual one. Perhaps more troubling still, the place of the physical temple in this reading is also the place of the sacrificial system that it housed. Jesus's death in this reading becomes a sacrifice that replaces—or supersedes—temple sacrifice" (Duran, "'Not One Stone,'" 315). I think Jesus' saving death certainly does do this, though not in the sense of a negation. To my mind, the Gospels share in Paul's confession of "the redemption which is in Christ Jesus, whom God put forward as an expiation by his blood, to be received by faith" (Rom 3:24-25).

76. Marcus, *Way of the Lord*, 123.

77. Regev, *Temple in Early Christianity*, 121.

78. See Pitre, *Jesus and the Last Supper*. See also S. C. Smith, *House of the Lord*; as well as Congar, *Mystery of the Temple*.

the temple and its cult. Christ does this "in order to fill the earth with God's temple presence."[79]

In this sense, Gray's portrait of an "alternative temple cult" is fully on target. At the same time, I agree with Regev that neither Mark nor Mark's Jesus has "an anti-Temple stance."[80] For Regev, this means that "Mark and his readers are not ready for Jewish life without the Temple"[81]; whereas I think that Mark understood himself to be living in the fulfilled temple in Christ.[82] Regev cautions against taking "the concept of community as a Temple from Paul" and attributing it to Mark's Gospel.[83] He argues that it is significant that the accusers of Jesus who are bearing "false witness" are the ones who report: "We heard him say, 'I will destroy this temple that is made with hands, and in three days I will build another, not made with hands'" (Mark 14:58). According to Regev, Mark put these words into the mouth of the false witnesses in order not only to reject the notion that Jesus

---

79. S. C. Smith, *House of the Lord*, 240. See also Smith's discussion of the prophecy of Zechariah regarding the Messiah and the forgiveness of sins, in *House of the Lord*, 230–35. Summing up the overall vision of the prophets, Smith underscores that the fulfillment anticipated by the prophets has Edenic overtones: "A sanctified Jerusalem and a restored Temple would draw all to it, and to God. A wave of holiness would radiate over the earth. The coming of God's messiah would be nothing less than a renewal of Paradise" (*House of the Lord*, 240).

80. Regev, *Temple in Early Christianity*, 124.

81. Regev, *Temple in Early Christianity*, 124. Regev states, "Mark associates Jesus with the Temple when he repeats several times that Jesus acts and teaches at the Temple.... The reason Mark ties Jesus to the Temple in these various ways is not a polemic against the Temple and the sacrificial cult, but, on the contrary, an attempt to associate Jesus with the Temple" (*Temple in Early Christianity*, 125–26). I agree that no polemic against the Temple per se is intended, but I hold that the primary purpose of the association of Jesus with the Temple is to show how he fulfills the Temple and its sacrifices and thus how he is the eschatological temple. For Regev, "The context of Jesus's partaking of the Passover sacrifice reveals that Mark does not perceive any tension between consuming Jesus's flesh and blood and the nature of the sacrificial cult. The Last Supper is complementary to the traditional sacrifices and actually builds upon it" (*Temple in Early Christianity*, 121). Again, this is accurate, but Jesus' bringing the temple and its sacrifices to fulfillment (as the eschatological Messiah) still needs to be accounted for.

82. Writing for a contemporary Christian audience that includes "proponents of a literal third temple," Daniel Hays emphasizes: "Perhaps even more troublesome in taking Ezekiel 40–48 literally is that one would be reestablishing the Levitical blood-sacrifice system. The New Testament is not ambiguous about this: the Levitical sacrificial system has been totally and completely abrogated and abolished by the once-and-for-all sacrifice of Jesus Christ" (J. D. Hays, *Temple and the Tabernacle*, 182). Indeed, the abrogation of the temple sacrifices is clear in the Letter to the Hebrews, and this fits with the tenor of the New Testament as a whole—although the apostles are glad to proclaim the gospel in the temple. The gospel of Jesus means that atonement has been accomplished (and will be shared in) through the eschatological temple that is Christ's body.

83. Regev, *Temple in Early Christianity*, 123.

sought to destroy the temple in Jerusalem, but also to call into question the notion of a temple "not made with hands."[84] But I do not think that Mark is questioning the latter notion. In Mark's Gospel, Jesus is in fact the temple not made by human hands, and Jesus prophesies the coming destruction of the Jerusalem temple.[85]

Thus, I hold that what we find in Mark—Jesus as the eschatological Son of Man who offers himself as the perfect sacrifice for sins and whose death tears the temple veil, thereby making available the divine glory to the whole world[86]—is the same reality that undergirds Paul's understanding of the eschatological temple in Christ. When Paul proclaims that "Christ, our paschal Lamb, has been sacrificed," and when he goes on to urge Christians to "celebrate the festival" in Christlike "sincerity and truth" (1 Cor 5:7-8), Paul's statements are in accord with the words of the one who "came . . . to give his life as a ransom for many" (Mark 10:45). Paul is urging the moral purification of believers, whom he has earlier described as "God's temple" due to the indwelling of the Holy Spirit (1 Cor 3:16).[87] As Fitzmyer remarks, this description "does not imply any antagonism for the Jerusalem Temple," although neither is the Jerusalem temple needed, since Christians are "God's very dwelling place."[88]

The Letter to the Hebrews

The Letter to the Hebrews portrays Christ entering the heavenly tabernacle and accomplishing, once and for all, the purpose of the temple sacrifices. But this does not entail a negative view toward the temple in Jerusalem. On the contrary, as Benjamin Ribbens has shown, the author of Hebrews has a "positive view of levitical sacrifices" and affirms their "principle that

---

84. See Regev, *Temple in Early Christianity*, 122-23.

85. Regev agrees with the latter point.

86. Theologically, my position on the tearing of the temple curtain accords with Sylva, "Temple Curtain and Jesus' Death," but I am aware of the extensive exegetical debate on this topic.

87. See Fitzmyer, *First Corinthians*, 241-42. Fitzmyer draws especially upon Howard, "'Christ Our Passover.'"

88. Fitzmyer, *First Corinthians*, 202. He adds with regard to 1 Corinthians 3:17 ("For God's temple is holy, and that temple you are"): "Paul predicates of the Corinthian community the adjective *hagios*, a description often used in the OT to convey the character of persons or objects set apart for or dedicated to the service of God in the Jerusalem Temple. In fact, *hagion* is sometimes predicated of the Temple (Ps 11:4; 65:5; 79:1) and *to hagion* is used as the name for 'the temple' itself (LXX Num 3:38; Ezek 45:18). What was true of the sanctity of the Jerusalem Temple must be true also of the Corinthian community" (*First Corinthians*, 203).

the forgiveness of sins is dependent on the blood of sacrifice."[89] At the same time, Hebrews understands "Christ's sacrifice as not only validating the levitical sacrifices but also bringing them to an end (7:18; 8:13; 10:9, 18)"—a tension flowing from Hebrews's "eschatological and covenantal perspective" according to which the temple sacrifices are "anticipatory, prophetic, [and] pedagogical" vis-à-vis the sacrifice of Christ.[90]

Regev recognizes that Hebrews values the actual temple and its sacrifices, and in this respect he sees Hebrews as a clarification and enhancement of Paul's explanations. According to Regev, Hebrews views "Christ as a continuation and development of the priestly Law" and builds "on both the themes of high priesthood and atonement sacrifices which purify sin," as befits an author who "is highly attached to priestly ideas and the sacrificial cult."[91] I note that Hebrews teaches that Christ, the "high priest," sealed the new covenant by his own blood; Christ "entered once for all into the Holy Place, taking not the blood of goats and calves but his own blood, thus securing an eternal redemption" (Heb 9:11–12). Hebrews drives this point home: "For if the sprinkling of defiled persons with the blood of goats and bulls and with the ashes of a heifer sanctifies for the purification of the flesh, how much more shall the blood of Christ, who through the eternal Spirit offered himself without blemish to God, purify your conscience from dead works to serve the living God"? (Heb 9:13–14). Christ's sacrifice, unlike the

---

89. Ribbens, *Levitical Sacrifice*, 238–39.

90. Ribbens, *Levitical Sacrifice*, 238.

91. Regev, *Temple in Early Christianity*, 281. He concludes that the purpose of Hebrews was to show that *"Christianity is the direct successor of the sacrificial cult, not its suppressor.* The logic of sacrifice leads to the logic of Christ saving others from sin. If this interpretation is accepted, then Hebrews, being written after 70, does not reject the Temple cult but rather extends it into new realms led by an author devoted to the priestly tradition who nevertheless believes that a second, better phase awaits it" (*Temple in Early Christianity*, 283–84). By contrast, for criticism of Hebrews for its "anti-Judaism"—its fostering of "the view that Judaism was an inferior religion, a temporary guide prior to Christ"—see Pamela Eisenbaum's introduction and annotations to Hebrews in Levine and Brettler, *Jewish Annotated New Testament*, 406–26, at 407. See also Ribbens's point that "the heavenly cult in Second Temple Judaism always validates the earthly cult.... [W]hile the heavenly cult could critique improper worship, it did not diminish the earthly, levitical cult; rather, the heavenly cult served to legitimize its earthly counterpart. The early worship that coordinated with the heavenly worship—i.e., the worship that was properly performed—was pleasing to God and efficacious" (Ribbens, *Levitical Sacrifice*, 137). Ribbens here is arguing that the Levitical sacrifices were efficacious in doing what God promised they would do because they participated (along sacramental lines) in "the heavenly sacrifice, the sacrifice of Christ": in other words, the Levitical sacrifices were *"external rituals sacramentally signifying an atoning efficacy that was achieved later by Christ and applied proleptically to levitical sacrifices"* (*Levitical Sacrifice*, 138).

daily sacrifice of the temple priests, never needs be repeated and suffices for the purification of all sinners (see Heb 10:10-14).[92]

Summary: The Messianic Temple

For Christians, therefore, the temple and its sacrifices remain important, but now as fulfilled and reconfigured by Jesus Christ. Paul fought against anything that implies that Christian believers are required for salvation to observe Torah (inclusive of the temple sacrifices), but he and other early Christian leaders continued to understand themselves as faithful Jews, although now as Jews whose Messiah has come. As faithful Jews, the Jerusalem temple was their place.[93] Their understanding of messianic fulfillment involved reconfiguring Israel in crucial ways, including the fact that the temple's animal sacrifices are no longer needed. This reconfiguration is seen as the eschatological perfecting of the temple and its sacrifices, rather than as a negation. Even the fact that the temple's animal sacrifices come to an end, as Hebrews presupposes, does not entail a negative view of the temple

---

92. In Regev's view, "Hebrews' brilliant and innovative linkage of Christology with the sacrificial cult, however, is not easily reconciled with the theology of the cross. When Hebrews pictures Christ's offering as a sacrifice in heaven (9:25-28), it somewhat marginalizes the meaning of his death on the cross as the symbolic image of the belief in Christ (1 Cor 1:23; 6:12-14). Jesus' death on the cross, including the shedding of his blood there (Col 1:20), is no longer the occasion of his sacrificing himself for the sake of others (Col 2:14) but merely the locus of Jesus's prayers and supplications (5:7), where the process of exaltation and sacrifice only begins. Furthermore, while many NT passages regard Jesus's ascension to heaven as a consequence of his sacrificial death ('for us') on the cross, Hebrews reverses the sequence. His death on earth grants him his exaltation in heaven, and only then does he also offer himself and his blood as a sacrifice in heaven" (*Temple in Early Christianity*, 281-82). I think that this overstates the temporal differentiation: the two levels of the action, Christ's earthly sacrifice and his heavenly sacrifice, are related spiritually rather than temporally (even if one can certainly say, as Ribbens does, that "the sacrificial process began on earth and concluded in heaven," since the reconciliation of heaven and earth is the whole point [*Levitical Sacrifice*, 139]). Ribbens's work on Hebrews's participatory ontology is important here.

93. Regev argues that "even if Christ atones for one's sins, the Temple is not necessarily superfluous. A Jew who believes in Jesus may nevertheless feel the need to visit the Temple and offer sacrifices to fulfill other aspects of cultic worship. It is also not inconceivable that some people would prefer to pursue multiple means of atonement at one and the same time" (*Temple in Early Christianity*, 5). The latter approach certainly is not "inconceivable"; indeed Paul warns sharply in Galatians and elsewhere against just such an approach. Christ's atoning cross fulfills all "aspects of cultic worship." Paul is clear that visiting the temple and participating in certain ways in its cult is appropriate for a Jew who is Christian. The problem would come only if Jewish believers in Christ supposed that his atoning sacrifice was not superabundantly sufficient for atonement and salvation.

sacrifices but rather underscores that the animal sacrifices were always open to fulfillment and reconfiguration by Israel's Messiah.[94]

In *The Temple in Early Christianity*, Regev comments: "It is commonly argued that there are at least four ways in which the Temple is superseded in the NT texts: the church is the new Temple, the individual believer is the Temple, the Temple is in heaven, and the Temple is Jesus's body. Some commentators even assume that . . . the Historical Jesus already regarded himself or the church as the new Temple."[95] I count myself among those commentators. Yet, Regev and I agree that the New Testament authors intended "to create a *continuation* of contemporary Jewish ideas relating to the Temple."[96] The temple is not "external or remote" to the worldview of the early Christians.[97] Rather, the early Christians were Jews—Jews who believed that Jesus was the Messiah of Israel. Regev rightly emphasizes that "early Christian authors draw heavily on the Temple as a major Jewish institution as well as on the concepts of the Temple and the sacrificial cult. They do so while minimally discrediting the legitimacy of the Jerusalem Temple and the sacrifices, even as they propose alternatives after its destruction."[98]

---

94. Regev's remarks are instructive: "Hebrews is the only NT text that sets out a clear, systematic alternative to the Temple; it is only in Hebrews that Christ takes the place of the high priest and the Temple cult. Yet its driving force is *not* a belief in the Temple's irrelevance or profanity. To the contrary, the Temple and the high priest are necessary to an explanation of Christ's role and purpose. Assuming that the epistle was written when the Temple was already in ruins, we might say that Hebrews carries on the priestly tradition in a new way—one, we should note, that hews much closer to the original than do many Jewish substitutions, such as prayer or Torah study" (Regev, *Temple in Early Christianity*, 290). See also, for a similar emphasis on continuity/fulfillment, my "Blood, Death, and Sacrifice."

95. Regev, *Temple in Early Christianity*, 3. As examples, Regev points to Wardle, *Jerusalem Temple*; Fassbeck, *Der Tempel der Christen*; Beale, *Temple and the Church's Mission*. Many more could be named. For Regev, "The Historical Jesus is certainly interested in the Temple, but only when he arrives in Jerusalem" (*Temple in Early Christianity*, 285)—a perspective that strikes me as a misunderstanding.

96. Regev, *Temple in Early Christianity*, 314.

97. Regev, *Temple in Early Christianity*, 314.

98. Regev, *Temple in Early Christianity*, 315. For example, Regev argues that "Matthew takes as its aim the enhancement of Temple practices and sensibilities after 70. For him, the Temple holds important symbolic value, which he in turn uses to reinforce Christianity's Jewish origins" (*Temple in Early Christianity*, 287). Regev contends against those who imagine that in Jesus' day the Temple was less important (due to priestly corruption and to the development of synagogues): "If the Temple had become less important, why do Paul, 1 Peter, Hebrews, and Revelation build so heavily upon it as a concept in order to convince their readers that their new ideas about Christ cohere with or continue old cultic conceptions?" (*Temple in Early Christianity*, 316). For analysis of temple-fulfillment imagery (the Church as the true temple) in 1 Peter, see Macaskill, *Union with Christ*, 159–62. Macaskill shows that 1 Peter 2:5 conveys "the

In sum, the temple was a highly important place for the first Christians. They believed that the temple had been fulfilled and reconfigured in Christ; but fulfillment, as such, is incomprehensible without love of God's temple in Jerusalem. Just as Regev says, therefore, the temple "fosters new avenues of thinking about Christ, his authority, closeness to God, and sacredness, while at the same time these ideas are expressed within a Jewish matrix."[99] The New Testament does not offer a replacement theology of the temple if by this is meant a negation of one thing to make way for an entirely discontinuous thing. The temple in Jerusalem prepares for and is always (even now) interiorly related to the eschatological temple established by the Messiah. In this sense, Regev is correct when he remarks about the New Testament authors: "They neither want the Temple to disappear nor do they want to replace it; rather, they want to recreate the Temple and its cult in a new and symbolic manner."[100]

III. Contemporary Jewish and Catholic Critiques of the Temple's Animal Sacrifices

Jewish Perspectives: Guy Stroumsa and Jonathan Sacks

Unfortunately, this highly positive view of the temple and its sacrifices—even if now fulfilled by Christ—is not widely shared in modern scholarship. For example, the Jewish scholar Guy Stroumsa, an expert in comparative religion, has recently investigated the epochal shift in Roman attitudes toward sacrifice that took place in the first centuries after Christ. As Stroumsa remarks, pagan philosophers in this period disagreed with each other about

---

activity of the Spirit in constituting the new temple and the holy priesthood within it," and he adds that for 1 Peter "this new temple, while itself the fulfilment of prophetic expectation, is also but the partial realization of a hope still to be brought to consummation" (*Union with Christ*, 162).

99. Regev, *Temple in Early Christianity*, 315. Or as Regev goes on to observe: "The Temple and the sacrificial cult are a symbolic field with ample meaning for the early Christians, and with substantive polishing and reshaping it makes sense of their new, radical belief in Jesus.... [T]he narratives, imagery, and ideas of the NT authors attest to the richness of the Temple as an institution and as an inspiring symbol. When Paul and the authors of the gospel of John, Revelation, and Hebrews need to explain who or what Christ is, to formulate new and radical Christologies, and to make them comprehensible to audiences who have at least some knowledge of the Hebrew/Greek Bible, they turn to the Temple and the sacrificial cult" (*Temple in Early Christianity*, 316).

100. Regev, *Temple in Early Christianity*, 317.

the value of sacrifices. Lucian of Samosata and Porphyry denounced animal sacrifices, whereas Iamblichus supported animal sacrifices, if only on the (rather tepid) grounds that non-philosophers need a bodily cult. In the mid-fourth century, Emperor Julian (the Apostate) sought to reinstate both pagan and Jewish animal sacrifices. He was influenced by his teacher Sallustius, who affirmed animal sacrifices on the grounds that they "represent our own lives, which we are symbolically offering. And prayers detached from sacrifices are worth nothing, because they are nothing but words, whereas if pronounced during sacrifices, they become animated words."[101] As it turned out, however, Julian and Sallustius were the last serious proponents of the cult of sacrificial animals in the Roman world.[102]

Stroumsa argues that this transformative cultural movement away from animal sacrifice would not have happened without the destruction of the temple in Jerusalem in 70 AD. In his view, the temple's destruction was a good thing for the Jewish people, at least with regard to freeing them from animal sacrifice. He states boldly: "The Jews should no doubt pay thanks to Titus, whose memory they hold in contempt, for having destroyed their temple for the second time, for imposing on them the need to free themselves from sacrifice and its ritual violence, before any other society."[103]

Stroumsa is well aware, of course, that "sacrifice" retains a place in the two religions that emerged from the destruction of the temple, namely, Rabbinic Judaism and Christianity. But repeated bloody sacrifices no longer have a cultic function, and for Stroumsa this is a very good thing. He argues that it contributed in a highly positive way to "the democratization and spatial explosion of Jewish worship" due to the end of the priestly caste and of the unique sacred space in Jerusalem.[104] Although prayers for the rebuilding of the temple never ceased, he notes that some rabbinic sages made clear that "the study of Torah, the *Talmud Torah*, has replaced sacrifices."[105] He

---

101. Stroumsa, *End of Sacrifice*, 62.

102. In part, this was because of an intense campaign of persecution and destruction (of shrines) that Christians unleashed after Julian's early death. On this topic, see Kirsch, *God against the Gods*.

103. Stroumsa, *End of Sacrifice*, 63.

104. Stroumsa, *End of Sacrifice*, 63–65. Stroumsa explains further: "The rabbis are teachers, but they are not priests and have no liturgical role. A group of ten adult men may constitute a community and may without any other condition celebrate public worship. God, who has lost his palace, his own habitation, now 'stays with the locals,' as it were. The divine presence, the *shekhina* (from the root *shakhan*, to inhabit) whose specific place had been in the Temple, is now found (according to a well-known midrash) in 'the four cubits of the *halakha* alone'" (*End of Sacrifice*, 65). In Stroumsa's view, this shift represents "a privatization of [Jewish] religion" (*End of Sacrifice*, 66).

105. Stroumsa, *End of Sacrifice*, 67. For Stroumsa, "the study of the Torah represents

also cites the liturgical prayers that replaced the temple sacrifices, as well as certain notable rabbinic texts that suggest that prayer and fasting equal or supersede sacrifice in terms of their value in God's sight.

Stroumsa admits that the rabbis deeply mourned the loss of the temple. He quotes Rabbi Eleazar, who lived in the third century, to the effect that the Second Temple's destruction created a "barrier of separation" between Israel and God.[106] According to Rabbi Eleazar, this "separation" means that Israel can no longer expect its prayers to be answered. The Divine Presence is no longer there to protect Israel, although the Divine Presence can be invoked. But the lesson that Stroumsa draws is not the one intended by Rabbi Eleazar. Stroumsa argues that what is visible in Rabbi Eleazar's mourning is the invention of the interior religious landscape of modernity. He contends: "Thus it is a religion of alienation, of the absence of God, that was invented by the sages of Israel after the end of sacrifices."[107]

For Stroumsa, religious modernity has certain characteristic marks. These include a sense of God's absence, an overall emphasis on individual interiority, and a particular emphasis on sincerity of intention. Whereas the temple sacrifices had objective power, now "prayer, fasting, and charity"—replacing the animal sacrifices—"are all practiced in silence and in secret, and also without any certainty of recompense."[108] On this basis, Stroumsa also links the rise of Jewish mysticism to the end of the temple sacrifices.[109]

Jewish acceptance of the Greek value of the *scholē*" (*End of Sacrifice*, 67). Stroumsa directs attention to Michael I. Satlow's argument that the study of Torah replaced sacrifice for the rabbis: Satlow, "'And on the Earth You Shall Sleep.'" Stroumsa adds that "[t]he rabbis had succeeded in constructing a system in which individual daily praxis—the closed network of behavior according to the law, *halakhah*, and also, for the elites, hermeneutic reflection—has replaced the order of sacrifices. This transformation stressed the *story* of sacrifice, whose reactivated memory has now been invested with a new power. Ritual was transformed into the story of ritual" (*End of Sacrifice*, 67).

106. Babylonian Talmud, *Berakoth*, 32b, cited in Stroumsa, *End of Sacrifice*, 68. Stroumsa refers here to Bokser, "Wall Separating God and Israel."

107. Stroumsa, *End of Sacrifice*, 69.

108. Stroumsa, *End of Sacrifice*, 69. Stroumsa grants that the prophets likewise emphasized interior sincerity, but he thinks that the rabbis accentuated it still further.

109. He notes that Rachel Elior traces it a bit farther back, to the "Zadokite priests excluded from worship by the Hasmonaean usurpers in the second decade of the second century BCE" (Stroumsa, *End of Sacrifice*, 70). See Elior, *Three Temples*. Regarding Christianity, Stroumsa suggests that it retains a strong emphasis on sacrifice, both in the development of the liturgical cult (priests liturgically reenacting Christ's sacrifice in a perpetual cultic service), and in the glorification of martyrdom. He states, "The martyrs and virgins no longer bring the sacrifice—they *are* the sacrifice. In effect, Christianity offers to every man and woman the possibility of becoming the sacrifice" (*End of Sacrifice*, 77). He connects this with Islamist suicide bombers! Nonetheless he grants, "The repulsion proclaimed by Christians for sacrifices in general, and their horror at human

For Stroumsa, this interiorizing of Jewish religiosity was a major religious and cultural breakthrough, one that made it possible to live without the superstitions and cultic animal slaughter of the ancient world.

From a quite different perspective, Rabbi Jonathan Sacks arrives at the same conclusion that the destruction of the temple produced a very good result. Sacks observes that Jeremiah 7:22—"For in the day that I brought them out of the land of Egypt, I did not speak to your fathers or command them concerning burnt offerings or sacrifices"—posed a serious difficulty to rabbinic commentators, who generally found ways to interpret it against its plain sense. For example, Maimonides holds that what God is saying here is that the sacrifices were only a means to the goal of knowing God properly.[110] Because God did in fact command the Israelites to offer animal sacrifices (according to Exodus, Leviticus, and Deuteronomy), Maimonides takes the exegetical opportunity provided by Jeremiah 7:22 as a justification for proposing that the animal sacrifices were only temporary and were intended by God to cease once the Jewish people knew the true God more fully. Maimonides's idea is that although the Jewish people prior to the temple's destruction tended to conceive of the sacrifices as intrinsically necessary for relating to God, in fact the sacrifices never were so.

Sacks is sympathetic to Maimonides's position, but he notes that a few rabbinic commentators went even further. These rabbis found a way to fully embrace the plain sense of Jeremiah 7:22. Sacks names Rabbi Isaac ben Judah Abravanel (1437–1508) as an example.[111] Abravanel considers that God

---

sacrifices in particular, would play a significant role in the eradication of human sacrifices in the Mediterranean world" (*End of Sacrifice*, 73). He also notes that some church fathers—and later Maimonides (and some early modern thinkers as well)—supposed that "the sacrifices formerly offered in the Jerusalem Temple represented a concession permitted by God to a stiff-necked people, overly influenced by the practices of pagan peoples such as Egyptians, among whom they had long sojourned" (*End of Sacrifice*, 80). For his discussion of Christian sacrifice he relies upon anti-sacrificial studies, such as Daly, *Christian Sacrifice*; Theissen, *Theory of Primitive Christian Religion*, chapter 8; Heyman, *Power of Sacrifice*; Bowersock, *Martyrdom and Rome*. Bowersock draws a connection to Islam at the conclusion of his book: "With the ultimate exclusion of suicide . . . Christian martyrdom was deprived of its most militant, its most Roman feature. But ironically it was that feature that was conspicuously to survive in Islam, when the heirs of the prophet Muhammad ruled in the land where Jesus was crucified" (*Martyrdom and Rome*, 74).

110. Indebted to Maimonides, Thomas Aquinas holds that, while God has no need of sacrifices (see Isa 1:11), God "wished them to be offered to Him, in order to prevent idolatry—in order to signify the right ordering of man's mind to God—and in order to represent the mystery of the Redemption of man by Christ" (Thomas Aquinas, *Summa theologiae* I-II, q. 102, a. 3, ad 1).

111. For discussion of Abravanel's thought and life, see Borodowski, *Isaac Abravanel*; and Netanyahu, *Don Isaac Abravanel*. Borodowski reminds us that in the victory

in Jeremiah 7:22 is teaching that "[t]he entire sacrificial system was not part of the original divine intention" but was commanded only after the tragic episode of the golden calf.[112] According to Abravanel, had it not been for Israel's demonstrated proclivity toward idolatrous worship (Exod 32), God would never have instituted animal sacrifices. When Israel had finally been weaned from this proclivity, God brought animal sacrifices to an end by allowing the temple to be destroyed and not rebuilt.

In Sacks's view, Abravanel's interpretation is essentially accurate. God only gave the sacrificial system to Israel after the golden calf, as a way of enabling the Israelites to experience his divine closeness or presence, "but in such a way that they were not blinded by His light, deafened by His voice, overwhelmed by His infinity."[113] According to Sacks, since the destruction of the temple, this same purpose been fulfilled by "the synagogue, study, and prayer."[114] Now that the people of Israel have the latter practices as a mode of fulfilling the Torah's commandments about animal sacrifice, the animal sacrifices themselves are no longer needed and have been permanently displaced.

Discussing Rabbi Akiva's response to the destruction of the temple, Sacks contends that Rabbi Akiva brilliantly, under God's guidance, "turned one of the most tragic events in the history of Israel into a stunning disclosure of new spiritual possibility."[115] So long as the temple was in place, the people of Israel had recourse to the sacrificial system and the priesthood in order to obtain atonement for sins. The destruction of the temple allowed

---

of Isabella and Ferdinand's Spain over the Muslim kingdom of Granada in the 1480s, Abravanel played a crucial role due to his financial abilities and a personal loan that he gave to Isabella and Ferdinand. He rose in status, serving by 1491 as the financial advisor of the queen. Spain repaid his services by expelling all (non-Christian) Jews, including Abravanel, in 1492.

112. Sacks, *Leviticus*, 125. Joshua A. Berman comments that the view that "the command to erect the Tabernacle did not immediately follow the Revelation, but was issued only after the people sinned in the building of the Golden Calf" is a relatively common one in the rabbinic tradition and is linked with the supposition that "the Jewish people should have been prepared to worship God without physical representations of his presence" but were unable to do so (J. A. Berman, *Temple*, 217n18). As examples of this view, Berman cites "*Midrash Aggadah Terumah*, 27:1, *Shemot Rabbah* 33:3, *Tanchuma Terumah* 8, Seforno to Exodus 24:18, and Rabbeinu Bahya to Exodus 25, s.v. *ba-shamayim*" (J. A. Berman, *Temple*, 218n18). In the same endnote, Berman goes on to defend the need for the tabernacle and the temple, while differentiating them (at least for adherents of the above view) from the animal sacrifices. According to Berman, Exodus 32–35 shows the ongoing value of the temple and its sacrificial cult.

113. Sacks, *Leviticus*, 131.

114. Sacks, *Leviticus*, 131.

115. Sacks, *Leviticus*, 268.

the people to bypass priesthood and animal sacrifice. In this sense, the seeming calamity drew God closer to the people; no priestly intermediary was needed any longer. Each Jewish person can now become a high priest, and wherever Jews gather for prayer is now a temple. Sacks states approvingly, "Prayer took the place of sacrifice. Confession and remorse took the place of the scapegoat [Lev 16]. Instead of being connected to God through the words and deeds of the High Priest, each individual Jew now stood directly in the Divine Presence."[116]

For Sacks, this development was a wonderful change in the unfolding spiritual history of the Jewish people. He considers that Rabbi Akiva's position brings together the "priestly and prophetic traditions" in an "almost miraculous" manner, one that is profoundly salutary.[117] By offering a more direct path for observing the commandments regarding animal sacrifice, Rabbinic Jewish *teshuva* unites the priestly liturgical emphasis with the prophetic focus on interior righteousness. Sacks praises the forced (but providential) ending of the animal sacrifices as a great step forward for Judaism. He sums up, "Atonement was now not a sacrificial rite, but a turning—a *returning*—of the soul to God. This was always implicit in Judaism, but it took R. Akiva to see it and make it explicit. This is what he discovered: that all it takes for God to return to us is for us to return to God."[118]

In Rabbinic Judaism thus understood, interiority, appreciation for the priesthood of all believers, and a deeper awareness of God's presence have replaced the exterior and hierarchical system of animal sacrifice in the temple. The Romans sought to harm the Jewish people by destroying the temple, but in fact the Romans helped the Jewish people discover the already implicit deeper relationship into which God was calling them. On this view, the cessation of animal sacrifice was a spiritual leap forward into the fullness of Rabbinic Judaism. Along a similar path, though without intending to comment on the temple's destruction, Jon Levenson remarks that the prayers and practice of the Sabbath and the study of Torah offer a foretaste of "the eschatological temple," which is "the world-to-come.... The destruction of the Temple did not close the gates of heaven to those who walk the path of Sinai [Torah] up to the world of which Zion [the temple] is the symbol."[119]

---

116. Sacks, *Leviticus*, 286.
117. Sacks, *Leviticus*, 270.
118. Sacks, *Leviticus*, 271.
119. Levenson, *Sinai and Zion*, 184.

Catholic Perspectives: René Girard and Louis-Marie Chauvet

As will become clear, I think that Stroumsa and Sacks are overly negative toward the temple cult, even though I too am glad to avoid animal sacrifices. Here I note that just as Jewish thinkers have criticized the temple's bloody sacrifices and celebrated their cessation, so have Christian thinkers. Indeed, Christian thinkers have if anything done so more freely, given that Christians connect the destruction of the Jerusalem temple with the inauguration of the eschatological temple in Christ. Prior to the Second Vatican Council, however, Catholics affirmed the value of sacrifice per se, given that the liturgy of the Eucharist was seen as a sacrificial participation in Christ's saving sacrifice on the cross. Let me here set forth the positions of two influential postconciliar Catholic critics of sacrifice.

The great literary theorist René Girard rejects "the idea of Old Testament 'prefiguration' and christological 'fulfillment'" with regard to the temple's animal sacrifices.[120] Instead, for Girard, the two Testaments are united by a shared rejection of the scapegoat mechanism.[121] He holds that the sacrificial system of the temple—with its sin offerings, guilt offerings, peace offerings, burnt offerings, and so on—helped to "repress and moderate the kind of conflict that is inevitable with the working of mimetic desire."[122] Humans perpetually seek to murder a human scapegoat in order to "purify" the community, for psycho-social reasons that Girard describes.[123] Sacrifice of animals, therefore, is fundamentally a way to avoid the scapegoating and killing of humans. To this degree, Girard grants that the temple's animal

---

120. Girard, *I See Satan Fall*, 129.

121. For discussion of Girard's mimetic theory and his understanding of the scapegoat mechanism, see G. Kaplan, *René Girard, Unlikely Apologist*. See also the defense of Judaism and Christianity, partly in critical reply to Girard (and in favor of "the Christian end of sacrifice"), offered by Milbank, "Stories of Sacrifice," including his point that "scapegoating does not seem to be quite as widespread a phenomenon as Girard allows. Nor, when it occurs, does it always seem to be to do with the suppression of rivalry, but rather with the 'bearing away' of many different impurities, many of a simply ritual variety" (47; earlier quotation from 54).

122. Girard, *I See Satan Fall*, 90.

123. Girard comments, "Sacrificial rituals are scheduled just at the moment needed when there is a crisis to resolve, and for good reason. They are initially nothing other than the spontaneous resolution of all crises by means of unanimous violence, crises that occur unexpectedly in social existence. Not solely mimetic conflicts, there crises are birth and death, changes of season, famines, disasters of all kinds, and thousands of other things besides that, right or wrong, disturb the life of primitive peoples. Human communities constantly resort to sacrifice to try to ease their distress" (Girard, *I See Satan Fall*, 91).

sacrifices played a positive role, insofar as the sacrificial system prevented human scapegoating.

Various gruesome examples of human scapegoating appear in the Torah. For example, when the men of Ai gain victory over Joshua's army (after the entrance into the promised land), God is depicted as telling Joshua that the reason for this military defeat was that someone rebelled against the Lord's command to destroy all the "devoted things" (Josh 6:18). By lot, Joshua discovers the one man in the camp who has done this: Achan the son of Carmi. It is Achan, therefore, who has caused the entire people to be defeated in battle. Relief and restoration come when "all Israel stoned him with stones. . . . And they raised over him a great heap of stones that remains to this day; then the Lord turned from his burning anger" (Josh 7:26). This is the kind of scapegoating that Girard has in view. He argues that it is this kind of scapegoating that the animal sacrifices sought to defuse, as for instance when on the Day of Atonement, the entirety of Israel's sins were heaped upon the head of a goat, which was then sent "away into the wilderness" and which bore "all their iniquities upon him to a solitary land" (Lev 16:21–22).

According to Girard, Jesus Christ freely became the scapegoat—and was then raised and exalted by God—in order to show us the wickedness of the urge to scapegoat others. By placing himself in the position of the scapegoat, Christ reveals that it is the scapegoat, not the community that kills the scapegoat, who is vindicated and pure. Christ thereby stands athwart the cycle of scapegoating, the cycle of violence by which communities attempt to purify themselves through seizing upon scapegoats.[124] Once Christ has revealed the perversity of the scapegoat mechanism, the temple's system of animal sacrifices is not longer necessary.

For Girard, the people of Israel in the Old Testament were already moving in this direction through the prophets' insistence upon justice for God's poor and through the animal sacrifices that, at least, spared human victims. The prophetic insistence upon the vindication of God's poor reaches a high point in the figure of the suffering servant in the book of Isaiah. Girard states, "This death, the murder of the great prophet rejected by his people, is the equivalent of the Passion in the Gospels. As in the Gospels, the collective lynching of the prophet and the revelation of Yahweh make up one and the same event."[125]

---

124. For appreciative theological appropriations of Girard's viewpoint, see—among many others—Barron, *Priority of Christ*, 101–15; Alison, *Joy of Being Wrong*; and Heim, *Saved from Sacrifice*. More broadly, see Kirwan, *Girard and Theology*.

125. Girard, *I See Satan Fall*, 30.

I agree with Girard that scapegoating takes place in human communities. Moreover, Girard is surely correct that Jesus overcomes our fallen impulse to scapegoat, by showing us that God identifies with the scapegoat rather than with the murderous community. I would emphasize, however, that this is not all that Jesus' death accomplishes. In my view, Girard has neglected the positive work done by sacrifice. Christ's sacrifice *restores* justice; it does not simply display (God's) justice. Christ truly "atones" or "satisfies" for sin by shedding his blood on the cross in supreme love. By taking on sin's relational penalty of death (a penalty inscribed in the relational order of creation), Christ heals from within the interior wound of injustice and alienation from God that sinners possess. He does not merely reveal that crucifying innocent people (scapegoating) is wicked—though he does reveal this. What humans owe to God is our whole selves in love; and Christ offers to God all—and more—that God is justly owed by the entire human race, because he loves God supremely and hands over to God his bodily life as the incarnate Son, by contrast to Adam and Eve who sought to grasp immortality for themselves.

Likewise, insofar as the animal sacrifices of the temple are related to Christ's free sacrifice, the animal sacrifices are more than merely a way of displacing the scapegoating impulse. They offer a way of worshipping God that is indeed good. Although they do not rise to the level of Christ's free sacrifice out of love, still they represent the interior sacrifice of the person—his or her self-giving love toward God—and they embody the virtuous act of offering to God something that we possess, in gratitude for God's gifts to us. As Thomas Aquinas says, "sacrifice is a special act deserving of praise in that it is done out of reverence for God."[126]

Let me now turn to a second influential Catholic critique of sacrifice, that of the sacramental theologian Louis-Marie Chauvet. Chauvet raises some concerns with Girard's approach, but not in order to defend the temple sacrifices. Chauvet's concerns arise instead from his view that in this life, "the passage from sacrificial oldness to gospel newness, represented by the relation of the two testaments, a relation which itself expresses the difficult task of conversion that is incumbent upon every society and every human being, is never fully achieved."[127] He warns sharply against what he

---

126. Thomas Aquinas, *Summa theologiae* II-II, q. 85, a. 3. Note that Girard never claims that his theory accounts for everything. See also the criticisms of Girard found in my *Betrayal of Charity*, chapter 8. For a helpful defense of Girard, see Lusvardi, "Girard and the 'Sacrifice of the Mass.'" See also the valuable Thomistic reflections on sacrifice by Bonino, "Le sacerdoce comme"; and Hütter, *Bound for Beatitude*, chapter 6 (titled "The Preparation for Beatitude: Justice toward God—The Virtue of Religion").

127. Chauvet, *Symbol and Sacrament*, 307–8.

perceives to be the Church's sad reversion to "sacrificial oldness." In his view, such a declension happened to the Catholic Church beginning in the fourth century, with the rise of a cultic priesthood and a sacrificial Eucharist. He comments: "the Church, which is under the anti-sacrificial law of the Spirit, is always in danger of sliding back toward the sacrificial, that is, of again subjecting both God and humankind to its own very 'worthy cause' through a closed dogmatic system, either moral or ritualistic."[128] One can see here the old Protestant critique of Jewish and Catholic legalism.

For Chauvet, the Temple's thank-offerings (or "sacrifice of praise") alone constitute the basis for an acceptable theology of (unbloody) sacrifice, through which expiatory or reconciliatory sacrifices can be understood and relativized. Praise, rooted in grateful response to the divine gifting, is true reconciliation. Since this is so, he holds that it is not necessary to reject the temple sacrifices tout court. But these sacrifices must undergo an anti-sacrificial conversion in our understanding. Chauvet explains that the "*anti-sacrificial*" is "not the negation of the sacrificial or of a part of it (its dimension of reconciliation), but *the task to convert all the sacrificial to the gospel in order to live it, not in a servile, but in a filial (and hence brotherly and sisterly) manner.*"[129] All cultic elements that have not been "convert[ed] . . . to the gospel" are here strenuously avoided and ritual is found to be valuable only when fully reducible to (prophetic) ethics.[130] Chauvet holds that "the ethical practice of reconciliation between human beings . . . constitutes the premier place of *our* 'sacrifice.' That is what the anti-sacrifice of the Eucharist shows us and enjoins us to do."[131] The notion of sacrifice, as grounded in the temple's animal sacrifices (at least the vast majority of them), has here been dismissed as misleading and irrelevant for Catholics.

As should be clear, I cannot agree with this perspective. The temple sacrifices, and cultic sacrifice per se, are far richer than Chauvet supposes. In justice, humans owe a debt of worship to the Creator; and human sins wound the relational order of justice and require, from the human side, a renewed gift of what is due to God. Cultic sacrifice serves to represent such

---

128. Chauvet, *Symbol and Sacrament*, 308.

129. Chauvet, *Symbol and Sacrament*, 311.

130. Chauvet, *Symbol and Sacrament*, 311.

131. Chauvet, *Symbol and Sacrament*, 311. See also Daly, *Sacrifice Unveiled*; and Kilmartin, *Eucharist in the West*. For a response to the perspective of Kilmartin and Daly (among others), see Pomplun, "Post-Tridentine Sacramental Theology." For background, see the Introduction to my *Sacrifice and Community*. See also Milbank's challenge in "Stories of Sacrifice" to such construals of ethics, untethered as they are to any rich account of political community; and the response to Milbank, pushing back in certain ways, by Hedley, "For God's Sake."

self-offering, in the service of thanksgiving, atonement for sin, and resumption of communion—although the sufficient offering (which is the lodestar of all sacrifice) is found only in the self-offering in supreme love by the sinless Christ.

IV. Jonathan Klawans's Defense of the Temple and Its Sacrifices

The Jewish biblical scholar Jonathan Klawans has sharply challenged the paths taken by the above critiques of the temple sacrifices. Given my own serious concerns about the above critiques, I will survey his challenge here. With him, I wish to insist upon the value of the temple sacrifices. My perspective differs from his, both insofar as I am a Christian and with respect to some aspects of his interpretation of New Testament texts. Klawans will help me to define with more precision the kind of cultic "supersessionism" that I think necessary for Christianity.

In *Purity, Sacrifice, and the Temple*, Klawans observes that few scholars, whether Jewish or Christian, have many positive things to say about the animal sacrifices of biblical Israel. He notes that most Jewish interpretations, no less than the standard Christian interpretations, hold that "the temple cult was destined to be replaced—superseded—by other less bloody rituals that would prove to be of greater value, both spiritually and symbolically."[132] As noted above, I have no nostalgia for the cultic slaying of birds and livestock. I would not wish to be splattered with animals' blood as part of worshipping God. Klawans argues, however, that inquiry into the Jewish temple cult needs to attend to what its actual *practitioners* thought about it and also to what was remembered about it after the destruction of the temple. Such inquiry, he insists, should not be governed by "evolutionist theories" according to which "the gradual and eventually complete de-Judaization of religion" appears as "a positive development."[133] After all, the animal sacrifices had important religious meaning and were valued by ancient Jews for this meaning. He contends that "the ancient Israelite sacrificial rules" should "be analyzed as a symbolic system."[134]

---

132. Klawans, *Purity, Sacrifice, and the Temple*, 3. See also Klawans's earlier *Impurity and Sin in Ancient Judaism*, where he argues that "the distinction drawn between ritual and moral impurity in the Hebrew Bible—and in particular a correct understanding of the nature of moral impurity"—is crucial for avoiding major misunderstandings of Second Temple Jewish writings (vii-viii).

133. Klawans, *Purity, Sacrifice, and the Temple*, 7.

134. Klawans, *Purity, Sacrifice, and the Temple*, 5.

In his introduction, Klawans names some of his scholarly opponents. He states that "the fullest attack on the Jewish temple in current scholarship is to be found in the works of Robert G. Hamerton-Kelly, who, following René Girard, indicts the temple as a place of violence, vengeance, and victimage."[135] He is well aware that the negative portraits include influential Jewish ones, above all that of Maimonides. Klawans sums up Maimonides's position: "In his *Guide of the Perplexed* (III:32, 69b) Maimonides compares the sacrificial laws to mother's milk (cf. Hebrews 5:11–14!) and claims that God suffered sacrificial worship to remain as a 'divine ruse' whose purpose was to eliminate idolatry."[136] According to Klawans, Maimonides is a Jewish "supersessionist" with regard to the temple's animal sacrifices, just as Christians hold that the Eucharist supersedes the temple's animal sacrifices.

Klawans's summary of Girard's position is more negative than the one that I offered above. He explains that for Girard, fallen people naturally desire what other people have; and this desire leads to a violent attempt to claim another person's possessions as one's own. The resulting murder leads to a cycle of vengeance that spawns more and more violence until it is ended by the sacrifice of a scapegoat, who is someone unanimously chosen by the whole community to be the victim. This scapegoating, while profoundly unjust, does produce relief from the deadly cycle. As a result, people ritually re-enact the scapegoating. Girard thinks that they do this, in Klawans's words, by employing "an animal victim that can be more readily disposed of—because no one will seek vengeance for it."[137] Animal sacrifices arise from this rationale.

As Klawans points out, then, Girard holds that animal sacrifices serve a purpose, but Girard does not believe that animal sacrifices serve this purpose very well. At the root of animal sacrifices is the horror of scapegoating innocent victims. Given such a root, it is quite difficult to defend the temple's animal sacrifices as anything but a deeply unfortunate stop-gap measure. Animal sacrifices on this view function simply to conceal and tamp down the horrific scapegoating. They are practices rooted in deception and violence, and have no positive meaning in their own right. I agree with Klawans that this genealogy of sacrifice is very troubling indeed, not least because it is false.

---

135. Klawans, *Purity, Sacrifice, and the Temple*, 8. See Hamerton-Kelly, *Gospel and the Sacred*; and Hamerton-Kelly, *Sacred Violence*. See also Hamerton-Kelly, ed., *Violent Origins*. Hamerton-Kelly's reading of Girard reflects Girard's early work, and thus should not be taken as a portrait of Girard's mature position.

136. Klawans, *Purity, Sacrifice, and the Temple*, 8.

137. Klawans, *Purity, Sacrifice, and the Temple*, 23.

From a historical perspective, Klawans subjects Girard's proposal about the origin of animal sacrifice to a devastating critique. He shows that Girard is not an expert on the historical development of animal sacrifice or on the purposes that humans have assigned to animal sacrifice. In addition, he blames Girard for constructing a metanarrative that proposes to unveil the entire meaning of the Christian Bible, heretofore concealed.[138] He similarly blames Girard for not attending to the actual historical evidence about what ancient people thought they were doing when they offered sacrifice; and he fears that Girard's position implies that Girard is claiming to have seen through their (presumably unconscious) deception and concealment.

Klawans is even less impressed by the avowedly Christian elements of Girard's theory. Klawans argues, somewhat unfairly (given Girard's high view of the Israelite prophets), that "[t]he supersessionistic nature of Girard's project becomes most clear when he turns to Christian narratives and finds *only* in them the revelation of what all earlier myths and rituals conceal."[139] Girard finds the Jewish people collectively guilty for scapegoating—and thus murdering—the innocent Jesus.[140] Jesus reveals that the temple sacrifices have all along been nothing but a way of saving innocent lives that would otherwise have been threatened by the mob.

Klawans observes that in the same year that Girard published *Violence and the Sacred*, Walter Burkert published *Homo Necans: The Anthropology of Ancient Greek Sacrificial Ritual and Myth* with the goal of finding the concealed origins of animal sacrifice. Burkert's work is equally unsuccessful (he traces the origins to hunting), but Klawans considers it better than Girard's, since at least Burkert "recognizes the difference between scapegoat rites and whole burnt offerings, and . . . denies that a single explanation works for all sacrificial rites."[141] Lastly, Klawans treats the three-volume commentary on Leviticus by the Jewish scholar Jacob Milgrom. He finds that Milgrom attributes meaning to the purity laws but not to the sacrificial system. For Milgrom, sacrifice began with people believing that they thereby fed the gods; the Israelites inherited animal sacrifice without giving it a clear meaning, and it was destined to be replaced by prayer.

Klawans points out that earlier scholars such as William Robertson Smith, despite their rejection of the purity laws, presented sacrifice more positively, by linking it with communion (between worshippers and the

---

138. Lusvardi persuasively shows that Girard does not mean to do this.

139. Klawans, *Purity, Sacrifice, and the Temple*, 25.

140. In this section, Klawans draws upon the critique of Girard advanced by the biblical scholar Bruce Chilton, *Temple of Jesus*, 15–25, 163–72. Klawans focuses his attention upon Girard's influential early work *Violence and the Sacred*, especially 28–38.

141. Klawans, *Purity, Sacrifice, and the Temple*, 27. See Burkert, *Homo Necans*.

god, resulting also in a joyful communion with each other).[142] Another significant nineteenth-century work, by Henri Hubert and Marcel Mauss,[143] argues that "ancient sacrifice cannot be reduced to any single motive" and suggests that the purpose of sacrifice is to draw the worshipper into the realm of the gods.[144] But Hubert and Mauss's key ideas came from their own context, especially through the influence of Sylvain Lévi's research on Indian religion as well as the influence of their teacher Émile Durkheim. Durkheim also had some positive things to say about sacrifice, but Klawans notes that Durkheim's later followers focused on what Durkheim called "negative" cult (purity) and neglected what he had to say about "positive" cult (sacrifice).

Klawans points out that in recent years, some studies have appeared that are more promising. He names four: Edmund Leach's "The Logic of Sacrifice," Howard Eilberg-Schwartz's *The Savage in Judaism*, Bruce Chilton's *The Temple in Judaism*, and Mary Douglas's *Leviticus as Literature*. He appreciates Chilton's critique of Girard, but finds Chilton's argument (drawn from French classicists) that sacrifice is really about food to be unpersuasive.[145] By contrast, Klawans considers Douglas's treatment of animal sacrifice to be brilliant, and it significantly informs his own constructive proposals. Douglas argues that "the same tripartite scheme involved in the analogy between Sinai and the tabernacle can be mapped onto the carcass of an animal offered for sacrifice."[146] Her position is quite complex, but she makes clear that in Leviticus the laws regarding animal sacrifices have a rich symbolic meaning in their own right.[147]

In light of this background, Klawans offers his own account of the positive meaning of animal sacrifice in the temple. In part, he thinks that in the Temple, the priest's role was to imitate God in his power over life and death. Metaphorically, "[t]he offerer and the priest play the part of God, and the domesticated animals—from the herd and the flock—play the part of the people (and particularly Israel)."[148] He also thinks that sacrifice pertained to attracting and maintaining the divine presence. Overall, the animal sacrifices involved imitating God and ensuring his presence among the people, both highly positive purposes.

142. See W. R. Smith, *Lectures on the Religion of the Semites*.
143. See the opening chapter of Hubert and Mauss, *Sacrifice*. Mauss later developed a sophisticated account of the gift (focused on reciprocity).
144. Klawans, *Purity, Sacrifice, and the Temple*, 35.
145. See Klawans, *Purity, Sacrifice, and the Temple*, 44. Leach's essay appears in his *Culture and Communication*; and see Eilberg-Schwartz, *Savage in Judaism*.
146. Klawans, *Purity, Sacrifice, and the Temple*, 45.
147. She thereby goes beyond her groundbreaking *Purity and Danger*.
148. Klawans, *Purity, Sacrifice, and the Temple*, 67.

Klawans addresses the widely held view that Israel's prophets anticipated the replacement of the temple's animal sacrifices. He criticizes the sharp dichotomy made in older Protestant scholarship between prophets and priests. He focuses his attention on Jeremiah 7 and Ezekiel 40–48, along with passages such as 1 Samuel 15:22–23, "Has the Lord as great delight in burnt offerings and sacrifices, as in obeying the voice of the Lord? Behold, to obey is better than sacrifice, and to listen than the fat of rams"; Isaiah 1:11, "What to me is the multitude of your sacrifices? says the Lord; I have had enough of burnt offerings of rams and the fat of fed beasts; I do not delight in the blood of bulls, or of lambs, or of he-goats"; Hosea 6:6, "For I desire mercy and not sacrifice, the knowledge of God, rather than burnt offerings"; Amos 5:21–22, "I hate, I despise your feasts, and I take no delight in your solemn assemblies. Even though you offer me your burnt offerings and cereal offerings, I will not accept them, and the peace offerings of your fatted beasts I will not look upon"; Micah 6:6–8, "With what shall I come before the Lord, and bow myself before God on high? Shall I come before him with burnt offerings, with calves a year old? Will the Lord be pleased with thousands of rams, with ten thousands of rivers of oil? . . . He has showed you, O man, what is good; and what does the Lord require of you but to do justice, and to love kindness, and to walk humbly with your God?"; and Psalm 40:6, "Sacrifice and offering you do not desire. . . . Burnt offering and sin offering you have not required."[149]

In the view of John Barton, the books of many prophets operating in the eighth and seventh centuries BC were indeed hostile to the temple's animal sacrifices.[150] Barton argues that we should not be surprised that prophets were critical of the worship of their day—just as many later Christian thinkers have been critical of the worship of their own day. For Klawans, by contrast, passages such as the above mean solely to teach that God does not value animal sacrifices offered by *wicked* people. Klawans denies that any prophet or biblical text intended to relativize animal sacrifices to the point

---

149. Similarly, Psalm 50:9–15 says, "I [God] will accept no bull from your house, nor he-goat from your folds. For every beast of the forest is mine, the cattle on a thousand hills. I know all the birds of the air, and all that moves in the field is mine. If I were hungry, I would not tell you; for the world and all that is in it is mine. Do I eat the flesh of bulls, or drink the blood of goats? Offer to God a sacrifice of thanksgiving, and pay your vows to the Most High; and call upon me in the day of trouble; I will deliver you, and you shall glorify me"; and Psalm 51:15–17 remarks, "For you [God] take no delight in sacrifice; were I to give you a burnt offering, you would not be pleased. The sacrifice acceptable to God is a broken spirit; a broken and contrite heart, O God, you will not despise."

150. Barton, "Prophets and the Cult," 111.

of rendering them obsolete.¹⁵¹ Instead, the prophets were insisting upon justice as the prerequisite for efficacious sacrifice: ethics and cult cannot be separated.¹⁵² Klawans also offers the caveat that "prophets were prone to hyperbole. What seems like a categorical rejection can probably be better understood as a prioritization."¹⁵³

Klawans makes this more concrete by explaining that the prophets condemn "the practice of sacrificing to God *matériel* that has been acquired through immoral means."¹⁵⁴ Turning to Jeremiah 7:22, which is particularly troubling because (as we have seen) it suggests that the Sinai covenant did not include any commandments regarding animal sacrifices, he directs attention to the context of this verse—namely, Jeremiah's critique of the people's reliance on "the temple of the Lord, the temple of the Lord, the temple of the Lord" (Jer 7:4). The central point is that the covenantal relationship is conditional with respect to the temple and its sacrifices: without justice, Jeremiah is saying, "the temple and the sacrifice that is performed there will be of no avail," and indeed God will permit the temple's destruction.¹⁵⁵

To my mind, Barton has the stronger side of the controversy. Klawans has not perceived the depth of the pre-exilic prophets' critique. Even if the prophets can best be seen as prioritizing justice, they inevitably do relativize the animal sacrifices by their rhetoric.¹⁵⁶ Their rhetoric pokes fun at the

---

151. See also, for the same point, Heschel, *Prophets*, 250. Heschel goes on to explain that in the animal sacrifices, "The sacrificial act was a form of personal association with God, a way of entering into communion with Him. In offering an animal, a person was offering himself vicariously. It had the power of atonement" (Heschel, *Prophets*, 251). Yet it remains the case, as Heschel adds, that the prophets significantly relativized acts of sacrificing animals. With regard to this relativizing of animal sacrifice, Heschel notes that "all this grandeur and solemnity are declared to be second rate, of minor importance, if not hateful to God, while deeds of kindness, worrying about the material needs of widows and orphans, commonplace things, platitudinous affairs, are exactly what the Lord of heaven and earth demands!" (Heschel, *Prophets*, 251). For discussion of Heschel on the temple's animal sacrifices, see my *Sacrifice and Community*, 169–71.

152. Klawans adds that various later prophets, including Haggai, Zechariah, and Malachi, actively supported rebuilding the temple and restoring the animal sacrifices. As Barton grants, these "post-exilic prophetic books record prophetic approval for the sacrificial cult, though sometimes criticizing its existing form. Haggai and Zechariah are presented as being strongly in favour of the rebuilding of the Temple, which is hard to imagine if they were opposed to the sacrificial rituals which were housed in it" (Barton, "Prophets and the Cult," 112).

153. Klawans, *Purity, Sacrifice, and the Temple*, 81.

154. Klawans, *Purity, Sacrifice, and the Temple*, 86.

155. Klawans, *Purity, Sacrifice, and the Temple*, 91.

156. Barton is well aware that "it may be argued that the pre-exilic prophets were in reality far less badly disposed toward cultic religion than the texts, taken at face value, might seem to suggest. One line of argument . . . is that it is simply not conceivable that

people's attempts to appease God by such lowly offerings. Such things as the "fat of rams" and the "blood of bulls" completely pale next to justice and interior holiness. Of course, devout Israelites knew that the sacrifices were symbolic, that God was not appeased by animal blood per se. But the prophets' language portrays God as ridiculing the notion that he might be pleased by such things. The prophets thereby pave the way for wondering whether all this fat, blood, and killing is actually needed. This development follows predictable lines, present already in Micah 6:8's insistence that "what is good" and what is required is solely "to do justice, and to love kindness, and to walk humbly with your God" and Psalm 40:6's observation that "[s]acrifice and offering you do not desire. . . . Burnt offering and sin offering you have not required."[157]

Even so, Klawans is correct that animal sacrifice had deeply positive meanings in ancient Israel. He retrieves the view of Josephus and Philo that the temple is a microcosmos, with the priest offering symbolic sacrifices on behalf of the cosmos to ensure the people's encounter with the divine

---

anyone is ancient Israel could have been so radically anti-ritualistic as the texts seem to imply" ("Prophets and the Cult," 113). Those who take this line of argument, Barton notes, often combine it with the idea that Protestant interpreters read their biases back into the texts. Barton adds that a second line of argument consists in holding that "the prophets were opposed to ritual when offered by those with hands polluted by crime, rather than in itself" ("Prophets and the Cult," 114). Against the view that opposition to the sacrificial cult would have been impossible in ancient Israel, Barton notes Douglas, *Natural Symbols*, in which she shows that heavily ritualized societies can have anti-ritual members. Barton concludes: "the tension between those who seek formal observance in matters of religion, and those who are scornful of established custom and seek the freedom of the spirit, can be found in many religious cultures. So can the tension between those for whom true religion is *religio*, public observance, and those for whom it is, in the words of the Epistle of James, 'to care for orphans and widows in their distress, and to keep oneself unstained by the world' (Jas 1.27)" ("Prophets and the Cult," 121).

157. With reference to Psalm 40:6 (as well as to Psalms 50:13-14; 51:16-17; 69:30-31; and 141:2) and Micah 6:6-8—along with other texts such as Isaiah 1:11-17, Jeremiah 6:20, Hosea 6:6, and Amos 5:21-24—Timothy Wardle comments: "In a move similar to that already begun in the Old Testament, and continued at Qumran, many of the early Christians borrowed sacrificial language and applied it to their community, seeing prayer, obedience, and a life devoted to God as efficacious in a way formerly reserved for the animal sacrifices in the temple" (Wardle, *Jerusalem Temple*, 206). See also Wardle, "Pillars, Foundations, and Stones." In this article, Wardle shows that "the Qumran and early Christian communities appropriated not only what happened at the temple (the sacrifices) and the identity of those who oversaw these sacrifices (the priests), but they also applied the very notion of the temple to their understandings of communal life as the people of God. In describing themselves as the temple, these two communities staked a claim to the idea that each now served as the distinct dwelling place of the God of Israel" (Wardle, "Pillars, Foundations, and Stones," 292).

presence.[158] The notion of a temple in heaven, of which the earthly temple is a type, is found in Second Temple literature such as 1 Enoch, the Testament of Levi, the Songs of the Sabbath Sacrifice, and the Letter to the Hebrews (and perhaps the book of Revelation), as well as in rabbinic traditions. Klawans observes that the notion of a heavenly temple need not imply a negative view of the earthly temple sacrifices.

In the Dead Sea Scrolls, Klawans finds "the call to abandon the morally defiled temple *in advance* of its punitive destruction."[159] In other late Second Temple texts, he identifies warnings that the divine presence will depart and that the temple will be destroyed due to injustice (as Jesus believed). In all cases, however, the temple and its sacrificial cult are seen as good, even if defiled at present. In Klawans's view, there is a consistent interest in the purification of the temple and its cult, rather than a desire to get rid of the animal sacrifices.[160] Even in the one or two texts that can possibly be read as speaking of an atonement undertaken *apart* from the temple,[161] this action constitutes a *prelude* to the restoration of the temple and its animal sacrifices. Various texts from Qumran envision a "glorious new temple" possessed of such eschatological elements as "a golden wall," "jewel-encrusted structures," and "streets paved in white stone, alabaster, and onyx."[162] Qumran's *Temple Scroll* depicts the temple's outer court as essentially the same size as the city of Jerusalem. The vast size ensures that the entire people of Israel will be connected to the sacred precincts where the divine presence dwells.

Some scholars, such as Timothy Wardle, contend that "the sectarians at Qumran came to view their community as a metaphorical temple, a substitute sanctuary in which pleasing sacrifices could be offered to God sans the blood of animals."[163] For Klawans, it is a mistake to think of Qumran or

---

158. Philo's position here is more richly developed than Josephus's: see Klawans, *Purity, Sacrifice, and the Temple*, 114–23.

159. Klawans, *Purity, Sacrifice, and the Temple*, 152.

160. Klawans grants that "a number of challenges face interpreters of *4QFlorilegium*. It remains possible (but not likely) that the document imagines an eschatological temple consisting not of bricks and mortar but of people, where offerings consist not of tangible sacrifices but of righteous deeds" (*Purity, Sacrifice, and the Temple*, 164).

161. He notes that "the Qumran sectarians were by no means alone in describing various ritual behaviors in cultic terms, or in maintaining purity beyond the boundaries of the temple" (*Purity, Sacrifice, and the Temple*, 169).

162. Klawans, *Purity, Sacrifice, and the Temple*, 159.

163. Wardle, *Jerusalem Temple*, 139. Wardle recognizes with regard to Qumran: "The sectarian's physical removal from the temple, and the harsh polemic directed toward the Jerusalem priesthood, has often been thought to indicate a complete rift with the temple in Jerusalem. Nevertheless, there are hints that some sectarians may have still participated, albeit to a limited extent, in the temple cult" (*Jerusalem Temple*, 145).

other instances—such as synagogue worship—as being cut off in any definitive or supersessionist sense from the temple sacrifices. He comments, "The difference between speaking of the templization of synagogues or the 'sacrificialization' of prayer on the one hand and the spiritualization of sacrifice on the other is significant."[164] The "spiritualization of sacrifice" is supersessionist language, whereas "the templization of synagogues or the 'sacrificialization' of prayer" is imitation language. The latter does not presume a desire to do away with the Temple cult (the animal sacrifices); rather, it presumes a desire to imitate the Temple cult, and thus presumes a positive attitude toward the animal sacrifices. I agree with this point, but I note that the movement toward "the templization of the synagogues" and "the 'sacrificialization' of prayer" is indeed a movement, even if unconscious, toward doing without killing animals as a part of worshipping God. This is because once people discover that they can do without animal sacrifice, then—strengthened by the texts from the prophets and by the psalms that testify that God does not need the blood of animals—people may wish to worship God without animal sacrifice. What can be done without, logically can be superseded.

Nevertheless, the rabbis consistently express hope for the rebuilding of the temple. I note that numerous Jewish theologians today join the rabbis in expressing this hope. This is not surprising, given that devout Jews recite daily prayers for the temple's rebuilding. Michael Wyschogrod argues that "the rebuilding of the Temple will, in time, become thinkable.... [W]hile the rebuilding of the Temple and the re-establishment of sacrifice is not an immediate prospect, it must become a thinkable idea. It is a thinkable idea

---

Wardle grants, too, that "[t]he Qumran community's separation from Jerusalem was not due to rejection of temple and cult in itself, since in principle these retained their vital role in religious life" (*Jerusalem Temple*, 150). This is Klawans's central point. However, for Wardle it is important that in Qumran we "find descriptions of the sectarian community and its rituals acting as functional substitutes for the Jerusalem temple.... It is in the sacrifices of prayer and pious living that the sectarians are able to atone for sin and guilt" (*Jerusalem Temple*, 155-56). Wardle thinks that it is likely that the Qumran community "functioned as an interim temple, with prayer and worship substituting for the sacrifices in the temple.... Not only were the prayers of the righteous able to atone for sins, but the members of the community itself were understood to comprise a spiritual temple responsible for the praise of God. Moreover, the sectarians saw themselves as participants in the divine liturgy and angelic worship of God, and looked forward to the day when their 'temple of men' would give way to a glorious new temple established by God himself" (*Jerusalem Temple*, 159, 162). See also the helpful discussion of this point, comparing documents from Qumran to the ecclesiology of Ephesians, in Bergsma, *Jesus and the Dead Sea Scrolls*, 151-52, 199-202.

164. Klawans, *Purity, Sacrifice, and the Temple*, 172.

because it is commanded in the word of God."[165] Likewise, Joshua Berman retrieves Maimonides's perspective on this topic: although the time when the temple will be rebuilt cannot be anticipated before it happens, nonetheless "when the Jewish people perfect their state, culminating in the ascent of an effective and popular leader of Davidic descent, the time will be ripe for the Jewish people themselves to rebuild the Temple."[166] In Maimonides's view, a Davidic ruler who rebuilt the temple would thereby reveal himself to be the Messiah. Berman compares Maimonides's view with that of Rashi, who holds that a divinely rebuilt temple "will literally descend from the heavens onto the Temple Mount in completed and finished form."[167] Berman also mentions the view of the nineteenth-century Rabbi Joseph b. Moses Babad that the Jewish people "have an obligation to rebuild the Temple at the moment that the opportunity affords itself," without waiting for a Davidic king or for Levitical priests.[168]

In working toward the eventual rebuilding of the temple, Berman suggests that the Jewish people today should focus on becoming "ideal covenantal partners" of God, by building a society worthy of emulation in all respects and by achieving Jewish unity.[169] In his view, until the people of Israel show themselves to be fully "deserving of the covenantal symbol that is the Temple," the rebuilding of the temple could not accomplish the

---

165. Wyschogrod, *Body of Faith*, 246–47. Wyschogrod adds, "One of the necessary conditions for the resumption of sacrifice is the reappearance of prophecy in Israel. Only by means of prophecy will certain determinations be possible that are not possible at present. While most Jews have family traditions as to whether they are or are not members of the priestly class, these traditions are not fully reliable and only by prophecy will it be possible to make definitive determinations, a necessity if sacrifices are to be restored" (*Body of Faith*, 246). To my mind, any attempt to rebuild the temple would be cataclysmic because of the problems it would cause vis-à-vis Islam. On the Muslim holy sites on the Temple Mount—the Dome of the Rock and Al Aqsa Mosque—as well as their rationale (rooted in Sura 17 of the Qur'an), see Eliach, *Judaism, Zionism and the Land*, 147–48. For discussion of Christian (dispensationalist) and Jewish support for destroying the Dome of the Rock and rebuilding the Temple, see Goldman, *Zeal for Zion*, 304–8.

166. J. A. Berman, *Temple*, 204, citing *Yad, Hilkhot Melakhim* 11:1–4. David Novak, in *Zionism and Judaism*, 11, mentions the hope that, in relation to formalizing a liturgical celebration of the establishment of the State of Israel, "current or future Jewish teachers [will] persuade the Jewish people to return to authentic Jewish life (which will be epitomized by the messianic rebuilding of the Temple in one way or another)."

167. J. A. Berman, *Temple*, 204, citing Rashi to *Sukkah* 41a, s.v. *'i nami*, based on *Mekhilta* to Exodus 15:17.

168. J. A. Berman, *Temple*, 205, citing R. Joseph b. Moses Badad, *Minchat Chinukh* to *Sefer Ha-Chinukh*, commandment 95.

169. J. A. Berman, *Temple*, 207.

purposes for which the temple was originally built.[170] But he assumes that in due time the temple will be rebuilt and the animal sacrifices—which he prefers to call "*korbanot*" or "offerings," in order to emphasize the positive purpose that consists in the people's drawing close to God[171]—will resume.

Klawans bemoans the fact that Jewish scholars have often recounted the history of Jewish liturgy in supersessionist terms. In *Jewish Liturgy: A Comprehensive History*, for example, Ismar Elbogen declares, "Jewish liturgy has unparalleled importance in the history of religions, for it was the first to free itself completely from the sacrificial cult, thus deserving to be called 'The Service of the Heart.'"[172] Despite being highly critical of Elbogen and others who hold similar positions, Klawans grants that there is an element of truth to their claim. The element of truth is that "a number of rabbinic traditions—almost all of which can be dated to the amoraic period—do suggest that sacrifice is either equaled or in some cases even bettered by something else, whether it is the study of Torah (e.g., *b. Menahot* 110a), acts of loving-kindness (e.g., *Avot de-Rabbi Natan* 4), or prayer (e.g., *b. Berakhot* 32b)."[173] Yet Klawans pushes back against over-reading these rabbinic traditions. His argument is that Torah study, acts of loving-kindness, and prayer were always recognized to be spiritually valuable, both before and after the destruction of the temple. The rabbis do not present such acts as though they were in a zero-sum competition with the temple sacrifices. Klawans admits that there are rabbinic texts that maintain that "the goals of sacrifice

---

170. J. A. Berman, *Temple*, 206. For Berman, "we [Jews today] have the peculiar distinction of being the only Jews in history who have lived under their own government in their own land *without* a Temple standing atop Mount Moriah. . . . As covenantal partners with the Almighty, we must surely believe that it is His will that the Temple eventually stand atop Mount Moriah. If we see in our time that He does not allow the Temple to be rebuilt, then we ought not point a finger at others, but at ourselves. The very presence of the Dome of the Rock atop Mount Moriah is not the obstacle toward the rebuilding of the Temple. Its presence atop Mount Moriah is rather a *sign* to us that we are not yet deserving of the covenantal symbol that is the Temple. It is a *symptom* of the fact that we need arrange our own house, before the House of God is to be rebuilt" (J. A. Berman, *Temple*, 206).

171. See J. A. Berman, *Temple*, 115–16. Berman argues that Christianity distorted the meaning of "sacrifice." He explains, "With the rise of Christianity, the term *sacrifice* took on a new meaning. Christianity rejected the institution of animal sacrifice on two accounts. First, it contended that God had no use for them and that worship was to be expressed through piety and righteousness. Moreover, Jesus had offered the ultimate sacrifice—his own life—on behalf of mankind, rendering all further sacrifice irrelevant and unnecessary. . . . While Christianity shunned the notion of a deity that accepted physical gifts, it embraced the notion of renunciation—for its own sake and even without a recipient—as a religious act" (J. A. Berman, *Temple*, 115).

172. Elbogen, *Jewish Liturgy*, 3.

173. Klawans, *Purity, Sacrifice, and the Temple*, 204.

may be achieved by another means."[174] But he argues that a careful reading of such texts shows that they do not advocate the replacement of the temple sacrifices; they simply describe the goodness of acts that were already being done, in various contexts, well before the destruction of the temple.

Again, I note that once one accepts that prayer and acts of loving-kindness are more important than the temple sacrifices and do not require the ritual slaying of animals, then, logically, people are going to think of doing without animal sacrifices. Klawans insists that for the rabbinic tradition, "sacrifice cannot be superseded by prayer, because . . . sacrifice is to return."[175] Klawans and I agree that neither Second Temple Jews nor the early rabbis (post-70) desired to do without the temple sacrifices. Where we differ is how we interpret the biblical texts that downplay the significance of animal sacrifices. To my mind, once such texts make clear that the slaying of animals is profoundly secondary (even if still valuable) in God's eyes, it is a short logical step to prefer to do without animal sacrifices. This does not entail, of course, giving up on the eschatological rebuilding of the temple.

Klawans on the New Testament

In my view, Catholics should not see Jesus' symbolic actions at the Last Supper as expressing a "rejection of the temple cult."[176] Sacrifice fulfilled—a transcendent and free self-sacrifice in love—is radically different from sacrifice rejected. Given that Jesus' actions were a fulfillment rather than a rejection, we do not need to be surprised that, as Klawans says, "Jesus' followers did not separate themselves from the temple and its sacrificial worship."[177] What better place to celebrate the coming of the Messiah of Israel than the temple of Israel? Jesus did not come to reveal that the sacrificial cult of the temple was all a big mistake. As we have seen, however, the New Testament locates the saving sacrifice and new eschatological temple in the Messiah.[178]

---

174. Klawans, *Purity, Sacrifice, and the Temple*, 205.

175. Klawans, *Purity, Sacrifice, and the Temple*, 210. Klawans grants that according to some rabbinic texts, since the eschaton will bring an end to sin and repentance, all temple sacrifices other than thanksgiving sacrifices will no longer be present in the eschaton. Yet, in these texts the temple itself will continue forever, precisely in order to offer thanksgiving sacrifices. See also the insights of Balberg, *Blood for Thought*.

176. Klawans, *Purity, Sacrifice, and the Temple*, 217.

177. Klawans, *Purity, Sacrifice, and the Temple*, 217.

178. For Klawans, since Paul does not reject the temple cult (and indeed is willing to participate in it), it seems likely that Paul's views about Jewish rituals were misunderstood by his Gentile converts.

Klawans identifies what he deems to be three clear instances of "antitemple polemic" in the New Testament: the conclusion of Stephen's speech in Acts 7:48–50 (read in light of Acts 6:13–14); Revelation 21–22; and the Letter to the Hebrews (especially chapters 7–10). The problem with Revelation 21–22, in Klawans's view, is that these chapters assert that in the new Jerusalem there is no temple. As he says, "in this vision of the future, the temple holds no place, and the Jerusalem of the future will not suffer from its absence."[179] He thinks that this absence "repudiates" what otherwise was a standard assumption among the Jewish people, namely, that "there would be some sort of temple in any future age."[180] But I think that Klawans has missed the point. There *is* a new temple in the eschatologically consummated kingdom, and that new temple is Christ. This is not an anti-material hope, since Christ and his members will have their glorified bodies. The temple of the new Jerusalem (and the perfect sacrifice) is "the Lamb" (Rev 21:22). In fact, the whole new Jerusalem—identified as "the Bride, the wife of the Lamb" (Rev 21:9)—is a temple, filled radiantly with "the glory of God" (Rev 21:23) and symbolically structured with twelve gates (the twelve tribes of Israel) and twelve foundations (the twelve apostles). This is not rejection or supersession, but fulfillment.

The second passage is Stephen's speech in Acts 7. For Klawans, "when we find the assertion that God dwells *only* in the heavenly temple, and not in any earthly one, then clearly we have entered the realm of antitemple polemic"—a polemic that "undercuts an essential and common facet of ancient Jewish theology: that God's presence, glory, or name dwells in the Jerusalem temple."[181] But here it seems as though Klawans is insisting upon a localized presence in a manner that differs from 1 Kings 8:27. Stephen is not denying that God placed his name in the temple or that God's glory filled the temple. What Stephen is arguing is that the fulfillment of the temple is actually in Christ, whose body was not made by human hands. This fulfillment—which is "the glory of God" (Acts 7:55)—is what Stephen finds confirmed in his eschatological vision of Christ at the right hand of God the Father.

Lastly, the Letter to the Hebrews strikes Klawans as clearly supersessionist. Hebrews describes the earthly temple in Jerusalem as "a copy and a shadow of the heavenly sanctuary; for when Moses was about to erect the tent, he was instructed by God, saying, 'See that you make everything according to the pattern which was shown you on the mountain'" (Heb 8:5).

---

179. Klawans, *Purity, Sacrifice, and the Temple*, 243.
180. Klawans, *Purity, Sacrifice, and the Temple*, 243.
181. Klawans, *Purity, Sacrifice, and the Temple*, 242.

I note that many Second Temple Jews believed that the earthly temple was a lesser copy of the heavenly temple. The question, then, is whether Hebrews's suggestion that the temple's sacrifices are not the source of divine forgiveness is "antitemple" and "antisacrificial."[182] Hebrews teaches that the Jerusalem temple could "never, by the same sacrifices which are continually offered year after year, make perfect those who draw near" (Heb 10:1). This is an insight that was confirmed by the prophets as well. Why else would Isaiah have prophesied a suffering servant who "has borne our griefs and carried our sorrows" and on whom "the Lord has laid . . . the iniquity of us all" (Isa 53:4, 6), and why would Zechariah have proclaimed that on the eschatological day of the Lord "there shall be a fountain opened for the house of David and the inhabitants of Jerusalem to cleanse them from sin and uncleanness" (Zech 13:1)? Klawans's complaint is that the Jerusalem temple, in Hebrews, "is seen to be inherently inferior"; but how could it not be, if Hebrews is correct that the divine Son has entered into the world as Jesus Christ and has "made purification for sins" (Heb 1:3)?[183] For Klawans, it is anti-temple and supersessionist to affirm that, by comparison with Christ, "[e]verything that came before was simply inadequate."[184] But "inadequate" does not mean rejected or worthless. In the perspective of Hebrews, the temple is fulfilled by Christ, but the temple is eternally meaningful both because of the true worship that it enabled and because of the glorious fulfillment that it invited.

My argument is that it is not "anti-temple" to hold that the temple and its sacrifices can be and have been fulfilled by Jesus' sacrifice on the cross. Christianity retains sacrifice, but now as fulfilled in Christ's sacrifice; Christianity retains the temple, but now as Jesus' eschatological body. Admittedly, for Klawans, any viewpoint that holds that Israel's temple and its sacrifices are at some point no longer intended to be present—even if they

---

182. Klawans, *Purity, Sacrifice, and the Temple*, 243.

183. Klawans, *Purity, Sacrifice, and the Temple*, 243. Rowland comments aptly, "For the author of Hebrews, the heavenly sanctuary is the eschatological sanctuary, built (Heb. 8.2) along with the city by God at the end of the age, an age that has now arrived according to Heb. 1.2. The climax of history has now occurred as Jesus is the first to enter the heavenly sanctuary. . . . The cross thus becomes the moment when the unmediated access to God becomes a possibility" (Rowland, "Temple in the New Testament," 477). Similarly in chapter 21 of the book of Revelation, "Almighty God and the Lamb are the Temple. . . . If a Temple separates off a place of divine presence in the midst of a world, here the divine is immediately present and all-pervasive, which guarantees and identifies holiness" ("Temple in the New Testament," 478). Rowland finds it theologically important to emphasize that for Christianity, "Heaven and earth have met in the moment of the death of a crucified man and not in tabernacle or Temple, but outside the camp, a place of shame and reproach" ("Temple in the New Testament," 480–81).

184. Klawans, *Purity, Sacrifice, and the Temple*, 243.

are fulfilled eschatologically rather than negated through an evolutionary progression—is a "supersessionist" position. To my mind, this claim leaves no room for the crucial distinction between an eschatological fulfillment (in the Messiah, taking up rather than negating the core elements of temple and sacrifice), on the one hand, and a spiritualizing or evolutionary displacement, on the other.[185]

V. Conclusion

Matthew Tapie has pointed out that Christian "supersessionism" has been variously defined and understood by those who seek to reject it.[186] An influential definition comes from the Methodist theologian Kendall Soulen. He defines supersessionist Christianity as the position that although God elected Israel, God did so only to prepare for Jesus Christ; now that Christ has come, the Jewish people are no longer God's elect people. As Soulen explains this supersessionist perspective, "the special role of the Jewish people came to an end and its place was taken by the church, the new Israel."[187] For supersessionists, therefore, Jewish observance of Torah is no longer required and can even be sinful. Furthermore, Jewish rejection of Jesus means that God has "rejected the Jews and scattered them over the earth."[188]

Soulen goes on to divide supersessionism into three kinds: punitive, economic, and structural. Punitive supersessionism is the view that, due to their unbelief in Jesus Christ, the Jewish people are no longer elect. Rather, they are now specially cursed because they should have believed in Christ more easily than the Gentiles who had received far less preparation for his coming. Economic supersession is the view that, in God's economy of salvation, "Christ's advent brings about the obsolescence of carnal Israel and inaugurates the age of the spiritual church. Everything that characterized the economy of salvation in its Israelite form becomes obsolete and is

---

185. For the point that many Second Temple Jews produced "messiah texts," see Novenson, *Christ among the Messiahs*, 177. Put simply, Jews were looking for the fulfillment of the covenants and prophecies, going beyond what the temple and its sacrifices could accomplish. In his *Grammar of Messianism*, Novenson eschews the standard focus on the "messianic idea"—as found for instance in Fitzmyer, *One Who Is to Come*—and argues along plausible lines that "Jewish messianism—of which Christian messianism can be thought of as just an extraordinarily well-documented example—always and everywhere involves the interplay of biblical tradition and empirical circumstance" (*Grammar of Messianism*, 196).

186. See Tapie, *Aquinas on Israel and the Church*, 18.

187. Soulen, *God of Israel*, 1–2.

188. Soulen, *God of Israel*, 2.

replaced by its ecclesial equivalent."[189] Finally, structural supersessionism is a way of understanding the Christian Bible that foregrounds the doctrines of creation, fall, Christ, the Church, and the eschatological consummation. For structural supersessionism, one can understand the gospel without attending to the people of Israel. Soulen finds structural supersessionism exemplified in the creeds. Of course, all three kinds of supersessionism can be found together.

Behind Soulen's typology stands the Jewish historian Jules Isaac's groundbreaking work.[190] Isaac points to a "double movement of fulfillment and cancellation" of Jewish Torah observance.[191] Once Christ has fulfilled Torah, Jewish Torah observance is henceforth cancelled and obsolete.

It would appear that this is precisely the situation described by the Letter to the Hebrews. Hebrews states that Christ "abolishes the first [the Torah's sacrifices and offerings] in order to establish the second [the doing of God's will through Christ's self-offering]" (Heb 10:9). Hebrews also contends that in Christ, "On the one hand, a former commandment [Torah observance] is set aside, because of its weakness and uselessness (for the law

---

189. Soulen, *God of Israel*, 29.

190. See Isaac, *Teaching of Contempt*; and Isaac, *Jesus and Israel*. For further background, see Connelly, *From Enemy to Brother*. Tapie cites and discusses Connelly's important book, which demonstrates the impact of "race-thinking" (united to traditional Catholic anti-Judaism) in German-speaking lands in the 1930s. Even German-speaking Catholics who repudiated the Nazis held that "Jews lived under a curse and continued to be punished by God throughout their history" (*From Enemy to Brother*, 25). For example, George Bichlmair, SJ, who was arrested by the Nazis in 1939 for aiding Jewish converts to Catholicism, gave a speech in 1936 arguing that "baptism was powerless to cure Jews of moral defects that they carried in their genes" as a racial fruit of their spiritual errors (Connelly, *From Enemy to Brother*, 23); for further background to Bichlmair's mission to convert Jews and to his anti-Judaism, see Bernauer, *Jesuit Kaddish*, 35). In German-speaking lands, there were nevertheless some notable Catholics who spoke out against anti-Semitism—among them (to name a few) Dietrich von Hildebrand, Johannes (John) M. Oesterreicher (a Jewish convert), Karl Thieme, Augustin Rösch, SJ, Alfred Delp, SJ, Irene Harand, and Blessed Bernhard Lichtenberg. At the Second Vatican Council, influenced by Thieme's work during the 1950s, Oesterreicher drafted the crucial chapter 4 of *Nostra Aetate*. Connelly grants: "Most German Catholics had limited personal contacts with Jews, and their political organizations are on record as opposing antisemitism before 1933, both as discrimination and as violence" (*From Enemy to Brother*, 172). But in Connelly's view, echoing Jules Isaac (and citing Léon Bloy), the problem was "the old anti-Judaic vision, which made sense of the world for perpetrators but also for onlookers. That vision remained even when one 'absolved' the Jews of deicide, because the idea of Jews living under punishment was untouched. Therefore, Hitler could—and did—claim to be doing a service to Christianity by persecuting Jews, and Christianity did not have a language with which to oppose him" (*From Enemy to Brother*, 172–73).

191. Tapie, *Aquinas on Israel and the Church*, 21.

made nothing perfect); on the other hand, a better hope [Christ's sacrifice] is introduced, through which we draw near to God" (Heb 7:19). If these passages are not enough, then surely clarity is achieved by the commentary on Jeremiah 31 offered by Hebrews 8:13: "In speaking of a new covenant he [the Lord] treats the first as obsolete. And what is becoming obsolete and growing old is ready to vanish away."

It would seem that here the conditions for economic supersessionism have been met.[192] Yet, as repeatedly noted above, I consider it crucial to distinguish between holding that the sacrifices are superseded because of human cultural progress away from primitivism, on the one hand, and holding that they are superseded because the eschatological fulfillment of Torah and temple has been inaugurated by Israel's Messiah. As we have seen, this distinction is overlooked by Klawans. A messianic fulfillment and transformation of the temple sacrifices is a possibility that cannot be ruled out from within Judaism, both due to the relativizing of sacrifice that one finds in the prophets, and to the eschatological power of God and his Messiah.

Does this mean that God no longer wants Torah observance from his Jewish people, or that Torah observance as the Jewish people practice it is obsolete? Here, as noted in my Introduction, everything depends upon what God has willed for the ongoing Jewish people (his beloved chosen people) and also upon whether, as a whole, they are in a condition of culpable unbelief in the Messiah Jesus. From a Christian perspective, their covenants

192. See also the taxonomy of "supersessionism" recently offered by Douglas Farrow in *Theological Negotiations*, 219–33. I find Farrow's defense of "soft supersessionism" to be persuasive (*Theological Negotiations*, 222–23). He goes on to describe two forms of Messianic Jewish understanding, which he calls "anti-supersessionism": "1. The new covenant is a more perfect form of the old covenant, an alteration or mutation that is operative within it, not alongside it or in place of it. The old covenant remains in force; the 'new' covenant simply redirects it from within to the fulfillment accomplished by Jesus. On the basis of the achievements of Jesus, it is a covenant in which Gentiles may now participate, as Gentiles, in a new way, with their own distinct covenantal arrangements. 2. The new covenant is complementary to the old rather than an alteration of the old. There are two parallel covenants, in other words, one applying to Jews who do not believe in Jesus and one applying to anyone, Jew or Gentile, who does believe in Jesus. The believing Jew participates in both, while the believing Gentile participates in the latter only. As regards the believing Jew, there are two possibilities: either (a) he must live according to Torah and may live according to Jewish custom, or (b) he ought to live according to both Torah and Jewish custom" (Farrow, *Theological Negotiations*, 223–24). Citing Vatican II's Dogmatic Constitution on the Church, *Lumen Gentium* §9, Farrow rightly argues that "it is simply not possible within Christian orthodoxy to deny that the old covenant is taken up and transformed by the new" (*Theological Negotiations*, 223). I should add that both Farrow (in footnotes in this section) and D'Costa (in chapter 2 of his *Catholic Doctrines*) offer instructive answers to the problems sketched by Bruce D. Marshall in "Christ and Israel"; and Marshall, "Christ and the Cultures." See also Marshall, "Elder Brothers," 120–26.

have been fulfilled but not revoked. On the one hand, their observance *is* obsolete in the strict sense that the Messiah has come and reconfigured everything around himself. But, on the other hand, because the Jewish people legitimately do not recognize this fulfillment, their observance remains fully necessary, not obsolete at all. Paul already perceived that this situation is a "mystery" (Rom 11:26) in which the divine will is inscrutably involved—a "mystery" that, in my view, includes the terrible "hardening" of boastful Christians toward the Jewish people. Although God has sent his Messiah and most Jews do not recognize this, the Jewish people have not "stumbled so as to fall" (Rom 11:11). They remain God's elect people, profoundly beloved by God, "for the gifts and the call of God are irrevocable" (Rom 11:29), as God works out his plan to "have mercy upon all" (Rom 11:32).

Klawans insists upon the importance of temple and sacrifice, and so should Christians. As the Byzantine theologian Nicholas Cabasilas comments, the consecration of the eucharistic elements makes present the "sacrificed Lamb" and thereby enables the community's sharing in his saving sacrificial offering.[193] Klawans holds that the temple sacrifices were good; and so should Christians, even while holding—on grounds shared with the prophets of Israel—that they were imperfect and in need of messianic fulfillment in order to accomplish their purpose fully. Thus, the earliest "Jerusalem Christians remained strongly attached to the temple and involved in the cult even as they began to proclaim the existence of a new eschatological temple."[194] Without rejecting the temple in Jerusalem, Christians inevitably relativize it by claiming in Christ to be "the distinct dwelling place of the God of Israel."[195] The Church daily shares in the salvific Pasch of Christ. As members of Christ's body, indwelt by the Spirit, Christians are eucharistically taken up into the perfect offering that suffices once and for all as atonement for sins.

I agree with Klawans's concerns regarding "supersessionist" views of the temple sacrifices, insofar as such views amount to a negation of the value of the temple sacrifices. Christians should embrace sacrificial worship of God in Jesus Christ the eschatological temple, the perfect fulfillment—not negation—of the temple sacrifices.[196] Christians should do so with love and

---

193. Cabasilas, *Commentary on the Divine Liturgy*, 82.

194. Wardle, *Jerusalem Temple*, 226. For Aquinas, indebted to Augustine, the reason for the first Jewish Christians' ongoing participation in Torah and temple was to make clear that Torah and temple were from God.

195. Wardle, *Jerusalem Temple*, 207.

196. For further insight, see the argument of Harold Attridge that Hebrews depicts Christ's death as the fulfillment of Yom Kippur's atoning sacrifice, in a manner that blends Yom Kippur "with Sinai as a covenant inaugurating event": Attridge, "Uses of

reverence for the Jerusalem temple. With the Psalmist, then, let all believers beseech God: "Let them bring me to your holy hill and to your dwelling [the temple]! Then I will go to the altar of God, to God my exceeding joy; and I will praise you with the lyre, O God, my God" (Ps 43:3–4).

Antithesis in Hebrews," 280.

Chapter 6

LAND

I. Introduction

My Christian Israelology now moves in a somewhat different direction, though still focused on central realities of the people of Israel (land and king). As Robert Barron points out with respect to Genesis 1's testimony to God's original plan, "it pleases God to involve his human creatures in a kind of kingly fellowship, granting to them the privilege and responsibility of tending the garden in line with God's purposes."[1] God wants to make us his partners—and indeed to make us his "bride" or "members of his [Christ's] body" (Eph 5:30), sharing intimately in the divine life as "a holy temple in the Lord" (Eph 2:21). But prior to the eschatological consummation, although Christ and his Spirit ensure that the solemn teachings of the Church (the communication of the gospel, the handing on of Scripture) is preserved from error, the Church's leaders can and do err due to misunderstandings or cultural prejudices.[2]

In the final two chapters of this book, therefore, I examine Israel's promised land and Davidic kingship with an eye to the relation of the Catholic Church to the Jewish people and to the State of Israel (chapter 6), and the exercise of papal power vis-à-vis the Jewish people (chapter 7). In these two chapters, I undertake a Christian theological exploration of Israel's land and kingship in dialogue with Jewish theology, as I have done above for the exodus, Torah, and temple. But my focus will be upon Catholic theo-political

---

1. Barron, *2 Samuel*, 4.

2. Lest there be any misunderstanding, I am not here denying the authority of *Cantate Domino*, whose correct interpretation and application (vis-à-vis Catholics who observe Torah as necessary for salvation) I briefly explained above.

judgments vis-à-vis the Jewish people, as befits engagement with the theopolitical entity that is the covenantal people of Israel.

In engaging the doctrine of Israel's land, let me begin with the challenge issued by Eugene Korn. Rabbi Korn has called upon the Catholic Church to come to grips with the fact that Jewish survival now largely depends upon the survival of the Jewish State of Israel. Korn argues, "If the continued existence of the Jewish people is truly testimony to God's promise and His faithfulness that the Church holds dear . . . then it would seem that forcefully and unequivocally supporting the State of Israel—but not necessarily all its policies—from its existential enemies is a religious obligation devolving upon the Church."[3] Against the Catholic tendency to make a sharp separation between support for the Jewish people (a theological matter) and support for the State of Israel (a prudential or political matter), Korn speaks for many Jews when he argues that this sharp division is untenable. He maintains, "This is not a contingent political issue, but a theological necessity. Sensitive to the Church's political interests as well as to its responsibility for Christians in the Middle East, supporting Israel's security and existence must be done carefully. However there seems no theological justification for neutrality or diplomatic silence."[4]

---

3. E. B. Korn, "Jewish Response to 'Theological Questions,'" 4. See the observation of Rabbi Fred Morgan: "When . . . the social Gospel of human rights is applied to the Palestinian people to the profound detriment of the Jewish people—that is, without any acknowledgement of the covenantal relationship between the people Israel and the land of Israel—the Jewish community sees this as anti-Semitism in another form, a politicized expression of theological triumphalism. Many in the Jewish community—including many who themselves are very sympathetic to the cause of the Palestinian people and, following the model of Abraham Joshua Heschel, speak out on their behalf—feel deeply misunderstood when it comes to matters relating to Israel" (Morgan, "Jewish Perspectives," 17). This situation is in the background of the comments of Ronald Lauder, president of the World Jewish Congress, who reports that in a private audience in 2015 Pope Francis told him: "To attack Jews is anti-Semitism, but an outright attack on the State of Israel is also anti-Semitism. There may be political disagreements between governments and on political issues, but the State of Israel has every right to exist in safety and prosperity" (Gallagher, "Pope Celebrates Church Document"). See also Pope Benedict XVI's comments in 2009: "Let it be universally recognized that the State of Israel has the right to exist, and to enjoy peace and security within internationally agreed borders. Let it be likewise acknowledged that the Palestinian people have a right to a sovereign independent homeland, to live with dignity and to travel freely" ("Address at Ben Gurion Airport").

4. E. B. Korn, "Jewish Response to 'Theological Questions,'" 4. For the opposite view, see Neuhaus, "Moments of Crisis and Grace," 23: "During his visit to the Holy Land in May 2009, Pope Benedict XVI's insistence on clearly separating between the relationship with Jews and Judaism (spiritual, religious) and the attitude to the State of Israel (political), provides the basis for a coherent distinction in the dialogue with the Jews. The patrimony that Jews and Christians share is indeed vast and deeply significant for

How should the Catholic Church respond to Korn's challenge? Many official Christian statements affirm the Jewish people's covenantal connection with the land, but argue that the land promise cannot be identified simply with a particular parcel of land. Instead, on this view, the land promise signifies God's will to bless his people with life and security. As such, it follows that the land promise applies to all peoples, since all have a right to security in a land.

From a somewhat different but related angle, the Israeli Jewish biblical scholar David Frankel has argued in his *The Land of Canaan and the Destiny of Israel* that Genesis and Deuteronomy are in tension. In Deuteronomy, it is assumed that the people of Israel will have to conquer the peoples of the land. According to Frankel, however, in Genesis the "Priestly" author assumes that all descendants of Abraham, *including* Ishmael, have a share in the covenant and therefore all peoples whose lineage can be traced to Abraham, and who are willing to receive circumcision, are "included in the covenant."[5] By contrast to the Deuteronomist, who considered the Israelites alone to be God's holy nation and who called for the extermination of the peoples of the land due to their idolatry, Frankel finds that "the early Priestly covenant text of Gen 17 makes no mention of one kind or nation dominating the others. The early Priestly tradition . . . did not envision Israelite domination over the various circumcised peoples in the land at all."[6] Frankel holds that the Priestly author never granted possession of the land to the Israelites, since the land belongs to the Lord and he alone determines who will dwell there.

Catholics. However, Catholics cannot ignore the obligations of justice and peace with regard to the Palestinian people. . . . This message is not always a popular one especially when many Jews expect firm Catholic solidarity with Israel in the light of centuries of traumatic Catholic-Jewish relations." As Neuhaus says, the Catholic Church is "acutely aware of the significant problems that were created at the time of the establishment of the State of Israel in the heart of the predominantly Arab Muslim Middle East. Catholics are to be found among both the Arab peoples in general and among the Palestinian Arabs in particular and they have constantly called the Church to solidarity with the Palestinian people. An important lobby in the Church promotes an awareness of issues of justice and peace, and among the festering sores in this domain are the questions of the Palestinian refugees and Palestinian aspirations to statehood" (Neuhaus, "Moments of Crisis and Grace," 22). I note that the problems pre-existed the establishment of the State of Israel in 1948; but all can agree that the Jewish Zionist movement produced a set of problems that were not present in the region prior to the movement. The situation of the Palestinians has yet to be resolved—though the disagreements begin when one strives to conceive of possible solutions or to evaluate previous peace plans. See also the collection of Neuhaus's essays, *Writing from the Holy Land*.

5. Frankel, *Land of Canaan*, 350.
6. Frankel, *Land of Canaan*, 376.

On this view, it is not the covenant with Abraham that establishes the validity of the Israelites' dwelling in the land. Rather, whoever dwells in the land has to be worthy of dwelling in God's own land, where God dwells. The Canaanites proved themselves unworthy, and so did the Israelites, leading to their exile.[7] Frankel's conclusion is that "the book of Genesis to a very large extent promoted the formation of covenants of coexistence with the Canaanite population in the land."[8] He hopes that his scholarly reconstruction shows that at least some texts of the Bible can be used today to "promote religious tolerance and respect between peoples in the land."[9]

I am unpersuaded by Frankel's reconstruction and by his use of it. Yet, I should note that he does not deny God's covenantal gift of the land to the people of Israel. Instead he insists that the borders of the land are "meant to keep the Israelites in but not to keep the outsiders out," since "[b]iblical Israel's task is to 'captivate' the nations surrounding them—not in the political sense, by military force or territorial expansion, but in the spiritual sense,

---

7. See Frankel, *Land of Canaan*, 153. Frankel goes on to note another tension: "While some prophets insisted that in the eschatological era the nations of the world would worship the Lord in Jerusalem, others, such as the prophet of Isa 19, envisioned a day when the nations would worship the Lord on their own soil. . . . This, by the way, stands in contrast to the assertion that foreign territory is inherently impure and thus unfit for any cultic worship of the Lord (Josh 22:19)" (*Land of Canaan*, 157–58).

8. Frankel, *Land of Canaan*, 382–83. In considering the implications of his research for contemporary Jews in the State of Israel, he directs attention to three recent works in Hebrew, whose titles he gives in English: Shapira, ed., *Bible in Israeli Identity*; Sheleff, *Biblical Narratives and Israeli Chronicles*; and U. Simon, *Seek Peace and Pursue It*. See also Eisen, "Off the Center"; U. Simon and Louvish, "Place of the Bible in Israeli Society."

9. Frankel, *Land of Canaan*, 384. An example of how he undertakes this project is his interpretation of Deuteronomy 20: "there is no sense in the original law of Deut 20 that the Canaanite gods or forms of worship are in any way perverse or even alluring. There is no demand made to destroy the Canaanite shrines or cultic facilities, as in Exod 23, or to impose upon the Canaanites the worship of YHWH. The only potential threat that the Canaanites might pose in this text is military, not religious. In comparison with the ideological world of the law in Exod 23, against which it may be struggling—and even more so in comparison with the final form of the law in Deut 20, which requires the total annihilation of the Canaanites—the original form of the text as reflected in vv. 10–14 is quite broad-minded. It reflects a value system that implicitly promotes religious tolerance, political coexistence, and a sense of responsibility toward the 'other' in the land" (Frankel, *Land of Canaan*, 393). In defense of his approach, he cites a rabbinic midrash that "not only implies that parts of the Torah do not reflect the highest ideal but also that God himself may adopt opposing perspectives in the same Torah" (*Land of Canaan*, 389). For particularly concerning texts—whose plain sense the Rabbis resisted, as do modern commentators—he cites E. W. Davies, "Morally Dubious Passages."

by living in accordance with just laws that evoke awe and admiration."[10] Frankel is well aware of the argument that, due to injustice toward the Palestinian people, the State of Israel is currently violating God's covenantal land promise, for which the penalty is to be vomited out of the land.[11] This perspective on the State of Israel has become relatively widespread among "mainline" Christian churches in recent decades.[12] Clearly in response to this charge of injustice, Frankel hopes that his work will encourage among his fellow Israeli Jews an understanding of the land promise that is "strongly informed by universal ethical concerns."[13] Without offering particular political solutions, he wishes to focus the Jewish people on their vocation of dwelling in and governing the land in a manner that all the nations will admire, due to the justice that shines forth and glorifies God.

I consider that Frankel has not addressed the key issues, which pertain to the biblical "land of Canaan" (Gen 17:8; Gen 28:13; Deut 32:49 and elsewhere) and specifically to concrete issues of governance. Undoubtedly, there are conflictual elements intrinsic to the existence of a Jewish State in a land where non-Jews also live and have lived for millennia. In the years after the Second Vatican Council, the Catholic Church has affirmed that God's covenant with the people of Israel is still in force, and surely this covenant includes both the promise of a people chosen by God and the promise of a land given by God as that people's dwelling place. Yet, the official statements of the Catholic Church consistently avoid discussing the land promise.[14] As

---

10. Frankel, *Land of Canaan*, 398.

11. See Boys, *Has God Only One Blessing?*, 263. See also Leighton, "Presbyterian-Jewish Impasse"; Small, "Presbyterian Disestablishment"; Gregerman, "Israel as the 'Hermeneutical Jew'"; and Gregerman, "Comparative Christian Hermeneutical Approaches." For a further example, see the warnings to the State of Israel in the 2014 statement by Gushee and Stassen, "Open Letter to America's Christian Zionists." For Gregerman, the key unaddressed question is "the appropriateness of applying Scriptural promises to a secular nation-state" ("Comparative Christian Hermeneutical Approaches," 422).

12. See the influential work of Naim Stifan Ateek, recipient of the 2006 Episcopal Peace Fellowship's John Nevin Sayre Award and director of the Sabeel Ecumenical Liberation Theology Center in Jerusalem: Ateek, *Justice, and Only Justice*; and Ateek, *Palestinian Christian Cry for Reconciliation*. Along similar lines, see Raheb, *I Am a Palestinian Christian*. For discussion of the work of Ateek and Raheb, see Kuruvilla, *Radical Christianity*. For studies of Palestinian Christian readings of the Old Testament (and thus of the land promise), see C. H. Miller, "Hermeneutical Problems"; and Stalder, *Palestinian Christians and the Old Testament*. See also Patriarch Michel Sabbah's 1993 Pastoral Letter, "Reading the Bible Today."

13. Frankel, *Land of Canaan*, 399.

14. See for example *Catechism*, §72. In the Catechism's Index, there is an entry for "Israel" but no sub-entry or entry for "land." See also Gregerman, "Is the Biblical Land Promise Irrevocable?" Gregerman points out that there are some exceptions, such as

Eugene Korn recognizes, the Catholic Church prefers to discuss the State of Israel simply as a secular state, without taking up the Zionist issue of whether the land promise is still in force, given the complicated politics and the situation of Palestinian Catholics.

To complicate matters further, in academic circles, the Jewish State of Israel is broadly despised. Many universities have divested financially from any businesses associated with the State of Israel. Nadim Rouhana and Areej Sabbagh-Khoury, scholars at Tufts and Columbia respectively, express a widely shared academic viewpoint when they describe the establishment of the State of Israel in 1948 as an episode of "ethnic cleansing" in which "the land they had lived on was turned into the exclusive homeland of the Jewish people, enacted through the self-definition of the state as Jewish"—with the result that "foreign colonizers" succeeded in implementing "the destruction and Judaization" of Palestinian "cities and towns, accompanied by the looting of houses, stores, and farms."[15] In the same volume, Azmi Bishara asks a question that presses to the heart of the issue: "Why does Israel insist ... that it is a Jewish state?"[16] He answers, "Israel insists on this in order to get not

---

a 1984 statement by the Brazilian bishops that holds that Jews today are inheritors of the land promise made to Abraham's descendants but that is also careful to move from theological language to legal/political language in discussing the rights of Jews in the State of Israel to a secure political existence. Another exception is the 2001 document of Pontifical Biblical Commission, "Jewish People." Gregerman notes that this document "presents a detailed and nuanced discussion of the land promise in the biblical covenant. The authors insist that this aspect cannot be ignored by Catholics when studying Scripture, and they situate this particular topic within a broader study of the ongoing Jewish covenant. On the issue of the land, there is nothing remotely similar in official statements on Jewish-Catholic relations, nor does this statement seem to have had any influence on later statements" ("Is the Biblical Land Promise Irrevocable?," 151). Cardinal Walter Kasper, who led the Pontifical Commission for Religious Relations with the Jews from 2001–2010, spoke extensively about the unrevoked "covenant" during these years, but only once—and then only in passing—mentioned the land promise.

15. Rouhana and Sabbagh-Khoury, "Memory and the Return of History," 412–13. See also Rouhana, *Palestinian Citizens*; Sabbagh-Khoury, "Palestinians in Palestinian Cities in Israel." For side-by-side histories describing the twentieth-century conflict, with the even-numbered pages presenting the history from an Israeli point of view and the odd-numbered pages presenting the history from a Palestinian point of view, see Adwan et al., eds., *Side by Side*. The massive divergence between the two perspectives, each of which is presented in a persuasive manner, becomes clear in this book, which was a project of the Peace Research Institute. See also Kimmerling and Migdal, *Palestinian People*.

16. Bishara, "Zionism and Equal Citizenship," 148. For mainline Protestant churches' critiques of Zionism and of the state of Israel—and for sharp criticism of these critiques—see Tooley, "Theology and the Churches." As background, Tooley cites Merkley, *Politics of Christian Zionism*; and see also Lewis, *Origins of Christian Zionism*. For discussion of pro- and anti-Zionist Christian viewpoints in the 1940s—including

only an Arab *de facto* recognition of Israel but also a retrospective recognition of the legitimacy of Zionism as an ideology and of the expulsion of the Arab majority in Palestine."[17]

By contrast, the Israeli scholar and peace activist Yossi Klein Halevi has argued in favor of the justice of the 1948 establishment of the State of Israel.[18] Halevi makes his case on historical, theological, and political grounds. He notes that "if by 'Zionism' one means the Jewish attachment to the land of Israel and the dream of renewing Jewish sovereignty in our place of origin, then there is no Judaism without Zionism. Judaism isn't only a set of rituals and rules but a vision linked to a place."[19] Ongoing Judaism has always involved a yearning for the restoration of the Jewish people to the land of Israel.

In addition, Halevi observes that now that a Jewish state has in fact been established, any misstep could involve extreme consequences for the Jewish people, especially given that a number of other states in the region

---

the Vatican's firm diplomatic opposition to a Jewish state in Palestine in 1943 (in the very midst of the Holocaust)—see Conway, "Founding of the State of Israel." Mainline Protestant churches, of course, have been in recent decades repudiating "supersessionism": on this point see Boys, "Covenant in Contemporary Ecclesial Documents," 95–100. See also the chapter on "Zionism and the State of Israel" in Kessler, *Introduction to Jewish-Christian Relations*; as well as Ateek et al., *Challenging Christian Zionism*.

17. Bishara, "Zionism and Equal Citizenship," 148.

18. See Halevi, *Letters to My Palestinian Neighbor*, 25–89. For a succinct historical account of the post-World War II events that led to the establishment of the State of Israel, including the United Nations General Assembly vote in favor of the partition plan on November 27, 1947 as well as David Ben-Gurion's declaration of independence on May 14, 1948 (just before the expiration of the British Mandate for Palestine) that established the State of Israel—along with the war that ended in 1949—see Stanislawski, *Zionism*, 57–66. For Protestant and Maronite Catholic scholarship defending the State of Israel, see McDermott, *Israel Matters*, 79–93; Nicholson, "Theology and Law"; Khalloul, "Theology and Morality." Regarding the justice of the establishment of the state of Israel in 1948, Khalloul draws attention to Morris, *One State, Two States*. See also Halevi, *At the Entrance*, with its deeply moving interfaith exchanges, such as the conversation between Halevi, Sheykh Abul-Rahim, and a settler rabbi on 308–10.

19. Halevi, *Letters to My Palestinian Neighbor*, 42. Halevi, writing to his "Palestinian neighbor," comments further: "When I see how my people and its story are portrayed in Palestinian media, I feel close to despair. It seems that the one idea unifying Palestinian media in all its ideological diversity is that the Jews are not a people and have no right to a state. That same message is conveyed in Palestinian schools and mosques. There was no ancient Jewish presence here—that is a Zionist lie. No Temple stood on the Mount. The Holocaust, too, is a Zionist hoax, invented to ensure Western support for Israel. According to the prevailing narrative on your side, I am a pathological liar without any history, a thief without rights to any part of this land, an alien who doesn't belong here" (*Letters to My Palestinian Neighbor*, 16–17).

have pledged to destroy the State of Israel.[20] Halevi suggests that the solution is for the Jews and Palestinians sincerely and publicly to accept the validity of each other's *maximalist* claims to the land. On this basis, each side can then freely renounce a portion of what it claims as its own. Halevi observes that academic or theological discussions of the State of Israel's legitimacy too easily neglect the reality that the State of Israel actually exists and that its termination would be devastating for most of the people who live in the state.[21]

The Catholic theologians Alain Marchadour and David Neuhaus, however, point out that the ongoing struggle over the land poses a painful dilemma for Christians. On the one hand, Christian treatment of the Jewish people in Christian-governed countries involved centuries of persecution and hatred, culminating in the Holocaust implemented by baptized (though often paganized) Christians.[22] On the other hand, there are a significant number of Palestinian Christians who are currently living in a situation of intense resentment toward the State of Israel as an oppressor-state, and they have grounds for their complaints.

In this light, Marchadour and Neuhaus recount the history of the United Nations' 1947 vote to divide the land of Palestine into two states. Jews then comprised about 35 percent of the population on the land. As Marchadour and Neuhaus tell the story, when this vote was rejected by the Arab states and the Palestinians, war ensued and "the majority of Muslim and Christian Palestinians became refugees (some fled and some were

20. Thus, Halevi remarks, "When Palestinian leaders call the creation of Israel one of the great crimes in history and refer to the 'seventy-year occupation' that began with its birth; when pro-Palestinian demonstrators around the world chant, 'From the river to the sea, Palestine will be free,' with the clear message that there is no place for a Jewish state—then the terms of the conflict aren't about policies but existence. Israel isn't just accused of committing crimes; it is a crime. From there, the next step is inevitable" (*Letters to My Palestinian Neighbor*, 185).

21. See also Langer, "Theologies of the Land."

22. See the earlier studies of the land by German-speaking scholars still dealing with the consequences of the Holocaust: Marquardt, *Die Juden*; and Rendtorff, *Israel und sein Land*. For the view that the progress sought by Rendtorff in German Protestantism has been accomplished, see Rosenhagen, "God Is Faithful." Rosenhagen states that in contemporary German Protestantism "the Christian church is no longer considered the heir of the biblical Israel and the Jewish people" ("God Is Faithful," 638)—but in my view this formulation is a disaster, since it would mean that Jesus is not the Messiah of Israel and thus Christianity is false at its core. It would also have the probable consequence of excising the Old Testament from the Christian Bible, and indeed the ultimate result would be the erasure of the New Testament. Still, there are many good developments noted by Rosenhagen, such as the affirmation of "Israel's continued chosenness, Christian witness for Jews in the light of the *Shoah*," and "God's faithfulness to Israel" ("God Is Faithful," 638).

forcibly evicted). After the war, they were prevented from returning to their homes. Due to the exit of the refugees and the great influx of Jewish immigrants following the establishment of the State of Israel, the Jews now made up almost 90 percent of the population."[23] Marchadour and Neuhaus consider this situation to be a "fundamental injustice" due to "the displacement of the Palestinians from their ancestral homeland."[24]

For Marchadour and Neuhaus, it is significant that there is no historical evidence that Abraham existed, though they affirm the people-forming significance of the biblical narratives. Archaeologically, they note that around the year 1200 BC there seems to have been an influx of new people into the land, especially around the territories of Ephraim, Benjamin, and Manasseh. At this same time, for whatever reason, pigs disappeared from these territories. They also note that some archaeological findings call into question whether Jerusalem really was a royal city (as distinct from a simple village) prior to the late eighth century BC. Having presented this historical-critical background—which grounds their conclusion that God's Word is not "found in the Bible in a raw, unmediated and pure state, normative in its most literal sense for our world today"[25]—they survey the recent history of Catholic dialogue with the Jewish people, remarking that the issue of the land has come to take center stage. In their view, "It is no longer a question of

23. Marchadour and Neuhaus, *Land, the Bible, and History*, 132–33. From a different perspective, see A. Beker, "Forgotten Narrative." See also Neuhaus, "Jewish-Christian Dialogue."

24. Marchadour and Neuhaus, *Land, the Bible, and History*, 133.

25. Marchadour and Neuhaus, *Land, the Bible, and History*, 189. They go on to argue, "The Land is promised to his [Abraham's] descendants as a place where hopefully they will succeed, unlike Adam and Eve, who failed in the Garden of Eden. In Abraham, the promise of a particular Land is linked to Abraham being a blessing for all the nations of the earth. The Land of promise where the Word of God is realized will begin the process of restoration by which all lands will once again become a space for holy living. . . . The Land that Israel is about to enter must be and must remain a Land of obedient fulfillment of the Law and covenant, where righteousness and justice between God and humanity and between man and man must reign. . . . With regard to the Land, the *Shabbat* serves to prevent Israel from forgetting its salvation history and transforming the Land into a land like all others. *Shabbat* guarantees remembering and acknowledging God as Creator and Redeemer but it also ensures that the powerful do not oppress brother or sister, widow, orphan, and disenfranchised without limit" (*Land, the Bible, and History*, 189–90). For Marchadour and Neuhaus, Scripture understands possession of the land to be a cause for mourning due to sin, and thereby a cause for exile and for rediscovery of God's fidelity: "The Land meant to be a space for holy living becomes a place of repeated transgression, both against God and against neighbor, especially the weakest among them. . . . Whereas the Land should provoke an attitude of thanksgiving to God for the blessings showered on the human person, it becomes a place where the human person congratulates himself on his prowess and bows down before the gods he has created" (*Land, the Bible, and History*, 190–92).

Catholic resistance to Jewish national sovereignty per se but rather Catholic concern for the application of principles of international law that guarantee justice for the Palestinians as well as rights and security for all Christians in the area."[26] They pay extensive attention to the writings of the then-Latin Patriarch of Jerusalem, Michel Sabbah, which bemoan Israeli military occupation of land belonging to the Palestinians and call for an end to violence on both sides, in hopes of attaining justice and security for all. They propose that the way forward might be "an authentic dialogue between indigenous Palestinian Catholics and Israeli Jews in Jerusalem."[27]

As Marchadour and Neuhaus observe, the Vatican was very slow to acknowledge the State of Israel in formal diplomatic terms.[28] The Vatican finally did so in 1994, and in 2000 and 2015 the Vatican formally recognized the Palestinian Liberation Organization and the Palestinian Authority, respectively.[29] For Marchadour and Neuhaus, it is not good that "Catholics from Europe and the United States, involved in dialogue with Jews, have pressured the Vatican to go further in recognizing Zionism as constituting an essential element in modern Jewish identity."[30] The problem is twofold, as the Vatican itself recognizes: Palestinian and Arab Christians in the Middle East would be deeply angered, and, even more importantly, there has

---

26. Marchadour and Neuhaus, *Land, the Bible, and History*, 170.

27. Marchadour and Neuhaus, *Land, the Bible, and History*, 172. On the surface of things, I am not optimistic about this proposal—unless it is the case (as it may be) that the Catholic Church in Jerusalem today has an understanding of Zionism that differs sharply from the negative views documented by Rioli, "'New Nazis'?" Rioli notes that things in fact became worse after the period she documents, due especially to the Six-Day War in 1967. See also Patriarch Michel Sabbah's collected essays and Pastoral Letters, *Faithful Witness*; and see also Khader and Neuhaus, "Holy Land Context for *Nostra Aetate*," including two Appendices: "Relations with Believers of Other Religions" at 74–83 (a document of the 1995–2000 Synod of the Catholic Churches of the Holy Land, published originally in: Assembly of Catholic Ordinaries in the Holy Land, *General Pastoral Plan*) and "Reflections on the Presence of the Church in the Holy Land'" at 84–88 (a 2003 Letter of Patriarch Michel Sabbah and the Theological Commission of the Latin Patriarchate of Jerusalem). For further background see Khader, "Christian-Jewish Dialogue" and Polyakov, "Christian-Jewish Dialogue." Unpromisingly, Khader and Neuhaus report: "For many of the Holy Land faithful, unfortunately, the Jew is often first and foremost a policeman, a soldier or a settler" ("Holy Land Context for *Nostra Aetate*," 70); and they deny that Palestinian Catholicism suffers from traditional anti-Judaism or anti-Semitism. See also the Palestinian Christian concerns set forth in Kassis, *Kairos for Palestine*.

28. See Cassidy, "Next Issues in Jewish-Catholic Relations."

29. For background, see Leonard Hammer's three articles: "2015 Comprehensive Agreement"; "Discerning Israel's Interpretation"; and "The Holy See-PLO Agreement." See also O'Mahony, "Vatican, Jerusalem, the State of Israel."

30. Marchadour and Neuhaus, *Land, the Bible, and History*, 183–84.

not yet been justice for the Palestinian people. Marchadour and Neuhaus suggest that the place to start is not with an affirmation of Jewish Zionism, but rather with a full accounting for the various elements that must be addressed by Christians in the face of conflicts in the Holy Land. They propose moving beyond "simplistic and single-minded ideologies" as well as beyond perspectives that focus solely upon Catholic-Jewish reconciliation or solely upon justice for the Palestinians.[31] The foundations of such an accounting, they argue, have been provided by Pope John Paul II's 1984 Apostolic Letter *Redemptoris Anno*.[32]

As a practical matter, their position ultimately involves understanding the land promise *only* in a Christian eschatological way.[33] For reasons that I will explain below, I do not think this is sufficient. As they observe, Christ has inaugurated his kingdom and has offered "his body as a meeting place for those called to lives of holiness from all lands."[34] Christians must demand justice and peace in all lands, bearing witness to the inauguration of the eschatological kingdom. The land promise, then, boils down to Christ's inauguration of "justice and peace in all lands." Christians call upon Scripture's teaching that "the Land that is God's must not become Egypt, the

---

31. Marchadour and Neuhaus, *Land, the Bible, and History*, 196.

32. See also, more recently, Pope Benedict XVI's 2012 *Ecclesia in Medio Oriente*; as well as Koch, "Press Conference."

33. In *Catholics, Jews and the State of Israel*, Anthony J. Kenny explores pro-Zionist positions taken by Catholic (and some non-Catholic) theologians since the Council. In Kenny's view, which seems right to me, the Church should not impose a particular *theological* understanding upon the Jewish people's return to the land and the establishment of the State of Israel. Yet, as Kenny says, the Church should welcome these events as evidence that God cares for his ongoing Jewish people and should rejoice that God has not allowed the Holocaust (or the wickedness of Christian persecution of the Jewish people over the centuries) to be the last word. Kenny emphasizes that "after the Holocaust the Jewish civilization of Europe is no more.... The State of Israel is the new form of Jewish existence, and any threat to Israel represents a threat to Jewish existence itself.... Catholic Magisterial silence on Israel is seen by Jews as calling into question the continuing existence of the State of Israel, and, consequently, it is interpreted as a threat to Jewish existence itself" (*Catholics, Jews and the State of Israel*, 117). Kenny calls for the establishment of formal diplomatic relations between the Vatican (the Holy See) and the State of Israel, and such diplomatic relations indeed were established shortly after the publication of his book. For discussion, see the essays in Breger, ed., *Vatican-Israel Accords*; as well as the background given by Irani, *Papacy and the Middle East*. Although Jonathan Sacks supported the establishment of diplomatic relations, he also notes that for many Jews, diplomatic relations with the Vatican are not desirable, given that "there are injuries too deep to be forgotten. The history of Jewish suffering in the Crusades, blood libels, inquisitions, ghettoes, and expulsions cannot be unwritten" (Sacks, *Faith in the Future*, 104).

34. Marchadour and Neuhaus, *Land, the Bible, and History*, 194.

land of a tyrannical Pharaoh,"[35] and Christians cannot offer support to any viewpoint that undermines justice and peace for all people. On this view, the main problem with Zionism is that it does not leave adequate room for justice for the Palestinian people who were the majority of the people in the land at the time of the United Nations' vote for partition. The only "Zionism" Marchadour and Neuhaus allow is one that recognizes that "[t]he Land is given to Israel as land is given to all people in order that it might become a land of fraternity, justice, and reconciliation"—in other words, in order that the eschatological kingdom might come to be, in which the injustices associated with nation-states are absent and the Palestinian people, along with the Jews and the Christian occupants of the land, are fully embraced in "fraternity, justice, and reconciliation."[36]

By contrast, for reasons that will become clear, I think that more attention needs to be given to Christian theological grounds for supporting the Jewish State of Israel. On a practical level, I think Halevi's proposal would

35. Marchadour and Neuhaus, *Land, the Bible, and History*, 190.

36. Marchadour and Neuhaus, *Land, the Bible, and History*, 200. Patriarch Michel Sabbah remarked in a 2003 speech devoted to Christian-Muslim relations in Palestinian society: "God is love and peace. Those who believe in God must live in love and peace. The person who lives in love and peace obtains all rights. For love and peace do not mean abandoning all rights; on the contrary, they are their best guarantee. But, we live in a reality that makes this language difficult to understand. Our reality is occupation, assassinations, demolition of houses, the destruction of our agriculture, contempt for human dignity, military barriers at which the Israeli army has its sport in humiliating the Palestinian human person. . . . And in human logic, which is not that of God, violence is met by violence and aggression is answered by aggression. And if someone cannot take revenge, his/her soul becomes filled with hatred while awaiting the time when revenge will be possible" (Sabbah, *Faithful Witness*, 138). In another 2003 speech, this time addressing Palestinian-Israeli relations, Sabbah bemoans the situation arising from the Israeli response to the Second Intifada: "In 2002, with the outbreak of the Second Intifada, Israel reoccupied most of the Territories, leaving the Palestinian Authority without any instrument of government. With this direct reoccupation, hard conditions prevailed in the daily life of Palestinians living in these occupied territories: Collective punishment measures inflicted upon them ranged from the general siege on towns and villages, to the demolition of access roads, to hundreds of military checkpoints, to curfews that are very frequently imposed impeding all movements inside the town, to the assassination of Palestinian leaders and activists, to the shelling and demolishing of houses and agricultural structures. This situation led to economic and social strangulation" (*Faithful Witness*, 142). He argues that terrorism will disappear once an independent, self-determining Palestinian state is established, and he blames Israel for refusing to make peace and for refusing the return to the 1967 borders. He insists that the Palestinians would be peaceful neighbors, no longer bearing hostility toward Israel, if only they were fully independent and self-determining. As he affirms: "Once the Palestinians are satisfied, once they are free and independent in their state, they will become friendly to Israel. Once the Palestinians are friendly to Israel, the other Arab peoples will be just as friendly" (*Faithful Witness*, 145).

be a good start. But on a theological level, Christians do not have to turn immediately to Christian eschatology in the manner that Marchadour and Neuhaus do. Instead, Christians should first look more closely into Jewish covenantal commitments. This would not mean turning a blind eye to the situations of the Palestinians, but it would involve a willingness to examine Christian theology and Christian history vis-à-vis the Jewish people more broadly.

As will become clear, my position is influenced by David Novak's two-fold argument regarding Zionism and the State of Israel. First, he holds that "[b]ecause the Jewish people have a definite need [in obedience to God's covenantal commandment] to acquire and settle the land God has given them to acquire and settle, and because that can be done in today's world of realpolitik only by having a sovereign state with the political, economic, and military power necessary for its survival in the world, the State of Israel has a justified claim on the support of the entire Jewish people."[37] On these grounds he supports the 1948 establishment of the State of Israel and the ongoing sustaining of the State of Israel as a Jewish state. He holds that its citizens, and "the entire Jewish people," must "risk life, limb, and property for the survival of the Jewish state."[38]

Second, however, Novak holds that "it is a great theological error to invest the humanly devised State of Israel with the sanctity of the land of Israel, and even more so, with the sanctity of the people of Israel."[39] Therefore, while insisting upon the theological necessity of Israel settling the land—and thus also upon the theological necessity of Jews' supporting the State of Israel and its ongoing existence—he does not conflate the State of Israel with God's covenantal people and their inheritance of the land.[40] The people and

---

37. Novak, *Zionism and Judaism*, 195-96.

38. Novak, *Zionism and Judaism*, 196. See also Berger, "Jewish-Christian Relations," 360-61: "the critical importance of Israel to Jewish survival extends far beyond its boundaries. So many Jews have become psychologically dependent upon the existence of the State—so many perceptions of Jewish history, Jewish identity, indeed of Judaism itself, have been linked to its success—that the destruction of Israel would mean not only the mass extermination of its inhabitants but the spiritual death of a majority of diaspora Jewry." Berger's essay originally appeared in 1983, but his point has even more resonance today. Berger adds that "non-Jews often fail to perceive the magnitude of the danger or to recognize the link between the threat to Israel and the threat to both Jewish lives and Jewish survival," and he fears that many non-Jews "are prepared to face the destruction of the Jewish people (not only the State of Israel) with relative equanimity" ("Jewish-Christian Relations," 361, 363).

39. Novak, *Zionism and Judaism*, 196.

40. Here Novak could agree with Pope Emeritus Benedict XVI, who argues that the establishment of the State of Israel as a homeland for the Jewish people "expresses God's faithfulness to the people of Israel," even though "[t]he nontheological character

land are divinely chosen in a way that the *State* of Israel, as a nation-state, is not. At the same time, the State of Israel is certainly a Jewish state. Novak holds that "gentile citizens of the state ought to acknowledge the raison d'être of the *Jewish* state they have chosen to live in," by publicly recognizing "the political legitimacy of the Jewish state in the land of Israel."[41] In return, Novak suggests that the State of Israel—in which non-Jewish citizens are presently second-class citizens in certain ways, despite the intentions of the State of Israel's Declaration of Independence[42]—could revive "the institution of the *ger toshav*, that is, giving true Jewish status to non-Jewish citizens of the Jewish state."[43]

In sum, Novak supports a Jewish polity in the land of Israel in which Jews retain "political power over gentiles," but he does not make the State of Israel, as such, into a theological entity with the divinely chosen status of

---

of the Jewish state means . . . that it cannot as such be considered the fulfillment of the promises of Scripture" (Benedict XVI, "Grace and Vocation," 179).

41. Novak, *Zionism and Judaism*, 207, 219. For the opposite perspective—describing "the settler-colonial structure of the Jewish state (or more accurately the Zionist state)" and condemning the "Zionist system that is built on the premise that the state established on their [the Palestinians'] homeland is actually the 'state of the Jewish people' and the homeland itself is the 'homeland of the Jewish people'" (xi)—see the essays in Rouhana, ed., *Israel and Its Palestinian Citizens*. Citing the *Haifa Declaration* of May 2007, to which he was a signator, Nadim N. Rouhana makes clear that in his view the problem consists in the 1948 event by which Palestinians, without their consent, became "citizens" of a new state of "Israel" in which they lacked equal rights. Along similar lines, see Masalha, *Bible and Zionism*. Masalha favors "a single, secular democratic framework in Palestine-Israel" (*Bible and Zionism*, 290; cf. 319), thus bringing the notion of a "Jewish state" to an end. In this vein see also Said, *Question of Palestine*; Said, *Politics of Dispossession*; Prior, *Zionism and the State of Israel*; Rogan and Shlaim, eds., *War for Palestine*; Masalha, *Imperial Israel and the Palestinians*; and Masalha, ed., *Catastrophe Remembered*.

42. See Masri, *Dynamics of Exclusionary Constitutionalism*. Novak notes that "Israel's Declaration of Independence speaks of 'equal rights for all citizens, regardless of religion, race, or gender'": *Zionism and Judaism*, 199. Novak recognizes that the question is "how in a true democracy can one people [the Jewish people] be so privileged? Aren't all the citizens of a democracy, their ethnicity notwithstanding, supposed to be equal across the board?" (*Zionism and Judaism*, 199).

43. Novak, *Zionism and Judaism*, 224. He goes on to say: "It is hard for many Jews to contemplate what should be the presence of non-Jews in the land of Israel or as citizens of the State of Israel. That is because of the experience of the Holocaust. For many Jews, the message that emerges from that shattering experience is that the State of Israel represents the Jewish reaction to the abandonment of the Jews by the nations-of-the-world during the Holocaust. So, why should Jews be concerned with gentiles who have been so unconcerned with the Jews, if not continually hostile to the Jews? I can well understand that kind of feeling, but I don't sympathize with it. It seems to me that it distorts the true raison d'être of a Jewish state in the land of Israel" (Novak, *Zionism and Judaism*, 224).

the people and the land.⁴⁴ Nor does he imagine that the return of the Jewish people to the land and the establishment of the State of Israel must be the harbingers or the vehicles of the eschaton. He recognizes that only God, in his absolute freedom, can bring about the "truly radical future (*l'atid la-vo*), which is the 'end of days' (*aharit ha-yamim*) or the *eschaton*."⁴⁵

The Catholic Church today affirms that the Jewish people are "the people of God of the Old Covenant, never revoked by God" and that the Jewish people are "the present-day people of the Covenant concluded with Moses."⁴⁶ If the Jewish people are the "people of the Covenant concluded with Moses," then this must include the land promise, since the pledge that God makes to Moses at the burning bush is that God will lead the Israelites "to a good and broad land, a land flowing with milk and honey, to the place of the Canaanites, the Hittites, the Amorites, the Perizzites, the Hivites, the Amorites, the Perizzities, the Hivites, and the Jebusites" (Exod 3:8). This land is the same land promised covenantally by God to Abraham, Isaac, and Jacob. The unrevoked covenant today, therefore, includes the promise of land—the actual land of Canaan where the biblical people of Israel dwelt (even if its dimensions are disputed and sometimes biblically unclear). In the words of Gavin D'Costa, "the promise of the land by God to his People remains intact, as part of the irrevocable covenant."⁴⁷

Christians know in faith, however, that this unrevoked covenant has been fulfilled by Christ. I agree with Marchadour and Neuhaus when they comment: "The fulfillment of the promises in Jesus Christ . . . implies a

---

44. Novak, *Zionism and Judaism*, 200. He thereby provides space for critique of the State of Israel in terms of its specific exercises of military power and whether or not it is acting justly in particular situations. He also provides theological space for "a non-Jewish polity within the land of Israel" (Novak, *Zionism and Judaism*, 223).

45. Novak, *Athens and Jerusalem*, 83. Novak argues that in this world "there is no potential but only a possibility" (in Aristotelian terms) for God's redemption to take place (*Athens and Jerusalem*, 83). The timing of the eschatological consummation is entirely up to God.

46. John Paul II, "Address to Representatives"; cited in D'Costa, "The Mystery of Israel," 941. Along the same positive lines, D'Costa also cites the *Catechism*, §839; Benedict XVI, "Address at the Synagogue of Rome"; and Pope Francis's 2013 Apostolic Exhortation *Evangelii Gaudium*.

47. D'Costa, *Catholic Doctrines*, ix. See also the recent reflections of Pope Emeritus Benedict XVI, in which he suggests that the formula "never-revoked covenant" does not get to the covenantal heart of the matter: "Yes, God's love is indestructible. But the covenant history between God and man also includes human failure, the breaking of the covenant and its internal consequences: the destruction of the temple, the scattering of Israel, and the call to repentance, which restores man's capacity for the covenant" (Benedict XVI, "Grace and Vocation," 183). No doubt this is right, but Christians have to be very careful to avoid overreading the past two thousand years of Jewish history, which Christians have interpreted falsely in the past with deadly consequences.

radical change concerning the place given to the Land in light of Jesus' life, death, and resurrection. The promise is no longer limited to one particular Land and to one specific people. Instead, it is addressed to the entire surface of the earth and to all of humanity."[48] Marchadour and Neuhaus have not thereby bypassed the land promise. Rather, they correctly perceive the New Testament's understanding that the land promise has been eschatologically fulfilled and thus transformed. In Romans 4:13, Paul teaches that the land promise was "the promise to Abraham and his descendants, that they should inherit the world." Paul was not alone in presuming that the eschatological fulfillment of the land promise must encompass the whole world (and indeed, for Paul, the whole cosmos): similar views of the land promise are found in Jubilees 19, 22, and 32; Philo's *On the Life of Moses*; and—in the Catholic Bible—Sirach 44:21. Carla Swafford Works points out that "Paul's language of inheriting the world, though bigger than land as territoried space, is congruent with other Hellenistic Jewish literature. Far from spiritualizing the promise of the land, this literature expands the physical space of inheritance to incorporate the whole earth."[49] Believing that the eschatological kingdom has been inaugurated by Jesus Christ, Christians believe that the land promise has been fulfilled so that Christ now reigns over the whole world and the whole cosmos, having inaugurated (but not consummated) the glorious renewal of all creation.

How, then, can Catholics affirm with the Jewish people that their covenant (including the land promise that is the basis of Jewish "Zionism," namely, Jewish return to the "land of Canaan" to dwell in and govern it) is *unrevoked* while at the same time affirming that Jesus Christ has *fulfilled* the land promise and established his reign, the inaugurated kingdom of God, *over the whole world*? I briefly explored this question in the second section of my book's Introduction, but I investigate it in more detail in this chapter.

The chapter proceeds in four steps. First, I examine the biblical testimony to the covenant of people and land, including the ways in which the prophets understood exile from the land and also the prophets' visions of an eschatological consummation involving the people and land. I highlight the problems that arose in biblical times for the doctrine of God's people and land, including the cataclysm of the Babylonian exile, as well as the tensions recorded in the New Testament between Christian and non-Christian Jews caused by the proclamation that the Messiah has come in Jesus of Nazareth.

48. Marchadour and Neuhaus, *Land, the Bible, and History*, 64.
49. Works, *Least of These*, 104. See also Byrne, *Romans*, 157; as well as Frankel, *Land of Canaan*, 395–96. For further discussion see Wazana, *All the Boundaries*; H. G. May, "Aspects of the Imagery of World Dominion"; and Blidstein, "Hast Thou Chosen Us to Rule?"

In this first section, I recognize that Christians retain a relation to the specific land of Canaan and to Jerusalem. But I make clear that "in and through the person and work of Christ all of God's promises have reached their *telos*," so that the true promised land is found in the "body of Christ" (the Church) and, thus, in the "new creation" (Gal 6:15) that Christ has inaugurated but not consummated.[50] For this reason, Christianity does not and cannot hold a Jewish Zionist view of the land.

Yet, Christian reflection on the promised land should not be limited to the perspective of Christian inaugurated eschatology, true though this eschatology is. My second section delves more deeply into part of the reason why Christian theologians must receive with utmost seriousness the Jewish people's covenantal claim to the land of Canaan. For centuries Christians treated the ongoing Jewish people as though the latter were a divinely cursed people doomed to wander until the final judgment without ever possessing their land again. In this second section, I briefly set forth some patristic and medieval instances of Christian persecution of Jews, before focusing on the horrific fact that in the decades prior to the Holocaust, Catholics closely linked to the Vatican were vigorously promoting the blood libel against the Jewish people.[51] As Joseph Ratzinger remarks with notable understatement:

---

50. O. R. Martin, *Bound for the Promised Land*, 170. Regarding the Abrahamic covenant and its land promise, Martin adds that "the flexibility of the geographical boundaries indicates that, although the boundaries initially delimit territory, the territory anticipates something more. That is, although it begins as a localized geographical plot, its rich theological associations and eschatological horizons actually extend beyond the territory itself" (*Bound for the Promised Land*, 75). Similarly, in the prophets "the promise of restoration goes far beyond what was previously experienced and is described in astonishing realities, for it includes not only the nation of Israel but also the nations, and not only the boundaries of the Promised Land but also the entire earth" (O. R. Martin, *Bound for the Promised Land*, 96).

51. Philip A. Cunningham and Didier Pollefeyt rightly warn against those who remark "that the Sinai covenant was 'often broken by the Israelites' without considering how often Christians may have 'broken' their covenantal life in Christ" ("Triune One," 188). Yet, I find Cunningham and Pollefeyt's soteriology to be inadequate from a Christian perspective, since they shy away from naming Jesus as the *Messiah of Israel* (although they name him "Christ") and since their account of salvation involves the Word's dwelling with his people but not salvation from sin and death (or from the covenantal curse). They state that "Jews do not need to share in the Christian experience of the Logos incarnated as Jesus to be participants in covenant with a saving God, since they continue to experience the indwelling of God within their community and people. From a Christian perspective, this indwelling necessarily involves the Logos, notwithstanding that the Word's incarnation in Jesus has not been revealed to Israel as a whole" (Cunningham and Pollefeyt, "Triune One," 199). What is missing here is the Messiah's redemptive suffering and death for Israel's sins and the sins of the whole world.

"the definitive nature of the unbreakable New Covenant . . . does not mean that [Christian] infractions of this Covenant are insignificant."[52]

Along lines sketched in my book's Introduction, therefore, the second section of this chapter develops the point that the Jewish people have been scandalized by Christian counter-witness, so that the Jewish people (as a whole) are in a state of "invincible ignorance" with regard to the claims that Christians make about Jesus.[53] This point affects Christian theological engagement with the doctrine of the land, because it means that even though Christ has fulfilled and transformed the land promise (establishing a cosmic kingdom), the ongoing Jewish people remain obligated to the original form of the covenant that God established with them, given that the covenant has not been revoked and the Jewish people legitimately do not know that the Messiah has come. On this basis, Christians should be able to recognize that

---

52. Ratzinger, *Many Religions—One Covenant*, 65. Ratzinger holds that, in a certain sense, for Christians "the Sinai covenant is indeed superseded," but only insofar as to follow Christ is "to keep the Torah, which has been fulfilled in him once and for all" (*Many Religions—One Covenant*, 70). For a critique of Ratzinger's position as "thoroughly supersessionist" because of his view that Jesus Christ fulfills Israel's covenants, see Boys, "Covenant in Contemporary Ecclesial Documents," 105. For Boys's two-track (or, indeed, multi-track) understanding of God's salvific purposes, see Boys, *Has God Only One Blessing?* See also the strong criticism of Ratzinger's position (and his *Many Religions—One Covenant*) offered by Moyaert and Pollefeyt, "Israel and the Church"; as well as by Aguzzi, "One Step Forward, Two Steps Back." Moyaert and Pollefeyt rightly criticize past Christian views about the ongoing Jewish people, but they lump together all "fulfillment" perspectives, including Ratzinger's, as "christomonist" and "ecclesiomonist" ("Israel and the Church," 160). They raise the concern: "what is the lasting significance of the first covenant if a more complete second covenant exists[?] Theologically speaking, what is the value of God's first covenant with Israel in light of the choice of God to make a new, unconditional, and more complete covenant through Christ?" (Moyaert and Pollefeyt, "Israel and the Church," 165). I hold that part of the answer is that Jesus, the Messiah, is a Jew. The new covenant, therefore, does not repudiate the earlier covenant but elevates it. The "lasting significance" of the new covenant requires the "lasting significance" of the first covenant. Moreover, the first covenant foresaw the possibility of its messianic and eschatological fulfillment; and the new covenant, as the inauguration of that messianic kingdom, also opens up to a consummation that goes far beyond what we can now imagine—and to an overcoming of present weaknesses and blind spots (this is what Aguzzi misses in Ratzinger, due to Aguzzi's critique of the "imperial" claims of the Catholic Church and to his view that Ratzinger has an overrealized eschatology). Moyaert and Pollefeyt are correct about the Church's teaching—but not correct in their criticism of it—when they remark: "The Church confirms Israel's intrinsic value but always within the borders of particular Christian *a priori's*, such as the uniqueness of Jesus as the universal savior" ("Israel and the Church," 166).

53. Gavin D'Costa notes that from a Christian perspective, "The objective truth is that the Messiah has come. The subjective truth of rabbinic Judaism is that he has not.... God permits 'invincible ignorance,' which is the condition of rabbinic Judaism's legitimate path of following God faithfully" ("Mystery of Israel," 974).

it is the Jewish people's covenantal duty to "declare in Zion the name of the Lord, and in Jerusalem his praise" (Ps 102:21) by dwelling in and governing the land of Canaan, until the "mystery" that Paul evokes (11:25–26) has come to fruition in the fullness of the eschaton.

Third, to enhance my understanding of the Jewish perspective on the land, I turn to the arguments of David Novak's *The Election of Israel* and *Zionism and Judaism*.[54] Novak considers that Christians should support the Jewish people's return to the land and should support the existence and flourishing of the Jewish State of Israel. His main reason is that the living God has covenantally obligated the Jewish people to dwell in and govern this particular land. As he emphasizes, the Jewish people are therefore striving, by God's grace, to obey their covenantal obligations.[55]

Notably, Novak rejects setting up a covenantal test for the legitimacy of the State of Israel, as though any human could declare the state to be *illegitimate* on covenantal grounds.[56] It would be especially irresponsible to claim to be able to make a negative theological judgment about the existential future of a state in which one does not live. Instead, Novak calls upon Christians simply to remember that, according to Christian theology itself, God has not revoked his covenants with the Jewish people.

54. I have chosen Novak as a representative of ongoing Judaism on this topic because of my admiration for his work. One might also see, for example, Heschel's *Israel*, written in response to the 1967 Six-Day War in which Arab armies led by Egypt blockaded the Gulf of Aqaba and attacked the State of Israel with the intention of destroying it—while "the world stood still. The world that was silent while six million died, was silent again, save for individual friends" (Heschel, *Israel*, 198). Trying to explain this silence, Heschel proposes that among other reasons, "[w]e have failed to clarify its [the State of Israel's] meaning, its value to our existence. We have failed to convey its significance to our Christian friends" (Heschel, *Israel*, 202).

55. Barron has similarly pointed out with regard to Christian participation in the new covenant: "*The* great mark of the disciple is obedience, abiding by the divine command; and the great mark of the anti-disciple is trying to master God" (Barron, *Strangest Way*, 35).

56. To my mind, Walter Brueggemann treads too far in this direction when he writes (in the context of the Israeli-Palestinian conflict) that "Christian appeal to biblical land traditions must insist that land possession is held, according to that tradition, only as land practices are under the discipline of neighbor practices grounded in the Torah. Any claim of land apart from that Torah tradition is deeply suspect and open to profound critique" (Brueggemann, *Land*, 203). This seems to imply that if Christians judge that the State of Israel is not following the Torah's "neighbor practices," Christians can determine that the State of Israel's existence (as such) is unjust. I do not see how Brueggemann's position comports with his earlier statement that "the urgency of the security of the contemporary state of Israel is readily acknowledged" (Brueggemann, *Land*, 203). It seems that his fundamental point is that "the Palestinian community also has a profound claim upon the land" (Brueggemann, *Land*, 203). I think this is correct, which is why I support a compromise two-state solution.

On the basis of the work of the first three sections, my fourth and final section offers a constructive Christian theological account of the land. I explain again why the Jewish view of the land cannot be the Christian one—even with regard to Jews who have become Christians.[57] Philip Cunningham accurately states, "The Land of Israel is not inextricably connected to Christian theology, it has no central place in the Christian effort to live as Christ"; and this is true even though the land of Israel retains "a sacramental aspect as the place where Jesus lived and died."[58] As the New Testament makes clear, for Christians the promised land is the body of Christ and the new creation, the renewed world and cosmos. Paraphrasing the Letter to the Hebrews, Robert Wilken remarks: "Christians have no abiding city. Their

---

57. For a differing viewpoint, see Kinzer, *Jerusalem Crucified, Jerusalem Risen*. Focusing on Luke and Acts, Kinzer argues that whereas the Gentile members of the Church are not obliged to keep the commandments of the Torah (other than the moral precepts), the Jewish members of the Church remain "obliged," as a matter of salvation and not simply as an optional pious practice, "to circumcise their sons, and to keep Torah" (*Jerusalem Crucified, Jerusalem Risen*, 205). I agree with Kinzer to the extent that I hold that, during the time period recorded by Acts, this question was a "live" one in the Christian community. But I think that theologically speaking, not only Luke-Acts but also the other books of the New Testament make clear that the answer is that Jewish Christians are not and indeed cannot be obligated as a matter of salvation to observe Torah in the form it had prior to Jesus Christ. For Kinzer, the covenantal land, too, is not reconfigured by Christ. He thinks that its eschatological consummation will involve the Jewish people (as distinct from the Gentiles) living and reigning in Jerusalem and its environs. He argues that the Church itself is meant to be "bilateral in composition and character, a united community with a twofold corporate expression—one Jewish, the other multi-national" (*Jerusalem Crucified, Jerusalem Risen*, 288; he is here appreciatively summarizing Dauermann, *Converging Destinies*, 188–90). For a critique of Kinzer's position that reflects my own concerns, see Farrow, "Jew and Gentile," 985–86, 990; as well as Farrow, *Theological Negotiations*, 249. For a position that extends Kinzer's views to political theology as a whole—and that relates also to Willitts, *Matthew's Messianic Shepherd-King*—see N. R. Brown, *For the Nation*; as well as, more broadly, Westerman, *Learning Messiah*. See also the irrefutable point made by Jonathan T. Pennington: "The Gospel proclaimed by Jesus is worldwide, encompassing the heavens and all the earth, including the Gentiles. Christianity from its earliest days is not just a Palestine- and land-based religion, but a universal one including all the nations of the earth" (J. T. Pennington, *Heaven and Earth in Matthew*, 326).

58. Cunningham, *Seeking Shalom*, 220. With regard to the "sacramental" aspect of the land, Cunningham directs attention to Lux, *Jewish People*. Like Lux, Cunningham recognizes that Palestinian Christians "have a distinctive self-understanding as being the 'living stones' whose church communities have continuously witnessed to the events of Jesus' life in the places where they physically occurred" (*Seeking Shalom*, 220–21; cf. Lux, *Jewish People*, chapter 4). Jewish Christians, too, often feel a deep connection to the land of Israel. But Cunningham is right to insist that "Christianity strongly emphasizes that God can be encountered anywhere" (*Seeking Shalom*, 221). See also Khoury, "History of Jerusalem," 9–20.

hope is set on a heavenly country, on the Jerusalem above, a city not made with human hands."[59]

Again, however, because God's covenants with the Jewish people have been fulfilled rather than revoked—and because Catholic persecution has obscured the face of Jesus for the Jewish people as a whole, meaning that the Jewish people continue to relate to God through their unrevoked covenant as they await the Messiah (in accord with the "mystery" of God's plan, and thus with a positive import)—I argue that Catholics should fully support Jews in their efforts to obey God's covenantal commandments in their original mode, including the commandment to dwell in and govern the land.

I do not intend here to minimize the fact that Catholics must also support a Palestinian state in the land alongside the Jewish state.[60] In this regard, it is appropriate for Catholics to raise concerns of justice in addressing both Israeli and Palestinian leaders, and to urge both sides to support two-state solutions with compromises on both sides, presuming that the security of both sides can be established.[61] But Catholic engagement with

---

59. Wilken, *Land Called Holy*, xii. Wilken is well aware of the tradition of Christian pilgrimage, and his book examines "how the land of the Bible, the land of Israel, the land of Canaan . . . became a Holy Land to Christians" between the fourth and seventh centuries, ending with the Muslim conquest in 640 AD (*Land Called Holy*, xiv). He also investigates "early Christian ideas that an earthly kingdom would be established in Jerusalem (millenarianism) and their importance in shaping initial Christian views of the Holy Land" (Wilken, *Land Called Holy*, xvi).

60. For a viewpoint that strikes me as extreme, however, see Masalha, *Palestine Nakba*. Masalha compares the Palestinian need for remembrance of the Nakba ("the destruction of historic Palestine" [*Palestine Nakba*, 2]) to the Jewish need for the remembrance of the Holocaust. Not atypically in works by Palestinian scholars, he emphasizes that "the root cause of the Palestine conflict is the Nakba," and the solution is insistence upon "the unity and territorial integrity of historic Palestine," which means the end of the Jewish State and the return of Palestinian refugees and exiles "to enjoy a normal and peaceful life on an equal basis in Palestine" (*Palestine Nakba*, 256). Masalha rejects the notion of the Jews' obligation to dwell in and govern the land as a biblical myth given prominence by Western Christianity. See also El-Hasan, *Is the Two-State Solution Already Dead?*, which focuses on Israeli injustices and denies that there is such a thing as the "Jewish people" descended from the biblical Jewish people. El-Hasan bemoans the "deep intra-Palestinian rift" (*Is the Two-State Solution Already Dead?*, 214) between Fatah and Hamas, and he contends that Israel is pretending to offer a two-state solution while in reality offering solely "a truncated, non-viable semi-sovereign state on part of the 'disputed lands' (occupied lands)" (*Is the Two-State Solution Already Dead?*, 219). For Jewish criticism of the State of Israel, see Gans, *Just Zionism*. See also the criticisms advanced by Kretzmer, *Occupation of Justice*.

61. See for example (although I disagree with him) John T. Pawlikowski, OSM's 2005 critique of Jewish leaders for focusing on "the safety and security of the State of Israel" and refusing to engage questions concerning "certain measures being taken by the Israeli government in the West Bank and Gaza" ("Challenge of *Tikkun Olam*," 236).

the doctrine of the promised land has notable theological reasons for supporting the Jewish people in dwelling and governing in the land of Canaan. To this extent, there can indeed be a Catholic version of Zionism.

As indicated in my Introduction and first chapter, the Catholic Church's perspective on the Jewish people began to change with *Nostra Aetate* and with Pope John Paul II's affirmation that God's covenant with Israel has never been revoked.[62] Never revoked does not mean untransformed: a Christian Israelology must affirm the eschatological fulfillment of the land promise by Jesus Christ. But this affirmation should now be joined to a theological commitment to supporting the Jewish people in living out their unrevoked covenantal obligation to dwell in and govern the land, in the context of a two-state solution. Given the Pauline "mystery" of Jews and Gentiles in God's plan of salvation and the impact of centuries of Christian persecution—an impact that will become painfully clear in this chapter—Catholics should support the existence and flourishing of the Jewish State of Israel.

II. Biblical Foundations: A Covenant and Its Tensions

Let me begin with a troubling question. If God wanted to establish a people in a promised land, why did God not do it in a simpler way, rather than through a promise to Abraham that was to be followed, some centuries later, by a bloody partial conquest? According to Scripture, Joshua tells the Israelites before they conquer Jericho, "Shout; for the Lord has given you the city" (Josh 6:17).[63] But even when they had finally conquered the land,

---

62. For Pope John Paul II's groundbreaking statement, see his "Address to Representatives," 60. Pope Pius X rejected Theodor Herzl's request in 1904 to lend his support to the Zionist movement, and Pope Pius XII did not support the establishment of the State of Israel in 1948 (see his encyclical *In Multiplicibus Curis*). See also Klein, "Vatican and Zionism" and Klein, "Vatican View of Jewry." For background to Herzl, see Avineri, *Theodor Herzl*. See also Small, "In Our Time."

63. For various Christian perspectives on these texts, see Billings, "*Israel Served the Lord*"; Walton and Walton, *Lost World of the Israelite Conquest*; Benedict XVI, *Verbum Domini*, §42. The Waltons argue that "Joshua's wars are recounted in terms of the typology of macrocosmic order and ongoing creation, but because of the literal nature of the land their actual actions take the form of military conquest" (*Lost World of the Israelite Conquest*, 169). They add that the author of Joshua used hyperbole and that the point was not actually to kill all the inhabitants but rather to destroy the previous communal identity of the peoples of the land so that now the land is identified as YHWH's. I think that the Waltons' reading makes historical and theological sense, especially if the actual settlement of the land by the people did not involve much full-scale conquest, as archaeological evidence suggests. For further discussion, see Bergsma and Pitre, *Old*

it turned out that the people of Israel still "dwelt among the Canaanites, the Hittites, the Amorites, the Perizzites, the Hivites, and the Jebusites; and they took their daughters to themselves for wives, and their own daughters they gave to their sons; and they served other gods" (Judg 3:5–6). What kind of gift of land is this?

Moreover, the book of Exodus makes clear that the people continually sought to worship other gods and complained about their God. When the people finally entered the promised land, almost immediately "they forsook the Lord, and served the Baals and Ashtaroth" (Judg 2:13). Most of the kings of Judah—and all the kings of Israel (the northern kingdom)—are presented as idolaters who do not care much for justice, let alone for the law of Moses or for the celebration of the liturgical feasts commanded by God. Nor are the common people of the two kingdoms (Israel and Judah) generally much better than their idolatrous kings. As the Psalmist says, "God looks down from heaven upon the sons of men to see if there are any that are wise, that seek after God. They have all fallen away; they are all alike depraved; there is none that does good, no, not one" (Ps 53:2–3).[64] Yet, it is also true that the yearning of the Israelites to obey God is often deeply moving and inspiring.

When we reach the time of Jeremiah, we find God accusing his people of doing a thing unheard of even in many pagan nations: "For cross to the coasts of Cyprus and see, or send to Kedar and examine with care, see if there has been such a thing. Has a nation changed its gods, even though they are no gods? But my people have changed their glory for that which does not profit" (Jer 2:10–11). The result, according to Jeremiah's prophecy, is that the people are going to be destroyed and the survivors exiled to a foreign land.[65] Nevertheless, God promises to restore the people to their land

---

Testament, 298–312.

64. For further discussion of the searing portraits of human sinfulness (and God's remedies) in Israel's Scriptures, see Boda, *Severe Mercy*; and Freedman, *Nine Commandments*.

65. Norman C. Habel describes Jeremiah's understanding of the land as follows: "The land is YHWH's chosen *naḥalah* from among all lands; the people are 'planted' in YHWH's personal plot of land. No other deity or power is tolerated in this union. . . . According to this ideology, when God's people violate their relationship with YHWH through cultic or social evils, they pollute the sacred land. The land becomes a tragic victim, suffering at the hands of God's people and God's anger. . . . The land suffers desolation and the people suffer exile" (Habel, *Land Is Mine*, 95). This historical-critical summary, while accurate in its way, contrasts with Walter Brueggemann's suggestion that for Jeremiah the land is Israel's covenantal inheritance from YHWH as Israel's "father"—so that Jeremiah's point is that Israel has failed properly "to acknowledge the giver of land and call him 'father'" and has thereby violated the meaning of being an heir (Brueggemann, *Land*, 113). Brueggemann finds that Jeremiah imports a positive meaning into the loss of the land: "That is, when Yahweh has willed land-loss, as he

after the exile. As Walter Brueggemann states with regard to a similar divine promise delivered through Ezekiel: "Yahweh will not forever be exiled from his place. Nor will he forever permit his people to be landless."[66]

Going beyond mere restoration to the land, God promises through Jeremiah that he will bring about a new covenant through which all the tribes of Israel and Judah will come to know God, to possess God's law as written on their hearts, and to receive complete forgiveness of their sins (Jer 31:31–34).[67] Still more boldly, God promises through Isaiah that "[o]n this mountain [Zion] the Lord of hosts will make for all peoples a feast of fat things, a feast of choice wines.... And he will destroy on this mountain the covering that is cast over all peoples, the veil that is spread over all nations. He will swallow up death for ever, and the Lord God will wipe away tears from all faces, and the reproach of his people he will take away" (Isa 25:6–8). At the end of the book of Isaiah, God promises that ultimately all nations will come to Jerusalem to see God's glory: "I am coming to gather all nations and tongues; and they shall come and shall see my glory, and I will set a sign among them.... And they shall bring all your brethren from all the nations as an offering to the Lord ... to my holy mountain Jerusalem" (Isa 66:18–20).[68]

Seemingly as a step toward the fulfillment of this promise, the people of Judah returned to Jerusalem from their Babylonian exile, thanks in part

---

surely has, to cling to the land is an act of rebellion that can only fail. That is a fresh departure in Israel's faith: (a) Landholding is an act of disobedience (see Num 14:39–45). (b) Land-loss is an act of faith. Exile is the way to new life in new land. One can scarcely imagine a more radical, less likely understanding of history. In covenantal categories, embrace of curse is the [way] to blessing. In New Testament categories, embrace of death is the way to life (Luke 9:23–27; Rom 6:1–11)" (Brueggemann, *Land*, 115; cf. 126).

66. Brueggemann, *Land*, 131.

67. Habel proposes that Jeremiah is here portraying "a 'new planting' in the land and a 'new heart' in the people of the land to re-establish the intimacy and purity of the original land-god-people relationship" (*Land Is Mine*, 96)—whereas I think the prophecy goes beyond the original relationship. He argues that for Jeremiah, "God's land is like Eden, a land of plenty (*karmel*) and pleasure (Jer. 2:7; 12:10)" (*Land Is Mine*, 78).

68. For discussion of Isaiah 40–66 on the land (and especially Jerusalem), see Wilken, *Land Called Holy*, 14–17. Wilken observes that the "sublime language and soaring images" of Isaiah "sowed the seeds for a new cartography of hope, expanding the horizon of human expectation.... Yet, his vision of the future, like all eschatological hope within Judaism, finally had its origin in a very particular promise: the descendants of Abraham would one day possess the land given to them by God" (*Land Called Holy*, 17). See also Brueggemann, *Land*, 138–41; and Middlemas, "Divine Reversal." Brueggemann reads the prophecies about the restoration of the people to the land as figuring resurrection to (eternal) life, as well as being about God's ability to start history afresh. Along somewhat similar lines, see Levenson, *Resurrection*.

to the leadership of Ezra and Nehemiah, and thanks also to the Persian conquest of Babylon. Yet, we should recall the painful ending of the book of Ezra. After the exiles have returned, Ezra finds that "[t]he sons of Israel and the priests and the Levites have not separated themselves from the peoples of the lands with their abominations, from the Canaanites, the Hittites, the Perizzites, the Jebusites, the Ammonites, the Moabites, the Egyptians, and the Amorites" (Ezra 9:1-2). Upon hearing this news, Ezra tears his robes and sits in ritual mourning. He commands that the people must separate themselves from their foreign wives, which involves a gruesome ripping apart of families. Likewise, toward the end of his life, Nehemiah finds many "Jews who had married women of Ashdod, Ammon, and Moab; and half of their children spoke the language of Ashdod, and they could not speak the language of Judah" (Neh 13:23-24). The pattern is clear: the sins of the people after the exile are similar to the sins of the people prior to the exile, and these sins continue to have disastrous consequences.[69]

After the time of Ezra and Nehemiah, the people of Israel continued on under increasing political strain, with various competing foreign kings and emperors taking turns invading the land and threatening the rebuilt temple. In the second century BC, some Jews, worn out by this strife and appreciative of Hellenistic culture, advocated accommodating themselves to the Gentile nations. They urged, "Let us go and make a covenant with the Gentiles round about us, for since we separated from them many evils have come upon us" (1 Macc 1:11). Other Jews persisted in obedience to the covenant, even to the point of martyrdom (1 Macc 1:62-63).[70]

It will be clear that the land promise always involved significant vulnerability. For this reason, Israel's doctrine of the covenantal people and land contains a strong eschatological dimension, as noted above in Isaiah. Through the prophets, God regularly promises the restoration of the people and their perfect dwelling with God in the land.

In the prophecy of Micah, God promises to gather the scattered people of Israel back to the land. God proclaims, "In that day . . . I will assemble the lame and gather those who have been driven away, and those whom I

---

69. See the analysis of the program of Ezra and Nehemiah in Brueggemann, *Land*, 145-50. His central point is that "Israel in the new history took seriously Yahweh's jealousy" (Brueggemann, *Land*, 150). For a theological reading of Ezra and Nehemiah, emphasizing Christians' profound debts to these leaders, see my *Ezra and Nehemiah*. For a sharp critique of Ezra and Nehemiah as offering a rationale for a chosen "people of God" undertaking a divinely sanctioned campaign against ethnic and religious "others" dwelling in the land, see (among other works, some of which I discuss in *Ezra and Nehemiah*) S. Johnson, "New Israel, New Canaan."

70. For helpful background, see Wilken, *Land Called Holy*, 23-29; Brueggemann, *Land*, 150-52.

have afflicted; and the lame I will make the remnant; and those who were cast off, a strong nation; and the Lord will reign over them in Mount Zion from this time forth and for evermore" (Mic 4:6–7). Similarly, through the prophet Zechariah, God exhorts his suffering people: "Sing and rejoice, O daughter of Zion; for behold, I come and I will dwell in the midst of you, says the Lord. And many nations shall join themselves to the Lord in that day, and shall be my people; and I [the Davidic king or Messiah] will dwell in the midst of you, and you shall know that the Lord of hosts has sent me to you" (Zech 2:10–11).[71] The eschatological fulfillment of the people and land will come about through God's wondrous dwelling in Jerusalem with his people.[72] Brueggemann sums up: "This hope for transformed land, renewed land, new land, became a central point for expectant Israel."[73]

What will the renewed land look like, and what will its boundaries be? Nili Wazana notes that many biblical texts include "[d]etailed geographical border descriptions: the 'land of Canaan' (Num 34:1–12), Ezekiel's vision of

---

71. On Zechariah see Wilken, *Land Called Holy*, 17–19, including the point that Zechariah is responsible for the term "holy land"—although the origins of the term go back to Ezekiel, whose "conception of the holy mountain on which stood the temple sanctioned the use of sacral language to depict the land as a whole" (Wilken, *Land Called Holy*, 19). In Zechariah, the "holy land" means Jerusalem and Judah. See also Brueggemann, *Land*, 143–44.

72. See the Pontifical Biblical Commission's 2001 document "Jewish People," §31: "After the return of the exiles, seen as imminent by Second Isaiah and soon to become a reality—but not in a very spectacular manner—the hope of *eschatological liberation* began to dawn: the spiritual successors of the exilic prophet announced the fulfilment, yet to come, of the redemption of Israel as a divine intervention at the end of time [cf. Isaiah 35:9–10 and 60:10–12]. It is as Saviour of Israel that the messianic prince is presented at the end of time (Mi 4:14–5:5)."

73. Brueggemann, *Land*, 156. Brueggemann embeds a sharp critique of the State of Israel in his book, accusing the State of Israel (under Ariel Sharon) of "undertaking an aggressive, brutalizing assault on the neighboring Palestinian population" (Brueggemann, *Land*, 158). Along lines that seem simplistic to me, he argues theologically that the State of Israel is violating the land promise by choosing "grasping" (through military force) rather than "waiting" upon God's gift as is required by God. He cites R. R. Ruether and H. J. Ruether, *Wrath of Jonah*. Adam Gregerman and others have shown that the Ruethers' work on the Israeli-Palestinian conflict retrieves numerous of the most odious Christian anti-Jewish tropes (including the view that the covenant of election and land is racist): see Gregerman, "Old Wine in New Bottles," 320, 322–23, 326–27, 329; J. K. Roth et al., "Ruethers' *Wrath of Jonah*." For an interpretation that is quite similar to Brueggemann's (including the motif of the goodness of landlessness for the Jews, about which the editors raise concerns), see Yoder, *Jewish-Christian Schism Revisited*. See also the work of the Mennonite scholar Weaver, "Sitting under the Vine"; as well as the response found in A. Levenson, "Four Brief Reflections." As Gregerman points out: "No author ever suggests that the Palestinians or any other people are truer to their own traditions when residing outside their ancestral land or under the sovereignty of others" ("Old Wine in New Bottles," 330). See also Ruether, "False Messianism."

the future land (Ezek 47:13–48:28), and the account of the tribal allocations (Joshua 15–19)."[74] However, as Wazana also points out, other biblical passages such as Zechariah 9:10, Psalm 2:8, and Psalm 72:8 envision a global Davidic kingdom.[75]

The latter perspective is that of Christian eschatology, insofar as the inaugurated kingdom (fulfilling the land promise) involves a transformed world and cosmos. When Jesus says the meek "shall inherit the earth" (Matt 5:5), he likely means that Jews and Gentile believers in Christ will inherit the whole world. As Ulrich Luz remarks regarding Matthew 5:5, "It is the earth, not only the land of Israel, that belongs to those who are kind [or meek], for the traditional promise of the land had long since been transposed into the cosmic realm."[76]

This inaugurated eschatological kingdom, the fulfillment of the land promise, stands at the heart of Christian faith. During Jesus' earthly ministry, some Jews hoped that he was the Messiah who would gather the scattered people, renew the temple, throw off the Roman yoke, and bring about the Spirit-filled eschatological kingdom that he himself announced. But when he was handed over to the Romans and crucified at the end of Passover week, he was abandoned even by almost all of his own disciples. To these very disciples, however, Jesus then showed his risen and glorified flesh. Christians believe that Jesus was and is the divine Messiah of Israel who has redeemed all peoples by his cross and resurrection. Thus, like Luz, Joseph Ratzinger/Pope Benedict XVI interprets Jesus' third beatitude, "Blessed are the meek, for they shall inherit the earth" (Matt 5:5) to mean that the whole earth eschatologically becomes God's, without national boundaries and supremely reflecting God's peace.[77]

In the *inaugurated* but not consummated kingdom of God, however, serious tensions remain. The tensions between the first Jewish followers of Jesus and their fellow Jews involved Christian understandings of the land promise, among other things.[78] As noted above, according to the Gospel

74. Wazana, *All the Boundaries*, 297.

75. Wazana notes that these latter passages likely "derive from Mesopotamian royal terminology, which depicts the reaches of imperial power as running 'from the upper to the lower sea.' In contrast to Mesopotamian documents, however, the biblical texts assert that true 'global power' belongs not to the king but to God. . . . The rule of the Davidic Dynasty as depicted in the Psalms is thus an image of God's reign as the Creator and guider of the world, who bestows on His earthly representative the authority to govern the whole earth" (*All the Boundaries*, 120–21).

76. Luz, *Matthew 1–7*, 194–95, citing Jubilees 22:14 and 32:19, along with Isaiah 60:21.

77. See Ratzinger, *Jesus of Nazareth* I.

78. See Pontifical Biblical Commission, "Jewish People," §41: "For Paul, Jesus'

of John, and indeed the New Testament as a whole, Jesus is the new temple (John 2:19–21). In Jesus Christ, the purpose of the land as the place where God will dwell with his people is fulfilled and reconfigured.[79] On the cross, Jesus goes to the Father in order to "prepare a place" for his followers and to take us to himself: "In my Father's house are many rooms" (John 14:2–3). In a similar vein, the Johannine book of Revelation expresses the eschatological reconfiguration of the land by depicting the "new heaven and . . . new earth"—the transformed and renewed cosmos—and "the holy city, new Jerusalem" (Rev 21:1–2). This eschatologically consummated land will need no temple, because the "new Jerusalem" will be the dwelling place of God and thus the new creation will be God's "temple."[80]

---

establishment of 'the new covenant in [his] blood' (1 Co 11:25) does not imply any rupture of God's covenant with his people, but constitutes its fulfilment. . . . Israel continues to be in a covenant relationship and remains the people to whom the fulfilment of the covenant was promised, because their lack of faith cannot annul God's fidelity (Rm 11:29). Even if some Israelites have observed the Law as a means of establishing their own justice, the covenant-promise of God, who is rich in mercy (Rm 11:26–27), cannot be abrogated. Continuity is underlined by affirming that Christ is the end and the fulfilment to which the Law was leading the people of God (Ga 3:24). . . . The Pauline Letters, then, manifest a twofold conviction: the insufficiency of the legal covenant of Sinai, on the one hand, and on the other, the validity of the covenant-promise. This latter finds its fulfilment in justification by faith in Christ, offered 'to the Jew first, but also to the Greek' (Rm 1:16)." See also §36: "The New Testament never says that Israel has been rejected. From the earliest times, the Church considered the Jews to be important witnesses to the divine economy of salvation."

79. For John's "Temple-Christology," emphasizing that "Divine space is now no longer located in a place but in a person," see Burge, *Jesus and the Land*, 52; cf. his broader discussion of "The Fourth Gospel and the land" at 43–57, as well as his summative point at 130 that "the New Testament applies to the person of Christ religious language formerly devoted to the Holy Land or Temple." Burge's main concern is to respond to evangelical Christian Zionism, which Burge considers to be not biblically warranted. For a critique of some aspects of Burge's book, see Bock, "Restoration of Israel," 168–77. Bock grants that there is "a lot of truth" in the view that "Jesus as Temple or as forming a new universal Temple community becomes the locus for holy space" and that "hope in the land is spiritualized to refer to a restored earth," but Bock argues that the New Testament teaches that there will come a "time when Israel responds to Jesus and God restores the nation"—a period where the Messiah (Jesus) reigns in Jerusalem and the twelve tribes are restored to their land. He directs attention to Fuller, *Restoration of Israel*. A better account of the restoration of Israel, in my view, is found in Pitre, *Jesus and the Last Supper*, 459–82.

80. Gregory Vall has argued that it is a mistake to view "the New Testament's handling of the Old Testament's theology of the land as an abrupt and arbitrary reinterpretation" (Vall, "'Man Is the Land,'" 150). Vall suggests that Davies comes close to this error, because he "treats the meanings that the New Testament authors assign to the traditional symbols of Judaism as extrinsic to those symbols and thus arbitrary," in a manner that leads to mere "replacement" rather than true fulfilment ("'Man Is the Land,'" 150). See W. D. Davies, *Gospel and the Land*; W. D. Davies, *Territorial Dimension*

Robert Wilken notes that among the early Christians, at least those who were not Gnostics, there was a general consensus that the new Jerusalem would be a heavenly Jerusalem come to earth, in accord with the book of Revelation as well as, arguably, with the imagery of Hebrews. Even after the Romans put an end to the Bar Kochba rebellion and exiled the Jewish people from Jerusalem (renamed Aelia Capitolina) in 135 AD, the Jewish people continued to hold that "there could be no full and God-pleasing Jewish life without the temple, without the city of Jerusalem, indeed without Jewish hegemony in the land."[81] Second-century Christians, too, often thought of the new Jerusalem (come down from heaven) as a city in the same earthly place that Jerusalem now stands. Justin Martyr and Irenaeus looked forward to a period of one thousand years in which Christ would reign in a newly adorned and enlarged Jerusalem. Prior to Origen—who interpreted the new Jerusalem as the whole new creation—"Christian eschatology remained wedded to the earth, retaining the realistic features of the [Jewish] restorationist tradition."[82]

Wilken is at his strongest in showing the difference between Christian eschatology pre- and post-Origen, a difference that other scholars have noted as well. But in *The Land Called Holy*, he does not do justice to the biblical grounding of the fulfilled land promise as the renewed world and renewed cosmos. The book of Revelation makes clear that all the blessed will dwell in the (impossibly vast) city, and that the city will neither possess a temple nor have any need for sun and moon—indeed there will be no night whatsoever, nor will there be a sea. This is a radically re-envisioned city and cosmos! Even if the language is symbolic, the thrust of the symbolism moves far beyond simply reinstating Jerusalem, now with Jesus as its king. As Ian Boxall observes, the "city" is "a symbol for the faithful Church,"

---

of Judaism. Vall notes, however, that Davies recognizes the value of the category of "sacrament" for understanding the New Testament's taking up of Jewish theologies of land. Vall argues that this "sacramental" model is already anticipated in the Old Testament itself. Vall corrects Wilken's contention that "[f]or the ancient Israelites *land* always referred to an actual land. Eretz Israel was not a symbol of a higher reality"; but he agrees with Wilken that the prophets' symbolic references to Jerusalem referred "to restoration of the actual city" (Wilken, *Land Called Holy*, 37, 41; cited in Vall, "'Man Is the Land,'" 146). See also Culbertson, "Eretz Israel"; as well as Karol Wojtyła's witness to the sacramentality of Israel's land, in John Paul II, *Place Within*, 111–18.

81. Wilken, *Land Called Holy*, 44.

82. Wilken, *Land Called Holy*, 59. See also Wilken, "*In novissimus diebus*," which shows that Wilken has a mastery of the complexities of the biblical and patristic discussion, especially the ways in which the church fathers were debating contemporaneous Jewish interpretations of the promises found in the prophets.

now enjoying "[t]he unmediated presence of God."[83] Wilken is correct that the "new heaven" and "new earth" will retain a link to the heaven and earth that we know, but the biblical images indicate that the differences will exceed our wildest imagination (as the prophets already made clear).[84]

Moreover, the fact that in the Christian view Christ reigns even now, not only in heaven but also on earth, shows the presence of some form of "spiritualization" (misleading though this term is), since most Jewish expectations of the Messiah were and are much more concrete in their hopes for immediate worldly peace and order. Some commentators argue that Christ's kingdom takes form on earth wherever economic and political justice is found — wherever we find that God "has put down the mighty from their thrones, and exalted those of low degree" (Luke 1:52).[85] Thus Walter Brueggemann comments on Luke 7:22: "The theme of radical inversion of landed and landless is presented as the central clue that the messianic age has dawned."[86] I recognize that care for the poor is a core teaching of Jesus

---

83. Boxall, *Revelation of Saint John*, 294-95. Emphasizing the symbolism, Peter J. Leithart remarks that "the heavenly city ... is *entirely* temple. It is an *enormous* cube, 12,000 stadia (1,500 miles) long, wide, and high, its walls 144 cubits (72 yards) thick. The city is like the mountain of Nebuchadnezzar's vision (Daniel 2), filling the earth. With a length and width measuring 12,000 stadia (v. 16), it has an area of 144,000,000 square stadia, enough not only for the 144,000 martyrs from the tribes of Israel who are the firstfruits of the city but also for the innumerable multitude from every tribe and nation that joins them. Then John records the vertical dimension, also 12,000 stadia, and thus gives us the volume of the city: 1,728,000,000,000,000" (Leithart, *Revelation 12-22*, 382). In addition, the gems that adorn the city (as well as the gold of its structures) connect with the precious stones that adorn the temple and the breastplate of the high priest. Note also, as Leithart says, that "[t]he Bridal city is not a temple for God; God is a temple for her" (Leithart, *Revelation 12-22*, 388).

84. See also Brueggemann's contention, against W. D. Davies, that in the New Testament "the land theme is more central than Davies believes and ... has not been so fully spiritualized as he concludes. It is more likely that the land theme can be understood in a dialectical way: in contexts of Gnosticism the land theme must be taken in a more physical, historical way; in contexts of politicizing the land theme must be taken in a more symbolic way" (Brueggemann, *Land*, 160).

85. See Brueggemann, *Land*, 161, citing Miranda, *Marx and the Bible*. Brueggemann grants that "it will not do to treat the New Testament as though it contains a simple promise of the land, as has been hinted by some liberation theologies informed by Marxist rhetoric" (*Land*, 164; cf. 204-5 on dialogue between Christian and Marxist views of land, though without sufficient awareness of the fallacies of Marxist economic theory).

86. Brueggemann, *Land*, 161. He goes on to interpret such passages as Luke 9:24, Luke 13:30, and Luke 14:11 as examples of "[t]he radical inversion of landed-landless arrangements" (Brueggemann, *Land*, 162). In my view, these passages are not about economics; but for Brueggemann they are, because they "reject the world of grasping and affirm the world of gifts" (Brueggemann, *Land*, 162). If the difference between a good economy and a bad one could be reduced solely to the difference between

and is central to the gospel.[87] But it is clear that if the dawn of the "messianic age" is really to be judged by the accomplishment of economic justice, then the messianic age has not yet been inaugurated. Besides, Jesus Christ insists that he is not a political king.

How then does Christ already reign in the eschatological land, so that it is true that he even now possesses "[a]ll authority in heaven and on earth" (Matt 28:18)? He reigns not by worldly power but by the hidden power of self-sacrificial love. He reigns through the outpouring of the Spirit and through the transformative working of grace and self-sacrificial love in believers, who even now have received "a kingdom that cannot be shaken" (Heb 12:28). Even now, believers in Christ have come to "the city of the living God, the heavenly Jerusalem" (Heb 12:22). Believers have done so because their "city" is held together by Christ's self-sacrificial love. Peter Leithart sums up: "Call it theosis; call it deification; call it theopoiesis: The end comes when men dwell in God, when God becomes the holy space for his image, created and glorified into his Bridal image."[88]

According to Hebrews, the wandering or pilgrim status for which Christians later mocked the Jewish people is the condition, *spiritually speaking*, that is blessed until the final eschatological consummation.[89] Hebrews praises people (beginning with Abraham and Sarah) who, desiring the promised inheritance, recognize that they cannot find it in this world and therefore act as "strangers and exiles on the earth," as people who "are

---

"grasping" and "gifting," then Brueggemann would be correct. Brueggemann's further assertion that "the proclamation of Jesus is about graspers losing and those open to gifts as receiving" (Brueggemann, *Land*, 164) is not a sufficient summary of Jesus' proclamation, although it contains an aspect of the proclamation.

87. See for example Works, *Least of These*, chapter 1. Works addresses Israel's "land" with appreciation for Brueggemann's perspective and drawing upon his book. Her conclusion seems apt to me: "*What is the promised inheritance that is being passed on to the Galatians as heirs?* In Galatians, the promise is directly related to at least three interrelated realities: life in the Spirit, the kingdom of God, and new creation. It is significant that all three of these synonymous realities employ land imagery" (*Least of These*, 101).

88. Leithart, *Revelation 12–22*, 388.

89. For an example of Catholic belief that Jews, due to their rejection of Christ and their supposed collective responsibility for his crucifixion, are doomed to be wanderers on the earth until the second coming of Christ—and are rightly kept separate from Christians due to their supposedly spiritually degraded state—see Philip A. Cunningham's description of the draft encyclical against the Nazis prepared in 1938 by John LaFarge, SJ (known for his 1937 book *Interracial Justice* condemning racism, with a particular focus on the American South), Gustave Desbuquois, SJ, and Gustuv Gundlach, SJ Fortunately, given its strongly anti-Jewish theology (despite its condemnation of the Nazi regime), this draft encyclical was never promulgated. See Cunningham, "Road Behind and the Road Ahead." For a fuller account, see Passelecq and Suchecky, *Hidden Encyclical of Pius XI*.

seeking a homeland" and who "desire a better country, that is, a heavenly one" (Heb 11:13–14, 16). It is this "better country" that Christ gives us by his self-offering on the cross, "securing an eternal redemption" and winning for us "the promised eternal inheritance" (Heb 9:12, 15). As Paul says, "our commonwealth is in heaven, and from it we await a Savior, the Lord Jesus Christ, who will change our lowly body to be like his glorious body, by the power which enables him even to subject all things to himself" (Phil 3:20–21).

In his letters, Paul does not explicitly mention the "land." He describes his care for the Church in Jerusalem, and he compares "the present Jerusalem" that "is in slavery with her children" to "the Jerusalem above" that "is free, and . . . is our mother" (Gal 4:25–26). He indicates that the true promised land is attained by dwelling in Christ, "where Christ is, seated at the right hand of God" (Col 3:1). But in Romans 4:13, as noted above, Paul reveals his understanding of the land promise.[90] For Paul, the original promise of land meant not merely the land of Canaan but rather the world as a whole; and Paul is here reflecting a common viewpoint among Second Temple Jews. The fulfilled promised land for Paul is none other than the new creation.

In the Gospels, Jesus suggests that the land of Canaan (Israel) will continue to have resonance in salvation history, even though he has inaugurated a worldwide eschatological kingdom. For example, in the Gospel of Luke he prophesies that "Jerusalem will be trodden down by the Gentiles, until the times of the Gentiles are fulfilled" (Luke 21:24).[91] In the Gospel of

---

90. See Works, *Least of These*, 102.

91. Michael Wolter interprets this passage in light of Tobit 14:15, and he proposes that "Luke limits the time of the trampling of Jerusalem by the Gentiles by limiting the 'time of the Gentiles' itself" (Wolter, *Gospel According to Luke*, 428). According to Wolter, "Luke makes unmistakably clear that the redemption that the Son of Man will bring at his parousia (vv. 27–28) will also include the reestablishment of Jerusalem. . . . At the same time, however, there should also be no doubt that in Jerusalem nothing will be like it was at the time when Jesus was in this city" (*Gospel According to Luke*, 428). The eschatological implication of Luke 21:24 is that at the end of the time of the Gentiles (or "nations"), Jesus will return in glory and renew Jerusalem and the whole world (see Gadenz, *Gospel of Luke*, 349). In the passage itself, however, Jesus does not draw a tight temporal connection between the end of the "time of the Gentiles" and the eschatological consummation. Given that the Gentiles (or "nations") today no longer govern Jerusalem, we can now know that the end of the "time of the Gentiles"—insofar as this means the end of the Gentiles' governance of Jerusalem—does not directly coincide with Jesus' coming in glory. Although the end of the "time of the Gentiles" surely prepares for Jesus' coming in glory, we do not possess a timetable for the latter event. See also Fitzmyer, *Gospel According to Luke*, 1346–47; as well as L. T. Johnson, *Gospel of Luke*, 324: "This temporal reference is only in Luke and replaces the assurance in Mark 13:20 about the times being shortened for the sake of the elect."

Matthew, he laments over Jerusalem: "Behold, your house is forsaken and desolate. For I tell you, you will not see me again, until you say, 'Blessed is he who comes in the name of the Lord'" (Matt 23:38–39). He anticipates both that Judaism will continue and that, when he returns in glory, he will be manifested to the Jewish people as a whole, presumably in the land of Israel.

Christians have consistently attacked the ongoing Jewish people as the wicked tenants of Jesus' parable and therefore as landless wanderers.[92] For Christians, as Joseph Fitzmyer says in commenting on Luke 20, Jesus Christ was rejected by his people and has become "the key figure in God's new building, the reconstituted Israel," namely the Church.[93]

Can the Church's status as the eschatological Israel be affirmed without denigrating the ongoing Jewish people? As noted above, Paul in Romans 11 admonishes Gentile Christians "to be humble" and to relate "in a deeply sympathetic manner to the 'holy tree', as the branch is related to the root."[94] Many Christians, however, have exalted themselves vis-à-vis the ongoing Jewish people and have oppressed and persecuted Jews rather than exhibiting the humble way of Christ.[95] In response, I do not think Christians

---

92. See the correction issued by Pontifical Biblical Commission, "Jewish People," §87: "it must be kept in mind that the New Testament polemical texts, even those expressed in general terms, have to do with concrete historical contexts and are never meant to be applied to Jews of all times and places merely because they are Jews. The tendency to speak in general terms, to accentuate the adversaries' negative side, and to pass over the positive in silence, failure to consider their motivations and their ultimate good faith, these are characteristics of all polemical language throughout antiquity, and are no less evident in Judaism and primitive Christianity against all kinds of dissidents."

93. Fitzmyer, *Gospel According to Luke*, 1282.

94. Von Balthasar, *Martin Buber and Christianity*, 19, 23. According to von Balthasar, the ongoing Jewish people and the Church are profoundly united in the crucified Christ, to whom both the Jewish people (unintentionally) and the Church bear witness. He states, "For the eyes of faith, the 'riddle of Israel' does not exist, not even the riddle of Israel's continued until the Last Judgment. The figure is legible, but only on Christian presuppositions. Israel and Christianity together form one single figure, carved in bold relief from the block of world-history—a figure whose higher centre is the God-Man" (von Balthasar, *Glory of the Lord* I, 658).

95. In this sense, Brueggemann's transposition of the land promise into a distinction between grasping and gift—so that the "landed" ones are spiritually "landless" because possession tends to be based upon defensive or aggressive grasping—would mean that during the centuries of Christendom, Jews were the true followers of Jesus; whereas now that Jews have power in the land of Israel, the true followers of Jesus are perhaps the Palestinians. Brueggemann states, "The meek, the ones claiming no home and living with homelessness, do indeed inherit the land" (*Land*, 172). Although it is clear that wealth, power, and "landedness" can be a spiritual snare—we must remember that we are pilgrims—Brueggemann's schema seems reductive to me; a fuller picture of life in Christ (and life under the Torah) is needed. To his credit, Brueggemann recognizes the danger (toward which his language tends) of making "landlessness a virtue instead of a

should adopt Zionism as Christian theology, because Christ has in fact fulfilled the land promise. Christians and Jews should continue to read Amos 9:14–15 differently: "I will restore the fortunes of my people Israel, and they shall rebuild the ruined cities and inhabit them. . . . I will plant them upon their land, and they shall never again be plucked up out of the land which I have given them" (Amos 9:14–15). Nevertheless, Christian engagement with Israel's doctrine of the promised land must today also reckon with how Christians treated the Jewish people during the centuries in which the Jewish people dwelt far from the land. To that task I now turn.

III. Christian Performative Contradiction: Hatred toward the Jewish People

In patristic references to the Jewish people, one often finds claims such as Origen's that the law of Moses "was dirty and enclosed in cheap and offensive meanings of the Jews until the Church should come from the Gentiles and take it up from the muddy and marshy places and appropriate it to itself within courts of wisdom and royal houses."[96] Minucius Felix, writing in the early third century prior to Origen, avers with regard to the scattered Jewish people that "by their wickedness they deserved this fortune, and . . . nothing happened which had not before been predicted to them, if they should persevere in their obstinacy."[97] For his part, Augustine often describes the Jewish people, including the Jews of his own day, as Christ-killers, despite the fact that Jesus' own disciples betrayed him and the Romans killed him.[98]

---

condition for receiving land"—a danger that would turn "poverty (landlessness)" into "virtue" (Brueggemann, *Land*, 205).

96. Origen, *Homilies on Genesis and Exodus*, 246. For discussion of Origen's treatment of the Jewish people in his biblical exegesis, emphasizing that Origen also attacks Marcion's rejection of the Old Testament, see Martens, *Origen and Scripture*. See also Wilken's observations on Origen in *Land Called Holy*, 67–72, especially his conclusion on 72: "In Origen's view the promise of the land signifies a spiritual conversion, that is, a return of 'those who have gone astray.' . . . When the psalmist says 'the meek shall possess the land and delight in much peace' [cf. Ps 37:11] he is referring to the 'pure land in the pure heaven,' not to a place located on the earth." Wilken adds, "Origen cheerfully acknowledges that in Christ the prophecies were not fulfilled in the way they were *thought* to take place" (*Land Called Holy*, 77).

97. Minucius Felix, *Octavius of Minucius Felix*, 194. Notably, Minucius is here attempting to justify the goodness and justice of Israel's God toward his covenantal people (the Jewish people).

98. For Augustine's harsh attacks upon the Jewish people, see Efroymson, "Whose Jews?"; Blumenkranz, *Die Judenpredigt Augustins*; as well as the succinct overview of the topic in Goodwin, "Jews and Judaism." See also Wilken, *Judaism*; Wilken, *John Chrysostom and the Jews*; Blumenkranz, *Les Auteurs chrétiens latins*; as well as Cohn-Sherbok,

In *City of God*, Augustine teaches that because the Jewish people "sinned by putting Christ to death," God ensured that they would be "dispersed over almost all the world, amongst all the nations."[99] Like many church fathers, he thinks that the Jews are destined to wander homelessly until the eschaton—much like Cain, who due to the murder of his innocent brother Abel became "a fugitive and a wanderer on the earth" (Gen 4:12).

Paula Fredriksen has argued that Augustine surpassed his Christian predecessors in some positive ways vis-à-vis the Jewish people.[100] Most importantly, indebted to Lactantius, he taught that the presence of ongoing Judaism among the nations is a good thing, because Jews unconsciously witness to the truth of Christianity, in a manner that reminds Christians of the truth of Christ.[101] The witness doctrine may have helped to ensure that later Christians did not undertake a sustained effort to annihilate the Jewish people. However, other scholars point out that many medieval rulers

---

"Church Fathers and Jewish Hatred."

99. Augustine, *City of God*, IV.34, p. 178.

100. See Fredriksen, *Augustine and the Jews*. For the view that Augustine's final writing on the Jews, his sermon "*Aduersus Iudaeos*," moves sharply in a conversionary direction and therefore undermines his earlier witness doctrine, see Hood, "Did Augustine Abandon His Doctrine?" Hood notes that "Roman winds were blowing in a decidedly anti-Jewish direction. As early as 414, the Patriarch of Constantinople seems to have expelled the Jews from the city. Five years later, imperial officials failed to prevent the destruction of synagogues in Syria, Palestine, and Trans-Jordan by Bar-Sauma and his followers. Nor did they protect the Jews of Minorca in 418 (or take retributive action afterward) when the island's Christians, inspired by Bishop Severus's anti-Jewish sermons, stormed their synagogue and effectively forced them to convert. Changes in law and imperial policy were more ominous still. For at least two hundred and fifty years—from the mid-second-century to the end of the fourth—Roman law consistently protected Judaism as a *religio licita*, permitted Jews to build synagogues and practice their faith, and exempted Jews from answering court summons on the Sabbath. In 408, Theodosius II issued a decree that forbade Jews from burning an effigy of Hamman on a cross during Purim, on the grounds that it constituted a mockery of Christ, and more generally warned Jews to cease insulting Christianity in their rites. . . . In October 415, the Emperors Honorius and Theodosius II formally demoted the Jewish Patriarch Gamaliel IV from the rank of Honorary Prefect and restricted his authority and powers. Almost as an afterthought, they also directed him to forbid Jews to construct new synagogues and ordered abandoned synagogues to be destroyed. This decree, a first in Roman history, was expanded by Theodosius II in 423 into an empire-wide prohibition on new synagogue construction. . . . Finally, in the summer of 425, Galla Placida, legislating in the name of her five-year-old son, Valentinian III, expelled Jews and pagans from the imperial administration, on the grounds that both were apt to misuse their power over Christians" (Hood, "Did Augustine Abandon His Doctrine?," 192).

101. Focusing on *City of God*, Gregory W. Lee shows that "in the wider context of Augustine's treatment of the two cities, the witness doctrine . . . underwrites Augustine's understanding of the Jews as a slave people that exists instrumentally for the sake of the church" (G. W. Lee, "Israel between the Two Cities," 526).

not only persecuted but also eventually expelled the Jewish people from their realms—thereby casting serious doubt on later Christian respect for the witness doctrine. Undeniably, Augustine's rhetorically powerful condemnations of the Jewish people as wandering Christ-killers contributed to deadly persecution over the centuries, even if his contrasting call to treat the Jewish people with humility and love (while seeking to convert them) had good effects at least in some instances.[102]

When Pope Innocent III, in his 1199 Constitution *Licet perfidia Iudaeorum*, has to insist that the Jews, despite their "faithlessness," "are not to be gravely oppressed by the faithful" and should not be physically assaulted or have their goods carried off by violence or be forcibly baptized or beaten or stoned during their religious rituals or have their graves violated, then something has clearly gone terribly awry, to say the least.[103] Many tragic examples of Christian persecution of the Jewish people in the twelfth and thirteenth centuries could be detailed. The fifteenth-century Council of Florence, in its Decree on Jews and Neophytes, commanded that bishops "depute persons well trained in scripture, several times a year, in the places where Jews and other infidels live, to preach and expound the truth of the

---

102. See Hood, "Did Augustine Abandon His Doctrine?," 194–95. On Augustine, Gregory, and medieval receptions of Augustine's teaching on the Jewish people, see also Goodwin, "Jews and Judaism"; J. Cohen, *Living Letters of the Law*; and Blumenkranz, *Juifs et chrétiens*.

103. Denzinger, *Compendium of Creeds*, nos. 772–773. See also the denigration of Jews (and advocacy of persecution against Jews) by Pope Innocent III in his papal bull *Etsi non displiceat Domino*, which is described in Tolan, "Of Milk and Blood." Tolan notes, "By the end of the Middle Ages, of course, Jews were often portrayed as a real physical threat to Christians" ("Of Milk and Blood," 141). For a valuable analysis and critique of medieval Christian anti-Jewish perspectives, see J. Cohen, *Living Letters of the Law*—although I think Cohen is overly negative in his assessment of Thomas Aquinas's position. Scandalized by Aquinas's view that "educated Jews who continued to observe their ceremonial law for its own sake" sinned mortally due to their "sinful intentions"—a point that Aquinas does not draw out in any detail, though he held it—Cohen argues that Aquinas's theology represents a major negative shift: "The postbiblical Jew of Augustinian theology differed little from the biblical Jew of Augustinian theology, one who rejected Christian salvation out of blind ignorance and lived on in Christendom as an instructive relic of the past. For Augustine, the Jew served that instructive purpose because he continued to observe and to embody the literal sense of the Old Testament. . . . For Aquinas, however, Jewish observance of the Mosaic commandments now amounts to nothing less than a repudiation of their literal sense" (J. Cohen, *Living Letters of the Law*, 388). I see much more ambiguity in Aquinas's position, and to this extent I agree with Tapie, *Aquinas on Israel and the Church*. See also the nuanced correction of Cohen's reading of Aquinas, arguing that Cohen is right about medieval anti-Judaism but that he misses the importance of Aquinas's rejection of Robert Grosseteste's positions, in Schenk, *Soundings in the History of a Hope*, 185–91. See also J. Cohen, "Supersessionism."

catholic faith in such a way that the infidels who hear it can recognise their errors. They [the bishops] should compel infidels of both sexes who have reached the age of discretion, to attend these sermons."[104] To enforce the attendance by Jews at these sermons, the council fathers decreed that any Jewish person who failed to show up should be barred from doing business with Catholics and should incur other penalties as well. Furthermore, the council fathers decreed that any Catholic who supported a Jewish person in avoiding these sermons should be stigmatized.

With unconscious irony, the council fathers also added that "the bishops and the preachers should behave towards them [Jews] with such charity as to gain them for Christ not only by the manifestation of the truth but also by other kindnesses."[105] That the bishops added this latter point suggests either that they feared they might not be acting charitably toward Jews or else that they really believed that bishops could find a way to compel Jews to listen to unwanted sermons, without thereby arousing feelings of profound resentment on the part of Jewish listeners.[106]

Let me now jump forward in time to a particularly painful and impactful episode, namely, Catholic denigration and slander of the Jewish people during the decades leading up to the Holocaust.[107] As David Kertzer notes, the Jesuit biweekly *Civiltà Cattolica*, founded in 1850, was published with a close link to the Vatican.[108] Kertzer points out that in the years 1880–1884 *Civiltà Cattolica* published a series of articles whose purpose was to urge Christian societies to protect themselves against Jewish influence.[109] Although

---

104. Council of Basel-Ferrara-Florence-Rome, "Decree on Jews and Neophytes," 483.

105. Council of Basel-Ferrara-Florence-Rome, "Decree on Jews and Neophytes," 483.

106. See also the essays in Nemes and Unowsky, eds., *Sites of European Antisemitism*. For further background to Christian anti-Judaism or anti-Semitism through the centuries, see such works as Finzi, *Anti-Semitism*; Almog, ed., *Antisemitism through the Ages*; and Katz, *Holocaust and Mass Death*. Katz holds that anti-Judaism is intrinsic to the New Testament and to Christianity.

107. For broader background and contextualization, see Brustein, *Roots of Hate*. Brustein treats the religious, racial, economic, and political roots of anti-Semitism in the nineteenth and early twentieth centuries, with some attention to the eighteenth century as well.

108. See Kertzer, *Popes Against the Jews*, 135.

109. See Kertzer, *Popes Against the Jews*, 134. See also the condemnation of *Civiltà Cattolica*'s anti-Semitism offered by Hannah Arendt, *Origins of Totalitarianism*, 102, cited in Dahl, "Anti-Semitism of *La Civiltà Cattolica*." Dahl's essay is an effort to absolve the Jesuits as much as possible, even while he recognizes that it is not fully possible by any means. He recognizes that "[t]he Italian Jesuits ... were not merely passively rejecting liberalism and Italian unification. They actively promoted an alternative Italian

the articles were unsigned (as were all articles in *Civiltà Cattolica*), we know that the author was Giuseppe Oreglia di Santo Stefano. Kertzer quotes a representative February 1881 article that, in light of the *Kulturkampf* and related attacks upon the Church's standing, defends the oppression of Jews by Christian states: "Every so often, as has recently happened in Germany, popular anti-Semitic exasperation erupts more or less violently. This could easily be avoided if only those few ancient laws of exception were brought back, laws which are as useful to the Jews themselves as they are to the Christians."[110] In this article, as Kertzer amply shows, Oreglia goes on to speak about the Jewish people in the most derogatory ways.

Regularly, Oreglia warns his readers not only against practicing Jews, but also against assimilated (non-practicing) Jews. The latter allegedly form the core of the "secret sects"—above all, the Freemasons[111]—that, in Oreglia's words, "express that anger, that vendetta and that satanic hate that the Jew harbors against those who . . . deprive him of that absolute domination

---

nation-building project. One of the strategies used in this struggle by members of *La Civiltà Cattolica* was to claim to represent the 'real' Catholic nation, while characterizing the liberal leadership, the 'legal' nation, as Jewish or foreign" ("Anti-Semitism of *La Civiltà Cattolica*," 220; citing Dahl, "Antisemitism of the Italian Catholics"; Dahl, "Role of the Roman Catholic Church"; and Taradel and Raggi, *La segregazione amichevole*. See also other studies cited by Dahl, including Starr, "Italy's Antisemites"; Klein, "Damascus to Kiev"; Luzzatto, "Aspetti di antisemitismo"; and Crepaldi, "L'omicidio rituale," 61–78. For a study of Jesuit anti-Judaism and anti-Semitism in the decades leading up to the Holocaust, see Bernauer, *Jesuit Kaddish*, especially chapter 2: "The Demonic Milieu."

110. Oreglia, "*Cronaca Contemporanea*" 489; cited in Kertzer, *Popes Against the Jews*, 134 (Kertzer omits the article's title). Kertzer observes, "As history had shown, the Jesuit wrote, 'if this foreign Jewish race is left too free, it immediately becomes the persecutor, oppressor, tyrant, thief, and devastator of the countries where it lives.' . . . Alas, wrote Father Oreglia, people [in the liberalizing nineteenth century] had not followed the Church's teachings and had come to regret it. 'The Jews—eternal insolent children, obstinate, dirty, thieves, liars, ignoramuses, pests and the scourge of those near and far— . . . immediately abused [their newfound freedom] to interfere with that of others. They managed to lay their hands on . . . all public wealth . . . and virtually alone they took control not only of all the money . . . but of the law itself in those countries where they have been allowed to hold public offices.' Yet, Father Oreglia continued, despite all this the Jews had the nerve to complain that they were being persecuted 'at the first shout by anyone who dares raise his voice against this barbarian invasion by an enemy race, hostile to Christianity and to society in general'" (*Popes Against the Jews*, 136–37).

111. Dahl points out that at least Pope Leo XIII's "encyclical *Humanum genus*, which he published against freemasonry in 1884, did not refer to Judaism. . . . If there was one thing that Oreglia had strived to achieve with his campaign, it was to render the connection of Freemasonry with Judaism commonly accepted" ("Anti-Semitism of *La Civiltà Cattolica*," 228–29).

over the entire universe that he Jewishly believes God gave him."[112] Writing about Oreglia, the historian David Lebovitch Dahl argues that he was "an old and unapproachable Jesuit who abused his seniority and relative independence to launch an idiosyncratic crusade against Jews."[113] This strikes me as unlikely, even if Oreglia's views represented a particularly extreme form of anti-Semitism. After all, both Oreglia's Jesuit superiors and the Vatican, despite the careful censorship in place at the time, allowed Oreglia "to diffuse hatred for months and years."[114]

Kertzer also documents the hate-filled articles against the Jewish people published in the 1890s in the *Civiltà Cattolica*. Among the examples that he cites, the work of Raffaele Ballerini stands out. Kertzer observes chillingly: "Ballerini cautioned that while the extermination of the Jews might seem to be an appealing solution to the problem, it was contrary to Christian teachings. As the people cursed by God, the Jews' continued degradation and their ceaseless wandering throughout the earth, with no land of their own, offered a precious witness to the New Testament's prophecies."[115] In addition, Kertzer draws attention to the sources employed by these Jesuit authors. He states, "The *Civiltà cattolica* articles and booklets quote approvingly from all the artificers of the modern anti-Semitic movement: Edouard Drumont in France, Adolf Stoecker in Germany, Karl Lueger in Vienna."[116]

---

112. Oreglia, *Civiltà Cattolica*, 1881, IV, 477; cited in Kertzer, *Popes Against the Jews*, 138–39. Dahl defends *Civiltà Cattolica* by reference to "the discovery in the Jesuit archives of a case of disagreement among the writers of the journal concerning the publication of anti-Jewish articles in the beginning of the 1880s" (Dahl, "Anti-Semitism of *La Civiltà Cattolica* Revisited," 222), a fact that Dahl also details in his "Case of Disagreement." Some Jesuit members of *Civiltà Cattolica* sought to persuade the Assistant General of the Jesuits to stop Oreglia's articles. Oreglia claimed to have support from the Vatican, and his articles were allowed to proceed until 1884. Dahl grants that "the fact that so many of Oreglia's articles were published is telling of what was considered acceptable in the Vatican at that time" ("Anti-Semitism of *La Civiltà Cattolica*," 229).

113. Dahl, "Anti-Semitism of *La Civiltà Cattolica*," 231.

114. Dahl, "Anti-Semitism of *La Civiltà Cattolica*," 231. See also the defense (which Dahl rightly finds inadequate) offered by Sale, "Antigiudaismo o antisemitismo?" Sale's essay is criticized by Kertzer in his "Anti-Semitism and the Vatican." See also Kertzer, "Roman Catholic Church." As Kertzer states against the formulations of *We Remember*, "The fact is that, in the wake of the granting of equal rights to Western Europe's Jews—a nineteenth-century development fiercely opposed by the Catholic Church—the church repeatedly tried to spread the alarm against a rapacious Jewish people bent on reducing all Christians to their slaves" ("Roman Catholic Church," 330).

115. Kertzer, *Popes Against the Jews*, 144.

116. Kertzer, *Popes Against the Jews*, 144. On the influence of Édouard Drumont's *La France juive*, see also Modras, *Catholic Church and Anti-Semitism*. John Connelly points out that France was less susceptible than were German-speaking countries to racist anti-Semitism (though not of course to anti-Judaism): see *From Enemy to*

A 1893 article in *Civiltà Cattolica* on "Jewish Morality" by Saverio Rondina displays how claims of Christian charity toward Jews were often mingled with slurs. Rondina states, "We do not write with any intention of sparking or fomenting any anti-Semitism in our country. Rather we seek to sound an alarm for Italians so that they defend themselves against those who, in order to impoverish them, dominate them, and make them their slaves, interfere with their faith, corrupt their morals, and suck their blood."[117] Kertzer points out that in August Rohling's 1871 *The Talmud Jew (Der Talmudjude)*, a central theme is "the claim that Jews were bound by their religion to murder Christian children for their blood."[118] Rohling remained a priest and professor of Catholic theology in Prague. In the early 1880s the Austrian government asked the archbishop, Fürst Cardinal Schwarzenberg, to curtail Rohling's anti-Semitic agitation—but this request was refused.[119] Rohling even sued Rabbi Josef Samuel Bloch for libel—un-

---

Brother, 80–81. Some Vichy leaders were racist anti-Semites, but they made a point of trying to deny that they were racists. In Connelly's view, "Karl Adam's type of Catholic, insistent on squaring racism with the central Catholic teaching of love of neighbor, was immeasurably more dangerous for Catholicism because it distorted Christianity's universalism" (*From Enemy to Brother*, 84). For a French critique of anti-Semitism from the 1930s, see de Férenzy, *Les Juifs et nous chrétiens*. Sixty bishops signed a letter congratulating him on the book, and de Férenzy's bi-monthly review *La Just Parole*, whose main goal was to attack anti-Semitism, was financially supported both by the French bishops and by Jewish groups.

117. Rondina, "La morale giudaica"; cited in Kertzer, *Popes Against the Jews*, 146. Rondina supposes that his "anti-Judaism" does not fall into "anti-Semitism," but it is clear that, in his hands at least, this is a distinction without a difference.

118. Kertzer, *Popes Against the Jews*, 158. Brustein traces the material in Rohling's pamphlet back to Johann Andreas Eisenmenger's 1710 book *Entdecktes Judenthum*. Brustein also directs attention to the mid-nineteenth century German theologians Sebastian Brunner and Bishop Konrad Martin as influential exponents of hatred toward Jews. See also Gross, *War Against Catholicism*. Gross mounts a persuasive case that "the nineteenth century in Germany with its particular confessional divide, modern rationalizing culture, and secularizing social currents was arguably more a century of anti-Catholicism" (*War Against Catholicism*, 1). Drawing upon Tal, *Christians and Jews in Germany*, 81–120, Gross shows that Jews generally supported the first phase of the Kulturkampf, but drew back after the introduction of the anti-Jesuit law.

119. Robert Michael provides a helpful overview of Austrian Anti-Semitism in the nineteenth and twentieth centuries, including a description of August Rohling's activities. In 1882 Rohling, originally from Germany, "testified as an expert witness at the Tísza-Eszlár murder trial. Fifteen members of the Jewish community of this Hungarian town were accused of murdering a Catholic child for her blood. . . . The trial was followed by pogroms in Hungary. . . . Although the accused Jews were all acquitted, Rohling attested that 'the religion of the Jews requires them to despoil and destroy Christianity in every way possible [and that] the shedding of a Christian virgin's blood is for the Jews an extraordinarily holy event'" (Michael, *History of Catholic Antisemitism*, 106). Michael observes that "[b]etween 1867 and 1914 there were a dozen

successfully of course—in response to Bloch's sharp critique of Rohling's writings on ritual murder.[120]

In June 1881, Oreglia took up the theme of ritual murder in *Civiltà Cattolica*. He grants that ritual murder had likely become rarer as the Jews assimilated, but he insists that ritual murder has not ceased to take place. In his view, it had once been prevalent, due to the Talmud's supposed command that Jews kill Christians. According to Oreglia, it is simply a fact that on Passover the Jews require the blood of a Christian child in order to produce their matzah. He gives credence to a recent report that the Jews of Egypt, able to find only Muslim children, baptized a Muslim child and then killed him for use in their Passover ritual. He even supposes that such actions must be commonplace in Egypt.

In 1893, Rondina published "Jewish Morality and the Mystery of the Blood" in *Civiltà Cattolica*. In Rondina's view, the evidence shows that Jews regularly engage in ritual murder of Christian children. Kertzer notes with dismay that "*L'Osservatore romano* offered a similar view. . . . A July 1892 article, commenting on a ritual murder trial then in progress in Germany, began: 'The trial . . . has barely begun, and it has already been established by many unimpeachable witnesses that Jews practice ritual homicides so that they can use Christian blood in making their Passover matzah.'"[121] A Milanese newspaper associated with the Vatican also took up the blood libel, publishing forty-four articles on the topic in March and April 1892, with graphic details that were picked up by many Catholic newspapers throughout Europe.[122]

---

ritual-murder trials in Austria-Hungary" (Michael, *History of Catholic Antisemitism*, 106).

120. Michael states, "Once Rohling's themes were picked up by the Jesuit journal *Civiltà Cattolica* in its late nineteenth-century antisemitic campaign, it was as if these Judeophobic ideas were awarded a papal imprimatur. Rohling was ultimately discredited by Jewish rabbi Joseph Bloch and had to resign his professorship, though his book continued to be sold, was translated into several languages (including Arabic), and served as a source for Nazi propaganda. In the end, Rohling was defrocked by the Church, not because of his fabrications and lying attacks on Jews and Judaism . . . but because of another heretical book of his" (*History of Catholic Antisemitism*, 106). See also Buchen, "'Herkules im antisemitischen Augiasstall.'"

121. "L'antisemitismo nel secolo decimonono"; cited in Kertzer, *Popes Against the Jews*, 162.

122. Kertzer adds that in August 1892, the French secular newspaper *Figaro* published an interview with Pope Leo XIII on the topic of the Catholic Church and anti-Semitism. In this interview, Pope Leo "stressed that violence directed at anyone was contrary to the teachings of the Church, and also stressed the Church's vision that all people, wherever they came from, were children of God, their souls made of the same essence" (Kertzer, *Popes Against the Jews*, 315–16).

Ulrich Wyrwa remarks that these articles "dramatically raised the [Milanese] *Osservatore Cattolico*'s profile far beyond the borders of Italy," but, fortunately, the articles "did not succeed in winning over Milanese and Italian opinion, but rather pushed the *Osservatore Cattolico* further to the margins."[123] Yet these margins contained many Catholics faithful to the Vatican's lead. Wyrwa connects the Catholic anti-Semitic campaign of the 1890s to Pope Leo XIII's appointment of Cardinal Mariano Rampolla, who had a reputation for vocal anti-Semitism, to the position of Vatican Secretary of State. When English Catholics protested the 1899 publication in *L'Osservatore Romano* of an article on Jewish ritual murder and requested that Pope Leo XIII repudiate the blood libel, Cardinal Rampolla assigned the inquiry to Cardinal Rafael Merry del Val, descended from a Spanish family that included a "saint" who had supposedly been ritually murdered for his blood.[124] Not surprisingly, his investigation found against the request of the English Catholics, in a decision approved by Pope Leo.[125]

Kertzer examines the series of articles on "the Jewish question" published in *L'Osservatore Romano* in 1892. According to these articles, Christian violence against Jews is the fault of Jews: when Jews exercise too much influence, the natural reaction of other people—given (supposedly) the rapacity and wickedness of the Jews—is to attack them physically. With

---

123. Wyrwa, "'L'Osservatore Cattolico,'" 71. See also Di Fant, "Don Davide Albertario."

124. Connelly reports, "As recently as 1928, Vatican Cardinal Secretary of State Merry del Val was dictating that the relation between Christians and Jews must be negative. 'Hebraism with all its sects inspired by the Talmud continues perfidiously to oppose Christianity,' he wrote in an internal opinion, accepted by Pius XI just before he banned Amici Israel.... Individual Jews might convert, but the Jewish people were damned. Worse: they were a danger from which Christians must be protected" (*From Enemy to Brother*, 170, citing Wolf, *Pope and Devil*, 105–6). Wolf's book draws upon the Vatican archives up to 1939. For the prayer for the conversion of the "perfidious Jews," found in Catholic Good Friday prayers from the seventh-century Gelasian Sacramentary through 1966, see P. Turner, "Jewish Dialogue and Christian Liturgy"—although Turner adds some proposals regarding the contemporary liturgy that I find to be mistaken.

125. See the additional discussion in Stow, *Jewish Dogs*, 49 and elsewhere. Stow traces the credence given to the blood libel in part to the work of the seventeenth-century Jesuit Bollandists of Antwerp and Leuven, who were responsible for a critical, multivolume *Acta Sanctorum*, in which they defended (with sincere belief in their research) the truth of the blood libel. Fortunately (even if too late), using the same critical tools but with more command of the sources, early "twentieth-century Bollandists... refuted the libel of ritual murder" (Stow, *Jewish Dogs*, 120). Regarding the seventeenth-century Bollandists, Stow notes that "Innocent III's apparent acceptance that Jews killed Christians clearly convinced them more than did Innocent IV's and Gregory X's denials that Jews used Christian blood or intentionally committed murder" (Stow, *Jewish Dogs*, 121). For further background to the blood libel, see also Taradel, *L'accusa del sangue*.

appreciation, however, Kertzer remarks that "the newspapers closest to the Pope were much less vocal on the Jewish question during Pius X's papacy."[126] At the same time, Kertzer still finds cause for concern. He notes that many of the clergy with whom Pius X partnered in the fight against Modernism were well known for anti-Semitism. An example is the Italian priest, Church historian, and journalist Umberto Benigni, founder of the Sodality of St. Pius V, which existed to spy on priests and laymen suspected of Modernist tendencies. Benigni wrote on June 3, 1891 in a newspaper he had founded: "If we keep up the way things have been going, within a few years the property and the businesses of all countries will be divided among a dozen exploitative Cyclops. Of these, eleven will belong to that worthy rabbinical race that still today in 1891 slits the throats of little Christians for the Synagogue's Passover."[127] Benigni rose to power and prestige under Pius X.

Pope Pius X's response to the 1913 trial of Mendel Beilis in Kiev for ritual murder raises similar concerns. In covering this trial, the Catholic press gave much additional fuel to the blood libel. A Catholic priest and theologian, Justinus Pranaitis, served as an expert witness against Beilis. He declared that the Catholic Church has long known that Jewish people regularly commit ritual murder. The newspaper *L'Unità Cattolica*—published in Florence and a leading advocate of Pope Pius X's anti-Modernist campaign—published numerous articles during the Beilis trial asserting the truth of the blood libel.[128] For its part, *Civiltà Cattolica* published two articles in 1914 by Paola Silva, arguing that "the Kiev case showed all the signs of a ritual murder performed by the Jews" in order to extract Christian blood needed for the Passover.[129] Indeed, according to Silva, Jews regularly

---

126. Kertzer, *Popes Against the Jews*, 225. Although Pope Pius X granted Theodore Herzl a private audience on January 26, 1904 to discuss the question of Zionism, Pius X emphasized in that audience that the Church could not favor a Jewish homeland in Palestine. The reason given by Pius X was that the Jewish people do not recognize Jesus as the Christ, and therefore Christians cannot recognize the Jewish people as the valid successor of the people from which Jesus was born.

127. Kertzer, *Popes Against the Jews*, 227.

128. Kertzer, *Popes Against the Jews*, 233.

129. Kertzer, *Popes Against the Jews*, 235. See also, on the "Protocols of the Elders of Zion," Kertzer, *Popes Against the Jews*, 265–67; and Brustein, *Roots of Hate*, 273–77. Father Umberto Benigni published the first Italian edition of the "Protocols" (in the journal *Fede e Ragione*) and spread it widely; while Father Ernest Jouin took the lead in spreading the "Protocols" in France. Jouin received commendations and honors from both Pope Benedict XV and Pope Pius XI. Brustein remarks, "In Germany at the time Hitler took power in 1933 [fourteen years after the first German edition of the "Protocols" appeared in 1919], the 'Protocols' had gone through thirty-three editions, with one popular edition alone selling roughly 100,000 copies" (Brustein, *Roots of Hate*, 277). For further background regarding the "Protocols of the Elders of Zion," see Segel,

drink human blood. Pope Pius X could have spoken out publicly or used his influence privately, but he did not, although he did write a private letter to a longtime Jewish friend expressing hope that the fanaticism of the Russian populace would not cause an injustice to be done to Mendel Beilis.[130]

Continuing his examination of papal history, Kertzer details Pope Pius XI's involvement in Italian politics and his sympathetic dealings with Benito Mussolini.[131] As he remarks, in 1922—when Mussolini and his fascist movement were poised to conquer Rome—*Civiltà Cattolica* "published a feature article titled 'The world revolution and the Jews,'" which argued that of the 500 leaders of the Bolshevik Revolution, Jews (supposedly) accounted for 447.[132] This article later became a cornerstone of Nazi propaganda. Moreover, when Mussolini imposed anti-Semitic laws in 1938, including "evicting all Jewish children from school, dismissing all Jewish teachers and professors, civil servants, etc.," these laws mirrored restrictive laws imposed in the Papal States prior to the Italian conquest of the Papal

---

Lie and a Libel; and Cohn, *Warrant for Genocide*.

130. For the equally bad (and at certain points worse) history of Protestant engagement with the Jewish people between 1517 and 1945, a place to start is Schramm and Stjerna, *Martin Luther*, including their brief excerpt from Luther's *On the Jews and Their Lies*, in which Luther commented: "So we are even at fault in not avenging all this innocent blood of our Lord and of the Christians which they shed for three hundred years after the destruction of Jerusalem, and the blood of the children they have shed since then (which still shines forth from their eyes and their skin). We are at fault in not slaying them" (*Martin Luther, the Bible, and the Jewish People*, 175). Some scholars argue that Luther began as a friend of the Jews (in his 1523 treatise *That Jewish Christ Was Born a Jew*) and ended as vitriolically anti-Jewish, but this view is challenged both by Schramm and Stjerna's compilation and by scholars such as Helmer, *How Luther Became the Reformer*, 83–98. By contrast, Thomas Kaufmann emphasizes "the tension between his writings of 1523 and 1543" and holds that "the form of anti-Semitism that aimed to eliminate the Jews, to kill them systematically, was completely alien to the historical Luther"; and he also differentiates Luther's anti-Judaism from "modern biology-inspired anti-Semitism" (Kaufmann, *Luther's Jews*, 9, 135). But Kaufmann admits: "The fact that Luther's preferred policies towards the Jews changed so fundamentally between 1523 and 1543 was not the result of any change to his theological convictions. Judaism in itself was not for him a tolerable religion at any stage of his life. He regarded it as something like a walking corpse. . . . Like Islam and Roman Catholicism, the Jewish religion embodied in his view the attempt by human beings to justify themselves before God" (*Luther's Jews*, 154). This last point is the thesis of Andreas Pangritz, who argues (engaging Kaufmann and many others along the way) that a particularly severe anti-Judaism follows inevitably from Luther's way of understanding the doctrine of justification: Pangritz, *Theologie und Antisemitismus*. For a defense of Luther that I find naïve, see Siemon-Netto, *Fabricated Luther*.

131. Kertzer, *Pope and Mussolini*.

132. Kertzer, "Roman Catholic Church," 330, citing Silva, "La rivoluzione mondiale."

States in 1870.¹³³ Worse still, "*Civiltà Cattolica* had been calling for exactly this kind of reimposition of restrictions on Italy's Jews in the years leading up to the racial laws."¹³⁴

Famously, the Jewish philosopher Hannah Arendt (among many others) faulted Pope Pius XII for not speaking out during the Holocaust. Although I understand the reasons why Pius XII chose this path—and I think that the attacks on Pius XII have been unfair in many ways—I agree with Arendt. Of course, Arendt did not know the extent of Pius XII's laudable activities, which included not only saving numerous Roman Jews by hiding them in the Vatican and elsewhere, but also actively encouraging a plot to assassinate Hitler.¹³⁵ Yet, when the Nuremberg laws forbade marriages between "Aryans" and persons of Jewish descent (including baptized Christians)—thereby denying the sacrament of marriage to Catholics who had a canonical right to it—the Vatican opposed these laws but did not discipline the German hierarchy for conforming to them. Some German bishops even encouraged the Nazi-required "segregation of Catholics of Jewish descent within the German Church," while the Vatican remained silent.¹³⁶ Pope Pius did not speak out against the death camps when he learned about them. Arendt concludes, "To be sure, no one can say what actually would have happened had the Pope protested in public. But . . . did no one in Rome realize what so many inside and outside the Church at that time realized, namely, that—in the words of Reinhold Schneider, the late German Catholic writer—a protest against Hitler 'would have elevated the Church to a position it has not held since the Middle Ages'?"¹³⁷ How right this point is!

133. Kertzer, "Roman Catholic Church," 331.
134. Kertzer, "Roman Catholic Church," 331.
135. See Riebling, *Church of Spies*; G. Thomas, *Pope's Jews*.
136. Arendt, *Responsibility and Judgment*, 224–25.
137. Arendt, *Responsibility and Judgment*, 225. It seems to me that Arendt achieves the right middle ground between attacking Pope Pius XII and acting as though his silence was not in fact a grave mistake. For more recent contributions to the controversy, see Cornwell, *Hitler's Pope*; Dalin, *Myth of Hitler's Pope*; Rychlak, *Righteous Gentiles*; Rychlak, *Hitler, the War, and the Pope*; Goldhagen, *Moral Reckoning*; Blet, *Pius XII and WWII*; and Dujardin, *L'Église catholique et le peuple juif*. While Dujardin treats Pius XII (in light of Kertzer's work), he also reflects more broadly upon the first-century Jewish-Christian schism, Christian anti-Judaism, and post-*Nostra Aetate* developments, with an eye to Christian mission, "dialogue," and God's will that ongoing Judaism continue until the eschaton. See also Zuccotti, *Under His Very Windows*, especially her balanced conclusions on 306–13, although I think she exaggerates what effective actions Pope Pius XII could have taken (see *Under His Very Windows*, 323, where she naively pictures a world waiting for the Pope to give "a word, a sign, an indication of how to respond" to the unfolding Holocaust). The best and most nuanced treatment is that of Ventresca, *Soldier of Christ*, chapters 5 and 6.

Even so, the popes were not the main problem. The main problem was rather the anti-Judaism or anti-Semitism of so many Catholics (and so many Europeans, Catholic or not).[138] To give an extreme example, in the very midst of the Holocaust (1943), the eminent German Catholic theologian Karl Adam "published an essay arguing that Jesus was racially not a Jew," as Susannah Heschel has noted.[139] Fortunately, Adam, who held that "Germany possessed a uniqueness in its unmatched expression of Catholicism" and was a sharp critic of neo-scholastic theology, was not representative of German Catholic priests.[140] Nevertheless the fact remains that the failures

138. Although "anti-Semitism" can be distinguished from "anti-Judaism" (the former contains within it nineteenth-century notions of race), nonetheless for most practical purposes, Christian van Gorder and Gordon Fuller are correct when they remark: "The term 'anti-Semitic' simply refers to that which is anti-Jewish" (van Gorder and Fuller, *Jews and Christians Together*, 114).

139. S. Heschel, *Aryan Jesus*, 133, with reference to K. Adam, "Jesus, der Christus." Heschel summarizes Adam's grounds for this claim, which had earlier been advocated by Fr. Richard Kleine: "Jesus came from Galilee, which was populated by non-Jews; Mary was conceived immaculately and thus did not possess Jewish moral or physical traits; and Jesus himself rejected Jewish law" (*Aryan Jesus*, 133). Heschel directs attention to Krieg, *Catholic Theologians in Nazi Germany*; Denzler, "Antijudaismus und Antisemitismus"; Connelly, "Catholic Racism"; and Bergen, *Twisted Cross*—and see also Krieg, *Karl Adam* and Krieg, "German Catholic Views of Jesus." Heschel makes clear that the Protestant churches—with the exception of the Confessing Church (with its Barmen Declaration)—were more compromised than the Catholic Church. Her book focuses on a Protestant undertaking, the Institute for the Study and Eradication of Jewish Influence on German Church Life. See also Ericksen, *Complicity in the Holocaust*; and the sad tale of priests compelled to serve (generally as chaplains and medics) in the German military, in Rossi, *Wehrmacht Priests*.

140. Spicer, *Hitler's Priests*, 184, with reference to K. Adam, "Deutsches Volkstum." In fact, Adam received a large amount of criticism, including from Msgr. Bernhard Lichtenberg, later to be executed by the Nazis (and beatified in 1996). In accepting an invitation in 1940 to join the small National Socialist priests' group founded by Fr. Richard Kleine—who, notably, identified Eugenio Pacelli as a strong opponent of Nazism and greeted with intense dismay his election as Pope Pius XII—Adam told Kleine: "As Germans who have been awakened by Hitler's genius to their full self, we particularly cannot bear being permanently separated from our brothers in the deepest and holiest respects. Therefore, change *has* to be brought about—if not by the Church leadership, then by us. There is as well a holy defiance and a holy revolution. . . . For this reason, I am happy to join your group'" (*Hitler's Priests*, 185, citing a May 29, 1940 letter preserved in the Johann-Adam-Möhler-Institut für Ökumenik). Spicer adds that in the same letter, "Adam also shared his belief that everything depended on 'whether we Catholics will succeed in establishing a truly German Catholicism. In my opinion, success can be hoped for *only* if the Führer issues a command to give us a German metropolitan who will possess sufficient energy to de-Romanize the entire teaching of the Church, including everything pertaining to the liturgy, catechesis, pastoral work, the education of theologians, etc., and to Germanize them.' Adam did add that this metropolitan 'must be as determinedly *Catholic* as German, and he must be appointed

of the popes generally reflected the anti-Judaism present among clergy laity. For centuries, regular Catholics, wielding little or no institutional power, were complicit in persecuting the Jewish people in Catholic countries in various ways, large and small.

As was clear to Vladimir Solovyov, the boasting directed by Christians from the outset against Jews who do not accept Jesus as Messiah has scandalized the Jewish people as a whole. Christians have given an abiding counter-witness to the Jewish people as a whole. As Paul says in a different context, "Then what becomes of our boasting? It is excluded" (Rom 3:27). It is in light of a realistic assessment of the extent of Christian boasting that Christian Israelology should reflect upon the land.

IV. David Novak's Theology of God's Choosing the People and Land

The next step is to attend to how ongoing Judaism understands its covenant of land, and to inquire into what contemporary Jewish scholars hope from Christians vis-à-vis the land promise. To do so, this third section will briefly examine David Novak's *The Election of Israel* and *Zionism and Judaism*.

In *The Election of Israel*, Novak argues that God's choosing of a people and land is ordered to the eschatological consummation of God's creation.[141] At the same time, he holds that until that final consummation—which God alone can accomplish, and which does not depend upon anything that the people of Israel can do—the purpose of God's choosing of the people of Israel is the relationship between God and his people. This relationship depends upon grace rather than upon merit. Even when the people fail to observe the *mishpatim* (the laws pertaining to universal moral justice), the relationship continues. The people's continued efforts to observe the *mishpatim* and to observe the *edot* (laws pertaining to Israel's worship) nourish the "collective relationship of Israel with the Lord and subsequently with each other."[142] The *ḥuqqim* or commandments whose purpose is shrouded

---

with Rome's *consent*'" (*Hitler's Priests*, 185). Note that Adam rejected the designation "National Socialist priests" as overly political (rather than nationalistic) and threatened to drop out of the group until Kleine reassured him; and that Adam in January 1934 had publicly criticized Nazi neo-paganism and as a result had been "barred by Nazi officials from teaching at the University of Tübingen until he promised to refrain from commenting on National Socialism and the Third Reich" (Krieg, "German Catholic Views of Jesus," 60).

141. See Novak, *Election of Israel*, 252.

142. Novak, *Election of Israel*, 251. The *mishpatim* are moral and judicial precepts that "justly govern interhuman relationships"; even if there been no election of Israel,

in obscurity also play a role in this relationship, by requiring Israel to realize humbly that not even God's chosen people can fully understand or master God and his ways.[143]

Novak emphasizes that while God's covenantal love means for Jews that "every effort must be made to practice that love [a response to God's love] towards every other Jew," Israel has the same requirements as do the other nations with regard to the *mishpatim*, the fundamental standards of justice between humans.[144] Jews must therefore relate to non-Jews with the same "peace, justice and righteousness" that God expects of all humans in their relations with each other.[145] In addition, "Israel cannot claim to be more redeemed than anyone else."[146] Far from allowing for boasting in any way, Israel's covenantal experience teaches that election and the relationship it entails emerge from God's freedom and cannot be a cause for pride.

In *Zionism and Judaism*, Novak observes that the first human community is that between Adam and Eve, who are addressed by God. Novak draws the conclusion that God created humans to be in communion with him. Our "religious" nature is thus related to our "political" nature; we are

---

reason still would dictate these precepts. The revelation of the *mishpatim* serves as a universal gift to all peoples, including God's chosen people, because the *mishpatim* reveal the moral "order of creation" (Novak, *Election of Israel*, 251). The *edot* are ceremonial precepts that "testify to covenantal events by symbolic celebration" and that structure Israel's worship (Novak, *Election of Israel*, 250). Novak explains that "[t]he *edot* are modes of Israel's active, responsive experience of God's electing and nurturing love for her in the covenant" (*Election of Israel*, 251). For a "Hebrew Catholic" appreciation of the *edot*, see Bardan, *Bride*.

143. For discussion of the *ḥuqqim* in the context of Greco-Roman theories of law, see C. Hayes, *What's Divine about Divine Law?*, chapter 6. As Hayes says about a tannaitic text commenting on Leviticus 18:4 (with its distinction between *mishpatim* and *ḥuqqim*), "On the one hand, the rabbinic author acknowledges that some divine laws are so arbitrary and illogical that no one would expect them to be a part of the divine Law. On the other hand, the rabbinic author takes pains to inform us that only an idolatrous or evil person—a person who does not accept the authority of the divine legislator—would actually *object* to these arbitrary and illogical laws" (*What's Divine about Divine Law?*, 248). An example of this kind of precept is God's command to Abraham to sacrifice Isaac. See the Jewish-Christian connections displayed by Kessler, *Bound by the Bible* (11–28), Bergant, "The Binding of Isaac," and Gellman, "*Akedah* and Covenant Today." For further discussion of the three kinds of commandments, see my *Jewish-Christian Dialogue*, 124–28.

144. Novak, *Election of Israel*, 254.

145. Novak, *Election of Israel*, 255.

146. Novak, *Election of Israel*, 255. Although Novak does not make it explicit, I think that he likely holds that Christians (due to their understanding of Christ and the Spirit) must consider themselves (as a group) "to be more redeemed than anyone else." I address the question of why Christians are such sinners in my "Sin and Grace in the Church."

supposed to be "one community under God and living for the sake of God" in a condition of justice.[147] Genesis teaches, however, that humans immediately fell away from a proper relationship with God, with disastrous results. The Tower of Babel symbolizes human efforts to be in communion with each other *without* God. The bitter fruit is the radical disruption of communion. Humans are now scattered upon the earth and unable to communicate easily with each other. It follows that "the desideratum of humankind ... to be united under God's universal sovereignty, becomes in scriptural teaching the eschatological desideratum only God can and will realize."[148] Humans cannot achieve this desideratum by their own power, but God promises that God will achieve it for us at the eschatological consummation.[149]

Novak suggests that given the scattered condition of fallen humans, it stands to reason that God must first relate to individuals who are separated from their political communities, whether Enoch (Gen 5:24) or Abraham (Gen 12). God chooses Abraham and commands him to go to the land of Canaan—an inhabited land—"there to found an altogether new sort of human community," uniting the "religious" and the "political" in a distinctive way.[150] This is not yet the kingdom of God in which God rules all humans (and in which all humans obey God), but it is better than the scattered condition in which God simply relates to individuals. Novak describes the new community that flows from Abraham as "a theological-political entity, one where the religious and political sides of human nature are interrelated, and where neither is neglected for the sake of the other."[151] It is a community that arises "through a covenant between God and this particular people, who become 'the unique nation [*goi ehad*] on earth' (1 Chronicles 17:21)."[152] Only God could have established such a community.

One question, though, is why God chose the land of Canaan for his theological-political community. Why not a less populated land, or a land less likely to be in the crosshairs of Egyptian, Assyrian, Babylonian, Persian, Hellenistic, and Roman imperialist ambitions? In Novak's view, some reasonable answer must be available. He first inquires into whether the

---

147. Novak, *Zionism and Judaism*, 123.

148. Novak, *Zionism and Judaism*, 125. For a different approach by a Jewish scholar to politics in the Hebrew Bible—one shaped by discomfort with and lack of belief in the Bible's God—see Walzer, *In God's Shadow*. For a more positive portrait than Walzer's, much closer to Novak's perspective, see Hazony, *God and Politics in Esther*.

149. In this regard Novak quotes Zechariah 14:9, "And the Lord will become king over all the earth; on that day the Lord will be one and his name one."

150. Novak, *Zionism and Judaism*, 126.

151. Novak, *Zionism and Judaism*, 126.

152. Novak, *Zionism and Judaism*, 126.

answer is simply that the people of Israel were the best people—and so God first chose the people and then chose a land near them. In response to this notion, he clarifies that it was not Israel's merit but rather God's grace (or freely bestowed love) that led God to choose Israel, which of itself has nothing to boast about.[153] As Moses tells the people prior to their entrance into the promised land, "Do not say in your heart, after the Lord your God has thrust them [the peoples of the land] out before you, 'It is because of my righteousness that the Lord has brought me in to possess this land'" (Deut 9:4). Moses explains that God chose the people Israel "for his own possession, out of all the peoples that are on the face of the earth" not because of any strength of theirs, but simply because God willed to do so: "the Lord loves you" (Deut 7:6, 8).

At the same time, Novak does not believe that the people were selected merely arbitrarily. He proposes that the reason for God's choice of the people was *prospective*, grounded in the eschatological future. If so, then the eschaton will shine a light on the past of God's people and make apparent how this particular people contributed to the eschatological accomplishment of his plan.[154]

---

153. Novak's position is in accord with Menachem Kellner's view that efforts "to ground Jewish chosenness in the claim that Jews are distinguished from others by some sort of innate characteristic, which makes them both different from and superior to other human beings, reflects a lack of religious self-confidence. . . . [T]he alternative view is that of Maimonides, according to which all human beings are equally made in the image of God. What distinguishes Jews from other human beings is nothing innate, ontological, metaphysical" (Kellner, "We Are Not Alone," 141–42). The Jewish theologian Ruth Langer comments along similar lines: "There is no question . . . that Israel's chosen status does not imply superiority. It is a calling to a particular service, one that is often not an easy one. But this is a service of God for God's mysterious reasons and it is particular to Israel. . . . Jews do serve God by serving the world, but this universal horizon comes from within Judaism's particularity and returns to it as well" (Langer, "Exploring the Interface," 291). Kellner grants that there are a "very small number of . . . rabbinic passages which could be construed as teaching that Jews are not only God's chosen people . . . but in some inherent sense truly distinct from and superior to non-Jews. But even such statements as BT *AZ* 22b, according to which only non-Jews carry the pollution which the Edenic snake cast into Eve (a statement the outer meaning of which Maimonides, *Guide*, ii.30, says is deeply disgraceful), and the various misanthropic statements attributed to R. Shimon bar Yohai, need not be read literally" (Kellner, "We Are Not Alone," 142fn4; see also Kellner, *Maimonides on Judaism*). Kellner also admits, with frustration, that due to the desire to keep Jews Jewish, "The view that Jews are in some serious way innately different from and superior to gentiles is deeply rooted in contemporary Judaism" ("We Are Not Alone," 147).

154. At the same time, Novak affirms the priority of the electing God. He states, "God's choices are not responses to any prior claims. God alone has absolute freedom of will, which is the prerogative of the Creator to initiate everything" (Novak, *Election of Israel*, 191).

But even if God's election of the people of Israel can be justified, why did God select this particular land? Is the reason simply that this land was close to Egypt and thus close to the people during their period of slavery, or some other historical accident of this kind? The pressing problem consists in the apparent divine sanction of the violence that, according to Scripture, was needed to conquer the land. Put simply, the habitable area between Babylon and Egypt was crowded.

Novak emphasizes that the Jews are not "a conquering people . . . , that is, a people dedicated to obliterating every other people's difference from them by absorbing these other people into the political and cultural domain of the Jews."[155] But although the people of Israel are not a conquering people, neither could they be—for God's theological-political project to work—an inherently homeless or landless people. They were not intended merely to bear witness to the homelessness and vulnerability of God's pilgrim people on earth, although at many points in their existence they have borne witness to this condition.[156]

Given that his chosen people must have a land, God could not allow the people to choose their own land or to dwell in a land that they might imagine had always been theirs. Had God done this, then the people would have understood themselves to be the *source* of their land; whereas, in fact, God is the source of all his covenantal gifts. God could not allow the people to think their claim to the land rested upon their own sufficiency. For this reason, rather than having a natural land (like the way in which the islands of Japan may seem always to have belonged to the Japanese, for example), and rather than being able to choose which land to settle, the people had to receive the land from God's own commandment and action. God's covenantal

---

155. Novak, *Zionism and Judaism*, 134. This makes the Jewish people different both from Christians and, even more clearly, from Muslims. Novak amplifies his point by means of two rhetorical questions: "wouldn't such a project turn Israel's dependence on God's redemption of us (and the rest of the world along with us) into Israel's presumptive redemption of the world and of God too along with the world? Wouldn't this compromise God's transcendence of the world by clearly implying that redemption (*ge'ulah*) is basically a matter of human initiation and projection, rather than properly asserting 'dominion [*ha-melukhah*] is the Lord's' (Obadiah 1:21)?" (*Zionism and Judaism*, 147). See also his reflections on 179: "choosing a land for themselves to be the base of an imperial project to conquer the world would be something that would make their worldly presence even further removed from the covenant with God that is envisioned to be fully consummated when God, not the people Israel acting as God's successors, 'becomes the King of the whole world' (Zechariah 14:9)."

156. *Pace* the view of John Howard Yoder (to name just one example; Novak himself does not give examples). See Yoder, *Jewish-Christian Schism Revisited*. I discuss Yoder's view in the Introduction to my *Ezra and Nehemiah*. See also Carl Roemer's critique of Yoder's position in "Wonder and Worries."

promise of *this* specific land implies that the people of Israel "have no right or claim to take any land because of what they have made of themselves."[157] When other nations become strong, they often seize land and add it to their nation, but in Israel's case the people cannot go beyond God's gift.

By the same logic, dwelling in the land that God has chosen is something that the people have an obligation to do. Emphasizing the theocentric character of Israel's doctrine of the promised land, Novak states: "The commandment is what God has chosen for them to do; the land of Israel is where God has chosen for them to do it."[158] If the choice of the land had been the people's, then it would not have reflected the people's dependence upon God. If it had been so, then today, too, the Jewish people "could decide there is no land here and now that suits them."[159] Or they could decide that, given the troubled politics of the Middle East, they should settle in a less occupied or less contentious part of the globe.[160] If the only connection of the Jewish people to the land of Israel were ancestral, then, clearly, the Palestinian people have the very same connection. According to Novak, however, the Jewish people are unique in being connected to the land by God's covenantal choice. They therefore make a "claim on the nations of the world to let them fulfill the duty God has placed upon them to acquire

157. Novak, *Zionism and Judaism*, 140.

158. Novak, *Zionism and Judaism*, 141. In light of an influential statement by Nachmanides (basing himself on Numbers 33:53), Novak later observes: "From this statement of the commandment to acquire the land and settle it, the following four points emerge: (1) It is obvious this is a Torah commandment, the point having been made several times in the Torah. (2) The importance of this commandment is emphasized by the sages, who determined the relative status of the commandments of the Torah, even elevating it to the highest status they could. It is not simply an isolated decree; hence it is especially important to understand its reason (*ta'amah shel mitsvah*). (3) This commandment is considered to be a positive commandment for perpetuity, like all such commandments directly revealed by God in the Torah. (4) This commandment obliges every individual Jew wherever and whenever he or she happens to be found" (Novak, *Zionism and Judaism*, 180). But Novak qualifies this in the following way: "Even if one thinks the words 'you shall acquire the land and settle it' (Numbers 33:53) to be a commandment having perpetual binding force, it is arguable whether it really devolves on each and every individual Jew. In fact, if you look at the context in which this commandment was given, and the context in which it was actually applied, it seems to be more of a communal obligation to be upheld by certain members of the community rather than a commandment each and every Jew is simply to take upon him- or herself to observe" (Novak, *Zionism and Judaism*, 187; see his further clarifications, aimed at allowing Jews to live in the diaspora while granting that it is better for Jews to live in Israel, on 188–91).

159. Novak, *Zionism and Judaism*, 141.

160. Indeed, as Novak points out, the Zionist leader Theodore Herzl briefly favored accepting the British government's offer that the Jewish people settle in a new nation in the region of Uganda.

and settle the land God has chosen for them."[161] No matter how outrageous such a claim might seem to be in the eyes of the nations, the commandment of God is unmistakably present in the Bible and the Jews have accepted that commandment covenantally for some thousands of years. If the covenant has not been revoked, then neither has the covenantal commandment regarding the land. During the many centuries in which the Jewish people could not live in the land due to various obstacles, the Jewish people never lost the hope or intention of living in the land that God chose for them.

As Novak points out, Christians believe in the covenantal validity of the original settlement of the land. Therefore, he thinks, Christians should also affirm the validity of Zionism, namely, the people's resettling in the land along with the establishment of the State of Israel that sustains this resettlement. For Novak, the reason that Christians should make this affirmation is twofold: belief in the divine revelation of God's choice of people and land, and the fact that God's choice—"God's covenant with the Jewish people and with the land of Israel as their inheritance"—has not been overturned, revoked, or replaced by Christ.[162] Novak argues that Christians can suitably claim that the coming of the Messiah has "supplemented" the covenantal standing of Israel, but Christians must not claim that the Jewish people no longer have covenantal standing as God's chosen people whose inheritance is the promised land.[163] To say the latter would be to hold that God has re-

---

161. Novak, *Zionism and Judaism*, 142. Novak emphasizes that the relationship of the Jewish people to the land is not merely a "subjective" stance (as distinct from more "objective" reasons that could be given). Rather, the "claim is based on revelation, and revelation is taken by them [the Jewish people] to be a higher, objective reality, whose Author has ultimate authority over them" (Novak, *Zionism and Judaism*, 142n54). Certainly the claim will seem merely subjective to those who do not believe in the divine revelation. But the viewpoint of the skeptics cannot be shown to be more reasonable or "objective" than the viewpoint of believers.

162. Novak, *Election of Israel*, 143. As the late Catholic biblical scholar and theologian Francis Martin puts it, "The Church has not replaced Israel; Israel has been fulfilled in the Church, and yet most of the Jewish people still find their identity relating to God through their ancient covenant that has never been revoked. From one point of view the resolution of this tension is eschatological. From another point of view this same tension is at least partially resolvable through a new mode of relating that undoes two millennia of fear and mistrust—an enormous spiritual task—and which, at the same time, forces us to a deeper discernment into the action of God in history, one faithful to God's word and to a more profound and mutual understanding of our traditions" (F. Martin, "Election, Covenant, and Law," 890).

163. Novak, *Election of Israel*, 143. In an instructive essay that accords with my own viewpoint, Novak explains the difference between what he calls "hard" and "soft" Christian supersessionism: "Soft supersessionism does not assert that God terminated the covenant of Exodus-Sinai with the Jewish people. Rather, it asserts that Jesus came to fulfill the promise of the old covenant, first for those Jews *already* initiated into the

jected his people and, correspondingly, to allow no theological space (other than that of rejection and repudiation) to the ongoing Jewish people. With regard to the covenantal standing of the Jewish people and their land, Novak holds that Christians must maintain, if they are to be "faithful to their own tradition," that both aspects of the covenant with Israel are "everlasting and forever valid."[164]

My position is somewhat different from Novak's. As explained above, I think that Christians, believing that Israel's Messiah has fulfilled the land promise, cannot strictly speaking be theological Zionists—since this would imply objectively that Christ's coming did not eschatologically fulfill the Abrahamic covenant by which the Jewish people were obligated to dwell in the land. At the same time, distinguishing between fulfillment and revocation, Christians must recognize that the ongoing Jewish people are still God's chosen people: their covenants have not been revoked. In addition, Christians must take into account the facts that Christians for centuries mocked the Jewish people as landless and that for the ongoing Jewish people the proclamation of "Christ" has almost from the outset been heard as one of hatred and pride—culminating, as we have seen, in the horrific libels leading up to the Holocaust.

Given these points, I can agree with the basic case that Novak makes, though with some added elements. Christians must assume that, due to Christian boasting, the Jewish people as a whole legitimately do not recognize Jesus as the Messiah and thus remain bound to obey God's covenant in its original mode. Therefore, theologically speaking, Christians must support the Jewish people in obeying their unrevoked covenant. Besides, on

---

covenant, who *then* accepted his messiahhood as that covenant's fulfillment. *And*, it asserts that Jesus came to both initiate and fulfill the promise of the covenant for those Gentiles whose sole connection to the covenant is through him. Hence, in this kind of supersessionism, those Jews who do not accept Jesus' messiahhood are still part of the covenant in the sense of 'what God has joined together let no one put asunder.' Nevertheless, they are out of step with the fulfillment of the covenant which Jesus began already and which he shall return to totally compete. For hard supersessionism, though, the old covenant is dead. The Jews by their sins, most prominently their sin of rejecting Jesus as the Messiah, have forfeited any covenantal status.... Despite the deep specific differences between soft and hard supersessionists in Christianity, it seems to me that Christianity must be generically supersessionist. In fact, I question the Christian orthodoxy of any Christian who claims he or she is not a supersessionist at all. The reason for my suspicion is as follows: If Christianity did not come into the world to bring something better than what Judaism did not or could not bring itself, then why shouldn't anyone who wants a concrete relationship with the God of Abraham, Isaac, and Jacob—and their descendants—either remain within normative Judaism or convert to it?" (Novak, "Covenant in Rabbinic Thought," 66–67).

164. Novak, *Election of Israel*, 143.

practical grounds—which are also theological ones, given God's love for his chosen people (a love that Christians must share!)—the destruction of the existing Jewish State of Israel would be a cataclysmic disaster for the Jewish people. To remain faithful to the God who emphatically has not "rejected his [Jewish] people" (Rom 11:1), Christians should support Jewish Zionism in the sense that Novak understands it.

V. Catholics and the Land of Israel

Let me unpack the above paragraph further, given the density of the claims I am making. Catholics cannot simply adopt a Jewish view of the promised land. Christ has fulfilled and reconfigured God's covenant of people and land around himself.[165] Christ unites Jews and Gentiles in one body (his own)—and, as Ephesians 2:11–22 emphasizes, the change is significant. Consider again Paul's claims that "[h]e is a Jew who is one inwardly, and

---

165. For Messianic Jewish views that differ from my perspective in this regard, see Kinzer, *Searching Her Own Mystery*; Kinzer, *Postmissionary Messianic Judaism*; and the essays in Rudolph and Willitts, eds., *Introduction to Messianic Judaism*. When Kinzer proposes that "the prayer of observant Jews is mysteriously tied to the sacrifice of Jesus and his continuing priestly work of intercession in the heavenly sanctuary"—on the grounds that in the *Amidah* prayer (connected with the temple sacrifices) "Jews set their faces toward Jerusalem and pray for the full restoration of Israel and the coming of God's universal reign" (*Searching Her Own Mystery*, 137, 141)—I agree that, from a Christian perspective, there may be an implicit connection between the ongoing Jewish people's eschatological prayer (the *Amidah*) and Christian eschatological prayer (the Eucharist). I likewise agree with Kinzer that the Church has been "wounded by its attitude to Jews and Judaism" (*Searching Her Own Mystery*, 169)—and Kinzer's splendid knowledge of Christianity's Jewishness and of the beauty of Rabbinic Judaism shows how much has been neglected. But I disagree with Kinzer's view that Jews who are Christians must or may continue to observe the *mitsvot* as *necessary* for their salvation, or that there should be an ongoing structurally embodied separation between Gentiles and Jews in the Catholic Church (so as to preserve Jewish Christians' *necessary* task of observing the *mitsvot*). This position misses what Paul and other New Testament writings proclaim, namely, that all people are now called to observe the *mitsvot* in Christ Jesus, in a reconfigured way that draws the Gentiles fully into the people of God (Israel) as the body of Christ. Similarly, although I agree with Gerald McDermott that Jesus Christ "was living Torah and invited human beings to become one with him and thus one with Torah" and that the Torah "looks different now because he has shown us the inner meaning of it" (McDermott, *Israel Matters*, 99–100), I am not persuaded that Paul "saw Torah as binding on [Christian] Jews in all of its commandments" in the sense that "even if Jews and gentiles were one in Christ as brothers and sisters in Abraham's family ... they had different relationships to Jewish law" (McDermott, *Israel Matters*, 68, 77). Although Paul permitted (and at times practiced) Jewish Torah observance, he insisted that such observance could not be deemed necessary for salvation for any Christian, Jew or Gentile.

real circumcision is a matter of the heart, spiritual and not literal" (Rom 2:29); and Paul's emphasis that both Jews and Gentiles are justified by faith in Christ (Rom 3:30; Gal 2-3), now that Christ has created "in himself one new man in place of the two," thereby breaking "down the dividing wall of hostility" (Eph 2:14-15) and making Gentiles "fellow citizens with the saints and members of the household of God" (Eph 2:19).[166] Catholics believe that the covenants with Israel have been fulfilled and taken up by Christ in ways that transform them.[167]

Yet, as I have repeatedly emphasized, Catholics must not suppose that God's election of the Jewish people has been revoked or negated by the coming of Christ. The covenants with Israel *still exist*, even if now they are to be obeyed *in a messianic mode*. Recall that Paul says of the Jewish people who did not accept Jesus as the Messiah: "As regards the gospel they are enemies of God, for your sake; but as regards election they are beloved for the sake of their forefathers. For the gifts and call of God are irrevocable" (Rom 11:28-29). Christians and Jews cannot agree "as regards the gospel," but it is possible for Christians and Jews to agree "as regards election"—if this means the election of the Jewish people (as distinct from election in Christ).[168]

166. For the contrasting view that Christians are those who are called "to serve God as Gentiles" and to do so "in a Gentile way" and as "the Gentile Church," see van Buren, "When Christians Meet Jews," 57, 65. See also chapters 4 and 5 of Fredriksen, *Paul: The Pagans' Apostle*.

167. Kinzer argues that "Jewish disciples of Jesus" who observe the *mitsvot* thereby become "a sacramental sign of the spiritual bond joining the *ecclesia* to genealogical Israel" (*Searching Her Own Mystery*, 175), but he has missed the power of Paul's claim. For Paul, all who are incorporated into the Messiah are now a sacramental sign of this "spiritual bond," since all Christians—Jews and Gentiles—have become "children of the promise" (Rom 9:8; cf. Gal 2:7). Paul holds that the Jewish people according to the flesh are still God's covenantal people (Rom 11:1-2, 28-32). Yet, Paul also holds that in Christ, Gentiles fully share in every aspect of the messianically fulfilled and reconfigured "Israel of God" (Gal 6:16; cf. Luke 3:8). For a critique of Messianic Judaism from Jewish perspectives, see Langer, "Exploring the Interface," 293-94 (in response to Rutishauser, "'Old Unrevoked Covenant'"); and Larry Behrendt's remarks in Le Donne and Behrendt, *Sacred Dissonance*, 23. See also David Novak's insistence that Messianic Jews "should not be regarded as any kind of 'bridge' between the Jewish community and the church" (Novak, "Covenant and Mission," 52). For my concern that Kinzer's proposal in *Postmissionary Messianic Judaism* may involve a twofold supersession (of Judaism and Christianity), see my *Jewish-Christian Dialogue*, chapter 1, indebted to Novak's "When Jews Are Christians." For the view that Messianic Jews should be included within the bounds of the Jewish community rather than excluded as apostates (though without agreeing with Messianic Judaism), see Cohn-Sherbok, *Messianic Judaism*; and similarly—against the strict identification markers separating "Jew" from "Christian" in traditional "Jewish-Christian dialogue"—see Ariel, "A Different Kind of Dialogue?"

168. Christian Rutishauser seeks to collapse this tension by suggesting that the Jewish people are not opponents of the gospel of Jesus Christ: "When Judaism and

What Hans Urs von Balthasar calls "the frightful anti-Semitism running through the Church's history" has operated by rejecting the validity of Paul's command to embrace the Jewish people as beloved "as regards election."[169]

As I made clear in my book's Introduction, I consider (going beyond Paul, but along his lines) that Catholics have been "consigned ... to disobedience" (Rom 11:32) with respect to their interactions over the centuries with God's elect Jewish people. Here I note that during his Universal Day of Pardon in the Jubilee Year of 2000, Pope John Paul II asked forgiveness for the sins that Catholics have committed "against the People of Israel."[170]

---

the church face each other it means that faith meets faith, not heresy or false belief" (Rutishauser, "'Old Unrevoked Covenant,'" 230.) Among ongoing Judaism's firm beliefs, however, is the claim that Christians are mistaken to identify Jesus as the divine Messiah. For ongoing Judaism, as Ruth Langer makes clear in her response to Rutishauser, the Church is built upon a number of false beliefs about Jesus of Nazareth (and about God). Rutishauser asks, "What are the repercussions of the statement that Jesus is the messiah of the Jews? And how are we to regard the biblical verses describing Jesus as having fulfilled the covenant and as the aim of the law (Matt. 5:17; Rom. 10:4)?" ("'Old Unrevoked Covenant,'" 232). In answer, he proposes that Jewish Messianism should be differentiated sharply from Christian Christology (a solution that is not tenable with regard to the New Testament!), and he considers Jesus to be a fulfillment of the Jewish covenant only in the sense that Jesus is the Torah-observant Jew who enables the Gentiles to receive a covenantal life with God, "without dissolving the covenant of Mount Sinai" (Rutishauser, "'Old Unrevoked Covenant,'" 238)—so that the Gentiles have Christ and the Jews have Sinai. Rutishauser recognizes that if the New Testament is true, Jesus must in some sense be the Savior of all people. He argues that the solution is that Jesus *will be* the savior of all people (Jews and Gentiles) at the eschaton, and also perhaps that Jews may come to find "a brother in Jesus" without being "expected to embrace the church's christology" ("'Old Unrevoked Covenant,'" 248). I note that it is clear from the New Testament that if indeed Jesus *will be* the Savior of all people at the eschaton, he *is* the Savior of all people now.

169. Von Balthasar, "Church and Israel," 290. As noted above, von Balthasar describes this condition as an "interim state of blindness" that, rooted in God's purposes of mercy toward all peoples, gives Christians (largely Gentiles who were "formerly blind") no "right to mockery, revenge, persecution, anti-Semitism" ("Church and Israel," 292). After all, the whole human race, Jews and Gentiles, is united both in disobedience and in God's overarching will to save, a point that Paul himself makes by telling the Gentile Christians that "[j]ust as you were once disobedient to God but now have received mercy because of their disobedience, so they have now been disobedient in order that by the mercy shown to you they also may receive mercy" (Rom 11:30–31). As von Balthasar comments along Barthian lines, for Paul "[h]uman guilt is certainly present within the all-embracing act of God, but it does not determine this act, and this is shown by the fact that it is embraced by the act of election and reconciliation as by that of reprobation and condemnation" ("Church and Israel," 291).

170. See John Paul II, "Universal Prayer—Day of Pardon." After discussing this prayer, Patrick J. Ryan asks: "How can a faith tradition or those who bear that tradition repent? Is it possible for the bearers of a faith tradition to revise their understanding of themselves and of their faith? Are there both faithful and faithless revisions of faith

Specifically, he apologized for the "sins committed by not a few [Catholics] against the people of the covenant and the blessings."[171] The apology was warranted (to say the least), given that the history of Catholics sinning against the Jewish people has had the result that for most Jews over the centuries, as the Jewish scholar Larry Behrendt observes, Christianity is "something to fear," to the point that "we Jews would rather not deal with you Christians."[172]

Rabbi Michael Cook puts the same point even more powerfully: "Ask a mixed group of Christians and Jews, 'What does the Cross mean to you?' Christians may say that it signals Christ's incomparable gift of his life so that they might be saved; Jews may counter that it symbolizes unspeakable terror."[173] More sharply still, Eliezer Berkovits has commented in a manner that Christians must hear and respect with great sorrow: "we [the Jewish people] are not as yet ready to enter into a fraternal dialogue with a church, a religion, that has been responsible for so much suffering, and which is ultimately responsible for the murder of our fathers and mothers, brothers and sisters in the present generation . . . . All we want of Christians is that they keep their hands off us and our children!"[174] I find his position to be profoundly understandable.

---

traditions?" (Ryan, *Amen*, 125). He answers that prophetic voices, generally treated as outsiders, have been able to produce repentance that "makes revision possible in the root sense of that word: seeing anew the claims of truth" (Ryan, *Amen*, 125). Although he sums up his point by criticizing those (Catholics) who hold that "nothing important has ever changed or ever can change" (Ryan, *Amen*, 125), I would suggest that the key to the distinction between "faithful and faithless revisions" is distinguishing rightly between what can and cannot change in a faith tradition, which (not least) requires an account of truth-claims that pertain definitively to the faith tradition in question. For just such an account with regard to Catholic doctrine on the Jewish people, see D'Costa, *Vatican II*, 10–58, 113–59; as well as Norris, "Jewish People at Vatican II." See also D'Costa, "*Nostra Aetate*"; as well as the introduction of Lamb and Levering, eds., *Reception of Vatican II*.

171. John Paul II, "Universal Prayer—Day of Pardon."

172. Le Donne and Behrendt, *Sacred Dissonance*, 6, 23. See also Hansen, "Why Some Jews Fear the Passion," cited in Le Donne, *Near Christianity*, 89. In conversation with Abraham Foxman, Hansen recalls the history of the passion plays and the anti-Jewish violence that resulted, as well as Hitler's 1934 praise for the Oberammergau Passion Play. See also Waddy, *Oberammergau in the Nazi Era*.

173. As quoted (without citing the source) by Le Donne, *Near Christianity*, 77. See also the parallel that Le Donne draws (see *Near Christianity*, 92–96) between Luther's counsels regarding specific modes of persecuting the Jewish people and Elie Wiesel's description of Jewish sufferings under the Nazis in Weisel, *Night*.

174. Berkovits, "Judaism in the Post-Christian Era," 290, 293. Philip A. Cunningham quotes this text and then comments: "Christians certainly have little basis to be offended by such sentiments. Our mutual history has been too painful and prolonged

The fact that the Jewish people have been scandalized by "'Christian' hatred of Jews in the name of Christ"[175] has significant Christian theological implications—above all, as I have frequently pointed out in this book, that Catholics cannot fault the Jewish people for not recognizing Jesus as the Messiah. From the Jewish perspective, however, my emphasis on this point may seem strange. After all, most Jews simply do not think that Jesus did what the Messiah must do. Look at the condition of the world and all the persecution of the Jewish people over the past two millennia! Similarly, most Jews think that it does not make sense for God to become man or for the one God to be three "Persons." From a Jewish perspective, the worry about whether the Jewish people as a whole should be held "culpable" for rejecting Jesus may seem ludicrous or offensive.

It may make more sense if the question is turned around and Jews are asked whether Christians should be held "culpable" for worshipping a man as God and for worshipping three divine Persons. From a Jewish perspective, worshipping a man as God surely is idolatry, which both the Torah and the prophets repeatedly indicate will receive the strongest punishment. Likewise, despite Christian responses, most Jews consider the worship of the Trinity to be in fundamental violation of the Shema: "Hear, O Israel: The Lord our God is one Lord" (Deut 6:4). Are Jewish Christians and Gentile

---

to anticipate the immediate establishment of *shalom* between the two communities. All that we Christians can do is undertake to reform our tradition's failure to heed Paul's warnings against arrogance and to commit ourselves to behaving as a covenantal people should" (Cunningham, "Paul's Letters," 159). Hannah Arendt is of course correct that "Catholic anti-Semitism had two limitations which it could not transgress without contradicting Catholic dogma and the efficacy of the sacraments—it could not agree to the gassing of the Jews any more than it could agree to the gassing of the mentally ill, and it could not extend its anti-Jewish sentiments to those who were baptized" (Arendt, *Responsibility and Judgment*, 224). I agree with the signers of *Dabru Emet*—and thus with its lead author David Novak—that "Nazism itself was not an inevitable outcome of Christianity" (David Novak et al., "*Dabru Emet*").

175. McDermott, *Israel Matters*, 132. McDermott and I agree about Christian sins against the Jewish people causing invincible ignorance, although he does not use the phrase. He states, "What about the myriads of Jews down through history who have loved the God of Israel—who Jesus taught us is the only true God—but who have been unable to see Jesus as Messiah? These are the Jews of whom Paul seems to have been writing when he said that God sent a 'hardening on part of Israel' (Rom. 11:25). In many cases this was because 'Christians' were killing Jews in the name of 'Christ.' Can we blame them for not seeing *this* Christ as their friend? Before he went to Damascus, Paul did not have Christians attacking him, yet he tells us later that God had mercy on him because he had 'acted ignorantly in unbelief' (1 Tim. 1:13). If God had mercy on Paul because of his ignorance, might God not have mercy on Jews who are ignorant of Jesus because of 'Christian' hatred of Jews in the name of 'Christ'?" (*Israel Matters*).

Christians culpable for idolatry, which is the gravest possible sin, deeper even than Christian oppression of the Jewish people?

For Jewish-Christian dialogue to gain traction, it would seem that ongoing Judaism would need to develop ways of identifying Christians as something other than idolaters, despite the fact that most Rabbinic Jews hold (as the Talmud makes clear) that Christians are objectively speaking in a state of grave error and that Jews who become Christians are apostates, cut off from God's people until they renounce their error. Ongoing Judaism would have to be able to conceive of Christians both as guilty of error (and of persecution) and somehow *also* as people to whose faith Jews owe a basic respect. Otherwise, ongoing Judaism would simply dismiss Christians as culpable idolaters, deserving of grave punishment and (to limit the spread of such odious errors) also of persecution.

The same point, *mutatis mutandis*, holds for Christians vis-à-vis the ongoing Jewish people. Christians should affirm, on the basis of Romans 11, that God has not revoked his covenant with the Jewish people and that the ongoing Jewish people remain God's chosen people, beloved of God, even though Christ has fulfilled and transformed the covenant. But from a Christian perspective, the ongoing Jewish people (i.e. those who are not Christians) reject Jesus' true identity as Messiah and Lord, and do so despite the fact that "[t]hey are Israelites, and to them belong the sonship, the glory, the covenants, the giving of the law, the worship, and the promises; to them belong the patriarchs, and of their race, according to the flesh, is the Christ, who is God over all" (Rom 9:4-5). From a Christian perspective, Jesus *should* be attractive to the Jewish people since he is their Messiah, the suffering servant, the one through whom the fountain of mercy is established. Christ accomplished the redemption of Israel, and "there is no other name under heaven given among men by which we must be saved" (Acts 4:12). Just as Jews must ask why it is that Christians do not stand under the curse of the most pernicious idolatry, Christians must ask why it is that Jews do not stand under the curse of rejecting their own Messiah, an error for which Jesus weeps (Luke 19:41) and Paul cries out in "great sorrow and unceasing anguish" (Rom 9:2).

This is why I have devoted considerable reflection upon the issue of culpability—not that I want to suggest that Christians should go around thinking about how guilty Jewish people are (indeed, that is a recipe for self-righteous disaster, as the Church has discovered too late), but rather because Christians need a theological way of accounting for the large-scale Jewish "no"—just as Jews need a way of accounting for the seemingly idolatrous "yes" on the part of so many Gentiles and of some Jews.

As I have argued, the path forward for Christians on this matter is found in Romans 11, with its agonized warnings about Gentile Christian boasting and its insistence—not heeded for centuries—that the Jewish people remain beloved. Romans 11 also perceives that the situation is a "mystery" of God's saving will, according to which somehow "God has consigned all men to disobedience, that he may have mercy upon all" (Rom 11:32). By reflecting on these realities (Christian counter-witness, ongoing Jewish election, and the "mystery" that is God's plan of mercy), Christian reflection on the unrevoked but fulfilled Jewish covenants will find a theological path for supporting the ongoing Jewish effort to obey God's covenant.

Lest my point be misunderstood, I recognize that it remains possible for particular Jewish people to reject Jesus culpably, especially in the sense of consciously turning their back upon God—as for instance by committing adultery or murder. Indeed Christians regularly turn away culpably, when, even while believing in Jesus, we act in greed, lust, pride, and so on. But whereas we Christians are guilty of consciously rejecting our Lord, no one can culpably reject Jesus Christ if, in his or her (communally inflected) experience, the very name of Jesus Christ recalls acts of vile persecution rather than love. This is where it is helpful to recognize the "invincible ignorance" caused by the boastful counter-witness of Christians.

Given this situation of scandal, and as part of the positive "mystery" of God's plan, the original mode of the covenant is in force for the Jewish people as a whole who legitimately do not know Jesus Christ. Thus Catholics must presume that the Jewish people as a whole are acting in good faith when they strive to obey the original obligations of the covenant. Among these obligations are, insofar as possible, dwelling in and governing the land of Israel, which the Jewish people who live in the State of Israel now do.[176] Since these obligations come from the living God whose word is true, Catholics should encourage the ongoing Jewish people (presuming they do not know Jesus as the Christ) in obeying the commandment of God, just as Novak urges. Indeed, what could be more important for God's people to do, while they await the Messiah?

---

176. Novak adds the point that "the Jewish people are centered in the land of Israel; they are not confined there, however. Though inferior to Jewish life in the land of Israel, Jewish life outside Israel, in the Diaspora (*golah*) has Jewish legitimacy. Moreover . . . the land of Israel is not confined to Jews. As such, Jews can recognize the right of non-Jews to live in the land of Israel: either as individual citizens in a Jewish state there, or *even* having a state of their own within the boundaries of the entire land of Israel. That is because, even though the land of Israel has been given to the Jews to govern, inhabit, and primarily develop, nonetheless they may not regard that land to be their own possession to do with as they please, to act in their *own* perceived self-interest" (Novak, *Election of Israel*, 147–48).

Of course, Catholics also must not forget to proclaim our own belief that since the Messiah has come in Jesus of Nazareth, the ecclesial body of Christ is God's dwelling place. Now that Christ has come, the "land" where all people are called to settle is the body of Christ, which at the eschaton will constitute the fullness of the new creation.[177] But in affirming this point about Christ's reconfiguration of the covenants around himself, Catholics must not deny or oppose—indeed Catholics must support—Jewish obedience to their still existent covenants.

For much of the twentieth century, the Catholic Church was antagonistic toward or deeply distrustful of the State of Israel. Philip Cunningham points out that during the drafting of *Nostra Aetate*, "Some Council fathers argued that any positive statement about Judaism would be seen as favoring the State of Israel and might bring retaliation upon the Christian minorities living in predominantly Muslim countries."[178] Even more so today, support for the State of Israel as a Jewish state is taken as an affront to Palestinians who lost their land and homes during the war following the establishment of the Jewish State of Israel. Note that I take it to be an evident fact

---

177. McDermott considers that the return of the people of Israel to the land and the spread of Christians across the globe have eschatological significance, as the fulfillment of biblical prophecies. He envisions the eschaton as "a renewed earth, with Israel at the center. Christ will be the King indeed, but it will be far more than simply an invisible rule of Jesus over minds and souls scattered around the world" (*Israel Matters*, 108; cf. 100–101). On this view, Jesus will reign over a renewed Jerusalem and the nations will stream to Jerusalem. I think that this view of the eschatological imagery of Scripture does not sufficiently allow for the transcendent fulfillment, the unimaginable new creation, that is the world-to-come. For background to various forms of evangelical Christian dispensationalism and premillennialism, see Ryrie, *Dispensationalism*. Novak points out that there was "an early rabbinic debate as to whether the Exodus will be no longer a point of reference at all, or whether it will remain as a secondary point of reference" in the world-to-come; and he observes that even for the proponents of the *latter* position, which is the majority position, "the Torah of the redeemed future . . . will be radically changed" (Novak, *Election of Israel*, 155). Although some Jews hold that eschatologically "Israel will dominate the nations of the world either politically or spiritually," Novak thinks it more theologically adequate to hold that "it will be persuasion or inspiration, not force, that ultimately reconciles Israel and the world under God" (*Election of Israel*, 158). See also the reflections of Mittleman, "Messianic Hope." Mittleman advocates for the adoption of Lenn Goodman's "realist messianism": see L. E. Goodman, *On Justice*. According to this view, "an ever more devoted acceptance of the Torah's moral tutelage" can bring about a (non-utopian and demythologized) messianic age (Mittleman, "Messianic Hope," 239). For a position that, from a different theological direction, similarly underestimates the freedom and transcendent power of God's action of eschatological consummation, see Shlomo Riskin's argument that "Universal Redemption . . . can only come about if the nations of the world accept fundamental biblical morality" (Riskin, "Covenant and Conversion," 106).

178. Cunningham, *Seeking Shalom*, 222.

that Palestinians who live in Israel today find themselves in a very difficult situation.[179]

Cunningham observes that in Vatican documents, therefore, a "highly nuanced distinction" is made "between the theological and politico-historical aspects of Christian attitudes toward the State of Israel," with the goal being that "Catholics should respect and seek to understand Jewish attachment to *Eretz Yisrael*, but the existence of the modern State of Israel . . . should not be interpreted by Catholics primarily in religious or biblical categories, but according to international legal principles."[180] Is this position the most that Catholics, including Palestinian Catholics (for whom this issue hits home the hardest), can or should be expected to affirm?

I do not think it is, although I acknowledge the political quandaries, far beyond the ability of a theologian to resolve. As Novak makes clear, although the modern State of Israel should not be invested with the covenantal significance of the people and land, it is also now true that the only way that the Jewish people can obey God's commandment to dwell in and govern the land is by constituting a state. Put otherwise, the Jewish people's political identity cannot be separated from their religious identity, given the nature of their covenants. Thus, once one grants that the ongoing Jewish people are

---

179. For stories of Palestinian Catholics (among others), see Burge, *Whose Land? Whose Promise?*, 246–51. These stories help one to understand the level of Palestinian anger, including Palestinian Catholic anger. Burge's book is written to persuade his fellow evangelical Christians to reduce their support for Christian Zionism, but he also affirms that "the protection of political Israel is a moral duty because of what happened to the Jews in European history" (*Whose Land? Whose Promise?*, 290). For realism regarding the military forces of the state of Israel—including both targeted killings and soldiers protesting such killings, with a focus on "the war between Israel and the Palestinians that broke out in September 2000 [the 'Second Intifada']—a war of continual retaliations of suicide bombings and targeted killings," perhaps even including the poisoning of Yasser Arafat, see Bergman, *Rise and Kill First*, 563. Bergman sums up, along lines that could be equally applied to American (and Russian) military operations in recent decades: "Thanks to its streamlined targeted killing apparatus, the Israeli intelligence community triumphed over something that for many years had been considered unbeatable: suicide terrorism. . . . The use of targeted killings, however, had heavy concomitant costs. The price was paid, first and foremost, by the innocent Palestinians who became 'coincidental damage' of the assassinations. Many innocent people were killed, and thousands, including many children, were wounded and left disabled for life. Others were mentally scarred or homeless. . . . The targeted killing campaign also did a great deal to further marginalize and delegitimize Israel in the eyes of the world" (*Rise and Kill First*, 563–64).

180. Cunningham, *Seeking Shalom*, 223. For the distinction between the land and the State of Israel, see Pontifical Commission, "Notes." To my mind, this distinction is necessary in one sense (so as not to sacralize the state of Israel) but not possible in another sense (insofar as the State of Israel is indeed the Jewish state on a portion of the land that God covenantally gave to his people).

bound to their covenantal obligation to dwell in the land if possible, then this has implications for the post-1948 State of Israel. One can and should avoid sacralizing the modern State of Israel; and one can and should deny that the State of Israel should occupy the entirety of the promised land in its (disputed) geographical dimensions.[181] But Catholic thinking about the modern State of Israel cannot simply bracket the biblical covenant of land. Again, this is so even when one recognizes that, in Christ, the covenant of people and land has been fulfilled and reconfigured so that for Christians (including Jewish Christians) there is no need to dwell in and govern the land.[182]

I concur with Cunningham, therefore, that for Catholics who are engaging the modern State of Israel, "the religious and secular realms cannot be fully separated," although the two must be distinguished (as Novak does).[183] As Cunningham aptly points out: "to suddenly claim that a renewed Jewish presence in the Land is devoid of religious meaning after alleging for centuries that Jewish exile from the Land was theologically significant seems capriciously inconsistent."[184] Again, as Novak cautions, this does not

---

181. With regard to the latter point, Cunningham notes that the book of Joshua offers contradictory descriptions of the geographical dimensions of the land of Israel (see Joshua 1, 11, and 13; as well as Genesis 15:18). As Cunningham rightly concludes, Catholics cannot "argue that 'God gave the Land of Israel to the Jews' as if this should settle all contemporary geopolitical disputes" (*Seeking Shalom*, 226).

182. Bruce D. Chilton argues, "Israel within Jesus' activity is not a matter of definition but an imperative of transformation. Those who offer of their own, forgiving and being forgiven, join in that eschatological Israel that benefits even non-Jews. Jesus' position is difficult to compare with other definitions of Israel current in his period because he provided for no clear social structure" (Chilton, "Israel of James," 118). Chilton considers that the fulfillment and reconfiguration that I describe is not rooted in Jesus' own perspective; and in making this point Chilton moves "from the strictest model of Israel as centered on the Temple (in the circle of James), through the reflection of severe tension within Israel as a result of Jesus' movement (in Q), and on to the conviction that God's spirit is available through Christ to those outside Israel as well as to those within (in the circle of Peter)" (Chilton, "Israel of James," 119–20). In my view, he has not apprehended correctly the teaching and symbolic actions of Jesus with regard to the Twelve and to the temple (and thus with regard to the inauguration of the kingdom).

183. Cunningham, *Seeking Shalom*, 224. For Novak's firmly non-messianic theological interpretation of the establishment and development of the State of Israel, see Novak, *Zionism and Judaism*, 232–49. For a perspective similar to Novak's in celebrating the establishment and flourishing of the State of Israel while refusing to sacralize the State of Israel, see Hartman, *Living Covenant*, 281. For Hartman, the success of Zionism is so spiritually important as to be set alongside Sinai and the post-70 emergence of Rabbinic Judaism, even if he does not consider the establishment of the State of Israel to have messianic import: see Hartman, *Conflicting Visions*, 48–49. Richard Lux discusses Hartman's views in Lux, *Jewish People*, 86–90. See also Tal et al., *Religious Zionism*.

184. Cunningham, *Seeking Shalom*, 224.

mean that people (whether Jews or Christians) should construe the Jewish people's return to the land as a step toward bringing about the eschatological consummation. Such a viewpoint falls into the error of exceeding what humans can know of God's timing, even in light of biblical prophecies.[185] But while we should deny that the return of the Jewish people to dwell in and govern the land is necessarily eschatologically significant, we cannot deny that it is theologically significant. It is the latter because the Jewish people, as a theological-political entity, are *obeying a divine commandment* that has not been revoked (even if Christians know that it has been messianically fulfilled and reconfigured).

During a news conference after a 2010 Synod on the Middle East at the Vatican, the Melkite Catholic Archbishop Cyril Bustros made the following claim: "As Christians, we cannot talk about a 'promised land' for the Jews. We talk about a 'promised land' which is the Kingdom of God. That's the promised land, which encompasses the entire earth with a message of peace and justice and equality for all the children of God. . . . There's no 'chosen people' any longer for Christians."[186] This statement caused understandable consternation. One problem is that Archbishop Bustros failed to acknowledge that the ongoing Jewish people are still the "chosen people" of God (see Rom 11:28–29). The archbishop also failed to appreciate that the Jewish people, not recognizing Jesus as the Messiah (and not culpable for this), are doing exactly what Christians should expect and wish them to do: striving

---

185. I differ here from McDermott, as noted above. For McDermott (an Anglican), Christians should give a positive answer to the following questions: "Was the establishment of the state of Israel a part of that prophesied history? Is this part of what Jeremiah, Ezekiel, and other prophets meant by their predictions that Jews would return to the land from all over the world? Does this mean that the massive ingathering of Jews to the land in the nineteenth century and then their organization of a protective state are somehow part of the fulfillment of not only Old Testament prophecies but also apostolic expectation of a time of *palingenesia* and *apokatastasis*?" (McDermott, "New (and Old) Scandal of Particularity," 434). McDermott adds, "To believe that the state of Israel is an ambiguous and partial—but real—fulfillment of prophecy does not require belief that this is the last state or the final goal of biblical prophecy" ("New (and Old) Scandal of Particularity," 435). See also Moseley, *Nationhood, Providence, and Witness*. My position coheres with Gavin D'Costa's proposal for a "minimalist Zionism, eschewing all eschatological and messianic signs connected with the land" (D'Costa, "Developing the Conversation," 441).

186. Allen, "Thinking Straight about Israel," cited in Cunningham, *Seeking Shalom*, 227. Surprisingly to me, Rabbi David Meyer suggests that the Jewish people are relinquishing the notion of a "chosen people." He states that the twenty-first century is "a time when the Jewish concept of Israel as the 'chosen people' is in radical retreat in Jewish thought. I do not know of any Jewish thinkers today who overtly proclaim the Jews to be 'God's chosen people'" (Meyer, "*Nostra Aetate*," 125). By contrast, I know a number of Jewish thinkers who affirm that the Jewish people are God's chosen people.

to obey God's command that they dwell in and govern the promised land. This does not mean that the claims of the Palestinian people to the land can be ignored by Catholics, but it means that the status of the "promised land" is not so easily dealt with as the archbishop thinks.[187]

To date, however, the Catholic Church has not found a way to express theological support for the Jewish state. Without expressing such support himself, Philip Cunningham rightly observes that "Christians cannot develop their own theology of the Land in isolation from Jews who are wrestling today with similar questions."[188] The wrestling that we found in Novak's writings on the topic of the land may therefore help to chart a path. For Novak, what is accomplished by the Jewish people's return to the land is, ideally, a covenantal witness to theocentric humility, through the practice of obedience to God's command in humble appreciation of God's gifts. Certainly, this witness is compromised by human fallenness, just as is the witness of the Catholic Church.

Is the notion of theocentric humility a mere stand-in for claiming land to which others have a better or more exigent claim? Christians cannot think this to be the case. Obeying Israel's God, for Christians, is indeed an act of humility—even in a situation as thorny as the promised land has always been. As Novak says, the Jewish people had to receive from God a place to dwell with God; they could not make such a place for themselves. The same thing holds for Christians, who could only receive—not make—the body of Christ. Perceiving this connection, Thomas Weinandy comments that the "Church has begun to recognize and acknowledge the revelational

---

187. As Gavin D'Costa remarks, no Catholic "affirmation of the Land [can] be at the cost of a Palestinian homeland. Since 1974 the Vatican has supported this, and in 2015 it formally recognized a Palestinian State" (D'Costa, "Developing the Conversation," 441; he cites Andrej Kreutz's pro-Palestinian *Vatican Policy on the Palestinian-Israeli Conflict*). See also Arendt, "Peace or Armistice in the Near East?," written in 1948 in the aftermath of the Arab-Jewish war, where she comments: "Against Jewish determination to regard the outcome as final stands the determination of the Arabs to view it as an interlude. . . . For more than twenty-five years, Jews and Arabs have made perfectly incompatible claims on each other. The Arabs never gave up the idea of a unitary Arab state in Palestine, though they sometimes reluctantly conceded limited minority rights to Jewish inhabitants. The Jews, with the exception of the Revisionists, for many years refused to talk about their ultimate goals, partly because they knew only too well the uncompromising attitude of the Arabs and partly because they had unlimited confidence in British protection. The Biltmore Program of 1942 for the first time formulated Jewish political aims officially—a unitary Jewish state in Palestine with the provision of certain minority rights for Palestinian Arabs who then still formed the majority of the Palestinian population. At the same time, the transfer of Palestinian Arabs to neighboring countries was contemplated and openly discussed in the Zionist movement" (Arendt, "Peace or Armistice in the Near East?," 429–30).

188. Cunningham, *Seeking Shalom*, 233.

significance of the land of Israel," and he hopes that the Church will work "to acknowledge, preserve, and cultivate Jewish identity, an identity that is literally rooted in Israel, both within and outside the Church."[189] He bemoans the fact that Catholics have so often displayed toward the Jewish people "an extreme arrogance and even a malicious animosity and poisonous hatred."[190]

For Weinandy, it is important to work for the conversion of the whole Jewish people to Jesus Christ prior to the eschaton. By contrast, though I greatly value Jewish converts (and Jewish Christians), I think that the conversion of the whole Jewish people will only be accomplished by the Messiah in his coming. Moreover, this eschatological event will involve a "conversion" also on the part of Christians, as the infinite depths of Christ's love and mercy gloriously shine forth, far beyond what we Christians can now know (but not in contradiction to what we now know).[191] Because I think that the conversion of the Jewish people *as a whole* will not take place until the eschaton—and because I do not wish to divide Jews and Gentiles who belong to Christ's messianically reconfigured Israel (i.e. divide them into a Jewish ekklesia and a Gentile ekklesia, let alone suppose that Christian Jews must observe the laws of Rabbinic Judaism as a salvific requirement)—I deny that the Church's theological mandate need involve preserving distinctive Jewish identity *within* the Church, except in the sense that the Church itself has a Jewish identity in the Messiah.

Nevertheless, Weinandy and I agree that Catholics should not treat the land of Israel as though it lacked theological significance. Its theological significance is grounded in the original covenant that the ongoing Jewish people—understandably not believing in Jesus—continues to strive to obey. Its Christian theological significance, after centuries of degrading the Jewish people, consists not least in our responsibility to support the Jewish people

---

189. Weinandy, "Jews and the Body of Christ," 423.

190. Weinandy, "Jews and the Body of Christ," 415.

191. For Weinandy, the conversion of the Jewish people "must be achieved historically and visibly if the biblical vision is to be fulfilled," and therefore it must not simply occur at the end of time (Weinandy, "Jews and the Body of Christ," 418–19). He holds that the Jewish people should specifically convert to Jesus Christ in the Catholic Church: "only if Jewish believers in Jesus are united to the Catholic Church under the authority of the Pope and the bishops in union with him will the Jewish presence within the Body of Christ be truly and fully beneficial to that Body" ("Jews and the Body of Christ," 419). But he adds that "while there needs to be a full integration of Jewish and Gentile Christians within the Body of Christ, Jewish believers should not lose their distinctive Jewishness" ("Jews and the Body of Christ," 419). I think this would make impossible a "full integration," in part by implying that Gentiles truly cannot become "Israelites" in Christ.

in living out the covenant. Palestinian Catholics, too, can appreciate this theological mandate, without minimizing the concern for justice. I believe it would greatly help the cause of seeking justice for Palestinians in the land if Palestinian Catholics were to perceive the Catholic theological grounds for affirming Jewish Zionism.

Thanks in part to the efforts of Abraham Joshua Heschel during the conciliar process,[192] *Nostra Aetate* began to heal the centuries-long scandal of Catholics treating the Jewish people as though they were not "beloved" or possessed of an irrevocable vocation. As noted above, I hold that over the centuries, the Church never lacked its attribute of holiness or its bond of charity, despite the fact that the visible Church often suffered from the grave corruption of people who claimed to be Catholics but either were not interiorly united to Christ or were in a condition of invincible ignorance. God permitted the members of his Church to fail profoundly with regard to their treatment of the Jewish people, at times explicitly in the name of the Church.[193] For almost two millennia, Catholics showed "ingrained hostility

---

192. See Furnal, "Abraham Heschel and *Nostra Aetate*"; and Fleischner, "Heschel's Significance," 153–59. Fleischner points out earlier that for the progress of Jewish-Christian dialogue, Heschel's "first 'precept' is: No more mission to the Jews. All attempts to convert Jews must be abandoned, for they are a call to Jews to betray their people's tradition, and proof of the failure to accept Judaism as a way of truth, a way to God, valid in its own right" ("Heschel's Significance," 148). For Heschel, the Christian invitation to conversion is tantamount to saying that it would be good if there were no more Judaism in the world. On this point, see Heschel, "No Religion Is an Island." I disagree with Heschel here. Yet, Christian history is full of the kind of proselytism that Heschel rightly fears, namely, threats of "convert or else face persecution." Heschel recognizes that Christianity has always understood itself to be intrinsically missionary, but he argues that Christianity is now shifting from "mission" to "dialogue": see Heschel, "From Mission to Dialogue."

193. Theologically speaking, the holiness of the Church does not mean that the Church has escaped every kind of error or wrong path. See Congar, *True and False Reform*; as well as Ratzinger, "Church's Guilt," and Levering, *Engaging the Doctrine of the Holy Spirit*, chapter 7. Ratzinger notes that in confessing the sins that have marred the Church in the past, Catholics are not arrogantly judging earlier Catholics, but rather are attempting to understand our own sins and the weaknesses that beset our Church as it has come to be over the course of history. Ratzinger also observes that "a Christian *confessio peccati* always has to go hand in hand with a *confessio laudis*. In any honest examination of conscience we can see that for our part in every generation we have done much that is evil. Yet we can also see that, in spite of our sins, God has always purified and renewed the Church and has always entrusted great things to fragile vessels.... It would be failing in honesty to see only our evil and not the good that God has effected through the faithful—in spite of their sins" ("Church's Guilt," 282–83). I should note that Congar's *True and False Reform*, published after the Holocaust, identifies true reform as a midpoint between the extremes of "Pharisaism" and the "temptation to become 'synagogue'"—thus indicating Congar's own debt to the anti-Jewish Christian attitudes of his day, despite the fact that Congar made an important contribution to

to Jews as a profound political and moral threat to human society."[194] This error reached a sort of climax in the nineteenth- and early-twentieth century anti-Semitism that we saw in *Civiltà Cattolica* and *L'Osservatore Romano*. Now that Catholics today recognize the Jewish people as "beloved" and as possessed of an "irrevocable" vocation (Rom 11:28–29), Catholics should respond positively to Novak's call to affirm "God's covenant with the Jewish people and with the land of Israel as their inheritance."[195] As Yves Congar observed already in 1955:

> [A]nti-semitism strikes at the roots of Christianity itself in several important respects. It destroys the very notion of God; it destroys charity, it destroys the biblical movement, that is to say revelation as it has been given to us. Consequently it is impossible to discuss Israel adequately except in a religious context.... We can equally well see, in the rise of a reconstituted, free Jewish state or a Jewish nation, the end result of innumerable prayers addressed to God by the Jews, especially since A.D. 70, the year of the capture of Jerusalem by Titus. We have no compelling reason to suppose that prayer of such fidelity, fervour and long duration must go unanswered.[196]

Nostra Aetate. The same highly negative view of ongoing Judaism appears in Congar, "Paul's Casuistry," 62. See Groppe, "Revisiting Vatican II's Theology," 596–600.

194. Pawlikowski, "Jews and Christians," 161.

195. Novak, *Election of Israel*, 143.

196. Congar, "Religious Significance," 445–46. For Congar, given that God's covenantal promises have been fulfilled in Christ and given that (at the same time) Paul states that the Jewish people are still the subject of God's promises, the establishment of the State of Israel may pertain to the ingathering of the Jewish people that is needed prior to their eschatological embrace of Christ. Congar does not think that it is possible for Christians to conceive of the establishment of the State of Israel as, in itself, the fulfillment of divine promises or prophecies—since these have been fulfilled in Christ. Admittedly, Congar lacks much of a sense of the ongoing Jewish people as God's chosen people. But he speculates, "It does not seem unlikely that military or diplomatic events may one day reinstate the Jews in the holy places of the old city and in the courts of the Temple" (Congar, "Religious Significance," 459), prompting a desire to rebuild the temple and reestablish the priesthood—which may lead the Jewish people to reevaluate Jesus' prophetic sign regarding the temple. To my mind, this is overly speculative, even if possible. It should suffice for Christians to recognize that the Jewish people still is God's covenantal people (even if Christ has fulfilled the covenants) and that this people, in the course of the "mystery" of God's plan for it, should be supported in fulfilling its covenantal obligation to dwell in and govern the land, given that Christians have no basis for claiming that the Jewish people as a whole should be able to recognize (in Christians) the inaugurated eschatological kingdom of the Messiah. Indebted to Louis Bouyer, Congar provides a helpful definition of the patristic meaning of "mystery": "a mystery is essentially that which is a part of the realization of God's plan. The Fathers call everything 'mystery' which represents a stage or an incident in that realization and

VI. Conclusion

I began this chapter by surveying the biblical teachings about the covenantal land promise, including the New Testament's understanding of the eschatological fulfillment and transformation of this promise by Jesus Christ. In Christ, the eschatological fulfillment has only been inaugurated, not consummated. The fullness of the new creation or New Jerusalem has not yet arrived. But the land promise is now understood by Christians to be the "body of Christ" rather than simply the land of Canaan.

Since Christians believe that the eschaton has been inaugurated but not yet consummated, there is space for a deeper Christian appreciation of the perspective of the Jewish people.[197] The Catholic Church today bears responsibility for a shameful history of scandalizing our Jewish brethren, God's chosen people. As with other human sins, this should be cause not for despair but for repentance and for the theocentric humility promoted by Novak. Christians should follow the example of Peter, who repeatedly recognized how weak he was by comparison with Jesus and who "fell down at Jesus' knees, saying, 'Depart from me, for I am a sinful man, O Lord'" (Luke 5:8). Jesus never gave up on Peter, but he did correct him sharply on more than one occasion—and Paul did the same. Peter's ministry of service remained intact nevertheless. In the words of George Hunsinger, humbled

---

which consequently derives its meaning from its relation to the consummation of that plan: that is, what we call eschatology" (Congar, "Religious Significance," 446).

197. Philip Cunningham and Didier Pollefeyt have observed, "Many Christians have wondered why Jews don't enter into covenant with God through the Logos incarnated in the glorified Jesus for the salvation of all humanity. But today we must seriously wrestle with the implications of the possibility that the mysterious providential plan includes the Jewish and Christian communities living in covenant with God throughout historic time according to two organically connected modalities. If we take seriously the Apostle Paul's intuition that God was responsible for a general Jewish lack of receptivity to his preaching of the Good News (Rom. 11:7-8, 25-26), then the existence of two distinct communities in covenant with God is not the result of some sort of mistake. Rather, it was God's will. If the continuing existence of two communities walking in covenant was the will of God, then their interrelationship must be viewed as having a positive meaning" (Cunningham and Pollefeyt, "Triune One," 200). As noted above, I think that God does will "Jewish and Christian communities living in covenant with God throughout historic time according to two organically connected modalities," in a manner that can and should have "a positive meaning." Yet, in itself, it is not positive that Jews do not recognize Jesus as their Messiah, given that Jesus is indeed such. Cunningham and Pollefeyt risk ironing away all tension from the relationship between Jews and Christians. In this regard see the warning given by Joseph B. Soloveitchik: "Standardization of practices, equalization of dogmatic certitudes, and the waiving of eschatological claims spell the end of the vibrant and great faith experience of any religious community" (Soloveitchik, "Confrontation," 101-2).

Christians must help the Jewish people be "less terrified, less isolated, less vulnerable to existential threats in the world."[198]

A large portion of the Jewish people recognizes that the Palestinian people also have a legitimate claim to a state within the boundaries of the biblical promised land. At present, it seems clear that a one-state solution (comprising Jews and Palestinians) would quickly make the Jewish people into a minority incapable of governing the land. If so, then a two-state solution appears to be the answer.[199] As Gavin D'Costa has affirmed, "There is no question that there must be some form of governance for Jewish people in the land of Israel."[200] D'Costa specifies that whatever form the State of Israel takes, it should be a form that ensures the ongoing existence of the Jewish people in the land. It should also be a form that opens the door to the flourishing of a Palestinian state in the land.[201]

---

198. Hunsinger, "After Barth," 61. On peace and justice grounds, Hunsinger distances himself firmly from any "uncritical" solidarity with the Jewish people if this is taken to mean uncritical support of the State of Israel.

199. For efforts to split the difference between a one-state solution and a two-state solution, see Shenhav, *Beyond the Two-State Solution*. In a Foreword to this book (vii–xvii), the Palestinian thinker Lama Abu Odeh argues: "Israel itself is nothing short of a huge settlement project that was founded upon the displacement of hundreds of thousands of Palestinians and the systematic expropriation of the land they left behind" (*Beyond the Two-State Solution*, vii). For Odeh, everything therefore depends upon the right of return. Shenhav, a Jewish scholar, intentionally operates at a utopian level in hopes of hitting upon a solution—but in my view his utopianism makes his analysis less than helpful (see, *Beyond the Two-State Solution*, 140–44, 154–59).

200. D'Costa, "Catholic Zionism," 19.

201. For the problem of "religious nationalism," to which Catholics are no strangers (having acted in religious-nationalist ways at many points over the centuries), see R. R. Ruether and H. J. Ruether, *Wrath of Jonah*, although the Ruethers take a different position than I do with regard to the conflict. In his 1992 book, Edward Said states, "Israel categorically refuses to commit itself to what all the Arabs have agreed to: an exchange of territory for secure peace" (Said, *Question of Palestine*, 243). I think that Israel came to make significant offers in this regard, but they were not reciprocated. Said says, "some Israelis and non-Israeli Jews have in fact understood that if Israelis and Palestinians can have any decent future it must be a common one, not based on the nullification of one by the other" (*Question of Palestine*, 244). In my view, the "common" future must specifically involve two separate states, both of which must fully affirm the right to exist of the other. See also the evangelical New Testament scholar Gary Burge's *Whose Land? Whose Promise?*, especially his statement that he seeks to be "pro-Israel, pro-Palestine, and pro-Jesus" (291). Burge fears that today a "two-state solution is impossible because West Bank settlers have destroyed even the possibility of a genuine Palestinian state" (*Whose Land? Whose Promise?*, 297). By contrast, Eugene Korn contends that "[o]nly a minuscule percentage of Israelis believe that settlement of [all] the land is more important than democracy, peace, and political compromise with Israel's Arab neighbors" (E. B. Korn, *Jewish Connection to Israel*, 121). For background to Israeli concerns regarding the good faith of peace negotiations, which have now broken off, see E. B. Korn, *Jewish*

LAND

The State of Israel is home to millions of people, most of them Jews. At present, debates about the justice of its founding often come down to the question of whether it is just and right that the State of Israel continue to exist as a *Jewish* state. If the state were redefined territorially and if, in a full democracy, Palestinians became the majority of voters in the state, then Israel would cease to be a Jewish state. Some theorists and activists are interested in the construction of such a state, with various hopes in view. Some think it might provide a new example of Jewish-Muslim harmony; some envision a recovery of justice for the Palestinians through a right of return that would turn Palestinians into the majority population of the State of Israel; and some hope for a more gradual reestablishment of Muslim governance of the entire land.

I do not see how any of the above hopes can be adopted by Catholics—even by Palestinian Catholics. In times past, before millions of Jews emigrated to the land, before the (British) Peel Commission in 1937 recommended the partition of Palestine into two states, before the Holocaust, before the United Nations voted in 1947 in favor of establishing distinct Jewish and Arab states in the land, and before the establishment in 1948 of the State of Israel (for practical purposes, as a Jewish state[202]), Christians might have had grounds to treat these matters theoretically and to arrive at divergent conclusions about whether there should be a Jewish state in the promised land. But even then, the theological points noted in this chapter would have applied. Today, in light of the existence of the State of Israel, Christians have both theological and practical reasons for opposing political proposals that would bring an end to the Jewish state.[203]

Connection to Israel, 126–41.

202. The meaning and purpose of a "Jewish state," of course, is debated among the Jewish citizens of Israel. After moving permanently to Israel in 1986, Yoram Hazony discovered that his contemporaries had become exhausted and had begun to wonder, "Why should the Jewish state exist at all?" (Hazony, *Jewish State*, xvii). By 1994, he found that "[t]he 'post-Jewish' condition had become a matter of national policy—to the point that one could easily imagine the Jewish state, for which such a fantastic price had been paid in sweat and blood, actually being dismantled in favor of a *non*-Jewish state: a political state for which the ideals and memories, traditions and interests of the Jews would be—simply irrelevant" (Hazony, *Jewish State*, xx). The situation is quite different today. For cognate concerns about Judaism in the United States, arguing that the traditional Jewish concept of *tikkun olam* has been hijacked to favor a political vision that "give[s] sanction to anti-Zionism and assimilation," see also Neumann, *To Heal the World?*, quotation from xvii.

203. See also Marquardt, "Kingdom for Israel?," 99, envisioning "a time when Israel can breathe easily, and phases where, through the activity of the friends of Jesus, the nations are won over *for* Israel, instead of always being diabolically put against it."

Admittedly, when Catholics look at the State of Israel, they can perceive a number of sins committed by that state against the Palestinian people. The list of sins sometimes includes the following (among others): taking land originally intended by the United Nations for the Arab state; building onerous and oppressive barbed-wire fences and checkpoints; siphoning water; police and military brutality toward Palestinians; unjustly imprisoning Palestinian leaders or targeting them for death. I accept that the State of Israel, like all states, has acted in unjust ways, though the specific list of these ways is a matter of debate. When Catholics look at the State of Israel, however, Catholics should also see the Jewish people's efforts to obey God's covenantal commandment. Catholics should be humbled by the centuries of persecution that the Jewish people endured in Catholic states. Perceiving these things will help Catholics appreciate why the Jewish state is not, in the mystery of God's plan, out of place even after Christ has inaugurated his kingdom. A Christian Israelology should support the existence of a Jewish state, the State of Israel, in the land.

Chapter 7

KING

I. Introduction

The four volumes of *The Destructive Power of Religion: Violence in Judaism, Christianity, and Islam*, published in 2004 with a foreword by the esteemed University of Chicago professor Martin Marty and a testimonial from Archbishop Desmond Tutu, are filled with essays by notable scholars on topics such as "The Violent Jesus." In his editor's preface to the four volumes, Harold Ellens remarks: "There can be no question that the God of the Hebrew Bible, and the God who is reported to have killed Jesus because, after getting ticked off at the human race, he could not get his head screwed on right again unless he killed us or somebody else, is abusive in the extreme."[1] I have strongly contested every element of this sentence elsewhere.[2] I note it here, however, as a forceful example of the claim that religion (when it is joined to temporal power) promotes violence—or more specifically that Judaism and Christianity promote violence, whenever their

---

1. Ellens, "Preface," in *Sacred Scriptures, Ideology, and Violence*, xvii–xix, at xix. For similar charges, see D. Barker, *God*. In a more nuanced fashion, James W. Laine raises a similar concern: "whether India would be more Buddhist or Hindu, whether Rome more pagan or Christian, whether China more Confucian or Buddhist, were all matters of great struggle—intellectual, spiritual, political, military. These struggles were real fights, and most often resulted in bloody conflict. If we attend to the teachings of Jesus, Confucius, and the Buddha, but ignore conflict, we are constructing portraits of religion that are perhaps beautiful and inspiring, but surely false and misleading" (Laine, *Meta-Religion*, 234). I think Laine is missing the distinction between Jesus' teachings and the transmission of those teachings. The teachings are not false or misleading simply because they will be transmitted by fallen human beings in a fallen world.

2. See for example my *Engaging the Doctrine of Creation*, introduction and chapter 7; and my *Betrayal of Charity*, especially chapters 1–2.

sacred texts are taken seriously by devout believers who have the power of the sword.

The biblical scholar John J. Collins is more temperate than Ellens. He remarks that even if the use of Scripture to justify violence is an instance "of the devil citing scripture for his purpose," believers should admit that "the devil does not have to work very hard to find biblical precedents for the legitimation of violence."[3] However, he adds that not everything described in the Bible receives ultimate divine approval. And he praises the Bible for giving "an unvarnished picture of human nature and of the dynamics of history, and also of religion and the things that people do in its name."[4] Certainly, as Collins says, people have done terrible things in the name of religion, including (as noted above) in the name of Christianity.[5]

---

3. Collins, "Zeal of Phinehas," 11. Charles Selengut holds that "belief in one's own absolute religious truth leads to intolerance and dissonance, which calls forth violent means" (Selengut, *Sacred Fury*, 67). I agree that this can and has happened, but I deny that the problem is cognitively knowable divine revelation. He warns against "an absolute and objective standard of Christian Catholic faith, doctrine, and practice" (*Sacred Fury*, 66), and he likewise warns that "[t]he church prior to the Enlightenment and subsequent widespread secularization saw itself as *the* vehicle for salvation and took seriously its responsibility to maintain an orthodoxy" (*Sacred Fury*, 67). But in my view, the problem is not the Church's effort to preserve, communicate, and understand more deeply the divine word that Christ has bestowed upon the Church; just as the problem with Judaism is not that God communicated certain truths (for example, the truth of Israel's unique covenantal election) to the people of Israel. Instead, the problem, when it occurs, consists in a failure to uphold the justice and charity that are at the center of divine revelation itself. This is an unavoidable problem in communities of fallen humans. In addition, communities that reject religious truth entirely—one thinks of Maoism, Stalinism, and Nazism but also less well known exemplars—expose the fully *secular* persistence of intolerance, dissonance, and brutal violence.

4. Collins, "Zeal of Phinehas," 25. Collins adds, "The biblical portrayal of human reality only becomes pernicious when it is vested with authority and assumed to reflect, without qualification or differentiation, the wisdom of God or the will of God. The Bible does not demystify or demythologize itself. But neither does it claim that the stories it tells are paradigms for human action in all times and places" (Collins, "Zeal of Phinehas," 25). This sentence needs nuancing, especially since much depends upon which biblical texts one is dealing with, but nevertheless Collins's point about "qualification or differentiation" is a needed one.

5. William T. Cavanaugh makes an important argument in this regard: "The idea that religion has a tendency to promote violence is part of the conventional wisdom of Western societies, and it underlies many of our institutions and policies, from limits on the public role of churches to efforts to promote liberal democracy in the Middle East. . . . I have no doubt that ideologies and practices of all kinds—including, for example, Islam and Christianity—can and do promote violence under certain conditions. What I challenge as incoherent is the argument that there is something called religion—a genus of which Christianity, Islam, Hinduism, and so on are species—which is necessarily more inclined toward violence than are ideologies and institutions that are identified as secular" (Cavanaugh, *Myth of Religious Violence*, 3, 5). Cavanaugh sums

Theologically, Yves Congar explains how this could happen even among a sanctified people. Even though God has given his Church the priesthood and the Magisterium, these gifts are exercised by people who "cannot escape being mixed up in some kind of compromise or blemish" and who are conditioned in part by the current "state of ideas and morals, politics, and even economics"—in other words, by habits and prejudices that do not belong intrinsically to Christianity and that, indeed, obscure the true reality of the Church of Christ.[6]

This final chapter of my Christian Israelology seeks to develop a Christian doctrine of Israel's kingship by reflecting upon abuse of power by divinely appointed leaders. I explore an example of the use of papal power against the Jewish people: the forcible removal of the six-year-old boy Edgardo Mortara from his loving Jewish parents by Pope Pius IX in June 1858. I evaluate this action from a Christian theological perspective informed by the writings of Thomas Aquinas. More broadly, I address the topic of Christian religious power in light of the divinely appointed role and multiple failures of the Davidic kings, and also by benefiting from David Novak's insights into contemporary Jewish appraisals of the religious meaning of the State of Israel.

Ephraim Radner has remarked that in the past half century, the Church—by which he means a wide array of Christian communities—has "for the first time in her history, begun to face the greatest failure of her navigation of collective identity," namely, "her relationship to the Jews."[7]

---

up his main argument: "My hypothesis is that religion-and-violence arguments serve a particular need for their consumers in the West. The arguments are part of a broader Enlightenment narrative that has invented a dichotomy between the religious and the secular and constructed the former as an irrational and dangerous impulse that must give way in public to rational, secular forms of power" (*Myth of Religious Violence*, 4–5). In support of the expansive "rational" state that Cavanaugh describes, see Brian Leiter's argument that no *religious* claim of conscience, as such, merits an exemption from the state's laws, in Leiter, *Why Tolerate Religion?* See also, in broad accord with Cavanaugh's perspective, D'Costa's *Christianity and World Religions*, chapters 3 and 4.

6. Congar, *True and False Reform*, 106.

7. Radner, *Church*, 9. Note that I do not think that all Christians are thereby "responsible" for anti-Semitism or anti-Judaism, since not all Christians fell into it and, besides, there were degrees of complicity. Hannah Arendt makes a good point with regard to political entities (even if it does not apply in the same way to the Church, whose unity is theologically much deeper): "Our political concepts, according to which we have to assume responsibility for all public affairs within our reach regardless of personal 'guilt,' because we are held responsible as citizens for everything that our government does in the name of the country, may lead us into an intolerable situation of global responsibility. The solidarity of mankind may well turn out to be an unbearable burden, and it is not surprising that the common reactions to it are political apathy, isolationist nationalism, or desperate rebellion against all powers that be rather than

The Holocaust, in which a third of the world's Jews were killed, inspired the Church's much needed and overdue reassessment. As Gavin D'Costa says, prior to the Holocaust, the existence of "a general Catholic anti-Semitic culture is indisputable."[8] In a process that is still ongoing, the Catholic Church has had to face and seek to understand its "complicity and cultural nurturing of anti-Semitism, often fueled through aspects of anti-Jewish theology."[9]

Joseph Ratzinger makes the same point, calling it "an occasion for a constant examination of conscience."[10] Regarding the Holocaust, Ratzinger notes that the fact that the Nazi leaders hated Christianity "does not change the fact that baptized people were responsible" for the Holocaust, and he acknowledges that "Christian anti-Semitism had prepared the soil to a certain degree.... There was Christian anti-Semitism in France, in Austria, in Prussia, in all European countries, and thus the ground was fertile."[11]

The Church has had to face its past anti-Semitism while at the same time navigating a world in which respect for its authority and sacraments has been decreasing. Unfortunately, sometimes the Church's legitimate defense of sacramental efficacy has intersected with the Church's treatment of the Jewish people. Seeking in the mid-nineteenth century to defend the truth of the Catholic sacrament of baptism, Pope Pius IX caused an international uproar by forcibly removing the Jewish boy Edgardo Mortara from his loving family, due to his alleged baptism as an infant by a nanny (without Edgardo's parents knowing about the nanny's action). As the ruler of the Papal States, Pope Pius never returned the boy to his family. Edgardo lived in the Vatican and received an education that, in addition to teaching him the tenets of the Catholic faith, taught him that the Jewish people were degraded Christ-killers.[12]

---

enthusiasm or a desire for a revival of humanism" (Arendt, "Karl Jaspers," 83). See also Jaspers, *Question of German Guilt*.

8. D'Costa, *Vatican II*, 114. He cites Connelly, *From Enemy to Brother*, 11–93, as well as Bauman, *Modernity and the Holocaust*.

9. D'Costa, *Vatican II*, 114.

10. Ratzinger, *Salt of the Earth*, 251.

11. Ratzinger, *Salt of the Earth*, 251.

12. The Catholic author Justus George Lawler has attempted to discredit Kertzer's *Popes Against the Jews*: see Lawler, *Were the Popes Against the Jews?* While Lawler is certainly right that no one has found "an actual declaration of a reigning pope" that supports the libel of Jewish ritual murder (*Were the Popes Against the Jews?*, 97), Lawler is unable to respond to the key point, namely, the repeated presence in *L'Osservatore Romano* and *Civiltà Cattolica* of articles supporting the blood libel. Given the importance of the so-called "Jewish question" at that time, it is not tenable to hold that the popes would have been unaware of these articles. Lawler's polemical work is undermined by

At the time, due to the growing influence of liberal or secularized Christians in Europe, the Catholic defenders of Pope Pius IX's action "regarded all those who questioned the wisdom of the Pope or the righteousness of canon law as anti-Christians, infidels, and worse."[13] More recently, some Catholics in the United States have defended Pius IX's action. Like Pope Pius IX and the earlier supporters of his action, they too tend to interpret "criticism of his action as . . . a veiled attack on religious conviction," and in particular an attack on the papacy and the sacramental doctrine of the Catholic Church.[14]

In addressing such matters, my chapter proceeds in four steps. First, I propose that Catholics can learn something from the biblical narratives about the Davidic kingship.[15] The Davidic kings failed in various grave ways, but God's covenantal promise and fidelity remained in place. As Keith Bodner remarks, God's promise to David "is sorely tested but never retracted, because, like the promise to Abraham, it is not predicated on exemplary

---

other contemporary scholarship (beyond Kertzer's books) on these matters. For his part, Vittorio Messori's "The Mortara Case," makes repeated efforts to discredit Kertzer, *Kidnapping of Edgardo Mortara*, but Messori's concealment of the many changes that he made in Mortara's text undermines his credibility.

13. B. W. Korn, *American Reaction*, 19. See for example Winock, "Louis Veuillot et l'antijudaïsme français."

14. Duffy, *Saints and Sinners*, 290. In *Kidnapping of Edgardo Mortara*, 75, Kertzer notes that in the first years of his pontificate, Pope Pius IX "abolished the much-reviled forced sermons" in the Jewish ghettoes. Pope Pius IX also symbolically tore down the ghetto walls and "put an end to the centuries-old humiliating public spectacle of vassalage requiring the officers of Rome's Jewish community on the first Saturday of Carnival to pay an annual tribute to the Senator of Rome as a large, raucous crowd jeered and mocked them": see Kertzer, *Pope Who Would Be King*, 98. However, like almost all Catholics of his day, Pius IX believed "in the divine punishment meted out to the Jews for their historical role in the killing of Christ, and in the perniciousness of the Jews' own religious beliefs and practices. . . . Not only did the Pope in the 1850s resist calls to give the Jews equal rights; he angrily denounced moves by other Italian states to do so. When the old regime of the Grand Duke was restored in Tuscany and the new constitution was nullified, the Pope was infuriated to learn that the constitutional provisions giving Jews equal rights, including the right to attend the university, was to remain in force" (*Pope Who Would Be King*, 81–82).

15. As David Novak observes, Baruch Spinoza wrongly understood the Bible to be "an antiquarian book" (Novak, *Election of Israel*, 112). Novak emphasizes "the continuing and uninterrupted historical connection of the people of Israel with the Bible *by* and *through* tradition, a tradition both theirs and that of the Bible itself"; and he adds that "historical research must always be secondary precisely because the Bible is the book that Jews have never stopped reading. It is a book addressed to them in all their generations" (*Election of Israel*, 112–13). What Novak has to say about Jewish reading of the Bible applies to proper Christian reading of the Bible as well.

human conduct."[16] In light of the biblical narratives about the failures of Judah's divinely established royal leaders, Catholics can gain insight into how to understand papal abuse of power.[17]

Second, arguing that Catholic truth-claims do not in themselves result in abuse of power but can be distorted in application, I examine the forcible baptism of Jewish children. I set forth Aquinas's critique of the practice of forcibly baptizing Jewish children, an action that he rejects on the grounds that it violates natural justice and natural law and also discredits the Church. Aquinas is aware that the forcible baptism of Jewish children has been relatively frequently done by Catholics, though not approved of by popes. Indeed, Blessed John Duns Scotus approved the practice. I argue that Catholics today should respond to this history neither by defending the abusive practice nor by denying God's fidelity in enabling his Church to be "the pillar and bulwark of the truth" when the Church solemnly teaches what pertains to Christian faith and morals (1 Tim 3:15).[18]

In my third section, I argue that Pope Pius IX's forcible removal of Edgardo Mortara was profoundly mistaken—in this respect much like abuses in the history of Israel's kingship. I provide historical background to Pius IX's action, showing that in earlier periods the forcible removal of Jewish children (baptized against their parents' will before the children were old enough to decide on their own) was all too common. Unfortunately, in recent decades contemporary Catholic writers such as Garry Wills and James Carroll have used Pius IX's action as a way of attacking the papacy and the Catholic sacraments, thereby sowing confusion. On seven grounds, I argue that Pius IX's action clearly constituted a grave abuse. I do so with an eye to the question raised by my first section: namely, what does it mean when divinely legitimated leaders of God's people gravely abuse their power? Is there a way for Catholics to criticize grave errors made even by saintly popes (such as St. Pope John Paul II's defense of Fr. Marcial Maciel) without calling into question the Church's faithful mediation of the apostolic teaching and sacraments?

My fourth and final section addresses such questions regarding divinely legitimated power and its abuse by taking up David Novak's treatment of various Jewish positions on Zionism and the State of Israel. Twentieth-century Jews experienced both the worst possible powerlessness (the Holocaust) and the establishment of a powerful Jewish state in the land of Israel.

16. Bodner, *Theology of the Book of Kings*, 230.

17. For the same point, see Duffy, *Saints and Sinners*. See also the dreadful stories—dreadful even if only half of them were accurate (and I suspect that not only are most of them true but many other worse ones are known to God)—in Noel, *Renaissance Popes*.

18. See *Lumen Gentium*, §25, in Tanner, ed., *Trent to Vatican II*, 869.

In studying Jewish theological evaluation of this conjunction of powerlessness and power, Novak identifies three representative viewpoints: Jews who *blame Jewish Zionists* for the Holocaust because they dared to return to the land without waiting for the coming of the Messiah; Jews who *blame God* for the Holocaust because, while awaiting the coming of the Messiah, the Jewish people were utterly exposed to their enemies; and, lastly, Jews who *attribute messianic significance to the State of Israel* in inaugurating the process of redemption.[19] Novak argues that no human actions in the realm of temporal politics (even temporal politics intimately bound to the survival and flourishing of God's people) can be decisive for God's eschatological plan.[20]

Applying Novak's point to the issue of papal abuse of power, I arrive at the following conclusion. Catholics cannot know why God permits some popes to abuse their power (consciously or unconsciously) in particular instances, but we can know in faith that God has not abandoned his people and that God will accomplish what he has promised for his people the Church. For almost two millennia, the leaders and members of the Catholic Church acted toward the Jewish people with a deadly arrogance and contempt. Faced with this history, some Catholics respond *by rejecting the Catholic Church* or at least its hierarchy; other Catholics respond by *rejecting God (and Christ)* for allowing such abuse of power against the Jewish people; and still other Catholics respond by arguing that the Church's supernatural mandate somehow *justifies the injustice against non-Catholics*. None of these responses are suitable. Instead, Catholics must repudiate the terrible abuses of power without thereby repudiating the good news of salvation that God enables the Church to proclaim and enact in the world. In theocentric humility, Catholics should not imagine that the prudential failures or successes of a pope can stand in the place of God's own work in bringing about his plan for Christ's coming in glory. "So do not become proud, but stand in awe" (Rom 11:20).

---

19. For a Catholic argument for the eschatological significance of the establishment and flourishing of the State of Israel, arguing that the State of Israel plays an identifiable positive role in ushering in the consummation of all things—and also arguing that the Holocaust paid the debt of punishment (for rejecting the Messiah) for which the ongoing Jewish people had been in exile for almost two millennia—see Lévy, *Jewish Church*, 337–43. As will be clear, I do not agree with Lévy on these matters.

20. Like Novak, I distinguish between temporal politics and what Scott Bader-Saye has called "the politics of election," that is, the covenantal life of God's people. See Bader-Saye, *Church and Israel after Christendom*. Bader-Saye remarks that "always the church's political calling and highest blessing will be its witness to the New Jerusalem that is coming and indeed now is, among those who have been chosen to embody God's reign on earth" (*Church and Israel after Christendom*, 148).

II. Israel's Davidic Kingship

By binding himself covenantally to the Davidic kingship (2 Samuel 7), God made himself present to his people in an especially concretized way. But by doing so, God risked being associated with the inevitable and deplorable sins of the kings who reigned in Jerusalem. The biblical scholar Jacob Wright considers the narratives about King David to be so negative toward David that they could not have been written prior to the Babylonian exile: "No Judahite king would have countenanced such a report of his beloved forefather's life, let alone condoned it or even commissioned it."[21] The narratives are powerful and instructive precisely in their willingness to criticize the man whom God appointed "as prince over Israel, the people of the Lord" (2 Sam 6:21).

Israel's doctrine of kingship has King David as its paradigm, although the model for kingship was articulated by Moses. At the height of his career, David's royal power was also priestly: "So David went and brought up the ark of God from the house of Obed-edom to the city of David with rejoicing; and when those who bore the ark of the Lord had gone six paces, he sacrificed an ox and a fatling. And David danced before the Lord with all his might; and David was belted with a linen ephod" (2 Sam 6:14-15).[22] Thus, David prepares for and prefigures his descendant Jesus, the messianic Davidic King who is also the great "high priest" holding "his priesthood permanently" (Heb 7:24, 26). But the exercise of power by the Davidic kings (including David) was often wrongheaded. God's linking himself to the royal house of David, therefore, may be compared to Christ's linking his Church to the Petrine office, since over the centuries there have been multiple grave missteps in the papacy's exercise of temporal power and in the behavior of popes.

---

21. J. L. Wright, *David, King of Israel*, 223. Wright holds that "the Tanakh's sources gradually accumulated overlapping layers of accretions" (*David, King of Israel*, 226), and the earliest biblical accounts of David say nothing about Israel but speak only about Judah. For Baruch Halpern, by contrast, "a great deal of what the books of Samuel and the first chapters of 1 Kings have to say about David is contemporary, or very nearly contemporary, with that king, in the 10th century B.C.E." (*David's Secret Demons*, 4). See also McKenzie, *King David*.

22. David Novak underscores that kingship, as such, derives from the Gentile nations, although Israel adopted it. He states that "beginning with the adoption of the admittedly non-Jewish type of polity of monarchy early in the history of ancient Israel, it became clear that a covenantal community who had accepted the law of God for herself could very well live under almost any type of regime" (Novak, *Natural Law in Judaism*, 181). Yet, I note that in the Davidic covenant, God claims the Davidic monarchy for himself in a very decisive fashion.

In the book of Deuteronomy, Moses tells the people of Israel that God will permit them to have a king, so long as the king recognizes himself to be humbly subservient to the word of God.[23] Moses states on behalf of God, "When you come to the land which the Lord your God gives you, and you possess it and dwell in it, and then say, 'I will set a king over me, like all the nations that are round about me'; you may indeed set as king over you him that the Lord your God will choose" (Deut 17:14–15). On this view of kingship, it is God who chooses Israel's king, and therefore Israel can be permitted to have a king without compromising God's sovereignty. But Moses adds some caveats. First, no non-Israelite can be king over God's people. Second and more tellingly, the king "must not multiply horses for himself, or cause the people to return to Egypt in order to multiply horses" (Deut 17:16). The multiplication of horses signifies a standing military force; and returning to Egypt signifies the oppression or even near-enslavement of the people in order to financially support the king's soldiers. Moses also requires that the king "shall not multiply wives for himself, lest his heart turn away; nor shall he greatly multiply for himself silver and gold" (Deut 17:17). The multiplication of royal wives is a way of sealing relationships with neighboring kings, and the multiplication of silver and gold comes about through taxation.

Most importantly, Moses commands that when the king "sits on the throne of his kingdom, he shall write for himself in a book a copy of this law [the Torah], from that which is in the charge of the Levitical priests" (Deut 17:18).[24] By copying out the Torah, the king will know *that* he is subservient and *to whom* he is subservient, namely to the God of Israel. The king must "learn to fear the Lord his God, by keeping all the words of this law and those statutes, and doing them" (Deut 17:19). Moses states that the king's task of copying, reading, and doing the law has the purpose of ensuring that the king's "heart may not be lifted up above his brethren"

---

23. Telford Work reads this passage (Deuteronomy 17:14–20) somewhat differently, if I understand him correctly. He states, "This passage does not recommend a king (cf. 1 Sam. 8). Instead, accepting that a jealous Israel will appropriate its neighbors' monarchy . . . it demands to choose the leader from among Israel's own people and for the Torah—not Gentile ways—to be his constitution" (Work, *Deuteronomy*, 171). I read the passage more positively: when Moses says, "you may indeed set as king over you him whom the Lord your God will choose" (Deut 17:15), I take this to indicate divine approval of Israel's establishing a kingship. Work is attempting to square the passage with God's negative response in 1 Samuel 8 to Israel's desire for a kingship.

24. From a source-critical perspective, Jeffrey Stackert finds that "[f]or D, the written text has triumphed decisively over the oral message of the prophet, and it is this prophetic text that endures in D's centralized locale as a basis for future society and rule" (Deut 17:18–20)" (Stackert, *Prophet Like Moses*, 143). Stackert, however, draws a sharp line between historical-critical scholarship and theological reflection on the biblical texts, a line that imposes methodological atheism upon biblical-studies discourse.

(Deut 17:20). In this way, the king of Israel will know himself to be under the sovereignty of God, and the king will humbly strive to implement God's word in governing the land. The king must be humble, not "presuming to speak for God or in place of God" (in Novak's words).[25]

As Walter Brueggemann comments, therefore, "Kingship in Israel is authorized for the practice of Torah. . . . Where kings depart from their true Yahwistic vocation, however, the monarchy may use power exploitatively and abusively."[26] Brueggemann understands the "practice of Torah" to mean loving God (avoiding idolatry) and loving neighbor (avoiding oppression).[27] Kingship ideally involves "the right deployment of public power for all members of the community," although Israel's kings did not generally live up to this vocation.[28]

In naming what Israel's kings must avoid doing, Deuteronomy 17:16–17 points forward to the disastrous decisions of King Solomon and his son. Solomon multiplied horses, foreign wives, and riches for himself, and the result was idolatry in his old age (1 Kgs 11:1–8). After Solomon's death, his son Rehoboam refused to lessen the crippling tax burden that Solomon had imposed upon the northern ten tribes (1 Kgs 12:1–15). The result of King Rehoboam's intransigence was the division of Israel into the ten northern tribes (Israel)—which never returned from Assyrian exile in 722 BC—and the two southern tribes (Judah). Without referencing the misdeeds of Solomon and his son, Karen Armstrong all too aptly concludes that "an intimate

---

25. Novak, *Zionism and Judaism*, 249. From an evangelical Christian perspective, Christopher J. H. Wright comments: "A radically different, consciously distinct, and counter-cultural model of political leadership is offered here. It is a model that limits military power, prestige, and private gain and puts all political executive authority firmly under the authority of the law itself" (*Deuteronomy*, 210). I agree with this, and yet it is noteworthy that the "counter-cultural model" remains a model of *kingship*. God knows that human kings will fall into sin, and yet still he associates himself with royal rule.

26. Brueggemann, *Theology of the Old Testament*, 697.

27. Aaron Wildavsky comments upon the numerous specific commandments: "The commandments are made up, as their very number suggests, of detailed prescriptions (for food, for clothes, for prayer, for the rhythm of daily life). Rulers as well as ruled are subject to these laws. Hence the commandments are incompatible with the arbitrary power of slave regimes, which set themselves up above the law. Rulers are not to be gods, followers not to be slaves. These innumerable prescriptions are also incompatible with a life of anarchy in which people feel free to follow rules of their own making, rules that can be remade when new bargains become more advantageous" (Wildavsky, *Moses as Political Leader*, 241).

28. Brueggemann, *Theology of the Old Testament*, 697.

association with government can badly compromise a faith tradition," at least in certain ways.[29]

In a passage that is in tension with Deuteronomy 17:14-20, God warns the prophet Samuel that the people of Israel, by asking to have a king, have rejected God's reign over them (1 Sam 8:7).[30] This statement is surprising given that Samuel's sons, whom Samuel had made "judges over Israel," "took bribes and perverted justice" (1 Sam 8:1, 3) and therefore deserved to be shunned by the people. God commands Samuel to instruct the people about the abusive power and pride that are associated with human kingship. Speaking to the people on behalf of God, Samuel tells them: "These will be the ways of the king who will reign over you: he will take your sons and appoint them to his chariots and to be his horsemen. . . . He will take your daughters to be perfumers and cooks and bakers. He will take the best of your fields and vineyards and olive orchards and give them to his servants" (1 Sam 8:11, 13-14). Samuel foretells that the king will be exactly what Moses warned against: a king who abusively concentrates all power and wealth in his hands.

In response, the people of Israel insist even more strongly that they want a king. They again say that they want to "be like all the nations" (1 Sam 8:20). Heeding their request, God requires Samuel to accept the demand of the people: "Listen to their voice, and make them a king" (1 Sam 8:22).[31]

---

29. Armstrong, *Fields of Blood*, 398. Armstrong's book presents the diverse world religions as products of human ingenuity, but she is an erudite interpreter of these religious traditions and, despite the book's title, she shows that they each contain (to varying degrees of course) a significant critique of violence. She also shows that the rise of the secular nation-state has certainly not inhibited violence, but, if anything, has amplified it.

30. Francesca Aran Murphy comments: "Requesting a king is not original sin, and statehood is not fallenness. But, historically, statehood occurs within the context of human fallenness. This is why, in 1 Sam. 8-15, our author advertently recalls voices that speak for and against monarchy . . . As a matter of ethics, monarchy can be put in the service of the city of God to the extent that the monarch puts himself at the service of God. The author of Deuteronomy was aware of this ambiguity, recognizing both that monarchy lays great temptation in the paths of the governing class and that, if its rulers dedicate their kingdom to God, monarchy can work" (Murphy, *1 Samuel*, 69).

31. Stephen B. Chapman is representative of many other scholars in finding here a choice: either God is king, or a human being is king. See Chapman, *1 Samuel as Christian Scripture*, 101. To my mind, however, the Davidic covenant underscores that God does not will to reign "alone" over his people, but wills to employ human royal and priestly mediators. Chapman may well agree with me on this, but I think that his insistence "that God alone is king over Israel—apart from any human viceroy or partner" (*1 Samuel as Christian Scripture*, 101) needs to allow for the fact that God, in his Davidic covenant, does not will to stand "*apart from* any human viceroy or partner," even though God clearly transcends and reigns over "any human viceroy or partner."

With God's approval, the people choose the tallest and most royal-looking young person to be king. The first thing that we learn about Saul is that "there was not a man among the sons of Israel more handsome than he; from his shoulders upward he was taller than any of the people" (1 Sam 9:2). At first, Saul appears humble, proclaiming that his family is "the humblest of all the families of the tribe of Benjamin" (1 Sam 9:21). Equally humbly, Saul hides when they try to choose him as king (1 Sam 10:22). In addition, Saul also receives the "spirit of God" (1 Sam 10:10) and prophesies with the prophets of God.

Reassuring the people, Samuel tells them that now that God has given them a king (Saul), they can flourish: "If you will fear the Lord and serve him and listen to his voice and not rebel against the commandment of the Lord, and if both you and the king who reigns over you will follow the Lord your God, it will be well" (1 Sam 12:14). At the same time, however, Samuel also condemns the people, telling them that by requesting a king, they showed that their "wickedness is great" (1 Sam 12:17). When the people respond with contrition, Samuel again reassures them. He exhorts them to be faithful to God and to remember God's steadfast faithfulness: "Fear not; you have done all this evil, yet do not turn aside from following the Lord, but serve the Lord with all your heart; and do not turn aside after vain things which cannot profit or save, for they are vain" (1 Sam 12:20–21). God's fidelity, Samuel promises, will never be in doubt.

Even though King Saul worships God and builds altars to God, and even though God grants Saul military victories, the fact that Saul attempts to manipulate sacred things—and does so without repentance—means that Saul's kingship cannot ultimately be blessed by God. God therefore has Samuel anoint David secretly (1 Sam 16:1–13), and the conflict between David and Saul's family continues after Saul's death in battle against the Philistines. After David wins the civil war, he is anointed king over all Israel (2 Sam 5:3) and he brings the ark of the covenant to his newly conquered capital city, Jerusalem (2 Sam 6).

To this point, God's relationship to kingship has at best been a strained one. Shockingly, therefore, in 2 Samuel 7 God covenantally binds himself to David and his family. Through the prophet Nathan, God promises David: "When your days are fulfilled and you lie down with your fathers, I will raise up your offspring after you, who shall come forth from your body, and I will establish his kingdom. He shall build a house for my name, and I will establish the throne of his kingdom for ever" (2 Sam 7:12–13). This promise seems to fly in the face of everything we have learned previously about kings and about God's view of kings. Kings are proud, and God knows it; kings use their power to presume to speak and act for God. Yet, God now binds himself to a royal family whose throne will endure forever in the presence of God. God embraces the very institution that God knows is rife with pride and idolatry.

King David responds with humility. Praising God for the gift of this covenant, he asks God, "Who am I, O Lord God, and what is my house, that you have brought me thus far?" (2 Sam 7:18). Humbly, David proclaims to God: "you are great, O Lord God; for there is none like you, and there is no God besides you" (2 Sam 7:22). David goes on to praise God for what God has done for the people of Israel by redeeming them from Egyptian slavery and by establishing them in the land. He concludes by praying that God will bring about what God has promised David. David tells God: "do as you have spoken; and your name will be magnified for ever, saying, 'The Lord of hosts is God over Israel,' and the house of your servant David will be established before you" (2 Sam 7:25–26).

In the narrative of 1 and 2 Samuel, there are earlier signs of David's humility. The young David recognizes the army of Israel to be the army of God, not of King Saul (1 Sam 17:26). Likewise, in his combat with Goliath, David trusts in God as his deliverer, rather than trusting in his own military strength (1 Sam 17:37). Similarly, after he becomes a rogue chieftain opposed to King Saul, David still regularly emphasizes his respect for the life of Saul as "the Lord's anointed" (1 Sam 24:6). David's humility continues even after his sins multiply and begin to catch up with him. For example, in response to the divine condemnation of his actions against Uriah, a condemnation delivered by the prophet Nathan (2 Sam 12:13), David publicly repents.

Nevertheless, as David's royal line continues, it becomes increasingly difficult to fathom why God covenantally linked himself to David. Solomon in his old age "went after Ashtoreth the goddess of the Sidonians, and after Milcom the abomination of the Ammonites" (1 Kgs 11:5). Solomon even "built a high place for Chemosh the abomination of Moab, and for Molech the abomination of the Ammonites, on the mountain east of Jerusalem" (1 Kgs 11:7). Twice God appeared to Solomon and commanded him not to worship other gods, but Solomon's "heart had turned away from the Lord" and "he did not keep what the Lord commanded" (1 Kgs 11:9–10). King Rehoboam was the son of "Naamah the Ammonitess"; thus it comes as no surprise that the worship of Ammonite gods proliferated (1 Kgs 14:21). Typical of David's royal line is King Jehoram, who marries a daughter of the northern king (Ahab)—a devout worshipper of Baal.

Indeed, although God called forth some notable prophets during the period of the Davidic kingship, almost all the Davidic kings were disasters who, far from being humble or devoted to the word of God, seem to have paid no real attention to the God of Israel. A rare exception is Hezekiah, who ruled in the late eighth century BC and saved Judah from the Assyrian army that carried the northern kingdom into exile. But after his death, things reverted to normal: his son Manasseh "did what was evil in the sight of the Lord, according to the abominable practices of the nations whom the Lord drove out before the people of Israel" (2 Kgs 21:2). Manasseh worshipped Baal and Asherah, built altars in the temple grounds for the worship of other gods, and "burned his son as an offering and practiced soothsaying and augury" (2 Kgs 21:6).

In 2 Kings 22, Hilkiah, the high priest, discovers the dusty and forgotten book of the law stored away in the temple. After this shocking (to the reader at least) turn of events, Hilkiah sends the book of the law to King Josiah. When Shapan, the king's secretary, reads him the book of the law, Josiah tears his clothes (2 Kgs 22:11). He immediately perceives how deeply the people of Israel had failed over the centuries in which the Davidic kings had reigned. King Josiah undertook a massive reform, but God told him that it was too late: the people of Judah would be punished for their apostasy. The punishment duly takes place, despite the valiant efforts of various prophets to forestall it. Nebuzaradan, acting on behalf of the Babylonian King Nebuchadnezzar, broke down Jerusalem's walls and "burned the house of the Lord, and the king's house and all the houses of Jerusalem," and "carried into exile" the people of Jerusalem (2 Kgs 25:9, 11). Although the people of Israel returned from Babylonian exile after fifty years, the Davidic kingship never resumed in its previous form, although some hope was briefly placed in Zerubabbel (see Neh 12:1; Haggai 1–2; Zech 4).

In the prophet Ezekiel's exilic eschatological vision, God promises that "I will save my flock, they shall no longer be a prey; and I will judge between sheep and sheep. And I will set up over them one shepherd, my servant David, and he shall feed them.... And I, the Lord, will be their God, and my servant David shall be prince among them" (Ezek 34:22–24). Ezekiel makes clear that this is an eschatological vision of the restoration of Israel. Joseph Blenkinsopp remarks, "The Jeremiah passage on which Ezekiel's shepherd discourse appears to be based (Jer. 23:1–8) also predicts the 'raising up' of a future Davidic ruler who will rule wisely, exercising justice and righteousness over a reunited Israel."[32] In Ezekiel, this vision involves a complete end to the present world's misery. As Blenkinsopp notes, in the final seven verses of Ezekiel 34, we find not only "the prospect of the restoration of order and justice under the Davidic ruler," but also a "vision of a world in which there

---

32. Blenkinsopp, *Ezekiel*, 160.

will be no more beasts of prey, no more oppression and enslavement," and no more cause for fear.[33]

Numerous messianic texts that today instruct both Jews and Christians could be cited. Some of these texts refer not distinctly to a Davidic king, but to a priestly or prophetic leader, or to a "son of man." For my purposes, it is enough to observe the strong association of messianic hopes with a coming Davidic king and with God reigning in Jerusalem over the whole world.[34] Insofar as messianic hopes were connected with the Davidic kingship, this brings to mind the long line of Davidic kings, most of whom failed miserably in their kingship but through all of whom God continued his work of preparing his people Israel for the consummation of his covenantal promises.

Christians believe, of course, that the Messiah has indeed come in Jesus of Nazareth (descended from David), who rose from the dead and now reigns as King at the right hand of the Father. At present, the risen and ascended King Jesus is leading his people to himself on the new exodus journey, on which his people are configured to his royal and priestly self-sacrificial love and are nourished by him as the new Passover lamb. When Christians think of the Davidic kingship, we think of Jesus Christ. But, inevitably, at least some Christians also think about how temporal power is exercised in the Church of Christ.

III. Catholic Truth, Justice, and Charity

Within his eschatological people, so Catholics believe, Jesus—the eschatological Davidic king—has bestowed a special office upon Peter and his successors. In response to Peter's confessing Jesus to be "the Christ, the Son of the living God" (Matt 16:16), Jesus promises Peter a unique share in his royal messianic authority. He says to Peter, "I will give you the keys of

---

33. Blenkinsopp, *Ezekiel*, 160. These exilic texts are not deemed "messianic" by some biblical scholars, who limit properly "messianic" texts to those that speak explicitly "of an awaited or future *anointed* agent of God" or "an awaited *anointed* human figure sent by God for the deliverance of His people" (Fitzmyer, *One Who Is to Come*, 4–5 [emphasis added]). But in Second Temple Judaism and the New Testament, texts such as Ezekiel 34:11–31 with its prophecy of "a divinely sent Davidic figure who shepherds and saves the scattered sheep of Israel" were interpreted messianically (Bird, *Are You the One?*, 134).

34. See Cohn-Sherbok, *Jewish Messiah*, although Cohn-Sherbok holds that "[i]n the modern world, these ancient doctrines can be superseded by a new vision of Jewish life which is human-centred in orientation. Rather than await the coming of a divinely appointed deliverer who will bring about peace and harmony on earth, Jews should themselves strive to create a better world for all peoples" (*Jewish Messiah*, 171).

the kingdom of heaven, and whatever you bind on earth shall be bound in heaven, and whatever you loose on earth shall be loosed in heaven" (Matt 16:19).[35] Catholics believe that the successors of Peter as bishop of Rome will not distort the truth of the gospel in any definitive way prior to the glorious coming of Christ to judge all things. Thus, God has bound himself in the freedom of his Holy Spirit to a human priestly hierarchy.

In believing this about the Church, can Catholics really be humble? Concerned about the temptation to use religion to undertake the "conquest and domination of others,"[36] David Novak warns against religious claims to have "the whole truth," on the grounds that such claims may lead believers to persecute those whom they think either lack truth or impede the victory of the truth.[37] Rabbi Jonathan Sacks makes the same point in a striking manner: "If there is only one truth, and you have it, then others do not. They live in error, and to save them from that error you can claim religious justification for conquering, converting or even killing them."[38]

---

35. For an Anglican historical-critical analysis of the figure of Peter, see Bockmuehl, *Simon Peter*. Bockmuehl states that "the opening and closing of the door to the kingdom of heaven is about *teaching authority* and how it is exercised.... The majority view among exegetes, which draws on widespread Jewish parallels, is that Peter exercises the unique teaching authority within the community to declare what is permitted and what is not permitted, probably including the exercise of discipline and excommunication. Peter, then, assumes in these verses the role of an empowered representative, who is entrusted with the charge of his master's business—the kingdom of heaven. Matthew's Peter alone is unique among the Twelve as the one on whom the Messiah's church is founded, and his teaching is the authoritative basis for the life of believers" (Bockmuehl, *Simon Peter*, 76). Yet, Bockmuehl considers that there is no ongoing Petrine office envisioned in the Gospel of Matthew—even though in his view "this need not rule out a priori the potential legitimacy of a later Roman *relecture* (rereading) of Matt. 16:18–19 in papal terms, particularly when this is linked with other NT passages such as John 21, but such an argument would need to be established in open reflection on well-documented patristic alternatives" (Bockmuehl, *Simon Peter*, 76). Such an argument has been made, though with a biblical rather than patristic focus, by Ratzinger, "Primacy of Peter," 47–74; see also Newman, *Essay on the Development of Doctrine*, 148–65; Rist, *What Is Truth?*, chapter 4; and von Balthasar, *Office of Peter*, 60–89. For the concerns raised by the Orthodox, see Siecienski, *Papacy and the Orthodox*; and for Protestant concerns see Powell, *Papal Infallibility*.

36. Novak, *Election of Israel*, 161.

37. Novak, *Election of Israel*, 161.

38. Sacks, *Future Tense*, 134. Sacks, however, maintains in *Dignity of Difference*, 55: "Religion is the translation of God into a particular language and thus into the life of a group, a nation, a community of faith. In the course of history, God has spoken to mankind in many languages: through Judaism to Jews, Christianity to Christians, Islam to Muslims. Only such a God is truly transcendental—greater not only than the natural universe but also than the spiritual universe articulated in any single faith, any specific language of human sensibility." This view of multiple revelations and multiple (equal) paths of salvation runs into difficult problems, given that the revelations are in certain

I agree that when the claim to possess truth is detached from self-sacrificial love and humility, it becomes very dangerous indeed—whether this truth is religious truth or simply truth about the world (for example, technological knowledge). The virtue of studiousness reminds us that we cannot rightly master truth; we can wonder at it and proclaim its goodness and beauty, but we cannot turn it into something that is "ours" or turn our supposed "mastery" of it into a weapon against others.[39] With religious rationalism and pride in view, Hans Urs von Balthasar cautions aptly: "Man is always trying to assemble the multifarious aspects of truth under a single principle that he can grasp."[40] Even in his self-revelation, God is not a principle whom we can grasp and master.

Nevertheless, as has been apparent throughout this book, Christians and Jews both claim to have truth that others do not have, and neither Christians nor Jews can rightly back down from this claim. For example, many people in the world deny that God elected his people Israel, but Christians and Jews affirm this truth and believe that, in this regard at least, those who deny it "live in error." Novak holds that God has communicated much truth to the Jewish people, including the truth of God's covenantal election of Israel and the truth of God's commandment that his people dwell in and govern the promised land. On the basis of this commandment, Novak (like Sacks) insists upon "the legitimacy of the collective enterprise of the Jewish state with its exercise of political, military, and economic power."[41] My point is that there is no warrant for jumping from the fact that truth-claims can be used to justify persecution and pride, to the quite different claim that truth and power must simply be renounced by believers.

For Christians, Christ is truth-in-person, and the mark of following his truth is to "love one another as I have loved you" (John 15:12) by laying

---

crucial ways mutually contradictory. Nor is "translation of God" a proper understanding of divine revelation. I agree with Charles Taylor when he approvingly quotes Sacks, "'Those who are confident in their faith are not threatened but enlarged by the different faith of others'" and when he links this to the fact that a person of faith moves toward an eschatological fullness that is unfathomable (C. Taylor, "Space of Exchange," 127; cf. 129). Taylor cites Sacks, *Dignity of Difference*, 65–66. Menachem Kellner puts the matter well when he says, "While not giving up on the idea that revelation (be it Jewish, Christian, or Muslim) teaches truth in some hard, exclusivist sense, putative addressees of revelation ought to be modest about how much of it they understand, and restrained in the claims they make on behalf of revelation and about adherents of other religions" (Kellner, "We Are Not Alone," 152).

39. For further discussion, see chapter 6 of my *Aquinas's Eschatological Ethics*.

40. Von Balthasar, *Truth Is Symphonic*, 25. While Catholics know truth about the content of faith and morality, they do not know truth in an exhaustive way or in a manner that gives them the ability to judge others interiorly or to lord it over others.

41. Novak, *Zionism and Judaism*, 185.

down our lives for each other. The path of the messianic King is not one of persecuting others but of serving others. After washing his disciples' feet in order to teach them about true royal rule, he explains to them: "You call me Teacher and Lord; and you are right, for so I am. If I then, your Lord and Teacher, have washed your feet, you also ought to wash one another's feet. For I have given you an example, that you also should do as I have done to you" (John 13:13–15).

It follows that Christians who obey the evangelistic command of the risen Jesus to "make disciples of all nations" (Matt 28:19) need not fall into pridefully claiming to know "the whole truth." Christ in person is the whole truth, and this truth is not only inexhaustible, but also knowable only in self-sacrificial love and humility. Likewise, Christians are not wrong to seek to instill Christian values in the world, including in the nations in which Christians live. The error instead comes when Christians seek to "enforce uniformity of belief"[42] and thereby seek to establish the kingdom of God through power rather than through love. Generally, one knows persecution when one sees it, but Jesus gives us even more clarity. In his parable of the Sheep and the Goats, he puts himself in the place of the neighbor in distress. He states that when we act with love toward our vulnerable neighbor, we are acting with love toward the messianic King. In the parable, Christ tells the blessed, "Come, O blessed of my Father, inherit the kingdom prepared for you from the foundation of the world; for I was hungry and you gave me food, I was thirsty and you gave me drink, I was a stranger and you welcomed me, I was naked and you clothed me, I was sick and you visited me, I was in prison and you came to me" (Matt 25:34–36). Jesus commands his followers to give particular care to vulnerable persons. The special place of the vulnerable comes about because, as David Martin says, "The drama of redemption is one of descent into limitation without which there can be no ascent into glory."[43]

Persecution takes place when people with power (including religious power) act to deprive the vulnerable of what is due to them in justice as human beings.[44] Thomas Aquinas identifies a case of grave persecution when he states, as two *objections* to his own perspective, that "kings and princes have the power to do what they will with Jewish children" and that "it is not unjust if Jewish children be taken away from their parents, and consecrated

---

42. Sacks, *Not in God's Name*, 5. Sacks goes on to say, "To invoke God to justify violence against the innocent is not an act of sanctity but of sacrilege" (*Not in God's Name*, 5).

43. D. Martin, *Religion and Power*, 62. Martin argues that the gospel is intrinsically pacifist, a point with which I disagree: see my *Betrayal of Charity*, chapter 7.

44. See Tranzillo, *John Paul II on the Vulnerable*.

to God in baptism."[45] In responding, Aquinas argues first that the Church already would have sanctioned this practice if it were "at all reasonable," whereas in fact the Church has never sanctioned it.[46] He goes on to explain that "it is against natural justice. For a child is by nature part of its father: thus, at first, it is not distinct from its parents as to its body, so long as it is enfolded within its mother's womb; and later on after birth, and before it has the use of its free-will, it is enfolded in the care of its parents, which is like a spiritual womb."[47] Before children have the use of reason and can freely make their own choices, the parents justly have care of the child, including care of the child's spiritual welfare. Aquinas concludes that because "according to the natural law, a son, before coming to the use of reason, is under his father's care," it follows that "it would be contrary to natural justice, if a child, before coming to the use of reason, were to be taken away from its parents' custody, or anything done to it against its parents' wish."[48] He reiterates this point even more strongly when he says that "no one ought to break the order of the natural law, whereby a child is in the custody of its father, in order to rescue it from the danger of everlasting death."[49]

In response to the objection that because every child belongs to God it is appropriate to seize Jewish children and baptize them, Aquinas answers by again asserting the dignity of the natural order and the fact that the Christian supernatural order does not achieve its ends by violating the natural law. He states, "Man is directed to God by his reason, whereby he can know Him. Hence a child before coming to the use of reason, in the natural order of things, is directed to God by its parents' reason, under whose care it lies by nature: and it is for them to dispose of the child in all matters relating to God."[50] He makes the same point in his discussion of the sacrament of baptism. Prior to attaining to the use of reason and freely choosing a religious faith, the child "is ordained to God, by a natural order, through the reason of its parents, under whose care it naturally lies."[51] Baptizing a Jewish child against the will of the parents has the same standing as baptizing

---

45. Thomas Aquinas, *Summa theologiae* II-II, q. 10, a. 12, obj. 3 and 4. I have standardized some capitalizations. For further background to the issues involved here, Weed, "Aquinas on the Forced Conversion of the Jews"; Weed, "Faith, Salvation, and the Sacraments."

46. Thomas Aquinas, *Summa theologiae* II-II, q. 10, a. 12. For discussion see Moschella, *To Whom Do Children Belong?*, 28 and elsewhere.

47. Thomas Aquinas, *Summa theologiae* II-II, q. 10, a. 12.

48. Thomas Aquinas, *Summa theologiae* II-II, q. 10, a. 1

49. Thomas Aquinas, *Summa theologiae* II-II, q. 10, a. 12, ad 2.

50. Thomas Aquinas, *Summa theologiae* II-II, q. 10, a. 12, ad 4.

51. Thomas Aquinas, *Summa theologiae* III, q. 68, a. 10, ad 3.

an adult against his or her will. Namely, it is a grave sin against justice. He repeats his insistence that no one should "infringe the order of the natural law, in virtue of which a child is under the care of its father, in order to rescue it from the danger of eternal death."[52]

In warning against overturning the natural order of the parents' care for their children, Aquinas notes that one reason not to do this is that such an action will often backfire. This is because the order of nature is generally strong, with the result that children who are forcibly baptized are "liable to lapse into unbelief, by reason of their natural affection for their parents."[53] Aquinas suggests here that the Church's longs-tanding "custom" of not forcibly baptizing Jewish children is anchored in a solid and salutary respect for the natural order.[54]

In his discussion of justice, Aquinas helps us to understand such persecution more clearly. Indebted to Aristotle, Aquinas defines justice as "a habit whereby a man renders to each one his due by a constant and perpetual will."[55] But what if charity toward a person requires doing something that otherwise might seem unjust (as in the case, perhaps, of baptizing a Jewish infant against the will of his or her parents)? Should not justice be defined as Augustine does, namely, as "love serving God alone"?[56] Aquinas replies that the relationship between charity and justice does not involve a conflict, although justice is best defined in terms of the natural order, taken up and fulfilled in charity. He explains, "Just as love of God includes love of our neighbor . . . so too the service of God includes rendering to each one his due."[57] Love of God does not mean overturning justice toward one's neighbor. Indeed, Aquinas states that "whoever does an injustice sins mortally," by breaking with the love of God and neighbor.[58]

In a family, it is just that the parents raise their child in their religion, at least until the child reaches the age of reason and is able to decide on his or her own. The charitable person owes it to the parents of the child (and to the child) to ensure that they receive what is due to them in justice, namely,

---

52. Thomas Aquinas, *Summa theologiae* III, q. 68, a. 10, ad 1.
53. Thomas Aquinas, *Summa theologiae* III, q. 68, a. 10.
54. Thomas Aquinas, *Summa theologiae* III, q. 68, a. 10. Aquinas's use of the term *custom* here is important; see his remark in I-II, q. 97, a. 3 that "when a thing is done again and again, it seems to proceed from a deliberate judgment of reason. Accordingly, custom has the force of a law, abolishes law, and is the interpreter of law."
55. Thomas Aquinas, *Summa theologiae* II-II, q. 58, a. 1. I have removed the italics. See also Franks, "Aristotelian Doctrines."
56. Thomas Aquinas, *Summa theologiae* II-II, q. 58, a. 1, obj. 6.
57. Thomas Aquinas, *Summa theologiae* II-II, q. 58, a. 1, ad 6.
58. Thomas Aquinas, *Summa theologiae* II-II, q. 59, a. 4; cf. I-II, q. 88, a. 2.

the raising of their child in their religion. The order of charity and the order of the natural law are not in conflict, but work together in harmony.[59]

The historian John Y. B. Hood has commented on the issue of forced baptism: "Aquinas stands his ground: The parent-child bond is inviolable, even if the consequences include allowing the child to suffer eternal alienation from God.... No doubt his position reflects his deep commitment to natural law and his absolutist insistence that no consequence, however heinous, can justify a morally wrong act."[60] Hood adds that Blessed John Duns Scotus "also believed in natural law, and he simply invoked hierarchy to conclude that Jewish children should be baptized: God's *dominium* supersedes all others, including that of parents."[61] For Scotus, the supernatural order can and does override and negate the natural law. Unlike Aquinas, Scotus considers that an action that is unjust in itself can rightly be done in the name of Christ's charity.

IV. The Edgardo Mortara Case

What Aquinas would have thought about the Mortara case will never be known, although six-year-old Edgardo certainly was not of an age to decide freely about his situation. The Pope commanded his police to take the boy because in the Papal States, the parents of a baptized child were legally bound to raise and educate the child in the Catholic faith—as parents who baptize their children today are still canonically bound to do.[62] Edgardo's parents, being Jews, could not do this. Therefore, the priest-inquisitor who investigated the case, and eventually the Pope himself, deemed that the Church (or the Papal States) must take the child from his parents and raise the child.[63]

---

59. For discussion of how Aquinas and John Duns Scotus understand cases where God himself appears to have worked outside the natural law, see my "God and Natural Law."

60. Hood, *Aquinas and the Jews*, 92.

61. Hood, *Aquinas and the Jews*, 92. See also N. L. Turner, "Jewish Witness."

62. In asking for (or in emergencies administering) the sacrament of baptism to children below the age of reason, the parents do so in the faith of the Church and with promises that bind them to raise the child in the faith. See also Tapie, "*Spiritualis Uterus*," 290, referencing the 1983 *Codex iuris canonici*, canon 868. In this canon, the Church teaches that for baptism to be licit, "the parents or at least one of them or the person who legitimately takes their place must consent" and "there must be a founded hope that the infant will be brought up in the Catholic religion," but nonetheless "an infant of Catholic parents or even of non-Catholic parents is baptized licitly in danger of death even against the will of the parents" (*Code of Canon Law*, pp. 285–86).

63. In his memoirs as edited and translated by Messori, Father Mortara indicates

Background to the Mortara Case

Lest there be a misunderstanding with regard to the motivations or perspective of Pope Pius IX, let me briefly sketch some historical background regarding the baptism of Jews in Catholic lands and in the Papal States. Beginning especially in the early medieval period, Catholic rulers not infrequently issued "ultimatum[s] that Jews of the kingdom either convert or be expelled from the country," and forced baptism of Jews also became an issue.[64] Some influential Catholic bishops responded sharply against such practices. For example, at the Fourth Council of Toledo in 633, Isidore of Seville delivered a sharp rebuke to King Sisebut's forced baptisms of Jews, insisting in canon 57 that no one should be forced to believe in Christ by threats and punitive measures.[65] Canon 57, however, also required that "those who had been baptized by force must remain Christian," and canon 60 adds the point that

---

his agreement with this course of action. He notes first of all, "The Mortaras profess the Jewish religion, which is contradictory and surpassed by history. Consequently, the parental authority of Signor and Signora Mortara is diminished, disabled, and is not in full possession of its rights, nor does it know its duties" (Mortara, "Mortara Case and Pius IX," 159). Second, Mortara sets the scene: "God guides and impels the hand of that girl, places her at the foot of the Cross of the divine Redeemer, from whose pierced Heart flows and separates a drop of His adorable blood. Mixed with the baptismal water, this drop regenerates, purifies, and sanctifies that soul, which men do not appreciate because they do not know it; but God loves, predestines, and protects it because it cost all the blood of God. What rights can be asserted by the parents of the child who has been abandoned by men and welcomed by God? Who interfered here; who profaned the sacred power of liberty; who did violence to the will of that child? All the 'blame', if 'blame' there be, belongs to God. There is no doubt that God's rights are superior to those of parental authority, which in this case happens to be completely destitute even of merely apparent rights" ("Mortara Child and Pius IX," 160). As a third step, he appeals to the civil laws as well: "We repeat: the civil laws in a Christian state are explicit in this case. The Mortara child must be separated from his parents. Of course, if the gentler, more conciliatory measures do not obtain the hoped-for result, and if the moral perversion of the child is evident and inevitable, the laws justify, command, and prescribe sequestration. And this is exactly what Pius IX did. He neither stole nor kidnapped a child from his parents, as the anti-Catholic press repeated tirelessly. After resorting to all possible methods of persuasion and conciliation, after proposing gentle paternal measures to the parents . . . Pius IX proceeded to separate the child. He was then seven years old and had attained the use of reason" (Mortara, "Mortara Child and Pius IX," 162). In fact, he was not yet seven years old.

64. Tapie, "*Spiritualis Uterus*," 295, drawing here upon N. Roth, *Jews, Visigoths, and Muslims*; as well as upon Linder, *Jews in the Legal Sources*, and the essays (including work on forced conversion) in Tolan et al., eds., *Jews in Early Christian Law*. In this section, I am indebted to Tapie's essay.

65. See Tapie, "*Spiritualis Uterus*," 295.

"forcibly baptized children ... must receive a Christian education" and must therefore be removed from their (Jewish) families.[66]

The removal of baptized children from their Jewish families thus has a long Catholic pedigree. Even so, forcing Jews to become Catholics continued to be condemned. Matthew Tapie notes that many popes rejected "forcible conversion of Jews ..., as indicated by the well-known letter of Gregory IV (r. 827–844), which cites the prohibition of the practice in canon 57 of Toledo IV."[67] There seems to have been general acceptance that, once forcibly baptized, baptized Jews were under compulsion to live as Catholics. Yet even in this regard there were some notable exceptions. For example, Tapie reports that "Pope Alexander II (1061–1073) permitted all Jews baptized by force during the First Crusade of 1096 to return to practicing Judaism."[68]

By the late twelfth century, canonists had begun to distinguish between absolute and conditional coercion. In the former case, no consent whatsoever is given by the recipient of baptism; in the latter case, under threat of violence or other harm, the recipient gives consent. For thirteenth-century canonists, the latter case—despite its occurring under severe duress—constitutes a valid baptism, even if canonists also held that it is a grave sin to administer forced baptism. The former case, however, does not constitute a valid baptism.

In the eighteenth century, Pope Benedict XIV reiterated the Church's teaching that Jewish children should not be baptized without their parents' consent, an action that seems to have been happening relatively frequently in the Rome of his day.[69] But Benedict XIV made exception for two cases: when a Christian finds a Jewish child in danger of death, and when a Jewish child is found alone outset the Jewish ghetto and thus has possibly been abandoned by his or her parents. Benedict XIV also described other instances in which Jewish children could receive baptism without the consent of both parents. Tapie explains, "Jewish children could be baptized in the following circumstances: if the Jewish parents were absent, and their guardians consented; if the Jewish father commanded it, even if the mother were unwilling; or if a Jewish convert to Christianity made 'offering' of a Jewish family member to the Church."[70] These exceptions were made on the

66. Tapie, "*Spiritualis Uterus*," 296.

67. Tapie, "*Spiritualis Uterus*," 297.

68. Tapie, "*Spiritualis Uterus*," 298, citing E. H. Flannery, *Anguish of the Jews*, 76.

69. Kleinberg, "Depriving Parents" and Ravid, "Forced Baptism of Jewish Minors." Both of these are cited in Tapie, "*Spiritualis Uterus*," 294. For background to the standing of the blood libel during this period, see Caffiero, "Alle Origini dell'Antisemitismo Politico."

70. Tapie, "*Spiritualis Uterus*," 302, indebted to Kleinberg, as well as to Caffiero,

canonical principle of acting in favor of the faith, much as in the case of Pauline privilege in marital law. It became standard practice in the Papal States that if such a baptism was known to have occurred, "the police removed the Jewish child from the parents' home and sent it to the House of the Catechumens."[71] Normally, these children were relatives of a recent male Jewish convert to Catholicism, but this of course does not excuse the action.

Against Pope Pius IX's Action

Like the Catholics who today praise Pope Pius IX's action,[72] I affirm that Catholics must cherish and defend the supernatural greatness of the sacraments, against the supposition that the sacraments are mere rituals or that there is no such thing as sacramental grace. Expositing the meaning of baptism, Colman O'Neill aptly speaks of "the active intervention of the heavenly Christ in the ceremony of baptism," an intervention that, through the sacred sign, causes an enduring ontological relationship of the baptized person to Christ—no matter whether, in the exercise of his or her freedom, the person goes on to live in such a way as to "correspond to this sacramental

---

Forced Baptisms. For Pope Benedict XIV's teachings on this matter, see his *Lettera a Monsignor Archivescovo* and his *Lettera della Santità di Nostro Signore,* translations of his Papal Bulls (published on the same dates) *Postremo mense* and *Probe te meminisse.* See also K. Pennington, "Law's Violence," 40-43. For background to the conditions for a licit and valid baptism in the nineteenth century (in the context of the Mortara case), see P. Turner, "Considering the Baptism of Mortara," 6: "A laywoman could baptize a Jewish child without parental consent in the nineteenth century only under certain conditions: if she determined that the child was in danger of death, if she had no recourse to an available priest or deacon to perform the ceremony, if she used the correct words, if she performed the correct actions, and if she had the right intention."

71. Tapie, "*Spiritualis Uterus*," 303-4

72. The discussion was spurred by Cessario, "Non Possumus," a review of the English translation of Messori, ed., *Kidnapped by the Vatican?*. In favor of Pope Pius IX's action, see also Roy Schoeman's preface to Messori, ed., *Kidnapped by the Vatican?*, vii-xi. A convert to Catholicism from Judaism, Schoeman argues along lines that reflect Pope Pius IX's self-understanding: "Pope Pius IX stood as a bulwark against this secularizing trend that was transforming Italy and all Europe. The Mortara case provided an ideal opportunity for his opponents to attack him personally, as well as the authority of the Church and the very idea of a confessional state. For one's view of the morality of his actions depends on one's acceptance, or rejection, of the truths of the Catholic faith. In the light of the faith, what the pope did can be seen as not only legally justified but also morally justified; in the darkness of a total rejection of the faith, it appears unconscionable" (Messori, ed., *Kidnapped by the Vatican?*, ix). For background, observing that the "Mortara case . . . ensured the papacy's loss of favor in European public opinion," see Foa, "Difficult Apprenticeship of Diversity," 50.

incorporation into Christ."[73] The power of baptism is such that in this sacrament, the risen Christ "sends the Spirit to transform the whole person of the believer" and "incorporates the believer into his sacramental body."[74] Roger Nutt remarks in the same vein, "The teaching of the Magisterium insists that the sacraments have an intrinsic causal power and that contact with the sacraments is operative in the outpouring of grace on the soul.... Grace is conferred in the sacraments, as long as the rite is properly celebrated."[75] In my view, O'Neill and Nutt—neither of whom has the Mortara case in mind, because they are simply stating Catholic doctrine—are completely correct.

Fortunately, the practice of forcibly removing young baptized Jewish children from their families is not a necessary element in the defense of Catholic sacramental doctrine or practice. Since the practice has been approved and undertaken by Catholics, however, let me attend to it here with regard to the Mortara case. I will offer seven considerations, each of which could be much expanded.

(1) Natural law and natural justice were violated by Pope Pius IX's action. In his discussion of charity in the *Summa theologiae*, Aquinas holds that "the aspect under which our neighbor is to be loved, is God, since what we ought to love in our neighbor is that he may be in God."[76] But to do an injustice to a person, even with the goal of ordering him toward God, is in Aquinas's view a sin. As Novak observes in his *Natural Law in Judaism*, often justice is the most that one can expect, but "in the covenant, justice is only the minimum. The covenant transcends nature, but as something more not less than it."[77] Charity cannot involve something less than natural justice. In *Caritas in Veritate*, Pope Benedict XVI affirms this point: "*Charity goes beyond justice* ... but it never lacks justice.... If we love others with charity, then first of all we are just towards them. Not only is justice not extraneous to charity, not only is it not an alternative or parallel path to

---

73. O'Neill, *Sacramental Realism*, 125, 135.

74. O'Neill, *Sacramental Realism*, 136. O'Neill rightly critiques human-centered (rather than God-centered) theologies of the sacraments: see *Sacramental Realism*, 140–42. The key, O'Neill observes, is affirming "God's objective way of acting in the world," or what O'Neill also calls "sacramental realism" (*Sacramental Realism*, 142).

75. Nutt, *General Principles of Sacramental Theology*, 110. See also Lynch, *Cleansing of the Heart*.

76. Thomas Aquinas, *Summa theologiae* II-II, q. 25, a. 1.

77. Novak, *Natural Law in Judaism*, 47. For further reflection on natural law, see the essays that David Novak and I wrote for our co-authored book with Anver Emon, *Natural Law*. See also Novak, *Covenantal Rights*; and my *Biblical Natural Law*. For further exposition, reflecting our somewhat different approaches but also our agreement regarding the basic precepts of natural law, see Novak, "Natural Law and Divine Command"; and my *Jewish-Christian Dialogue*, chapter 4: "Natural Law and Noahide Law."

charity: justice is inseparable from charity, and intrinsic to it. Justice is the primary way of charity."⁷⁸

Yet, what about the canonical expectation that once a child has been baptized (even against the will of his parents), the Church must ensure that the child is raised and educated in the Catholic faith, as was legally required in the Papal States? Can this justify doing a natural injustice to the child's Jewish parents—and to the child who has a natural right to be raised by his parents—in the name of Christian charity toward the child? Assuming that the infant Edgardo *was* secretly baptized by the servant Anna Morisi, this was a secret baptism of an infant without the consent of his parents. Even if one were to insist that Christian charity may require doing a natural injustice to the parents and to the child as an unfortunate effect of doing the child the supernatural good of raising him as a Christian, there would be pertinent distinctions to be made with regard to the sacramental order. A secret baptism against the will of an infant's parents needs to be distinguished from a normal baptism with respect to expectations about education in the faith. It does not make sense to argue that because a good in the supernatural order has been bestowed, there must then follow a severe injustice in the natural order toward the parents who are the natural caretakers of the child as well as toward the child who has a natural right in justice to be raised by his parents. The sacramental order can recognize diverse circumstances and can adjust its legal requirements accordingly.

After all, Catholics would be utterly appalled if our children were forcibly removed by state power from our homes, in order to be educated in the faith of a confessional non-Catholic state or by an atheistic state that deemed unacceptable the inculcation of Catholic beliefs. As the Apostle Paul says, Christian "love does no wrong to a neighbor" (Rom 13:10). Forcibly taking away a child from his parents, unless absolutely necessary due to insanity or physical abuse on the part of the parents, does a grievous wrong to a neighbor.⁷⁹

---

78. Benedict XVI, *Caritas in Veritate*, §6.

79. Cessario argues, "No one who considers the Mortara affair can fail to be moved by its natural dimensions. It is a grievous thing to sever familial bonds. But the honor we give to mother and father will be imperfect if we do not render a higher honor to God above. Christ's authority perfects all natural institutions—the family as well as the state. This is why he said that he came bearing a sword that would sunder father and son. One's judgment of Pius will depend on one's acceptance of Christ's claim" ("Non Possumus," 58). For Cessario, it was an act of charity (and justice) toward the boy Edgardo, once he had (supposedly) been baptized secretly, to ensure that he be educated as a Christian—and the enactment of this charity (and justice) sadly required separating him from his loving Jewish parents. Cessario suggests that anyone who disagrees with Pope Pius IX's action has rejected the supernatural order and reign of Christ.

(2) To violate the order of the natural law in this manner causes scandal and undermines the public credibility of both the natural and the supernatural order, and therefore is deeply imprudent. Aquinas recognizes that forcible baptism of Jewish children "would be detrimental to the faith" because, under normal circumstances, the parents would later be able to demonstrate to the children (once they had reached the age of reason) that an injustice had been done in the name of the Catholic faith. He notes that this would be likely to discredit the Catholic faith in the eyes of children who naturally love their parents, unless this natural love had been stamped out in the interim.[80] Today—and in 1858—affirming that a secret baptism of an infant against the will of his parents mandates the forcible removal of the boy from his family discredits the Church, even if anti-Jewish sentiment previously allowed such things in Catholic cultures.

(3) Defenders of the forcible removal of the boy Edgardo affirm that this action was necessary in order to ensure that Edgardo was educated in the Catholic faith.[81] But this excuse for violating the natural justice (and charity) due to Edgardo and his parents does not hold up under theological scrutiny. Aquinas teaches, "The physician of souls, i.e. Christ, works in two ways. First, inwardly, by himself: and thus he prepares man's will so that it works good and hates evil."[82] The interior mission of the incarnate Word takes place whenever and to whomever Christ wills. Assuming Edgardo was validly baptized, the interior missions of the Son and Spirit could have operated within him and borne fruit efficaciously after he had reached the age of reason.[83] Those who claim that he would otherwise likely never have enjoyed the supernatural grace of his baptism neglect the fact that not only could God have continued to work interiorly in Edgardo, but also God

---

80. Thomas Aquinas, *Summa theologiae* II-II, q. 10, a. 12.

81. Edgardo Mortara himself, of course, held this position. I note that attention needs to be paid here to a phenomenon described by Jonathan Sacks, who points out that Jews, including Jews who convert to Christianity, have been among the prominent advocates of persecution of Jews. Sacks offers some notable examples: see Sacks, *Leviticus*, 216–17.

82. Thomas Aquinas, *Summa theologiae* III, q. 68, a. 4, ad 2; cf. I, q. 43, a. 5.

83. Cessario comments in defending Pope Pius IX's action: "Allow me to recall that, according to Catholic teaching, the character of baptism does not work like magic. The new life that Catholics believe baptism brings requires instruction in the faith of the Catholic Church. Such instruction precedes baptism for adults. On the other hand, baptized children require rearing in the faith just as any child requires instruction in order to develop his or her human capacities" ("Romanus Cessario, O.P., replies," 4). Of course this is so, but the question is whether there is an alternative to removing a child, (supposedly) baptized as an infant without his parents' knowledge, from his loving parents.

could have used many external instruments to awaken the *adult* Edgardo to the supernatural grace of his baptism.[84]

(4) Some Catholics have contended that because Pope Pius IX has been declared "Blessed," his prudential decision in this case should be accepted as an exercise of virtuous prudence, given that Pius IX repeatedly reaffirmed the rightness of what he did to Edgardo Mortara and his family, and given that his beatification "preclude[s] the view that Pius IX was an unrepentant sinner committed to violations of the natural law."[85] But even saints can adhere to grievous prudential error, for example by persistently misunderstanding the elements of a case due to unconscious cultural prejudices.[86] The idea that no one declared "Blessed" could have persisted in a serious prudential error is not credible, either theologically or historically.

(5) According to David Kertzer, Pope Pius IX was given plausible evidence that indicated that Anna Morisi did not tell the truth about what she claimed to have done. Edgardo's parents stated that she was never alone with the baby Edgardo. The Mortara's family doctor, Pasquale Saragoni, "testified that at the time that Anna Morisi said she performed the baptism

---

84. See also Thomas Aquinas, *De veritate*, q. 14, a. 11, ad 1. For diverse perspectives, see Garrigou-Lagrange, "On those who are invincibly ignorant"; Nicolas, *Synthèse dogmatique*, 706–18.

85. Cessario, "Romanus Cessario, O.P., replies," 4. Messori makes a similar point more than once. He remarks, "Much more of a pastor than a politician, much more candid than astute, this pontiff was incapable of falsehood. He was a priest who made painful, rigorous examinations of conscience, trusting in the mercy of Christ, whose vicar he was, and at the same time afraid of not living up to the gospel, knowing that he was supposed to be the greatest witness to it. Nevertheless, this sincere, scrupulous man, although beset by the storm that was raging halfway around the world, never had any hesitation, and years later he coolheadedly confirmed it on a public, solemn occasion: 'What we did for that boy, We had the right and the duty to do. And if the opportunity presented itself, We would do it again.' The Church has proclaimed this pope Blessed, declaring his heroic virtues and proposing him therefore to the faithful as a role model and an intercessor. The tranquility of this pope's conscience says something, does it not, to Catholics at least?" (Messori, "The Mortara Case," 32). Messori is mistaken to suggest that Catholics need to defend all the prudential decisions made and defended by sainted popes. Cessario recognizes that "a beatification does not endorse every political decision of the blessed" ("Romanus Cessario, O.P., replies," 4), but Cessario suggests that the fact that Pius IX repeatedly confirmed this decision means that it should be embraced.

86. See Sherwin, *On Love and Virtue*, 176; Thomas Aquinas, *Summa theologiae* II-II, q. 47, a. 14, ad 1. See also McHugh and Callan, *Moral Theology*, 21, 28; Maritain, *Distinguish to Unite*, Appendix VII: "Speculative" and "Practical," 481–89, especially 488; as well as the discussion of the errors committed by even saintly Church leaders in exercising their functions in the Church, in Nicolas, *Synthèse dogmatique*, 700–704; and Maritain, *On the Church of Christ*, 135–242.

of the sick child, she herself was very ill and confined to bed."[87] Maria Capelli, a Catholic, supported Saragoni's testimony secondhand by reporting what her mother, a daytime servant of the Mortaras, had told her. Another Catholic servant, Ippolita Zacchini, also confirmed Saragoni's account; as did both her daughter, Marianna Zacchini, and the seamstress Giuseppina Borghi, who lived in the floor below the Mortara family. Anna Morisi claimed that she had asked a local grocer, Cesare Lepori, how to baptize a child, but Lepori denied that he had spoken to Anna or that he even knew the procedure for baptizing. Furthermore, many testified that Anna Morisi was not trustworthy in her overall behavior.[88]

(6) The signification of the sacrament of baptism, insofar as it is associated with the forcible removal of a Jewish child from his parents, is undermined. Christians affirm that "all of us who have been baptized into Christ Jesus were baptized into his death" (Rom 6:3). Paul states, "For as many of you as were baptized into Christ have put on Christ" (Gal 3:27). Given that baptism is an efficacious sign of our sharing in Christ's death and our configuration to Christ, the action of forcibly removing a child secretly baptized by a servant functions inevitably as a counter-sign, expressive not of union with the crucified Christ but of an act of overweening temporal power.

(7) Kertzer has demonstrated that many positive details put forward by the Catholic press of the day were fabrications intended to paint the Church in a better light.[89] He has also demonstrated that the recent Italian edition

---

87. Kertzer, *Kidnapping of Edgardo Mortara*, 97.

88. Father Mortara, in his "Mortara Child and Pius IX," presents Morisi as a devout Catholic, well instructed in her faith and knowledgeable in the mode of baptism, and he also insists that he (as an infant) was indeed on the point of death: "The child Edgardo was seriously ill; the doctors had lost all hope of saving him. His parents, confronted with all the most unequivocal signs of a fatal end of the incident, abandoned themselves to a desperate sorrow. The child was on the point of taking his last breath; only a few moments more and he would be in Eternity. . . . In such a terrible predicament, the Morisi woman, who had been appropriately instructed, knew her catechism well and the manner and form for administering the Sacrament of Baptism to a dying person. She took a glass of water, dipped her hand into it, and baptized the child. . . . [S]hortly afterward, the child miraculously recovered and was completely restored to health" (153–54).

89. For example, Kertzer notes, "The part of the memoir that the conservative Catholic media is most loudly trumpeting today is Edgardo's description of how, after learning of the baptism but before Edgardo was taken away, Pius IX repeatedly tried to arrange some kind of compromise with his parents. In Edgardo's original account, the pope proposed sending him to a Catholic boarding school in Bologna, for, 'That way, his parents would be able to visit him whenever they wanted.' The Inquisitor, Edgardo writes, repeatedly went to the Mortara home to convince his parents to accept the pope's thoughtful plan. . . . Yet this account is pure invention—and not by Messori, but by Edgardo himself. The Inquisitor went on trial in 1860 on charges of kidnapping the

of Edgardo Mortara's memoirs, along with the recent English edition, has been heavily doctored by Vittorio Messori in order to make the Church look better.[90] Romanus Cessario remarks: "If Catholics are to respond effectively to David Kertzer's allegations in *The Kidnapping of Edgardo Mortara* ... they might strengthen their grasp on certain facets of the question.... Evaluation of Pope Pius IX's actions ... should be based on the most accurate detailing of the facts that political, legal, and religious history can provide."[91] Surely this is so, but Cessario is naming his own deficiency. He does not recognize the doctored state of the memoirs, and he demonstrates little knowledge of the ambiguities of the case—including the reasons for doubting Anna Morisi's story. He also takes at face value, without researching further, that "the chief rabbi of Rome, Sabatino Scazzocchio, wrote a private letter praising 'the benign and charitable nature' of Pius while lamenting the interference of the secular press. When Rome's Jews were invited to join Garibaldi's

---

boy; trial transcripts offering hundreds of pages of firsthand accounts—from the boy's parents, the police, and the Inquisitor—all make clear that the Inquisitor never spoke with the Mortaras before the papal police took Edgardo away. The appearance of the police that night in June 1858 came as a complete shock to the Mortaras. The only offer that Church authorities ever made came *after* the boy was already securely in Rome in the House of the Catechumens, the Church institution dedicated to converting the Jews. Edgardo's parents were then told that if they themselves were to enter the House of Catechumens along with the rest of their children, and accept baptism, they would once again be able to live together as a family—a Christian family" (Kertzer, "Doctored 'Memoir'"). For further details about Edgardo's kidnapping and its immediate aftermath, see Kertzer's *Kidnapping of Edgardo Mortara*, especially 3–73, 83–117.

90. Kertzer points out, "In Messori's version of the memoir, the reader is treated to a heartwarming story of a six-year-old child who is overjoyed to be taken from his parents so that he can become a Catholic.... But this is not the narrative Edgardo actually wrote. The happy version instead emerges from numerous changes to the original, including the addition and deletion of entire paragraphs—changes that are common to both published versions of the Edgardo Mortara memoir in Italian and English. A case in point is the addition of a 300-word paragraph, presented seamlessly with the rest of the text. It offers a justification for Pius IX's action in ordering Edgardo's removal from his family, and also describes the touching scene of the Inquisitor, Father Feletti, the man responsible for ordering the boy taken, going to see little Edgardo. 'In Rome, with great pleasure and tears in his eyes,' Messori's version of the memoir reads, 'Father Feletti hugged the Mortara child, for whose eternal salvation he had suffered so much, and he always had a special affection for him. Father Mortara will always hold very dear the memory of this respectable friar, who was one of those who more closely intervened in the spiritual regeneration and rehabilitation of his soul.' Neither this scene, nor the rest of the paragraph in which it appears, are to be found in Edgardo's original memoir" (Kertzer, "Doctored 'Memoir'"). Kertzer goes on to show that Messori softened the anti-Semitic remarks that Mortara makes in the memoir, language that leaves "the impression that Church mentors may have filled a Jewish child's mind with anti-Semitic ideas" ("Doctored 'Memoir'").

91. Cessario, "Romanus Cessario, O.P., replies," 4–5.

campaign against Pope Pius, they declined."[92] He implies that this means that the Roman Jews appreciated Pope Pius's motivations. Even the slightest study of the actual situation in Rome and the tenuous situation of the Jews there, as well as their outrage over Pius's actions, makes clear how farfetched this interpretation is. In addition, he approvingly quotes Edgardo Mortara's praise of Pius IX, where Mortara describes the Jewish (and non-Jewish) critics of Pius IX as low-life calumniators and Christ-killers: "There will come a day, yes, and it is not far away, in which, once they have stopped listening to the calumnies and the '*Crucifige*' (shouts of 'Crucify!') of the dregs of humanity, posterity will accept the poor arguments of the Mortara child."[93] This description of the Jews as demanding the crucifixion of Christ and as "the dregs of humanity" is a classic example of Catholic anti-Semitism.[94]

Unfortunately, as noted above, some Catholic scholars have made papal abuses of power into an excuse for denigrating the Catholic Church's priesthood and sacramental doctrine. For example, in his chapter on "Priestly Imperialism" in *Why Priests? A Failed Tradition*, Garry Wills argues that most sacraments are about "the priestly controlling of life."[95] He concludes that "[t]he great scandal of Christians is the way they have persecuted fellow Christians," largely due to "the jealousy of prerogative, the pride

---

92. Cessario, "Non Possumus," 58.

93. Mortara, *Mortara Child and Pius IX*, 175, cited in Cessario, "Non Possumus," 58. Shortly earlier, Mortara states similarly: "Ah! Amid your cackling, in the middle of the whirlpool of your hatreds and resentments, over the thick cloud and the dense fogs of your ignorance and pride, high above the movement of the base, treacherous passions that the infernal Serpent awakens and provokes in your ignoble hearts, arises, ascends and towers, like a new Moses on Sinai, at the summit of the Vatican, the great admirable, immortal Pontiff of the Immaculate and of the *Syllabus*. The flash of his glance, together with the thunder of his sublime '*Non possumus*', silences your '*Tolle, tolle, crucifige eum*' (Away with him, away with him, crucify him) (Jn 19:15) and leaves Pius IX on a throne that is still great, still noble, and unvanquished. . . . The accusers of Pius IX, like those of Jesus, of whom he is the visible vicar, are squashed under the weight of their inconsistent, ridiculous calumnies" (Mortara, *Mortara Child and Pius IX*, 174).

94. Cessario concludes "Romanus Cessario, O.P., replies" with the following words: "My review of a book that reports the story of a man who died in 1940 does not in any way purport to compromise what, in 1965, Blessed Paul VI set down in *Nostra Aetate*, especially no. 4: 'In her rejection of every persecution against any man, the Church, mindful of the patrimony she shares with the Jews and moved not by political reasons but by the Gospel's spiritual love, decries hatred, persecutions, displays of anti-Semitism, directed against Jews at any time and by anyone'" (5). See also the response to Cessario by Kertzer, "Enduring Controversy over the Mortara Case." Kertzer fills in further historical details about Father Mortara's life and ministry, with assistance from Pizzorusso, "Il caso Mortara"; and Mancini, "Pier Gaetano Feletti."

95. Wills, *Why Priests?*, 236. See also Wills, *Papal Sin*.

in exclusivity, the desire to define one's own Jesus as the only Jesus, that the priesthood fostered through the centuries" as "a way of fortifying the [priestly] monopoly on sacred things."[96] I note that to blame Catholic sinfulness upon the priesthood in this way is an act of scapegoating that offers Catholic laity, themselves a sinful people, a free pass.

Toward the end of his *Constantine's Sword: The Church and the Jews: A History*, James Carroll proposes a similarly anti-clerical solution to the wrongs committed by Catholics against the Jewish people over the centuries: "The Church's own experience—in particular, of its grievous sin in relation to the Jews—proves how desperately in need of democratic reform the Church is.... Vatican III must restore the broken authority of the Church by locating authority in the place where it belongs, which is with the people through whom the Spirit breathes."[97] On this view, if Catholic laypeople had been in charge, such abuses of power against the Jewish people would not have occurred. This blaming of priestly power is absurd, given the level of anti-Semitism that characterized the broad Catholic populace.[98] Besides, when one sees the misdeeds of Catholic laypeople—their all too frequent corruption, incompetence, negligence, and moral failings—one is appalled by the hypocrisy of Catholic attacks upon the Catholic priesthood.

What is needed instead is a deeper sense of the fact that God has willed to mediate his revelation through the instrumentality of sinful human beings. Jesus Christ, who "knew no sin" (2 Cor 5:21), communicates his life, death, and resurrection—his saving power and presence—to us through the mediation of the apostles and their successors, all of whom have been sinners. In the Gospel of Luke, Peter falls down "at Jesus' knees, saying, 'Depart from me, for I am a sinful man, O Lord'" (Luke 5:8). Paul accuses both Barnabas and Peter of acting with "insincerity" in their relationships with Gentiles (Gal 2:13). The disciples characteristically debated with each other about who among them "was the greatest" (Mark 9:34). The followers of Jesus, unlike the Messiah-king himself, have never been sinless.

The wrong lesson would be learned, therefore, if Catholics simply rejected the papacy as such or Blessed Pope Pius IX because he gravely abused

---

96. Wills, *Why Priests?*, 258.

97. Carroll, *Constantine's Sword*, 598. See also the documentation in Nicholls, *Christian Antisemitism*, especially 204-6. For further documentation see Marcus, *Jews in the Medieval World*. See also Ratzinger, "Church's Guilt," 280-81.

98. Robert Louis Wilken notes, "'Anti-Judaism' accents religious and theological factors, 'anti-Semitism' racial aspects of antipathy to the Jews" (Wilken, "Something Greater Than the Temple," 179). Wilken cautions that the application of the term "anti-Judaism" to Christianity, while in a certain way necessary, should not be allowed to obscure the significance of Christianity's rejection of truly anti-Jewish Marcionism and Gnosticism.

his power against the Mortaras. Christ freely willed to associate himself with the authority of the Petrine office and to ensure that it faithfully hands on the contents of the gospel, but insofar as this office is exercised by fallen humans it can be and has been abused. A simple-minded "anti-Roman attitude" blames the bishop of Rome for all the Church's (or world's) woes.[99] But as Hans Urs von Balthasar remarks, "there is—and always has been among Catholics—a healthy popular sentiment that is faithful to Rome without being blind to the faults and human failings of the curia and even of the pope."[100]

Even so, von Balthasar raises the key issue: "Can we trust an authority that has failed so often, failed so humanly? Which has also failed frequently in those universal instructions which, though not in the 'infallible' category in the narrower theological sense, were influential in shaping history?"[101] Seeking to respond to this issue, let me turn for help, in my chapter's final section, to David Novak's reflections on the meaning of the State of Israel.[102]

V. David Novak and Eschatological Humility

In *Zionism and Judaism*, Novak notes that according to some Jewish thinkers, the establishment of the State of Israel was a corrupt effort to accomplish the Messiah's eschatological work for him, rather than waiting upon

99. Von Balthasar, *Office of Peter*, 29.

100. Von Balthasar, *Office of Peter*, 29. For these human failings, see also Norwich, *Absolute Monarchs*.

101. Von Balthasar, *Office of Peter*, 19.

102. Ironically, Daniel Jonah Goldhagen, in calling for radical changes that he associates with Catholic "progressive voices," suggests that the solution might be to inflate the papacy's role so that a Pope can reject core teachings of Scripture and Tradition and force the whole Church to go along with his decisions. In a classically liberal vein, he proposes that a Pope might remake the Catholic Church around the "Church's core moral doctrines" while getting rid of most of the other doctrines and structures: "The Church is a resilient institution, having remade itself many times in many ways because of its formidable and admirable internal intellectual culture, which (its historical blind spots regarding Jews notwithstanding) nurtures a thirst for, and a drive to seek, enlightenment, truth, and goodness.... If a man becomes Pope who sees the necessity of completing the journey of the Church's postwar trajectory, listens to the progressive voices, takes into his own heart the immense goodness of the faithful's hearts, applies the Church's core moral doctrines, and seeks to remake the Church according to all of this, or if such a man just comes to see that the Church does have the duty to perform restitution, then he would have the authority (at least until he himself undoes it) to transform the Church into the pluralist, tolerant, publicly self-critical, anti-antisemitic institution that the twenty-first century demands" (Goldhagen, *Moral Reckoning*, 291–92). I note that no changes implemented by such a tyrant-Pope would have doctrinal value.

God to send the Messiah and restore the Jewish people to the land. Novak refers to these Jews as "pietists." The leading proponent of this perspective on the establishment of the State of Israel was Joel Teitelbaum, who died in 1979 and served as the "Rebbe" of the Satmar Hasidim.[103] In his *Concerning Redemption and Its Counterfeit Substitute*, published in Hebrew in 1956, Teitelbaum accuses the Zionist movement of attempting to restore the Jewish people to the land on human terms rather than on God's own messianic terms.[104] Teitelbaum even blames the Zionist movement for causing the Holocaust—which he construes as divine punishment for Zionism's eschatological presumption. On this view, just as God punished the Jewish people for *wanting* a state by allowing them to undergo the Holocaust, so also God will punish them by means of some future disaster for having dared—after the Holocaust—to establish the State of Israel in the land.

Whereas Teitelbaum (among others) blames Zionist Jews for the Holocaust, Novak notes that a different set of Jewish thinkers blame God himself for the Holocaust. On this view, the Holocaust proves that God cannot be counted upon to send the Messiah at the right time. Thus, Richard

---

103. Note, however, that in the nineteenth century, "[b]efore the rise of Zionism, the ... scholar and leader of German Jewish Orthodoxy, Samson Raphael Hirsch, argued that it is forbidden actively to accelerate divine deliverance. In light of such teaching, Zionism was perceived by the strictly Orthodox as a conspiracy against God's will and equated with pseudo-messianism. Preeminent among such Orthodox figures was Zadok of Lublin who stated that he prayed to the Lord for the day of redemption, but was unwilling to settle in Palestine out of fear that such an act could be interpreted as condoning the Zionist movement" (Cohn-Sherbok, *Jewish Messiah*, 158). Cohn-Sherbok reports that the "ultra-Orthodox group, *Agudat Israel*, was formed in 1912 to unite rabbis and laity against the Zionist movement. Although the Torah maintains that it is the duty of religious Jews to return to the Holy Land, these Orthodox critics emphasized that such an ingathering of the exiles must be preceded by messianic redemption.... In Palestine itself ultra-Orthodox Jews joined with *Agudat Israel* in its struggle against Zionism. Frequently its leaders protested to the British government and the League of Nations about the Zionist quest to create a national home in Palestine.... Between the end of the War [World War II] and the founding of the Jewish State a zealous extreme group, the *Neturei Karta* ('Guardians of the City') in Jerusalem accused the *Agudat* of succumbing to the Zionist cause. Headed by Amram Blau and Aharon Katzenellenbogen, these extremists were supported by the followers of rabbis in Brisk (Poland) and Szatmar (Hungary) who had emigrated to the United States and other Western countries. According to the *Neturei Karta*, those who accepted the Jewish State were apostates" (Cohn-Sherbok, *Jewish Messiah*, 158–61).

104. See Teitelbaum, *Concerning Redemption*. For further discussion of Teiltelbaum and especially the Satmar Hasidim, who adopted an isolationist stance in their small town of Kiryas Joel, New York, see Batnitzky, *How Judaism Became a Religion*, 186–90. For English translations of some of Rabbi Teitelbaum's writings, including his blaming of the Holocaust on Zionism (Teitelbaum himself narrowly escaped being sent to Auschwitz along with hundreds of thousands of other Hungarian Jews), see Batnitzky and Bafman, eds., *Jewish Legal Theories*, 146–59. See also Levenson, "What Are They?"

Rubenstein argues that no sin of the people could have warranted the Holocaust and therefore (in Novak's words) "no relationship with the covenantal God is possible ever again."[105] God has failed the people of Israel and can no longer be trusted. For Rubenstein, whatever protection that the State of Israel has given to Jews has come too late. Had the God of Israel been a true covenant partner, God would surely have established the State of Israel (or sent the eschatological Messiah) in time to defeat the plans of the Nazis and spare the Jewish people from the Holocaust. Rubenstein therefore rejects the God of Israel because, despite his covenantal promises and his pledges regarding the Messiah, God left the Jewish people radically vulnerable to obliteration. God did not protect his people at their gravest hour of need.

Teitelbaum and Rubenstein represent two extremes in the interpretation of Israel's doctrine of kingship. Rubenstein condemns God for not sending the Messiah or restoring the earthly power of the State of Israel soon enough, whereas Teitelbaum requires the Jewish people to do nothing prior to God's decision (in God's own time) to send the Messiah in order to gather all Jews to a restored Israel. Both conclude that the Holocaust has to do with an eschatological failure, whether a failure on the part of God (Rubenstein) or a failure on the part of the many Zionists among the Jewish people (Teitelbaum).

A third and increasingly prominent view, which Novak terms "religionationalist," is that God allowed the Holocaust in order to bring about the establishment of the State of Israel as the inauguration of the messianic process of redemption.[106] Anticipating this viewpoint, some influential

---

105. Novak, *Zionism and Judaism*, 232, with reference to Rubenstein, *After Auschwitz*, 157–76.

106. Mention should also be made of Michael Wyschogrod's perspective. Responding to Emil Fackenheim, Wyschogrod argues that the Holocaust, as a negative event, cannot be central to the people of Israel in the ways that God's acts of redemption are. Wyschogrod states, "There is no salvation to be extracted from the Holocaust, no faltering Judaism can be revived from it, no new reason for the continuation of the Jewish people can be found in it" ("Faith and the Holocaust," 294). Yet, Wyschogrod adds: "For believing Israel, the Holocaust is not just another mass murder but, perhaps, the final circumcision of the people of God" ("Faith and the Holocaust," 293). Wyschogrod thereby lends some credence to viewing the Holocaust as eschatologically significant. He argues that the eschatological value of Israel's suffering is that "Israel suffers and, thereby, God's presence is drawn into human history and redemption enters the horizon of human existence" ("Faith and the Holocaust," 293). Israel's suffering is always intrinsically related to the eschatological redemption of the world. At the same time, Wyschogrod grants "the inscrutability of God's will" ("Faith and the Holocaust," 288), a claim that is at the core of Novak's position. Wyschogrod notes that Fackenheim (like Novak) mounts a strong critique of Richard Rubenstein's position, but Wyschogrod pushes back against Fackenheim (without, of course, adopting Rubenstein's position): "Fackenheim's lack of sympathy for Rubenstein's total rejection of the 'for our sins we

mid-nineteenth-century Jewish leaders, motivated by eschatological considerations, called for a Zionist resettling of the land of Israel. For example, the Ashkenazic rabbi Zvi Kalischer (d. 1874) and the Sephardic rabbi Judah Alakalai (d. 1878) interpreted the *Talmud Yerushalmi* to mean that the redemption of the Jews will come through a gradual process rather than through an apocalyptic event. They concluded that the Jews must populate the land of Israel in order to begin this gradual eschatological process. Similarly, Rabbi Isaac Jacob Reines (d. 1915) founded the *Mizrahi* Zionist movement explicitly in order to initiate an eschatological redemption that would come about through worldly action rather than through direct divine intervention.

For contemporary advocates of this perspective, "the messianic reality is a process that begins with the reestablishment of the State of Israel and is to culminate in the full messianic reign in the land of Israel and beyond."[107] Novak observes that a liturgical prayer composed for the State of Israel in 1948 and recited in most Orthodox synagogues today lends support to this perspective. The prayer "asks God to bless the state [of Israel] as 'the beginning of the growth of our redemption' (*ge'ulteinu*)."[108]

Among the twentieth-century proponents of this perspective, Novak identifies especially Abraham Isaac Kook (the Ashkenazic Chief Rabbi of Palestine who died in 1935) and his son Tzvi Yehudah Kook, also an influential rabbi.[109] The latter, who died in 1982 and who, unlike his father,

---

are punished' theology would make good sense if Fackenheim could see his way to embracing this standpoint, a standpoint which is, after all, not unhallowed by Jewish history. The fact of the matter, however, is that Fackenheim, too, finds it impossible to embrace the theology of 'for our sins we are punished.' . . . This being so, what is so dreadfully wrong with Rubenstein's rejection of the biblical God once he found himself rejecting the view that, in Hitler, Israel was once more feeling the scourge of God?" ("Faith and the Holocaust," 287). See Fackenheim, *God's Presence in History*.

107. Novak, *Zionism and Judaism*, 232.

108. Novak, *Zionism and Judaism*, 232.

109. For background to Tzvi Yehudah Kook (also spelled Zvi Yehuha Kook) and his father, see Goldman, *Zeal for Zion*, 274–89 and Stanislawski, *Zionism*, 87–88. Goldman sums up: "The Rabbis Kook, father and son, transformed religious Zionism into an activist movement inspired by messianic expectations" (*Zeal for Zion*, 288). The real impressiveness of the theological-mystical vision of Abraham Isaac Kook becomes clear in Jonathan Sacks's "Abraham Isaac Kook." Sacks concludes that Kook "left the dynamics of history to fill the gap at the heart of his system. Torah *would* fill the whole of Jewish culture with light, as fringes on the corners of a garment reveal the sanctity of the garment in its totality. The redemptive process would see a higher synthesis emerge, even if we could not yet precisely specify the steps to be taken to bring it about. As such, his thought is utopian, a vision without a programme. This makes it no less inspiring, no less one of the great contributions of all time to the development of Jewish spirituality" (Sacks, "Abraham Isaac Kook," 31). Cohn-Sherbok provides a helpful reflection

lived after 1948 in the State of Israel (rather than in the British territory of Palestine), expressly viewed the State of Israel as sacred. For Tzvi Yehudah Kook, the suffering endured by Jews in the Holocaust served to make the Jews worthy of such a divine gift. According to Tzvi Yehudah Kook, the divine gift of the State of Israel is in fact the beginning of the eschatological final days. The Jews of Israel and their supporters are "in the vanguard of the emerging messianic process in history leading toward history's true goal: the 'End of Days' (*aharit ha-yamim*)."[110]

Novak compares this viewpoint with the Jewish anti-Zionist view. The "religio-nationalists" see the victims of the Holocaust as a "burnt offering" that opens the path to the messianic future, whereas the anti-Zionists see the victims of the Holocaust as a "guilt offering" for the (pre-World War II) Zionist Jewish past.

---

upon Yehuda Alkalai (Novak spells this name "Judah Alakalai"), Zwi [or Zvi] Kalischer, and Abraham Isaac Kook in his *Jewish Messiah*, 154–58. Stanislawski is not atypical in drawing a rather sharp distinction between father and son: "[Abraham Isaac] Kook's messianism was entirely theoretical, but soon the subterranean messianic tension latent in his teachings bred a far more overt and activist theology in the ranks of his students. Led by his son, Rabbi Zvi Yehuda Kook, this ideology advanced an interpretation of Rabbi Kook's thought in which the conquest of the Holy Land was regarded as a divine act heralding the advent of the messianic age, 'quickly and in our day,' as the liturgy had traditionally put it. In the years before 1967, this radical theology became more and more popular among younger National Religious Party activists, who founded Gush Emunim, which put forth an entirely unprecedented variation on Jewish messianism: a messianic movement without a messiah" (Stanislawski, *Zionism*, 88).

110. Novak, *Zionism and Judaism*, 237. See also Inbari, *Messianic Religious Zionism*, chapter 1, "Zionist Perceptions in the Thought of Rabbi Zvi Yehuda Kook." Deeming Kook to be a Jewish "fundamentalist," Inbari summarizes Kook's position on the state of Israel: "His sanctification of statism led him to adhere to the belief that redemption precedes repentance; accordingly, he attributed an element of sanctity to Israeli reality and to the army as part of this reality. . . . Kook claimed after the [1967] war that the situation was no longer one of the 'beginning of redemption,' or the initial phase of messianic realization; rather, this process was already in its middle phase" (*Messianic Religious Zionism*, 29–30). For theological discussion, see Weissman, "Zionism as Jewish Hope," especially 270–78. Weissman points to the study by Ravitzky, *Messianism*, as well as to Scholem, *Messianic Idea in Judaism*. For an especially balanced analysis, see Sacks, *Arguments*, 175–78. Sacks observes that "messianism has led to opposite extremes. Neturei Karta and Gush Emunim share the view that the messianic idea is central to Judaism and that the State of Israel can only be understood in relation to it. For Neturei Karta the messianic process has not yet begun; therefore the state is a heresy. For Gush Emunim the process *has* begun; therefore the state is, wittingly or otherwise, holy and the instrument of redemption" (Sacks, *Arguments*, 177). He notes that "moderate religious Zionism," of the kind he himself supports, has garnered little popular support among Orthodox Israelis: "Apocalyptic images speak more directly to Israeli hopes and fears than the language of diplomacy or moderation or subtle halakhic interpretation" (*Arguments*, 178).

In response, Novak emphasizes that God's people must not mistake their own actions in temporal matters for God's work of bringing about the eschatological consummation. Neither their good actions nor their sins can trigger the Messiah's consummation of all things. The glorious coming of the Messiah will be a gift, even if at the eschaton we will also see how the actions of the people have prepared for it. While differing from Teitelbaum, Novak thinks that Teitelbaum at least was correct that no human political action can bring about the eschatological consummation that only God can accomplish. A divine gift can only come from God. Novak insists, "The reign of the Messiah is not the culmination of a discernible process within history leading to its end. Instead, the coming of the Messiah is one event, and it will have no active preconditions on the part of any human being. There is no potential in the world for the coming of the Messiah."[111]

When God's eschatological work is conceived as flowing from "worldly processes," Novak fears, we have the recipe for forms of fanaticism that abuse the name of God.[112] I agree with this concern. Novak is right to warn against "the pretensions of this-worldly projects" and against "totalizing schemes in the world" that claim to be doing God's work for him.[113] We cannot assume that we know what God's purposes are for allowing this or that event; we cannot take it on ourselves to justify God or to reveal God's plans. Novak quotes a statement of Abraham Joshua Heschel: "The State of Israel is not an atonement. It would be blasphemy to regard it as a compensation."[114]

Instead, Novak advocates what he calls "transcendent messianism."[115] This messianism does not pretend that human institutions, however valuable, can be simply identified with God's own eschatological action. Theodicy, too, is not possible prior to the eschaton; only God can justify himself, including with regard to the Holocaust. Jews who survived the Holocaust or who are descended from survivors do not need to justify either God or their own existence. They can simply note that God's "fundamental covenantal promise" has not been falsified, because Jews have survived (and now

---

111. Novak, *Zionism and Judaism*, 239. See also Novak, *Covenantal Rights*, 74–75, in which Novak discusses the radically transformed world of the eschaton and comments that "without the messianic kingship, eschatology tends to become a trajectory of lone individuals who no longer need any full earthly community, but who simply enjoy God all for themselves, all by themselves" (*Covenantal Rights*, 75).

112. Novak, *Zionism and Judaism*, 240.

113. Novak, *Zionism and Judaism*, 240.

114. Novak, *Zionism and Judaism*, 244. Novak does not provide a source.

115. Novak, *Zionism and Judaism*, 245.

also have thrived) and because Jews still obey Torah as God's covenantal people.[116]

If we leave Jewish eschatology and the Holocaust to the side for now, then a comparable reflection can be undertaken with regard to the Catholic Church and the sins of its members and leaders. Over the centuries, many popes, bishops, and other members of the Catholic Church have contributed in various ways to a widespread and wicked culturally ingrained Christian anti-Jewish attitude. This anti-Jewish attitude fueled irreparable acts of injustice toward the Jewish people. It was exploited by, and laid significant groundwork for, the neo-pagan Nazi reign of terror against the Jewish people, culminating in the Holocaust.

In response, Catholics must repent and work to ensure that no such attitude reemerges in the Catholic Church. But Catholics should not respond by blaming God for not preserving the Church from this anti-Jewish attitude. Catholics should also not respond by blaming the leaders of the Church so strongly as to presume that God's promises in Christ to his Church have failed. The promises of God in Christ, including those pertaining to the Petrine ministry, have not failed. It remains true that, as *Lumen Gentium* says, "revelation is transmitted integrally either in written form or in oral tradition through the legitimate succession of bishops and above all through the watchful concern of the Roman Pontiff himself; and through the light of the Spirit of truth it is scrupulously preserved in the Church and unerringly explained."[117] If believers have placed their hope in the leaders of the Church or have expected the Church to embody the holiness of the *consummated* kingdom, then believers have failed to place their hope where it must be placed, namely, in Christ, who by his Spirit sustains the Church's definitive teachings and sacraments for the salvation of the world but who also allows the Church, in various ways, to fall into grievous sins and errors. The Church, prior to Christ's coming, will always be in need of repentance and renewal. Renewal does not mean rejecting Christ's promises and teachings, but rather it means living in a greater dependence upon Christ's power and mercy.

In *Zionism and Judaism*, Novak concludes that Jews should rejoice in the establishment of the State of Israel by celebrating a "holy day" and by saying the psalms of praise that are said on holy days. They can rightly do so, however, not because of any this-worldly messianic schema, but rather because the establishment of the State of Israel stands as a manifest

---

116. Novak, *Zionism and Judaism*, 247.

117. Vatican Council II, *Lumen Gentium*, §25. See also Vatican II's Dogmatic Constitution on Divine Revelation, *Dei Verbum*, §7.

demonstration that Hitler and his collaborators did not attain their goal. Insofar as the people of Israel not only survived but also established the State of Israel in the land, it can rightly be said that "God gave the victory to the Jewish people."[118] Thus, if the Holocaust tempts some Jews to give up on the God of the covenant because of their powerlessness, and if the establishment of the State of Israel tempts some Jews to replace the God of the covenant because of their power, then the solution is that the two events should temper each other. The Jewish people must continue to trust in the God of the covenant, without claiming a God's-eye perspective on events. What is necessary, says Novak, is simply that "Jews (and their friends) are able to speak to God and of God in the world, without presuming to speak for God or in place of God. That is the true task of Jewish theology at this juncture of history—nothing more and nothing less."[119]

Of course, Jews can in a sense "speak for God" in proclaiming the truth of what God has spoken to the Jewish people—for example, the truth of the covenantal election of the people. Likewise, the pope, and the Catholic Church led by the pope, can in a sense "speak for God" in solemnly proclaiming the truth of the Gospel, the apostolic deposit of faith communicated by Christ and sustained in the Church by the Holy Spirit. Catholics can never, however, speak rightly "in place of God." Rather than rejecting God because of the weakness and failure of the popes or becoming proud due to the power of the Church, Catholics must learn theocentric humility. God will accomplish his promises in his own ways, while permitting—and judging—human abuse of power in the Church, including the history of persecuting the Jewish people.

VI. Conclusion

David Novak disagrees, of course, with the Christian claim that Israel's Davidic kingship finds its fulfillment in the humility of Jesus of Nazareth who reveals himself to be the Messiah and who, as the incarnate Son filled with the Spirit, is the eschatological temple.[120] As Novak says, Rabbinic Jews agree in being "on guard against any pseudo-messianism that declared the

---

118. Novak, *Zionism and Judaism*, 247.

119. Novak, *Zionism and Judaism*, 249.

120. Novak's position vis-à-vis Christianity has been spelled out afresh in his recent "Supersessionism Hard and Soft." Against syncretism, Novak notes that "we must respect the essentially different existential decisions we make as to *who* Jesus of Nazareth *is* and *what* he means for the covenant between God and His people, Israel" ("Supersessionism Hard and Soft," 30).

kingdom of God to be now with us and that much of the present Torah, therefore, is to be presently abrogated."[121] In describing this "pseudo-messianism," he is describing Christianity.[122] Novak and Christians can agree, however, that the meaning of Israel's kingship is now a fundamentally eschatological one. For both Jews and Christians, too, God has truly bound himself to human structures, and yet God transcends and judges the human structures to which he binds himself. God alone can bring about the eschatological consummation through the coming of his Messiah, even if here and now God's people can and should testify (by their words and by their lives) to the truth of what the God of Israel, who alone is God, has done and is doing for the salvation of the world.

As Rabbi Gil Student has remarked, Pope Pius IX's action toward the Mortara family pertains to why "cultural memories of the danger to Jewish families once posed by the Catholic Church still run deep."[123] Given that

---

121. Novak, *Zionism and Judaism*, 249.

122. See also Cohn-Sherbok, *Jewish Messiah*, 61–79. As Cohn-Sherbok puts it, "according to Judaism it is obvious that Jesus did not fulfil the messianic expectations as recorded in Scripture, post-biblical literature, and as elaborated by the rabbis. He did not restore the kingdom of David to its former glory; nor did he gather in the dispersed ones of Israel and restore all the laws of the Torah that were in abeyance (such as the sacrificial cult). He did not compel Israel to walk in the way of the Torah, nor did he rebuild the Temple and usher in a new order in the world and nature. In other words, Jesus did not inaugurate a cataclysmic change in history. Universal peace, in which there is neither war nor competition, did not come about on earth" (Cohn-Sherbok, *Jewish Messiah*, 76). Novak adds that in the view of Rabbinic Judaism, "the redeemed future must be an event so messianically self-evident that it would not entail the type of dispute that led to the schism of the Christian community" (Novak, *Zionism and Judaism*, 156).

123. Student, "Letter to the Editor." The "cultural memories" of Jews and Catholics will inevitably be different, but Catholics should be aware of and sensitive to the truth of Jewish "cultural memories" of Catholic rule. For example, medieval political life was of a much richer character than later critics assume, and there is much to commend in it; yet, the saintly Catholic King Louis IX ordered the burning of thousands of copies of the Talmud and other Jewish writings; more than once made initial plans to arrest the Jews or to expel them from France; and compelled the Jews to wear a red badge on the back and front of their shirt. Andrew Willard Jones defends Louis IX's treatment of the Jews on the grounds that usury was a grave sin and that "Jews who did not commit these crimes were to be protected" (A. W. Jones, *Before Church and State*, 99). But a "protection" that involved all Jewish people wearing a badge and that also involved the immolation of Jewish sacred books is not protection but persecution, as Catholics could perceive if they imagined themselves in the situation endured by the Jews. See also Geiger, "What Happened to Christian Hebraism?," 62n47. For discussion of the Talmud Trial that took place in 1240 in Paris and the burning of the copies of the Talmud in 1241, see Y. Schwartz, "Authority, Control, and Conflict"; as well as the helpful essays in Dahan, ed., *Le Brûlement du Talmud*. See also Grayzel, *Church and the Jews*; Grayzel, *Church and the Jews*, vol. II: *1254-1314*. In vol. II: *1254-1314*, Grayzel includes

Pope Pius IX was the pope under whose pontificate the dogma of papal infallibility was defined, it is perhaps fitting that his action puts the lie to ultramontanist notions of papal infallibility that imply that whatever a pope does or says in exercising his office is to be applauded.[124] The sacramental character given by baptism does not require forcibly removing a Jewish child from his parents' home when a servant claims to have secretly baptized the infant child. The loss of the Papal States, an event that arguably resulted from Pope Pius's action, has in many ways been a boon for the Church, not least because the Papal States were often deplorably misgoverned.[125]

When God is associated with powerful human structures, the temptation toward human pride easily arises. The biblical witness to God's covenantal association with the Davidic kingship provides a powerful corrective to such pride, but this corrective does not consist in agnosticism about God's gifts to his people. Rather, humility is shown in the manner of our reception and exercise of God's gifts.[126]

Pope Alexander IV's papal bull "*In Sacro Generali*" (September 3, 1258), which orders the Duke of Burgundy to confiscate all copies of the Talmud and to ensure that Jews wear the badge and do not receive public office (these latter two persecutory measures comprise canons 68 and 69 of the Fourth Lateran Council). Earlier in the same volume Grayzel remarks that "a partial expulsion of Jews from the French royal domain took place ... in 1252 and ... in 1254.... The Jews were permitted to return in 1257 or 1258, and King Louis restored to them property that was considered unlikely to have been gained through usury (e.g., synagogues and homes)" (Grayzel, *Church and the Jews* II, 62n3). See also Stow, *Popes, Church, and Jews*, chapter 3, "Papal and Royal Attitudes toward Jewish Lending in the Thirteenth Century"; as well as Jordan, *French Monarchy and the Jews*. Stow shows that Louis IX took a much stricter line than did the popes, who allowed for moderate interest to be collected on loans. On the expulsion of the Jews from England, see Mundill, *England's Jewish Solution*.

124. See Page, *What Will Newman Do?*

125. Von Balthasar considers the Papal States to have caused numerous problems that otherwise would not have arisen: "How many unnecessary humiliations could have been spared the papacy in more modern times, such as the absurd situation where the rigid Caraffa Pope invoked the aid of the Sultan against the equally rigid Spaniard, Philip II, or Gregory XIII's sanction, expressed to the same Philip, of political assassination in the confessional wars" (*Office of Peter*, 257).

126. The Jewish scholar Samuel Fleischacker, in distinguishing Written and Oral Torah, makes the following important point about the reception of God's revelation: "Revelation and its reception thus belong together by *contrast*; the relationship is lost if we ignore their differences. That is a mistake shared by progressive religious movements and their fundamentalist opponents. Progressive religious movements, over the past two centuries, have come to see sacred scriptures simply as human attempts to grasp God's will; they therefore regard the process of interpreting these texts as continuous with the process by which they were produced. Partly in reaction to this view, some traditionalists have insisted that not just the scriptures themselves but the established pre-modern interpretations of them are direct communications from God, which cannot be challenged in the name of what seem reasonable to us. Both of these views erase

Jews and Catholics believe that God has bound himself to human structures. Otherwise, there could be no possibility of a divinely appointed Davidic king—or a divinely instituted Church led by an episcopal hierarchy headed by the successor of Peter. Yet, God does not ensure that the leaders of his people will necessarily be prudent in their exercise of power. In the Catholic view, God's gifts are not intended to enable his people to build the perfect earthly kingdom. The Second Vatican Council teaches in *Gaudium et Spes*, "Christ did not bequeath to the Church a mission in the political, economic, or social order: the purpose he assigned to it was a religious one. But this religious mission can be the source of commitment, direction, and vigor to establish and consolidate the community of men according to the law of God."[127] The Jewish people received a law and a land. As Jonathan Sacks says, "Judaism cannot... coherently imagine a divorce between Torah and the Jewish people, or between either and the place of their redemption,

---

the distinction between revelation and its reception. The first dissolves revelation into its reception; the second freezes reception into an additional revelation" (Fleischacker, *Good and the Good Book*, 98). I agree with this insistence upon a distinct divine revelation, which Catholics call the apostolic deposit of faith. According to Catholic faith, the Holy Spirit guides the Church in choosing between major forks in the road in the interpretation of this divine revelation (for example, revelation would have an entirely different meaning had Arius's views prevailed). The dogmatic and moral teaching of the Church enables revelation to be communicated faithfully in every era, not by acquiring additional revelation, but by interpreting truly the revelation that has been given for the salvation of all.

127. Vatican II, *Gaudium et Spes*, §42, 942. In the Reformed theologian David Fergusson's *Church, State and Civil Society*, Fergusson addresses more directly "the end of Christendom" in which "western societies have severed in important respects their earlier connections with the Christian churches" (193). Fergusson notes that "the church now finds itself in an altered social location. Yet, although more detached from political society, it has not ceased to be publicly significant.... Faith communities that continue to offer meaning, vision and an account of human well-being will provide a necessary contribution not only to their own adherents, but also to wider public debates about how we should organise our common life" (*Church, State and Civil Society*, 192). This stance, however accurate, strikes me as rather weak: surely Vatican II's "commitment, direction, and vigor to establish and consolidate the community of men according to the law of God" hopes for more. Andrew Jones is correct to fear that contemporary Christians, aware of the sins of Christendom, have gone to the other extreme and despaired about the power of grace among social animals such as ourselves. As Jones puts it, "Charity and Faith might remain ideals, but the ideal is shifted exclusively to an otherworldly realm: to heaven, entrance to which is no longer something that mankind finds through struggle and with the aid of sacramental grace through actual transformation to virtue, but rather something that is or is not given to him regardless of a life lived entirely in the realm of sin, which, with the possibility of supernatural virtue removed, is all there is in this life" (A. W. Jones, *Before Church and State*, 442). The balance between hope and presumption is a delicate one.

the land of Israel."[128] But the Jewish people have never established a perfect polity in the land, nor should they be expected to do so. Scripture mandates humility with regard to the expectations that we have for the exercise of political power on the part of the leaders of God's people.

I agree with David Bentley Hart that no society "has ever more than partially embodied... a political order wholly subordinate to divine charity, to verities higher than any state, and to a justice transcending every government or earthly power"; it follows that in this sense, "Christendom" was "always defective."[129] But Hart adds a clarification of this point, against the temptation to veer from triumphalism to despair. He notes that Christianity, rooted in Israel's Scriptures and in Christ's teachings, has always recognized in principle—and often also recognized in practice—the value of weak and vulnerable persons in the sight of the God who, as Creator and Redeemer, is infinite Love. As a result, the systemic failure of Christians to act charitably and justly toward the Jewish people over the centuries can be judged by the application of the divinely given principles that Christians (and Jews) espouse.

Because of the truth and goodness of the teachings of Christ, *Gaudium et Spes* is quite right that Christianity can, has, and should provide "commitment, direction, and vigor to establish and consolidate the community of men according to the law of God." Yet, in defending the truth of the Church's mediation of divine revelation and its goodness for the world, there is inevitably a temptation to go too far and to argue that what may seem to be Christian political deviations from justice are actually a higher form of obedience to the call of supernatural charity, or that Christians alone possess political wisdom. What is needed, as Novak perceives, is theocentric humility about the earthly work of God's people. The cautionary scriptural accounts of Israel's Davidic kingship are ever instructive.

The long line of the successors of Peter, like the long line of the Davidic kings, contains many who failed miserably. Somehow, even through the more despicable popes, God has managed to sustain the work of handing on the saving realities of faith. Of course, the link that I am drawing between the Davidic kings and the popes has evident limitations. There are

---

128. Sacks, *Arguments*, 186.

129. Hart, *Atheist Delusions*, 213. In Hart's view, Jesus Christ condemned any and all "storing up of earthly wealth"—any and all possessions or private property (Hart, "What Lies Beyond Capitalism?," 36). I disagree with Hart in this regard; for a more nuanced account of Christ's teaching (and early Christian practice) on private property and almsgiving, see G. A. Anderson, *Sin: A History*, 164–88. See also Walzer, "Justice, Justice," 82–84; and the nuances provided by Halbertal, "Addressing the Needs of Others?"

obviously numerous major points of difference, including most notably that Jesus Christ himself fulfilled the Davidic kingship. The popes are not in the line of David, except insofar as, like all Christians, they are adopted sons in the Son. The point rather is that in the new covenant too, God establishes a concrete human authority to lead his people, despite the fact that God well knows the failings of human rulers.

Because such a task is too much for any fallen human being, all popes will fail in the exercise of their temporal or prudential power, although some will fail more spectacularly than others. Von Balthasar comments, "it is *God* who puts the officeholders in the 'last' place," so that the office cannot ultimately be a point of pride; and indeed "[t]he fact that there is an office in the community is certainly a cross for the community too."[130] It is especially painful when a pope fails by acts of persecution against the Jewish people, who should be "beloved" to Christians "as regards election" (Rom 11:28). Von Balthasar observes that during his visit to Jerusalem, Pope Paul VI "spoke about the 'traitor Peter' and made a public confession of Christendom's sins, and particularly the sins of the papacy."[131] Catholics today feel great sadness about the repeated "anti-Semitic failures" endured by the Jewish people for centuries under Catholic and papal rule.[132]

130. Von Balthasar, *Office of Peter*, 355. Von Balthasar remarks along the same lines, "The pope can strive to discharge his office as humbly and as competently as possible—but Paul too was competent and yet had to take the 'last' place. . . . The irreversible duality between the office and the man who holds it, between the dignity of the office and the unworthiness of the officeholder ('Depart from me . . .': 'Henceforth you will be catching men'; Lk 5:8, 10) is bridged by the office itself" (von Balthasar, *Office of Peter*, 354).

131. Von Balthasar, *Office of Peter*, 57.

132. Benedict XVI, "Grace and Vocation," 166. David Novak cautions that something similar could happen in the Jewish world, unless a proper understanding of the Torah is maintained. Responding to Michael Wyschogrod's view that the Torah is given for Israel as God's elect (rather than Israel being elected so as to observe the primordial Torah), Novak explains that "if the people of Israel is the sole raison d'être of the Torah, there is no room left for any higher standard in it by which nationalistic self-interest can be judged. But clearly, the prophets of Israel taught otherwise. In their teaching, the Lord of nature and history judges Israel as he judges the whole world. Thus the standard of divine judgment (*mishpat*) must be seen as transcending what is being judged by it. . . . The practical implication of assuming that the Torah is solely for the sake of affirming the election of Israel is to see no transcendent standard governing Israel's relationships with the nations of the world. The only relationship possible, then, is one where gentiles accept Jewish sovereignty and dominance, be it political or only 'religious.' That does not mean, of course, that this theological stance necessarily leads to political programs where Jews are to dominate non-Jews coercively" (Novak, *Election of Israel*, 247–48). I assume that Wyschogrod would share Novak's concerns. For example, Wyschogrod urges, "Our deepest solidarity is with our fellow human beings because they are created in the image of God (Gen. 1:26). . . . If the result of the election

As I have noted repeatedly in this book, Paul urgently warned the Gentile Christians of Rome not to "boast over the branches" and not to "become proud" vis-à-vis Paul's "fellow Jews" who have not embraced Jesus as the Messiah (Rom 11:14, 18, 20). At the end of his probing of this mysterious development in the covenantal history of God and his people, Paul suggests that somehow the reason is that "God has consigned all men to disobedience, that he may have mercy upon all" (Rom 11:32). As I have made clear above, I believe that this verse can be applied to the centuries of Christian "disobedience" through persecuting the Jewish people.

In his action against the Mortara family, Pope Pius IX fell into this "disobedience," presumably unconsciously. His misdeed does not mean that "the gates of Hades" have prevailed against the Church or that the rock of Peter has broken down (Matt 16:18). As Ratzinger remarks, Catholics do not excuse our disobedience when we insist that "the Church, in spite of it all, has been and still remains an instrument of salvation."[133] God has chosen to work out his eschatological plan for the salvation of Israel and the world not only through the sinless Christ, but also through sinful humans. In praying the penitential psalms (like God's people Israel) and calling upon God's forgiveness in Christ, Catholics confess (in Ratzinger's words) that "our history, too, is of the kind the psalms are describing—a history of rebellion, of sins, of shortcomings."[134]

---

in Abraham is an alienation of Israel from the rest of humanity, then the election has achieved the opposite of its intended result" (Wyschogrod, "Dialogue with Christianity," 236). See also Novak, *Athens and Jerusalem*, 81.

133. Ratzinger, "Church's Guilt," 281. Ratzinger notes that admitting the Catholic Church's stains of sin was complicated at the Reformation by the Protestant charge that the Church had "become an instrument of the Antichrist" and, later, by the Enlightenment focus on "the Crusades, the Inquisition, the burning of witches" ("Church's Guilt," 280–81). Now, however, given the atrocities committed in the twentieth century by people (such as the Nazis, the Communists, and so on) who firmly rejected the Church, the Church can confess the sins that have caused such stain upon the Church without seeming to imply that the world would be better off without God's gifts through the Church. As Ratzinger concludes, "The Church Fathers saw this paradox of guilt and grace as being summed up in the words of the Bride in the Song of Song: '*Nigra sum sed formosa*' (Song 1:4). 'I am stained with sins, yet beautiful'—beautiful through your grace and through what you have done. The Church is able to confess the sins of the past and of the present in all openness and confidence, in the knowledge that evil will never completely ruin her; in the knowledge that the Lord is stronger than our sins and renews his Church again and again" (Ratzinger, "Church's Guilt," 283).

134. Ratzinger, "Church's Guilt," 278. Ratzinger notes that the point of this confession is not to damn earlier Catholics as though we today are better, but rather "to recognize ourselves and to open ourselves up for the purifying of our memory and for our being renewed" ("Church's Guilt," 278). For further discussion, see Štrukelj, "Purification of Memory." Štrukelj points out that "acknowledgment of the failings of

Unwilling to be appropriately critical of Catholic abuses of power (too often against the Jewish people), Catholic triumphalists mirror Jewish triumphalists. Wyschogrod describes the problem from the Jewish side: "Many times, Israel has found it hard to believe that its election is not the fruit of its virtue, that the endless love God bestows on this people is not richly deserved."[135] As Wyschogrod goes on to say, however, "The unfaithfulness of Israel is, however, only part of the truth, though it is the part Israel likes to forget and the nations like to remember. The other part of the truth is Israel's faithfulness.... If it is true that Israel is not worthy of its election, it is also true that God's election is not in vain."[136] This point, too, is true about the Catholic Church.

Pope Pius IX's action stands in sharp contrast with the praise that Cardinal Joseph Ratzinger offered in the year 2000 to "our Jewish brothers, who despite all the difficulties of their history have maintained to this day their faith in this God and bear witness to him before other peoples."[137] In his remarks, Ratzinger bemoaned the presence among Catholics of "anti-Jewish attitudes" that have produced "lamentable acts of violence" over the centuries; and he called for "a sincere intention of overcoming every kind of anti-Jewish attitude" and also for "a greater esteem for this people, the Israelites, a greater love for them" among all Christians.[138] In this work of sincere

---

the Church's sons and daughters in the past can foster renewal and reconciliation in the present" ("Purification of Memory," 92).

135. Wyschogrod, "Israel, the Church, and Election," 181.

136. Wyschogrod, "Israel, the Church, and Election," 181.

137. Ratzinger, "Heritage of Abraham," 271.

138. Ratzinger, "Heritage of Abraham," 272. In his essay "Incarnation and God's Indwelling in Israel," Michael Wyschogrod remarks, "There are those Christians who stress Israel's transgressions and its remoteness from God. There are those who stress the Jewish 'no' to Jesus and Jewish secularism and materialism. And there are those who—without overlooking Israel's failures—sense the overwhelming love with which God relates to this people and who find it possible to participate in that love" (Wyschogrod, "Incarnation and God's Indwelling in Israel," 175). The last named path is the right one. In his "Why Was the Theology of Barth of Interest?," 224, Wyschogrod puts the point more sharply in assessing Barth's theology of Israel: "To see Barth struggling toward the sign that is Israel, to see him fighting against his gentile nature that demands antipathy to the people of election, to see this nature yield to the Word of God and to Barth's love for that Jew whom he loves above all others, is to see the miraculous work of God. The work is incomplete. There remains a dark side, an emphasis on Israel's disobedience which, as we have said, is not the whole truth. But even more important is this final point. Whatever Israel's problems with its God may be, however great Israel's sin and God's wrath may be, the quarrel is a family one, between Israel and God, its father. For strangers to intervene, to point out the shortcomings of the son, to revel in them, to make a theology of them, to feel superior because of them, is a very, very dangerous strategy. However terrible the anger of a father toward his son may be, it is

repentance, it will be important for the Church to reaffirm that Catholics can trust the papacy's role in the faithful handing on of Christ's gifts (teaching, sacraments, and offices), while, at the same time, openly confessing the papacy's grievous sins against the Jewish people, including the Mortaras. One way to do this is to reflect upon parallels with the Davidic kingship, while recognizing the differences as well.

Again, to admit the failures of papal governance is not to deny that God enables the pope and the bishops to hand on divine revelation truthfully, but it is to subject Church leaders' prudential words and deeds to appropriate critique.[139] Guided by Scripture's history of God's people, Catholics can understand better both the failures—prominent among them the treatment of the Jewish people—and the successes of leadership within the inaugurated kingdom of Christ. At many moments of the history of the Church, we can say with Bishop Robert Barron: "Who is so blind not to see that the pressing need of our time is a purification of the Church?"[140] And, equally, we can be assured that God has not abandoned his Church. When we cry out for Christ to have mercy upon us by sending his Spirit to unite us to himself, we will experience "new works of the Spirit" that bring forth new fruits of the gospel.[141] Yet, we must not rush ahead in hopes of avoiding penance. Let

---

an anger that he can afford because underneath it is a love that is a father's. . . . I will therefore be frank. It is not for gentiles to see the sins of Israel. It is not for gentiles to call Israel to its mission, to feel morally superior to it and to play the prophet's role towards it. It is for gentiles [Christians] to love this people if need be blindly, staunchly, not impartially but partially and to trust the instincts of this people whom God has chosen as his own." I agree with Wyschogrod that "strangers" (Christians) should not "revel" in the Jewish people's "shortcomings" or "feel morally superior" or "play the prophet" toward the Jewish people.

139. My perspective accords with Joseph Ratzinger's emphasis on the pope's "personal responsibility," which inevitably means that "the cross is the real *locus* of the vicar of Christ" (Ratzinger, "Papal Primacy," 42). But whereas Ratzinger's focus is the necessity of the obedience of the pope to Christ, my focus is on the inevitability, for fallen human beings, of (conscious or unconscious) disobedience to Christ in the exercise of power, even if such disobedience does not negate the gifts of divine revelation that God has willed to hand on through the Church.

140. Barron, *Letter to a Suffering Church*, 96. Elsewhere Barron comments: "The last twenty-five years have been bad ones for religion in general and Catholicism in particular. The clerical sexual scandals, which have rocked the entire Catholic world, have amounted to a perfect storm, undermining the work of the Church in practically every way. They have lead to an enormous loss of credibility in priestly leadership" (Barron, *Arguing Religion*, 109).

141. Barron, *Letter to a Suffering Church*, 96. Edward Kessler remarks from a Jewish perspective that, for Paul, "[t]he church's election derives from that of Israel, but this does not mean that God's covenant with Israel is broken. Rather, it remains unbroken—irrevocably (Rom 11:29). For Paul, the mystery of Israel is that her rejection and her stumbling do not mean that she ceases to be accepted by God. Rather, Israel allows the

us instead pause a bit, with grievous mourning mingled with confidence in God, and cry out to God: "Restore us to yourself, O Lord, that we may be restored! Renew our days as of old! Or have you utterly rejected us? Are you exceedingly angry with us?" (Lam 5:21–22).

Gentiles to participate in the peoplehood of Israel. . . . Of course, one could argue that if Jews have not kept faith with God, then God has a perfect right to cast them off. It is interesting that Christians who argue this way have not often drawn the same deduction about Christian faithfulness, which has not been a notable characteristic of the last two millennia. Actually, God seems to have a remarkable ability to keep faith with both Christians and Jews, when they have not kept faith with God, a point of which Paul is profoundly aware in Romans 9–11" (Kessler, "'I Am Joseph,'" 70).

Conclusion

On the floor of the Second Vatican Council in 1964, Cardinal Richard Cushing of Boston asked "whether we ought not to confess humbly before the world that Christians, too frequently, have not shown themselves as true Christians, as faithful to Christ, in their relations with their Jewish brothers?"[1] Humbly making this confession today, Christian theologians need to be in an active conversation with our Jewish brethren, just as were the drafters of *Nostra Aetate*.[2] After all, as Mary Boys says, "There is simply no way to talk about Christianity without reference to Judaism."[3]

---

1. F. Anderson, ed., *Council Daybook*, 71, cited in Connelly, *From Enemy to Brother*, 253. According to Connelly, the Council's focus on Romans 9–11 implicity rejected the remainder of the New Testament's teaching about the Jewish people. I do not agree with this claim, but it nonetheless is evident that, as Connelly says, "[w]ithout Romans and its confirmation of God's promises to the Jews as well as the eschatological hope for unity in an unspecified future, the church would not have had a language to talk about the Jews after the Holocaust," given that Romans 9–11 represents "Paul's *only* pastoral letter directly instructing believers about his people" (Connelly, *From Enemy to Brother*, 256).

2. For the influence of Jewish scholars, among them Ernst Ludwig Erlich and Abraham Joshua Heschel, see Connelly, *From Enemy to Brother*, 255–58.

3. Boys, *Has God Only One Blessing?*, 7. Boys expresses concern that even now, "Jewish-Christian dialogue is peripheral in the church," which continues to tell the story "of the loving Christ against legalistic Jews" (*Has God Only One Blessing?*, 8–9). As she recognizes, liberation and feminist theologies frequently contain anti-Jewish caricatures. In addition, she correctly notes that "[t]he presence of Jews when we read the Second (New) Testament often means we are struck by passages that had never before impressed themselves on us. Certain texts then assume a problematic character they had not had before" (Boys, *Has God Only One Blessing?*, 27). In part, of course, this is because the texts bring us face to face with real disagreements (for example, about Jesus' identity). It is difficult to know how to handle such disagreements without either smoothing them out of existence or devolving into the mutual polemics of the past—but Christians learn how to engage the disagreements while eschewing both the polemics and the false irenicism.

CONCLUSION

Yet, the question is how, in Christian dogmatic reflection, one can read Israel's Scriptures in light of Jesus Christ and the Church without either denigrating ongoing Judaism or fatally weakening Christian truth-claims about the Messiah of Israel and his inaugurated kingdom. Bemoaning the influence of early twentieth-century biblical scholars (and Nazi sympathizers) such as Gerhard Kittel and Martin Noth, John Pawlikowski observes that if any Judaism worthy of the name ceased with the rejection of Jesus in the first century—as Kittel and Noth supposed—then it would follow that "the Jewish people and its tradition no longer have a role to play in the Church's theological understanding of Jesus' ministry."[4] The present book has rejected such a viewpoint, in accord with Pawlikowski's contention that "an understanding of Judaism is integral to an authentic interpretation of Christian doctrine as such, not merely for a theology of Christian-Jewish relations."[5]

At the same time, I have made clear that I do not receive post-biblical Jewish texts (Oral Torah) as inspired by God, no more than I would expect Jewish theologians to suppose that the New Testament is inspired by God. I do not hold that (outside Christ) "Judaism is *complete, coherent* and *comprehensive*," although I believe that ongoing Judaism has its own "integrity and meaning."[6] Appreciation for Jewish theology and biblical scholarship

---

4. Pawlikowski, "Reflections on Covenant and Mission," 66. For further discussion see Ericksen, *Theologians under Hitler*. Kittel distinguished sharply between secular Jews and religious Jews, seeing the former as the source of societal decay with the aim of world domination. Unfortunately, his perspective was all too common among Christian theologians and intellectuals (Protestant and Catholic) in the nineteenth and early twentieth centuries. In *Jews and the Christian Imagination*, Stephen R. Haynes demonstrates the connections between how pro- and anti-Nazi theologians conceived of the Jewish people, a point made also by Talmage, *Disputation and Dialogue*. Simon Schoon cites Haynes's book, and he also treats Friedrich-Wilhelm Marquardt's view that "[n]ever again should Christians make Israel the object of their theology. Jews can speak as subjects for themselves and should not be made mute" (Schoon, "'The New People of God,'" 107).

5. Pawlikowski, "Reflections on Covenant and Mission," 88. This does not mean that one cannot formulate authentic Christian doctrine without understanding ongoing Judaism. Obviously, authentic Christian doctrine and authentic Christian faith are quite possible without understanding ongoing Judaism, but the latter understanding is indeed a desideratum.

6. Morgan, "Jewish Perspectives," 5–6. Morgan observes that Christians view Judaism "through a prism of Christian theology. It is seen for what it means to Christianity.... Judaism is viewed as a precursor of the Christian religion" ("Jewish Perspectives," 6). In my view, from a Christian perspective it is impossible not to think about Jesus and about historical Christianity when thinking of ongoing Judaism. The "prism of Christian theology" cannot be removed—and certainly not in a Christian dogmatic project such as the one I have undertaken here. But one can still seek to learn as much as possible about ongoing Judaism as it understands itself, and to try not to distort this

should not lead the Church to reduce, weaken, or apologize for the confession of Jesus as the divine Messiah of Israel and universal Savior. I also consider that the rejection of Jesus by most of the Jewish people, even if mysteriously in accord with God's will (for positive purposes), was a tragic event. After all, if Jesus really was and is the Messiah, then no Jewish person would be glad that the Jewish people as a whole failed to embrace him! It is unhelpful for Christians to imagine that God granted a blessing to the Jewish people by allowing most of them not to recognize the Messiah of Israel. Furthermore, Christians cannot rightly deny that in Christ, Jews and Gentiles together are "a royal priesthood, a holy nation, God's own people" (1 Pet 2:9).[7]

Nevertheless, the notion that God has thereby rejected the ongoing Jewish people, abandoning them and cursing them for the past two millennia, is woefully mistaken! Jesus Christ has fulfilled the covenants and promises. But, as Paul says, "God has not rejected his people" (Rom 11:2)—and not only because some Jews became or today become Christians. For Paul, certainly, God has "hardened" a "part of Israel" (Rom 11:7, 25), but we cannot take this to mean that the past two thousand years of Jewish history are merely a negation. Paul confirms that the Jewish people (meaning those who have not accepted Jesus) have not "stumbled so as to fall" even though he charges them with a "failure" to recognize Jesus (Rom 11:11–12). Indeed, Paul makes clear that he cannot interpret what has happened with full clarity, since God's purpose in this "mystery" is "mercy upon all" and since the Gentile Christians themselves are already showing signs of "boast[ing] over the branches" (Rom 11:18, 25, 32).

We must underscore Paul's sense that here we are in the realm of something "unsearchable" and "inscrutable," in which there is much that we do not understand but with regard to which we can be confident God is working for good (Rom 11:33). Instructed by the Church's Magisterium, I have highlighted Paul's insistence that "the gifts and the call of God are

---

self-understanding in communicating it in a Christian context. Morgan knows that Jews likewise see Christianity through the prism of ongoing Judaism. He states that the members of his synagogue exhibit "powerful preconceptions about Christianity.... These preconceptions were built on cultural and historical constructs, the stories that comprise centuries-old Jewish memory as well as more recent experiences of anti-Semitism including the horrors of the Nazi Holocaust. The past is a scene not of dialogue but rather of disputation, coercion and destructive conflict. Because of these memories and experiences, often quite personal, it is difficult for Jews to see Christianity as a religion with integrity and meaning of its own" ("Jewish Perspectives," 6).

7. For concerns about the Church's claim to be the people of God—concerns that I share regarding "replacement" but not regarding "fulfillment"—see Schoon, "'New People of God.'" See also Brockway et al., *Theology of the Churches*.

irrevocable," despite the universality of human "disobedience" (Rom 11:29, 32). This point should guide us.

It follows that as the Jewish scholar Edward Kessler says—echoing Catholic Magisterial statements from 1974 onward—"Christians need to understand Judaism as a living faith."[8] As Vladimir Solovyov stated in the midst of the anti-Semitic hysteria of the late nineteenth century: "The actions of Jews are not worse than ours, and it is not for us to blame them."[9] Recall that Solovyov denounces Christian failure to act toward the Jewish people in accordance with charity, and he deplores the terrible scapegoating to which Christians have subjected the Jewish people.

On the Way to the Marriage of God and Creation

The basic idea behind my book is the following:

God, having created all things for the purpose of the marriage of God and creation, prepares for this "marriage" through his people Israel. At the center of Israel's Scriptures and Israel's life are the realities of the Creator God, the redemptive exodus, the Torah and the constitution of the nation, the temple and its sacrifices, the promised land, and the Davidic kingship. All these are profoundly instructive for the inauguration of the marriage of God and humanity in Jesus Christ and his eschatological Church.

Christian claims about these aspects of Israel's Scriptures inevitably impinge upon Jewish understandings of the same aspects. Adam Gregerman points out that the problem can be "a Christian casting of Jews in roles they might not recognize or choose" and—worse—the fact that "the Jews' own perceptions are irrelevant in all of these theological narratives."[10] My ac-

---

8. Kessler, "'I Am Joseph,'" 50, citing the Pontifical Commission, "Guidelines," 744: "On the practical level in particular, Christians must therefore strive to acquire a better knowledge of the basic components of the religious tradition of Judaism; they must strive to learn by what essential traits the Jews define themselves in the light of their own religious experience."

9. Solovyov, "Jews and the Christian Problem," 122. He goes on to say that, from a Christian perspective, if the Jews have a problem it is that they do not accept Jesus as the Messiah; but, as he immediately adds, they are perfectly justified in remaining Jews given the scandalous behavior of Christians. As he puts it, "The Jews are certainly not going to accept Christianity so long as it is rejected by the Christians themselves" (Solovyov, "Jews and the Christian Problem," 122–23). He has hopes that eschatologically, Christians will fully unite in one Church (overcoming the scandalous divisions between Christian communities) and a portion of the Jewish people will then join this fully unified Christian Church.

10. Adam Gregerman, "Interpreting the Pain of Others," 456. Gregerman is here writing about how the two popes, in their statements about the Holocaust, have

count of the various aspects of Israel's Scriptures is an explicitly Catholic one. In envisioning the inauguration of the marriage of God and humanity in Christ, I think in terms of the new exodus in Christ, the embodiment of Torah in Christ, the fulfillment of the temple sacrifices in Christ (and the Eucharist). I investigate creation and scriptural ambiguity in light of a Christian understanding of the theo-drama. My presentation of Israel's promised land and Davidic kingship explores Christian failures vis-à-vis the ongoing Jewish people, while also affirming that Christ has fulfilled and transformed the land promise and the kingship.

Nevertheless, despite evident theological differences, I hold that "Jews' own perceptions" (and ongoing covenantal life) are important for contemporary Christian development of the doctrine of Israel. I began this book with a chapter on Jewish-Christian dialogue and continued, in each chapter, to engage Jewish interlocutors at length.[11] In my view, Nancy Duff is cor-

---

Catholic concerns and categories foremost in mind. He remarks with concern, for example, that "the popes' claims of a shared vulnerability of Jews and Catholics/Christians to Nazi hatred, while perhaps grounded in a genuine sense of Nazi peril to both, nonetheless minimized the significance of Jews' experiences. In other contexts, such historical speculation may be appropriate; for example, it is not incorrect to note Nazi hostility to Catholicism. However, by repeatedly highlighting a debatable claim about the Nazis' broader intention to eliminate Christianity eventually, the popes too quickly skirted past what really *did* happen in order to speculate about what *might* have happened. Especially when speaking in places such as a former death camp or a destroyed ghetto, this speculation is inappropriate. Theological claims of a shared threat minimize or obfuscate the actual evidence of different losses" ("Interpreting the Pain of Others," 457). This point seems correct to me.

11. See the helpful explanation of such "dialogue" offered by the Pontifical Commission, "Guidelines," 744: "[S]uch relations as there have been between Jew and Christian have scarcely ever risen above the level of monologue. From now on, real dialogue must be established. Dialogue presupposes that each side wishes to know the other, and wishes to increase and deepen its knowledge of the other. It constitutes a particularly suitable means of favoring a better mutual knowledge and, especially in the case of dialogue between Jews and Christians, of probing the riches of one's own tradition. Dialogue demands respect for the other as he is; above all, respect for his faith and his religious convictions." The Pontifical Commission does not envision a contradiction between dialogue (thus understood) and mission. As the Pontifical Commission says, "In virtue of her divine mission, and her very nature, the Church must preach Jesus Christ to the world"; while at the same time it is crucial that "the witness of Catholics to Jesus Christ" gives no offense to the Jewish people (Pontifical Commission, "Guidelines," 744). For discussion from a Jewish perspective of this document and two later ones produced by the Pontifical Commission, see Kessler, "Jewish-Christian Relations." In "'I Am Joseph'" Kessler notes "dialogue" is not well defined: "A casual conversation between Jews and Christians that may add up to no more than a loose restatement of entrenched theological positions is sometimes claimed to be dialogue. . . . In reality, dialogue consists of a direct meeting of two people and involves a reciprocal exposing of the full religious consciousness of the one with the Other" ("'I Am Joseph,'" 52–53,

rect that Christians who today wish to address the doctrine of Israel "need to have at least a basic knowledge of Jewish traditions and of the history of Christian anti-Semitism and anti-Judaism."[12] Conversations with Jewish thinkers can and should enrich Christian theology, leading not to a capitulation (on either side) but to more understanding of realities of faith (without minimizing the differences). Jonathan Sacks's emphasis on the exodus as the political founding of a nation reminded me that no account of the new exodus makes sense unless it centrally involves the founding of a holy nation. Joseph B. Soloveitchik's concern that halakhah bring the heavenly Torah to earth reminded me that the Christian life is an embodied imitation of Torah incarnate (Christ). Jonathan Klawans's insistence that the temple's animal sacrifices should not be denigrated reminded me that Christian worship has Christ's free self-sacrifice, and our participation in it, at its center. David Novak's appreciation for the Jewish people's covenantal obligation to dwell in the land, along with Novak's resistance to presumptuous links between the founding of the State of Israel and the coming of the eschaton, reminded me that Christian understanding of the inaugurated kingdom must do justice both to the reality of the gifts that God has given and to the gravity of ongoing Christian sinfulness. It is through such theocentric humility that the Church prepares for the glorious coming of the humble Lord—the eschatological wedding feast.

Absent healthy Jewish-Christian dialogue, Christians will be unable to understand the truth of the New Testament without, all too often, consciously or unconsciously carrying forward its first-century polemic against "the Jews."[13] At the same time, Christians—in order to be Christian—must believe in the truth of the revelation contained in the New Testament as handed on in the Church. As Nancy Duff puts it, Christians can and should confess the Church's historical sins, but if a Christian "decides that Christianity is *essentially* anti-Semitic or even anti-Judaic, perhaps that person should consider giving up the Christian faith."[14] Duff points out that discarding core Christian truth-claims on the grounds that they are allegedly anti-Judaic is not a feasible Christian path forward in the dialogue. With Rosemary Radford Ruether's work in view, Duff states: "Such efforts to

---

indebted to Franz Rosenzeig).

12. Duff, "Christians Preparing for Conversation," 245.

13. Edward Kessler asks, "can Christians view Judaism as a valid religion on its own terms (and vice versa)?" ("'I Am Joseph,'" 54). I think the answer is, for both Christians and Jews, yes with qualifications.

14. Duff, "Christians Preparing for Conversation," 246.

redeem the Christian faith from anti-Judaism and anti-Semitism by ripping the heart out of its core beliefs are counterproductive."[15] I very much agree.

The New Testament was largely written by Jews. It was written in an exciting but tense situation, marked by persecution of (mainly Jewish) Christians by their fellow Jews, in which Christian Jews were insisting that the Messiah of Israel had come and had been rejected by the Jewish leaders, leading to his crucifixion by the Romans and, ultimately, to his resurrection and ascension.[16] Edward Kessler notes that the first-century "disputes were serious, vigorous, and often bitter" and "were between Jews, about a Jew, or about Jewish issues (even when they concerned Gentile converts)."[17] Intense debates about the Abrahamic covenant and the status of Gentile converts took place within the early Christian community. The Jewish members of the early Church, along with all the authors of writings that became part of the New Testament, insisted upon reading Israel's Scriptures through a christological lens. Richard Hays comments, "each Evangelist carries forward and renarrates the story of *Israel* through intertextual references to Scripture"; and "each Evangelist draws on scriptural stories and images to interpret the world-changing significance of *Jesus*."[18]

---

15. Duff, "Christians Preparing for Conversation," 246. Duff adds that "a strong relationship between Christianity and Judaism cannot be built on guilt" ("Christians Preparing for Conversation," 246). It seems to me that John Pawlikowski's urging that Christians must "reformulate basic Christian self-understanding in the key areas of Christology and ecclesiology" is well-intentioned but mistaken (Pawlikowski, "Fifty Years of Christian-Jewish Dialogue," 100). Pawlikowski draws attention here to his *Restating the Catholic Church's Relationship*.

16. Kessler comments: "Most of his [Jesus'] contemporaries, of course, had never heard of Jesus" ("'I Am Joseph,'" 63–64). The preaching of the apostles and of the Jews who accepted the gospel caused many more Jews to be aware of Jesus after his death and resurrection than were aware of him during his public ministry.

17. Kessler, "'I Am Joseph,'" 64. In Kessler's view, therefore, "The problem of polemic is magnified greatly when we read the passages as if they were 'Christian' arguments against 'Jews.' To read them this way is to misread them and this misreading contributed to the Christian teaching of contempt. Since the ministry of Jesus can only be understood in the context of first-century Palestinian Judaism, it is essential to emphasize that the concerns of Jesus and his followers are Jewish concerns; that despite the disagreements, much of the polemic reflects the situation in which the Gospels were written when Jews and Jewish followers of Jesus had come to view each other in terms of hostility and disagreement" (Kessler, "'I Am Joseph,'" 64). Kessler thinks this applies to Jesus' conflicts with the Pharisees, whereas I tend to think that these conflicts belong to Jesus' own day. Still, the conflicts of Jesus' day could be emphasized even more in a post-70 context, as Kessler supposes, when Jewish Christians and the successors of the Pharisees were in conflict regarding the future of the Jewish people after the destruction of the Temple.

18. R. B. Hays, *Echoes of Scripture*, 14.

These two moves assisted in developing an understanding of the Church grounded by Israel's Scriptures. But they also made for intense controversy among first-century Jews (Christian and non-Christian), a controversy that carried forward into the largely Gentile Christian communities founded by the apostles. After all, the Gospels are polemically charged works of testimony that compel a choice. Hays concludes: "There is only one reason why the Evangelists' christological interpretation of the Old Testament is not a matter of stealing or twisting Israel's sacred texts: the God to whom the Gospels bear witness, the God incarnate in Jesus, is the same as the God of Abraham, Isaac, and Jacob. Either that is true, or it is not. If it is not, the Gospels are a delusional and pernicious distortion of Israel's story."[19]

Given the radical character of this claim, it is not surprising that the battle lines quickly formed and that the evidence of these battles is present throughout the New Testament. The long history of Christian persecution and denigration of the ongoing Jewish people was in part caused by interpreting the polemical New Testament language and the destruction of the Jerusalem Temple by the Romans as meaning that the ongoing Jewish people are now spiritually dead. This mistaken conclusion needs to be fixed not by Christians denying core truths about Christ and the Church, but by Christians entering more deeply into Christianity's core truths.

For example, in seeking to understand who Christ is, Christians benefit greatly from relearning that we are on exodus with him. Christians need to retrieve the fact that he is our Passover; he is our manna and our rock; his Spirit is the pillar of cloud that guides us; and we are journeying with

---

19. R. B. Hays, *Echoes of Scripture*, 364–65. I have removed the italics. Along lines with which I largely agree, Nancy Duff maintains: "While some people believe no christological hermeneutic should be employed by Christians reading the Old Testament, I disagree. As long as Christians seek to understand an Old Testament text in its specific biblical context and acknowledge that the original writers had no christological notions in mind, and as long as Christians acknowledge that Jewish interpretations of the Hebrew texts carry their own integrity for Judaism, a christological hermeneutic that grows from the unity of both Testaments for Christians is an acceptable hermeneutic" (Duff, "Christians Preparing for Conversation," 249). I demur only in that I think that some of the original writers (such as some of the prophets) did have "christological notions in mind." Rightly, too, Duff underscores that "while 'Hebrew Bible' is the standard language of the academy, it is not the language of Christian or Jewish worship. Many Christian worshippers will not, in fact, know what the term means, any more than they would understand reference to the New Testament as the 'Greek Bible.' Also, because there is no inherent connection between the Hebrew Bible and the New Testament, the two Testaments are unwittingly divorced from one another when 'Hebrew Bible' is employed by Christians. Hence, replacing the Old Testament with 'Hebrew Bible' leads unwittingly to a form of Marcionism by suggesting that the Old Testament belongs *exclusively* to Judaism" (Duff, "Christians Preparing for Conversation," 249).

him to the promised land, the new creation which he has inaugurated and in which he reigns in merciful love and perfect justice at the right hand of the Father. We make this new exodus not merely as individuals seeking relief from suffering and death, though in the risen Christ we have hope for everlasting freedom from suffering and death. Rather, on the new exodus we are formed into a holy nation in Christ, a mystical body in which when one suffers we all suffer and when one rejoices we all rejoice. We are meant to call the whole of humanity into this new exodus journey. The holy nation or inaugurated kingdom has as its purpose the embodiment of the hope and life of Christ's Passover. Yet, we are still sinners and so, as Duff contends (and as the church fathers sometimes affirmed), "[a]ny words of judgment against Israel in the Old Testament should now be considered by Christians as words of judgment against us."[20]

Likewise, in seeking to understand Christ, Christians need to relearn that he is the embodiment of Torah, divine wisdom whose truth is supreme love. The forgetfulness of Torah can lead Christians to imagine the moral life to be simply a matter of getting by in this world. Instead, we are called to bring the heavenly Torah (the risen and ascended Christ) to earth, and to instantiate his cruciform reign—his mercy, justice, and love—in the world. We are called to a profoundly intimate dwelling with God through incarnate Torah (Christ). This means not an ecstatic ethereal spirituality, but rather a concrete, embodied spirituality of daily life, in which each and every thing we do is done in Christ. In the daily routine of grace-filled obedience to Christ, we experience the presence of the God who has covenantally elected us, and we look forward to the eschatological consummation in which incarnate Torah (Christ) will be reflected in a perfectly full way. It is a privilege to live the "burden" of obedience to Christ—a burden that is "light" (Matt 11:30). When we fail in following Christ, we know how to start anew, confident that God has given us a path by which to rise from sinful alienation. In

---

20. Duff, "Christians Preparing for Conversation," 249. She adds: "Furthermore, while the New Testament portrays Pharisees as self-righteous and legalistic, it is historically inaccurate to define all Pharisees with such a description. In the story of Jesus healing on the Sabbath, Christians should know that Jewish tradition has always given priority to saving a life—even animal life—over strict adherence to the law. The only way to preserve the integrity of such texts is to criticize legalistic attitudes among *Christians*, while avoiding caricature of all Pharisees in history, or the charge that contemporary Judaism fits this caricature now" ("Christians Preparing for Conversation," 249–50). I agree with Duff, although I would offer the caveat that Jesus' condemnations of the Pharisees to whom he was speaking should stand, without our applying his condemnations to *all* Pharisees (let alone to ongoing Judaism). After all, it is reasonable—given the presence today of Christian hypocrisy and legalism—to suppose that Jesus' opponents included leading figures who had similar problems to what we see today among Christians.

all of the above we should insist, as Pawlikowski says, that "the Jewishness of Jesus" is "theologically significant for the interpretation of his message today."[21]

To understand Christ, furthermore, we need to appreciate the temple and its animal sacrifices. Otherwise we will not be able to understand the sacrificial significance of his Passover-linked action on the cross. We will certainly not be able to understand his symbolic purposes at the Last Supper or his aims with respect to our eucharistic sharing in his Pasch. Nor will we be able to understand why God placed his name upon the temple and what it means to say that Jesus Christ is the eschatological temple. As Jonathan Klawans shows, it is easy today to assume that the ritual shedding of animal blood was primitive and disgusting, full stop. Learning from Jewish thinkers to value the Temple cult, Christians gain insight into the value of Jesus' work and into the meaning of the eucharistic sacrifice.

Engaging the (Christian) doctrine of Israel, then, deepens our understanding of who the Messiah of Israel is and what it means today to be united to him.[22] It stands to reason that the Messiah would fulfill and embody the

---

21. Pawlikowski, "Reflections on Covenant and Mission," 67. Without affirming it himself, Pawlikowski broaches the notion of "an understanding of the Jewish-Christian relationship within a multi-covenant framework" ("Reflections on Covenant and Mission," 74), with reference to Marcus Braybrooke's reflections in *Jewish-Christian Dialogue*. This seems to me, however, to be a path toward jettisoning the teaching of the New Testament. Pawlikowski argues that the view that Jesus Christ brings the covenants and promises of Israel to fulfillment entails that ongoing Judaism must be "a second class religion" (Pawlikowski, "Reflections on Covenant and Mission," 75). As I have indicated above, I think Pawlikowski is mistaken here. Rejecting the categories of "first class" versus "second class" would negate Judaism itself, since the election of Israel in a certain sense elevated the Jewish people above the nations and their (pagan) worship. Fortunately, Pawlikowski rejects the view that "the Christ Event is only one of several authentic revelations with no particular universal aspect," but he adopts the odd idea that perhaps "the Church can speak about the universal significance of the Christ Event in a way that allows for its articulation through religious symbols not directly connected with Christology" (Reflections on Covenant and Mission," 80, 82). If he solely meant that ongoing Judaism can in certain ways be connected to Jesus Christ without explicitly confessing him, then of course this is true.

22. Stephen Haynes considers the "witness doctrine" to be a myth to which Christians recur: according to this "myth," the Jews, as God's elect people, have a world-historical mission in which their sins lead to dreadful sufferings and their good deeds to salvific advancement. As an example, he offers Charles Journet's "Mysterious Destinies of Israel." Haynes criticizes Journet's essay on the grounds that it is locked into the same mentality that has caused so much trouble already: "Journet's article represents the thinking of a Christian philosemite—one who cherishes Israel because Israel is God's first love. But despite all his moving language about the unique place of Israel in the heart of God, despite his talk of Israel's unique capacity to unveil the mysteries of God's presence in the mundane, Journet remains convinced that Israel will ultimately recognize the Messiah it has rejected. In this way the 'Israel of exile' will someday be

great covenantal aspects of Israel's life: the exodus, the Torah, the temple, the land, the Davidic kingship. The Messiah does this in a transcendent way, so that in inaugurating and sustaining the new exodus, he is himself the destination toward which we are journeying. The Messiah reveals himself to be Torah incarnate in whom believers now fulfill Torah, and the Messiah establishes the eschatological temple and its cult. The Messiah, as the everlasting Davidic king who makes his people just and establishes them in the fullness of life, fulfills and transforms the land promise, now broadened (in accord with biblical and Second Temple texts) to encompass the renewed world and cosmos.

Attention to ongoing Judaism and its spiritual vitality enables Christians to avoid the pitfalls of seeing the new exodus simply as the salvation of the individual believer, or of seeing life in Christ as essentially lawless, or of seeing sacrificial worship as a mere relic. The Christian doctrine of Israel assists Christians in pondering the Israel-shaped work of the Messiah of Israel and the Israel-shaped patterns of life in the Messiah. Christians cannot be Christians without understanding themselves to be the messianic "Israel of God," bearing "the marks of Jesus" (Gal 6:16–17).

Again, however, fulfillment in Christ does not mandate a flip side according to which the Jewish people have "stumbled so as to fall," as though it were not true that "the gifts and the call of God are irrevocable" (Rom 11:11, 29) or as though it were not true that God's plan envisions "mercy upon all" (Rom 11:32). Thus engaging the Christian doctrine of Israel in

---

metamorphosed into the 'Israel of reintegration.' As Barth, Bonhoeffer, and Niemöller did in the 1930s, and as Christian fundamentalists continue to do in the 1990s, Journet proffers a version of Israel's nature and destiny consciously designed to combat Christian anti-Judaism. But because it is so steeped in the language and concepts of the witness-people myth, Journet's attempt to speak anew of Israel is doomed from the outset" (*Jews and the Christian Imagination*, 175). See Bonhoeffer, "Church and the Jewish Question," where Bonhoeffer presumes that the Jewish people remain under a permanent curse due to rejecting and killing Jesus. Haynes calls for Christians "to think of Jews and the Jewish state in utterly normal terms" (Haynes, *Jews and the Christian Imagination*, 178). If by this he means thinking of Jews as human beings, and of the Jewish State of Israel as a nation-state that has normal strengths and weaknesses, then this is indeed necessary! But I fear that by "utterly normal" he means "not God's chosen people." Thus he goes on to criticize Jewish thinkers, whom he finds "are as likely as their Christian counterparts to speak of chosenness, to exult in the miraculous nature of Jewish survival and the redemptive aspects of Jewish restoration in Israel, and to assign theological meaning to the persistence of anti-Semitism" (*Jews and the Christian Imagination*, 179). I agree with Haynes that Christians must avoid making Jews "objects of unnatural expectations, religious projections, and irrational fantasies" (*Jews and the Christian Imagination*, 182), but we disagree about the "witness doctrine" and the "chosen people." For Christian "irrational fantasies" about Jews, see Maccoby, *Judas Iscariot*. Maccoby himself, however, blames a Jew: see Maccoby, *Mythmaker: Paul*.

dialogue with Jewish scholars invites Christians to a more adequate awareness of Christian sinfulness.[23] Over the centuries, the Catholic Church has shown itself to be filled with conscious and unconscious corruption in addition to manifesting the fruits of grace. Just as the Jewish people in the Old Testament (and over their entire history) have been wondrously honest and open about their failings in God's sight, so too the Catholic Church must be similarly honest and open, without despairing about the reality of the eschatological outpouring of the Spirit and inauguration of the kingdom.

I focused my chapters on Israel's promised land and Israel's Davidic kingship on grappling with Christian persecution of the ongoing Jewish people. These chapters did not simply talk about Christian sins, of course. Rather, I offered extensive biblical reflection upon the promised land, its eschatological scope, and the tensions that arose in biblical times vis-à-vis the land. Likewise, I examined the biblical narratives that treat the failures (and successes) of Israel's Davidic kings, despite their covenantally sealed divine mandate to govern the people. Drawing upon the spiritual resources of ongoing Judaism, both chapters also explored David Novak's analysis of religion and power, Zionism and eschatology, and Israel's covenantal obligation to dwell in and govern the land. In both chapters, too, I pressed forward my Israel-shaped doctrinal exploration of Christ and the Church. For Catholics, the promised land is the eschatological new creation rather than any territory on earth, because Christ has established his reign (in sacrificial love) over the whole earth. Similarly, for Catholics Jesus is the eschatological Davidic king foretold by the prophets.

Nevertheless, my chapter on Israel's promised land had centrally in view Christian "boast[ing] over the branches" (Rom 11:18). In addition to the well-known Catholic taunting of the Jewish people as accursed Christ-killers and permanently landless wanderers, I drew attention to the fact that little more than a century ago, in the decades leading up to the Holocaust, influential Catholic newspapers closely linked to the Vatican were proclaiming the libel that the Jewish people require the blood of a Christian boy in order to make their Passover bread. What a terrible sin on the part of Catholics! In light of Catholic obscuring of the face of Christ vis-à-vis the Jewish people, Catholics cannot expect the Jewish people as whole to

---

23. For emphasis that Christians must always conceive of ourselves in relation to the Jewish people—and therefore with awareness of the history of Christian failure to love that people—see Littell, *Crucifixion of the Jews*. The opposite perspective is taken by A. Roy Eckhardt, who argues that the only way forward is for Christians to cease entirely from offering theologies of Judaism or Israelologies. See Eckhardt, *Jews and Christians*. Stephen Haynes discusses the approaches of Eckhardt and Littell in the conclusion to his *Jews and the Christian Imagination*.

perceive Jesus' identity as the Messiah ("invincible ignorance"). Thus Catholics should support the Jewish people in obeying their original covenantal obligations, which have been fulfilled and transformed by Christ but have not been revoked. Engaging the doctrine of Israel's promised land is an occasion not simply for Christians to ponder the blessing of Christ's inauguration of the new creation. It is also an occasion for Christians to offer support to the State of Israel (within a hoped-for two-state framework) as the mode by which the Jewish people, for so many centuries taunted by Christians as permanent wanderers, obey their unrevoked (even if, in Christ, fulfilled and transformed) covenantal obligations to the living God.[24]

I made similar points in my chapter on Israel's Davidic kingship, which had centrally in view the treatment of the Jewish people by the popes and, specifically, the treatment of Edgardo Mortara and his family by Pope Pius IX. Attempts to defend this treatment end up praising actions that, if done by non-Catholics to a Catholic family, would immediately be recognized as unjust and deplorable. It violates natural justice—and obscures Christian witness to supernatural charity—to remove a young boy from his loving family simply because a servant claims to have baptized him. When one looks deeper, the injustice is amplified by plausible testimony that the servant actually never baptized him, and the injustice is further amplified by anti-Semitic language that the adult Edgardo Mortara, as a Catholic priest, considered suitable to employ in telling his own story, even if we still lack an accurate English or Italian version of this story and many of Mortara's claims are contradicted by evidence set forth in contemporaneous testimony.

In my view, the conjunction of religion and power needs to be examined from a perspective shaped by the narratives about Israel's Davidic kings. This will assist Catholics in refusing to go to either of two extremes: blindly approving everything done by popes, on the one hand, or renouncing the truth of the Catholic mediation of the salvific gospel through solemn teaching, on the other. David Novak's measured assessment of the Jewish state can help Catholics achieve a balance in thinking about the conjunction of (Catholic) religion and power, granted the theological distinctives and assurances that pertain to the papacy.

24. Kessler is correct that as a practical matter, "it has been easier for Christians to condemn anti-Semitism as a misunderstanding of Christian teaching than to come to terms with the reestablishment of the Jewish state" ("'I Am Joseph,'" 65). In part, he suggests, this is because Catholics are used to the image of the Jewish people as a suffering minority. Kessler also observes, "In the first decade of the 21st century, relations between the Holy See and the state of Israel have become strained, epitomized by the lack of agreement over juridical and tax issues. Occasional bilateral talks have failed to produce agreement over 'the fundamental accord' that has been sought since 1993" ("'I Am Joseph,'" 67).

God is the one of whom it can be said, "The heavens are yours, the earth also is yours; the world and all that is in it, you have founded them. The north and the south, you have created them" (Ps 89:11–12). Isaiah is not offering a biblically incongruous thought when he states, "Have you not known? Have you not heard? The Lord is the everlasting God, the creator of the ends of the earth" (Isa 40:28). Yet, why is it that for long stretches of the Torah, God's standing as Creator is not even mentioned? When God names himself to Moses at the burning bush, it might seem that this would be an opportune time to proclaim himself the Creator of all things. But God does not mention it; instead he names himself solely "I am who I am" and "the God of your fathers, the God of Abraham, the God of Isaac, and the God of Jacob" (Exod 3:14–15).[25] Likewise, when God introduces himself to Abraham, he does not name himself as Creator, and indeed he does not name himself at all. We read simply: "Now the Lord said to Abram, 'Go from your country and your kindred and your father's house to the land that I will show you'" (Gen 12:1).

In giving the Decalogue, God mentions his standing as Creator when explaining why Israel must keep the Sabbath: "for in six days the Lord made heaven and earth, the sea, and all that is in them, and rested on the seventh day; therefore the Lord blessed the sabbath day and hallowed it" (Exod 20:11). But even here, God's speaking the Ten Commandments begins by God naming himself as the one who brought the people "out of the land of Egypt, out of the house of bondage" (Exod 20:2), rather than by naming himself as the Creator who *also* is the Redeemer from Egyptian slavery.

Undoubtedly, God is the Creator not merely in the sense that God molds all things, but in the sense that the finite being of each and every existing thing derives utterly from God and is sustained in existence by the Creator God. Without this backdrop, God could not properly be understood as the One who miraculously accomplishes the exodus, or who gives Israel the Torah, temple, land, and kingship. Why then does Genesis 1 contain ambiguity on this central doctrinal point? My second chapter argued that the answer is that the Bible intends not only to provide true propositional judgments about divine realities, although it does provide such judgments. Instead, through the biblical word, God invites Scripture's hearers or readers into an ongoing theo-drama in which the hearers or readers are active participants. As the rabbis (and church fathers) proposed, the Bible contains ambiguities in order to stimulate mystical and metaphysical pondering, in the awareness that we must strive to know truth about God from within a relationship with God and from within God's people. Biblical language

---

25. See Saner, *"Too Much to Grasp."*

invites us into the depths of the divine speech, awakening us to the presence of a divine "language" in every creature, and awakening us to the unfathomable depths of the God who speaks all things into existence.

Envoi: Psalms and Providence

According to David Novak, God's providence is a constant and all-encompassing reality. Novak considers it is axiomatic that "[n]othing just happens, even though we humans do not know why most events in our world occur the way they do. That is because God is continually concerned with all His creation, for which God freely assumes responsibility, even for intervening in nature when needed."[26] Of course, this does not mean that all that happens is good, let alone that all that happens is what God would prefer to take place. Such a view could not account for such horrors as the Holocaust.

As originally conceived, the present book contained a chapter on divine providence with a focus on the Psalms. The Reformed theologian David Fergusson rightly remarks: "Among the books of the Bible, the Psalter offers the richest reflections on providence."[27] On the one hand, the Psalter confesses God's providential power, trustworthiness, and consistency. On the other hand, the Psalter gives a significant place to the conflicts that God permits and against which God strives. Regarding divine providence, therefore, the book of Psalms contains an "unresolved tension" and "resist[s] any simple systematization."[28] Ellen Charry notes that there is a "theodicy

26. Novak, *Athens and Jerusalem*, 60. For concerns, see Fergusson, *Providence of God*, 7. See also my response to Fergusson's book, forthcoming in *International Journal of Systematic Theology*.

27. Fergusson, *Providence of God*, 26. According to Réginald Garrigou-Lagrange, OP, "*The infallibility of providence* touching everything that happens, including even our present and future free actions, is stressed in the Old Testament no less clearly than its universal extent" (Garrigou-Lagrange, *Providence*, 164). Garrigou-Lagrange cites numerous psalms in defense of this claim, and in my view he is correct. But, as Fergusson says, there are also numerous psalms that indicate that God is engaged in a struggle and does not always have the upper hand. These latter psalms do not thereby reject God's absolute providence, which in fact they often affirm, but nonetheless their perspective is quite different. For discussion of the perception of divine providence in Christian experience, see Elliott, *Providence Perceived*.

28. Fergusson, *Providence of God*, 22, 27. For an edited volume that includes essays denouncing the God of Israel (and the God of Jesus Christ) as wicked and unreliable alongside essays affirming the goodness and justice of the God of Israel (and the God of Jesus Christ), see Bergmann et al., eds., *Divine Evil?* Each of the essays has a response from scholar who differs sharply from the author of the essay. I note that scriptural complexity ultimately directs us to questions of canon and community as decisive for how we understand and integrate scriptural texts. Helpful in this regard is Christopher

question at the heart of the Psalter," given that many psalms "contend with grief, humiliation, and God-abandonment."[29] Yet it is also the case that "the Psalter promotes the notion that the God of Israel is the Lord of the universe" and strongly affirms "the power and goodness of God."[30]

I had to excise my planned chapter on providence due to the fact that my book had become too lengthy. Providentially, therefore, I will bring my Christian Israelology to a close by drawing upon the Psalms as testimony to the divine providence that unfolds in creation, exodus, Torah, temple, land, and kingship—and thus in Christ and his Church. Put simply, how can the Creator God's sovereign power over history, so evident in the above realities, be squared with so much agony, including the disastrous relationship of Christians over the centuries to the ongoing Jewish people?

The Psalms testify firmly to the sovereignty of God. It is no wonder that Jews, in times of trouble, turn to the comfort of reciting the psalms[31]—and that Christians do the same. Consider, for example, Psalm 61:3's testimony that "you [God] are my refuge, a strong tower against the enemy." According to numerous psalms, God has been, is, and will be the Redeemer. Psalm 66:2 urges the people, "Say to God, 'How awesome are your deeds! So great is your power that your enemies cringe before you'"; and the psalm continues by bearing witness: "Come and see what God has done: he is awesome in his deeds among men" (Psalm 66:5). Over and over again, we find the strongest insistence that God reigns even now. An eminent example is Psalm 97:1–5, "The Lord reigns; let the earth rejoice; let the many islands be glad! Clouds and thick darkness are round about him; righteousness and justice are the foundation of his throne. Fire goes before him, and burns up his adversaries round about. . . . The mountains melt like wax before the Lord, before the Lord of all the earth." God is "from everlasting," with an everlasting throne

---

Seitz's observation in his "Canon and Conquest," 299–300: "To read the Bible as a container of sentences and paragraphs, to be held up for approval or justification, is to raise questions of hermeneutics and the consideration of canonical form. It is also to read the Bible independently of those communities which recognized its canonical form (as Tanak or Christian scripture) as ingredient in the proper handling of its complex world of discourse. So from a Biblical Theological perspective, this volume [*Divine Evil?*] raises the question of *what kind of Bible* is being proposed for discussion." See also, for a similar point, Barron, *Priority of Christ*, 47.

29. Charry, *Psalms 1–50*, xviii–xix.

30. Charry, *Psalms 1–50*, xix, xxiv. For helpful overviews of modern historical-critical reflection upon the Psalms and the contributions that such reflection has made to understanding the Psalms, see Wenham, *Psalms as Torah*, chapter 2; Hunter, *Introduction to the Psalms*.

31. See Magonet, *Rabbi Reads the Psalms*, 6–7.

(Ps 94:2).[32] His power cannot be challenged even in the slightest, when he wills to exercise it.

According to many psalms—whose perspective I strongly affirm—we are entirely in the hand of the Creator God, due to the awe-inspiring power God possesses. Psalm 95:6-7 exhorts, "O come, let us worship and bow down, let us kneel before the Lord, our Maker! For he is our God, and we are the people of his pasture, and the sheep of his hand" (cf. Ps 100:3).[33] The sea often is an image of chaos in Scripture. But God does not merely control and mark off the bounds of the sea; rather, "The sea is his, for he made it; for his hands formed the dry land" (Ps 95:5). God sees everything and knows everything (Ps 94:7-11). As Psalm 103:19 says, "The Lord has established his throne in the heavens, and his kingdom rules over all." As Patrick Miller remarks, furthermore, "That Psalm 104 is a self-conscious elaboration of the basic claim 'Maker of heaven and earth' is evident from the start."[34]

32. For God's relation to time according to the Psalms, see P. D. Miller, *Lord of the Psalms*, 44-45. Miller argues that in the Psalms, "what distinguishes God from us relative to temporality and eternity is the perdurance of the experience of God's love and faithfulness as well as God's rule of this finite world. . . . While God's eternity may be categorically different from our temporality, it is at the same time the ground for the security of human temporality that God's love and faithfulness shall never end because God never ends and God's rule is for all time" (*Lord of the Psalms*, 45). By contrast, for an argument in favor of divine temporality see Novak, *Election of Israel*. Against Judah Halevi and Moses Maimonides, Novak states: "both God and Israel are temporally related. The difference between them is that Israel, like any creature, is ultimately engulfed by death as the personal dissolution that time entails for her, whereas God is not engulfed by it. Thus the time of Israel as a creature is limited (finite); the time of God as creator is unlimited (infinite). . . . In Biblical-Rabbinic Judaism, it makes no sense to speak of eternity. Even God is not eternal, but, rather, *everlasting*. An *eternal* God, in the classical philosophic sense of unchanging and hence unresponsive Being, bears little or no resemblance to the creator God who associates himself with Abraham, Isaac, and Jacob and their progeny, who, in the unforgettable characterization of my late revered teacher Abraham Joshua Heschel, is a 'God of pathos'" (Novak, *Election of Israel*, 201-3). For a critique of Heschel (and thus also of Novak) on this point, see Weinandy, *Does God Suffer?*, 64-68.

33. As Zenger says, "Psalm 100 shares with Psalms 93, 95*, 96, 98, 99 the perspective that YHWH's reign over the world can be experienced in the present" (Zenger, "God of Israel's Reign," 174).

34. P. D. Miller, *Lord of the Psalms*, 47. Miller adds, "Psalm 104 is a theological grounding of the large claim of Genesis 1 that heaven and earth, everything that God had made, is good indeed *very good*. In Genesis 1 this point is underscored as the evaluating judgment of the Creator. In Psalm 104, the goodness of creation is elaborated from beginning to end. The outcome is joy in the creation (vv. 15, 31, 34) and praise of the Creator (vv. 1, 24, 33-35)" (*Lord of the Psalms*, 49; see also 97-98). Moreover, Psalm 104 closely links creation and providence: "What is very clear from Psalm 104 is that there is little distinction between creation and providence in that God's creative work continues in the provision of water and grass and food and plants" (*Lord of the Psalms*,

CONCLUSION

In his powerful providence, God is the only hope of sinners. The psalmist proclaims in this regard, "O Israel, hope in the Lord! For with the Lord there is mercy, and with him is plenteous redemption" (Ps 130:7). If God forgives Israel or forgives the sins of one of his people, then these sins will truly be washed away. Hope in God does not disappoint. The fact is that "[w]hatever the Lord pleases he does, in heaven and on earth, in the seas and all deeps" (Ps 135:6). All things belong to his providential plan, his "book" of history. The psalmist maintains, "Your eyes beheld my unformed substance [in the womb]; in your book were written, every one of them, the days that were formed for me, when as yet there was none of them" (Ps 139:16). Even before we speak (or think) a word, God knows what it is going to be (Ps 139:2-4). Can evildoers, even powerful rulers, disrupt God's providential plan? Certainly not! In fact, threats from wicked kings cause God no worry at all, since God will accomplish his plan no matter what wicked humans might try: "He who sits in the heavens laughs; the Lord has them in derision" (Ps 2:4).

All the above is true. And yet, as Jews and Christians know, this same God is shockingly permissive of trials. This is the "weak" God, the God who permits so many horrific and tragic things to happen. For instance, Psalm 10 begins, "Why do you stand afar off, O Lord? Why do you hide yourself in times of trouble?" (10:1). God allows his righteous people to despair or at least seemingly to have good reason to despair, while the wicked exult. Psalm 10:10 reports, "The hapless is crushed [by the wicked], sinks down, and falls by his might." The psalmist comes near to giving up hope that God will ever come to his aid. He asks in deepest agony, "How long, O Lord? Will you forget me for ever?" (Ps 13:1).

In Psalm 44, the extremity of the situation facing God's people is revealed. The psalmist complains to God: "You have made us like sheep for slaughter, and have scattered us among the nations. You have sold your

---

51). Jon D. Levenson similarly emphasizes the connection between Genesis 1 and Psalm 104. After pointing out that Psalm 104:26 is the only biblical text that explicitly proclaims God to be the creator of Leviathan, Levenson observes that Genesis 1 goes a step further and mentions only the creation of the sea creatures rather than mentioning Leviathan per se. In addition, Levenson finds other parallels: "Just as God's first creative act in Genesis is the creation of light, so does Psalm 104 begin with the image of YHWH majestically donning his 'robe of light.' As God in Genesis 1:6 next makes an expanse or firmament 'in the midst of the water, that it may separate water from water,' that is, the sky, which was thought to intervene between the supernal and the terrestrial waters, so does YHWH in Psalm 104:3-4 'set the rafters on His lofts in the waters' and use the clouds as his chariot" (Levenson, *Creation*, 55). Psalm 104 concludes, "Let sinners be consumed from the earth, and let the wicked be no more!" (104:35). Levenson takes this as an indication that Psalm 104's "bright and cheerful vision of the created order . . . is not fully in force so long as people resist the creator's will" (*Creation*, 58).

people for a trifle, demanding no high price for them. You have made us the taunt of our neighbors" (Ps 44:11–13). These are strong charges indeed, but they become even stronger. The psalmist insists that, in fact, none of this suffering has come about due to Israel's sinful actions. The suffering has come about simply because God has not been present. The psalmist says, "All this has come upon us, though we have not forgotten you or been false to your covenant. Our heart has not turned back, nor have our steps departed from your way" (Ps 44:17–18).

Why has God permitted such suffering, which the psalmist compares to being attacked by jackals and to being submerged in total darkness? Here indeed is the weak God, weak in the sense of mysteriously "abandoning" his innocent people for a purpose that is humanly inscrutable. The psalmist can only conclude that "for your sake we are slain all the day long, and accounted as sheep for the slaughter" (Ps 44:22). Psalm 55 provides yet another example. The psalmist speaks about being overcome by trouble, being in anguish, experiencing overpowering "terrors of death," and wishing that he had "wings like a dove" so as to be able to flee from his troubles (Ps 55:4, 6). Again, in Psalm 59 the psalmist declares himself innocent of any sin but bemoans that he is under mortal threat from "bloodthirsty men" (Ps 59:2). He asks plaintively why God is not bothering to help him.

The "weakness" of God appears still more vividly in Psalm 74's description of the destruction of the temple, especially since God is also presented by this psalm as the sovereign Creator.[35] After a somewhat half-hearted remark about God's anger (implying that the people have sinned), the main section of the psalm devotes itself to a heartbreaking account of what God has caused or allowed to be done. Israel is the "sheep of [God's] pasture" and God has made Israel his "heritage" and Zion his dwelling place (Ps 74:1–2). What has happened to this people, then, is hardly comprehensible. Gentile idolaters, the enemies of God, have conquered the temple, chopped to pieces its wooden beams, and burned it to the ground.

Psalm 77 reveals a particular depth of despair. The psalmist actually raises the possibility that God's strength has ended forever and God will never again come to his people's aid. Whether or not the people's sins are the reason, the psalmist has reached the end of his rope. He asks, "Will the Lord spurn for ever, and never again be favorable?" (Ps 77:7). Psalm 83 sounds an equally urgent note. The psalmist warns God that the enemies of God are "lay[ing] crafty plans against your people," genocidal plans: "'Come, let us wipe them out as a nation; let the name of Israel be remembered no more!'"

---

35. For discussion see Batto, "Divine Sovereign," 117.

(Ps 83:3–4).[36] Obviously, this would be horrific, an unthinkable defeat of God.

In Psalm 89, which contains some of the most forceful praises of God's absolute power and faithfulness to Israel, the psalmist also bitterly laments that God has hidden himself and abandoned his people. The psalmist even charges God with the great sin of covenant infidelity: "You have renounced the covenant with your servant; you have defiled his crown in the dust. You have breached all his walls; you have laid his strongholds in ruins. . . . You have removed the scepter from his hand, and cast his throne to the ground" (Ps 89:39–40, 44).

In sum, in the Psalms we find both amazing testimony to God's absolute providential power, and deeply troubling testimony to God's de facto providential "weakness." Arguably, we can perceive both God's sovereignty and God's seeming weakness in the post-biblical histories of Jews and Christians.

Catholics rejoice in the lives of countless saints around the world and in the reality of the charity spread by Christ and his Spirit in and through the Church. In the words and deeds of such figures as Ignatius of Antioch, Athanasius, Macrina, Monica, and through the centuries, God's sovereign care for his messianic people in Christ is clearly displayed, even (and especially) in their configuration to the death of Christ. Yet at the same time Catholics have been such sinners! Surely, the gravest Christian sin—which quickly became a "blindness"—has been "boast[ing] over the branches" (Rom 11:18), that is, over ongoing Judaism.[37] God did not cause this failure, but how could God have allowed it?

---

36. Regarding the silence of God faced by the psalmist (and the people of Israel) as described in Psalm 83, see Nicholas Wolterstorff, "Silence of the God Who Speaks," 215. Wolterstorff argues that the fall and its aftermath signal that "things have gone awry with reference to God's creating and maintaining intent," in other words, God's providence ("Silence of the God Who Speaks," 222). He rightly warns (against what he terms "soul-making theodicy"), "The God who kills children for the sake of the chastisement or spiritual growth of parents, the God who kills millions of Jews for the sake of the chastisement or spiritual growth of the survivors, is a grotesque parody of the biblical God. And should someone suggest that the early death of the child represents the punishment of the child for the child's own sins, and that the early death of the victims of the Holocaust represents the punishment of the victims for the victims' own sins, we must, emboldened by God's own book of Job, reject this suggestion as blasphemy against the justice of God and grotesquely libelous of those we loved" ("Silence of the God Who Speaks," 223). Wolterstorff concludes that in the face of "untimely death and . . . unredemptive suffering," we can only learn from "the biblical silence of the biblical God. We shall have to live in the silence" ("Silence of the God Who Speaks," 227). See also Wolterstorff's *Lament for a Son*.

37. Björn Krondorfer testifies to a situation that I too have lived through. In the mid-1990s, when I was a doctoral student, Jewish-Christian relations were still a hot

Christians cannot solve this puzzle, even as we affirm both God's sovereignty and God's seeming "weakness." Rather, Christians must engage this puzzle as active participants in the theo-drama in which God has placed us, whose dramatic form is self-surrendering love.[38] The new exodus is our corporate journey in Christ who nourishes us as the Passover lamb and whose Spirit guides us; but the presence of Christ and the Spirit does not make it an easy journey, because we still have to face the trials of life and the temptations of "Egypt," and we still have to be configured to incarnate Torah in self-sacrificial love, which requires faith, repentance, and frequently starting anew. The author of the Letter to the Hebrews exhorts us: "Therefore lift your drooping hands and strengthen your weak knees, and make straight paths for your feet, so that what is lame may not be put out of joint but rather be healed" (Heb 12:12-13). We are lame, drooping, weak, and in need of healing.

If so, then what does it mean to say that Jesus (and his "body" the Church) is the eschatological temple, filled with the presence of the Spirit and united to God through his perfect sacrifice of atonement and thanksgiving? It does not mean that Christians are yet what we should be (the consummated kingdom), but rather it means that God in Christ has provided the ongoing healing and transformation that we need (the inaugurated kingdom). As noted above, Hebrews urges Christians to recall that we "have come to Mount Zion and to the city of the living God, the heavenly Jerusalem, and to innumerable angels in festal gathering, and to innumerable angels in festal gathering, . . . and to Jesus, the mediator of a new covenant, and to the sprinkled blood that speaks more graciously than the blood of Abel" (Heb 12:22-24). We do not make the new exodus journey alone; we

---

topic; whereas today the topic is somewhat passé. Krondorfer puts it this way, based on his experience with his students: "their interests have shifted to other issues of cultural and religious diversity. They see themselves as spiritual seekers, not committed to particularity. . . . Also, since the events of 9/11, focus has shifted to Muslim-Christian and Muslim-Jewish dialogue and, more generally, to conversations with the Asian religious traditions," in which truth-claims are more fluid (Krondorfer, "Art of Dialogue," at 305). In the end, Krondorfer strives to build dialogue on the basis of social justice concerns: for example, he states, "In encounters with Palestinians, I can testify to the kind of responsibility I have toward Jewish Israelis because of my link to the Holocaust without having to expect that Palestinians will share my view or that, therefore, the value of the Naqba is diminished" ("Art of Dialogue," 316). But this kind of Jewish-Christian dialogue cannot sustain the theological truth-claims needed to keep the dialogue relevant. Among liberal Christians, it has therefore been replaced by other social justice issues, other religious identities, and other dialogues. The future of Jewish-Christian dialogue, from the Christian side, will be among doctrinally committed evangelicals and Catholics: see for example Phelan, *Separated Siblings*; and Mayfield, *Unto Us a Child Is Born*.

38. This is a central theme of my *Achievement of von Balthasar*.

CONCLUSION

make it while already caught up into the new temple as "living stones" (1 Pet 2:5) and while sharing sacramentally in Christ's saving sacrifice. As Torah incarnate, Christ reveals God's law to be embodied love and he reveals the divine lawgiver to be infinite mercy, humility, and love, enabling us to cleave to the One who perfectly fulfills Torah for us. Christ is the divine Davidic king, "the great shepherd of the sheep" (Heb 13:20), who leads us to "the city which is to come" (Heb 13:14).

Does this claim ease the scandal of Christian sins against the Jewish people? On the contrary, it intensifies the scandal. Learning about the long and grim history of Christian persecution of the Jewish people—a history that many Christians do not know, but that Jews know well—Christians come face to face with our need for Christ: we are truly sinners in need of the Savior. In fact, it is only when we are on our knees asking for God's mercy that we can understand how it might be that "neither death, nor life, nor angels, nor principalities, nor things present, nor things to come, nor powers, nor height, nor depth, nor anything else in all creation, will be able to separate us from the love of God in Christ Jesus our Lord" (Rom 8:38-39). Christ's love is a love for sinners—not to encourage us to remain sinners, but to call us to his reconciling and redeeming love, to a union so intimate with the holy Trinity as to be marital.[39]

---

39. See Jon D. Levenson, *Love of God*. For Levenson, God is king over the whole cosmos, and his covenantal partner (Israel) pledges an exclusive relationship with him. Within this exclusive relationship, covenantal fidelity is shown by means of acts of love, including obeying his commandments and worshipping him alone. Since each commandment offers an opportunity to express love, every aspect of Israel's life is marked by this covenantal relationship. Love is embodied in deeds, rather than being merely feeling or eros; love involves fidelity. Admittedly, the fullness of love (given human sinfulness) will require God's eschatological intervention, but that is no reason for not striving to observe Torah now. The practice of Torah, moreover, stimulates interior love of God. Levenson adds that the Abrahamic covenant is gratuitous, sheer grace without stipulations. The Mosaic covenant comes with stipulations—reflecting the mature person's awareness that the gift of life bears moral obligations with it. When Israel accepts God's Torah at Sinai—admittedly after briefly giving up on Moses and God—the two covenants come together in "love made practical, reliable, reciprocal, and socially responsible through law, divine law observed in love" (*Love of God*, 57). Levenson's understanding of history—and thus of Israel and the providence of God—opens up to a theology of martyrdom. Discussing a midrash from *Siphre Deuteronomy* 32, Levenson comments that people cannot cleave to their own life as the highest good, but must instead "subordinate their own instincts to the love of God, redirecting themselves and their assets to his service" (*Love of God*, 73). On this view, history can have horrors without God's providence and God's covenantal love necessarily being at stake. In the midst of the horrors, the Jewish people can act with faithful covenantal love for God, and this is in fact the purpose of life. At the same time, the people also have to face their own sinfulness, rather than (as Levenson puts it) "luxuriat[ing] in the comforting thought, 'God loves me'" (*Love of God*, 113).

In preparation for the marriage feast of the Lamb, let Christians today join the apostles who, despite having betrayed and abandoned the Lord prior to his crucifixion, receive instruction and comfort from the risen Christ. The apostles urge the risen Christ to bring about the fullness of the kingdom immediately, but he reminds them: "It is not for you to know times or seasons which the Father has fixed by his own authority" (Acts 1:7). With their typical eagerness to bypass the cross, the apostles had been hoping to reign immediately with Jesus Christ! Instead he calls them to follow his own path, which is the path of the cross. To sustain them on this new exodus in which, while remaining imperfect, they will be configured to his cruciform self-offering in love, he pours out the Holy Spirit upon them.

What does the Holy Spirit do? Configuring us to the cross, the Spirit calls us into resurrection life, a life of joy and gratitude for the mercies of God. All at once, the cross no longer becomes a path of fear. It becomes a path of love, a path of mercy, a path of service. It becomes a path, God willing, of learning from others in humility--including from Jewish brethren who gift us with their friendship and wisdom. For Christians, the cross is the place of our new exodus, our participation in incarnate Torah and in the eschatological temple. It is a path of reconciliation, of marital intimacy with the Creator, of divine praise. We can say with Paul: "far be it from me to glory except in the cross of our Lord Jesus Christ" (Gal 6:14).

"Praise the Lord! Praise God in his sanctuary; praise him in his mighty firmament! Praise him for his mighty deeds; praise him according to his exceeding greatness!" (Ps 150:1-2). "And they worshiped him, and returned to Jerusalem with great joy, and were continually in the temple blessing God" (Luke 24:52).

Bibliography

Adam, Andrew K. M. "Matthew's Readers, Ideology, and Power." In *SBL 1994 Seminar Papers*, edited by E. H. Lovering Jr., 435–49. Atlanta: Scholars, 1994.
Adam, Karl. "Deutsches Volkstum und katholisches Christentum." *Theologische Quartalschrift* 114, no. 1 (1933) 40–63.
———. "Jesus, der Christus und wir Deutsche." *Wissenschaft und Weisheit* 10 (1943) 73–103.
Adwan, Sami, Dan Bar-On, and Eyal Naveh, eds. *Side by Side: Parallel Histories of Israel-Palestine*. New York: New, 2012.
Aguzzi, Steven D. "One Step Forward, Two Steps Back: Supersessionism and Pope Benedict XVI's Eschatological Ecclesiology Concerning Israel and the Jewish People." *Journal of Ecumenical Studies* 49, no. 4 (September 2014) 601–12.
Aitken, James K. "What Does Christianity in Jewish Terms Mean?" In *Challenges in Jewish-Christian Relations*, edited by James K. Aitken and Edward Kessler, 203–17. New York: Paulist, 2006.
Albright, William F., and C. S. Mann. *Matthew*. Garden City, NY: Doubleday, 1971.
Alexander IV. "*In sacro generali*." September 3, 1258. In Solomon Grayzel, *The Church and the Jews in the XIIIth Century*, vol. 2: *1254–1314*, edited by Kenneth R. Stow, 64–66. New York: The Jewish Theological Seminary of America, 1989.
Alison, James. *The Joy of Being Wrong: Original Sin through Easter Eyes*. New York: Crossroad, 1998.
Allen, John L., Jr. "Thinking Straight about Israel, the Jews, and the Archbishop." *National Catholic Reporter Online*, October 27, 2010. www.ncronline.org.
Almog, Shmuel, ed. *Antisemitism through the Ages*. Translated by Nathan H. Reisner. Oxford: Pergamon, 1988.
Anderson, Bernhard W. *Creation versus Chaos: The Reinterpretation of the Mythical Symbolism in the Bible*. Philadelphia: Fortress, 1987.
Anderson, Floyd, ed. *Council Daybook, Vatican II, Session 3: Sept. 14 to Nov. 21, 1964*. Washington, DC: National Catholic Welfare Conference, 1965.
Anderson, Gary A. *Christian Doctrine and the Old Testament: Theology in the Service of Biblical Exegesis*. Grand Rapids: Baker Academic, 2017.
———. "*Creatio ex nihilo* and the Bible." In *Creation ex nihilo: Origins, Development, Contemporary Challenges*, edited by Gary A. Anderson and Markus Bockmuehl, 15–35. Notre Dame, IN: University of Notre Dame Press, 2018.
———. *The Genesis of Perfection: Adam and Eve in Jewish and Christian Imagination*. Louisville, KY: Westminster John Knox, 2001.

———. *Sin: A History.* New Haven, CT: Yale University Press, 2009.
Anderson, Gerald H. "The Church and the Jewish People: Some Theological Issues and Missiological Concerns." *Missiology: An International Review* 2, no. 3 (July 1974) 279–93.
Apostolic Constitutions. In *Ante-Nicene Fathers*, vol. 7, edited by Alexander Roberts, James Donaldson and Cleveland Coxe, translated by James Donaldson, 385–508. Buffalo, NY: Christian Literature, 1886.
Arendt, Hannah. "Cui Bono?" In *The Jewish Writings*, edited by Jerome Kohn and Ron H. Feldman, 150–52. New York: Schocken, 2007.
———. "Karl Jaspers: Citizen of the World?" In *Men in Dark Times*, 81–94. New York: Harcourt Brace & Co., 1968.
———. "Moses or Washington." In *The Jewish Writings*, edited by Jerome Kohn and Ron H. Feldman, 149–50. New York: Schocken, 2007.
———. *The Origins of Totalitarianism.* New York: Meridian, 1958.
———. "Peace or Armistice in the Near East?" In *The Jewish Writings*, edited by Jerome Kohn and Ron H. Feldman, 423–50. New York: Schocken, 2007.
———. *Responsibility and Judgment.* Edited by Jerome Kohn. New York: Schocken, 2003.
Ariel, Yaakov. "A Different Kind of Dialogue? Messianic Judaism and Jewish-Christian Relations." *Cross Currents* 62, no. 3 (September 2012) 318–27.
Armstrong, Karen. *Fields of Blood: Religion and the History of Violence.* New York: Alfred A. Knopf, 2014.
Arnold, Bill T. *Genesis.* Cambridge: Cambridge University Press, 2009.
———. "The Genesis Narratives." In *Ancient Israel's History: An Introduction to Issues and Sources*, edited by Bill T. Arnold and Richard S. Hess, 23–45. Grand Rapids: Baker Academic, 2014.
Assembly of Catholic Ordinaries in the Holy Land. *The General Pastoral Plan.* Jerusalem: 2001.
Ateek, Naim Stifan. *Justice, and Only Justice; A Palestinian Theology of Liberation.* Maryknoll, NY: Orbis, 1989.
———. *A Palestinian Christian Cry for Reconciliation.* Maryknoll, NY: Orbis, 2009.
Ateek, Naim Stifan, Cedar Duaybis, and Maurine Tobin. *Challenging Christian Zionism: Theology, Politics and the Israel-Palestine Conflict.* London: Melisende, 2005.
Attridge, Harold. "The Uses of Antithesis in Hebrews 8–10." In *Essays on John and Hebrews*, 273–80. Grand Rapids: Baker Academic, 2012.
Augustine. "*Aduersus Judaeos.*" Translated by Marie Liguori. In vol. 27 of *The Fathers of the Church*, 387–414. Washington, DC: Catholic University of America Press, 1955.
———. *Answer to Faustus, a Manichean.* Translated by Ronald Teske. Hyde Park, NY: New City, 2007.
———. *City of God.* Translated by Henry Bettenson. New York: Penguin, 1984.
———. *Enchiridion on Faith, Hope, and Charity.* Translated by Bernard M. Peebles. In vol. 2 of *The Fathers of the Church*, 369–472. New York: Fathers of the Church, 1947.
———. *On Christian Doctrine.* Translated by D. W. Robertson Jr. New York: Macmillan, 1958.

———. "Sermon 10." *The Works of Saint Augustine: A Translation for the 21st Century*: Part III: Sermons, vol. I: *Sermons 1–19*. Translated by Edmund Hill, 282–92. Brooklyn, NY: New City, 1990.

Austin, J. L. *How to Do Things with Words*. 2d ed. Edited by J. O. Urmson and Marina Sbisà. Oxford: Oxford University Press, 1975.

Avineri, Shlomo. *Theodor Herzl and the Foundation of the Jewish State*. London: Weidenfeld & Nicolson, 2014.

Bader-Saye, Scott. *Church and Israel after Christendom: The Politics of Election*. Boulder, CO: Westview, 1999.

Bahktin, Mikhail. *Problems of Dostoevsky's Poetics*. Translated by Caryl Emerson. Minneapolis: University of Minnesota Press, 1984.

Bahnsen, Greg L. "The Theonomic Reformed Approach to Law and Gospel." In *The Law, the Gospel, and the Modern Christian: Five Views*, edited by Willem VanGemeren, 93–143. Grand Rapids: Zondervan, 1999.

Balberg, Mira. *Blood for Thought: The Reinvention of Sacrifice in Early Rabbinic Literature*. Oakland, CA: University of California Press, 2017.

Balch, David L. "Response to Daryl D. Schmidt: Luke-Acts Is Catechesis for Christians, Not Kerygma to Jews." In *Anti-Judaism and the Gospels*, edited by William R. Farmer, 97–110. Harrisburg, PA: Trinity International, 1999.

Baldwin, Joyce C. *Haggai, Zechariah, Malachi*. Downers Grove, IL: InterVarsity, 1972.

Barclay, John M. G. *Obeying the Truth: Paul's Ethics in Galatians*. Edinburgh: T. & T. Clark, 1988.

———. *Paul and the Gift*. Grand Rapids: Eerdmans, 2015.

Bardan, Channah. *The Bride: One Woman's Walk Through Judaism and Catholicism: The Sabbath, Marriage, Mass, and the World to Come*. Saint Louis, MO: Miriam, 2017.

Barker, Dan. *God: The Most Unpleasant Character in All Fiction*. New York: Sterling, 2016.

Barker, Margaret. *King of the Jews: Temple Theology in John's Gospel*. London: SPCK, 2014.

———. *Temple Mysticism: An Introduction*. London: SPCK, 2011.

Barnett, Victoria J. *Bystanders: Conscience and Complicity During the Holocaust*. Westport, CT: Praeger, 1999.

Barron, Robert. *Arguing Religion: A Bishop Speaks at Facebook and Google*. Park Ridge, IL: Word on Fire, 2018.

———. *Letter to a Suffering Church: A Bishop Speaks on the Sexual Abuse Crisis*. Park Ridge, IL: Word on Fire, 2019.

———. *The Priority of Christ: Toward a Postliberal Catholicism*. Grand Rapids: Brazos, 2007.

———. *The Strangest Way: Walking the Christian Path*. Maryknoll, NY: Orbis, 2002.

———. *2 Samuel*. Grand Rapids: Brazos, 2015.

Barth, Karl. *Church Dogmatics*. 4 vols. Edited by G. W. Bromily and T. F. Torrance. Translated by G. W. Bromiley et al. Edinburgh: T. & T. Clark, 1936–1975.

Barth, Markus. *Jesus the Jew: What Does It Mean That Jesus Is a Jew? Israel and the Palestinians*. Translated by Frederick Prussner. Atlanta: John Knox, 1978.

Bartholomew, Craig G. *The God Who Acts in History: The Significance of Sinai*. Grand Rapids: Eerdmans, 2020.

Barton, John. "The Prophets and the Cult." In *Temple and Worship in Biblical Israel*, edited by John Day, 111–22. London: T. & T. Clark, 2007.

Batnitzky, Leora. "Dialogue as Judgment, Not Mutual Affirmation: A New Look at Franz Rosenzweig's Dialogical Philosophy." *Journal of Religion* 79, no. 4 (October 1999) 523–44.

———. *How Judaism Became a Religion: An Introduction to Modern Jewish Thought*. Princeton, NJ: Princeton University Press, 2011.

———. *Idolatry and Representation: The Philosophy of Franz Rosenzweig Reconsidered*. Princeton, NJ: Princeton University Press, 2000.

———. "Jesus in Modern Jewish Thought." In *Jesus Among the Jews: Representation and Thought*, edited by Neta Stahl, 159–70. London: Routledge, 2012.

Batnitzky, Leora, and Yonatan Y. Brafman, eds. *Jewish Legal Theories: Writings on State, Religion, and Morality*. Waltham, MA: Brandeis University Press, 2018.

Batto, Bernard F. "The Ancient Near Eastern Context of the Hebrew Ideas of Creation." In *In the Beginning: Essays on Creation Motifs in the Ancient Near East and the Bible*, 7–53. Winona Lake, IN: Eisenbrauns, 2013.

———. "The Divine Sovereign: The Image of God in the Priestly Creation Account." In *In the Beginning: Essays on Creation Motifs in the Ancient Near East and the Bible*, 96–138. Winona Lake, IN: Eisenbrauns, 2013.

Bauckham, Richard. *The Jewish World around the New Testament*. Grand Rapids: Baker Academic, 2010.

Baum, Gregory. "Catholic Dogma after Auschwitz." In *Anti-Semitism and the Foundations of Christianity*, edited by Alan Davies, 137–50. New York: Paulist, 1979.

Bauman, Zygmunt. *Modernity and the Holocaust*. Ithaca, NY: Cornell University Press, 1989.

Bayfield, Tony. *Being Jewish Today: Confronting the Real Issues*. London: Bloomsbury, 2019.

Bea, Augustin, SJ. *The Church and the Jewish People: A Commentary in the Second Vatican Council's Declaration on the Relation of the Church to Non-Christian Religions*. Translated by Philip Lovetz. London: Geoffrey Chapman, 1966.

Beale, G. K. *The Temple and the Church's Mission: A Biblical Theology of the Dwelling Place of God*. Downers Grove, IL: InterVarsity, 2004.

Beck, Norman A. *Mature Christianity: The Recognition and Repudiation of the Anti-Jewish Polemic of the New Testament*. Selinsgrove, PA: Susquehanna University Press, 1985.

Becker, Adam, and Annette Yoshiko Reed, eds. *The Ways That Never Parted: Jews and Christians in Late Antiquity and the Early Middle Ages*. Tübingen: Mohr Siebeck, 2003.

Bede. *On Ezra and Nehemiah*. Translated by Scott DeGregorio. Liverpool: Liverpool University Press, 2006.

Beker, Avi. "The Forgotten Narrative: Jewish Refugees from Arab Countries." *Jewish Political Studies Review* 17, no. 3/4 (October 2005) 3–19.

Beker, J. Christiaan. "The New Testament View of Judaism." In *Jews and Christians: Exploring the Past, Present and Future*, edited by James H. Charlesworth, 60–69. New York: Crossroad, 1990.

Bellis, Alice Ogden, and Joel S. Kaminsky, eds. *Jews, Christians, and the Theology of the Hebrew Scriptures*. Atlanta: SBL, 2000.

Belloc, Hillaire. *The Jews*. London: Constable & Co., 1922.

Benedict XIV. *Lettera a Monsignor Archivescovo di Tarso Vicegerente sopra il Battesimo degli Ebrei o infanti o adulti.* February 28, 1747.

———. *Lettera della Santità di Nostro Signore Benedetto Papa XIV a Monsignor Pier Girolamo Guglielmi Assessore del Sant'Officio sopra l'Offerta fatta dall'Avia Neofita di alcuni suoi Nipoti infanti Ebrei alla Fede Christiana.* December 15, 1751.

———. *Postremo mense.* February 28, 1747.

———. *Probe te meminisse.* December 15, 1751.

Benedict XVI. "Address of His Holiness Benedict XVI: 'Ben Gurion' International Airport—Tel Aviv." May 15, 2009. Vatican.va.

———. "Address of His Holiness Benedict XVI: Visit to the Synagogue of Rome." January 17, 2010. Vatican.va.

———. *Caritas in Veritate.* 2009. Vatican.va

———. *Ecclesia in Medio Oriente: Post-Synodal Apostolic Exhortation of His Holiness Pope Benedict XVI to the Patriarchs, Bishops, Clergy, and Consecrated Persons and the Lay Faithful on the Church in the Middle East: Communion and Witness.* September 14, 2012. Vatican.va.

———. "Grace and Vocation without Remorse: Comments on the Treatise *De Iudaeis*." Translated by Nicholas J. Healy Jr. *Communio* 45 (Spring 2018) 163-84.

———. *Spe Salvi.* San Francisco, CA: Ignatius, 2008.

———. *Verbum Domini.* Vatican translation. Boston: Pauline, 2010.

Benedict XVI and Arie Folger. "Briefwechsel Benedikt XVI. - Rabbi Arie Folger." *Internationale katholische Zeitung Communio* 47, no. 6 (November, 2018) 611-17.

Bergant, Dianne. "The Binding of Isaac: Hermeneutical Reflections." In *Two Faiths, One Covenant? Jewish and Christian Identity in the Presence of the Other*, edited by Eugene B. Korn and John T. Pawlikowski, 29-34. Lanham, MD: Rowman and Littlefield, 2005.

Bergen, Doris L. *Twisted Cross: The German Christian Movement in the Third Reich.* Chapel Hill, NC: University of North Carolina Press, 1996.

Berger, David. "Anti-Semitism: An Overview." In *History and Hate: The Dimensions of Anti-Semitism*, edited by David Berger, 3-14. Philadelphia: Jewish Publication Society, 1986.

———. "Christians, Gentiles, and the Talmud: A Fourteenth-Century Jewish Response to the Attack on Rabbinic Judaism." In *Persecution, Polemic, and Dialogue: Essays in Jewish-Christian Relations*, 158-76. Boston: Academic Studies, 2010.

———. "*Dabru Emet*: Some Reservations about a Jewish Statement on Christians and Christianity." In *Persecution, Polemic, and Dialogue: Essays in Jewish-Christian Relations*, 392-98. Boston: Academic Studies, 2010.

———. "From Crusades to Blood Libels to Expulsions: Some New Approaches to Medieval Anti-Semitism." In *Persecution, Polemic, and Dialogue: Essays in Jewish-Christian Relations*, 15-39. Boston: Academic Studies, 2010.

———, ed. and trans. *The Jewish-Christian Debate in the High Middle Ages: A Critical Edition of the Nizzahon Vetus.* Philadelphia: Jewish Publication Society of America, 1979.

———. "Jewish-Christian Relations: A Jewish View." In *Persecution, Polemic, and Dialogue: Essays in Jewish-Christian Relations*, 333-66. Boston: Academic Studies, 2010.

———. "Jews, Christians, and *The Passion*." In *Persecution, Polemic, and Dialogue: Essays in Jewish-Christian Relations*, 399-416. Boston: Academic Studies, 2010.

———. "On *Dominus Iesus* and the Jews." In *Persecution, Polemic, and Dialogue: Essays in Jewish-Christian Relations*, 378–84. Boston: Academic Studies, 2010.

———. "Reflections on Conversion and Proselytizing in Judaism and Christianity." In *Persecution, Polemic, and Dialogue: Essays in Jewish-Christian Relations*, 367–77. Boston: Academic Studies, 2010.

———. "Revisiting 'Confrontation' after Forty Years: A Response to Rabbi Eugene Korn." In *Persecution, Polemic, and Dialogue: Essays in Jewish-Christian Relations*, 385–91. Boston: Academic Studies, 2010.

———. "Texts, Values, and Historical Change: Reflections on the Dynamics of Jewish Law." In *Radical Responsibility: Celebrating the Thought of Chief Rabbi Lord Jonathan Sacks*, edited by Michael J. Harris, Daniel Rynhold, and Tamra Wright, 201–16. New Milford, CT: Maggid, 2012.

Bergman, Ronen. *Rise and Kill First: The Secret History of Israel's Targeted Assassinations*. New York: Random House, 2018.

Bergmann, Michael, Michael J. Murray, and Michael C. Rea, eds. *Divine Evil? The Moral Character of the God of Abraham*. Oxford: Oxford University Press, 2011.

Bergsma, John. *Jesus and the Dead Sea Scrolls: Revealing the Jewish Roots of Christianity*. New York: Random House, 2019.

Bergsma, John, and Brant Pitre. *The Old Testament*. Vol. 1 of *A Catholic Introduction to the Bible*. San Francisco: Ignatius, 2018.

Berkman, Joyce Avrech. "Esther and Mary: The Uneasy Jewish/Catholic Dynamic in the Work and Life of Edith Stein." *Journal of Feminist Studies in Religion* 32, no. 1 (April 2016) 55–73.

Berkovits, Eliezer. "Judaism in the Post-Christian Era." In *Disputation and Dialogue: Readings in the Jewish-Christian Encounter*, edited by F. E. Talmage, 284–95. New York: KTAV, 1975.

Berman, Joshua A. *Created Equal: How the Bible Broke with Ancient Political Thought*. Oxford: Oxford University Press, 2008.

———. "The History of Legal Theory and the Study of Biblical Law." *Catholic Biblical Quarterly* 76, no. 1 (January 2014) 19–39.

———. *The Temple: Its Symbolism and Meaning Then and Now*. Eugene, OR: Wipf & Stock, 2010.

Berman, Morris. *Wandering God: A Study of Nomadic Spirituality*. Albany, NY: State University of New York Press, 2000.

Bernardin, Joseph. "Anti-Semitism: The Historical Legacy and Challenge for Christians." In *A Legacy of Catholic-Jewish Dialogue: The Joseph Cardinal Bernardin Jerusalem Lectures*, edited by Thomas A. Baima, 1–17. Chicago: Liturgy Training, 2012.

Bernauer, James, SJ. *Jesuit Kaddish: Jesuits, Jews, and Holocaust Remembrance*. Notre Dame, IN: University of Notre Dame Press, 2020.

Berthe, Pierre-Marie. "Pourquoi l'Église ne devrait pas avoir peur de l'histoire." *Nova et Vetera* 95, no. 3 (2020) 317–29.

Berwick, Robert C., and Noam Chomsky. *Why Only Us: Language and Evolution*. Cambridge, MA: MIT Press, 2016.

Bieringer, R. B., D. Pollefeyt, and F. Vandecasteele-Vanneuville, eds. *Anti-Judaism and the Fourth Gospel*. Louisville, KY: Westminster John Knox, 2001.

Billings, Rachel M. *"Israel Served the Lord": The Book of Joshua as Paradoxical Portrait of Faithful Israel*. Notre Dame, IN: University of Notre Dame Press, 2013.

Bird, Michael F. *Are You the One Who Is to Come? The Historical Jesus and the Messianic Question*. Grand Rapids: Baker Academic, 2009.

———. *Colossians and Philemon: A New Covenant Commentary*. Eugene, OR: Cascade, 2009.

———. "Salvation in Paul's Judaism?" In *Paul and Judaism: Crosscurrents in Pauline Exegesis and the Study of Jewish-Christian Relations*, edited by Reimund Bieringer and Didier Pollefeyt, 15–40. London: Bloomsbury, 2012.

Birnbaum, Pierre. *Antisemitism in France: A Political History from Leon Blum to the Present*. Oxford: Oxford University Press, 1992.

Bishara, Azmi. "Zionism and Equal Citizenship: Essential and Incidental Citizenship in the Jewish State." In *Israel and Its Palestinian Citizens: Ethnic Privileges in the Jewish State*, edited by Nadim N. Rouhana, 137–55. Cambridge: Cambridge University Press, 2017.

Blackwell, Ben C. *Christosis: Engaging Paul's Soteriology with His Patristic Interpreters*. Grand Rapids: Eerdmans, 2016.

Blenkinsopp, Joseph. *Ezekiel*. Louisville, KY: John Knox, 1990.

Blet, Pierre, SJ. *Pius XII and the Second World War: According to the Archives of the Vatican*. Translated by Lawrence J. Johnson. New York: Paulist, 1999.

Blidstein, G. J. "Hast Thou Chosen Us to Rule? The Political Dimension of Israel's Election in the Sages' Literature." In *Chosen People, Elect Nation and Universal Mission*, edited by Shmuel Almog and Michael Heyd, 99–120. Jerusalem: The Zalman Shazar Center for Jewish History, 1991.

Block, Daniel I. *Beyond the River Chebar: Studies in Kingship and Eschatology in the Book of Ezekiel*. Eugene, OR: Cascade, 2013.

———. *For the Glory of God: Recovering a Biblical Theology of Worship*. Grand Rapids: Baker Academic, 2014.

Blowers, Paul M. *Drama of the Divine Economy: Creator and Creation in Early Christian Theology and Piety*. Oxford: Oxford University Press, 2012.

Blumenkranz, Bernhard. *Les Auteurs chrétiens latins du moyen âge sur les juifs et le judaïsme*. Paris: Mouton, 1963.

———. *Die Judenpredigt Augustins*. Basel: Helbing & Lichtenhahn, 1946.

———. *Juifs et chrétiens dans le monde occidental, 430–1096*. Paris: Mouton, 1960.

Boadt, Lawrence, CSP, and Kevin di Camillo, eds. *John Paul II in the Holy Land: In His Own Words. With Christian and Jewish Perspectives by Yehezkel Landau and Michael McGarry*. Mahwah, NJ: Paulist, 2005.

Boccaccini, Gabriele. *Paul's Three Paths to Salvation*. Grand Rapids: Eerdmans, 2020.

Bock, Darrell. "The Restoration of Israel in Luke-Acts." In *Introduction to Messianic Judaism: Its Ecclesial Context and Biblical Foundations*, edited by David Rudolph and Joel Willitts, 168–77. Grand Rapids: Zondervan, 2013.

Bockmuehl, Markus. "The Idea of Creation out of Nothing: From Qumran to Genesis Rabbah." In *Visualising Jews through the Ages: Literary and Material Representations of Jewishness and Judaism*, edited by Hannah Ewence and Helen Spurling, 17–31. New York: Routledge, 2015.

———. "Introduction." In *Creation* ex nihilo: *Origins, Development, Contemporary Challenges*, edited by Gary A. Anderson and Markus Bockmuehl, 1–13. Notre Dame, IN: University of Notre Dame Press, 2018.

———. *Jewish Law in Gentile Churches: Halakhah and the Beginning of Christian Public Ethics*. London: T. & T. Clark, 2000.

———. *Simon Peter in Scripture and Memory: The New Testament Apostle in the Early Church.* Grand Rapids: Baker Academic, 2012.
Boda, Mark J. *Haggai, Zechariah.* Grand Rapids: Zondervan, 2004.
———. *The Heartbeat of Old Testament Theology: Three Creedal Expressions.* Grand Rapids: Baker Academic, 2017.
———. *A Severe Mercy: Sin and Its Remedy in the Old Testament.* Winona Lake, IN: Eisenbrauns, 2009.
Bodner, Keith. *The Theology of the Book of Kings.* Cambridge: Cambridge University Press, 2019.
Bokser, Baruch M. "The Wall Separating God and Israel." *Jewish Quarterly Review* 73, no. 4 (April 1983) 349–74.
Bolton, David J. "Catholic-Jewish Dialogue: Contesting the Covenants." *Journal of Ecumenical Studies* 45, no. 1 (January 2010) 37–60.
Bonald, Louis de. "De l'origine du langage." In *Recherches philosophiques sur les premiers objets des connaissances morales*, 119–259. Brussels: La Sociéte nationale, 1845.
Bonhoeffer, Dietrich. "The Church and the Jewish Question." In *Dietrich Bonhoeffer Works*, vol. 12: *Berlin: 1932–1933*, 361–70. Minneapolis: Fortress, 2009.
Bonino, Serge-Thomas, OP. "Le sacerdoce comme institution naturelle selon saint Thomas d'Aquin." *Revue Thomiste* 99, no. 1 (1999) 33–57.
Borgen, Peder. "Polemic in the Book of Revelation." In *Anti-Semitism and Early Christianity: Issues of Polemic and Faith*, edited by Craig A. Evans and Donald A. Hagner, 199–211. Minneapolis: Fortress, 1993.
Borodowski, Alfredo Fabio. *Isaac Abravanel on Miracles, Creation, Prophecy, and Evil: The Tension Between Medieval Jewish Philosophy and Biblical Commentary.* New York: Peter Lang, 2003.
Borowitz, Eugene. *Choices in Modern Jewish Thought.* New York: Behrman House, 1983.
Boustan, Ra'anan S. "Augustine as Revolutionary? Reflections on Continuity and Rupture in Jewish-Christian Relations in Paula Fredriksen's *Augustine and the Jews.*" *Jewish Quarterly Review* 99, no. 1 (January, 2009) 74–87.
Bouteneff, Peter C. *Beginnings: Ancient Christian Readings of the Biblical Creation Narratives.* Grand Rapids: Baker Academic, 2008.
Bouyer, Louis. *The Church of God: Body of Christ and Temple of the Spirit.* Translated by Charles Underhill Quinn. San Francisco: Ignatius, 2011.
Bowersock, Glen W. *Martyrdom and Rome.* Cambridge: Cambridge University Press, 1995.
Boxall, Ian. *Discovering Matthew: Content, Interpretation, Reception.* Grand Rapids: Eerdmans, 2014.
———. *The Revelation of Saint John.* London: A. & C. Black, 2006.
Boyarin, Daniel. *Socrates and the Fat Rabbis.* Chicago: University of Chicago Press, 2009.
Boys, Mary C. "The Covenant in Contemporary Ecclesial Documents." In *Two Faiths, One Covenant? Jewish and Christian Identity in the Presence of the Other*, edited by Eugene B. Korn and John T. Pawlikowski, 81–110. Lanham, MD: Rowman and Littlefield, 2005.
———. *Has God Only One Blessing? Judaism as a Source of Christian Self-Understanding.* New York: Paulist, 2000.

———. "The *Nostra Aetate* Trajectory: Holding Our Theological Bow Differently." In *Never Revoked: Nostra Aetate as Ongoing Challenge for Jewish-Christian Dialogue*, edited by Marianne Moyaert and Didier Pollefeyt, 133–57. Leuven: Peeters, 2010.

———. *Redeeming Our Sacred Story: The Death of Jesus and Relations between Jews and Christians*. New York: Paulist, 2013.

———, ed. *Seeing Judaism Anew: Christianity's Sacred Obligation*. Lanham, MD: Rowman & Littlefield, 2005.

Branick, Vincent P. "The Sinful Flesh of the Son of God (Rom 8:3): A Key Image of Pauline Theology." *Catholic Biblical Quarterly* 47, no. 2 (April 1985) 246–62.

Braybrooke, Marcus. *Jewish-Christian Dialogue: The Next Steps*. London: SCM, 2000.

Breger, Marshall J. "A Reassessment of Rav Soloveitchik's Essay on Interfaith Dialogue: 'Confrontation.'" *Studies in Christian-Jewish Relations* 1 (2005–2006) 151–69.

———, ed. *The Vatican-Israel Accords: Political, Legal, and Theological Contexts*. Notre Dame, IN: Notre Dame University Press, 2004.

Briggs, Richard S. *Theological Hermeneutics and the Book of Numbers as Christian Scripture*. Notre Dame, IN: University of Notre Dame Press, 2018.

Brill, Alan. "Elements of Dialectical Theology in Rabbi Soloveitchik's View of Torah Study." In *Study and Knowledge in Jewish Thought*, vol. 1, edited by Howard Kreisel, 265–96. Beer Sheva: Ben-Gurion University The Negev, 2006.

———. *Judaism and Other Religions: Models of Understanding*. New York: Palgrave Macmillan, 2010.

Brockway, Allan, Paul van Buren, Rudolf Rendtorff, and Simon Schoon. *The Theology of the Churches and the Jewish People*. Geneva: WCC, 1988.

Brooks, Roger, and John Collins, eds. *Hebrew Bible or Old Testament? Studying the Bible in Judaism and Christianity*. Notre Dame, IN: University of Notre Dame Press, 1990.

Brosend, William F., II. *James and Jude*. Cambridge: Cambridge University Press, 2004.

Browe, Peter. *Die Judenmission im Mittelalter und die Päpste*. Rome: SALER, 1942.

Brown, Nicholas R. *For the Nation: Jesus, the Restoration of Israel, and Articulating a Christian Ethic of Territorial Governance*. Eugene, OR: Pickwick, 2016.

Brown, Raymond S., SS. *The Death of the Messiah, from Gethsemane to Grave: A Commentary on the Passion Narratives in the Four Gospels*. 2 vols. New York: Doubleday, 1994.

———. *The Gospel According to John (i–xii)*. Garden City, NY: Doubleday, 1966.

Brueggemann, Walter. *A Commentary on Jeremiah: Exile and Homecoming*. Grand Rapids: Eerdmans, 1998.

———. "Dialogue between Incommensurate Partners: Prospects for Common Testimony." *Journal for Ecumenical Studies* 38, no. 4 (September 2001) 383–98.

———. *Genesis*. Louisville, KY: Westminster John Knox, 2010.

———. *The Land: Place as Gift, Promise, and Challenge in Biblical Faith*. 2d ed. Minneapolis: Fortress, 2002.

———. *Theology of the Old Testament: Testimony, Dispute, Advocacy*. Minneapolis: Fortress, 1997.

Brustein, William I. *Roots of Hate: Anti-Semitism in Europe before the Holocaust*. Cambridge: Cambridge University Press, 2003.

Buber, Martin. *I and Thou*. Translated by Ronald Gregor Smith. New York: Charles Scribner's Sons, 1958.

———. *Two Types of Faith*. Translated by Norman P. Goldhawk. New York: Macmillan Co., 1951.

Buchen, Tim. "'Herkules im antisemitischen Augiasstall': Joseph Samuel Bloch und Galizien in der Reaktion auf Antisemitismus in der Habsburgermonarchie." In *Einspruch und Abwehr: Die Reaktion des europäischen Judentums auf die Entstehung des Antisemitismus (1879-1914)*, edited by Ulrich Wyrwa, 193-214. Frankfurt am Main: Campus, 2010.

Bulgakov, Sergius. *The Bride of the Lamb*. Translated by Boris Jakim. Grand Rapids: Eerdmans, 2002.

Bullivant, Stephen. "*Sine Culpa?* Vatican II and Inculpable Ignorance." *Theological Studies* 72, no. 1 (March 2011) 70-86.

Burge, Gary M. *Jesus and the Land: The New Testament Challenge to "Holy Land" Theology*. Grand Rapids: Baker Academic, 2010.

———. *Whose Land? Whose Promise? What Christians Are Not Being Told about Israel and the Palestinians*. 2d ed. Cleveland, OH: Pilgrim, 2013.

Burke, Trevor J. *Adopted into God's Family: Exploring a Pauline Metaphor*. Downers Grove, IL: IVP Academic, 2006.

Burkert, Walter. *Homo Necans: The Anthropology of Ancient Greek Sacrificial Ritual and Myth*. Translated by Peter Bing. Berkeley, CA: University of California Press, 1983.

Burrell, David B., CSC. "Creation in St. Thomas Aquinas's *Super Evangelium S. Joannis Lectura*." In *Reading John with St. Thomas Aquinas: Theological Exegesis and Speculative Theology*, edited by Michael Dauphinais and Matthew Levering, 115-26. Washington, DC: Catholic University of America Press, 2005.

Busch, Eberhard. "Karl Barth and the Jews: The History of a Relationship." In *Karl Barth, the Jews, and Judaism*, edited by George Hunsinger, 24-36. Grand Rapids: Eerdmans, 2018.

———. *Unter dem Bogen des einen Bundes: Karl Barth und die Juden 1933-1945*. Neukirchen-Vluyn: Neukirchener Verlag, 1996.

Byrne, Brendan, SJ. *Romans*. Collegeville, MN: Liturgical, 1996.

Cabasilas, Nicholas. *A Commentary on the Divine Liturgy*. Translated by J. M. Hussey and P. A. McNulty. Crestwood, NY: St. Vladimir's Seminary, 1998.

Caffiero, Marina. "Alle Origini dell'Antisemitismo Politico. L'Accusa di Omicidio Rituale nel Sei-Settecento tra Autodifesa degli Ebrei e Pronunciamenti Papali." In *Les Racines chrétiennes de l'antisémitisme politique (fin XIXe—XXe siècle)*, edited by Catherine Brice and Giovanni Miccoli, 25-59. Rome: Ecole française de Rome, 2003.

———. *Forced Baptisms: Histories of Jews, Christians, and Converts in Papal Rome*. Translated by Lydia G. Cochrane. Berkeley, CA: 2012.

Caird, G. B. *The Language and Imagery of the Bible*. Grand Rapids: Eerdmans, 1997.

Campbell, William S. "Covenantal Theology and Participation in Christ: Pauline Perspectives on Transformation." In *Paul and Judaism: Crosscurrents in Pauline Exegesis and the Study of Jewish-Christian Relations*, edited by Reimund Bieringer and Didier Pollefeyt, 41-60. London: Bloomsbury, 2012.

———. *Paul and the Creation of Christian Identity*. London: T. & T. Clark International, 2008.

Capéran, Louis. *Le Salut des infidels*. Paris: Beauchesne, 1912.

Carroll, James. *Constantine's Sword: The Church and the Jews: A History*. Boston: Houghton Mifflin, 2001.

Carter, Craig A. *Interpreting Scripture with the Great Tradition: Recovering the Genius of Premodern Exegesis*. Grand Rapids: Baker Academic, 2018.
Carter, Warren. "Response to Amy-Jill Levine." In *Anti-Judaism and the Gospels*, edited by William R. Farmer, 47–62. Harrisburg, PA: Trinity International, 1999.
Cassidy, Edward Idris. "The Next Issues in Jewish-Catholic Relations." *Journal of Ecumenical Studies* 34, no. 3 (1997) 362–69.
Catalano, Rosann M. "A Matter of Perspective: An Alternative Reading of Mark 15:38." In *Seeing Judaism Anew: Christianity's Sacred Obligation*, edited by Mary C. Boys, 187–99. Lanham, MD: Rowman & Littlefield, 2005.
Catechism of the Catholic Church. 2d ed. Vatican City: Libreria Editrice Vaticana, 1997.
Catherine of Siena. *The Dialogue*. Translated by Suzanne Noffke. New York: Paulist, 1980.
Cavanaugh, William T. *The Myth of Religious Violence: Secular Ideology and the Roots of Modern Conflict*. Oxford: Oxford University Press, 2009.
Center for Jewish-Christian Understanding and Cooperation. "To Do the Will of Our Father in Heaven: Toward a Partnership between Jews and Christians." December 3, 2015. https://www.cjcuc.org/2015/12/03/orthodox-rabbinic-statement-on-christianity/.
Cessario, Romanus, OP. "Non Possumus." Review of *Kidnapped by the Vatican?*, by Vittorio Messori. *First Things* 280 (February 2018) 55–58.
———. "Romanus Cessario, O.P., replies." *First Things* 282 (April 2018) 4–5.
Chalmers, Aaron. *Interpreting the Prophets: Reading, Understanding and Preaching from the Worlds of the Prophets*. Downers Grove, IL: IVP Academic, 2015.
Chambers, Nathan. *Reconsidering Creation Ex Nihilo in Genesis 1*. University Park, PA: Eisenbrauns, 2020.
Chanikuzhy, Jacob. *Jesus, the Eschatological Temple: An Exegetical Study of Jn 2,13–22 in the Light of the Pre-70 C.E. Eschatological Temple Hopes and the Synoptic Temple Action*. Leuven: Peeters, 2012.
Chapman, Stephen B. *1 Samuel as Christian Scripture: A Theological Commentary*. Grand Rapids: Eerdmans, 2016.
Charry, Ellen T. "The Doctrine of God in Jewish-Christian Dialogue." In *The Oxford Handbook of the Trinity*, edited by Gilles Emery and Matthew Levering, 559–72. Oxford: Oxford University Press, 2011.
———. *Psalms 1–50: Sighs and Songs of Israel*. Grand Rapids: Brazos, 2015.
———. "Response to Joseph B. Tyson." In *Anti-Judaism and the Gospels*, edited by William R. Farmer, 259–64. Harrisburg, PA: Trinity International, 1999.
———. "Toward Ending Enmity." In *Karl Barth, the Jews, and Judaism*, edited by George Hunsinger, 147–71. Grand Rapids: Eerdmans, 2018.
Chauvet, Louis-Marie. *Symbol and Sacrament: A Sacramental Reinterpretation of Christian Existence*. Translated by Patrick Madigan and Madeleine Beaumont. Collegeville, MN: Liturgical, 1995.
Chazan, Robert. *Barcelona and Beyond: The Disputation of 1263 and Its Aftermath*. Berkeley, CA: University of California Press, 1992.
———. *Fashioning Jewish Identity in Medieval Western Christendom*. Cambridge: Cambridge University Press, 2009.
———. "Medieval Christians and Jews: Divergences and Convergences." In *A Legacy of Catholic-Jewish Dialogue: The Joseph Cardinal Bernardin Jerusalem Lectures*, edited by Thomas A. Baima, 131–49. Chicago: Liturgy Training, 2012.

Chester, Andrew. *Messiah and Exaltation: Jewish Messianic and Visionary Traditions and New Testament Christology.* Tübingen: Mohr Siebeck, 2007.

Chester, Stephen. "Paul and the Galatian Believers." In *The Blackwell Companion to Paul*, edited by Stephen Westerholm, 63–78. Oxford: Wiley-Blackwell, 2011.

Childs, Brevard S. *Biblical Theology of the Old and New Testaments: Theological Reflection on the Christian Bible.* Minneapolis: Fortress, 1993.

———. *The Book of Exodus: A Critical, Theological Commentary.* Louisville, KY: Westminster, 1974.

———. *Myth and Reality in the Old Testament.* London: SCM, 1962.

Chilton, Bruce. "The Israel of James, the Community of Q, and Peter." In *The Body of Faith: Israel and the Church*, by Jacob Neusner and Bruce D. Chilton, 118–33. Valley Forge, PA: Trinity International, 1996.

———. *The Temple of Jesus: His Sacrificial Program within a Cultural History of Sacrifice.* University Park, PA: Pennsylvania State University Press, 1992.

Chilton, Bruce, and Jacob Neusner. *Judaism in the New Testament: Practices and Beliefs.* London: Routledge, 1995.

Chrysostom, John. *Discourses Against Judaizing Christians.* Vol. 68 of *The Fathers of the Church.* Translated by Paul W. Harkins. Washington, DC: Catholic University of America Press, 2014.

———. *Homilies on the Gospel of St. Matthew.* Vol. 10 of *Nicene and Post-Nicene Fathers*, edited by Philip Schaff. Translated by George Prevost and M. B. Riddle. Peabody, MA: Hendrickson, 1995.

Church, Philip. *Hebrews and the Temple: Attitudes to the Temple in Second Temple Judaism and in Hebrews.* Leiden: Brill, 2017.

Clement VIII. "*Caeca et obdurate Hebraeorum perfidia.*" February 25, 1593.

Clifford, Richard J., SJ. "*Creatio ex nihilo* in the Old Testament/Hebrew Bible." In *Creation ex nihilo: Origins, Development, Contemporary Challenges*, edited by Gary A. Anderson and Markus Bockmuehl, 55–76. Notre Dame, IN: University of Notre Dame Press, 2018.

———. *Creation Accounts in the Ancient Near East and in the Bible.* Washington, DC: Catholic Biblical Association, 1994.

Code of Canon Law: Latin-English Edition. Translated by the Canon Law Society of America. Washington, DC: Canon Law Society of America, 1999.

Codex iuris canonici. Vatican City: Libreria Vaticana Editrice, 1983.

Cohen, Jeremy. *Living Letters of the Law: Ideas of the Jew in Medieval Christianity.* Berkeley, CA: University of California Press, 1999.

———. "Revisiting Augustine's Doctrine of Jewish Witness." *Journal of Religion* 89, no. 4 (October, 2009) 564–78.

———. "'Slay Them Not': Augustine and the Jews in Modern Scholarship." *Medieval Encounters* 4, no. 1 (1998) 78–92.

———. "Supersessionism, the Epistle to the Romans, Thomas Aquinas, and the Jews of the Eschaton." *Journal of Ecumenical Studies* 52, no. 4 (2017) 524–53.

Cohen, Mark. *Under Crescent and Cross: The Jews in the Middle Ages.* Princeton, NJ: Princeton University Press, 1994.

Cohen, Shaye J. D. "'Anti-Semitism' in Antiquity: The Problem of Definition." In *History and Hate: The Dimensions of Anti-Semitism*, edited by David Berger, 43–47. Philadelphia: Jewish Publication Society, 1986.

———. *From the Maccabees to the Mishnah*. 2d ed. Louisville, KY: Westminster John Knox, 2006.

Cohn, Norman. *Warrant for Genocide: The Myth of the Jewish World-Conspiracy and the Protocols of the Elders of Zion*. London: Eyre & Spottiswoode, 1967.

Cohn-Sherbok, Dan. "The Church Fathers and Jewish Hatred." In *The Crucified Jew: Twenty Centuries of Christian Anti-Semitism*, 25–37. Grand Rapids: Eerdmans, 1997.

———. *The Crucified Jew: Twenty Centuries of Christian Anti-Semitism*. Grand Rapids: Eerdmans, 1997.

———. *The Jewish Messiah*. Edinburgh: T. & T. Clark, 1997.

———. *Messianic Judaism*. London: Continuum, 2000.

———. "The Resurrection of Jesus: A Jewish View." In *Resurrection Reconsidered*, edited by Gavin D'Costa, 184–200. Oxford: Oneworld, 1996.

Collins, John J. "The Exodus and Biblical Theology." In *Jews, Christians, and the Theology of the Hebrew Scriptures*, edited by Alice Ogden Bellis and Joel S. Kaminsky, 247–61. Atlanta: SBL, 2000.

———. "The Zeal of Phinehas, the Bible, and the Legitimation of Violence." In *The Destructive Power of Religion: Violence in Judaism, Christianity, and Islam*, vol. 1: *Sacred Scriptures, Ideology, and Violence*, edited by J. Harold Ellens, 11–33. Westport, CT: Praeger, 2004.

Coloe, Mary L. *God Dwells with Us: Temple Symbolism in the Fourth Gospel*. Collegeville, MN: Liturgical, 2001.

Compton, Jared, and Andrew David Naselli, eds. *Three Views on Israel and the Church: Perspectives on Romans 9–11*. Grand Rapids: Kregel Academic, 2018.

Concannon, Cavan W. *"When You Were Gentiles": Speakers of Ethnicity in Roman Corinth and Paul's Corinthian Correspondence*. New Haven, CT: Yale University Press, 2014.

Conference of European Rabbis and The Rabbinical Council of America. "Between Jerusalem and Rome." August 31, 2017. https://www.cjcuc.org/2017/08/31/between-jerusalem-and-rome/.

Congar, Yves, OP. *Lay People in the Church: A Study for a Theology of the Laity*. Translated by Donald Attwater. London: Geoffrey Chapman, 1985.

———. *The Mystery of the Temple*. New York: Newman, 1962.

———. "Paul's Casuistry." In *A Gospel Priesthood*, translated by P. J. Hepburne-Scott, 49–73. New York: Herder and Herder, 1967.

———. "The Religious Significance of the Restoration of the Jewish State and Nation in the Holy Land." In *Dialogue between Christians: Catholic Contributions to Ecumenism*, translated by Philip Loretz, 445–61. Westminster, MD: The Newman, 1966.

———. *True and False Reform in the Church*. Translated by Paul Philibert. Collegeville, MN: Liturgical, 2011.

Congregation of the Doctrine of the Faith (CDF). *"Dominus Iesus": On the Unity and Salvific Universality of Jesus Christ and the Church*. 2000. Vatican.va.

Connelly, John. "Catholic Racism and Its Opponents." *Journal of Modern History* 79, no. 4 (December, 2007) 813–47.

———. *From Enemy to Brother: The Revolution in Catholic Teaching on the Jews, 1933–1965*. Cambridge, MA: Harvard University Press, 2012.

Consultation of the National Council of Synagogues and delegates of the [United States] Bishops Committee for Ecumenical and Interreligious Affairs. "Reflections on Covenant and Mission." August 12, 2002. www.usccb.org/beliefs-and-teachings/ecumenical-and-interreligious/jewish/upload/Reflections-on-Covenant-and-Mission.pdf.

Conway, John S. "The Founding of the State of Israel and the Responses of the Christian Churches." *Kirchliche Zeitgeschichte* 12, no. 2 (1999) 459–72.

Cornwell, John. *Hitler's Pope: The Secret History of Pius XII*. New York: Viking, 1999.

Coudert, Allison P., and Jeffrey S. Shoulson, eds. *Hebraica Veritas? Christian Hebraists and the Study of Judaism in the Early Modern Period*. Philadelphia: University of Pennsylvania Press, 2004.

Council of Basel-Ferrara-Florence-Rome. "Decree on Jews and Neophytes." In *Decrees of the Ecumenical Councils*, vol. 1: *Nicaea I to Lateran V*, edited by Norman P. Tanner, 483–85. Washington, DC: Georgetown University Press, 1990.

Cousar, Charles B. *A Theology of the Cross: The Death of Jesus in the Pauline Letters*. Minneapolis: Fortress, 1990.

Craigie, Peter C., and Marvin E. Tate. *Psalms 1–50*. 2d ed. Nashville, TN: Thomas Nelson, 2004.

Crane, Richard Francis. "Jacques Maritain, the Mystery of Israel, and the Holocaust." *The Catholic Historical Review* 95, no. 1 (January 2009) 25–56.

———. *Passion of Israel: Jacques Maritain, Catholic Conscience and the Holocaust*. Scranton, PA: University of Scranton Press, 2010.

Cranfield, C. E. B. "Light from Saint Paul on Christian-Jewish Relations." In *Karl Barth, the Jews, and Judaism*, edited by George Hunsinger, 128–37. Grand Rapids: Eerdmans, 2018.

Crepaldi, Francesco. "L'omicidio rituale nella 'moderna' polemica antigiudaica di *Civiltà Cattolica* nella seconda metà del XIX secolo." In *Les Racines chrétiennes de l'antisémitisme politique (fin XIXe—XXe siècle)*, edited by Catherine Brice and Giovanni Miccoli, 61–78. Rome: Ecole française de Rome, 2003.

Culbertson, Philip. "Eretz Israel: Sacred Space, Icon, Sign, or Sacrament?" *Shofar* 6 (April 1988) 9–17.

Culpepper, R. A. "The Gospel of John as a Threat to Jewish-Christian Relations." In *Overcoming Fear Between Jews and Christians*, edited by James H. Charlesworth, 21–43. New York: Crossroad, 1992.

Cunningham, Philip A. "Celebrating Judaism as a 'Sacrament of Every Otherness." In *The Theology of Cardinal Walter Kasper: Speaking Truth in Love*, edited by Kristin M. Colberg and Robert A. Krieg, 223–40. Collegeville, MN: Liturgical, 2014.

———. "Covenant and Conversion." In *Seeing Judaism Anew: Christianity's Sacred Obligation*, edited by Mary C. Boys, 151–62. Lanham, MD: Rowman & Littlefield, 2005.

———. "Gifts and Calling: Coming to Terms with Jews as Covenantal Partners." *Studies in Christian-Jewish Relations* 12, no. 1 (March 2017) 1–18.

———. "Paul's Letters and the Relationship between the People of Israel and the Church Today." In *Paul and Judaism: Crosscurrents in Pauline Exegesis and the Study of Jewish-Christian Relations*, edited by Reimund Bieringer and Didier Pollefeyt, 141–62. London: Bloomsbury, 2012.

———. "The Road Behind and the Road Ahead: Catholicism and Judaism." In *Catholicism and Interreligious Dialogue*, edited by James L. Heft, 23–42. Oxford: Oxford University Press, 2012.

———. *Seeking Shalom: The Journey to Right Relationship Between Catholics and Jews*. Grand Rapids: Eerdmans, 2015.

Cunningham, Philip A., and Didier Pollefeyt. "The Triune One, the Incarnate Logos, and Israel's Covenantal Life." In *Christ Jesus and the Jewish People Today: New Explorations of Theological Interrelationships*, edited by Philip A. Cunningham et al., 183–201. Grand Rapids: Eerdmans, 2011.

Dahan, Gilbert, ed. *Le Brûlement du Talmud à Paris, 1242–1244*. Paris: Cerf, 1999.

Dahl, David Lebovitch. "The Antisemitism of the Italian Catholics and Nationalism: 'The Jew' and 'the Honest Italy' in the Rhetoric of *La Civiltà Cattolica* during the Risorgimento." *Modern Italy* 17, no. 1 (February 2012) 1–14.

———. "The Anti-Semitism of *La Civiltà Cattolica* Revisited." In *"The Tragic Couple": Encounters Between Jews and Jesuits*, edited by James Bernauer and Robert A. Maryks, 219–31. Leiden: Brill, 2014.

———. "A Case of Disagreement among the Jesuits of *La Civiltà Cattolica* over Anti-Jewish Propaganda around 1882." *Rivista di Storia del Cristianesimo* 7, no. 1 (2010) 181–201.

———. "The Role of the Roman Catholic Church in the Formation of Modern Anti-Semitism: *La Civiltà Cattolica*, 1850–1879." *Modern Judaism* 23, no. 2 (2003) 180–97.

Dalin, David G. *The Myth of Hitler's Pope: How Pope Pius XII Rescued Jews from the Nazis*. New York: Regnery, 2005.

Daly, Robert J., SJ. *Christian Sacrifice: The Judaeo-Christian Background before Origen*. Washington, DC: Catholic University of America Press, 1978.

———. *Sacrifice Unveiled: The True Meaning of Christian Sacrifice*. New York: T. & T. Clark International, 2009.

Daube, David. *The Exodus Pattern in the Bible*. London: Faber and Faber, 1963.

Dauermann, Stuart. *Converging Destinies: Jews, Christians, and the Mission of God*. Eugene, OR: Cascade, 2017.

Davies, Alan, ed. *Anti-Semitism and the Foundations of Christianity*. New York: Paulist, 1979.

Davies, Daniel. "Reason, Will, and Purpose: What's at Stake for Maimonides and His Followers in the Doctrine of Creation." In *Creation ex nihilo: Origins, Development, Contemporary Challenges*, edited by Gary A. Anderson and Markus Bockmuehl, 213–31. Notre Dame, IN: University of Notre Dame Press, 2018.

Davies, Eryl W. "The Morally Dubious Passages of the Hebrew Bible: An Examination of Some Proposed Solutions." *Currents in Biblical Research* 3, no. 2 (April 2005) 197–225.

Davies, W. D. *The Gospel and the Land: Early Christianity and Jewish Territorial Doctrine*. Berkeley, CA: University of California Press, 1974.

———. "Paul and the New Exodus." In *The Quest for Context and Meaning: Studies in Biblical Intertextuality in Honor of James A. Sanders*, edited by Craig A. Evans and Shemaryahu Talmon, 443–463. Leiden: Brill, 1997.

———. *The Territorial Dimension of Judaism, with a Symposium and Further Reflections*. Minneapolis: Fortress, 1991.

Davies, W. D., and Dale C. Allison Jr. *Commentary on Matthew VIII–XVIII*. Vol. 2 of *A Critical and Exegetical Commentary on the Gospel According to Saint Matthew*. London: T. & T. Clark International, 2004.

———. *Commentary on Matthew XIX–XXVIII*. Vol. 3 of *A Critical and Exegetical Commentary on the Gospel According to Saint Matthew*. London: T. & T. Clark International, 2004.

Davis, Ellen F. "Becoming God's People—Exodus 16–40." In *Opening Israel's Scriptures*, 50–61. Oxford: Oxford University Press, 2019.

———. *Getting Involved with God: Rediscovering the Old Testament*. Lanham, MD: Rowman & Littlefield, 2001.

———. "Losing a Friend: The Loss of the Old Testament to the Church." In *Jews, Christians, and the Theology of the Hebrew Scriptures*, edited by Alice Ogden Bellis and Joel S. Kaminsky, 83–94. Atlanta: SBL, 2000.

———. *Opening Israel's Scriptures*. Oxford: Oxford University Press, 2019.

Davison, Andrew. "'He Fathers-Forth Whose Beauty Is Past Change,' but 'Who Knows How?': Evolution and Divine Exemplarity." *Nova et Vetera* 16 (2018) 1067–1102.

D'Costa, Gavin. "Between Doctrine and Discernment: The Question of the Jewish People and the Development of Doctrine Arising from Vatican II." In *The Past, Present, and Future of Theologies of Interreligious Dialogue*, edited by Terrence Merrigan and John Friday, 64–80. Oxford: Oxford University Press, 2017.

———. *Catholic Doctrines on the Jewish People after Vatican II*. Oxford: Oxford University Press, 2019.

———. "Catholic Zionism." *First Things* 229 (January 2020) 18–24.

———. *Christianity and World Religions: Disputed Questions in the Theology of Religions*. Oxford: Wiley-Blackwell, 2009.

———. "Developing the Conversation: A Divine Messiah and a Catholic Zionism." *Pro Ecclesia* 27, no. 4 (2018) 437–43.

———. "The Mystery of Israel: Jews, Hebrew Catholics, Messianic Judaism, the Catholic Church, and the Mosaic Ceremonial Laws." *Nova et Vetera* 16, no. 3 (2018) 939–77.

———. "Nostra Aetate." In *The Reception of Vatican II*, edited by Matthew L. Lamb and Matthew Levering, 425–58. Oxford: Oxford University Press, 2017.

———. "Supersessionism: Harsh, Mild or Gone for Good?" *European Judaism* 50, no. 1 (March 2017) 99–107.

———. *Vatican II: Catholic Doctrines on Jews and Muslims*. Oxford: Oxford University Press, 2014.

———. "What Does the Catholic Church Teach about Mission to the Jewish People?" *Theological Studies* 73, no. 3 (September 2012) 590–613.

Deines, Roland. *Die Pharisäer: Ihr Verständnis im Spiegel der christlichen und jüdischen Forschung seit Wellhausen und Graetz*. Tübingen: Mohr Siebeck, 1997.

Denzinger, Heinrich. *Compendium of Creeds, Definitions, and Declarations on Matters of Faith and Morals*. 43rd ed. German edition revised, enlarged, and edited by Peter Hünermann and Helmut Hoping, English edition edited by Robert Fastiggi and Anne Englund Nash. San Francisco: Ignatius, 2012.

Denzler, Georg. "Antijudaismus und Antisemitismus in der Theologie unserer Jahrhunderts: Karl Adam, Michael Schmaus, und Anton Stoner." *Law and Politics* 1, no. 1 (1997) 11–20.

De Susannis, Marquardus. *De Iudaeis et aliis infidelibus*. Venice, 1558.

Di Fant, Annalisa. "Don Davide Albertario propagandista antiebraico. L'accusa di omicidio ritual." *Storicamente* 7, no. 21 (May 2011). www.storicamente.org.

Di Segni, Riccardo. "Progress and Issues of the Dialogue from a Jewish Viewpoint." In *The Catholic Church and the Jewish People: Recent Reflections from Rome*, edited by Philip A. Cunningham, Norbert J. Hofmann, and Joseph Sievers, 12–22. New York: Fordham University Press, 2007.

Donaldson, Terence L. *Judaism and the Gentiles: Jewish Patterns of Universalism*. Waco, TX: Baylor University Press, 2008.

Doolan, Gregory T. "Aquinas on the Divine Ideas and the Really Real." *Nova et Vetera* 13 (2015) 1059–92.

———. *Aquinas on the Divine Ideas as Exemplar Causes*. Washington, DC: Catholic University of America Press, 2008.

Dorff, Elliot. "Halakhic Man: A Review Essay." *Modern Judaism* 6, no. 1 (February 1986) 91–98.

Douglas, Mary. "The Eucharist: Its Continuity with the Bread Sacrifice of Leviticus." *Modern Theology* 15, no. 2 (April 1999) 209–24.

———. *Natural Symbols: Explorations in Cosmology*. 2d ed. London: Routledge, 1996.

———. *Purity and Danger: An Analysis of the Concepts of Pollution and Taboo*. London: Routledge and Kegan Paul, 1966.

Dozeman, Thomas B. *Exodus*. Grand Rapids: Eerdmans, 2009.

Drumont, Édouard. *La France juive*, 2 vols. 115th ed. Paris: C. Marpon & E. Flammarion, 1887.

Duff, Nancy J. "Christians Preparing for Conversation: Jewish-Christian Relations." *Theology Today* 74, no. 3 (October 2017) 243–51.

Duffy, Eamon. *Saints and Sinners: A History of the Popes*. 4th ed. New Haven, CT: Yale University Press, 2014.

Dujardin, Jean. *L'Église catholique et le peuple juif. Un autre regard*. Paris: Calmann-Lévy, 2003.

Dulles, Avery, SJ. "The Covenant with Israel." *First Things* 157 (November, 2005). http://www.firstthings.com/article.php3?id_article=256.

———. "Who Can Be Saved?" In *Church and Society: The Laurence J. McGinley Lectures, 1988–2007*, 522–34. New York: Fordham University Press, 2008.

Dunn, James D. G. "Anti-Semitism in the Deutero-Pauline Literature." In *Anti-Semitism and Early Christianity: Issues of Polemic and Faith*, edited by Craig A. Evans and Donald A. Hagner, 151–65. Minneapolis: Fortress, 1993.

———. *Jesus Remembered* (2003). Vol. 1 of *Christianity in the Making*. Grand Rapids: Eerdmans, 2003/2015.

———. *The Theology of Paul's Letter to the Galatians*. Cambridge: Cambridge University Press, 1993.

———. *The Theology of Paul the Apostle*. Grand Rapids: Eerdmans, 1998.

Duran, Nicole Wilkinson. "'Not One Stone Will Be Left on Another': The Destruction of the Temple and the Crucifixion of Jesus in Mark's Gospel." In *Sacrifice, Cult, and Atonement in Early Judaism and Christianity: Constituents and Critique*, edited by Henrietta L. Wiley and Christian A. Eberhart, 311–25. Atlanta: SBL, 2017.

Eckhardt, A. Roy. *Jews and Christians: The Contemporary Meeting*. Bloomington, IN: Indiana University Press, 1986.

Efroymson, D. P. "Whose Jews? Augustine's Tractatus on John." In *A Multiform Heritage: Studies on Early Judaism and Christianity in Honor of Robert A. Kraft*, edited by Benjamin G. Wright, 197–211. Durham, NC: Duke University Press, 1999.

Ehrensperger, Kathy. "Trajectories and Future Avenues in Pauline Studies and Jewish-Christian Relations: The Relevance of William S. Campbell's Approach to Paul." *Journal of Beliefs and Values* 38, no. 2 (May 2017) 153–58.

Eilberg-Schwartz, Howard. *The Savage in Judaism: An Anthropology of Israelite Religion and Ancient Judaism*. Bloomington, IN: Indiana University Press, 1990.

Eisen, A. M. "Off the Center: The Concept of the Land of Israel in Modern Jewish Thought." In *The Land of Israel: Jewish Perspectives*, edited by L. A. Hoffman, 263–96. Notre Dame, IN: University of Notre Dame Press, 1986.

Eisenmenger, Johann Andreas. *Entdecktes Judenthum*. Königsberg, 1711.

Elbogen, Ismar. *Jewish Liturgy: A Comprehensive History*. Translated by Raymond P. Scheindlin. Philadelphia: Jewish Publication Society, 1993.

El-Hasan, Asan Afif. *Is the Two-State Solution Already Dead?* New York: Algora, 2010.

Eliach, Yotav. *Judaism, Zionism and the Land of Israel*. Washington, DC: Dialog, 2018.

Elior, Rachel. *The Three Temples: On the Emergence of Jewish Mysticism*. Oxford: Littman Library of Jewish Civilization, 2004.

Ellens, J. Harold, ed. *Sacred Scriptures, Ideology, and Violence*. Vol. 1 of *The Destructive Power of Religion: Violence in Judaism, Christianity, and Islam*. Westport, CT: Praeger, 2004.

Elliott, Mark W. "The Character of the Biblical God." In *The Identity of Israel's God in Christian Scripture*, edited by Don Collett, Mark Elliott, Mark Gignilliat, and Ephraim Radner, 47–64. Atlanta: SBL, 2020.

———. *Providence Perceived: Divine Action from a Human Point of View*. Berlin: de Gruyter, 2015.

Ellul, Jacques. *The Humiliation of the Word*. Translated by Joyce Main Hanks. Grand Rapids: Eerdmans, 1985.

Elukin, Jonathan. *Living Together, Living Apart: Rethinking Jewish-Christian Relations in the Middle Ages*. Princeton, NJ: Princeton University Press, 2007.

Emery, Gilles, OP. *The Trinitarian Theology of Saint Thomas Aquinas*. Translated by Francesca Aran Murphy. Oxford: Oxford University Press, 2007.

Emon, Anver M., Matthew Levering, and David Novak. *Natural Law: a Jewish, Christian, and Islamic Trialogue*. Oxford: Oxford University Press, 2014.

Ephrem the Syrian. *Hymns on Paradise*. Translated by Sebastian Brock. Crestwood, NY: St. Vladimir's Seminary, 1990.

Ericksen, Robert P. "Christian Complicity? Changing Views on German Churches and the Holocaust." Joseph and Rebecca Meyerhoff Annual Lecture, November 8, 2007. Washington, DC: United States Holocaust Memorial Museum, 2009. https://www.ushmm.org/m/pdfs/Publication_OP_2009-11.pdf.

———. *Complicity in the Holocaust: Churches and Universities in Nazi Germany*. Cambridge: Cambridge University Press, 2012.

———. *Theologians under Hitler*. New Haven, CT: Yale University Press, 1985.

Estelle, Bryan D. *Echoes of Exodus: Tracing a Biblical Motif*. Downers Grove, IL: IVP Academic, 2018.

Eubank, Nathan. *First and Second Thessalonians*. Grand Rapids: Baker Academic, 2019.

Eugenius IV. *Cantate Domino*. In *Decrees of the Ecumenical Councils*, vol. 1: *Nicaea I to Lateran V*, edited by Norman P. Tanner, 567–82. Washington, DC: Georgetown University Press, 1990.

Fackenheim, Emil L. *God's Presence in History: Jewish Affirmations and Philosophical Reflections*. New York: Harper & Row, 1972.

———. "Jewish-Christian Relations after the Holocaust: Toward Post-Holocaust Theological Thought." In *A Legacy of Catholic-Jewish Dialogue: The Joseph Cardinal Bernardin Jerusalem Lectures*, edited by Thomas A. Baima, 19–38. Chicago: Liturgy Training, 2012.

Farrow, Douglas. "Jew and Gentile in the Church Today." *Nova et Vetera* 16, no. 3 (2018) 979–93.

———. *Theological Negotiations: Proposals in Soteriology and Anthropology*. Grand Rapids: Baker Academic, 2018.

Fassbeck, G. *Der Tempel der Christen: Traditionsgeschichtliche Untersuchungen zur Aufnahme des Tempelkonzepts im frühen Christentum*. Tübingen: Francke, 2001.

Feingold, Lawrence. *The Mystery of Israel and the Church*. 4 vols. St. Louis, MO: Miriam, 2010.

Feldman, Louis H. "Anti-Semitism in the Ancient World." In *History and Hate: The Dimensions of Anti-Semitism*, edited by David Berger, 15–42. Philadelphia: Jewish Publication Society, 1986.

Feldmeier, Reinhard, and Hermann Spieckermann. *God of the Living: A Biblical Theology*. Translated by Mark E. Biddle. Waco, TX: Baylor University Press, 2011.

Férenzy, Oscar de. *Les Juifs et nous chrétiens*. Paris: 1935.

Fergusson, David. *Church, State and Civil Society*. Cambridge: Cambridge University Press, 2004.

———. *The Providence of God: A Polyphonic Approach*. Cambridge: Cambridge University Press, 2018.

Feuerbach, Ludwig. *The Essence of Christianity*. Translated by George Eliot. Amherst, NY: Prometheus, 1989.

Finzi, Roberto. *Anti-Semitism: From Its European Roots to the Holocaust*. New York: Interlink, 1999.

Fischer, Heinz-Joachim. *Päpste und Juden: Die Wende unter Johannes Paul II und Benedikt XVI*. Berlin: LIT, 2012.

Fishbane, Michael. "The 'Exodus' Motif: The Paradigm of Historical Renewal." In *Text and Texture: Close Readings of Selected Biblical Texts*, 121–40. New York: Schocken, 1979.

Fisher, Eugene J. "Are the Gospels Anti-Semitic?" In *Faith without Prejudice: Rebuilding Christian Attitudes Toward Judaism*, 2d ed., 56–71. New York: Crossroad, 1993.

———. "Heschel's Impact on Catholic-Jewish Relations." In *No Religion Is an Island: Abraham Joshua Heschel and Interreligious Dialogue*, edited by Harold Kasimow and Byron L. Sherwin, 3–22. Maryknoll, NY: Orbis, 1991.

———. *A Life in Dialogue: Building Bridges Between Catholics and Jews: A Memoir*. St. Petersburg, FL: Mr. Media, 2017.

———. "What Does *Dominus Iesus* Say about Judaism? Actually, Nothing." *Shofar* 22, no. 2 (January 2004) 33–43.

Fisher, Eugene J., and Leon Klenicki, eds. *The Saint for Shalom: How Pope John Paul II Transformed Catholic Jewish Relations: The Complete Texts 1979–2005*. New York: Crossroad, 2011.

Fitzmyer, Joseph A., SJ. "Antisemitism and the Cry of 'All the People' (Matt xxvii 25)." *Theological Studies* 26, no. 4 (December 1965) 667–71.

———. *First Corinthians: A New Translation with Introduction and Commentary.* New Haven, CT: Yale University Press, 2008.

———. *The Gospel According to Luke (X–XXIV).* Garden City, NY: Doubleday, 1985.

———. *The One Who Is to Come.* Grand Rapids: Eerdmans, 2007.

Flannery, Austin, OP, ed. *The Conciliar and Post Conciliar Documents*, rev. ed. Vol. 1 of *Vatican Council II: Constitutions, Degrees, Declarations.* Northport, NY: Costello, 1996.

Flannery, Edward H. *The Anguish of the Jews: Twenty-Three Centuries of Antisemitism.* New York: Macmillan, 1965.

———. *The Anguish of the Jews: Twenty-Three Centuries of Antisemitism.* 2d ed. Mahwah, NJ: Paulist, 2004.

———. "The Finaly Case." In *The Bridge: A Yearbook of Judeo-Christian Studies*, vol. 1, edited by John M. Oesterreicher, 306–13. New York: Pantheon, 1955.

———. "Israel, Jerusalem, and the Middle East." In *Twenty Years of Jewish-Catholic Relations*, edited by Eugene J. Fisher, A. James Rudin, and Marc H. Tenenbaum, 73–86. New York: Paulist, 1986.

Fleischacker, Samuel. *Divine Teaching and the Way of the World: A Defense of Revealed Religion.* Oxford: Oxford University Press, 2011.

———. *The Good and the Good Book: Revelation as a Guide to Life.* Oxford: Oxford University Press, 2015.

Fleischner, Eva. "Heschel's Significance for Jewish-Christian Relations." In *Abraham Joshua Heschel: Exploring His Life and Thought*, edited by John C. Merkle, 142–64. New York: Macmillan, 1985.

Foa, Anna. "The Difficult Apprenticeship of Diversity." In *The Catholic Church and the Jewish People: Recent Reflections from Rome*, edited by Philip A. Cunningham, Norbert J. Hofmann, and Joseph Sievers, 41–53. New York: Fordham University Press, 2007.

Forte, Bruno. "Israel and the Church—The Two Explorers of the Promised Land: Toward a Christian Theology of Judaism." In *The Catholic Church and the Jewish People: Recent Reflections from Rome*, edited by Philip A. Cunningham, Norbert J. Hofmann, and Joseph Sievers, 73–91. New York: Fordham University Press, 2007.

Fowl, Stephen. "Learning to Be a Gentile: Christ's Transformation and Redemption of Our Past." In *Christology and Scripture: Interdisciplinary Perspectives*, edited by Andrew T. Lincoln and Angus Paddison, 22–40. London: T. & T. Clark, 2007.

Francis, Pope. "Address to members of the 'International Council of Christians and Jews.'" June 30, 2015. Vatican.va.

———. *Evangelii Gaudium.* Vatican trans. Boston: Pauline, 2013. Vatican.va.

Frankel, David. *The Land of Canaan and the Destiny of Israel: Theologies of Territory in the Hebrew Bible.* Winona Lake, IN: Eisenbrauns, 2011.

Franks, Christopher A. "Aristotelian Doctrines in Aquinas's Treatment of Justice." In *Aristotle in Aquinas's Theology*, edited by Gilles Emery and Matthew Levering, 139–66. Oxford: Oxford University Press, 2015.

Fredriksen, Paula. *Augustine and the Jews: A Christian Defense of Jews and Judaism.* 2d ed. New Haven, CT: Yale University Press, 2010.

———. *Paul: The Pagans' Apostle.* New Haven, CT: Yale University Press, 2017.

———. "*Secundum Carnem*: History and Israel in the Theology of St. Augustine." In *The Limits of Ancient Christianity: Essays on Late Antique Thought and Culture in Honor of R. A. Markus*, edited by W. Klingshirn and M. Vessey, 26–41. Ann Arbor, MI: University of Michigan Press, 1999.

———. *When Christians Were Jews: The First Generation*. New Haven, CT: Yale University Press, 2018.

Freedman, David Noel. *The Nine Commandments: Uncovering the Hidden Pattern of Crime and Punishment in the Hebrew Bible*. Edited by Astrid B. Beck. New York: Doubleday, 2000.

Freyne, Sean. "Vilifying the Other and Defining the Self: Matthew's and John's Anti-Jewish Polemic in Focus." In *"To See Ourselves as Others See Us": Christians, Jews, "Others" in Late Antiquity*, edited by Jacob Neusner and E. Frerichs, 117–43. Chico, CA: Scholars, 1985.

Friedman, Richard Elliott. *The Exodus*. New York: HarperCollins, 2017.

Frymer-Kensky, Tikva. "The Emergence of Jewish Biblical Theologies." In *Jews, Christians, and the Theology of the Hebrew Scriptures*, edited by Alice Ogden Bellis and Joel S. Kaminsky, 109–21. Atlanta: SBL, 2000.

Frymer-Kensky, Tikva, David Novak, Peter Ochs, David Fox Sandmel, Michael A. Signer. "A Jewish Statement on Christians and Christianity." In *Christianity in Jewish Terms*, edited by Tikva Frymer-Kensky et al., xvii–xx. Boulder, CO: Westview, 2000.

———. "What of the Future? A Jewish Response." In *Christianity in Jewish Terms*, edited by Tikva Frymer-Kensky et al., 366–73. Boulder, CO: Westview, 2000.

Frymer-Kensky, Tikva, David Novak, Peter Ochs, and Michael A. Signer. "Jewish-Christian Dialogue: Jon D. Levenson and Critics." *Commentary* 113, no. 4 (April 2002) 8–21.

Fuhr, Richard Alan, Jr., and Gary E. Yates. *The Message of the Twelve: Hearing the Voice of the Minor Prophets*. Nashville, TN: B&H Academic, 2016.

Füllenbach, Elias H. "Shock, Renewal, Crisis: Catholic Reflections on the Shoah." In *Antisemitism, Christian Ambivalence, and the Holocaust*, edited by Kevin P. Spicer, 201–34. Bloomington, IN: Indiana University Press, 2007.

Fuller, Michael E. *The Restoration of Israel: Israel's Regathering and the Fate of the Nations in Early Jewish Literature and Luke-Acts*. Berlin: de Gruyter, 2006.

Furnal, Joshua. "Abraham Joshua Heschel and *Nostra Aetate*: Shaping the Catholic Reconsideration of Judaism During Vatican II." *Religions* 7, no. 6 (June 2016). https://doi.org/10.3390/rel7060070.

Furstenberg, Yair. "Defilement Penetrating the Body: A New Understanding of Contamination in Mark 7.15." *New Testament Studies* 54, no. 2 (April 2008) 176–200.

Fyall, Robert. "A Curious Silence: The Temple in 1 and 2 Kings." In *Heaven on Earth: Temple in Biblical Theology*, edited by T. Desmond Alexander and Simon Gathercole, 49–58. Waynesboro, GA: Paternoster, 2004.

Gadenz, Pablo T. *The Gospel of Luke*. Grand Rapids: Baker Academic, 2018.

Gager, John G. *The Origins of Anti-Semitism: Attitudes Towards Judaism in Pagan and Christian Antiquity*. Oxford: Oxford University Press, 1983.

Gale, Aaron M. "Introduction and Annotations." In *The Jewish Annotated New Testament*, edited by Amy-Jill Levine and Marc Zvi Brettler, 1–54. Oxford: Oxford University Press, 2011.

Gallagher, Delia. "Pope Celebrates Church Document That Turned Jews 'From Enemies' Into Friends." CNN International Edition. October 28, 2015. https://edition.cnn.com/2015/10/28/world/pope-jews.

Gane, Roy E. *Old Testament Law for Christians: Original Context and Enduring Application*. Grand Rapids: Baker Academic, 2017.

Gans, Chaim. *A Just Zionism: On the Morality of the Jewish State*. Oxford: Oxford University Press, 2008.

Gaon, Saadia. *The Book of Beliefs and Opinions*. Translated by Samuel Rosenblatt. New Haven, CT: Yale University Press, 1948.

Garrett, Susan R. "Exodus from Bondage: Luke 9:31 and Acts 12:1–24." *Catholic Biblical Quarterly* 52, no. 4 (October 1990) 656–80.

———. "The Meaning of Jesus' Death in Luke." *Word and World* 12, no 1. (1992) 11–16.

Garrigou-Lagrange, Réginald, OP. "On those who are invincibly ignorant of the preaching of the Catholic faith." In *De revelatione per ecclesiam proposita*, 5th ed., 500–502. Rome: Desclée, 1950.

———. *Providence*. Translated by Bede Rose. Rockford, IL: TAN, 1998.

Garrigues, Jean-Miguel, OP. "Un seul peuple en deux assemblées: la Synagogue et l'Église." In Jean-Miguel Garrigues et al., *L'unique Israel de Dieu*, 59–72. Limoges: Criterion, 1987.

Gärtner, Bertil. *The Temple and the Community in Qumran and the New Testament: A Comparative Study in the Temple Symbolism of the Qumran Texts and the New Testament*. Cambridge: Cambridge University Press, 1965.

Geiger, Ari. "What Happened to Christian Hebraism in the Thirteenth Century?" In *Jews and Christians in Thirteenth-Century France*, edited by Elisheva Baumgarten and Judah D. Galinsky, 49–63. New York: Palgrave Macmillan, 2015.

Gellman, Yehuda (Jerome). "The *Akedah* and Covenant Today." In *Two Faiths, One Covenant? Jewish and Christian Identity in the Presence of the Other*, edited by Eugene B. Korn and John Pawlikowski, 35–42. Lanham, MD: Rowman & Littlefield, 2005.

Gerdmar, Anders. *Roots of Theological Anti-Semitism: German Biblical Interpretation and the Jews, from Herder and Semler to Kittel and Bultmann*. Leiden: Brill, 2009.

Giambrone, Anthony, OP. Review of *When Christians Were Jews: The First Generation*, by Paula Fredriksen. *Nova et Vetera* 19 (2021) 303–309.

Gilbert, Martin. *Auschwitz and the Allies*. New York: Holt, Rinehart, and Winston, 1980.

Girard, René. *I See Satan Fall Like Lightning*. Translated by James G. Williams. Maryknoll, NY: Orbis, 2001.

———. *Violence and the Sacred*. Translated by Patrick Gregory. Baltimore: Johns Hopkins University Press, 1977.

Glenn, Susan A. "The 'Kidnapping' of Hilda McCoy: Child Adoption and Religious Conflict in the Shadow of the Holocaust." *Jewish Social Studies* 24, no. 3 (2019) 80–123.

Goldhagen, Daniel Jonah. *The Devil That Never Dies: The Rise and Threat of Global Antisemitism*. New York: Back Bay, 2013.

———. *Hitler's Willing Executioners: Ordinary Germans and the Holocaust*. New York: Knopf, 1996.

———. *A Moral Reckoning: The Role of the Catholic Church in the Holocaust and Its Unfulfilled Duty of Repair*. New York: Knopf, 2002.

Goldin, William B. "St. Thomas Aquinas and Supersessionism: A Contextual Study and Doctrinal Application." STD Thesis, Angelicum, 2017.

Goldingay, John. *Israel's Faith*. Vol. 2 of *Old Testament Theology*. Downers Grove, IL: InterVarsity, 2006.

———. *Israel's Gospel*. Vol. 1 of *Old Testament Theology*. Downers Grove, IL: InterVarsity, 2003.

———. *Israel's Life*. Vol. 3 of *Old Testament Theology*. Downers Grove, IL: InterVarsity, 2009.

Goldman, Shalom. *Zeal for Zion: Christians, Jews, and the Idea of the Promised Land*. Chapel Hill, NC: University of North Carolina Press, 2009.

Goldstein, Jonathan A. *II Maccabees: A New Translation with Introduction and Commentary*. Garden City, NY: Doubleday, 1983.

Goodman, Lenn E. "Judaism and the Problem of Evil." In *The Cambridge Companion to the Problem of Evil*, edited by Chad Meister and Paul K. Moser, 193–209. Cambridge: Cambridge University Press, 2017.

———. *On Justice: An Essay in Jewish Philosophy*. Oxford: The Littman Library of Jewish Civilization, 2008.

Goodman, Martin. "The Temple in First Century CE Judaism." In *Temple and Worship in Biblical Israel*, edited by John Day, 459–68. London: T. & T. Clark, 2007.

Goodwin, Deborah L. "Jews and Judaism." In *The Oxford Guide to the Historical Reception of Augustine*, vol. 3, edited by Karla Pollmann, 1214–18. Oxford: Oxford University Press, 2013.

Gordis, David M., and Peter C. Phan. "Catholics and Jews: Looking Ahead." In *Toward the Future: Essays on Catholic-Jewish Relations in Memory of Rabbi León Klenicki*, edited by Celia M. Deutsch, Eugene J. Fisher, and James Rudin, 215–24. New York: Paulist, 2013.

Goris, Harm. "Theology and Theory of the Word in Aquinas: Understanding Augustine by Innovating Aristotle." In *Aquinas the Augustinian*, edited by Michael Dauphinais, Barry A. David, and Matthew Levering, 62–78. Washington, DC: Catholic University of America Press, 2007.

Gorman, Michael J. *Inhabiting the Cruciform God: Kenosis, Justification, and Theosis in Paul's Narrative Soteriology*. Grand Rapids: Eerdmans, 2009.

Goshen-Gottstein, Alan. "Judaisms and Incarnational Theologies: Mapping Out the Parameters of Dialogue." *Journal of Ecumenical Studies* 39, no. 3 (2002) 219–47.

Graves, Michael. *The Inspiration and Interpretation of Scripture: What the Early Church Can Teach Us*. Grand Rapids: Eerdmans, 2014.

Gray, Alyssa M. "The People, Not the Peoples: The Talmud Bavli's 'Charitable' Contribution to the Jewish-Christian Conversation in Mesopotamia." *The Review of Rabbinic Judaism* 20, no. 2 (August 2017) 137–67.

Gray, Timothy C. *The Temple in the Gospel of Mark*. Tübingen: Mohr Siebeck, 2008.

Grayzel, Solomon. *The Church and the Jews in the XIIIth Century: A Study of Their Relations During the Years 1198–1254, Based on the Papal Letters and the Conciliar Decrees of the Period*. Rev. ed. New York: Hermon, 1966.

———. *The Church and the Jews in the XIIIth Century*. Vol. 2: *1254–1314*. Edited by Kenneth R. Stow. New York: Jewish Theological Seminary in America, 1989.

Green, Joel B. *1 Peter*. Grand Rapids: Eerdmans, 2007.

Greenberg, Irving. *For the Sake of Heaven and Earth: The New Encounter Between Judaism and Christianity*. Philadelphia: Jewish Publication Society, 2004.

———. "Judaism and Christianity: Covenants of Redemption." In *Christianity in Jewish Terms*, edited by Tikva Frymer-Kensky et al., 141–58. Boulder CO: Westview, 2000.

———. "Judaism and Christianity: Their Respective Roles in the Strategy of Redemption." In *Visions of the Other: Jewish and Christian Theologians Assess the Dialogue*, edited by Eugene J. Fisher, 7–27. New York: Paulist, 1994.

Greenberg, Moshe. *Ezekiel 21–37: A New Translation with Introduction and Commentary*. New York: Doubleday, 1997.

Gregerman, Adam. "Biblical Prophecy and the Fate of the Nations in Early Jewish and Christian Interpretations of Isaiah." In *'What Does the Scripture Say?': Studies in the Function of Scripture in Early Judaism and Christianity*, vol. 1: *The Synoptic Gospels*, edited by Craig A. Evans and H. Daniel Zecharias, 212–40. London: Bloomsbury, 2012.

———. *Building on the Ruins of the Temple: Apologetics and Polemics in Early Christianity and Rabbinic Judaism*. Tübingen: Mohr Siebeck, 2016.

———. "Comparative Christian Hermeneutical Approaches to the Land Promises to Abraham." *Cross Currents* 64, no. 3 (September 2014) 410–24.

———. "Interpreting the Pain of Others: John Paul II and Benedict XVI on Jewish Suffering in the *Shoah*." *Journal of Ecumenical Studies* 48, no. 4 (September 2013) 443–66.

———. "Israel as the 'Hermeneutical Jew' in Protestant Statements on the Land and State of Israel: Four Presbyterian Examples." *Israel Affairs* 23, no. 5 (September 2017) 773–93.

———. "Is the Biblical Land Promise Irrevocable? Post-*Nostra Aetate* Catholic Theologies of the Jewish Covenant and the Land of Israel." *Modern Theology* 34, no. 2 (April 2018) 137–58.

———. "Jewish Theology and Limits on Reciprocity in Catholic-Jewish Dialogue: A Response to Cardinal Kurt Koch's October 30, 2011 Keynote Address at Seton Hall University during the 10th Annual Meeting of the Council of Centers on Christian-Jewish Relations." *Studies in Christian-Jewish Relations* 7, no. 1 (May 2012) 1–13.

———. "Old Wine in New Bottles: Liberation Theology and the Israeli-Palestinian Conflict." *Journal of Ecumenical Studies* 41, no. 3–4 (Fall 2004) 313–40.

———. "Reverence Despite Rejection: The Paradox of Early Christian Views of Biblical Authority." *Cross Currents* 59, no. 2 (2009) 176–90.

———. "Superiority without Supersessionism: Walter Kasper, *The Gifts and the Calling of God Are Irrevocable*, and God's Covenant with the Jews." *Theological Studies* 79, no. 1 (2018) 36–59.

Groppe, Elizabeth. "Revisiting Vatican II's Theology of the People of God after Forty-Five Years of Catholic-Jewish Dialogue." *Theological Studies* 72, no. 3 (September 2011) 586–619.

———. "Toward the Future as People of God and Partners in Covenant." In *Toward the Future: Essays on Catholic-Jewish Relations in Memory of Rabbi León Klenicki*, edited by Celia M. Deutsch, Eugene J. Fisher, and James Rudin, 69–81. New York: Paulist, 2013.

———. "The Tri-Unity of God and the Fractures of Human History." In *Christ Jesus and the Jewish People Today: New Explorations of Theological Interrelationships*, edited by Philip A. Cunningham, et al., 164–82. Grand Rapids: Eerdmans, 2011.

Gross, Michael B. *The War Against Catholicism: Liberalism and the Anti-Catholic Imagination in Nineteenth-Century Germany*. Ann Arbor, MI: University of Michigan Press, 2004.
Guarino, Thomas G. *The Disputed Teachings of Vatican II: Continuity and Reversal in Catholic Doctrine*. Grand Rapids: Eerdmans, 2018.
Guelich, Robert A. "Anti-Semitism and/or Anti-Judaism in Mark?" In *Anti-Semitism and Early Christianity: Issues of Polemic and Faith*, edited by Craig A. Evans and Donald A. Hagner, 80–101. Minneapolis: Fortress, 1993.
Gunneweg, Antonius H. J. *Biblische Theologie des Alten Testaments. Eine Religionsgeschichte Israels in biblisch-theologischer Sicht*. Stuttgart: Kohlhammer, 1993.
Gupta, Nijay K. *Paul and the Language of Faith*. Grand Rapids: Eerdmans, 2020.
Gushee, David P., and Glen Stassen. "An Open Letter to America's Christian Zionists." New Evangelical Partnership For The Common Good. September 19, 2011. http://www.newevangelicalpartnership.org/.
Guttmann, A. "The End of the Jewish Sacrificial Cult." In *Origins of Judaism*, vol. 6: *History of the Jews in the First Century of the Common Era*, edited by Jacob Neusner, 229–40. New York: Garland, 1990.
Habel, Norman C. *The Land Is Mine: Six Biblical Land Ideologies*. Minneapolis: Fortress, 1995.
Hagner, Donald A. "Paul's Quarrel with Judaism." In *Anti-Semitism and Early Christianity: Issues of Polemic and Faith*, edited by Craig A. Evans and Donald A. Hagner, 128–50. Minneapolis: Fortress, 1993.
Hahn, Scott W. *The Kingdom of God as Liturgical Empire: A Theological Commentary on 1–2 Chronicles*. Grand Rapids: Baker Academic, 2012.
———. *Kinship by Covenant: A Canonical Approach to the Fulfillment of God's Saving Promises*. New Haven, CT: Yale University Press, 2009.
The Haifa Declaration. Mada al-Carmel. May 2007. https://mada-research.org/wp-content/uploads/2007/09/watheeqat-haifa-english.pdf.
Halbertal, Moshe. "Addressing the Needs of Others: What Is the Stance of Justice?" In *Radical Responsibility: Celebrating the Thought of Chief Rabbi Lord Jonathan Sacks*, edited by Michael J. Harris, Daniel Rynhold, and Tamra Wright, 95–109. New Milford, CT: Maggid, 2012.
Halevi, Yossi Klein. *At the Entrance to the Garden of Eden: A Jew's Search for Hope with Christians and Muslims in the Holy Land*. New York: HarperCollins, 2002.
———. *Letters to My Palestinian Neighbor*. New York: HarperCollins, 2018.
Halpern, Baruch. *David's Secret Demons: Messiah, Murderer, Traitor, King*. Grand Rapids: Eerdmans, 2001.
Hamerton-Kelly, Robert G. *The Gospel and the Sacred: Politics of Violence in Mark*. Minneapolis: Fortress, 1994.
———. *Sacred Violence: Paul's Hermeneutic of the Cross*. Minneapolis: Fortress, 1992.
———, ed. *Violent Origins: Walter Burkert, René Girard, and Jonathan Z. Smith on Ritual Killing and Cultural Formation*. Stanford, CA: Stanford University Press, 1987.
Hammele, Matthias. *Das Bild der Juden im Johannes-Kommentar des Thomas von Aquin. Ein Beitrag zu Bibelhermeneutik und Wissenschafts-geschichte im 13. Jahrhundert*. Stuttgart: Bibelwerk, 2012.

Hammer, Leonard. "Discerning Israel's Interpretation of the 1993 Holy See-Israel Fundamental Agreement." In *The Vatican-Israel Accords: Political, Legal, Theological Contexts*, edited by Marshall J. Breger, 67–96. Notre Dame, IN: University of Notre Dame Press, 2004.

———. "The Holy See-PLO Agreement and Its Significance for Israel." In *The Vatican-Israel Accords: Political, Legal, Theological Contexts*, edited by Marshall J. Breger, 150–67. Notre Dame, IN: University of Notre Dame Press, 2004.

———. "2015 Comprehensive Agreement Between the Holy See and the Palestinian Authority: Discerning the Holy See's Approach to International Relations in the Holy Land." *Oxford Journal of Law and Religion* 6, no. 1 (February 2017) 162–79.

Hammer, Reuven. *Akiva: Life, Legend, Legacy*. Philadelphia: Jewish Publication Society, 2015.

Hansen, Collin. "Why Some Jews Fear the Passion." *Christianity Today*, August 8, 2008. http://www.christianitytoday.com/ch/news/2004/feb20.html.

Hare, Douglas R. A. "The Rejection of the Jews in the Synoptic Gospels and Acts." In *Anti-Semitism and the Foundations of Christianity*, edited by Alan T. Davies, 28–32. New York: Paulist, 1979.

Harkins, Angela Kim. "Biblical and Historical Perspectives on 'the People of God.'" In *Transforming Relations: Essays on Jews and Christians throughout History in Honor of Michael A. Signer*, edited by Franklin T. Harkins, 319–39. Notre Dame, IN: University of Notre Dame Press, 2010.

Harkins, Franklin T. "*Primus Doctor Iudaeorum*: Moses as Theological Master in the *Summa Theologiae* of Thomas Aquinas." *The Thomist* 75, no. 1 (2011) 65–94.

———, ed. *Transforming Relations: Essays on Jews and Christians throughout History in Honor of Michael A. Signer*. Notre Dame, IN: University of Notre Dame Press, 2010.

Harley, David C. "The Church and the Jewish People: A Theological Perspective." *International Bulletin of Missionary Research* 11, no. 3 (July 1987) 117–20.

Harrington, Daniel J., SJ. *First and Second Maccabees*. Collegeville, MN: Liturgical, 2012.

Hart, David Bentley. *Atheist Delusions: The Christian Revolution and Its Fashionable Enemies*. New Haven, CT: Yale University Press, 2009.

———. *The Experience of God: Being, Consciousness, Bliss*. New Haven, CT: Yale University Press, 2013.

———. *The New Testament: A Translation*. New Haven, CT: Yale University Press, 2017.

———. *That All Shall Be Saved*. New Haven, CT: Yale University Press, 2019.

———. "What Lies Beyond Capitalism? A Christian Exploration." *Plough Quarterly* no. 21 (August 2019) 32–38.

Hartman, David. *Conflicting Visions: Spiritual Possibilities of Modern Israel*. New York: Schocken, 1990.

———. *Israelis and the Jewish Tradition: An Ancient People Debating Its Future*. New Haven, CT: Yale University Press, 2000.

———. *A Living Covenant: The Innovative Spirit in Traditional Judaism*. Woodstock, VT: Jewish Lights, 1997.

Hasan-Rokem, Galit, and Alan Dundes. *The Wandering Jew: Essays in the Interpretation of a Christian Legend*. Bloomington, IN: Indiana University Press, 1986.

Hauerwas, Stanley. *Against the Nations: War and Survival in a Liberal Society*. Notre Dame, IN: University of Notre Dame Press, 1992.

———. *In Good Company: The Church as Polis*. Notre Dame, IN: University of Notre Dame Press, 1995.

Hayes, Christine. *What's Divine about Divine Law? Early Perspectives*. Princeton, NJ: Princeton University Press, 2015.

Hayes, Peter. *Why? Explaining the Holocaust*. New York: W. W. Norton, 2017.

Haynes, Stephen R. *Jews and the Christian Imagination: Reluctant Witnesses*. Louisville, KY: Westminster John Knox, 1995.

Hays, J. Daniel. *The Temple and the Tabernacle: A Study of God's Dwelling Places from Genesis to Revelation*. Grand Rapids: Baker, 2016.

Hays, Richard B. *Echoes of Scripture in the Letters of Paul*. New Haven, CT: Yale University Press, 1989.

———. *First Corinthians*. Louisville, KY: John Knox, 1997.

———. *The Moral Vision of the New Testament: Community, Cross, New Creation: A Contemporary Introduction to New Testament Ethics*. New York: HarperCollins, 1996.

Hayward, C. T. R. *The Jewish Temple: A Non-Biblical Sourcebook*. London: Routledge, 1996.

Hazony, Yoram. *God and Politics in Esther*. 2d ed. Cambridge: Cambridge University Press, 2016.

———. *The Jewish State: The Struggle for Israel's Soul*. New York: Basic, 2000.

———. *The Philosophy of Hebrew Scripture*. Cambridge: Cambridge University Press, 2012.

Head, Peter. "The Temple in Luke's Gospel." In *Heaven on Earth: Temple in Biblical Theology*, edited by T. Desmond Alexander and Simon Gathercole, 101–19. Waynesboro, GA: Paternoster, 2004.

Healy, Mary. *Hebrews*. Grand Rapids: Baker Academic, 2016.

Hector, Kevin. *Theology without Metaphysics: God, Language, and the Spirit of Recognition*. Cambridge: Cambridge University Press, 2011.

Hedley, Douglas. "For God's Sake: Why Sacrifice? Mediating Reflections on Peter Jonkers and John Milbank." *Neue Zeitschrift für systematische Theologie und Religionsphilosophie* 50 (2008) 301–17.

Heim, S. Mark. *Saved from Sacrifice: A Theology of the Cross*. Grand Rapids: Eerdmans, 2006.

Held, Shai. *The Heart of Torah*, vol. 1: *Essays on the Weekly Torah Portion: Genesis and Exodus*. Philadelphia: Jewish Publication Society, 2017.

Heldt, Petra. "Bibliography of Dialogue between Orthodox Christians and Jews." *Immanuel* 26/27 (1994) 240–50.

———. "A Brief History of the Dialogue between Orthodox Christians and Jews." *Immanuel* 26/27 (1994) 211–24.

Hellman, John. "The Jews in the 'New Middle Ages': Jacques Maritain's Anti-Semitism in Its Times." In *Jacques Maritain and the Jews*, edited by Robert Royal, 89–103. Mishawaka, IN: American Maritain Association, 1994.

Helmer, Christine. *How Luther Became the Reformer*. Louisville, KY: Westminster John Knox, 2019.

Hendel, Ronald S. *Remembering Abraham: Culture, Memory, and History in the Hebrew Bible*. Oxford: Oxford University Press, 2005.

Henrix, Hans Herman. "The Son of God Became Human as a Jew: Implications of the Jewishness of Jesus for Christology." In *Christ Jesus and the Jewish People Today: New Explorations of Theological Interrelationships*, edited by Philip Cunningham et al., 114–43. Grand Rapids: Eerdmans, 2011.

Heschel, Abraham Joshua. *The Earth Is the Lord's: the Inner World of the Jew in Eastern Europe*. 1st paperback ed. Woodstock, VT: Jewish Lights, 1995.

———. "From Mission to Dialogue." *Conservative Judaism* 21, no. 3 (Spring 1967) 1–11.

———. *God in Search of Man: A Philosophy of Judaism*. New York: Farrar, Straus and Giroux, 1955.

———. *Heavenly Torah: As Refracted through the Generations*. Edited and translated by Gordon Tucker. New York: Continuum, 2005.

———. *Israel: An Echo of Eternity*. New York: Farrar, Straus and Giroux, 1969.

———. "No Religion Is an Island." *Union Seminary Quarterly Review* 21 (1966) 117–34.

———. *The Prophets*. New York: HarperCollins, 2001.

———. *The Sabbath: Its Meaning for the Modern Man*. New York, NY: Farrar, Straus and Giroux, 2005.

Heschel, Susannah. *The Aryan Jesus: Christian Theologians and the Bible in Nazi Germany*. Princeton, NJ: Princeton University Press, 2008.

Heyman, George. *The Power of Sacrifice: Roman and Christian Discourses in Conflict*. Washington, DC: Catholic University of America Press, 2007.

Hibbs, Pierce Taylor. *The Speaking Trinity and His Worded World: Why Language Is at the Center of Everything*. Eugene, OR: Wipf & Stock, 2018.

Higgins, George G. "Twenty Years of Catholic-Jewish Relations: *Nostra Aetate* in Retrospect." In *Twenty Years of Jewish-Catholic Relations*, edited by Eugene J. Fisher, A. James Rudin, and Marc H. Tanenbaum, 19–38. New York: Paulist, 1986.

Hirshman, Marc. *A Rivalry of Genius: Jewish and Christian Biblical Interpretation in Late Antiquity*. Translated by Batya Stein. New York: SUNY, 1996.

Hocken, Peter. "The Jewish People and the Unity of the Church." *Louvain Studies* 33, no. 3 (March 2008) 304–18.

Hoffman, Karl W. *Ursprung und Anfängstatigkeit der ersten Päpstlichen MissionInstituts, ein Beitrag zur Geschichte der katholische Juden und Mohammedanermission im sechzehnten Jahrhundert*. Munster: Aschendorff, 1923.

Hood, John Y. B. *Aquinas and the Jews*. Philadelphia: University of Pennsylvania Press, 1995.

———. "Did Augustine Abandon His Doctrine of Jewish Witness in *Aduersus Iudaeos*?" *Augustinian Studies* 50, no. 2 (2019) 171–95.

Hopkins, Martin K., OP. "Jewish-Catholic Relations after Vatican II." *Perkins School of Theology Journal* 23, no. 1 (Fall 1970) 15–21.

Hoskins, Paul M. *Jesus as the Fulfillment of the Temple in the Gospel of John*. Eugene, OR: Wipf & Stock, 2007.

Howard, J. K. "'Christ Our Passover': A Study of the Passover-Exodus Theme in 1 Corinthians." *Evangelical Quarterly* 41 (1969) 97–108.

Hruby, Kurt. "The Future of Jewish-Christian Dialogue: A Christian View." Translated by Francis McDonagh. In *Christians and Jews*, edited by Hans Küng and Walter Kasper, 87–92. New York: Seabury, 1975.

Hubert, Henri, and Marcel Mauss. *Sacrifice: Its Nature and Functions*. Translated by W. D. Halls. Chicago: University of Chicago Press, 1964.

Huizenga, Leroy A. *The New Isaac: Tradition and Intertextuality in the Gospel of Matthew*. Leiden: Brill, 2009.

Hummel, Daniel G. "*His Land* and the Origins of the Jewish-Evangelical Israel Lobby." *Church History* 87, no. 4 (December 2018) 1119–51.

Humphrey, Edith M. *And I Turned to See the Voice: The Rhetoric of Vision in the New Testament*. Grand Rapids: Baker Academic, 2007.

Hünermann, Peter. "Jewish-Christian Relations: A Conciliar Discovery and Its Methodological Consequences for Dogmatic Theology." In *The Catholic Church and the Jewish People: Recent Reflections from Rome*, edited by Philip A. Cunningham, Norbert J. Hofmann, and Joseph Sievers, 113–26. New York: Fordham University Press, 2007.

Hunsinger, George. "After Barth: A Christian Appreciation of Jews and Judaism." In *Karl Barth, the Jews, and Judaism*, edited by George Hunsinger, 60–74. Grand Rapids: Eerdmans, 2018.

Hunter, Alastair G. *An Introduction to the Psalms*. London: T. & T. Clark, 2008.

Hurowitz, Victor Avigdor. *I Have Built You an Exalted House: Temple Building in the Bible in Light of Mesopotamian and Northwest Semitic Writings*. Sheffield: Sheffield Academic, 1992.

———. "Yhwh's Exalted House—Aspects of the Design and Symbolism of Solomon's Temple." In *Temple and Worship in Biblical Israel: Proceedings of the Oxford Old Testament Seminar*, edited by John Day, 63–110. New York: T. & T. Clark, 2007.

Hütter, Reinhard. *Bound for Beatitude: A Thomistic Study in Eschatology and Ethics*. Washington, DC: Catholic University of America Press, 2019.

Imbelli, Robert P. "The Reaffirmation of the Christic Center." In *Sic et Non: Encountering Dominus Iesus*, edited by Stephen J. Pope and Charles Hefling, 96–106. Maryknoll, NY: Orbis, 2002.

———. *Rekindling the Christic Imagination: Theological Meditations for the New Evangelization*. Collegeville, MN: Liturgical, 2014.

Imes, Carmen Joy. *Bearing God's Name: Why Sinai Still Matters*. Downers Grove, IL: IVP Academic, 2019.

Inbari, Motti. *Messianic Religious Zionism Confronts Israeli Territorial Compromises*. Cambridge: Cambridge University Press, 2012.

Innocent III. "*Etsi non displiceat Domino*." January 1205. In *The Apostolic See and the Jews*. Vol. 1: *492–1404*, edited by Shlomo Simonsohn, 82–83. The Pontifical Institute of Mediaeval Studies, 1988.

———. *Licet perfidia Iudaeorum* (1199). In Heinrich Denzinger. *Compendium of Creeds, Definitions, and Declarations on Matters of Faith and Morals*, German edition revised, enlarged, and edited by Peter Hünermann and Helmut Hoping, English edition edited by Robert Fastiggi and Anne Englund Nash, 43rd edition, nos. 772–773. San Francisco: Ignatius, 2012.

Irani, George E. *The Papacy and the Middle East: The Role of the Holy See in the Arab-Israeli Conflict, 1962–1984*. Notre Dame, IN: University of Notre Dame Press, 1986.

Isaac, Jules. *Jesus and Israel*. Translated by Claire Huchet Bishop. New York: Holt, Rinehart and Winston, 1971.

———. *The Teaching of Contempt: Christian Roots of Anti-Semitism*. Translated by Helen Weaver. New York: Holt, Rinehart and Winston, 1964.
Isbell, Charles David. *The Function of Exodus Motifs in Biblical Narratives: Theological Didactic Drama*. Lewiston, NY: Edwin Mellen, 2002.
———. *Sermons from a Southern Rabbi*. Eugene, OR: Wipf & Stock, 2009.
Ivy, Alfred L. "Maimonides on Creation." In *Creation and the End of Days: Judaism and Scientific Cosmology*, edited by David Novak and Robert Samuelson, 185–209. Lanham, MD: University Press of America, 1986.
Jacobs, Louis. "The Significance of the Law: In Judaism." In *Christians and Jews*, edited by Hans Küng and Walter Kasper, 17–24. New York: Seabury, 1975.
Jaffé, Dan. *Le judaïsme et l'avènement du christianisme. Orthodoxie et hétérodoxie dans la literature talmudique, Ier-IIe siècle*. Paris: Cerf, 2005.
Jasper, David. *A Short Introduction to Hermeneutics*. Louisville, KY: Westminster John Knox, 2004.
Jaspers, Karl. *The Question of German Guilt*. Translated by E. B. Ashton. New York: Doubleday, 1947.
Jenkins, Philip. *Laying Down the Sword: Why We Can't Ignore the Bible's Violent Verses*. New York: HarperCollins, 2011.
Jenson, Robert W. "Toward a Christian Theology of Judaism." In *Jews and Christians: People of God*, edited by Carl E. Braaten and Robert W. Jenson, 1–13. Grand Rapids: Eerdmans, 2003.
———. *The Triune Story: Collected Essays on Scripture*. Edited by Brad East. Oxford: Oxford University Press, 2019.
Jewish Publication Society. *The Jewish Study Bible*, edited by Adele Berlin and Marc Zvi Brettler. Oxford: Oxford University Press, 2004.
Jipp, Joshua W. *The Messianic Theology of the New Testament*. Grand Rapids: Eerdmans, 2020.
Jocz, Jakob. *A Theology of Election*. New York: Macmillan, 1958.
John Paul II. "Address to Representatives of the West German Jewish Community." Mainz, West Germany. November 17, 1980. In *The Saint for Shalom: How Pope John Paul II Transformed Catholic Jewish Relations: The Complete Texts 1979–2005*, edited by Eugene J. Fisher and Leon Klenicki, 58–61. New York: Crossroad, 2011. https://www.ccjr.us/dialogika-resources/documents-and-statements/roman-catholic/pope-john-paul-ii/jp2-8onov17.
———. *The Place Within: The Poetry of Pope John Paul II*. Translated by Jerzy Peterkiewicz. New York: Random House, 1994.
———. "Universal Prayer—Day of Pardon." Vatican Basilica, March 12, 2000. Vatican. va.
Johnson, Luke Timothy. *Among the Gentiles: Greco-Roman Religion and Christianity*. New Haven, CT: Yale University Press, 2009.
———. *Constructing Paul: The Canonical Paul*, vol. 1. Grand Rapids: Eerdmans, 2020.
———. *The Gospel of Luke*. Collegeville, MN: Liturgical, 1991.
———. "The New Testament's Anti-Jewish Slander and the Conventions of Ancient Polemic." *Journal of Biblical Literature* 108, no. 3 (1989) 419–41.
Johnson, Mark. "Did St. Thomas Aquinas Attribute a Doctrine of Creation to Aristotle?" *New Scholasticism* 63, no. 2 (May 1989) 129–55.
Johnson, Sylvester. "New Israel, New Canaan: The Bible, the People of God, and the American Holocaust." *Union Seminary Quarterly Review* 59 (2005) 25–39.

Jones, Andrew Willard. *Before Church and State: A Study of Social Order in the Sacramental Kingdom of St. Louis IX*. Steubenville, OH: Emmaus Academic, 2017.
Jones, E. Michael. *Catholics and the Jew Taboo*. South Bend, IN: Fidelity, 2018.
———. *Jewish Fables: Darwinism, Materialism, and Other Jewish Fables*. South Bend, IN: Fidelity, 2018.
———. *Jewish Privilege*. South Bend, IN: Fidelity, 2019.
———. *The Jewish Revolutionary Spirit*. South Bend, IN: Fidelity, 2008.
———. *The Jews and Moral Subversion*. Edited by John Beaumont. South Bend, IN: Fidelity, 2016.
Jones, Priscilla Dale. "The Finaly Affair: Issues and Implications." *Religion* 13, no. 3 (July 1983) 177–203.
Jordan, William Chester. *The French Monarchy and the Jews: From Philip Augustus to the Last Capetians*. Philadelphia: University of Pennsylvania Press, 1989.
Joseph, Simon J. *Jesus and the Temple: The Crucifixion in Jewish Context*. Cambridge: Cambridge University Press, 2018.
Joslyn-Siemiatkoski, Daniel. *The More Torah, the More Life: A Christian Commentary on Mishnah Avot*. Leuven: Peeters, 2018.
Journet, Charles. "The Mysterious Destinies of Israel." In *The Bridge: A Yearbook of Judeo-Christian Studies*, vol. 2, edited by John M. Oesterreicher, 35–90. New York: Pantheon, 1956.
Joyce, Paul M. "Temple and Worship in Ezekiel 40–48." In *Temple and Worship in Biblical Israel: Proceedings of the Oxford Old Testament Seminar*, edited by John Day, 145–63. New York: T. & T. Clark, 2007.
Kalmin, Richard Lee. "Christians and Heretics in Rabbinic Literature of Late Antiquity." *Harvard Theological Review* 87, no. 2 (April 1994) 155–69.
———. *Jewish Babylonia between Persia and Roman Palestine*. Oxford: Oxford University Press, 2006.
Kaminsky, Joel S. "Paradise Regained: Rabbinic Reflections on Israel at Sinai." In *Jews, Christians, and the Theology of the Hebrew Scriptures*, edited by Alice Ogden Bellis and Joel S. Kaminsky, 15–43. Atlanta: SBL, 2000.
———. *Yet I Loved Jacob: Reclaiming the Biblical Concept of Election*. Nashville, TN: Abingdon, 2007.
Kaminsky, Joel S., and Mark Reasoner. "The Meaning and Telos of Israel's Election: An Interfaith Response to N. T. Wright's Reading of Paul." *Harvard Theological Review* 112, no. 4 (October 2019) 421–46.
Kampen, John. *Matthew within Sectarian Judaism*. New Haven, CT: Yale University Press, 2019.
Kanarfogel, Ephraim, and Dov Schwartz, eds. *Scholarly Man of Faith: Studies in the Thought and Writings of Rabbi Joseph B. Soloveitchik*. New York: KTAV, 2018.
Kaplan, Grant. *René Girard, Unlikely Apologist: Mimetic Theory and Fundamental Theology*. Notre Dame, IN: University of Notre Dame Press, 2016.
Kaplan, Jacob. *Justice pour la foi juive*. Paris: Centurion, 1977.
Kaplan, Lawrence. "Rabbi Joseph B. Soloveitchik's Philosophy of Halakhah." *The Jewish Law Annual* 7 (1988) 139–97.
———. "The Religious Philosophy of Rabbi Joseph Soloveitchik." *Tradition* 14, no. 2 (October 1973) 43–64.
Kärkkäinen, Veli-Matti. *Doing the Work of Comparative Theology*. Grand Rapids: Eerdmans, 2020.

Kasper, Walter. "Paths Taken and Enduring Questions in Jewish-Christian Relations Today: Thirty Years of the Commission for Religious Relations with the Jews." In *The Catholic Church and the Jewish People: Recent Reflections from Rome*, edited by Philip A. Cunningham, Norbert J. Hofmann, and Joseph Sievers, 3–11. New York: Fordham University Press, 2007.

Kassis, Rifat Odeh. *Kairos for Palestine*. Ramallah: Baydal/Alternatives, 2011.

Katz, Steven T. *The Holocaust and Mass Death before the Modern Age*. Vol. 1 of *The Holocaust in Historical Context*. Oxford: Oxford University Press, 1994.

Kaufman, Philip S. *The Beloved Disciple: Witness against Anti-Semitism*. Collegeville, MN: Liturgical, 1991.

Kaufmann, Thomas. *Luther's Jews: A Journey into Anti-Semitism*. Translated by Lesley Sharpe and Jeremy Noakes. Oxford: Oxford University Press, 2017.

Keating, Daniel. *First and Second Peter, Jude*. Grand Rapids: Baker Academic, 2011.

Keener, Craig S. *Acts: An Exegetical Commentary*, vol. 2: *3:1–14:28*. Grand Rapids: Baker Academic, 2013.

———. *Acts: An Exegetical Commentary*, vol. 3: *15:1–23:35*. Grand Rapids: Baker Academic, 2014.

———. *The Gospel of John: A Commentary*, vol. 1. Grand Rapids: Baker Academic, 2003.

———. *The Gospel of John: A Commentary*, vol. 2. Grand Rapids: Baker Academic, 2003.

———. *The Mind of the Spirit: Paul's Approach to Transformed Thinking*. Grand Rapids: Baker Academic, 2016.

———. *Miracles: The Credibility of the New Testament Accounts*, vol. 1. Grand Rapids: Baker Academic, 2011.

Keesmaat, Sylvia C. "Exodus and Romans 8:14–30." *Journal for the Study of the New Testament* 54 (1994) 29–49.

Keith, Chris. *Jesus against the Scribal Elite: The Origins of the Conflict*. Grand Rapids: Baker Academic, 2014.

Kellner, Menachem. *Maimonides on Judaism and the Jewish People*. 2d ed. Albany, NY: SUNY, 1991.

———. "We Are Not Alone." In *Radical Responsibility: Celebrating the Thought of Chief Rabbi Lord Jonathan Sacks*, edited by Michael J. Harris, Daniel Rynhold, and Tamra Wright, 139–53. New Milford, CT: Maggid, 2012.

Kelly, J. N. D. *Golden Mouth: The Story of John Chrysostom—Ascetic, Preacher, Bishop*. Ithaca, NY: Cornell University Press, 1995.

Kenneally, Christine. *The First Word: The Search for the Origins of Language*. New York: Viking, 2007.

Kenny, Anthony J. *Catholics, Jews and the State of Israel*. New York: Paulist, 1993.

Kepnes, Steven. "'Turn Us to You and We Shall Return': Original Sin, Atonement, and Redemption in Jewish Terms." In *Christianity in Jewish Terms*, edited by Tikva Frymer-Kensky et al., 293–304. Boulder CO: Westview, 2000.

Kerr, Alan R. *The Temple of Jesus' Body: The Temple Theme in the Gospel of John*. Sheffield: Sheffield Academic, 2002.

Kerr, Gaven. *Aquinas and the Metaphysics of Creation*. Oxford: Oxford University Press, 2019.

Kertzer, David I. "Anti-Semitism and the Vatican: On Anti-Judaism, Anti-Semitism, and the Holocaust." *Kirchliche Zeitgeschichte* 16, no. 1 (January 2003) 76–91.

———. "The Doctored 'Memoir' of a Jewish Boy Kidnapped by the Vatican." *The Atlantic*, April 15, 2018. https://www.theatlantic.com/international/archive/2018/04/edgardo-mortara-doctored-memoir/554948/.

———. "The Enduring Controversy over the Mortara Case." *Studies in Christian-Jewish Relations* 14, no. 1 (April 2019) 1–10.

———. *The Kidnapping of Edgardo Mortara*. New York: Alfred A. Knopf, 1997.

———. *The Pope and Mussolini: The Secret History of Pius XI and the Rise of Fascism in Europe*. New York: Random House, 2014.

———. *The Popes Against the Jews: The Vatican's Role in the Rise of Modern Anti-Semitism*. New York: Alfred A. Knopf, 2001.

———. *The Pope Who Would Be King: The Exile of Pius IX and the Emergence of Modern Europe*. New York: Random House, 2018.

———. "The Roman Catholic Church, the Holocaust, and the Demonization of the Jews: Response to 'Benjamin and us: Christianity, its Jews, and history' by Jeanne Favret-Saada." *HAU Journal of Ethnographic Theory* 4, no. 3 (December 2014) 329–33.

Kessler, Edward. *Bound by the Bible: Jews, Christians and the Sacrifice of Isaac*. Cambridge: Cambridge University Press, 2005.

———. "*Dabru Emet* and Its Significance." In *Challenges in Jewish-Christian Relations*, edited by James K. Aitken and Edward Kessler, 195–202. New York: Paulist, 2006.

———. "'I Am Joseph, Your Brother': A Jewish Perspective on Christian-Jewish Relations Since *Nostra Aetate* No. 4." *Theological Studies* 74, no. 1 (February 2013) 48–72.

———. *An Introduction to Jewish-Christian Relations*. Cambridge: Cambridge University Press, 2010.

———. "Jewish-Christian Relations in the Global Society: What the Institutional Documents Have and Have Not Been Telling Us." In *Jews and Christians in Conversation: Crossing Cultures and Generations*, edited by Edward Kessler, John Pawlikowski, and Judy Banki, 53–73. Cambridge: Orchard Academic, 2002.

———. "A Jewish Response to Gavin D'Costa." *Theological Studies* 73, no. 3 (September 2012) 614–28.

Khader, Jamal. "Christian-Jewish Dialogue in Palestine/Israel." In *Coexistence and Reconciliation in Israel: Voices for Interreligious Dialogue*, edited by Ronald Kronish, 86–99. New York: Paulist, 2015.

Khader, Jamal, and David Neuhaus, SJ. "A Holy Land Context for *Nostra Aetate*." *Studies in Christian-Jewish Relations* 1, no. 1 (2006–2007) 67–88.

Khalloul, Shadi. "Theology and Morality: Is Modern Israel Faithful to the Moral Demands of the Covenant in Its Treatment of Minorities?" In *The New Christian Zionism: Fresh Perspectives on Israel and the Land*, edited by Gerald R. McDermott, 281–301. Downers Grove, IL: IVP Academic, 2016.

Khoury, Rafiq. "The History of Jerusalem: A Christian Perspective." In *The Spiritual Significance of Jerusalem for Jews, Christians and Muslims*, edited by Hans Ucko, 9–20. Geneva: World Council of Churches, 1994.

Kilmartin, Edward J., SJ. *The Eucharist in the West: History and Theology*. Edited by Robert J. Daly. Collegeville, MN: Liturgical, 1998.

Kimelman, Reuven. "Rabbis Joseph B. Soloveitchik and Abraham Joshua Heschel on Jewish-Christian Relations." *The Edah Journal* 4, no. 2 (2004). http://www.edah.org/backend/JournalArticle/4_2_Kimelman.pdf.

Kimmerling, Baruch, and Joel Migdal. *The Palestinian People: A History*. Cambridge, MA: Harvard University Press, 2003.

Kinman, Brent. *Jesus' Entry into Jerusalem: In the Context of Lukan Theology and the Politics of His Day*. Leiden: Brill, 1995.

Kinzer, Mark S. *Jerusalem Crucified, Jerusalem Risen: The Resurrected Messiah, the Jewish People, and the Land of Promise*. Eugene, OR: Cascade, 2018.

———. *Postmissionary Messianic Judaism: Redefining Christian Engagement with the Jewish People*. Grand Rapids: Brazos, 2005.

———. *Searching Her Own Mystery: Nostra Aetate, the Jewish People, and the Identity of the Church*. Eugene, OR: Cascade, 2015.

Kirsch, Jonathan. *God against the Gods: The History of the War Between Monotheism and Polytheism*. New York: Penguin, 2004.

Kirwan, Michael. *Girard and Theology*. New York: T. & T. Clark, 2009.

Kister, Menahem. "*Tohu wa-Bohu*, Primordial Elements and *Creatio ex Nihilo*." *Jewish Studies Quarterly* 14, no. 3 (January 2007) 229–56.

Klawans, Jonathan. *Impurity and Sin in Ancient Judaism*. Oxford: Oxford University Press, 2000.

———. *Purity, Sacrifice, and the Temple: Symbolism and Supersessionism in the Study of Ancient Judaism*. Oxford: Oxford University Press, 2006.

Klein, Charlotte. "Damascus to Kiev: Civiltà Cattolica on Ritual Murder." *The Wiener Library Bulletin* 27 (1974) 18–25.

———. "Vatican and Zionism, 1897–1967." *Christian Attitudes on Jews and Judaism* 36–37 (June–August 1974) 11–16.

———. "Vatican View of Jewry, 1939–1962, in the Mirror of *Civiltà Cattolica*." *Christian Attitudes on Jews and Judaism* 43 (1976) 12–16.

Kleinberg, Aviad M. "Depriving Parents of the Consolation of Children: Two Legal Consilia on the Baptism of Jewish Children." In *De Sion exibit lex et verbum domini de Hierusalem: Essays on Medieval Law, Liturgy and Literature in Honour of Amnon Linder*, edited by Yitzhak Hen, 129–44. Turnhout: Brepols, 2001.

Kluger, Jerzy, and Gianfranco Di Simone. *The Pope and I: How the Lifelong Friendship Between a Polish Jew and John Paul II Advanced the Cause of Jewish-Christian Relations*. Translated by Matthew Sherry. Maryknoll, NY: Orbis, 2012.

Knierim, Rolf P. *The Task of Old Testament Theology: Method and Cases*. Grand Rapids: Eerdmans, 1995.

Koch, Kurt, Cardinal. "Theological Questions and Perspectives in Jewish-Catholic Dialogue: October 30, 2011 Keynote Address at Seton Hall University during the 10th Annual Meeting of the Council of Centers on Christian-Jewish Relations." *Studies in Christian-Jewish Relations* 7, no. 1 (2012) 1–12.

———. "Press Conference to Present the Meeting of the Holy Father Francis with the Heads of the Churches and Christian Communities of the Middle East in Bari." March 7, 2018. Vatican.va.

Kolbrener, William. *The Last Rabbi: Joseph Soloveitchik and the Talmudic Tradition*. Bloomington, IN: Indiana University Press, 2016.

———. "The Transcendent Pharisee, Rabbi Joseph Soloveitchik: Israel and the Poverty of Politics." *Toronto Journal of Theology* 35 (2019) 176–88.

Kook, Abraham Isaac. *The Lights of Penitence, Lights of Holiness, The Moral Principles, Essays, Letters, and Poems*. Translated by Ben Zion Bokser. London: SPCK, 1979.

Korn, Bertram Wallace. *The American Reaction to The Mortara Case: 1858–1859.* Cincinnati: The American Jewish Archives, 1957.

Korn, Eugene B. *The Jewish Connection to Israel, the Promised Land: A Brief Introduction for Christians.* Woodstock, VT: Jewish Lights, 2008.

———. "A Jewish Response to 'Theological Questions and Perspectives in Jewish-Catholic Dialogue' by Cardinal Kurt Koch." *Studies in Christian-Jewish Relations* 7, no. 1 (May 2012) 1–7.

———. "The Man of Faith and Religious Dialogue: Revisiting 'Confrontation'," *Modern Judaism* 25, no. 3 (October 2005) 290–315.

Kosmala, Hans. "'His Blood on Us and on Our Children': The Background of Mat. 27, 24–25." *Annual of the Swedish Theological Institute* 7 (1968–69) 94–126.

Kösters, Christoph, and Mark Edward Ruff, eds. *Die katholische Kirche im Dritten Reich: Eine Einführung.* 2d ed. Freiburg im Breisgua: Herder, 2018.

Krajewski, Stanislaw. "The Reception of *Nostra Aetate* and Christian Jewish Relations in Poland." *Kirchliche Zeitgeschichte* 29, no. 2 (January 2016) 292–303.

Kreitzer, Larry J. "The Messianic Man of Peace as Temple Builder: Solomonic Imagery in Ephesians 2.13–22." In *Temple and Worship in Biblical Israel: Proceedings of the Oxford Old Testament Seminar,* edited by John Day, 484–512. New York: T. & T. Clark, 2007.

Kretzmer, David. *The Occupation of Justice: The Supreme Court of Israel and the Occupied Territories.* Albany, NY: State University of New York Press, 2002.

Kreutz, Andrej. *Vatican Policy on the Palestinian-Israeli Conflict: The Struggle for the Holy Land.* New York: Greenwood, 1990.

Krieg, Robert A. *Catholic Theologians in Nazi Germany.* New York: Continuum, 2004.

———. "German Catholic Views of Jesus and Judaism, 1918–1945." In *Antisemitism, Christian Ambivalence, and the Holocaust,* edited by Kevin P. Spicer, 50–75. Bloomington, IN: Indiana University Press, 2007.

———. *Karl Adam: Catholicism in German Culture.* Notre Dame, IN: University of Notre Dame Press, 1992.

Krokus, Christian S. *The Theology of Louis Massignon: Islam, Christ, and the Church.* Washington, DC: Catholic University of America Press, 2017.

Krondorfer, Björn. "The Art of Dialogue: Jewish-Christian Relations in a Post-Shoah World." *Cross Currents* 62, no. 3 (September 2012) 301–17.

Kugel, James. *The Bible as It Was.* Cambridge, MA: Harvard University Press, 1997.

———. *The Kingly Sanctuary: An Exploration of Some Underlying Principles of Judaism, for a Jewish Student Who Has Become Disillusioned.* Scotts Valley, CA: CreateSpace, 2014.

———. *On Being a Jew.* San Francisco, CA: HarperSanFrancisco, 1990.

Küng, Hans. "Introduction." In *Christians and Jews,* edited by Hans Küng and Walter Kasper, 9–16. New York: Seabury, 1974–1975.

Kuruvilla, Samuel J. *Radical Christianity in Palestine and Israel: Liberation and Theology in the Middle East.* London: I. B. Tauris, 2013.

Kushner, Aviya. *The Grammar of God: A Journey into the Words and Worlds of the Bible.* New York: Random House, 2015.

Kutsko, John E. *Between Heaven and Earth: Divine Presence and Divine Absence in the Book of Ezekiel.* Winona Lake, IN: Eisenbrauns, 2000.

Kysar, Robert. "Anti-Semitism in the Gospel of John." In *Anti-Semitism and Early Christianity: Issues of Polemic and Faith*, edited by Craig A. Evans and Donald A. Hagner, 113-27. Minneapolis: Fortress, 1993.
LaFarge, John, SJ. *Interracial Justice: A Study of the Catholic Doctrine of Race Relations*. New York: Arno, 1978.
Laine, James W. *Meta-Religion: Religion and Power in World History*. Oakland, CA: University of California Press, 2014.
Lamb, Matthew L., and Matthew Levering, eds. *The Reception of Vatican II*. Oxford: Oxford University Press, 2017.
Lamberigts, Mathijs, and Leo Declerck. "Vatican II on the Jews: A Historical Survey." In *Never Revoked: Nostra Aetate as Ongoing Challenge for Jewish-Christian Dialogue*, edited by Marianne Moyaert and Didier Pollefeyt, 13-56. Leuven: Peeters, 2010.
Langer, Ruth. "Constructing Memory in Jewish Liturgy." In *Toward the Future: Essays on Catholic-Jewish Relations in Memory of Rabbi León Klenicki*, edited by Celia M. Deutsch, Eugene J. Fisher, and James Rudin, 117-28. New York: Paulist, 2013.
———. "Exploring the Interface of Dialogue and Theology: A Jewish Response to Christian Rutishauser, Thomas Norris, and Liam Tracey." In *Christ Jesus and the Jewish People Today: New Explorations of Theological Interrelationships*, edited by Philip A. Cunningham et al., 287-95. Grand Rapids: Eerdmans, 2011.
———. "Theologies of the Land and State of Israel: The Role of the Secular in Christian and Jewish Understandings." *Studies in Christian-Jewish Relations* 3, no. 1 (April 2008) 1-17.
"L'antisemitismo nel secolo decimonono." *L'Osservatore romano*, 10 July 1892.
Lapide, Pinchas E. *The Last Three Popes and the Jews*. London: Souvenir, 1967.
Laras, Guiseppe. "Jewish Perspectives on Christianity." In *The Catholic Church and the Jewish People: Recent Reflections from Rome*, edited by Philip A. Cunningham, Norbert J. Hofmann, and Joseph Sievers, 23-28. New York: Fordham University Press, 2007.
Larsson, Göran. *Bound for Freedom: The Book of Exodus in Jewish and Christian Traditions*. Peabody, MA: Hendrickson, 1999.
Lasker, Daniel J. *Jewish Philosophical Polemics against Christianity in the Middle Ages*. New York: KTAV, 1977.
Lawler, Justus George. *Were the Popes Against the Jews? Tracking the Myths, Confronting the Ideologues*. Grand Rapids: Eerdmans, 2012.
Leach, Edmund. *Culture and Communication: The Logic by Which Symbols Are Connected*. Cambridge: Cambridge University Press, 1976.
Le Donne, Anthony. *Near Christianity: How Journeys along Jewish-Christian Borders Saved My Faith in God*. Grand Rapids: Zondervan, 2016.
Le Donne, Anthony, and Larry Behrendt. *Sacred Dissonance: The Blessing of Difference in Jewish-Christian Dialogue*. Peabody, MA: Hendrickson, 2017.
Lee, Gregory W. "Israel between the Two Cities: Augustine's Theology of the Jews and Judaism." *Journal of Early Christian Studies* 24, no. 4 (2016) 523-51.
———. *Today When You Hear His Voice: Scripture, the Covenants, and the People of God*. Grand Rapids: Eerdmans, 2016.
Lee, Michelle V. *Paul, the Stoics, and the Body of Christ*. Cambridge: Cambridge University Press, 2006.
Lefebvre, Marcel. *Collections, Codes, and Torah: The Re-characterization of Israel's Written Law*. New York: T. & T. Clark, 2006.

———. *I Accuse the Council!* 2d ed. Translated by Jaime Pazat de Lys. Kansas City, MO: Angelus, 1998.
Lehming, Hanna, Joachim Liss-Walther, Matthias Loerbroks, and Rien van der Vegt, eds. *Wendung nach Jerusalem: Friedrich-Wilhelm Marquardts Theologie im Gespräch*. Gütersloh: Kaiser, 1999.
Leighton, Christopher. "The Presbyterian-Jewish Impasse." In *Studies in Contemporary Jewry*, edited by Jonathan Frankel and Ezra Mendelsohn, 106–25. Oxford: Oxford University Press, 2010.
Leiter, Brian. *Why Tolerate Religion?* Princeton, NJ: Princeton University Press, 2013.
Leithart, Peter J. *Revelation 12–22*. London: Bloomsbury, 2018.
———. *Traces of the Trinity: Signs of God in Creation and Human Experience*. Grand Rapids: Brazos, 2015.
Leo XIII. *Humanum genus: Encyclical of Pope Leo XIII on Freemasonry*. April 20, 1884. Vatican.va.
Levenson, Alan. "Four Brief Reflections on *The Jewish-Christian Schism Revisited*." *The Journal of Scriptural Reasoning* 16 (November 17, 2017). http://jsr.shanti.virginia.edu/?s=Four+Brief+Reflections.
Levenson, Jon D. *Creation and the Persistence of Evil: The Jewish Drama of Divine Omnipotence*. Princeton, NJ: Princeton University Press, 1994.
———. *The Death and Resurrection of the Beloved Son: The Transformation of Child Sacrifice in Judaism and Christianity*. New Haven, CT: Yale University Press, 1993.
———. "The Exodus and Biblical Theology: A Rejoinder to John J. Collins." In *Jews, Christians, and the Theology of the Hebrew Scriptures*, edited by Alice Ogden Bellis and Joel S. Kaminsky, 263–75. Atlanta: SBL, 2000.
———. *The Hebrew Bible, the Old Testament, and Historical Criticism*. Louisville, KY: Westminster John Knox, 1993.
———. "How Not to Conduct Jewish-Christian Dialogue." *Commentary* 112, no. 5 (December 2001) 31–37.
———. *Inheriting Abraham: The Legacy of the Patriarch in Judaism, Christianity, and Islam*. Princeton, NJ: Princeton University Press, 2012.
———. "Liberation Theology and the Exodus." In *Jews, Christians, and the Theology of the Hebrew Scriptures*, edited by Alice Ogden Bellis and Joel S. Kaminsky, 215–30. Atlanta: SBL, 2000.
———. *The Love of God: Divine Gift, Human Gratitude, and Mutual Faithfulness in Judaism*. Princeton, NJ: Princeton University Press, 2016.
———. "The Perils of Engaged Scholarship: A Rejoinder to Jorge Pixley." In *Jews, Christians, and the Theology of the Hebrew Scriptures*, edited by Alice Ogden Bellis and Joel S. Kaminsky, 239–46. Atlanta: SBL, 2000.
———. *Resurrection and the Restoration of Israel: The Ultimate Victory of the God of Life*. New Haven, CT: Yale University Press, 2006.
———. "Review of *Exodus*," by Thomas Joseph White. In *The Thomist* 82, no. 3 (July 2018) 476–80.
———. *Sinai and Zion: An Entry into the Jewish Bible*. New York: Harper & Row, 1985.
———. "The Universal Horizon of Biblical Particularism." In *Ethnicity and the Bible*, edited by Mark Brett, 143–69. Leiden: Brill, 1996.
———. "What Are They? Modernity and Jewish Self-understanding." Review of *How Judaism Became a Religion: An Introduction to Modern Jewish Thought*. *Commonweal* 139, no. 4 (February 2012) 21–24.

———. "Why Jews Are Not Interested in Biblical Theology." In *The Hebrew Bible, the Old Testament, and Historical Criticism: Jews and Christians in Biblical Studies*, 33–61. Louisville, KY: Westminster John Knox, 1993.

Levering, Matthew. *The Achievement of Hans Urs von Balthasar: An Introduction to His Trilogy*. Washington, DC: Catholic University of America Press, 2019.

———. "Aquinas and Supersessionism One More Time: A Response to Matthew A. Tapie's *Aquinas on Israel and the Church*." *Pro Ecclesia* 25, no. 4 (November 2016) 395–412.

———. *Aquinas's Eschatological Ethics and the Virtue of Temperance*. Notre Dame, IN: University of Notre Dame Press, 2019.

———. "Aristotle and the Mosaic Law." In *Aristotle in Aquinas's Theology*, edited by Gilles Emery and Matthew Levering, 70–93. Oxford: Oxford University Press, 2015.

———. *The Betrayal of Charity: The Sins That Sabotage Divine Love*. Waco, TX: Baylor University Press, 2011.

———. *Biblical Natural Law: A Theocentric and Teleological Approach*. Oxford: Oxford University Press, 2008.

———. "Blood, Death, and Sacrifice in the Epistle to the Hebrews According to Thomas Aquinas." In *So Great a Salvation: A Dialogue on the Atonement in Hebrews*, edited by Jon C. Laansma, George H. Guthrie, and Cynthia Long Westfall, 120–143. London: T. & T. Clark, 2019.

———. *Christ's Fulfillment of Torah and Temple: Salvation According to Thomas Aquinas*. Notre Dame, IN: University of Notre Dame Press, 2002.

———. *Did Jesus Rise from the Dead?* Oxford: Oxford University Press, 2019.

———. *Dying and the Virtues*. Grand Rapids: Eerdmans, 2018.

———. *Engaging the Doctrine of Creation: Cosmos, Creatures, and the Wise and Good Creator*. Grand Rapids: Baker Academic, 2017.

———. *Engaging the Doctrine of the Holy Spirit: Love and Gift in the Trinity and the Church*. Grand Rapids: Baker Academic, 2016.

———. *Engaging the Doctrine of Revelation: The Mediation of the Gospel through Church and Scripture*. Grand Rapids: Baker Academic, 2014.

———. *Ezra and Nehemiah*. Grand Rapids: Brazos, 2007.

———. "God and Natural Law: Reflections on Genesis 22." *Modern Theology* 24, no. 2 (April 2008) 151–77.

———. *An Introduction to Vatican II as an Ongoing Theological Event*. Washington, DC: Catholic University of America Press, 2017.

———. *Jesus and the Demise of Death: Resurrection, Afterlife, and the Fate of the Christian*. Waco, TX: Baylor University Press, 2012.

———. *Jewish-Christian Dialogue and the Life of Wisdom: Engagements with the Theology of David Novak*. New York: Continuum, 2010.

———. *Mary's Bodily Assumption*. Notre Dame, IN: University of Notre Dame Press, 2015.

———. *Paul in the* Summa Theologiae. Washington, DC: Catholic University of America Press, 2014.

———. *Predestination: Biblical and Theological Paths*. Oxford: Oxford University Press, 2011.

———. Response to *The Providence of God: A Polyphonic Approach*, by David Fergusson. *International Journal of Systematic Theology*. Forthcoming.

———. Review of *Another Reformation: Postliberal Christianity and the Jews*, by Peter Ochs. *International Journal of Systematic Theology* 17, no. 2 (April 2015) 234–37.

———. *Sacrifice and Community: Jewish Offering and Christian Eucharist*. Malden, MA: Blackwell, 2005.

———. *Scripture and Metaphysics: Aquinas and the Renewal of Trinitarian Theology*. Oxford: Blackwell, 2004.

———. "Sin and Grace in the Church according to Paul and Aquinas." In *Thomas Aquinas, Biblical Theologian*, edited by Michael Dauphinais and Roger Nutt, 185–206. Steubenville, OH: Emmaus Academic, 2021.

———. "Thomas Aquinas." In *The Decalogue through the Centuries: From the Hebrew Scriptures to Benedict XVI*, edited by Jeffrey P. Greenman and Timothy Larsen, 67–80. Louisville, KY: Westminster John Knox, 2012.

Levering, Matthew, and Tom Angier, eds. *The Achievement of David Novak: A Catholic-Jewish Dialogue*. Eugene, OR: Pickwick, 2021.

Levine, Amy-Jill. "Anti-Judaism and the Gospel of Matthew." In *Anti-Judaism and the Gospels*, edited by William R. Farmer, 9–36. Harrisburg, PA: Trinity International, 1999.

———. "Matthew, Mark, and Luke: Good News or Bad?" In *Jesus, Judaism, and Christian Anti-Judaism: Reading the New Testament after the Holocaust*, edited by Paula Fredriksen and Adele Reinhartz, 77–98. Louisville, KY: Westminster John Knox, 2002.

———. *The Misunderstood Jew: The Church and the Scandal of the Jewish Jesus*. San Francisco: HarperSanFrancisco, 2006.

———. *Short Stories by Jesus: The Enigmatic Parables of a Controversial Rabbi*. New York: HarperCollins, 2014.

Levine, Amy-Jill, and Marc Zvi Brettler, eds. *The Jewish Annotated New Testament*. Oxford: Oxford University Press, 2011.

Lévy, Antoine, OP. *Jewish Church: A Catholic Approach to Messianic Judaism*. Lanham, MD: Lexington, 2021.

Lewis, Donald M. *The Origins of Christian Zionism: Lord Shaftesbury and Evangelical Support for a Jewish Homeland*. Cambridge: Cambridge University Press, 2010.

Lincicum, David. *Paul and the Early Jewish Encounter with Deuteronomy*. Grand Rapids: Baker Academic, 2013.

———. "Sacraments in the Pauline Epistles." In *The Oxford Handbook of Sacramental Theology*, edited by Hans Boersma and Matthew Levering, 97–108. Oxford: Oxford University Press, 2015.

Lindbeck, George. "The Church as Israel: Ecclesiology and Ecumenism." In *Jews and Christians: People of God*, edited by Carl E. Braaten and Robert W. Jenson, 78–94. Grand Rapids: Eerdmans, 2003.

———. "Postmodern Hermeneutics and Jewish-Christian Dialogue: A Case Study." In *Christianity in Jewish Terms*, edited by Tikva Frymer-Kensky et al., 106–13. Boulder CO: Westview, 2000.

———. "What of the Future? A Christian Response." In *Christianity in Jewish Terms*, edited by Tikva Frymer-Kensky et al., 357–66. Boulder CO: Westview, 2000.

Linder, Amnon. *The Jews in the Legal Sources of the Early Middle Ages*. Detroit: Wayne State University Press, 1997.

Lindsay, Mark R. *Barth, Israel and Jesus: Karl Barth's Theology of Israel*. Aldershot, England: Ashgate, 2007.

———. *Covenanted Solidarity: The Theological Basis of Karl Barth's Opposition to Nazi Antisemitism and the Holocaust.* New York: Peter Lang, 2001.

———. "Jewish-Christian Dialogue from the Underside: Markus Barth's Correspondence with Michael Wyschogrod (1962–84) and Emil Fackenheim (1965–80)." *Journal of Ecumenical Studies* 53, no. 3 (June 2018) 313–47.

———. *Reading Auschwitz after Barth: The Holocaust as Problem and Promise for Barthian Theology.* Eugene, OR: Wipf & Stock, 2014.

Littell, Franklin. *The Crucifixion of the Jews: The Failure of Christians to Understand the Jewish Experience.* Macon, GA: Mercer University Press, 1986.

Lohfink, Norbert, SJ. "Covenant and Torah in the Pilgrimage of the Nations (The Book of Isaiah and Psalm 25)." In Norbert Lohfink and Erich Zenger, *The God of Israel and the Nations: Studies in Isaiah and the Psalms,* 33–84. Translated by Everett R. Kalin. Collegeville, MN: Liturgical, 2000.

———. *The Covenant Never Revoked: Biblical Reflections on Christian-Jewish Dialogue.* New York: Paulist, 1991.

———. "The Concept of 'Covenant' in Biblical Theology." In Norbert Lohfink and Erich Zenger, *The God of Israel and the Nations: Studies in Isaiah and the Psalms,* 11–31. Translated by Everett R. Kalin. Collegeville, MN: Liturgical, 2000.

Lohfink, Norbert, SJ, and Erich Zenger. "The Theological Context: The New Relationship Between the Church and Israel." In *The God of Israel and the Nations: Studies in Isaiah and the Psalms,* translated by Everett R. Kalin, 1–9. Collegeville, MN: Liturgical, 2000.

———. "Theological Relevance: The Drama of Covenant History." In Norbert Lohfink and Erich Zenger, *The God of Israel and the Nations: Studies in Isaiah and the Psalms,* translated by Everett R. Kalin, 191–98. Collegeville, MN: Liturgical, 2000.

Lohr, Joel N. *Chosen and Unchosen: Conceptions of Election in the Pentateuch and Jewish-Christian Interpretation.* Winona Lake, IN: Eisenbrauns, 2009.

Lonergan, Bernard, SJ. *Verbum: Word and Idea in Aquinas.* Edited by Frederick E. Crowe and Robert M. Doran. Toronto: University of Toronto Press, 1997.

Louth, Andrew, et al. *Five Views on the Extent of the Atonement,* edited by Adam Johnson. Grand Rapids: Zondervan, 2019.

Lowe, Malcom, ed. *Orthodox Christians and Jews on Continuity and Renewal: the Third Academic Meeting Between Orthodoxy and Judaism: Including a History and Bibliography of Dialogue Between Orthodox Christians and Jews.* Jerusalem: Ecumenical Theological Research Fraternity in Israel, 1994.

Lusvardi, Anthony R., SJ. "Girard and the 'Sacrifice of the Mass': Mimetic Theory and Eucharistic Theology." *Journal of Violence, Mimesis, and Culture* 24, no. 1 (April 2017) 159–90.

Luther, Martin. *Commentary on Romans.* Translated by J. T. Mueller. London: Zondervan, 1954.

———. "On the Jews and Their Lies (1543)." In *Martin Luther, the Bible, and the Jewish People: A Reader,* edited by Brooks Schramm and Kirsi I. Stjerna, 164–176. Minneapolis: Fortress, 2012.

———. "That Jesus Christ Was Born a Jew." In *Martin Luther, the Bible, and the Jewish People: A Reader,* edited by Brooks Schramm and Kirsi I. Stjerna, 76–83. Minneapolis: Fortress, 2012.

Lux, Richard C. *The Jewish People, the Holy Land, and the State of Israel: A Catholic View.* New York: Paulist, 2010.

Luz, Ulrich. *Matthew 1-7: A Commentary*. Translated by James E. Crouch. Minneapolis: Fortress, 2007.

Luzzatto, Gadi. "Aspetti di antisemitismo nella 'Civiltà Cattolica' dal 1881 al 1903." *Bailamme* 1, no. 2 (1987) 125–38.

Lynch, Reginald M. *The Cleansing of the Heart: The Sacraments as Instrumental Causes in the Thomistic Tradition*. Washington, DC: Catholic University of America Press, 2017.

Łysiak, Anna. "Rabbinic Judaism in the Writings of Polish Catholic Theologians, 1918–1939." In *Antisemitism, Christian Ambivalence, and the Holocaust*, edited by Kevin P. Spicer, 26–49. Bloomington, IN: Indiana University Press, 2007.

Macaskill, Grant. *Living in Union with Christ: Paul's Gospel and Christian Moral Identity*. Grand Rapids: Baker Academic, 2019.

———. *Revealed Wisdom and Inaugurated Eschatology in Ancient Judaism and Early Christianity*. Leiden: Brill, 2007.

———. *Union with Christ in the New Testament*. Oxford: Oxford University Press, 2013.

Maccoby, Hyam. *Judas Iscariot and the Myth of Jewish Evil*. New York: Free, 1992.

———, ed. and trans. *Judaism on Trial: Jewish-Christian Disputations in the Middle Ages*. Rutherford, NJ: Fairleigh Dickinson University Press, 1982.

———. *The Mythmaker: Paul and the Invention of Christianity*. New York: Barnes & Noble, 1998.

Madges, William. "Covenant, Universal Mission, and Fulfillment." *Studies in Christian-Jewish Relations* 12, no. 1 (March 2017) 1–13.

Magister, Sandro. "'Oremus Pro Conversione Judaeorum.' Cardinal Kasper Takes the Field." Translated by Matthew Sherry. 2008. http://chiesa.espresso.repubblica.it/articolo/197381bdc4.html?eng=y.

Magonet, Jonathan. "Jewish-Catholic Relations Today." *European Judaism* 50, no. 1 (March 2017) 108–12.

———. *A Rabbi Reads the Psalms*. 2d ed. London: SCM, 2004.

———. *Talking to the Other: Jewish Interfaith Dialogue with Christians and Muslims*. London: I. B. Tauris, 2003.

Maier, Johann. *Jesus von Nazareth in der Talmudischen Überlieferung*. Darmstadt: Wissenschaftliche Buchgesellschaft, 1978.

Maimonides, Moses. *The Guide of the Perplexed*. Translated by Shlomo Pines. Chicago: University of Chicago Press, 1963.

Mancini, Massimo, OP. "Pier Gaetano Feletti e l'affare Mortara." In *Dominikaner und Junen*, edited by Eias H. Füllenback and Gianfranco Miletto, 421–37. Berlin: De Grutyer, 2015.

Mansini, Guy, OSB. *Ecclesiology*. Washington, DC: Catholic University of America Press, 2021.

———. *Fundamental Theology*. Washington, DC: Catholic University of America Press, 2018.

March, Eugene W. *Israel and the Politics of the Land: A Theological Case Study*. Louisville, KY: Westminster John Knox, 1994.

Marchadour, Alain, and David Neuhaus, SJ. *The Land, the Bible, and History: Toward the Land That I Will Show You*. New York: Fordham University Press, 2007.

Marcus, Jacob. *The Jews in the Medieval World: A Sourcebook, 315–1791*. New York: Jewish Publication Society, 1938.

Marcus, Joel. *The Way of the Lord: Christological Exegesis of the Old Testament in the Gospel of Mark.* Edinburgh: T. & T. Clark, 1993.

Margaroni, Mary. "The Blood Libel on Greek Islands in the Nineteenth Century." In *Sites of European Antisemitism in the Age of Mass Politics, 1880–1918,* edited by Robert Nemes and Daniel Unowsky, 178–96. Waltham, MA: Brandeis University Press, 2014.

Maritain, Jacques. *Distinguish to Unite, or, The Degrees of Knowledge,* rev. ed. Translated from the 4th French edition by Gerald B. Phelan. Notre Dame, IN: University of Notre Dame Press, 1995.

———. "The Mystery of Israel." In *Ransoming the Time,* translated by Harry Lorin Binsse, 141–179. New York: Charles Scribner's Sons, 1941.

———. *On the Church of Christ: The Person of the Church and Her Personnel.* Translated by Joseph W. Evans. Notre Dame, IN: University of Notre Dame, 1973.

Marmur, Dow. *The Star of Return: Judaism after the Holocaust.* New York: Greenwood, 1991.

Marquardt, Friedrich-Wilhelm. "Elements Unresolved in Leo Baeck's Criticism of Adolf von Harnack." In *Theological Audacities: Selected Essays,* edited by Andreas Pangritz and Paul S. Chung, translated by Don McCord et al., 31–47. Eugene, OR: Pickwick, 2010.

———. "'Enemies for Our Sake': The Jewish No and Christian Theology." In *Theological Audacities: Selected Essays,* edited by Andreas Pangritz and Paul S. Chung, translated by Don McCord et al., 3–30. Eugene, OR: Pickwick, 2010.

———. *Die Entdeckung des Judentums für christliche Theologie: Israel im Denken Karl Barths.* Munich: Kaiser, 1967.

———. *Die Juden und ihr Land.* Hamburg: Siebenstern Taschenbuch, 1975.

———. "When Will You Restore the Kingdom for Israel?" In *Theological Audacities: Selected Essays,* edited by Andreas Pangritz and Paul S. Chung, translated by Don McCord et al., 85–99. Eugene, OR: Pickwick, 2010.

———. "Why the Talmud Interests Me as a Christian." In *Theological Audacities: Selected Essays,* edited by Andreas Pangritz and Paul S. Chung, translated by Don McCord et al., 68–84. Eugene, OR: Pickwick, 2010.

Marshall, Bruce D. "Christ and Israel: An Unresolved Problem in Catholic Theology." In *The Call of Abraham: Essays on the Election of Israel in Honor of Jon D. Levenson,* edited by Gary Anderson and Joel Kaminsky, 330–50. Notre Dame, IN: University of Notre Dame Press, 2013.

———. "Christ and the Cultures: The Jewish People and Christian Theology." In *The Cambridge Companion to Christian Doctrine,* edited by Colin Gunton, 81–100. Cambridge: Cambridge University Press, 1997.

———. "Do Christians Worship the God of Israel?" In *Knowing the Triune God: The Work of the Spirit in the Practices of the Church,* edited by James J. Buckley and David S. Yeago, 231–64. Grand Rapids: Eerdmans, 2001.

———. "Elder Brothers: John Paul II's Teaching on the Jewish People as a Question to the Church." In *John Paul II and the Jewish People: A Jewish-Christian Dialogue,* edited by David G. Dalin and Matthew Levering, 113–29. Lanham, MD: Rowman & Littlefield, 2008.

———. "Religion and Election: Aquinas on Natural Law, Judaism, and Salvation in Christ." *Nova et Vetera* 14, no. 1 (2016) 61–125.

Martens, Peter W. *Origen and Scripture: The Contours of the Exegetical Life*. Oxford: Oxford University Press, 2012.

Martin, David. *Religion and Power: No Logos without Mythos*. Burlington, VT: Ashgate, 2014.

Martin, Francis. "Election, Covenant, and Law." *Nova et Vetera* 4 (2006) 857-90.

Martin, Oren R. *Bound for the Promised Land: The Land Promise in God's Redemptive Plan*. Downers Grove, IL: InterVarsity, 2015.

Martin, Ralph. "Ad Gentes." In *The Reception of Vatican II*, edited by Matthew L. Lamb and Matthew Levering, 266-91. Oxford: Oxford University Press, 2017.

———. *Will Many Be Saved? What Vatican II Actually Teaches and Its Implications for the New Evangelization*. Grand Rapids: Eerdmans, 2012.

Masalha, Nur. *The Bible and Zionism: Invented Traditions, Archaeology and Post-Colonialism in Israel-Palestine*. London: Zed, 2007.

———, ed. *Catastrophe Remembered: Palestine, Israel and the Internal Refugees: Essays in Memory of Edward W. Said*. London: Zed, 2005.

———. *Imperial Israel and the Palestinians: The Politics of Expansion*. London: Pluto, 2000.

———. *The Palestine Nakba: Decolonising History, Narrating the Subaltern, Reclaiming Memory*. London: Zeb, 2012.

Masri, Mazen. *The Dynamics of Exclusionary Constitutionalism: Israel as a Jewish and Democratic State*. Portland, OR: Hart, 2017.

Massie, Alban. *Peuple prophétique et nation témoin: Le peuple juif dans le* Contra Faustum manichaeum *de saint Augustin*. Paris: Institut d'Études Augustiniennes, 2011.

Matera, Frank J. *II Corinthians: A Commentary*. Louisville, KY: Westminster John Knox, 2003.

Matter, Ann E. "Wandering to the End: The Medieval Christian Context to the Wandering Jew." In *Transforming Relations: Essays on Jews and Christians Throughout History in Honor of Michael A. Signer*, edited by Franklin T. Harkins, 224-40. Notre Dame, IN: University of Notre Dame Press, 2010.

May, Gerhard. *Creatio ex Nihilo: The Doctrine of "Creation out of Nothing" in Early Christian Thought*. Translated by A. S. Worrall. Edinburgh: University of Edinburgh Press, 1994.

May, H. G. "Aspects of the Imagery of World Dominion and World State in the Old Testament." In *Essays in Old Testament Ethics*, edited by James L. Crenshaw and J. T. Willis, 57-76. New York: KTAV, 1974.

Mayfield, Tyler D. *Unto Us a Child Is Born: Isaiah, Advent, and Our Jewish Neighbors*. Grand Rapids: Eerdmans, 2020.

McDermott, Gerald R. *Israel Matters: Why Christians Must Think Differently about the People and the Land*. Grand Rapids: Brazos, 2017.

———. "A New (and Old) Scandal of Particularity." *Pro Ecclesia* 27 (September 2018) 430-36.

McDonald, Margaret Y. *Colossians and Ephesians*. Collegeville, MN: Liturgical, 2008.

McDonough, Sean M. *Christ as Creator: Origins of a New Testament Doctrine*. Oxford: Oxford University Press, 2009.

McFarland, Ian. *From Nothing: A Theology of Creation*. Louisville, KY: Westminster John Knox, 2014.

BIBLIOGRAPHY

McGarry, Michael B. "Can Catholics Make an Exception? Jews and the New Evangelization." https://www.bc.edu/content/dam/files/research_sites/cjl/texts/cjrelations/resources/articles/mcgarry.htm.

———. "The Land of Israel in the Cauldron of the Middle East: A Challenge to Christian-Jewish Relations." In *Seeing Judaism Anew: Christianity's Sacred Obligation*, edited by Mary C. Boys, 55–79. Lanham, MD: Rowman & Littlefield, 2005.

McHugh, John A., OP, and Charles J. Callan, OP. *Moral Theology: A Complete Course Based on St. Thomas Aquinas and the Best Modern Authorities*. Revised and enlarged by Edward P. Farrell. Vol. 2. Edited by Paul A. Böer. N.p.: Veritatis Splendor, 2014 (originally published 1929).

McKenzie, Steven L. *King David: A Biography*. Oxford: Oxford University Press, 2000.

McKnight, Scot. *Kingdom Conspiracy: Returning to the Radical Mission of the Local Church*. Grand Rapids: Brazos, 2014.

———. "A Loyal Critic: Matthew's Polemic with Judaism in Theological Perspective." In *Anti-Semitism and Early Christianity: Issues of Polemic and Faith*, edited by Craig A. Evans and Donald A. Hagner, 55–79. Minneapolis: Fortress, 1993.

McNicol, Allan J. "Response to Daryl D. Schmidt." In *Anti-Judaism and the Gospels*, edited by William R. Farmer, 111–19. Harrisburg, PA: Trinity International, 1999.

Medoff, Rafael. *The Jews Should Keep Quiet: Franklin D. Roosevelt, Rabbi Stephen S. Wise, and the Holocaust*. Philadelphia: The Jewish Publication Society, 2019.

Meier, John P. *Companions and Competitors*. Vol. 3 of *A Marginal Jew: Rethinking the Historical Jesus*. New York: Doubleday, 2001.

———. *Law and Love*. Vol. 4 of *A Marginal Jew: Rethinking the Historical Jesus*. New Haven, CT: Yale University Press, 2009.

———. *Matthew*. Wilmington, DE: Michael Glazier, 1980.

———. *Mentor, Message, and Miracles*. Vol. 2 of *A Marginal Jew: Rethinking the Historical Jesus*. New York: Doubleday, 1994.

Merkle, John C. "The God of Israel and Christian Worship." In *Seeing Judaism Anew: Christianity's Sacred Obligation*, edited by Mary C. Boys, 177–86. Lanham, MD: Rowman & Littlefield, 2005.

Merkley, Paul Charles. *Christian Attitudes towards the State of Israel*. Montreal: McGill and Queens University Press, 2001.

———. *The Politics of Christian Zionism, 1891–1948*. London: Routledge, 1998.

Merrigan, Terrence. "Introduction: Rethinking Theologies of Interreligious Dialogue." In *The Past, Present, and Future of Theologies of Interreligious Dialogue*, edited by Terrence Merrigan and John Friday, 1–13. Oxford: Oxford University Press, 2017.

Messori, Vittorio. "The Mortara Case." In *Kidnapped by the Vatican? The Unpublished Memoirs of Edgardo Mortara*, edited by Vittorio Messori, 1–67. San Francisco: Ignatius, 2017.

———, ed. *Kidnapped by the Vatican? The Unpublished Memoirs of Edgardo Mortara*. San Francisco: Ignatius, 2017.

Metz, Johann Baptist. "Facing the Jews: Christian Theology after Auschwitz." In *The Holocaust as Interruption*, edited by Elisabeth Schüssler-Fiorenza and David Tracy, 26–42. Edinburgh: T. & T. Clark, 1984.

Meyer, David. "*Nostra Aetate*: Past, Present, and Future. A Jewish Perspective." In *Never Revoked: Nostra Aetate as Ongoing Challenge for Jewish-Christian Dialogue*, edited by Marianne Moyaert and Didier Pollefeyt, 117–32. Leuven: Peeters, 2010.

Meyers, Carol L. *Exodus*. Cambridge: Cambridge University Press, 2005.
Meyers, Carol L., and Eric M. Meyers. *Haggai, Zechariah 1-8*. New York: Doubleday, 1987.
Michael, Robert. *A History of Catholic Antisemitism: The Dark Side of the Church*. New York: Palgrave Macmillan, 2008.
Middlemas, Jill. "Divine Reversal and the Role of the Temple in Trito-Isaiah." In *Temple and Worship in Biblical Israel*, edited by John Day, 164-87. London: T. & T. Clark, 2007.
Milbank, John. "Stories of Sacrifice." *Modern Theology* 12 (1996) 27-56.
Miles, Jack. *God: A Biography*. New York: Vintage, 1996.
Miller, Charles H. "Hermeneutical Problems for a Palestinian Catholic Reading the Old Testament and Current Pastoral Responses." *ARAM* 18-19 (2006-2007) 307-24.
Miller, Patrick D. *The Lord of the Psalms*. Louisville, KY: Westminster John Knox, 2013.
Minucius Felix, Marcus. *The Octavius of Minucius Felix*. Translated by Robert Ernest Wallis. Vol. 4 of the *Ante-Nicene Fathers Series: Tertullian, Part Fourth; Minucius Felix; Commodian; Origen, Parts First and Second*, edited by Alexander Roberts, James Donaldson, and A. Cleveland Coxe, 173-98. Peabody, MA: Hendrickson, 1995.
Miranda, José Porfirio. *Marx and the Bible: A Critique of the Philosophy of Oppression*. Translated by J. Eagleson. Maryknoll, NY: Orbis, 1974.
Mitch, Curtus, and Edward Sri. *The Gospel of Matthew*. Grand Rapids: Baker Academic, 2010.
Mittleman, Alan. "Messianic Hope." In *Covenant and Hope: Christian and Jewish Reflections: Essays in Constructive Theology*, edited by Robert W. Jenson and Eugene B. Korn, 222-43. Grand Rapids: Eerdmans, 2012.
Moberly, R. W. L. *The Bible, Theology, and Faith*. Cambridge: Cambridge University Press, 2000.
———. "The Bible, the Question of God, and Christian Faith." In *The Bible, Theology, and Faith: A Study of Abraham and Jesus*, 1-44. Cambridge: Cambridge University Press, 2000.
———. "Miracles in the Hebrew Bible." In *The Cambridge Companion to Miracles*, edited by Graham Twelftree, 57-74. Cambridge: Cambridge University Press, 2010.
———. *The Old Testament of the Old Testament : Patriarchal Narratives and Mosiac Yahwism*. Minneapolis: Fortress, 1992.
———. *Old Testament Theology: Reading the Hebrew Bible as Christian Scripture*. Grand Rapids: Baker Academic, 2013.
———. *The Theology of the Book of Genesis*. Cambridge: Cambridge University Press, 2009.
Modras, Ronald. *The Catholic Church and Anti-Semitism: Poland, 1932-1939*. Chur, Switzerland: Harwood Academic, 1994.
Morales, Isaac Augustine, OP. "Baptism and Union with Christ." In *"In Christ" in Paul: Explorations in Paul's Theology of Union and Participation*, edited by Michael J. Thate, Kevin J. Vanhoozer, and Constantine R. Campbell, 157-79. Grand Rapids: Eerdmans, 2018.
———. "Paul and the Gift of Sonship." *Nova et Vetera* 17, no. 2 (2019) 215-28.
Morales, L. Michael. *Exodus Old and New: a Biblical Theology of Redemption*. Downers Grove, IL: InterVarsity, 2020.

———. "The New Exodus in the Gospel of John." In *Exodus Old and New: a Biblical Theology of Redemption*, 159–72. Downers Grove, IL: InterVarsity, 2020.

———. "The Spirit of the New Exodus." In *Exodus Old and New: a Biblical Theology of Redemption*, 173–84. Downers Grove, IL: InterVarsity, 2020.

———. *The Tabernacle Prefigured: Cosmic Mountain Ideology in Genesis and Exodus*. Leuven: Peeters, 2012.

———. *Who Shall Ascend the Mountain of the Lord? A Biblical Theology of the Book of Leviticus*. Downers Grove, IL: InterVarsity, 2015.

Morales, Rodrigo J. *The Spirit and the Restoration of Israel: New Exodus and New Creation Motifs in Galatians*. Tübingen: Mohr Siebeck, 2010.

Morali, Ilaria. "Catholic Theology vis-à-vis Religions and Dialogue Fifty Years after Vatican II." In *The Past, Present, and Future of Theologies of Interreligious Dialogue*, edited by Terrence Merrigan and John Friday, 81–91. Oxford: Oxford University Press, 2017.

Morgan, Fred. "Jewish Perspectives on Jewish-Christian Dialogue over Five Decades." *European Judaism* 48, no. 2 (October 2015) 3–22.

Morris, Benny. *One State, Two States: Resolving the Israeli/Palestinian Conflict*. New Haven, CT: Yale University Press, 2009.

Mortara, Edgardo, CRL. "The Mortara Case and Pius IX: The Autobiographical Account of the 'Mortara Case' Written by the Protagonist, Reverend Father Pio Maria Mortara, C. R. L." In *Kidnapped by the Vatican? The Unpublished Memoirs of Edgardo Mortara*, edited by Vittorio Messori, translated by Andrea Vannicelli and Vittorio Messori, 77–175. San Francisco, CA: Ignatius, 2017.

Moschella, Melissa. *To Whom Do Children Belong? Parental Rights, Civic Education, and Children's Autonomy*. Cambridge: Cambridge University Press, 2016.

Moseley, Carys. *Nationhood, Providence, and Witness: Israel in Modern Theology and Social Theory*. Eugene, OR: Wipf and Stock, 2013.

Mosès, Stéphane. *System and Revelation: Philosophy of Franz Rosenzweig*. Translated by Catherine Tihanyi. Detroit: Wayne State University Press, 1992.

Moyaert, Marianne. "'The Gifts and the Calling of God Are Irrevocable' (Rom 11:29): A Theological Reflection." *Irish Theological Quarterly* 83, no. 1 (February 2018) 24–43.

Moyaert, Marianne, and Didier Pollefeyt. "Israel and the Church: Fulfillment Beyond Supersessionism?" In *Never Revoked: Nostra Aetate as Ongoing Challenge for Jewish-Christian Dialogue*, edited by Marianne Moyaert and Didier Pollefeyt, 159–83. Leuven: Peeters, 2010.

Mundill, Robin R. *England's Jewish Solution: Experiment and Expulsion, 1262–1290*. Cambridge University Press, 1998.

Murphy, Francesca Aran. *1 Samuel*. Grand Rapids: Brazos, 2010.

Naeh, Schlomo. "Freedom and Celibacy: A Talmudic Variation on Tales of Temptation and Fall in Genesis and Its Syrian Background." In *The Book of Genesis in Jewish and Oriental Christian Interpretation*, edited by Judith Frishman and Lucas Van Rompay, 73–90. Leuven: Peeters, 1997.

Nanos, Mark D. *Collected Essays of Mark D. Nanos*. 4 vols. Eugene, OR: Cascade, 2017.

———. "Paul and Judaism: Why Not Paul's Judaism?" In *Paul Unbound: Other Perspectives on the Apostle*, edited by Mark Douglas Given, 117–60. Peabody, MA: Hendrickson, 2009.

———. "Paul's Relationship to Torah in Light of his Strategy 'to Become Everything to Everyone' (1 Corinthians 9.19–23)." In *Paul and Judaism: Crosscurrents in Pauline Exegesis and the Study of Jewish-Christian Relations*, edited by Reimund Bieringer and Didier Pollefeyt, 106–40. London: Bloomsbury, 2012.

———. *Reading Romans within Judaism: Collected Essays of Mark D. Nanos*, vol. 2. Eugene, OR: Cascade, 2018.

Nardoni, Enrique. *Rise Up, O Judge: A Study of Justice in the Biblical World*. Translated by Seán Charles Martin. Grand Rapids: Baker Academic, 2010.

Nemes, Robert, and Daniel Unowsky, eds. *Sites of European Antisemitism in the Age of Mass Politics, 1880–1918*. Waltham, MA: Brandeis University Press, 2014.

Netanyahu, Benzion. *Don Isaac Abravanel: Statesman and Philosopher*. Philadelphia: Jewish Publication Society, 1982.

Neuhaus, David, SJ. "Jewish-Christian Dialogue and the Question of the Land of Israel." *Recherches de science religieuse* 103 (2015) 397–418.

———. "Moments of Crisis and Grace: Jewish-Catholic Relations in 2009." *One in Christ* 43, no. 2 (2010) 6–24.

———. *Writing from the Holy Land*. Jerusalem: Studium Theologicum Salesianum, 2017.

Neuman, Kalman. "Political Hebraism and the Early Modern '*Respublica Hebraeorum*': On Defining the Field." In *Political Hebraism: Judaic Sources in Early Modern Political Thought*, edited by Gordon Schochet, Fania Oz-Salzberger, and Meirav Jones, 57–71. Jerusalem: Shalem, 2008.

Neumann, Jonathan. *To Heal the World? How the Jewish Left Corrupts Judaism and Endangers Israel*. New York: St. Martin's, 2018.

Neusner, Jacob. *Christian Faith and the Bible of Judaism: The Judaic Encounter with Scripture*. Grand Rapids: Eerdmans, 1987.

———. *From Politics to Piety: The Emergence of Rabbinic Judaism*. Englewood Cliffs, NJ: Prentice Hall, 1973.

———. "How We Meet God in the Torah." In Jacob Neuser and Bruce Chilton. *Revelation: The Torah and the Bible*, 50–75. Valley Forge, PA: Trinity International, 1995.

———. "Israel as Kingdom of Priests and Holy Nation." In *The Body of Faith: Israel and the Church*, by Jacob Neusner and Bruce D. Chilton, 31–48. Valley Forge, PA: Trinity International, 1996.

———. *Judaism: The Evidence of the Mishnah*. Chicago: University of Chicago Press, 1981.

———. "Mr Maccoby's Red Cow, Mr Sanders's Pharisees—and Mine." *Journal of Semitic Studies* 23, no. 1 (1991) 81–98.

———. *Performing Israel's Faith: Narrative and Law in Rabbinic Theology*. Waco, TX: Baylor University Press, 2005.

———. *A Rabbi Talks with Jesus: An Intermillennial, Interfaith Exchange*. New York: Doubleday, 1993.

———. *Telling Tales: Making Sense of Christian and Judaic Nonsense*. Louisville, KY: Westminster John Knox, 1993.

Neusner, Jacob, and Bruce Chilton. *The Body of Faith: Israel and the Church*. Valley Forge, PA: Trinity International, 1996.

———. *Jewish-Christian Debates: God, Kingdom, Messiah*. Minneapolis: Fortress, 1998.

———. *Revelation: The Torah and the Bible*. Valley Forge, PA: Trinity International, 1995.

Newman, John Henry. "Bodily Suffering." In *Parochial and Plain Sermons*, 568–77. San Francisco: Ignatius, 1987.

———. *An Essay on the Development of Christian Doctrine*. 6th ed. Notre Dame, IN: University of Notre Dame Press, 1989.

Nicholls, William. *Christian Antisemitism: A History of Hate*. Northvale, NJ: Jason Aronson, 1993.

Nicholson, Robert. "Theology and Law: Does the Modern State of Israel Violate Its Call to Justice in the Covenant by Its Relation to International Law?" In *The New Christian Zionism: Fresh Perspectives on Israel and the Land*, edited by Gerald R. McDermott, 249–80. Downers Grove, IL: IVP Academic, 2016.

Nicolas, Jean-Hervé, OP. *Synthèse dogmatique. De la Trinité à la Trinité*. Paris: Beauchesne, 1985.

Niehaus, Jeffrey J. *God at Sinai: Covenant and Theophany in the Bible and the Ancient Near East*. Grand Rapids: Zondervan, 1995.

Ninow, Friedbert. *Indicators of Typology within the Old Testament: The Exodus Motif*. Frankfurt: Peter Lang, 2001.

Nixon, R. E. *The Exodus in the New Testament*. London: Tyndale, 1963.

Noel, Gerald. *The Renaissance Popes: Statesmen, Warriors and the Great Borgia Myth*. New York: Carroll & Graf, 2006.

Norris, Thomas J. "The Jewish People at Vatican II: The Drama of a Development in Ecclesiology and Its Subsequent Reception in Ireland." In *Christ Jesus and the Jewish People Today: New Explorations of Theological Interrelationships*, edited by Philip A. Cunningham et al., 251–67. Grand Rapids: Eerdmans, 2011.

Norwich, John Julius. *Absolute Monarchs: A History of the Papacy*. New York: Random House, 2011.

Novak, David. *Athens and Jerusalem: God, Humans, and Nature*. Toronto: University of Toronto Press, 2019.

———. "Avoiding Charges of Legalism and Antinomianism in Jewish-Christian Dialogue." In *Talking with Christians: Musings of a Jewish Theologian*, 26–45. Grand Rapids: Eerdmans, 2005.

———. "Before Revelation: The Rabbis, Paul, and Karl Barth." In *Talking with Christians: Musings of a Jewish Theologian*, 108–26. Grand Rapids: Eerdmans, 2005.

———. *Covenantal Rights: A Study in Jewish Political Theory*. Princeton, NJ: Princeton University Press, 2009.

———. "Covenant and Mission." In *Covenant and Hope: Christian and Jewish Reflections: Essays in Constructive Theology from the Institute for Theological Inquiry*, edited by Robert W. Jenson and Eugene Korn, 41–57. Grand Rapids: Eerdmans, 2012.

———. "The Covenant in Rabbinic Thought." In *Two Faiths, One Covenant? Jewish and Christian Identity in the Presence of the Other*, edited by Eugene B. Korn and John Pawlikowski, 65–80. Lanham, MD: Rowman & Littlefield, 2005.

———. *The Election of Israel: The Idea of a Chosen People*. Cambridge: Cambridge University Press, 1995.

———. "The End of the Law: A Significant Difference between Judaism and Christianity." In *Essays on Jews and Christians Throughout History in Honor of Michael A. Signer,* edited by Franklin T. Harkins, 34-49. Notre Dame, IN: University of Notre Dame Press, 2010.

———. "Franz Rosenzweig's Theology of the Jewish-Christian Relationship." In *Jewish-Christian Dialogue: A Jewish Justification,* 93-113. Oxford: Oxford University Press, 1989.

———. "From Supersessionism to Parallelism in Jewish-Christian Dialogue." In *Talking with Christians: Musings of a Jewish Theologian,* 8-25. Grand Rapids: Eerdmans, 2005.

———. "How Jewish Was Karl Barth?" In *Karl Barth, the Jews, and Judaism,* edited by George Hunsinger, 1-23. Grand Rapids: Eerdmans, 2018.

———. "Introduction: What to Seek and What to Avoid in Jewish-Christian Dialogue." In *Christianity in Jewish Terms,* edited by Tikva Frymer-Kensky et al., 1-6. Boulder, CO: Westview, 2000.

———. *Jewish-Christian Dialogue: A Jewish Justification.* New York: Oxford University Press, 1989.

———. "The Jewish Mission." *First Things* 227 (November 2012) 39-43.

———. "Karl Barth on Divine Command: A Jewish Response." In *Talking with Christians: Musings of a Jewish Theologian,* 127-45. Grand Rapids: Eerdmans, 2005.

———. "Law and Eschatology: A Jewish-Christian Intersection." In *The Last Things: Biblical and Theological Perspectives on Eschatology,* edited by Carl E. Braaten and Robert W. Jenson, 90-112. Grand Rapids: Eerdmans, 2002.

———. "Mitsvah." In *Christianity in Jewish Terms,* edited by Tikva Frymer-Kensky et al., 115-26. Boulder CO: Westview, 2000.

———. "Natural Law and Divine Command: Some Thoughts on *Veritatis Splendor.*" In *John Paul II and the Jewish People: A Jewish-Christian Dialogue,* edited by David G. Dalin and Matthew Levering, 61-79. Lanham, MD: Rowman & Littlefield, 2008.

———. *Natural Law in Judaism.* Cambridge: Cambridge University Press, 1998.

———. "Supersessionism Hard and Soft." *First Things* 290 (February 2019) 27-31.

———. "What Does Edith Stein Mean for Jews?" In *Talking with Christians: Musings of a Jewish Theologian,* 146-66. Grand Rapids: Eerdmans, 2005.

———. "What Is Jewish Theology?" In *The Cambridge Companion to Jewish Theology.* Forthcoming.

———. "When Jews Are Christians." In *Talking with Christians: Musings of a Jewish Theologian,* 218-28. Grand Rapids: Eerdmans, 2005.

———. *Zionism and Judaism: A New Theory.* Cambridge: Cambridge University Press, 2015.

Novak, David, Tikva Frymer-Kensky, Peter Ochs, and Michael Alan Signer. "*Dabru Emet*: A Jewish Statement on Christians and Christianity." *First Things* 107 (November 2000) 39-41.

Novenson, Matthew V. *Christ among the Messiahs: Christ Language in Paul and Messiah Language in Ancient Judaism.* Oxford: Oxford University Press, 2012.

———. *The Grammar of Messianism: An Ancient Jewish Political Idiom and Its Users.* Oxford: Oxford University Press, 2017.

Nutt, Roger W. *General Principles of Sacramental Theology.* Washington, DC: Catholic University of America Press, 2017.

Oakes, Peter. "Πίστις as Relational Way of Life in Galatians." *Journal for the Study of the New Testament* 40, no. 3 (2018) 255-75.

Ochs, Peter. *Another Reformation: Postliberal Christianity and the Jews.* Grand Rapids: Baker Academic, 2011.

———. *Religion without Violence: The Practice and Philosophy of Scriptural Reasoning.* Eugene, OR: Cascade, 2019.

———. "To Love Tanakh Is Love Enough for the Jews." In *Karl Barth, the Jews, and Judaism*, edited by George Hunsinger, 75–102. Grand Rapids: Eerdmans, 2018.

O'Collins, Gerald, SJ. *The Second Vatican Council on Other Religions.* Oxford: Oxford University Press, 2013.

Oesterreicher, Johannes M. "Declaration on the Relation of the Church to Non-Christian Religions." In *Commentary on the Documents of Vatican II*, vol. 3, edited by Herbert Vorgrimler, 1–154. London: Burns & Oates, 1968.

———. "Dr. Eberle zur Judenfrage." *Die Erfüllung* 3 (September 1936) 134–35.

Olson, Dennis T. *Numbers.* Louisville, KY: John Knox, 1996.

O'Mahony, Anthony. "The Vatican, Jerusalem, the State of Israel, and Christianity in the Holy Land." *International Journal for the Study of the Christian Church* 5, no. 2 (July 2005) 123–46.

O'Neill, Colman E., OP. *Sacramental Realism: A General Theory of the Sacraments*, edited by Romanus Cessario. Chicago: Midwest Theological Forum, 1998.

Oort, Johannes van. "Jews and Judaism in Augustine's *Sermones*." *Instrvmenta Patristica et Mediaevalia* 53 (2009) 213–65.

O'Regan, Cyril. "Thomism in Ecstasy: Olivier-Thomas Venard on the Wording of Theology and the Expropriation of Cultural Discourses." *Nova et Vetera* 18 (2020) 695–707.

Oreglia, Guiseppe, di Santo Stefano, SJ. *La Civiltà Cattolica.* Roma.

———. "Cronaca Contemporanea." *Civiltà Cattolica* 11.5, no. 736 (February 19, 1881) 482–90.

Origen of Alexandria. *Homilies on Genesis and Exodus.* Translated by Ronald E. Heine. Washington, DC: Catholic University of America Press, 1982.

———. *On First Principles.* Translated by G. W. Butterworth. Gloucester, MA: Peter Smith, 1973.

Ounsworth, Richard. *Joshua Typology in the New Testament.* Tübingen: Mohr Siebeck, 2012.

Ozar, Alex. "The Emergence of Max Scheler: Understanding Rabbi Joseph Soloveitchik's Philosophical Anthropology." *Harvard Theological Review* 109, no. 2 (April 2016) 178–206.

Paddison, Angus. "Christology and Jewish-Christian Understanding: Reading the Fourth Gospel as Scripture." In *Christology and Scripture: Interdisciplinary Perspectives*, edited by Andrew T. Lincoln and Angus Paddison, 41–57. London: T. & T. Clark, 2007.

Page, John R. *What Will Dr. Newman Do? John Henry Newman and Papal Infallibility, 1865–1875.* Collegeville, MN: Liturgical, 1994.

Pangritz, Andreas. *Theologie und Antisemitismus: Das Beispiel Martin Luthers.* Frankfurt am Main: Peter Lang, 2017.

———. *Vergegnungen, Umbrüche und Aufbrüche: Beiträge zur Theologie des christlich-jüdischen Verhältnisses.* Leipzig: Evangelische Verlagsanstalt, 2015.

———. "Wendung nach Jerusalem: Zu Friedrich-Wilhelm Marquardts Arbeit an der Dogmatik." In *Vergegnungen, Umbrüche und Aufbrüche: Beiträge zur Theologie des christlich-jüdischen Verhältnisses*, 167–86. Leipzig: Evangelische Verlagsanstalt, 2015.

Pannenberg, Wolfart. *Systematic Theology*. Vol. 3. Translated by Geoffrey W. Bromiley. Grand Rapids: Eerdmans, 1993.

Pao, David W. *Acts and the Isaianic New Exodus*. Grand Rapids: Baker Academic, 2002.

Papademetriou, George C. "Jewish Rite in the Christian Church: Ecumenical Possibility." *Scottish Journal of Theology* 26, no. 4 (November 1973) 466–87.

Passelecq, Georges, and Bernard Suchecky. *The Hidden Encyclical of Pius XI*. Translated by Steven Rendall. New York: Harcourt, Brace, 1997.

Paul IV. "*Cum nimis absurdum*." July 14, 1555.

Pawlikowski, John T., OSM. "Can We Speak of a Theological Bond between Christians and Jews? A Dialogue with Michael Signer." In *Transforming Relations: Essays on Jews and Christians throughout History in Honor of Michael A. Signer*, edited by Franklin T. Harkins, 385–404. Notre Dame, IN: University of Notre Dame Press, 2010.

———. "A Catholic Response to Gavin D'Costa." *Theological Studies* 73, no. 3 (September 2012) 629–40.

———. "The Challenge of *Tikkun Olam* for Jews and Christians." In *Seeing Judaism Anew: Christianity's Sacred Obligation*, edited by Mary C. Boys, 227–38. Lanham, MD: Rowman & Littlefield, 2005.

———. "A Christian-Jewish Dialogical Model in Light of New Research on Paul's Relationship with Judaism." In *Paul and Judaism: Crosscurrents in Pauline Exegesis and the Study of Jewish-Christian Relations*, edited by Reimund Bieringer and Didier Pollefeyt, 163–73. London: Bloomsbury, 2012.

———. "Christian Theological Concerns after the Holocaust." In *Visions of the Other: Jewish and Christian Theologians Assess the Dialogue*, edited by Eugene J. Fisher, 28–51. New York: Paulist, 1994.

———. *Christ in the Light of Christian-Jewish Dialogue*. New York: Paulist, 1982.

———. "Christology and the Jewish-Christian Dialogue: A Personal Theological Journey." *Irish Theological Quarterly* 72, no. 2 (May 2007) 147–67.

———. "Fifty Years of Christian-Jewish Dialogue—What Has It Changed?" *Journal of Ecumenical Studies* 49, no. 1 (January 2014) 99–106.

———. *Jesus and the Theology of Israel*. Wilmington, DE: Michael Glazier, 1989.

———. "Jews and Christians: Their Covenantal Relationship in the American Context." In *Two Faiths, One Covenant? Jewish and Christian Identity in the Presence of the Other*, edited by Eugene B. Korn and John Pawlikowski, 155–65. Lanham, MD: Rowman & Littlefield, 2005.

———. "Reflections on Covenant and Mission: Forty Years after *Nostra Aetate*." In *Never Revoked: Nostra Aetate as Ongoing Challenge for Jewish-Christian Dialogue*, edited by Marianne Moyaert and Didier Pollefeyt, 57–91. Leuven: Peeters, 2010.

———. *Restating the Catholic Church's Relationship with the Jewish People: The Challenge of Super-Sessionary Theology*. Lewiston, NY: Edwin Mellen, 2013.

———. "The Significance of the Christian-Jewish Dialogue and Holocaust Studies for Catholic Ethics." *Political Theology* 13, no. 4 (March 2012) 444–57.

———. "The Uniqueness of the Christian-Jewish Dialogue: A Yes and a No." *Studies in Christian-Jewish Relations* 12, no. 1 (March 2017) 1–14.

Pennington, Johnathan T. *Heaven and Earth in the Gospel of Matthew*. Grand Rapids: Baker Academic, 2009.

Pennington, Johnathan T., and Sean M. McDonough, eds. *Cosmology and New Testament Theology*. London: T. & T. Clark, 2008.

Pennington, Kenneth. "The Law's Violence against Medieval and Early Modern Jews." *Rivista Internazionale di Diritto Comune* 23 (2012) 23–44.

Perrier, Emmanuel, OP. "The Election of Israel Today: Supersessionism, Post-Supersessionism, and Fulfilment." *Nova et Vetera* 7, no. 2 (2009) 485–504.

Perrin, Nicholas. *Jesus the Priest*. Grand Rapids: Baker Academic, 2018.

Peterson, Erik. "The Church from Jews and Gentiles." In *Theological Tractates*, edited and translated by Michael J. Hollerich, 40–67. Stanford, CA: Stanford University Press, 2011.

Peterson, Paul Silas. *The Early Hans Urs von Balthasar: Historical Contexts and Intellectual Formation*. Berlin: de Gruyter, 2015.

Peter the Venerable. *Against the Inveterate Obduracy of the Jews*. Translated by Irven M. Resnick. Washington, DC: Catholic University of America Press, 2013.

Phan, Peter C. "Jesus as the Universal Savior in the Light of God's Eternal Covenant with the Jewish People: A Roman Catholic Perspective." In *Seeing Judaism Anew: Christianity's Sacred Obligation*, edited by Mary C. Boys, 127–37. Lanham, MD: Rowman & Littlefield, 2005.

———. "Judaism and Christianity: Reading Cardinal Koch's Address Between the Lines and Against the Grain: A Response to Cardinal Kurt Koch's October 30, 2011 Keynote Address at Seton Hall University during the 10th Annual Meeting of the Council of Centers on Christian-Jewish Relations." *Studies in Christian-Jewish Relations* 7, no 1. (May 2012) 1–7.

Phayer, Michael. *The Catholic Church and the Holocaust, 1930–1965*. Bloomington, IN: Indiana University Press, 2000.

Phelan, John E., Jr. *Separated Siblings: An Evangelical Understanding of Jews and Judaism*. Grand Rapids: Eerdmans, 2020.

Phythian-Adams, W. J. *The People and the Presence*. Oxford: Oxford University Press, 1942.

Pinay, Maurice. *Complotto contro la Chiesa*, Rome: s.n 1962.

Pitkänen, Pekka, M. A. *Central Sanctuary and the Centralization of Worship in Ancient Israel from the Settlement to the Building of Solomon's Temple*. Piscataway, NJ: Gorgias, 2003.

———. "From Tent of Meeting to Temple: Presence, Rejection and Renewal of Divine Favour." In *Heaven on Earth: Temple in Biblical Theology*, edited by T. Desmond Alexander and Simon Gathercole, 23–24. Waynesboro, GA: Paternoster, 2004.

Pitre, Brant James. *Jesus and the Last Supper*. Grand Rapids: Eerdmans, 2015.

———. *Jesus, the Tribulation, and the End of the Exile: Restoration Eschatology and the Origin of the Atonement*. Grand Rapids: Baker Academic, 2005.

Pitre, Brant James, Michael P. Barber, and John A. Kincaid. *Paul, a New Covenant Jew: Rethinking Pauline Theology*. Grand Rapids: Eerdmans, 2019.

Pius XII. *In Multiplicibus Curis: Encyclical of Pope Pius XII on Prayers for Peace in Palestine*. October 24, 1948. Vatican.va.

Pixley, Jorge V. "History and Particularity in Reading the Hebrew Bible: A Response to Jon D. Levenson." In *Jews, Christians, and the Theology of the Hebrew Scriptures*, edited by Alice Ogden Bellis and Joel S. Kaminsky, 231–37. Atlanta: SBL, 2000.

———. *On Exodus: A Liberation Perspective*. Translated by Robert R. Barr. Maryknoll, NY: Orbis, 1987.

Pizzorusso, Giovanni. "Il caso Mortara: due libri e un documento Americano." *Il Veltro* 42 (1998) 134–41.
Plen, Matt. "Rabbi Soloveitchik: A Teacher, Writer, and Community Leader Who Helped to Shape Modern Orthodoxy in America." February 2007. *myjewishlearning.com*.
Pollefeyt, Didier, ed. *Jews and Christians, Rivals or Partners for the Kingdom of God? In Search of an Alternative for the Theology of Substitution*. Grand Rapids: Eerdmans, 1997.
Polyakov, Emma O'Donnell. "Christian-Jewish Dialogue in the Monasteries of Jerusalem: An Evolution of Monastic Interreligious Dialogue." *Journal of Ecumenical Studies* 53, no. 4 (2018) 521–40.
Pomis, David de. *Enarratio brevis, de senum affectibus praecavendis, atque curandis . . .* Venice: 1588.
Pomplun, Trent. "Post-Tridentine Sacramental Theology." In *The Oxford Handbook of Sacramental Theology*, edited by Hans Boersma and Matthew Levering, 348–61. Oxford: Oxford University Press, 2015.
Pontifical Biblical Commission. "The Interpretation of the Bible in the Church." Vatican City: *Libreria Editrice Vaticana*, 1993. Vatican.va.
———. "The Jewish People and Their Sacred Scriptures in the Christian Bible." Vatican City: *Libreria Editrice Vaticana*, 2001. Vatican.va.
Pontifical Commission for Religious Relations with the Jews. "'The Gifts and the Calling of God Are Irrevocable' (Rom 11:29): A Reflection on Theological Questions Pertaining to Catholic-Jewish Relations on the Occasion of the 50th Anniversary of 'Nostra Aetate' (no. 4)." Vatican City: *Libreria Editrice Vaticana*, 2015. Vatican.va.
———. "Guidelines on Religious Relations with the Jews (n. 4) [1974]." In *Vatican Council II: Constitutions, Degrees, Declarations*, vol. 1: *The Conciliar and Post Conciliar Documents*, rev. ed., edited by Austin Flannery, 743–49. Northport, NY: Costello, 1996.
———. "Notes on the Correct Way to Present the Jews and Judaism in Preaching and Catechesis in the Roman Catholic Church." 1985. Vatican.va.
Pontifical Council for Interreligious Dialogue. "Dialogue in Truth and Charity: Pastoral Orientations for Interreligious Dialogue." Vatican City: *Libreria Editrice Vaticana*, 2014. Vatican.va.
Powell, Mark E. *Papal Infallibility: A Protestant Evaluation of an Ecumenical Issue*. Grand Rapids: Eerdmans, 2009.
Prior, Michael. *Zionism and the State of Israel: A Moral Inquiry*. London: Routledge, 1999.
Procario-Foley, Elena. "Fulfillment and Complementary: Reflections on Relationship in 'Gifts and Calling.'" *Studies in Christian-Jewish Relations* 12, no. 1 (March 2017) 1–12.
Prosic, Tamara. *The Development and Symbolism of Passover Until 70 CE*. London: T. & T. Clark, 2004.
Provan, Iain, V. Philips Long, and Tremper Longman III. *A Biblical History of Israel*. Louisville, KY: Westminster John Knox, 2003.
Radner, Ephraim. *A Brutal Unity: The Spiritual Politics of the Christian Church*. Waco, TX: Baylor University Press, 2012.
———. *Church*. Eugene, OR: Cascade, 2017.

———. *A Profound Ignorance: Modern Pneumatology and Its Anti-modern Redemption.* Waco, TX: Baylor University Press, 2019.
Raheb, Mitri. *I Am a Palestinian Christian.* Minneapolis: Fortress, 1995.
Ramban (Nachmanides). *Commentary on the Torah: Genesis.* Translated by Charles B. Chavel. New York: Shilo, 1999.
Rashkover, Randi. *Freedom and Law: A Jewish-Christian Apologetics.* New York: Fordham University Press, 2011.
———. *Revelation and Theopolitics: Barth, Rosenzweig and the Politics of Praise.* London: T. & T. Clark, 2005.
Ratzinger, Joseph. "The Church's Guilt: Presentation of the Document *Remembrance and Reconciliation* from the International Theological Commission." In *Pilgrim Fellowship of Faith: The Church as Communion*, edited by Vinzenz Pfnur, translated by Henry Taylor, 274–83. San Francisco: Ignatius, 2005.
———. *Daughter Zion: Meditations on the Church's Marian Belief.* Translated by John M. McDermott. San Francisco: Ignatius, 1983.
———. "The Heritage of Abraham." In *Pilgrim Fellowship of Faith: The Church as Communion*, edited by Vinzenz Pfnur, translated by Henry Taylor, 270–73. San Francisco: Ignatius, 2005.
———. *Jesus of Nazareth*, vol. 1: *From the Baptism in the Jordan to the Transfiguration.* Translated by Adrian J. Walker. New York: Doubleday, 2007.
———. *Many Religions—One Covenant: Israel, the Church, and the World.* Translated by Graham Harrison. San Francisco: Ignatius, 1999.
———. "The Papal Primacy and the Unity of the People of God." In *Church, Ecumenism and Politics: New Essays in Ecclesiology*, translated by Robert Nowell, 29–45. New York: Crossroad, 1988.
———. "The Primacy of Peter and the Unity of the Church." In *Called to Communion: Understanding the Church Today*, translated by Adrian Walker, 47–74. San Francisco: Ignatius, 1996.
———. *Salt of the Earth: Christianity and the Catholic Church at the End of the Millennium: An Interview with Peter Seewald.* Translated by Adrian Walker. San Francisco: Ignatius, 2017.
———. "The Sign of the Woman: An Introduction to the Encyclical 'Redemptoris Mater.'" Translated by Lothar Krauth. In *Mary: God's Yes to Man: Pope John Paul II's Encyclical Letter: Mother of the Redeemer*, 9–40. San Francisco: Ignatius, 1988.
———. *The Spirit of the Liturgy.* Translated by John Saward. San Francisco: Ignatius, 2000.
Ravid, Benjamin C. I. "The Forced Baptism of Jewish Minors in Early Modern Venice." *Italia: Studi e ricerche sulla cultura e sula letteratura degli ebrei d'Italia* 13 (2001) 259–301.
Ravitzky, Aviezer. *Messianism, Zionism, and Jewish Religious Radicalism.* Translated by Michael Swirsky and Jonathan Chipman. Chicago: University of Chicago Press, 1996.
———. "Rabbi J. B. Soloveitchik on Human Knowledge: Between Maimonidean and neo-Kantian Philosophy." *Modern Judaism* 6 (May 1986) 157–88.
Regev, Eyal. "Community as Temple: Revisiting Cultic Metaphors in Qumran and the New Testament." *Bulletin for Biblical Research* 28, no. 4 (2018) 604–31.
———. "Temple and Righteousness in Qumran and Early Christianity: Tracing the Social Differences Between the Two Movements." In *Text, Thought, and Practice*

in Qumran and Early Christianity, edited by D. R. Schwartz and R. A. Clements, 64–87. Leiden: Brill, 2009.

———. *The Temple in Early Christianity: Experiencing the Sacred*. New Haven, CT: Yale University Press, 2019.

Reinhartz, Adele. *Cast Out of the Covenant: Jews and Anti-Judaism in the Gospel of John*. Lanham, MD: Lexington, 2018.

———. "The Gospel of John: How the 'Jews' Became Part of the Plot." In *Jesus, Judaism, and Christian Anti-Judaism: Reading the New Testament after the Holocaust*, edited by Paula Fredriksen and Adele Reinhartz, 99–116. Louisville, KY: Westminster John Knox, 2002.

Reiser, Marius. *Jesus and Judgment: The Eschatological Proclamation in Its Jewish Context*. Translated by Linda M. Maloney. Minneapolis: Fortress, 1997.

Renan, Ernest. *De l'origine du langage*. Paris: Calmann-Lévy, 1883.

Rendtorff, Rolf. *Israel und sein Land: Theologische Überlegungen zu einem politischen Problem*. Munich: Kaiser, 1975.

Reno, R. R. "Loving the Law: What Christians Can Learn from Jews." In *Rav Shalom Banayikh: Essays Presented to Rabbi Shalom Carmy*, edited by Hayyim Angel and Yitzchak Blau, 239–54. Jersey City, NJ: KTAV, 2012.

Rensberger, David. "Anti-Judaism and the Gospel of John." In *Anti-Judaism and the Gospels*, edited by William R. Farmer, 120–57. Harrisburg, PA: Trinity International, 1999.

Reznick, Leibel. *The Holy Temple Revisited*. Northvale, NJ: Jason Aronson, 1990.

Ribbens, Benjamin J. *Levitical Sacrifice and Heavenly Cult in Hebrews*. Berlin: Walter de Gruyter, 2016.

Rice, Peter H. *Behold, Your House Is Left to You: The Theological and Narrative Place of the Jerusalem Temple in Luke's Gospel*. Eugene, OR: Pickwick, 2016.

Riebling, Mark. *Church of Spies: The Pope's Secret War Against Hitler*. New York: Basic, 2015.

Rioli, Maria Chiara. "The 'New Nazis' or the 'People of our God'? Jews and Zionism in the Latin Church of Jerusalem, 1948–1962." *Journal of Ecclesiastical History* 68, no. 1 (2017) 81–107.

Riskin, Shlomo. "Covenant and Conversion: The United Mission to Redeem the World." In *Covenant and Hope: Christian and Jewish Reflections: Essays in Constructive Theology from the Institute for Theological Inquiry*, edited by Robert W. Jenson, and Eugene Korn, 99–128. Grand Rapids: Eerdmans, 2012.

Rist, John M. *What Is Truth? From the Academy to the Vatican*. Cambridge: Cambridge University Press, 2008.

Roberts, Alastair J., and Andrew Wilson. *Echoes of Exodus: Tracing Themes of Redemption through Scripture*. Wheaton, IL: Crossway, 2018.

Rodríguez, Rubén Rosario. *Dogmatics after Babel: Beyond the Theologies of Word and Culture*. Louisville, KY: Westminster John Knox, 2018.

Roemer, Carl. "Wonder and Worries: An Appreciation and Critique of John Howard Yoder's *The Jewish-Christian Schism Revisited*." *The Journal of Scriptural Reasoning* 16 (2017). jsr.shanti.virginia.edu/back-issues/vol-16-no-1-november-2017-special-issue-honoring-the-work-of-stanley-hauerwas-and-his-friends/wonder-and-worries-an-appreciation-and-critique-of-john-howard-yoder's-The-Jewish-Christian-Schism-Revisited/.

Rogan, Eugene L., and Avi Shlaim, eds. *The War for Palestine: Rewriting the History of 1948*. Cambridge: Cambridge University Press, 2001.

Rondina, Saverio, SJ. "La morale giudaica e il mistero del sangue." *Civiltà cattolica* 1, no. 1022 (1892)145–56.

Rosen, David. "Jewish and Israeli Perspectives 40 Years after Vatican II." In *Nostra Aetate: Origins, Promulgation, Impact on Jewish-Catholic Relations*, edited by Uri Bialer, Neville Lamdan, and Alberto Melloni, 175–88. Berlin: LIT Verlag, 2007.

Rosenhagen, Ulrich. "God Is Faithful to God's People: The New Theology of Israel in Contemporary German Protestantism." *Journal of Ecumenical Studies* 46, no. 4 (September 2011) 621–38.

Rosenzweig, Franz. *The Star of Redemption*. Translated by Barbara E. Galli. Madison, WI: University of Wisconsin Press, 2005.

Rossi, Lauren Faulkner. *Wehrmacht Priests: Catholicism and the Nazi War of Annihilation*. Cambridge, MA: Harvard University Press, 2015.

Roth, John K., et al. "The Ruethers' *Wrath of Jonah*: An Essay-Review." *Continuum* 1 (1990) 105–36.

Roth, Norman. *Jews, Visigoths, and Muslims in Medieval Spain*. Leiden: Brill, 1994.

Rouhana, Nadim N. *Palestinian Citizens in an Ethnic Jewish State: Identities in Conflict*. New Haven, CT: Yale University Press, 1997.

———, ed. *Israel and Its Palestinian Citizens: Ethnic Privileges in the Jewish State*. Cambridge: Cambridge University Press, 2017.

Rouhana, Nadim N., and Areej Sabbagh-Khoury. "Memory and the Return of History in a Settler-Colonial Context: The Case of the Palestinians in Israel." In *Israel and Its Palestinian Citizens: Ethnic Privileges in the Jewish State*, edited by Nadim N. Rouhana, 393–432. Cambridge: Cambridge University Press, 2017.

Rowland, Christopher. "The Temple in the New Testament." In *Temple and Worship in Biblical Israel: Proceedings of the Oxford Old Testament Seminar*, edited by John Day, 469–83. New York: T. & T. Clark, 2007.

Rubenstein, Richard. *After Auschwitz*. 2d ed. Baltimore: Johns Hopkins University Press, 1992.

Rudin, A. James. "The Dramatic Impact of *Nostra Aetate*." In *Twenty Years of Jewish-Catholic Relations*, edited by Eugene J. Fisher, A. James Rudin, and Marc H. Tenenbaum, 9–18. New York: Paulist, 1986.

Rudolph, David, and Joel Willitts, eds. *Introduction to Messianic Judaism: Its Ecclesial Context and Biblical Foundations*. Grand Rapids: Zondervan, 2013.

Ruether, Rosemary Radford. "Anti-Judaism Is the Left Hand of Christology." In *Jewish-Christian Relations*, edited by Robert Heyer, 1–9. New York: Paulist, 1974.

———. "Anti-Semitism and Christian Theology." *Theology Today* 30, no. 4 (January 1974) 365–82.

———. *Faith and Fratricide: The Theological Roots of Anti-Semitism*. New York: Seabury, 1974.

———. "False Messianism and Prophetic Consciousness: Toward a Liberation Theology of Jewish-Christian Solidarity." In *Judaism, Christianity, and Liberation: An Agenda for Dialogue*, edited by Otto Maduro, 83–95. Maryknoll, NY: Orbis, 1991.

Ruether, Rosemary Radford, and Herman J. Ruether. *The Wrath of Jonah: The Crisis of Religious Nationalism in the Israeli-Palestinian Conflict*. 2d ed. Minneapolis: Fortress, 2002.

Ruff, Mark Edward. *The Battle for the Catholic Past in Germany, 1954–1980*. Cambridge: Cambridge University Press, 2017.

Rutishauser, Christian, SJ. *The Human Condition and the Thought of Rabbi Joseph B. Soloveitchik*. Jersey City, NJ: KTAV, 2013.

———. "'The Old Unrevoked Covenant' and 'Salvation for All Nations in Christ'—Catholic Doctrines in Contradiction." In *Christ Jesus and the Jewish People Today: New Explorations of Theological Interrelationships*, edited by Philip A. Cunningham et al., 229–50. Grand Rapids: Eerdmans, 2011.

Ryan, Patrick J., SJ *Amen: Jews, Christians, and Muslims Keep Faith with God*. Washington, DC: The Catholic University of America, 2018.

Rychlak, Ronald J. *Hitler, the War, and the Pope*. Rev. ed. Huntington, IN: Our Sunday Visitor, 2010.

———. *Righteous Gentiles: How Pius XII and the Church Saved Half a Million Jews from the Nazis*. Dallas, TX: Spence, 2005.

Rynhold, Daniel. "Science or Hermeneutics? Rav Soloveitchik's Scientific Method Revisited." In *Scholarly Man of Faith: Studies in the Thought and Writings of Rabbi Joseph B. Soloveitchik*, edited by Ephraim Kanarfogel and Dov Schwartz, 109–33. New York: KTAV, 2018.

Ryrie, Charles C. *Dispensationalism*. Rev. ed. Chicago: Moody, 2007.

Sabbagh-Khoury, Areej. "Palestinians in Palestinian Cities in Israel: A Settler Colonial Reality." In *The Palestinians in Israel: Readings in History, Politics and Society*, edited by Nadim N. Rouhana and Areej Sabbagh-Khoury, 103–20. Haifa, Israel: Mada al-Carmel—Arab Center for Applied Social Research, 2015.

Sabbah, Michael. "Reading the Bible Today in the Land of the Bible." 1993. https://www.lpj.org/.

———. *Faithful Witness: On Reconciliation and Peace in the Holy Land*, edited by Drew Christiansen and Saliba Sarsar. Brooklyn, NY: New City, 2008.

Sacks, Jonathan. "Abraham Isaac Kook: The Dynamic of Sanctification." In *Tradition in an Untraditional Age: Essays on Modern Jewish Thought*, 19–34. London: Valentine, Mitchell, 1990.

———. *Arguments for the Sake of Heaven: Emerging Trends in Traditional Judaism*. Northvale, NJ: Jason Aronson, 1991.

———. "Awakening from Above, Awakening from Below." In *Exodus: The Book of Redemption*, 271–76. Jerusalem: Maggid, 2010.

———. *The Dignity of Difference: How to Avoid the Clash of Civilizations*. New York: Continuum, 2002.

———. *Exodus: The Book of Redemption*. Vol. 2 of *Covenant and Conversation: A Weekly Reading of the Jewish Bible*. Jerusalem: Maggid, 2010.

———. *Faith in the Future*. London: Darton, Longman and Todd, 1995.

———. *Future Tense: Jews, Judaism, and Israel in the Twenty-First Century*. New York: Schocken, 2009.

———. *Genesis: The Book of Beginnings*. Vol. 1 of *Covenant and Conversation: A Weekly Reading of the Jewish Bible*. Jerusalem: Maggid, 2009.

———. *The Great Partnership: God, Science and the Search for Meaning*. London: Hodder & Stoughton, 2011.

———. *The Home We Build Together: Recreating Society*. London: Continuum, 2007.

———. "The Home We Make for God." In *Genesis: The Book of Beginnings*, vol. 1 of *Covenant and Conversation: A Weekly Reading of the Jewish Bible*, 199–206. Jerusalem: Maggid, 2009.

———. "Interview with Chief Rabbi Lord Jonathan Sacks, October 29, 2012." In *Jonathan Sacks: Universalizing Particularity*, edited by Hava Tirosh-Samuelson and Aaron W. Hughes, 105–39. Leiden: Brill, 2013.

———. "Joseph B. Soloveitchik: Conflict and Creation." In *Tradition in an Untraditional Age: Essays on Modern Jewish Thought*, 35–55. London: Valentine, Mitchell, 1990.

———. *A Letter in the Scroll: Understanding Our Jewish Identity and Exploring the Legacy of the World's Oldest Religion*. New York: Free, 2000.

———. *Leviticus: The Book of Holiness*. Vol. 3 of *Covenant and Conversation: A Weekly Reading of the Jewish Bible*. Jerusalem: Maggid, 2015.

———. "The Long Walk to Freedom." In *Genesis: The Book of Beginnings*, 67–71. Jerusalem: Maggid, 2009.

———. "A New Kind of Hero." In *Genesis: The Book of Beginnings*, 73–75. Jerusalem: Maggid, 2009.

———. *Not in God's Name: Confronting Religious Violence*. New York: Schocken, 2015.

———. *The Politics of Hope*. London: Jonathan Cape, 1997.

———. "Rabbi Joseph B. Soloveitchik: Halakhic Man." In *Tradition in an Untraditional Age: Essays on Modern Jewish Thought*, 267–85. London: Valentine, Mitchell, 1990.

———. "Rabbi Joseph B. Soloveitchik's Early Epistemology." In *Tradition in an Untraditional Age: Essays on Modern Jewish Thought*, 287–301. London: Valentine, Mitchell, 1990.

———. *To Heal a Fractured World: The Ethics of Responsibility*. New York: Schocken, 2005.

———. *Tradition in an Untraditional Age: Essays on Modern Jewish Thought*. London: Valentine, Mitchell, 1990.

Said, Edward W. *The Politics of Dispossession: The Struggle for Palestinian Self-Determination 1969–1994*. London: Vintage, 1995.

———. *The Question of Palestine*. 2d ed. with a new preface and epilogue. New York: Random House, 1992.

Saiman, Chaim N. *Halakhah: The Rabbinic Idea of Law*. Princeton, NJ: Princeton University Press, 2018.

Sale, Giovanni, SJ. "Antigiudaismo o antisemitismo? Le accuse contro la Chiesa e 'La Civiltà Cattolica.'" *Civiltà Cattolica* 3647 (June 1, 2002) 419–31.

Salier, Bill. "The Temple in the Gospel According to John." In *Heaven on Earth: The Temple in Biblical Theology*, edited by T. Desmond Alexander and Simon Gathercole, 121–34. Carlisle, UK: Paternoster, 2004.

Sanders, E. P. *Judaism: Practice and Belief, 63 BCE–66 CE*. London: SCM, 1992.

———. *Paul and Palestinian Judaism*. Philadelphia, PA: Fortress, 1977.

———. "Reflections on Anti-Judaism in the New Testament and in Christianity." In *Anti-Judaism and the Gospels*, edited by William R. Farmer, 265–86. Harrisburg, PA: Trinity International, 1999.

Sandmel, David Fox. "Israel, Judaism, and Christianity." In *Christianity in Jewish Terms*, edited by Tikva Frymer-Kensky et al., 159–67. Boulder, CO: Westview, 2000.

———. "Philosemitism and 'Judaizing' in the Contemporary Church." In *Transforming Relations: Essays on Jews and Christians throughout History in Honor of Michael*

A. Signer, edited by Franklin T. Harkins, 405–20. Notre Dame, IN: University of Notre Dame Press, 2010.

Sandnes, Karl Olav. *Belly and Body in the Pauline Epistles*. Cambridge: Cambridge University Press, 2002.

Sandt, Huub van de. "Acts 28, 28: No Salvation for the People of Israel? An Answer in the Perspective of the LXX." *Ephemerides Theologicae Lovanienses* 70, no. 4 (1994) 341–58.

Saner, Andrea. *"Too Much to Grasp": Exodus 3:13–15 and the Reality of God*. Winona Lake, IN: Eisenbrauns, 2015.

Saperstein, Marc. "Christians and Jews—Some Positive Images." *Harvard Theological Review* 79, no. 1–3 (Spring 1986) 236–46.

Sarna, Nahum M. *Exploring Exodus: The Origins of Biblical Israel*. New York: Schocken, 1996.

Satlow, Michael I. "'And on the Earth You Shall Sleep': Talmud Torah and Rabbinic Asceticism." *Journal of Religion* 83, no. 2 (April 2003) 204–25.

Shachar, Isaiah. *The Judensau: A Medieval Anti-Jewish Motif and Its History*. London: Warburg Institute, 1974.

Schacter, Jacob. "Halakhic Authority in a World of Personal Autonomy." In *Radical Responsibility: Celebrating the Thought of Chief Rabbi Lord Jonathan Sacks*, edited by Michael J. Harris, Daniel Rynhold, and Tamra Wright, 155–76. New Milford, CT: Maggid, 2012.

Schäfer, Peter. *Jesus in the Talmud*. Princeton, NJ: Princeton University Press, 2007.

———. *The Jewish Jesus: How Judaism and Christianity Shaped Each Other*. Princeton, NJ: Princeton University Press, 2012.

———. *Two Gods in Heaven: Jewish Concepts of God in Antiquity*. Princeton, NJ: Princeton University Press, 2020.

Scheinerman, Amy. *The Talmud of Relationships*. 2 vols. Philadelphia: Jewish Publication Society, 2018.

Schembri, Justin, OP. "On the Unity of the Two Testaments: In What Sense Is the Torah a Law for Christians?" *Nova et Vetera* 18 (2020) 1323–39.

Schenck, Kenneth L. *Cosmology and Eschatology in Hebrews: The Settings of the Sacrifice*. Cambridge: Cambridge University Press, 2007.

Schenk, Richard, OP. *Soundings in the History of a Hope: New Studies on Thomas Aquinas*. Ave Maria, FL: Sapientia, 2016.

Schlueter, C. J. *Filling Up the Measure: Polemical Hyperbole in 1 Thessalonians 2:14–16*. Sheffield: JSOT, 1994.

Schmid, Konrad. *A Historical Theology of the Hebrew Bible*. Translated by Peter Altmann. Grand Rapids: Eerdmans, 2019.

Schmidt, Daryl D. "Anti-Judaism and the Gospel of Luke." In *Anti-Judaism and the Gospels*, edited by William R. Farmer, 63–96. Harrisburg, PA: Trinity International, 1999.

Schnackenburg, Rudolf. *God's Rule and Kingdom*. Translated by John Murray. Edinburgh: Nelson, 1963.

———. *The Gospel of Matthew*. Translated by Robert R. Barr. Grand Rapids: Eerdmans, 2002.

Schoeman, Roy H. *Salvation Is from the Jews: The Role of Judaism in Salvation History from Abraham to the Second Coming*. San Francisco: Ignatius, 2003.

Scholem, Gershom. *The Messianic Idea in Judaism*. New York: Schocken, 1971.

———. *Sabbatai Sevi: The Mystical Messiah*. Princeton, NJ: Princeton University Press, 1973.
Schoon, Simon. "'The New People of God': A Protestant View." In *Never Revoked:* Nostra Aetate *as Ongoing Challenge for Jewish-Christian Dialogue*, edited by Marianne Moyaert and Didier Pollefeyt, 93–116. Leuven: Peeters, 2010.
Schramm, Brooks, and Kirsi I. Stjerna. *Martin Luther, the Bible, and the Jewish People: A Reader*. Minneapolis: Fortress, 2012.
Schreckenberg, Heinz. *Die christliche Adversus-Judaeos-Texte und ihr literarisches und historisches Umfeld (11.–13. Jh.)*. 3rd ed. Bern: Peter Lang, 1997.
Schremer, Adiel. *Brothers Estranged: Heresy, Christianity, and Jewish Identity in Late Antiquity*. Oxford: Oxford University Press, 2010.
Schwartz, Dov. *Religion and Halakha: The Philosophy of Rabbi Joseph B. Soloveitchik*, vol. 1. Leiden: Brill, 2007.
Schwartz, Yossef. "Authority, Control, and Conflict in Thirteenth-Century Paris: Contextualizing the Talmud Trial." In *Jews and Christians in Thirteenth-Century France*, edited by Elisheva Baumgarten and Judah D. Galinsky, 93–110. New York: Palgrave Macmillan, 2015.
Sciglitano, Anthony C., Jr. *Marcion and Prometheus: Balthasar Against the Expulsion of Jewish Origins from Modern Religious Dialogue*. New York: Crossroad, 2014.
Searle, John R. *Speech Acts: An Essay in the Philosophy of Language*. Cambridge: Cambridge University Press, 1969.
Segel, Binjamin W. *A Lie and a Libel: The History of the* Protocols of the Elders of Zion. Translated and edited by Richard S. Levy. Lincoln, NE: University of Nebraska Press, 1995.
Seitz, Christopher R. "Canon and Conquest: The Character of the God of the Hebrew Bible." In *Divine Evil? The Moral Character of the God of Abraham*, edited by Michael Bergmann, Michael J. Murray, and Michael C. Rea, 292–308. Oxford: Oxford University Press, 2011.
———. *The Character of Christian Scripture: The Significance of a Two-Testament Bible*. Grand Rapids: Baker Academic, 2011.
———. *The Elder Testament: Canon, Theology, Trinity*. Waco, TX: Baylor University Press, 2018.
Selengut, Charles. *Sacred Fury: Understanding Religious Violence*. 3rd ed. Lanham, MD: Rowman & Littlefield, 2017.
Senior, Donald. *Matthew*. Nashville, TN: Abingdon, 1998.
Shapira, Anita, ed. *The Bible in Israeli Identity*. Jerusalem: Magnes, 2005.
Shapiro, Paul A. "Faith, Murder, Resurrection: The Iron Guard and the Romanian Orthodox Church." In *Antisemitism, Christian Ambivalence, and the Holocaust*, edited by Kevin P. Spicer, 136–70. Bloomington, IN: Indiana University Press, 2007.
Shatz, David. "Contemporary Scholarship on Rabbi Soloveitchik's Thought: Where We Are, Where We Can Go." In *Scholarly Man of Faith: Studies in the Thought and Writings of Rabbi Joseph B. Soloveitchik*, edited by Ephraim Kanarfogel and Dov Schwartz, 135–96. New York: KTAV, 2018.
———. "Ego, Love, and Self-Sacrifice: Altruism in Jewish Thought and Law." In *Radical Responsibility: Celebrating the Thought of Chief Rabbi Lord Jonathan Sacks*, edited by Michael J. Harris, Daniel Rynhold, and Tamra Wright, 17–38. New Milford, CT: Maggid, 2012.

———. "Morality, Liberalism, and Interfaith Dialogue." In *New Perspectives on Jewish-Christian Relations in Honor of David Berger*, edited by Elisheva Carlebach and Jacob J. Schacter, 491–519. Leiden: Brill, 2012.

Sheleff, Leon. *Biblical Narratives and Israeli Chronicles*. Tel Aviv: Hakibbutz Hameuchad, 2002.

Shenhav, Yehouda. *Beyond the Two-State Solution: A Jewish Political Essay*. Cambridge, England: Polity, 2012.

Sheridan, Mark. *Language for God in Patristic Tradition: Wrestling with Biblical Anthropomorphism*. Downers Grove, IL: IVP Academic, 2015.

Sherwin, Byron, and Harold Kasimow, eds. *No Religion Is an Island: Abraham Joshua Heschel and Interreligious Dialogue*. Maryknoll, NY: Orbis, 1991.

Sherwin, Michael S., OP. *On Love and Virtue: Theological Essays*. Steubenville, OH: Emmaus Academic, 2018.

Shuler, Philip L. "Response to Amy-Jill Levine." In *Anti-Judaism and the Gospels*, edited by William R. Farmer, 37–46. Harrisburg, PA: Trinity International, 1999.

Siecienski, A. Edward. *The Papacy and the Orthodox: Sources and History of a Debate*. Oxford: Oxford University Press, 2017.

Siegal, Michal Bar-Asher. *Early Christian Monastic Literature and the Babylonian Talmud*. Cambridge: Cambridge University Press, 2013.

———. *Jewish-Christian Dialogues on Scripture in Late Antiquity: Heretic Narratives of the Babylonian Talmud*. Cambridge: Cambridge University Press, 2019.

Siemon-Netto, Uwe. *The Fabricated Luther: Refuting Nazi Connections and Other Modern Myths*. 2d ed. St. Louis, MO: Concordia, 2007.

Signer, Michael A. "Abraham: The One and the Many." In *Memory and History in Christianity and Judaism*, edited by Michael A. Signer, 204–12. Notre Dame, IN: University of Notre Dame Press, 2001.

———. "A Jewish Response to *Dominus Iesus: On the Unicity and Salvific Universality of Jesus Christ and the Church*." *Jewish-Christian Relations: Insights and Issues in the Ongoing Jewish-Christian Dialogue*. 2000. https://www.jcrelations.net/articles/article/a-jewish-response-to-dominus-iesus-on-the-unicity-and-salvific-universality-of-jesus-christ-and-the-church.html.

———. "Jews and Judaism in the New Catechism of the Catholic Church—An Intervention." In *Coming Together for the Sake of God: Contributions to Jewish-Christian Dialogue from Post-Holocaust Germany*, edited by Hanspeter Heinz and Michael A. Signer, 63–68. Collegeville, MN: Liturgical, 2007.

———. "The Rift That Binds: Hermeneutical Approaches to the Jewish-Christian Relationship." In *Ecumenism: Present Realities and Future Prospects*, edited by Lawrence S. Cunningham, 95–115. Notre Dame, IN: University of Notre Dame Press, 1998.

———. "Searching the Scriptures: Jews, Christians and the Book." In *Christianity in Jewish Terms*, edited by Tikva Frymer-Kensky et al., 85–98. Boulder, CO: Westview, 2000.

Signer, Michael A., and John Van Engen, eds. *Jews and Christians in Twelfth-Century Europe*. Notre Dame, IN: University of Notre Dame Press, 2001.

Silva, P. "La rivoluzione mondiale e gli ebrei." *La Civiltà Cattolica* 4 (1922) 111–21.

Simkovich, Malka Z. *The Making of Jewish Universalism: From Exile to Alexandria*. Lanham, MD: Lexington, 2017.

Simon, Uriel. *Seek Peace and Pursue It: Topical Issues in Light of the Bible; The Bible in Light of Topical Issues.* Tel Aviv: Yediot Aharonot, 2002.

Simon, Uriel, and David Louvish. "The Place of the Bible in Israeli Society: From National Midrash to Existential Peshat." *Modern Judaism* 19, no. 3 (1999) 155–77.

Simon, Yves R. *The Definition of Moral Virtue.* Edited by Vukan Kuic. New York: Fordham University Press, 1986.

Singer, David, and Moshe Sokol. "Joseph Soloveitchik: Lonely Man of Faith." *Modern Judaism* 2 (1982) 227–72.

Singer, Isaac Bashevis. *Satan in Goray.* Translated by Jacob Sloan. New York: Farrar, Straus and Giroux, 1996.

Sklba, Richard. "Covenant Renewed: Josef Ratzinger, Theologian and Pastor." In *Covenant and Hope: Christian and Jewish Reflections: Essays in Constructive Theology,* edited by Robert W. Jenson and Eugene B. Korn, 59–79. Grand Rapids: Eerdmans, 2012.

Small, Joseph D. "In Our Time: The Legacy of *Nostra Aetate* in Mainline Protestant Churches." In *A Jubilee for All Time: The Copernican Revolution in Jewish-Christian Relations,* edited by Gilbert S. Rosenthal, 77–95. Eugene, OR: Pickwick, 2014.

———. "Presbyterian Disestablishment." In *Let Us Reason Together: Christians and Jews in Conversation,* edited by Joseph D. Small and Gilbert S. Rosenthal, 163–75. Louisville, KY: Witherspoon, 2010.

Smiga, George. *Pain and Polemic: Anti-Judaism and the Gospels.* New York: Paulist, 1992.

Smith, Daniel Lynwood. "The Uses of 'New Exodus' in New Testament Scholarship: Preparing a Way Through the Wilderness." *Currents in Biblical Research* 14, no. 2 (February 2016) 207–43.

Smith, D. Moody. *First, Second, and Third John.* Louisville, KY: John Knox, 1991.

Smith, Steve. *The Fate of the Jerusalem Temple in Luke-Acts: An Intertextual Approach to Jesus' Laments Over Jerusalem and Stephen's Speech.* London: Bloomsbury, 2017.

Smith, Steven C. *The House of the Lord: A Catholic Biblical Theology of God's Temple Presence in the Old and New Testaments.* Steubenville, OH: Franciscan University Press, 2017.

Smith, William Robertson. *Lectures on the Religion of the Semites: The Fundamental Institutions.* 3rd ed. New York: Macmillan, 1927.

Sokolow, Moshe. *Reading the Rav: Exploring Religious Themes in the Thought of Rabbi Joseph B. Soloveitchik.* New York: Kodesh, 2018.

Soloveitchik, Joseph B. *Abraham's Journey: Reflections on the Life of the Founding Patriarch,* edited by David Shatz, Joel B. Wolowelsky, and Reuven Ziegler. New York: Toras HoRav Foundation, 2008.

———. "The Absence of God and the Community of Prayer." In *Worship of the Heart: Essays on Jewish Prayer,* 2d ed., edited by Shalom Carmy, 73–86. New York: Toras HoRav, 2002.

———. "The Community." In *Confrontation and Other Essays,* 1–23. New Milford, CT: Maggid, 2015.

———. "Confrontation." In *Confrontation and Other Essays,* 85–115. New Milford, CT: Maggid, 2015.

———. *Confrontation and Other Essays.* New Milford, CT: Maggid, 2015.

———. "Exaltation of God and Redeeming of the Aesthetic." In *Worship of the Heart: Essays on Jewish Prayer*, 2d ed., edited by Shalom Carmy, 51–72. New York: Toras HoRav, 2002.

———. *And From There You Shall Seek*. Translated by Naomi Goldblum. New York: Toras HoRav Foundation, 2008.

———. *Halakhic Man*. Translated by Lawrence Kaplan. Philadelphia: The Jewish Publication Society, 1983.

———. *The Halakhic Mind: An Essay on Jewish Traditional and Modern Thought*. Ardmore, PA: Seth, 1986.

———. *Halakhic Morality: Essays on Ethics and Masorah*. Edited by Joel B. Wolowelsky and Reuven Ziegler. New Milford, CT: Maggid, 2017.

———. "Intention (Kavvanah) in Reading Shema and in Prayer." In *Worship of the Heart: Essays on Jewish Prayer*, 2d ed., edited by Shalom Carmy, 87–106. New York: Toras HoRav, 2002.

———. *Kol Dodi Dofek: Listen—My Beloved Knocks*. Translated by David Z. Gordon. Edited by Jeffrey R. Woolf. New York: Yeshiva University Press, 2006.

———. *The Lonely Man of Faith*. 2d ed. New Milford, CT: Maggid, 2018.

———. "Reflections on the Amidah." In *Worship of the Heart: Essays on Jewish Prayer*, 2d ed., edited by Shalom Carmy, 144–82. New York: Toras HoRav, 2002.

———. "Religious Styles." In *Halakhic Morality: Essays on Ethics and Masorah*, edited by Joel B. Wolowelsky and Reuven Ziegler, 193–207. New Milford, CT: Maggid, 2017.

———. "Torah and Humility." In *Halakhic Morality: Essays on Ethics and Masorah*, edited by Joel B. Wolowelsky and Reuven Ziegler, 209–22. New Milford, CT: Maggid, 2017.

———. "Tzedakah: Brotherhood and Fellowship." In *Halakhic Morality: Essays on Ethics and Masorah*, edited by Joel B. Wolowelsky and Reuven Ziegler, 123–80. New Milford, CT: Maggid, 2017.

Solovyov, Vladimir. "The Jews and the Christian Problem." In *A Solovyov Anthology*, edited by S. L. Frank, 105–23. London: Saint Austin, 2001.

Somme, Luc-Thomas, OP. "L'adoption filiale des juifs de l'Ancienne Alliance selon saint Thomas d'Aquin." *Revue Thomiste* 106 (2006) 149–69.

Sommer, Benjamin D. *Revelation and Authority: Sinai in Jewish Scripture and Tradition*. New Haven, CT: Yale University Press, 2015.

Sonderegger, Katherine. *The Doctrine of God*. Vol. 1 of *Systematic Theology*. Minneapolis: Fortress, 2020.

———. *The Doctrine of the Holy Trinity: Processions and Persons*. Vol. 2 of *Systematic Theology*. Minneapolis: Fortress, 2020.

———. *That Jesus Christ Was Born a Jew: Karl Barth's "Doctrine of Israel."* University Park, PA: Pennsylvania State University Press, 1992.

Soulen, Kendall R. *Distinguishing the Voices*. Vol. 1 of *The Divine Name(s) and the Holy Trinity*. Louisville, KY: Westminster John Knox, 2011.

———. *The God of Israel and Christian Theology*. Minneapolis: Fortress, 1996.

———. "Israel and the Church: A Christian Response to Irving Greenberg's Covenantal Pluralism." In *Christianity in Jewish Terms*, edited by Tikva Frymer-Kensky et al., 167–74. Boulder, CO: Westview, 2000.

———. "The Priority of the Present Tense for Jewish-Christian Relations." In *In Between Gospel and Election: Explorations in the Interpretation of Romans 9–11*, edited by Florian Wilk and J. Ross Wagner, 497–504. Tübingen: Mohr Siebeck, 2010.

Spector, Stephen. *Evangelicals and Israel: The Story of American Christian Zionism*. Oxford: Oxford University Press, 2009.

Spicer, Kevin P., CSC. *Hitler's Priests: Catholic Clergy and National Socialism*. DeKalb, IL: Northern Illinois University Press, 2008.

———. *Resisting the Third Reich: The Catholic Clergy in Hitler's Berlin*. DeKalb, IL: Northern Illinois University Press, 2004.

Spillman, Joann. "Targeting Jews for Conversion: A Contradiction of Christian Faith and Hope." In *Seeing Judaism Anew: Christianity's Sacred Obligation*, edited by Mary C. Boys, 163–74. Lanham, MD: Rowman & Littlefield, 2005.

Stackert, Jeffrey. *A Prophet Like Moses: Prophecy, Law, and Israelite Religion*. Oxford: Oxford University Press, 2014.

Stalder, Will. *Palestinian Christians and the Old Testament: History, Hermeneutics, and Ideology*. Minneapolis: Fortress, 2015.

Stanislawski, Michael. *Autobiographical Jews: Essays in Jewish Self-Fashioning*. Seattle, WA: University of Washington Press, 2004.

———. *Zionism: A Very Short Introduction*. Oxford: Oxford University Press, 2017.

Starr, Joshua. "Italy's Antisemites." *Jewish Social Studies* 1, no. 1 (January 1939) 105–24.

Staub, Jacob J. "Gersonides and Contemporary Theories on the Beginning of the Universe." In *Creation and the End of Days: Judaism and Scientific Cosmology*, edited by David Novak and Robert Samuelson, 245–59. Lanham, MD: University Press of America, 1986.

Steigmann-Gall, Richard. "Old Wine in New Bottles? Religion and Race in Nazi Antisemitism." In *Antisemitism, Christian Ambivalence, and the Holocaust*, edited by Kevin P. Spicer, 285–308. Bloomington, IN: Indiana University Press, 2007.

Steinberg, Jonah Chanan. "Theosis through Works of the Law: Deification of the Earthly Righteous in Classical Rabbinic Thought." In *Crossing Boundaries in Early Judaism and Christianity: Ambiguities, Complexities, and Half-Forgotten Adversaries: Essays in Honor of Alan F. Segal*, edited by Kimberly B. Stratton and Andrea Lieber, 41–73. Leiden: Brill, 2016.

Stock, Augustine. *The Way in the Wilderness: Exodus, Wilderness, and Moses Themes in Old Testament and New*. Collegeville, MN: Liturgical, 1969.

Stockhausen, Carol Kern. *Moses' Veil and the Glory of the New Covenant: The Exegetical Substructure of II Cor. 3,1—4,6*. Rome: Pontifical Biblical Institute, 1989.

Stow, Kenneth R. *Alienated Minority: The Jews of Medieval Latin Europe*. Cambridge, MA: Harvard University Press, 1992.

———. *Catholic Thought and Papal Jewish Policy, 1555–1593*. New York: Jewish Theological Seminary of America, 1977.

———. *Jewish Dogs: An Image and Its Interpreters. Continuity in the Catholic-Jewish Encounter*. Stanford, CA: Stanford University Press, 2006.

———. *Popes, Church, and Jews in the Middle Ages: Confrontation and Response*. Aldershot: Ashgate, 2007.

Striet, Magnus. "Christliche Theologie im Angesicht des Judeseins Jesu." In Walter Homolka and Magnus Striet, *Christologie auf dem Prüfstand: Jesus der Jude— Christus der Erlöser*, 71–140. Freiburg: Herder, 2019.

Stroumsa, Guy G. *The End of Sacrifice: Religious Transformations in Late Antiquity*. Translated by Susan Emanuel. Chicago: University of Chicago Press, 2009.

Štrukelj, Anton. "The Purification of Memory." Translated by Michael J. Miller. *Communio* 45 (2018) 85–92.
Stubbs, David L. *Table and Temple: The Christian Eucharist and Its Jewish Roots*. Grand Rapids: Eerdmans, 2020.
Student, Gil. "Letter to the Editor." *First Things* 282 (April 2018) 3.
Stump, Eleonore. "The God of Abraham, Saadia and Aquinas." In *Referring to God: Jewish and Christian Philosophical and Theological Perspectives*, edited by Paul Helm 95–119. New York: St. Martin's, 2000.
Sullivan, Desmond. "New Insights into Matthew 27:24–25." *New Blackfriars* 73, no. 863 (September 1992) 453–57.
Sullivan, Francis, SJ. *Creative Fidelity*. New York: Paulist, 1996.
———. *Salvation outside the Church? Tracing the History of the Catholic Response*. London: Geoffrey Chapman, 1992.
Surh, Gerald D. "Duty and Ambivalence: The Russian Army and Pogroms, 1903–1906." In *Sites of European Antisemitism in the Age of Mass Politics, 1880–1918*, edited by Robert Nemes and Daniel Unowsky, 215–35. Waltham, MA: Brandeis University Press, 2014.
Svartvik, Jesper. "What If There Is Life on Other Planets? Reflections on Kurt Cardinal Koch's Lecture." *Studies in Christian-Jewish Relations* 7, no. 1 (May 2012) 1–12.
Sweeney, Marvin A. *Jewish Mysticism: From Ancient Times through Today*. Grand Rapids: Eerdmans, 2020.
Sylva, Dennis. "The Temple Curtain and Jesus' Death in the Gospel of Luke." *Journal of Biblical Literature* 105, no. 2 (June 1986) 239–50.
Sztuden, Alex. "The Identity of Love and Cognition in the Thought of R. Joseph Soloveitchik." In *Scholarly Man of Faith: Studies in the Thought and Writings of Rabbi Joseph B. Soloveitchik*, edited by Ephraim Kanarfogel and Dov Schwartz, 49–74. New York: KTAV, 2018.
Tal, Uriel. *Christians and Jews in Germany: Religion, Politics, and Ideology in the Second Reich, 1870–1914*. Translated by Noah Jonathan Jacobs. Ithaca, NY: Cornell University Press, 1975.
———. "The Future of Jewish-Christian Dialogue: A Jewish View." In *Christians and Jews*, edited by Hans Küng and Walter Kasper, 80–87. New York: Seabury, 1975.
Tal, Uriel, Simon Uriel, Janet Aviad, and Lawrence Kaplan. *Religious Zionism: Challenges and Choices*. Jerusalem: Oz VeShalom, 1985.
Talmage, Frank. *Disputation and Dialogue*. New York: Ktav, 1975.
Tanenbaum, Marc H. "A Jewish Viewpoint on *Nostra Aetate*." In *Twenty Years of Jewish-Catholic Relations*, edited by Eugene J. Fisher, A. James Rudin, and Marc H. Tenenbaum, 39–60. New York: Paulist, 1986.
Tanner, Norman P., SJ, ed. *Trent to Vatican II*. Vol. 2 of *Decrees of the Ecumenical Councils*. Washington, DC: Georgetown University Press, 1990.
Tapie, Matthew A. *Aquinas on Israel and the Church: The Question of Supersessionism in the Theology of Thomas Aquinas*. Eugene, OR: Pickwick, 2014.
———. "*Spiritualis Uterus*: The Question of Forced Baptism and Thomas Aquinas's Defense of Jewish Parental Rights." *Bulletin of Medieval Canon Law* 35, no. 1 (2018) 289–329.
Taradel, Ruggero. *L'accusa del sangue: Storia politica di un mito antisemita*. Rome: Editori Riuniti, 2002.

Taradel, Ruggero, and Barbara Raggi. *La segregazione amichevole: "La Civiltà Cattolica" e la questione ebraica 1850–1945*. Rome: Editori Riuniti, 2000.

Taylor, Charles. "The Space of Exchange." In *Radical Responsibility: Celebrating the Thought of Chief Rabbi Lord Jonathan Sacks*, edited by Michael J. Harris, Daniel Rynhold, and Tamra Wright, 127–38. New Milford, CT: Maggid, 2012.

Taylor, John B. "The Temple in Ezekiel." In *Heaven on Earth: Temple in Biblical Theology*, edited by T. Desmond Alexander and Simon Gathercole, 59–70. Waynesboro, GA: Paternoster, 2004.

Taylor, Miriam S. *Anti-Judaism and Early Christian Identity: A Critique of the Scholarly Consensus*. Leiden: Brill, 1995.

Taylor, N. H. "Luke-Acts and the Temple." In *The Unity of Luke-Acts*, edited by Joseph Verheyden, 709–21. Leuven: Peeters, 1999.

Teitelbaum, Joel. *Concerning Redemption and Its Counterfeit Substitute* [Hebrew]. Brooklyn, NY: Jerusalem Book Store, 1989.

Terrace, Herbert S. *Why Chimpanzees Can't Learn Language and Only Humans Can*. New York: Columbia University Press, 2019.

Thate, Michael J., Kevin J. Vanhoozer, and Constantine R. Campbell, eds. *"In Christ" in Paul: Explorations in Paul's Theology of Union and Participation*. Grand Rapids: Eerdmans, 2018.

Theissen, Gerd. *A Theory of Primitive Christian Religion*. Translated by John Bowden. London: SCM, 1999.

Thiessen, Matthew. *Contesting Conversion: Genealogy, Circumcision, and Identity in Ancient Judaism and Christianity*. Oxford: Oxford University Press, 2011.

———. *Jesus and the Forces of Death: The Gospels' Portrayal of Ritual Impurity within First-Century Judaism*. Grand Rapids: Baker Academic, 2020.

———. *Paul and the Gentile Problem*. Oxford: Oxford University Press, 2016.

———. "Paul, the Animal Apocalypse, and Abraham's Gentile Seed." In *The Ways That Often Parted: Essays in Honor of Joel Marcus*, edited by Lori Baron, Jill Hicks-Keeton, and Matthew Thiessen, 65–78. Atlanta: SBL, 2018.

Thomas Aquinas. *Commentary on the Gospel of John, vol. 1: Chapters 1–5*. Translated by Fabian Larcher and James Weisheipl. Washington, DC: Catholic University of America Press, 2010.

———. *Commentary on the Gospel of Matthew, Chapters 13–28*. Translated by Jeremy Holmes. Lander, WY: The Aquinas Institute for the Study of Sacred Doctrine, 2013.

———. *An Exposition of Jeremiah the Prophet*. Translated by Benjamin Martin. STL thesis, St. Mary of the Lake, 2019.

———. *Summa theologiae*. Translated by the Fathers of the English Dominican Province. Westminster, MD: Christian Classics, 1981.

———. *Truth* (Quaestiones disputatae De veritate). Translated by Robert W. Mulligan, J. V. McGlynn, and R. W. Schmidt. Chicago: Henry Regnery, 1952.

Thomas, Gordon. *The Pope's Jews: The Vatican's Secret Plan to Save Jews from the Nazis*. New York: St. Martin's, 2012.

Thomas, Matthew J. *Paul's 'Works of the Law' in the Perspective of Second Century Reception*. Tübingen: Mohr Siebeck, 2018.

Thompson, James W. *The Church according to Paul: Rediscovering the Community Conformed to Christ*. Grand Rapids: Baker Academic, 2014.

Thorsteinsson, Runar M. *Jesus as Philosopher: The Moral Sage in the Synoptic Gospels*. Oxford: Oxford University Press, 2018.

Tilling, Chris. *Paul's Divine Christology*. Grand Rapids: Eerdmans, 2012.

Tobias, Norman C. *Jewish Conscience of the Church: Jules Isaac and the Second Vatican Council*. New York: Palgrave Macmillan, 2017.

Tolan, John. "Of Milk and Blood: Innocent III and the Jews, Revisited." In *Jews and Christians in Thirteenth-Century France*, edited by Elisheva Baumgarten and Judah D. Galinsky, 139–49. New York: Palgrave Macmillan, 2015.

Tolan, John, et al., eds. *Jews in Early Christian Law: Byzantium and the Latin West, 6th–11th Centuries*. Turnhout: Brepols, 2014.

Tooley, Mark. "Theology and the Churches: Mainline Protestant Zionism and Anti-Zionism." In *The New Christian Zionism: Fresh Perspectives on Israel and the Land*, edited by Gerald R. McDermott, 197–219. Downers Grove, IL: IVP Academic, 2016.

Torrance, Thomas F. "The Divine Vocation and Destiny of Israel in World History." In *Karl Barth, the Jews, and Judaism*, edited by George Hunsinger, 118–27. Grand Rapids: Eerdmans, 2018.

Torrell, Jean-Pierre, OP. "Saint Thomas et les non-chrétiens." *Revue Thomiste* 106, no. 1/2 (2006) 17–49.

Trachtenberg, Joshua. *The Devil and the Jews: The Medieval Conception of the Jew and Its Relation to Modern Anti-Semitism*. Philadelphia: Jewish Publication Society, 2002.

Tranzillo, Jeffrey. *John Paul II on the Vulnerable*. Washington, DC: Catholic University of America Press, 2012.

Troeltsch, Ernst. "On the Possibility of a Liberal Christianity." In *Religion in History*, translated by James Luther Adams and Walter F. Bense, 343–59. Minneapolis: Fortress, 1991.

Tropper, Amram. *Wisdom, Politics, and Historiography: Tractate Avot in the Context of the Graeco-Roman Near East*. Oxford: Oxford University Press, 2004.

Turner, Nancy L. "Jewish Witness, Forced Conversion and Island Living: John Duns Scotus on Jews and Judaism." In *Christian Attitudes Towards the Jews in the Middle Ages: A Casebook*, edited by Michael Frassetto, 183–209. New York: Routledge, 2007.

Turner, Paul. "Considering the Baptism of Edgardo Mortara in the Context of Catholic Teachings and Rituals Then and Now." *Studies in Christian-Jewish Relations* 14, no. 1 (April 2019) 1–9.

———. "Jewish Dialogue and Christian Liturgy." *Worship* 90 (May 2016) 196–204.

Tyson, Joseph B., ed. *Luke-Acts and the Jewish People: Eight Critical Perspectives*. Minneapolis: Augsburg, 1988.

Unterseher, Lisa A. *The Mark of Cain and the Jews: Augustine's Theology of the Jews and Judaism*. Piscataway, NJ: Gorgias, 2009.

Vall, Gregory. "'Man Is the Land': The Sacramentality of the Land of Israel." In *John Paul II and the Jewish People: A Jewish-Christian Dialogue*, edited by David G. Dalin and Matthew Levering, 131–67. Lanham, MD: Rowman & Littlefield, 2008.

Van Buren, Paul M. *A Christian Theology of the People of Israel*. Vol. 2 of *A Theology of the Jewish-Christian Reality*. New York: Seabury, 1983.

———. *Discerning the Way*. Vol. 1 of *A Theology of the Jewish-Christian Reality*. New York: Harper & Row, 1980.

———. "When Christians Meet Jews." In *Visions of the Other: Jewish and Christian Theologians Assess the Dialogue*, edited by Eugene J. Fisher, 55–66. New York: Paulist, 1994.

Van Gorder, A. Christian, and Gordon Fuller. *Jews and Christians Together: An Invitation to Mutual Respect*. Eugene, OR: Cascade, 2020.

Vanhoozer, Kevin J. *Biblical Authority after Babel: Retrieving the Solas in the Spirit of Mere Protestant Christianity*. Grand Rapids: Brazos, 2016.

———. *The Drama of Doctrine: A Canonical-Linguistic Approach to Christian Theology*. Louisville, KY: Westminster John Knox, 2005.

———. "A Person of the Book? Barth on Biblical Authority and Interpretation." In *Karl Barth and Evangelical Theology: Convergences and Differences*, edited by Sung Wook Chung, 26–59. Grand Rapids: Baker Academic, 2006.

———. *Remythologizing Theology: Divine Action, Passion, and Authorship*. Cambridge: Cambridge University Press, 2010.

Vanlaningham, Michael G. "Should the Church Evangelize Israel? A Response to Franz Mussner and Other Sonderweg Proponents." *Trinity Journal* 22, no. 2 (October 2001) 197–217.

VanMaaren, John. "Does Mark's Jesus Abrogate Torah? Jesus' Purity Logion and Its Illustration in Mark 7:15–23." *Journal of the Jesus Movement in Its Jewish Setting* 4 (2017) 21–41.

Vatican Council II. *Ad Gentes*. In *Decrees of the Ecumenical Councils*, vol. 2: *Trent to Vatican II*, edited by Norman P. Tanner, 1011–42. Washington, DC: Georgetown University Press, 1990.

———. *Dei Verbum*. In *Vatican Council II: Constitutions, Degrees, Declarations*, vol. 1: *The Conciliar and Postconciliar Documents*, rev. ed., edited by Austin Flannery, 750–65. Northport: Costello, 1996.

———. *Gaudium et Spes*. In *Vatican Council II: Constitutions, Degrees, Declarations*, vol. 1: *The Conciliar and Postconciliar Documents*, rev. ed., edited by Austin Flannery, 903–1001. Northport: Costello, 1996.

———. *Lumen Gentium*. In *Decrees of the Ecumenical Councils*, vol. 2: *Trent to Vatican II*, edited by Norman P. Tanner, 849–900. Washington, DC: Georgetown University Press, 1990.

———. *Lumen Gentium*. In *Vatican Council II: Constitutions, Degrees, Declaration*, vol. 1: *The Conciliar and Postconciliar Documents*, rev. ed., edited by Austin Flannery, 350–426. Northport: Costello, 1996.

———. *Nostra Aetate*. In *Decrees of the Ecumenical Councils*, vol. 2: *Trent to Vatican II*, edited by Norman P. Tanner, 968–71. Washington, DC: Georgetown University Press, 1990.

———. *Unitatis Redintegratio*. In *Vatican Council II: Constitutions, Degrees, Declarations*, vol. 1: *The Conciliar and Postconciliar Documents*, rev. ed., edited by Austin Flannery, 452–70. Northport: Costello, 1996.

Venard, Olivier-Thomas, OP. *A Poetic Christ: Thomist Reflections on Scripture, Language and Reality*. Translated by Kenneth Oakes and Francesca Aran Murphy. London: T. & T. Clark, 2019.

———. *La Langue de l'ineffable. Essai sur les fondements théologiques du discourse métaphysique*. Geneva: Ad Solem, 2004.

Ventresca, Robert A. *Soldier of Christ: The Life of Pope Pius XII*. Cambridge, MA: Harvard University Press, 2013.

Vermès, Geza. *The Changing Faces of Jesus*. London: Allen Lane, 2000.
Vitoria, Francisco de. *De Indis recenter inventis, et De jure belli Hispanorum in barbaros*, edited by Walter Schötzel. Tübingen: Mohr, 1952 (1539).
Vlach, Michael J. "A Non-Typological Future-Mass-Conversion View." In *Perspectives on Romans 9–11*, edited by Jared Compton and Andrew David Naselli, 21–73. Grand Rapids: Kregel Academic, 2018.
Vogt, Brandon. *Saints and Social Justice: A Guide to Changing the World*. Huntington, IN: Our Sunday Visitor, 2014.
Volf, Miroslav. "The Lamb of God and the Sin of the World." In *Christianity in Jewish Terms*, edited by Tikva Frymer-Kensky et al., 313–19. Boulder, CO: Westview, 2000.
Volf, Miroslav, and Matthew Croasmun. *For the Life of the World: Theology That Makes a Difference*. Grand Rapids: Brazos, 2019.
Von Balthasar, Hans Urs. "Casta Meretrix." Translated by John Saward. In *Explorations in Theology*, vol. II: *Spouse of the Word*, 193–288. San Francisco: Ignatius, 1991.
———. "The Church and Israel." In *Explorations in Theology*, vol. II: *Spouse of the Word*, translated by A. V. Littledale with Alexander Dru, 289–98. San Francisco: Ignatius, 1991.
———. "The Claim to Catholicity." In *Explorations in Theology*, vol. 4: *Spirit and Institution*, translated by Edward T. Oakes, 65–121. San Francisco: Ignatius, 1995.
———. *The Glory of the Lord: A Theological Aesthetics*, vol. 1: *Seeing the Form*, edited by Joseph Fessio and John Riches. Translated by Erasmo Leiva-Merikakis. San Francisco: Ignatius, 1982.
———. *The Glory of the Lord: A Theological Aesthetics*, vol. 7: *Theology: The New Covenant*, edited by John Riches. Translated by Brian McNeil. San Francisco: Ignatius, 1989.
———. *Martin Buber and Christianity: A Dialogue between Israel and the Church*. Translated by Alexander Dru. New York: Macmillan, 1961.
———. *The Office of Peter and the Structure of the Church*. Translated by Andrée Emery. San Francisco: Ignatius, 1986.
———. *Theo-Drama: Theological Dramatic Theory*, vol. 1: *Prolegomena*. Translated by Graham Harrison. San Francisco: Ignatius, 1988.
———. *Theo-Drama: Theological Dramatic Theory*, vol. 2: *The Dramatis Personae: Man in God*. Translated by Graham Harrison. San Francisco: Ignatius, 1990.
———. *Theo-Drama: Theological Dramatic Theory*, vol. 3: *The Dramatis Personae: The Person in Christ*. Translated by Graham Harrison. San Francisco: Ignatius, 1989.
———. *Theo-Logic: Theological Logical Theory*, vol. 2: *Truth of God*. Translated by Adrian J. Walker. San Francisco: Ignatius, 2004.
———. *Theo-Logic: Theological Logical Theory*, vol. 3: *The Spirit of Truth*. Translated by Graham Harrison. San Francisco: Ignatius, 2005.
———. *Truth Is Symphonic: Aspects of Christian Pluralism*. Translated by Graham Harrison. San Francisco: Ignatius, 1987.
Von Hildebrand, Dietrich. *Memoiren und Aufsätze gegen den Nationalsozialismus, 1933–1938*, edited by Ernst Wenisch. Mainz: Matthias-Grünewald-Verlag, 1994.
Waddy, Helena. *Oberammergau in the Nazi Era: The Fate of a Catholic Village in Hitler's Germany*. Oxford: Oxford University Press, 2010.
Wahlberg, Mats. *Revelation as Testimony: A Philosophical-Theological Study*. Grand Rapids, MI: Eerdmans, 2014.

Walsh, Jerome T. *1 Kings*. Collegeville, MN: Liturgical, 1996.

Walton, John H. *The Lost World of Genesis One: Ancient Cosmology and the Origins Debate*. Downers Grove, IL: IVP Academic, 2009.

———. *Old Testament Theology for Christians: From Ancient Context to Enduring Belief*. Downers Grove, IL: IVP Academic, 2017.

Walton, John H., and D. Brent Sandy. *The Lost World of Scripture: Ancient Literary Culture and Biblical Authority*. Downers Grove, IL: InterVarsity, 2013.

Walton, John H., and J. Harvey Walton. *The Lost World of the Israelite Conquest: Covenant, Retribution, and the Fate of the Canaanites*. Downers Grove, IL: IVP Academic, 2017.

———. *The Lost World of the Torah: Law as Covenant and Wisdom in Ancient Context*. Downers Grove, IL: IVP Academic, 2019.

Walzer, Michael. *Exodus and Revolution*. New York: Basic, 1985.

———. *In God's Shadow: Politics in the Hebrew Bible*. New Haven, CT: Yale University Press, 2012.

———. "Justice, Justice Shalt Thou Pursue." In *Radical Responsibility: Celebrating the Thought of Chief Rabbi Lord Jonathan Sacks*, edited by Michael J. Harris, Daniel Rynhold, and Tamra Wright, 79–93. New Milford, CT: Maggid, 2012.

Wardle, Timothy. *The Jerusalem Temple and Early Christian Identity*. Tübingen: Mohr Siebeck, 2010.

———. "Pillars, Foundations, and Stones: Individual Believers as Constituent Parts of the Early Christian Communal Temple." In *Sacrifice, Cult, and Atonement in Early Judaism and Christianity: Constituents and Critique*, edited by Henrietta L. Wiley and Christian A. Eberhart, 289–309. Atlanta: SBL, 2017.

Warren, Donald. *Radio Priest: Charles Coughlin, the Father of Hate Radio*. New York: Free, 1996.

Warrior, Robert Allen. "Canaanites, Cowboys, and Indians: Deliverance, Conquest, and Liberation Theology Today." In *The Postmodern Bible Reader*, edited by David Jobling, Tina Pippin, and Ronald Schleifer, 188–94. Oxford: Blackwell, 2011.

Watson, Francis. *Paul and the Hermeneutics of Faith*. London: T. & T. Clark International, 2004.

Watts, Rikki E. *Isaiah's New Exodus in Mark*. Grand Rapids: Baker Academic, 1997.

———. "The New Exodus/New Creational Restoration of the Image of God: A Biblical-Theological Perspective on Salvation." In *What Does It Mean to Be Saved? Broadening Evangelical Horizons of Salvation*, edited by John G. Stackhouse Jr., 15–42. Grand Rapids: Baker Academic, 2002.

Wawrykow, Joseph. "Aquinas and Bonaventure on Creation." In *Creation ex nihilo: Origins, Development, Contemporary Challenges*, edited by Gary A. Anderson and Markus Bockmuehl, 173–93. Notre Dame, IN: University of Notre Dame Press, 2018.

Wazana, Nili. *All the Boundaries of the Land: The Promised Land in Biblical Thought in Light of the Ancient Near East*. Translated by Liat Qeren. Winona Lake, IN: Eisenbrauns, 2013.

Weaver, Alain Epp. "Sitting under the Vine: A Theology of Exile and Return." *Kairos: Canadian Ecumenical Justice Initiatives*. http://216.19.72.137/e/partners/mideast/israelPalestine/sittingVine.asp.

Webster, John. *Holy Scripture*. Cambridge: Cambridge University Press, 2000.

Weed, Jennifer Hart. "Aquinas on the Forced Conversion of the Jews." In *Jews in Medieval Christendom: "Slay Them Not,"* edited by Kristine T. Utterback and Merrall L. Price, 129–46. Leiden: Brill, 2013.

———. "Faith, Salvation, and the Sacraments in Aquinas: A Puzzle Concerning Forced Baptisms." *Philosophy, Culture, and Traditions* 10 (2014) 95–110.

Weinandy, Thomas G., OFM Cap. *Does God Change?* Petersham, MA: St. Bede's, 1985.

———. *Does God Suffer?* Notre Dame: University of Notre Dame Press, 2000.

———. "The Human Acts of Christ and the Acts That Are the Sacraments." In *Ressourcement Thomism: Sacred Doctrine, the Sacraments, and the Moral Life: Essays in Honor of Romanus Cessario, O.P.*, edited by Reinhard Hütter and Matthew Levering, 150–68. Washington, DC: Catholic University of America Press, 2010.

———. "The Jews and the Body of Christ: An Essay in Hope." *Pro Ecclesia* 27, no. 4 (September 2018) 412–24.

Weinfeld, Moshe. "Sabbath, Temple, and the Enthronement of the Lord: The Problem of the Sitz im Leben of Genesis 1.1–2.3." In *Mélanges bibliques et orientaux en l'honneur de M. Henri Cazelles*, edited by A. Caquot and M. Delcor, 501–12. Neukirchen-Vluyn: Neukirchener, 1981.

Weisel, Elie. *Night.* Translated by Stella Rodway. New York: Penguin, 1981.

Weissman, Deborah. "Zionism as Jewish Hope and Responsibility." In *Covenant and Hope: Christian and Jewish Reflections: Essays in Constructive Theology*, edited by Robert W. Jenson and Eugene B. Korn, 263–83. Grand Rapids: Eerdmans, 2012.

Wells, Bruce. "What Is Biblical Law? A Look at Pentateuchal Rules and Near Eastern Practice." *Catholic Biblical Quarterly* 70, no. 2 (April 2008) 223–43.

Wells, Jo Bailey. *God's Holy People: A Theme in Biblical Theology.* Sheffield: Sheffield Academic, 2000.

Wenham, Gordon J. *Psalms as Torah: Reading Biblical Songs Ethically.* Grand Rapids: Baker Academic, 2012.

Westerman, Edjan. *Learning Messiah: Israel and the Nations: Learning to Read God's Way Anew.* Eugene, OR: Wipf and Stock, 2018.

White, Thomas Joseph, OP. *Exodus.* Grand Rapids: Brazos, 2016.

———. "The Universal Mediation of Christ and Non-Christian Religions." *Nova et Vetera* 14, no. 1 (2016) 177–98.

Wicker, Brian. *The Story-Shaped World: Fiction and Metaphysics. Some Variations on a Theme.* Notre Dame, IN: University of Notre Dame Press, 1975.

Wildavsky, Aaron. *Moses as Political Leader.* 2d ed. Jerusalem: Shalem, 2005.

Wilder, William. *Echoes of the Exodus Narrative in the Context and Background of Galatians 5:18.* New York: Peter Lang, 2001.

Wilken, Robert Louis. "*Fides Caritate Formata*: Faith Formed by Love." *Nova et Vetera* 9, no. 4 (Fall 2011) 1089–1100.

———. "*In novissimus diebus*: Biblical Promises, Jewish Hopes and Early Christian Exegesis." *Journal of Early Christian Studies* 1, no. 1 (1993) 1–19.

———. *John Chrysostom and the Jews: Reality and Rhetoric in the Late Fourth Century.* Berkeley, CA: University of California Press, 1983.

———. *Judaism and the Early Christian Mind: A Study of Cyril of Alexandria's Exegesis and Theology.* New Haven, CT: Yale University Press, 1971.

———. *The Land Called Holy: Palestine in Christian History and Thought.* New Haven, CT: Yale University Press, 1992.

———. "Something Greater Than the Temple." In *Anti-Judaism and the Gospels*, edited by William R. Farmer, 176–202. Harrisburg, PA: Trinity International, 1999.
Williams, Delores. *Sisters in the Wilderness: The Challenge of Womanist God-Talk*. Maryknoll, NY: Orbis, 1993.
Williams, Rowan. *Luminaries: Twenty Lives That Illuminate the Christian Way*. London: SPCK, 2019.
Williams, Stephen N. *The Election of Grace: A Riddle without a Resolution?* Grand Rapids: Eerdmans, 2015.
Williamson, Clark M. *A Guest in the House of Israel: Post-Holocaust Church Theology*. Louisville, KY: Westminster John Knox, 1993.
———. "The Universal Significance of Christ." In *Seeing Judaism Anew: Christianity's Sacred Obligation*, edited by Mary C. Boys, 138–47. Lanham, MD: Rowman & Littlefield, 2005.
Williamson, Peter S. *Revelation*. Grand Rapids: Baker Academic, 2015.
Willitts, Joel. "Jewish Fish (ΙΧΘΥΣ) in Post-Supersessionist Water: Messianic Judaism within a Post-Supersessionistic Paradigm." *HTS Theological Studies* 72, no. 4 (2016) 1–5.
———. *Matthew's Messianic Shepherd-King: In Search of 'The Lost Sheep of the House of Israel.'* Berlin: De Gruyter, 2008.
Wills, Garry. *Papal Sin: Structures of Deceit*. New York: Doubleday, 2000.
———. *Why Priests? A Failed Tradition*. New York: Penguin, 2013.
Wilson, Todd A. "The Supersession and Superfluity of the Law? Another Look at Galatians." In *Introduction to Messianic Judaism: Its Ecclesial Context and Biblical Foundations*, edited by David Rudolph and Joel Willitts, 235–44. Grand Rapids: Zondervan, 2013.
Winner, Lauren F. *The Dangers of Christian Practice: On Wayward Gifts, Characteristic Damage, and Sin*. New Haven, CT: Yale University Press, 2018.
Winock, Michel. "Louis Veuillot et l'antijudaïsme français lors de l'affaire Mortara." In *Les Racines chrétiennes de l'antisémitisme politique (fin XIXe—XXe siècle)*, edited by Catherine Brice and Giovanni Miccoli, 79–88. Rome: Ecole française de Rome, 2003.
Wippel, John. "Aquinas on Creation and Preambles of Faith." *The Thomist* 78, no. 1 (2014) 1–36.
Witherington, Ben, III. *Jesus the Sage: The Pilgrimage of Wisdom*. Minneapolis: Fortress, 1994.
Wittman, Tyler R. *God and Creation in the Theology of Thomas Aquinas and Karl Barth*. Cambridge: Cambridge University Press, 2019.
Wolf, Hubert. *Pope and Devil: The Vatican's Archives and the Third Reich*. Translated by Kenneth Kronenberg. Cambridge, MA: Harvard University Press, 2010.
Wolter, Michael. *The Gospel According to Luke: Volume II (Luke 9:51—24)*. Translated by Wayne Coppins and Christoph Heilig. Waco, TX: Baylor University Press, 2017.
Wolterstorff, Nicholas. *Divine Discourse: Philosophical Reflections on the Claim that God Speaks*. Cambridge: Cambridge University Press, 1995.
———. *Lament for a Son*. Grand Rapids: Eerdmans, 1987.
———. "The Silence of the God Who Speaks." In *Divine Hiddenness: New Essays*, edited by Daniel Howard-Snyder and Paul K. Moser, 215–28. Cambridge: Cambridge University Press, 2002.
Work, Telford. *Deuteronomy*. Grand Rapids: Brazos, 2009.

Works, Carla Swafford. *The Least of These: Paul and the Marginalized.* Grand Rapids: Eerdmans, 2020.

Wright, Christopher J. H. *Deuteronomy.* Grand Rapids: Baker, 1996.

———. *Old Testament Ethics for the People of God.* Downers Grove, IL: InterVarsity, 2004.

Wright, Jacob L. *David, King of Israel, and Caleb in Biblical Memory.* Cambridge: Cambridge University Press, 2014.

Wright, N. T. *Colossians and Philemon.* Grand Rapids: Eerdmans, 1986.

———. *The Day the Revolution Began: Reconsidering the Meaning of Jesus's Crucifixion.* New York: HarperCollins, 2016.

———. *History and Eschatology: Jesus and the Promise of Natural Theology.* Waco, TX: Baylor University Press, 2019.

———. *Jesus and the Victory of God.* Minneapolis: Fortress, 1996.

———. "The Lord's Prayer as a Paradigm for Christian Prayer." In *Into God's Presence: Prayer in the New Testament,* edited by Richard N. Longenecker, 132–54. Grand Rapids: Eerdmans, 2001.

———. *Paul and the Faithfulness of God.* 2 vols. Minneapolis: Fortress, 2013.

———. "Romans." In *The New Interpreter's Bible,* vol. 10, edited by Leander Keck, 393–770. Nashville, TN: Abingdon, 2002.

Wright, William M., IV, and Francis Martin. *Encountering the Living God in Scripture: Theological and Philosophical Principles for Interpretation.* Grand Rapids: Baker Academic, 2019.

Wyrwa, Ulrich. "'L'Osservatore Cattolico' and Davide Albertario: Catholic Public Relations and Antisemitic Propaganda in Milan." In *Sites of European Antisemitism in the Age of Mass Politics, 1880–1918,* edited by Robert Nemes and Daniel Unowsky, 61–75. Waltham, MA: Brandeis University Press, 2014.

Wyschogrod, Michael. *The Body of Faith: God in the People Israel.* 2d ed. Northvale, NJ: Jacob Aronson, 1996.

———. "The Dialogue with Christianity and My Self-Understanding as a Jew." In *Abraham's Promise: Judaism and Jewish-Christian Relations,* edited by R. Kendall Soulen, 225–36. Grand Rapids: Eerdmans, 2004.

———. "Faith and the Holocaust: A Review Essay of Emil Fackenheim's *God's Presence in History.*" *Judaism* 20, no. 3 (July 1971) 286–94.

———. "Franz Rosenzweig's *The Star of Redemption.*" In *Abraham's Promise: Judaism and Jewish-Christian Relations,* edited by R. Kendall Soulen, 121–30. Grand Rapids: Eerdmans, 2004.

———. "The Impact of Dialogue with Christianity on My Self-Understanding as a Jew." *Abraham's Promise: Judaism and Jewish-Christian Relations,* edited by R. Kendall Soulen, 225–36. Grand Rapids: Eerdmans, 2004.

———. "Incarnation and God's Indwelling in Israel." In *Abraham's Promise: Judaism and Jewish-Christian Relations,* edited by R. Kendall Soulen, 165–78. Grand Rapids: Eerdmans, 2004.

———. "Israel, the Church, and Election." In *Abraham's Promise: Judaism and Jewish-Christian Relations,* edited by R. Kendall Soulen, 179–87. Grand Rapids: Eerdmans, 2004.

———. "A Jewish Perspective on the Incarnation." *Modern Theology* 12, no. 2 (April 1996) 195–209.

———. "Why Was and Is the Theology of Karl Barth of Interest to a Jewish Theologian?" In *Abraham's Promise: Judaism and Jewish-Christian Relations*, edited by R. Kendall Soulen, 211–24. Grand Rapids: Eerdmans, 2004.

Yadin-Israel, Azzan. "Concepts of Scripture in the Schools of Rabbi Akiva and Rabbi Ishmael." In *Jewish Concepts of Scripture: A Comparative Introduction*, edited by Benjamin D. Sommer, 47–63. New York: New York University Press, 2012.

———. *Scripture and Tradition: Rabbi Akiva and the Triumph of Midrash*. Philadelphia: University of Pennsylvania Press, 2015.

———. *Scripture as Logos: Rabbi Ishmael and the Origins of Midrash*. Philadelphia: University of Pennsylvania Press, 2004.

Yoder, John Howard. *The Jewish-Christian Schism Revisited*. Edited by Michael G. Cartwright and Peter Ochs. Grand Rapids: Eerdmans, 2003.

Yuval, Israel Jacob. *Two Nations in Your Womb: Perceptions of Jews and Christians in Late Antiquity and the Middle Ages*. Translated by Barbara Harshav and Jonathan Chipman. Berkeley, CA: University of California Press, 2008.

Zaas, Peter. "Guide to Reading [Colossians]." In *The Jewish Annotated New Testament*, edited by Amy-Jill Levine and Marc Zvi Brettler, 262–63. Oxford: Oxford University Press, 2011.

Zakovitch, Yair. *"And You Shall Tell Your Son . . .": The Concept of the Exodus in the Bible*. Jerusalem: Magnes, 1991.

Zellentin, Holger M. *Rabbinic Parodies of Jewish and Christian Literature*. Tübingen: Mohr Siebeck, 2011.

Zenger, Erich. "The Covenant That Was Never Revoked: The Foundations of a Christian Theology of Judaism." In *The Catholic Church and the Jewish People: Recent Reflections from Rome*, edited by Philip A. Cunningham, Norbert J. Hofmann, and Joseph Sievers, 92–112. New York: Fordham University Press, 2007.

———. "The God of Israel's Reign over the World (Psalms 90–106)." In Norbert Lohfink and Erich Zenger, *The God of Israel and the Nations: Studies in Isaiah and the Psalms*, translated by Everett R. Kalin, 161–90. Collegeville, MN: Liturgical, 2000.

Zuccotti, Suzan. *Under His Very Windows: The Vatican and the Holocaust*. New Haven, CT: Yale University Press, 2000.

Index

Abraham
    Children of, 66–67, 81–82, 84–87
    historicity of, 79–80, 330
    in the New Testament 80–87
    see also: Covenant, Abrahamic
Al Aqsa Mosque, 312
Anti-Semitism (Nazi), 71, 72
    see also: Christian anti-semitism and persecution of the Jewish people
Aquinas, Thomas, 27–28, 95, 116, 194–94, 272, 296, 301, 357, 400, 412–15, 419, 421
Arendt, Hannah, 150, 366
Atonement, 124, 126
    sacrificial rite, 297–98, 316, 316
    by Christ, 94, 98, 247–48, 288, 290–291, 301, 316
    Day of, 124, 126
    return to God, 298
Augustine, 99–100, 109, 112–13, 335
Auschwitz, 173–74, 177, 248, 428

Babylonian Exile, 337, 345, 408, see also, Exile
Baptism, 81–82, 84, 179–80, 241, 398, 398
    effect of, 418–19, 421, 423
    forced, 397–98, 400, 412–18
Barth, Karl, 30, 42, 47, 61, 136
Benedict XVI (Joseph Ratzinger), 87, 111–12, 165, 177, 189–91, 207–9, 336, 339, 348, 398, 419, 440–441
Blood libel, 338, 361–65, 362

Brisker Method of halakhic reasoning, 212

Canaan, 16, 184, 326, 336–37, 347, 353, 370
Canon Law, 195, 416
Cantate Domino, 263–64, 322
Christian anti-semitism and persecution of the Jewish people, 38, 68–74
    charge of deicide, 95, 99, 100, 106, 202
    in patristic exegesis, 355–57
    in the 19th and 20th centuries, 54, 358–68
    in the Middle Ages, 357–58
    papacy's complicity in, 357–67, 397–99
    see also, Mortara Case; Papal abuse of power; Polemic in the New Testament; Polemical, Anti-Jewish Christian interpretation of Scripture
Christian boasting over the branches, 19, 25–26, 28, 46, 68, 108, 382, 440
Christian life in Christ (Christian Halakhic man, 229–56, 452–53
Church
    as inaugurated kingdom, 23, 153–54
    as Israel, 50, 61, 86, 152–53, 177, 184–85, 190
    as promised land, 348
    as temple, 241–42, 282, 287–88

Church *(continued)*
  divinely instituted, 437, 440
  instrument of salvation, 440
  visible corporate form of, 184–88
Circumcision, 81, 84–86, 104, 156, 203, 263, 267, 324, 377
Civiltà Cattolica, 358–66
Clement VIII, 36
Cognitive man, 215–16
Conversion (of Jews to Christianity), 21–22, 27, 30, 33, 388–89
  coerced, 36, See also, baptism, coerced
Council of Florence, 28, 263, 357–58
Council of Jerusalem, 82
Council of Toledo IV, 416–17
Covenant
  Abrahamic, 77, 167, 191, 343, 370
  eschatological mode of observance by Christians, 15–20, 191, 376–77
  fulfilled in Christ, 10, 15–22, 48, 332, 336, 337, 348–55, 375–77
  Mosaic, 147, 167–68, 182, 191, 465
  New, 22, 182–83, 191, 439
  ongoing observation in original mode, 15–22, 214, 326, 327, 336, 339, 339–42, 375, 382
  unrevoked, 55, 60, 191, 319–20, 343, 375, 377, 382, 446
  with David, 406–7
  see also, land; law; Torah; Israel as chosen people; Israel, establishment as holy nation
Covenantal politics of Israel, 166, 169–70, 370
Creation, 2–3
  as divine speech, 118–20, 121–24, 135, 144
  as God's cosmic temple, 269–70
  as tzimtzum, 220, 240
  ex nihilo, 3, 5, 6, 110–16, 126, 135, 140, 144–46
  from preexistent matter/out of chaos, 112, 114, 124, 126, 135, 138
Cross
  as act self-giving love, 230, 247
  as manifestation of divine presence, 240
  Christians' participation in Christ's sacrifice, 252, 256
  Christ's fulfillment of the Torah on, 197, 201–2, 247, 251
  Christ's inauguration of the kingdom on, 183, 186, 192
  saving power of, 183, 192, 202, 213, 301
  used to justify persecution of Jews, 202, 248, 379
Crucifixion, 178–79, 183, 185, 192
Culpability for Jesus's death deicide, 55, 69, 99, 318, 355

David, 406
Davidic kingship, 11, 399–400, 402–9
  establishment of by God, 403–5
  failures of Israel's kings, 404–8
  fulfilled by Jesus, 48, 402, 409, 434
  God's covenant with David, 406–7
  messianic hopes for, 408–9, 435
De Iudaeis et aliis infidelibus, 36
Divine ideas, 122, 124
Divine Presence, 128, 130, 159, 173–75, 181, 185, 189, 215, 221, 226, 315
  in Jesus, 239–40
  in Torah observance, 173–74, 219
Divine providence, 458–66
Dome of the Rock, 312
Dominus Iesus, 24, 63

Eastern Orthodoxy, 13–15, 142
Elokim, 167
Eschatology
  Christian, 15–17, 20, 22, 187, 192, 219, 237–38, 255, 348–53, 370
  Jewish, 94, 152, 217, 276–78, 336, 383, 432
Eternal life, 192, 218, 282, 284, see also, Resurrection
Eucharist, 8, 187, 241
  as new manna, 177, 179, 193
  as participation in the body of the Lord, 255–56
  as participation in the new Passover, 183, 320, 453

INDEX

as sharing in Christ's perfect
  sacrifice, 265, 287, 299
as Temple sacrifice, 304, 320
see also, sacrifice
Evangelicals, 136
Exile
  Babylonian, 337, 345
  by Romans in 135 AD, 350
  Prophecy concerning, 344–46
Exodus
  from Egypt, 6, 147–49, 155–76
  historicity of, 148
  new exodus in Christ, 6, 147–48,
    151, 154, 176–93
  suffering in, 160–65, 193

First Crusade of 1096, 417

Gaudium et Spes, 437, 438
*Gifts and the Calling of God Are
  Irrevocable, the,* 31–33, 40–41
Girard, René, 299–301, 304–5
golden calf, 161, 297

halakah, 200, 204, 211–27
halakhic man, 216–27
  as participating in God creative
    work, 225–26
  Christian, 227–56
halakhic reasoning, 216–17
Hasidic Judaism, 221–22
Heschel, Abraham Joshua, 4–5, 117,
  124–36, 144, 223
Holocaust, 68–69, 71–73, 329, 366,
  398
  Jewish responses to, 427–29, 430
  and theodicy, 432, 434
Holy Spirit, 177, 179, 181, 183–84,
  193, 197, 241–42, 466
homo religiosus, 215–16, 218

Implicit faith, 24–25, 27–29
Incarnation of the Logos, 213, 215,
  316
  as divine contraction, 239–40, 284
Inclusivism and Exclusivism, 43–44,
  58–59
Innocent III, 357

Invincible ignorance, 10, 19,
  23–26, 28–29, 34, 264, 339, 375,
  380–382
Isaac, 78, 83–84
Isaac, Jules, 56, 318
Ishmael, 78, 83–84
Islam, 10, 66, 71, 88, 166, 168, 210,
  312, 396, 410
Israel (see also, state of Israel)
  chosen people, 50–52, 368–71
  Christ as, 191
  Church as, 50, 61, 86, 152–53, 177,
    184–85, 190
  Establishment as a holy nation,
    151–52, 155, 166–69, 172–74

Jerusalem, 330, 347, 350, 353
  heavenly or new, 350–353
Jewish-Christian dialogue, 52–66,
  108–9, 380–381, 449–50
Jewish Mysticism, 126, 127, 129, 135,
  221, 295
John Paul II (Karol Wojtyła), 11, 343,
  378, 379, 400
Josephus, 309–10
Josiah, 270, 408

Kabbalah, 129, 220–221, see also,
  Jewish mysticism
Kingdom of God
  consummated, 17, 20, 176, 188,
    255, 315, 337, 464
  inaugurated, 10–11, 15–17, 20,
    153–54, 176–77, 180–84,
    186–93, 203, 206, 206, 214,
    348–51, 464
Klawans, Jonathan, 4, 8, 303–11,
  313–17, 320
Kook, Abraham Isaac, 430
Kook, Tzvi Yehudah, 430–431

Land (Promised)
  and the State of Israel, 324–33
  Catholic theology of, 376–91
  covenantal Promise of land to
    Israel, 8–10, 373–74
  disputed dimensions and meaning,
    324–27, 330, 332–33

INDEX

Land (Promised) *(continued)*
  eschatological dimension in Old Testament account of, 344–48
  eschatological dimension in the New Testament account of, 348–55
  specific Land/chosen by God, 372–73
  Jewish obligation to settle, 372–75, 384–86
Last Supper, 147, 177, 182–83, 248, 286–87
Law (see also Torah)
  Christ's law of love, 251–53
  food laws, 203–6
  in Paul's theology, 82–84, 195, 201–3, 257, 281–83
  in the gospels, 202–9
  new, 192, 195, 208
  revealed at Sinai, 159, 164–66, 175, 217
Leo XIII, 362–63
Levenson, Jon D., 67, 79, 84–85, 114, 138, 152, 163–64, 269–70, 298, 465
L'Osservatore Romano, 362–63
Lumen Gentium, 28, 55, 433

Manna, 159–60, 193
Martyrdom, 295
Mary, 87, 188, 192
Messiah
  Jesus as, 258–59, 378, 380, 381, 453–54
  in Judaism, Jewish hope for, 258–60, 314, 380–381, 408–9
Messianic Judaism, 60, 209, 341, 376–77
Mission
  Christian mandate to proclaim the gospel, 30–32, 383, 412
  Christian mission to the Jews, 31–34
  mission v. proselytizing, 32, 412
Mitsvot, 197, 211
Mortara Case, 415–25
Mortara, Edgardo, 11, 397–98, 400, 415, 422, 424–25
Moses, 150, 155, 161–63, 166, 170

Jesus as new Moses, 178, 180
Mount Horeb, 155
Mount Sinai, 151, 159, 167–68, 180, 207, 209, 219
Mount Zion, 186, 187
Mussolini, Benito, 365

Nakba, 342
Nazism, 71–73, 365
Nebuchadnezzar, 270, 408
Nostra Aetate, 55, 73, 99, 264, 318, 343, 383, 389, 444
Novak, David, 1, 32, 37, 64, 74, 77, 110, 132, 197, 199–200, 209–10, 334–36, 340, 368, 419, 458
  The Election of Israel, 368–69
  Zionism and Judaism, 369–75
Nuremberg laws, 366

Oesterreicher, John, 44, 318
Ongoing Judaism, 18–19, 26, 38–43, 214, 319–20, 339–40, 354, 375, 378–82
  anticipated by Jesus, 354
  anticipated by Paul, 26, 38–43, 354
  see also Covenant, unrevoked; Romans 11
Oreglia, Guiseppe di Santo Stefano, 359–60, 362
Origen of Alexandria, 95, 112, 113, 350, 355

Palestine, 327, 329
Palestinian Authority, 331
Palestinian Liberation Organization, 331
Palestinian people, 323–25, 327, 329, 383–84, 392–94
Palestinian state, 342
Papacy, 11, 402, 409–10, 433, 438, 442
Papal abuse of power, 400–402, 438–39
  see also, Mortara case; Christian anti-semitism and persecution of the Jewish people
  anti-Roman responses to, 425–26
  responding with theocentric humility, 433–34
Papal infallibility, 410, 436

Passover, 157–58, 171
Passover Lamb, 157–58
  Jesus as, 177, 179, 182, 185, 187, 192, 284–87, 288, 320
  ritual, 158, 171, 287–88
Paul IV, 36
Paul VI, 439
Pentecost, 180–81, 243
Peter (Apostle), 181, 234, 242–43, 247, 254, 391, 409
Pharaoh, 150, 155–58, 164, 170–72, 268, 269, 333
Philo of Alexandria, 309–10, 337
Pius IX, 11, 397–98 400, 415, 419, 422, 424–26, 435–36
Pius X, 343, 364–65
Pius XI, 363
Pius XII, 343, 366
Polemic in the New Testament, 51–53, 89–90, 53, 101–9, 450–451
Polemical anti-Jewish Christian interpretation of Scripture, 95–100
  see also, Christian anti-Semitism and persecution of the Jewish people
Promised land, see land
Protestantism, classical liberal, 2, 136, 144, 189, 326

Qumran Community, 90, 93, 197, 258, 278, 309–11
Qumran documents, 278, 310–311

Rabbinic Judaism, 195–99, 211–12
Redemption
  from slavery in Egypt, 158, 165, 171, 178, 184
  from slavery to sin and death, 165, 171, 178–80, 184–85, 188, 193
Regev, Eyal, 278, 280–284, 286–89, 290–293
Rejection of Jesus as Messiah by Jews
  culpability for, 19, 21, 23–25, 207, 214, 263–64, 319, 380, 382, 386
  tragic event, 446
Resurrection, 178–81, 287
Revelation
  and creation, 119–20, 123–214
  as divine dialogue, 140–43
  at Sinai, 131–34, 159
  human language and the divine Word, 120–22
  propositional character of, 133, 137
Rohling, August, 361–62
Rondina, Saverio, 361–62
Rosenzweig, Franz, 4–5, 117–20, 144

Sabbath (Shabbat), 169–70, 181, 218, 223
Sacks, Jonathan, 4, 78, 151, 165–76, 181, 188–89, 223, 296–98
Sacraments, 16, 179, 183, 193, 241, 398, 418–19, see also, Baptism and Eucharist
Sacrifice
  acts of loving kindness as, 226, 312, 314
  animal, 8, 197, 217, 263, 286–87, 291, 294–301, 303–11, 313–14
  animal sacrifice positive purposes of, 306–10
  critics of temple sacrifice, 293–303
  cultic sacrifice as a spiritual work, 301, 303
  in prophetic texts, 307–10
  of Eucharist, 299, 304, 320
  perfect sacrifice of Jesus, 8, 286–92, 314, 316, 320
  prayer as, 220, 311, 313–14
  Torah study as, 220, 313–14
Saul, 406
Scapegoat, 299–301, 304–5
  Christ as, 300–301, 305
Scripture
  affirmation of communion of God and his creatures, 124, 127, 131, 136
  anthropomorphism in, 5, 117, 124–25, 127, 130–31, 135, 139–40, 142–44
  dialogical character, 137–43, 145–46
  divine inspiration of the biblical text, 128–29, 140, 145
  human origin of the biblical text, 120, 131–35, 139, 145
  perfect, 135

INDEX

Scripture interpretation
  Christological, 450–451
  Rabbi Akiva's School of interpretation/Mystical mode of interpretation, 117, 125–36, 144
  Rabbi Ishmael's School of Interpretation/Rational mode of interpretation, 117, 125, 126, 129–36
Second Temple Judaism, 198, 199
Second Vatican Council, 55–56, 73, 264, 299, 318, 437, 444
Separate existence, see, Ongoing Judaism, Romans 11
Sermon on the Mount, 180
Shekinah, See divine presence
Six-Day War, 331
Solomon, 268–70, 404, 407
Soloveitchik, Joseph B., 4, 113–14, 196, 200, 212–13, 215–27
Solovyov, Vladimir, 14–15, 447
State of Israel
  establishment of, 327–29, 393
  dispute over existence of, 322–36
  theological significance of, 9–10, 174, 384–89
  see also, Land, Zionism
Stephen, deacon (Acts 7), 178, 253, 315
Stroumsa, Guy, 293–96
Supersessionism, 210, 303, 311, 313, 314, 315, 316, 317
  Christian, 5, 8, 62, 152–53, 165, 210, 262–64, 292, 304–5, 315–19, 374–75
  Jewish, 210, 304

Tabernacle, 173, 175, 180, 269, 284, 289
Talmud, 3–4, 40, 85, 134, 195
Teitelbaum, Joel, 428–29, 432
Temple
  as microcosm, 309–10, 310
  Christ as eschatological temple, 8, 48, 94, 98, 283–87, 288–89, 291–92, 314–17, 320, 453
  community of Christian believers as temple, 241–42, 282, 287–88
  critics of, 293–98
  destruction of Second Temple, 51, 88, 90–94, 198, 220, 294, 296
  eschatological, 8, 93–94, 98, 177, 273–78
  in the New Testament, 279–93, 315
  Jesus's prophesy of its destruction, 279–80, 283–84, 286, 289
  Old Testament prophecy of its destruction, 271–73
  rebuilding of, 311–13
  Second Temple, 278–79
  Solomon's, 268–71
Ten Commandments, 159, 164, 168, 228
Theocentric humility, 37, 387, 391, 401, 434, 436, 438
Theodicy, 432, 434, 458–59, 461–64
Theo-drama, 137–38, 142–43, 145–46, 464
Thieme, Karl, 45, 318
Torah (see also, Law)
  Christ as embodiment/fulfillment of, 7, 48–49, 195, 197, 199–200, 203, 208–9, 452
  descent of God through, 219, 221
  Earthly Torah and Heavenly Torah, 132
  fulfillment mode, 49
  ongoing observance of, 206, 219–20, 223, 319–20
  Oral Torah, 49, 79, 87–88, 133, 142, 168–69, 194–95, 198–99, 211, 260, 445
  Paul on ongoing observance of, 282–83, 291
  sanctification of the world by, 219
  Written Torah, 79, 169, 197, 199
Tower of Babel, 172, 370
Transcendent messianism 432
Trinity, 240
  Jewish perception as idolatry, 380–381
Two-state solution, 340, 342, 392
tzimtzum, 220, 221
  divine indwelling in believers as, 239, 241
  Incarnation as, 239, 240

United Nations Partition Plan (1947), 328–29, 333, 393
Universal savior, Christ as, 24, 60–62, 224, 247, 377–78

Vanhoozer, Kevin, 117–18, 136–43, 145, 145
Venard, Olivier-Thomas, 117, 121–24, 144
von Balthasar, Hans Urs, 39–40, 40, 95, 106, 123, 187, 209–10, 214, 439

von Hildebrand, Dietrich, 44–45, 318
Wyschogrod, Michael, 143–44, 196–97, 201–3, 213, 311, 429, 441

Zionism, 8–10, 327–28, 331–33, 337
    Christian support for, 9–11, 374–94
    Jewish duty to settle the land God has chosen, 373–74
    messianic, 429–30
    Mizrahi Zionist movement, 430

www.ingramcontent.com/pod-product-compliance
Lightning Source LLC
Chambersburg PA
CBHW021229300426
44111CB00007B/481

* 9 781725 291102 *